PROVINCIAL JUSTICE
Upper Canadian Legal Portraits from the
Dictionary of Canadian Biography

In the formative years of Ontario's history, the law loomed large, as a profession, a preoccupation of legislators, a subject of debate and controversy, and a force that many citizens found themselves up against. Robert Fraser has drawn from the pages of the *Dictionary of Canadian Biography* the stories of seventy people who played roles in the legal history of Upper Canada.

The first group covers Upper Canadian officialdom, including such luminaries as the aristocratic Sir John Beverley Robinson, attorney general, and Robert Baldwin, a central figure on the road to responsible government. The second section includes members of the bar, among them William Warren Baldwin, father and political ally of Robert. Next are some of the most significant of those who stood accused before the law. One is Jacob Overholser, who was convicted of treason in the War of 1812. Another is Mary Thompson, whose conviction for infanticide in 1823 led to the reform of a notorious law. And finally there are those who came up against the law in various ways. Some were the centre of *causes célèbres*; others were critics of the judicial system, such as publisher Bartemas Ferguson, a champion of the liberty of the press and victim of the harsh laws of libel.

Told in a readable style that has been much praised, these portraits contain information that bears the authoritative stamp of the *DCB* volumes from which they come. They add a valuable personal dimension to Ontario's legal history.

ROBERT FRASER is an editor with the *Dictionary of Canadian Biography*.

Provincial Justice
Upper Canadian Legal Portraits from the *Dictionary of Canadian Biography*

Edited by
ROBERT L. FRASER

Published for The Osgoode Society by
University of Toronto Press
Toronto Buffalo London

© University of Toronto Press Incorporated 1992
Toronto Buffalo London
Introduction © The Osgoode Society 1992
Reprinted in paperback 2017
ISBN 978-0-8020-2896-9 (cloth)
ISBN 978-0-8020-7404-1 (paper)

Printed on acid-free paper

Canadian Cataloguing in Publication Data

Main entry under title:

Provincial justice

ISBN 978-0-8020-2896-9 (bound). — ISBN 978-0-8020-7404-1 (pbk.)

1. Law — Ontario — Biography. 2. Law — Ontario —
History — 18th century. 3. Law — Ontario — History
— 19th century. I. Fraser, Robert L. (Robert
Lochiel). II. Osgoode Society. III. Title: Dic-
tionary of Canadian Biography.
KE396.O5P76 1992   349.713'0922   C92-095598-3
KF345.Z9A1P76 1992

Illustration credits

Archives of Ontario: Rolph (S159); Robinson (S8503) **Queen's University Archives:** Hagerman (P6–K, 168–3) **Metropolitan Toronto Reference Library:** W.W. Baldwin (T31037); Sullivan (T15026); Bidwell (J. Ross Robertson collection [JRRC], T15345); Robert Baldwin (T10252); Jones (T16853); Campbell (JRRC, T16845); Sherwood (JRRC, T31455); Powell (T16859); Hagerman's law office (JRRC, T11263); Robinson's law office (JRRC, T12347); Home District court-house and jail 1827–40 (JRRC, T11963); Home District jail 1799–1827 (T32183); execution of Kain (TK343.K11) **Hamilton Public Library, Special Collections:** Gore District court-house and jail **Agnes Etherington Art Centre, Queen's University:** Midland District court-house (gift of Chancellor Agnes Benidickson 1987) **Royal Ontario Museum:** Pavilion Hotel, Niagara Falls (942.48.3) **Brant Historical Society:** Mohawk Village (Frank Adams collection, FA134)

For my father, Robert Lochiel Fraser,
who wanted me to be a lawyer
when I grew up.
And for my mother, Marion F. Fraser,
who limited her hope to the expectation
that I would grow up.

Contents

FOREWORD — xi

GENERAL INTRODUCTION — xiii

PREFACE — xv

'All the privileges which Englishmen possess':
Order, Rights, and Constitutionalism
in Upper Canada — xxi

Officialdom: The Judiciary and Crown Officers

Henry Allcock	3
Robert Baldwin	8
D'Arcy Boulton	39
Henry John Boulton	43
Sir William Campbell	51
William Henry Draper	64
John Elmsley	76
William Firth	79
Robert Isaac Dey Gray	83
Christopher Alexander Hagerman	85
Robert Sympson Jameson	100
Jonas Jones	104

Sir James Buchanan Macaulay 115
John Macdonell (Greenfield) 121
Archibald McLean 127
William Osgoode 129
William Dummer Powell 135
Sir John Beverley Robinson 153
Peter Russell 175
Thomas Scott 182
Levius Peters Sherwood 185
Robert Thorpe 188
John White 192
John Walpole Willis 195

The Legal Profession

William Warren Baldwin 201
Donald Bethune 222
Marshall Spring Bidwell 225
Robert Easton Burns 234
James Clark 236
George Mackenzie 239
William Birdseye Peters 243
Thomas Mabon Radenhurst 247
George Ridout 250
Walter Roe 253
John Rolph 256
James Hunter Samson 270
Robert Baldwin Sullivan 272
Simon Ebenezer Washburn 283
William Weekes 285

The Accused

Elijah Bentley 289
William Brass 293
Cornelius Albertson Burley 296
Joshua Gwillen Doan 301
William Kain 303
James Owen McCarthy 306
Edward McSwiney 310
Peter Matthews 314

Mary Osborn (London)	316
Jacob Overholser	320
Angelique Pilotte	327
George Powlis	332
Nils von Schoultz	337
Joseph Seely	340
Shawanakiskie	344
Henry Sovereene	346
Daniel Sullivan	348
Mary Thompson	351
Jack York	355

The Critics and the *Causes Célèbres*

Barnabas Bidwell	361
Francis Collins	370
Reuben Crandall	375
Bartemas Ferguson	378
William Forsyth	382
Charles French	392
Benajah Mallory	396
John Matthews	404
Peter Perry	410
Robert Randal	420
Joseph Willcocks	432
John Willson	443
CONTRIBUTORS	449
INDEX	453

PUBLICATIONS OF THE OSGOODE SOCIETY

1981 David H. Flaherty, ed., *Essays in the History of Canadian Law,* volume I
1982 Marion MacRae and Anthony Adamson *Cornerstones of Order: Courthouses and Town Halls of Ontario, 1784–1914*
1983 David H. Flaherty, ed., *Essays in the History of Canadian Law,* volume II
1984 Patrick Brode *Sir John Beverley Robinson: Bone and Sinew of the Compact*
1984 David Williams *Duff: A Life in the Law*
1985 James G. Snell and Frederick Vaughan *The Supreme Court of Canada: History of the Institution*
1986 Paul Romney *Mr Attorney: The Attorney General for Ontario in Court, Cabinet, and Legislature, 1791–1899*
1986 Martin L. Friedland *The Case of Valentine Shortis: A True Story of Crime and Politics in Canada*
1987 C. Ian Kyer and Jerome E. Bickenbach *The Fiercest Debate: Cecil A. Wright, the Benchers, and Legal Education in Ontario, 1923–1957*
1988 Robert Sharpe *The Last Day, the Last Hour: The Currie Libel Trial*
1988 John D. Arnup *Middleton: The Beloved Judge*
1989 Desmond Brown *The Genesis of the Canadian Criminal Code of 1892*
1989 Patrick Brode *The Odyssey of John Anderson*
1990 Philip Girard and Jim Phillips, eds., *Essays in the History of Canadian Law,* volume III, *Nova Scotia*
1990 Carol Wilton, ed., *Essays in the History of Canadian Law,* volume IV, *Lawyers and Business in Canada 1830–1930*
1991 Constance Backhouse *Petticoats and Prejudice: Women and Law in Nineteenth-Century Canada*
1992 Brendan O'Brien *Speedy Justice: The Tragic Last Voyage of His Majesty's Vessel 'Speedy'*
1992 Robert L. Fraser, ed., *Provincial Justice: Upper Canadian Legal Portraits from the 'Dictionary of Canadian Biography'*

Foreword

THE OSGOODE SOCIETY

The purpose of The Osgoode Society is to encourage research and writing in the history of Canadian law. The Society, which was incorporated in 1979 and is registered as a charity, was founded at the initiative of the Honourable R. Roy McMurtry, former Attorney-General for Ontario, and officials of the Law Society of Upper Canada. Its efforts to stimulate the study of legal history in Canada include the sponsorship of a fellowship, a research support program, and work in the fields of oral history and legal archives. The Society publishes (at the rate of about one a year) volumes of interest to the Society's members that contribute to legal-historical scholarship in Canada, including studies of the courts, the judiciary, and the legal profession, biographies, collections of documents, studies in criminology and penology, accounts of great trials, and work in the social and economic history of the law.

Current directors of The Osgoode Society are Jane Banfield, Brian Bucknall, Archie Campbell, J. Douglas Ewart, Martin Friedland, Howard Hampton, John Honsberger, Kenneth Jarvis, Allen Linden, James Lisson, Colin McKinnon, Roy McMurtry, Brendan O'Brien, Peter Oliver, James Spence, and Richard Tinsley. The annual report and information about membership may be obtained by writing to the Osgoode Society, Osgoode Hall, 130 Queen Street West, Toronto, Ontario, Canada, M5H 2N6. Members receive the annual volumes published by the Society.

It has always been the policy of The Osgoode Society to publish only original manuscripts, but in this case we are delighted to make an exception. By reprinting in a single volume a series of legal portraits of Upper Canadian figures previously published in the *Dictionary of Canadian Biography*, we are confident that we are making an important contribution to understanding Canadian legal culture. The *Dictionary of Canadian Biography* is an outstanding monument to historical scholarship in twentieth-century Canada which to date has published twelve monumental volumes dealing with Canadian lives from the years 1000 to 1900. All *DCB* entries have passed exacting tests of contemporary scholarship, and the *DCB* has won international acclaim for its scrupulous research, readable style, and high editorial standards. By putting together in a single volume the most interesting and significant portraits of Upper Canadian legal figures, this book makes the work of the *DCB* accessible to a new audience in a coherent and attractive manner. The volume includes seventy biographies of Upper Canadian officialdom (both the judiciary and Crown officers), members of the bar, critics of the judicial system, and those who stood before it. Among those included are Chief Justice Sir William Campbell; William Warren Baldwin, a lawyer who claimed in 1821 that 'there was no Society [referring to the Law Society of Upper Canada] for which the country should feel so deep an interest ... Without it, whose property was safe?'; Jacob Overholser (convicted of treason in 1814); Mary Osborn (the first woman executed in Upper Canada); Cornelius Burley (convicted of murder; his skull is now exhibited in a museum); Mary Thompson (whose conviction for infanticide in 1823 led to the reform of a notorious law); and many more.

We thank the volume editor, Dr Robert Fraser of the *DCB*, for supervising the entire project and for writing a sparkling introductory essay which places the biographies in their larger social and political contexts. Not the least of Dr Fraser's contributions is his authorship of many of the biographies reprinted here. And we thank as well our colleagues at the *DCB* and at University of Toronto Press who helped make possible this happy collaboration.

If *Provincial Justice* is well received, The Osgoode Society, the *Dictionary of Canadian Biography*, and University of Toronto Press may publish further works in this series.

R. Roy McMurtry
President

Peter N. Oliver
Editor-in-Chief

General Introduction

The *Dictionary of Canadian Biography* is pleased to be associated with The Osgoode Society in our first venture into the publication of thematic volumes. The Osgoode Society has played an indispensable role in encouraging scholarship in the field of legal history. Though the mandate of the *DCB* is a much broader one, legal figures have always been among the most numerous in our volumes. Bringing a selection of these figures together provides only one illustration of the historical world that the biographies in the *DCB* have created.

Provincial Justice: Upper Canadian Legal Portraits from the 'Dictionary of Canadian Biography,' selected from the first twelve volumes of the *Dictionary*, reveals the way that biography illuminates many of the dark corners of the past. Each life has its interest. But the context of family, society, politics, profession, and place turns biography into the history of society. Here the lives of those prominent in the legal life of Upper Canada – judges, lawmakers, lawyers, and lawbreakers – are set out in detail. Taken together the biographies also reveal an evolving legal system, and its workings, in these formative years of Canadian legal history.

Ramsay Cook
General Editor

Preface

This is the first book in The Osgoode Society's series to feature biographies taken from the *Dictionary of Canadian Biography*. It is, as well, the first time in which *DCB* material has been regrouped to focus on a particular theme. This subsidiary volume (to borrow a term used by the *Dictionary of New Zealand Biography*) concentrates on Upper Canadian lives which touched, in whole or in part, upon aspects of the administration of justice between 1791 and 1840.

Biography cannot, of course, satisfy all interests in Upper Canadian legal history. Yet this collective portrait will, it is hoped, introduce readers to some of the themes, personalities, structures, and issues that highlight the contours of the map of Upper Canadian legal history.

The idea of subsidiary volumes is almost as old as the *Dictionary* itself, but for a variety of reasons it was never acted upon. When it was raised again recently, however, Ramsay Cook, the *DCB*'s general editor, asked staff to suggest possibilities for purposes of discussion. As one whose doctorate is in Upper Canadian history and whose interest lies, at least partially, in the field of legal history, I thought the combination of area (Upper Canada) and focus (legal history) a natural. First, the *DCB* volumes include every major figure in Upper Canadian history and a host of minor ones. Secondly, as Professor Graeme Patterson of the University of Toronto pointed out in a recent review (he was commenting on the new directions taken by the Upper

Canadian biographies in the *DCB*): 'Interpretations such as these have yet to work their way into the larger and more general explorations of colonial history of which they are significantly contradictory ... One looks forward to the ferment of ideas.' Thirdly, collectively, the volumes provide a reasonably comprehensive introduction to the legal history of Upper Canada.

The present subsidiary volume has been arranged thematically to convey as coherently as possible the leading aspects of that history. The *Dictionary* contains the biographies of every justice (with one exception) of the Court of King's Bench, all the attorneys and solicitors general, a wide range of the greater and lesser members of the bar, a cross-section of the accused, and a good representation of the *causes célèbres*. And this brief description, in fact, encapsulates the present volume's thematic organization – officialdom, the judiciary and crown officials, the legal profession, and the accused and the *causes célèbres*. Because the numbers are relatively small, I decided to include all the justices and attorneys and solicitors general, and a sampling of the other areas.

When the idea of subsidiary volumes came up, it was decided that an introductory essay would be written to set the context. This has not been an easy task. The concept was the most difficult part. In the end, I decided to focus on what I thought was the most important theme in Upper Canadian legal history: the charge of partiality levelled against the administration of justice. Surprisingly (or, perhaps not), it is a touchy subject still – there are those who think that raising the subject is somehow subversive. But this is not an essay *engagé*; it is merely an essay in retrieval. Its sole purposes are to provide context for the emergence of law, justice, and the constitution as one of Upper Canada's most frequently fought-over battlegrounds and to offer some insight as to why this should have been so. As to whether the charge is true or not, that matter has not been resolved and awaits further research.

Readers are reminded that the *DCB*'s *Directives to Contributors* exhort biographers to take note of 'all stages of the career' but to discuss fully and evaluate 'the most significant aspects.' As countless contributors to *DCB* volumes have discovered, this is no mean feat, especially given the multifaceted careers of most people appearing within the project's pages. It is not, moreover, always possible. Legal history is a relative newcomer to the historical scene in this country. Thus, in biographies published in early volumes, the legal/judicial dimensions of some careers do not receive the treatment they would now and the focus rather is on political events.

For instance, the biography of John Beverley Robinson (solicitor general, attorney general, and chief justice), published in 1976, would be much different were it to be rewritten now. At the time, little work had been done on Robinson and Robert Saunders's entry for the *Dictionary* represented the best and most recent research. Since then, of course, a great deal has been written in Upper Canadian history, not the least of which is a full-length biography of Robinson (published by The Osgoode Society), as well as numerous articles on his judicial career, to say nothing of a study of the office of the attorney general. Indeed, as previously mentioned, a significant debate has emerged concerning the partiality of the administration of justice in the 1820s and Robinson emerges as the central figure in that debate. Entries in the *Dictionary* reflect current interests in historiography and, in certain cases, even encourage research in new fields. It is rare, however, for *DCB* entries to precede new historiographical developments.

As legal history develops, the lacunae in the *DCB* become more noticeable. I have, for instance, been taken to task twice for gaps in my own *DCB* articles: first, Peter Oliver, editor-in-chief of The Osgoode Society, noted the failure of the entry on Robert Baldwin Sullivan to consider his career on the bench; secondly, Carol Wilton, editor of a recent volume in the Osgoode series, consigned me and my collaborator to the historical woodshed for saying 'virtually nothing' in our biography of Robert Baldwin 'about his law practice or his contributions to the Law Society of Upper Canada.' Both criticisms are valid.

The biographies have been reprinted largely as they appear in the original volumes. Few changes have been made. Cross-referencing apparatus (asterisks, large and small capitals) has been removed. The introductory paragraph has been redesigned, while double columns and individual bibliographies have been omitted. Authors were asked for corrections of errors of fact and, happily, there have been only a few; these errors have been corrected.

Most of the biographies in this book appear in volumes 5 to 8, a series that is quite consistent in the presentation of style, place-names, and institutional names. Over the years, however, the *DCB* has changed its policies on such matters, two examples being the use of Upper Canada/Canada West or 'family compact'/Family Compact. It has been decided to let these minor inconsistencies stand.

The *Dictionary* has an elaborate set of policies regarding its editorial procedures. Readers wishing detailed information should consult the editorial notes which appear in the preliminary pages of every volume. It is worth repeating a few pertinent points. Persons have been entered under family name rather than title, pseudonym, popular name, nickname, or name in religion. Where possible the form of the surname is based on the signature, although contemporary usage is taken into account. Common variant spellings are included in parenthesis.

Where a signature was not available for a subject whose name began with Mc or Mac, the form Mac, followed by a capital letter, has been used. Married women have been entered under their maiden names. Names of indigenous peoples have presented a particular problem, since a person might be known by his/her own name (written in a variety of ways by people unfamiliar with native languages) and by a nickname or a baptismal name. Indian names have been used when they could be found, and, because it is impossible to establish original spellings, the form generally chosen is the one found in standard sources or the one linguists now regard as correct.

Place-names are generally given in the form used at the time of reference; where necessary, the modern name and/or the present name of the province, territory, state, or country in which the place is located have been included in parenthesis.

The wording, spelling, punctuation, and capitalization of original quotations are not altered unless it is necessary to do so for meaning, in which case the changes are made within square brackets.

As always, there are people who deserve mention for their contributions. Ian Montagnes, recently retired after many years with University of Toronto Press, broached the subject of *DCB* theme volumes early in 1991 with Ramsay Cook. After various discussions within the office, it was decided to pursue the matter further. In April 1991 Laura Macleod and I presented the idea to Peter Oliver of The Osgoode Society. He greeted it enthusiastically and suggested it to his board, which was equally supportive. Since then the indefatigable Marilyn MacFarlane of The Osgoode Society has flailed me unmercifully in her effort, as always, to ensure that the publication schedule was met. I owe her something and I am sure that it is thanks.

Thanks are due to Peter Oliver and the directors of The Osgoode Society for their support of this book, and, again, to Ian Montagnes and Laura Macleod of University of Toronto Press for their faith in the idea. *DCB* volumes are at heart collaborative efforts between the historical community that contributes biographies, the editors (at both the University of Toronto and Université Laval), and the translators. To the contributors whose work makes the project possible, I offer my thanks. Finally, the editorial standards of what H.V. Nelles once called the 'great cathedral to the biographical tradition' are among the highest in the world (I qualify the statement only out of concern that it might be considered less than objective were I to do otherwise). It is a privilege to be one of, and to work with, the members of that order which tends the cathedral.

To the *DCB*'s captain, Ramsay Cook, to Mary Bentley, and to Deborah Marshall, I offer particular thanks. In a volume such as this, it may not seem that the editorial staff of the *DCB* are directly engaged, and in a limited sense that it is true. But the quality of the entries in this volume owes as much to the editors (in both our Toronto and our Quebec City offices) as to the authors. As one who has worn both hats for this volume, I simply know it as a fact. My thanks go to Henri Pilon, Jane Graham, Stuart Sutherland, David Roberts, Susan Bélanger, and Phyllis Creighton in Toronto, to Jean Hamelin (the directeur adjoint), Michel Paquin, Huguette Filteau, Paulette Chiasson, Pierrette Desrosiers, and Réjean Banville in Quebec City, and to past members of the staff in both offices. The family of the *DCB* is a large one. Two former editors, now freelancers, have worked on this volume. Curtis Fahey edited the introduction and Elizabeth Hulse prepared the index. Both took on these assignments on short notice. I owe them my thanks. And finally, I wish to express my gratitude to the newest member of the *DCB* team, Peter G. White of Hollinger Inc., who is chairing the project's national fund-raising committee.

Several people read and commented upon the introduction. Peter Oliver pored over it as it inched its way towards conclusion. Paul Romney was everything one could wish for in an assessor. His remarks were as perceptive as they were constructive and supportive. I thank both with the usual proviso that neither is responsible for its remaining faults, errors, or omissions. Fortunately, the introduction has been my burden (a word that expresses my meaning exactly) and not my family's. On one recent occasion, however, I went back on a promise to take my son to a basketball game in order to squeeze in a few more hours' work at a critical juncture. Although not yet eleven, Robert negotiated a very generous compensation package for himself. There is therefore no need to thank him for his forbearance.

Robert L. Fraser
Hamilton, Ontario
July 1992

'All the privileges which Englishmen possess': Order, Rights, and Constitutionalism in Upper Canada

A Symbol

'An innocent man ... executed unjustly'
Michael Vincent, gallows address

'Bears, Wolves, Indians and Unbroken Forest' – this heading captured the gist of John Ryckman's recollections of the Hamilton area's early history. 'A hale, lively old gentleman of 82 winters,' he had ambled into the offices of the Hamilton *Spectator* on 30 September 1880, pulled up a chair, and reminisced with a reporter about the early days. For the most part, Ryckman, a justice of the peace of impeccable loyalist parentage, stuck to this and related topics. But one subheading ('Unpleasant Recollections') offered the newspaper's readers a more pungent slice of history – his memories of two executions. The first was the mass hanging in 1814 of War of 1812 traitors; the second was the execution of Michael Vincent, convicted in 1828 of the murder of his wife.

Hamilton, Upper Canada, 8 September 1828. The day was warm and sunny. By 10 a.m. a crowd had already formed around the still only partially constructed gallows. Three hours later, several thousand onlookers milled about in expectation of the day's event. A squadron of cavalry moved forward to hold the pressing throng at bay. Hawkers, in expectation of a lucrative day, mingled with the crowd peddling their wares. About 1:30 p.m., the appearance of a grim procession of local worthies signalled the beginning of the first public execution in Hamilton since the hangings for treason in 1814: the grand jury, the magistrates of the Gore District, and other leading men of Gore marched out from the court-house in double file. Minutes later, the convicted murderer, Michael Vincent, made his appearance accompanied by the district sheriff and a local minister, George Sheed. The crowd strained for a better view.

Most executions in Upper Canada offered spectators a gallows address by the condemned, usually contrite, felon exhorting them not to follow in his or her path.[1] Under strong and repeated pressure to conform to custom, Vincent consistently refused, steadfastly maintaining his innocence. Upon the scaffold, he asked permission to address the throng and the sheriff consented. The rope was adjusted around Vincent's neck; he gathered his thoughts and, 'in a firm voice,' declared: 'Gentlemen, you see before you an innocent man who is about to be executed unjustly – the witnesses against me have sworn falsely – I die innocent of the crime alledged [sic] against me – I declare before Almighty God, I am not guilty of the crime for which I am to suffer.' Sheed pressed him to recant and 'implored him to reflect on the consequences of dying with a falsehood on his lips.' Vincent, however, reiterated his innocence, this time as an oath before God. The clergyman then recited the Lord's Prayer. When he reached 'forgive us our trespasses,' the executioner let the trapdoor fall. As was often the case, the execution was bungled; the rope slipped under Vincent's chin, causing further suffering; he convulsed for about fifteen minutes before dying. His body was left hanging for an hour before being cut down and handed over to local surgeons for dissection.[2]

Public executions were intended as compelling symbols of the potency of the law and its administration, and were considered powerful deterrents to crime.[3] Michael Vincent's execution was certainly symbolic but the message derived from it was not altogether the intended one. It was beyond the ability of either crown officials or the judiciary to mould the public's response. Whether the grisly spectacle left the desired impression upon those who witnessed, heard, or read about it is not known. What is certain, however, is that the execution and, more important, the trial were both perceived and depicted by important reform-minded journalists, and others as well, as symbols – not of the impartiality of the judicial system – but rather of its failings and partiality. And it was this image that endured, not only in the journalists' accounts, but also in the minds of some witnesses. Fifty-two years after the event, the octogenarian John Ryckman, a magistrate himself, told the *Spectator*'s readers that he 'and many others were of opinion that he [Vincent] was innocent.'[4]

Why Ryckman believed Vincent's claim of innocence is not known. His reasons may have been connected to the disturbing suggestion expressed in some newspapers, such as Francis Collins's *Canadian Freeman*, that Vincent had lost his life probably as a result of a dramatic departure from judicial custom by the neophyte trial judge, Christopher Alexander Hagerman.

Hagerman's apparently stunning judicial novelty occurred during his address to the petit jury. Nearing the end of his summation, he observed that if the jurors agreed with Vincent's counsel, John Rolph, that Mrs Vincent had died during 'a fit,' they should acquit Vincent. Then, Hagerman boldly declared, 'I shall be always ready to share the responsibility with the jury ... my opinion is that the evidence is strongly against the man, and that you will see no possibility of returning a verdict of not guilty.'

Francis Collins reported that Rolph, 'seeing the Judge's charge so decidedly against the prisoner, with great humanity threw in a parley in favour of him.' Noting how 'irregular' it was 'to say any thing at this time,' Rolph was, none the less, impelled to do so because 'an unfortunate man's life was at stake.' The judge was 'impatient' and ordered counsel to be seated. Rolph, however, 'persisted' with his own deviation from customary behaviour, claiming that, 'from his knowledge of the [medical] profession' – Rolph was not only a leading member of the bar, but also an eminent medical practitioner – the evidence by the two doctors who had testified for the crown 'went to show that the deceased died of a fit.'

Hagerman dismissed this sally with the comment that his own 'opinion was quite the contrary, and the jury might give such weight as they pleased to their [Hagerman's and Rolph's] respective opinions.' After about an hour, the jury returned its verdict. Hagerman's position had won the day.[5] Three days later, Vincent was hanged.

Collins damned Hagerman, without reservation, for usurping the jury's role and thereby 'mis-construing the existing code with a view to increase its faults.'[6] Bartemas Ferguson, the determinedly moderate editor of a local Hamilton paper, the *Gore Balance*, also castigated Hagerman for his actions. A former critic of government in the late

1810s, Ferguson himself had stood before the courts and suffered during his subsequent incarceration. Although he had abandoned many of his earlier causes, he remained keenly interested in the administration of justice. Even in cases where the guilt of the accused was certain, the content of Hagerman's charge to the petit jury was, Ferguson thought, 'without example.'[7] Three years later, an unrelenting Collins reminded both his readers and Hagerman of the judge's responsibility for Vincent's execution: 'Let Mr. Hagerman remember, as a consoling thought when he lays his head upon his pillow, the charge that he delivered against an unhappy fellow who protested his innocence with his last breath.'[8] The image conveyed by this rhetoric was powerful. It arose from Vincent's claim to innocence from the moment of his arrest, and seems to have lasted for years after his execution.

The vaunted hallmarks of the British constitution and English justice had failed to protect the life of a man, possibly innocent. This course of events, in the mind of Francis Collins, was an indictment of the very system itself. Hagerman's place on the bench and his actions in Vincent's case illustrated the partiality that many believed undermined the rule of law in Upper Canada. The familiar nostrums regarding the superiority of British justice provided scant solace either to Vincent or to the system's critics. The trial had locked together in judicial combat the leading adversaries in the legal/constitutional/political battles that racked the province's political communities – Attorney General John Beverley Robinson had prosecuted the crown's case; John Rolph, a leading assemblyman and oppositionist, and one of the foremost members of the bar, had defended Vincent; and 'Kit' Hagerman, a bumptious Kingston lawyer, had presided on the bench. Within weeks of the trial, Rolph – recently re-elected to the House of Assembly in July 1828 – was planning a coordinated strategy for the reform-minded coalition of lawyers and politicians that included himself, the Baldwins (William Warren and Robert), and Marshall Spring Bidwell. The following year Robinson was elevated to the chief justiceship. Hagerman's appointment to the Court of King's Bench was not confirmed in England; he stepped down from the bench and became solicitor general.

The major figures in the Vincent case had all been party to various disputes during the 1820s (some of only several months' standing) concerning the alleged partiality of the legal system. The trial was another lost battle in a war waged both in the legislature and in courtrooms across Upper Canada.⁹ At no other point in this province's history has the judicial system been so embattled, so mired in controversy, so liable to the charges of partiality and maladministration, and so lacking in broad public legitimacy.¹⁰ And, more often than not, critics seized upon trials such as Vincent's both to prove and to assert their claims.

Loyalism and the Constitutional Context

>'Vive le Roi'
>*J.B. Robinson*

>'Making a due provision ... for that legal Aristocracy'
>*John Graves Simcoe*

How did Upper Canada reach this state? What explains the wars that raged around its political and legal institutions? Part of the answer can be found through an exploration of the colony's constitution, the aristocratic and hierarchical intentions that underlay it, and their subsequent defence by succeeding generations of political and administrative élites.

Paris, France, 24 August 1816. John Beverley Robinson, the young solicitor general of Upper Canada, walked in the gardens of the Tuileries palace. A crowd had gathered there hoping to catch a glimpse of the restored Bourbon monarch, Louis XVIII. Young Robinson, who as acting attorney general had prosecuted those charged with treason at the Ancaster Assizes in 1814, 'waited patiently among the rest.' When the king finally appeared at a window, 'hats were all taken off & I joined in the cry of "Vive le Roi."' ¹¹ Robinson was at a young age already prominent in his profession; he would become the most important legal and judicial figure in Upper Canadian history. The scene, as related in his diary, of him heartily cheering the apotheosis of the so-called *ancien régime*, a Bourbon monarch, evokes the purposes enshrined in the Constitutional Act of 1791. This statute gave Upper Canada its constitution, one that lasted fifty years. Although it is possible to exaggerate the significance of a youth caught up in the enthusiasm of the moment, Robinson's act embodies the monarchical and aristocratic faith of many members of the Upper Canadian élite and their commitment to a hierarchical social order.

The political traditions attached to the Constitutional Act were largely imported into the colony by the first lieutenant governor, John Graves Simcoe, and the administrators surrounding him such as Chief Justice William Osgoode. But the structure of the old regime was not easily realized in the wilderness of Upper Canada. The attempt to impose an aristocratic polity met with deep resistance from the outset of settlement. The political faith of the loyalists was hostile to hierarchy, the so-called late loyalists lacked even the attachment to monarchy that characterized their namesakes, and there was little in the subsequent waves of immigration to alter this attitude. The process of settlement in an uncleared land lacking even the basic rudiments of internal communication would, in itself, have presented an almost insurmountable obstacle to the planting of the old regime in Upper Canada. Emigrants came from different societies at different times. Only rarely was anything resembling an intact and hierarchical social structure imported. Moreover, in England aristocracy had its economic basis in large landed estates maintained by a tenant class. In Upper Canada land was plentiful and cheap, if not free. The economic conditions for aristocracy were altogether lacking, there was no established social structure, and the closest thing to a native political tradition was a disdain for monopoly, political or otherwise, which was evinced by most settlers, loyalist or otherwise, from the beginning.

The foremost historian of the political culture of British North America, S.F. Wise, perceived in the colonial origins of Canadian society an underlying conservative (a word, incidentally, unknown in the colony before 1828 and rarely used before 1836) consensus, a tradition informing the Canadian political fabric to the present. Central to Wise's thesis was the hothouse effect of Upper Canada's geography and demographics upon its political culture. Because of the colony's close geographical proximity to the United States, its political tradition was formed, he suggested, by the convergence of 'two streams of conservatism': 'One that was brought by the Loyalist founders of the colony: an emotional compound of loyalty to King and Empire, antagonism to the United States, and an acute, if partisan sense of recent history. To the conservatism of the émigré was joined another, more sophisticated viewpoint, first brought by Simcoe and his entourage, and crystallized in the Constitutional Act of 1791: the Toryism of late eighteenth century England.'[12]

This perceptive account delineates the shadings within the 'spectrum' of loyalist political opinion and recognizes a common and 'distinctively American attitude towards government and authority.' But on the essential point, Wise was adamant; the muted tones of American liberalism notwithstanding, the political language of loyalism was conservative. Most loyalists were, he thought, inclined to the government side and 'the liberal strain was rapidly subordinated to the values of the official political culture.' At the heart of this ethos were 'loyalty, order, stability.'[13]

For anyone who has read the loyalists' claims for compensation (from the British government) or their later petitions for free land grants (from the Upper Canadian Executive Council), there is a familiar, if undistinguished, pattern of language. Most loyalists were small farmers, often semi-literate, whose explanation of their decision to risk life, property, and family during the American revolution is probably subsumed in Nathaniel Pettit's declaration of 'his Sturdey Attachment To his most Gratious majestye and the british Constitution.'[14] The idea of loyalty to the crown is straightforward enough. It is possible, however, that this loyalty was sustained more by emotional attachment than by constitutional preference. What a man such as Pettit meant by the 'british Constitution' is not entirely clear.

Other loyalists were more illuminating. In January 1784 a group of Associated Loyalists from New York petitioned the governor of Quebec, Frederick Haldimand:

In as much as the said Associated Companies have for years past nobly contended for the support of that Constitution or Form of Government under which they have long Enjoyed Happiness, & for which they have at last sacrificed their All ... when they arrived at the Place destined for their Settlement would [Haldimand] be Pleased to Establish among them, a Form of Government as nearly similar to that which they Enjoyed in the Province of New York in the year of 1763.[15]

Here was a specific loyalist constitutional model taken neither from theory nor from English example but from the experience of pre-revolutionary provincial New York.

In the summer of 1784 parties of loyalists moved out of their refugee camps in the province of Quebec to the virtually uninhabited region of western Quebec (present-day southern Ontario).[16] Settling primarily in the areas of Cornwall and Kingston (then known as New Johnstown and Cataraqui), they were not content to live under the laws and institutions of Quebec. In 1785 loyalist leaders petitioned the king to the effect that: 'They were born British Subjects, and have ever been accustomed to the Government and Laws of England. It was to restore that Government, and to be restored to those Laws, for which from Husbandmen they became Soldiers.'[17] They wanted the 'Establishment of a liberal System of Tenure, Law, and Government in this new Settlement,' by which they meant British (to be more exact, English) rather than French institutions and civil law. Two years later, another loyalist petition urged the government, yet again, to bestow upon them the 'blessings of the British Constitution.'[18] By this phrase, they meant primarily that 'their Lands [be] granted according to English tenures' rather than French seigneurial tenure. In addition, they asked for assistance for the churches of Scotland and England, and help in establishing schools and in other matters relating mainly to local improvement.

The general thrust of loyalist constitutional concern, then, could be met by the simple introduction of English land tenure, civil law, and representative government. To the extent that it can be measured, loyalist sentiment had little to say about the desirability of an aristocratic hierarchy. If anything, the earliest manifestations of loyalist sentiment on this question were less than prepossessing. For instance, in the 1780s an aggrieved land surveyor, Patrick McNiff, was able to exploit discontents which erupted in the New Johnston area between 'Gentlemen officers enjoying half-pay from the Crown, and the Comonality.'[19] When in 1788 the government of Quebec erected four new administrative districts in the western part of the province, it was welcomed as a gesture in the loyalists' direction. Three years later, the establishment of the western portion as a separate colony with its own constitution satisfied general expectations with respect to separation from Quebec and its civil law. But with respect to their constitutional aspirations, the loyalists got something they had not bargained for.

The Canada or Constitutional Act of 1791 gave the new province of Upper Canada a constitution forged in the fires of English counter-revolutionary hopes. The French revolution, after all, was only two years old and England was its leading antagonist. The model for the act was not the New York colony in 1763; rather it was England, and the constitution conferred was the so-called mixed or balanced constitution composed of the three classical forms of polity: monarchy, aristocracy, and democracy, represented respectively by a lieutenant governor, an appointed legislative council, and an elected legislative assembly. These elements brought together within a system of checks and balances would, it was believed, prevent the natural tendency of political regimes to degenerate into their unconstitutional forms: tyranny, oligarchy, and anarchy. A proper aristocratic emphasis would allow the newly erected colonies to hold the democratic element of the constitution in check as had not been the case in colonies such as New York prior to the other revolution, the American one.

From a continental European perspective, the hallmark of this uniquely English constitutional arrangement was liberty, yet in an 'age of democratic revolution' the Constitutional Act, with its emphasis on monarchical and aristocratic elements, was counter-revolutionary. Wise insisted on the emotional impact of loyalism and the political tendencies that flowed from it. There is good reason, however, to emphasize the American aspect of loyalism in Upper Canada and its sustained impact. As it turned out, not all loyalists voted on the government side.[20] The strength of the counter-revolutionary experiment derived almost exclusively from the Constitutional Act. The loyalist experience may have had at its core a concern for order and stability but there was no intrinsic constitutional preference embodied in it. Powerful, non-loyalist merchants such as Robert Hamilton of Queenston were just as insistent upon the necessity of order and far more specific, in political terms, about its structure.[21]

Successive adherents of the counter-revolutionary tradition, whether English officeholders such as Chief Justice Osgoode or native-born administrators and politicians such as Robinson, breathed fire and force into the Constitutional Act and struggled consciously against hostile social reality to maintain it; for without it, there was no hope for what John Macaulay of Kingston referred to in 1850 as a 'government of gentlemen.'[22] Crucial to this creed and to the constitution's ultimate success was aristocracy. Lieutenant Governor John Graves Simcoe took measures, as he expressed it, for 'making a due provision of Power for that legal Aristocracy which the Experience of Ages has proved necessary to the Ballance and Permanency of her [Great Britain's] inestimable form of Government.'[23] To that end, he established lieutenants of counties (modelled on English practice) and conferred the office upon those 'who seem most respectable ... for their property, Loyalty, Abilities, and Discretion ... and who from a Combination of such Possessions and Qualities acquire that weight, respect, and public confidence which renders them the natural support of Constitutional Authority.'[24] But county lieutenants such as Joel Stone of

xxx 'All the privileges which Englishmen possess'

Gananoque were little more than semi-literate country bumpkins compared with their English equivalents.[25]

The undercurrent of popular animus against so-called 'noble' pretensions, first manifest in Patrick McNiff's machinations in the 1780s, erupted again. This time it was at the western end of the province. François Baby, a member of an old, wealthy, and powerful family, and an exemplar of a Roman Catholic, French-Canadian gentleman, protested to Simcoe. It seems that the congregation of Notre-Dame-de-l'Assomption bridled at his claim to a 'place of honour' – a pew granted him (in the manner of the French regime) as deputy lieutenant of the county. The congregation went so far as to have the 'distinctive pew' removed.[26]

The popular sentiment evident in the McNiff and Baby episodes would be a recurrent theme. Isaac Swayze, a loyalist of unsavoury repute, boasted in 1800 that he had been elected to the House of Assembly in 1792 by the 'farmers and general classes' who regarded him as their champion rather than the local 'nobles.'[27] Although the experiment with county lieutenancies was of brief duration – barely surviving the War of 1812 – it, like Robinson's cheer at the Tuileries in 1816, captured the essence of the counter-revolutionary tradition in Upper Canada, the attempt to found a traditional hierarchical polity, characteristic of both England and Europe in the early modern period, which revolution had forestalled in the Thirteen Colonies and destroyed in France.

In point of fact, the assumptions underlying the Constitutional Act were as old as Aristotle's *Politics*.[28] For the ancients, natural inequality was an invariant condition of human nature and the foundation for political inequality. The counter-revolutionary tradition further secured subordination by blessing it with the stamp of providential design and emphasizing the symbiotic relationship between throne and altar, sceptre and mitre.[29] The Constitutional Act also provided for an established church, the Church of England. As Robinson later expressed it, 'Religion is the only secure basis on which civil authority can rest.'[30] Above all, the order of society required the maintenance of a graded social structure and that structure's continuance was inseparable from aristocracy. The anomaly of the Upper Canadian situation was the want of an aristocracy. In the 1790s (and for several decades afterwards) the colony lacked a settled province-wide, as opposed to local or regional, social structure of any sort.[31] As the social order took shape, however, it became all too clear to Robinson, for instance, that the great experiment had been an abject failure. He observed in the late 1830s that recent English electoral reforms had occurred in spite of 'the vast patronage of Government ... with all the influence of ancient and venerable institutions, and the traditionary respect for rank and family – with all the substantial power of wealth, and the control of numerous landlords over a grateful tenantry.' If the combined power of these institutions could not frustrate democratic forces in England, then how would Upper Canada fare with, as Robinson put it, 'none of these counteracting checks.'[32]

The Constitutional Act established a political basis for an aristocracy in the appointed legislative council and made due provision for hereditary titles, although in the latter case little came of it. But in England the House of Lords represented the political, economic, and social reality of the aristocracy; indeed, the entire political structure including the House of Commons was highly restrictive and represented little more than John Macaulay's 'gentlemen.' The property limitations on the franchise ensured that representation in the House of Commons was largely confined to them.

In the absence of an indigenous hierarchy, proponents of church and state such as Robinson regarded the Legislative Council as the colony's best, if not only, hope. Any extension of the elective principle to the council would destroy it. Without gentlemen in the council, society would be deprived of countervailing institutions to democracy. The elective principle would preclude the crown 'from appointing a gentleman of high character, of large property, and of superior information' to the council.[33] Only the royal prerogative over council appointments maintained intact would provide a political role in society for the 'most worthy, intelligent, loyal, and opulent' inhabitants of the province.[34] Robinson argued that a reconstructed council with its power diminished would destroy its basis for independence. It was precisely because the council was not hereditary that the crown prerogative was vital. The Constitutional Act and the English constitutional example demanded the separation of the upper branch of parliament from the lower, as did – according to Robinson – the nature of monarchical government.[35]

Although there were restrictions upon the franchise in Upper Canada and even greater restrictions in other colonies such as New Brunswick, the availability of abundant, cheap land ensured a much more 'extensive' use of the franchise than in England.[36] The framers of the Constitutional Act had expected it to bring political stability to the

xxxii 'All the privileges which Englishmen possess'

Canadas and to avoid the political turbulence which, they thought, had led to the American revolution. But in Upper Canada, regardless of the exact percentage of political participation, the extent of the franchise, the pluralistic and local nature of colonial society, the absence of an aristocracy, the lack of sufficient executive-controlled patronage to manage the Legislative Assembly, and the internecine conflict between several political traditions rendered the political structure unworkable and, hence, unstable. It would take over fifty years to work out a new contractual basis for political stability, an essentially middle-class stability that would overturn the Constitutional Act and everything it represented and put into place a new political arrangement recognizing the essential minimum requirements of British North American pluralism – responsible government (meaning the responsibility of the executive to the assembly), the separation of church and state, and the separation of the judiciary from the executive and legislative functions of government.

Order, Hierarchy, and the Mythology of British Constitutionalism

> 'Order is heavens first law'
> J.B. Robinson

> 'One is formed to rule[,] another to obey'
> John Strachan

> 'Justice, under the British Constitution, confers more privileges ., than any system of Government the world has ever devised'
> Robert Stanton

In recent years Upper Canadian historians have focused on the attempts by early élites to foster myths surrounding the loyalists and the role of the militia in the War of 1812 in their collective search for a glue to hold together Upper Canadian society.[37] The loyalist myth, like that of the militia, enjoyed its greatest popularity in the mid and late nineteenth century. Astute participants in the life of early Upper Canada, such as John Strachan, the Church of England rector of York (Toronto), saw the potential in such myths. For instance, in 1813 Strachan wrote a short life of a British army officer, Cecil Bisshopp, recently killed during a raid upon an American fort. The raiding party consisted of British regulars, Upper Canadian militia, and natives.

Strachan had hopes of turning Bisshopp's death to political favour, but little came of it.³⁸ Loyalism and the militia ultimately failed to justify the rule of élites before the Act of Union. Their real appeal was to a later age.

A more compelling myth with much deeper roots both in Upper Canadian society and in the Anglo-American political inheritance was British constitutionalism and the rule of law. This myth had great appeal to officialdom, the judiciary, and their supporters. It proffered a constitution that was itself the legacy of, and sanctioned by, the ages; it boasted of individual rights, it enshrined the language of liberty, it assured the equality of all subjects before the law, and it trumpeted the Solomon-like role of the judiciary as the impartial guardian of the constitution and its benefits.

One of the first to give public expression to the myth was Strachan. In 1810 he penned a long pamphlet, ostensibly on the virtuous character of King George III. It was, as his former student Robinson observed, an attempt 'to make the disaffected among us loyal and contented.'³⁹ Although it met with 'little regard,' it was a notable attempt to defend the constitution from the 'wicked spirit of party.'⁴⁰ The body of the text consisted of adulatory pap about the character of the king and the royal family, whereas the footnotes contained incisive comments about the province's political institutions and recent history. Strachan's intended readership is uncertain but it is likely he had taken aim at the doubtful sympathies of a significant segment of the loyalists. Loyalist assemblymen such as Thomas Dorland, David McGregor Rogers, Ralph Clench, Peter Howard, and Ebenezer Washburn had figured at various times in the opposition to Lieutenant Governor Francis Gore.⁴¹ In the columns of Joseph Willcocks's *Upper Canadian Guardian*, such prominent loyalist families as the Secords of Niagara had disputed the administration's interpretation of loyalism, an interpretation that robbed it of its oppositionist content.⁴²

Strachan's task was to delineate the true meaning of liberty in relation to the constitution, a constitution that secured both liberty and property to all British subjects. It is not surprising that he thought liberty was best secured by the restraints of law, tradition, custom, religious education, and duty.⁴³ In a revolutionary age Britain alone had hallowed liberty in its constitution, a constitution that had received the approbation of the ages. He concluded that, guarded by a magnanimous king in the due exercise of his monarchical prerogative, the British nation was the freest on earth, sure in its property and rights.⁴⁴ The rallying standard was the constitution. 'It is not,' Strachan wrote, 'the work of a day; it rests upon old and tried foundations, the more durable, because visionary empiricks have not been allowed to touch them. No fine spun theories of metaphysicians, which promise much and end in misery, have shared in its formation; such men may destroy, but they can never build. All the privileges which Englishmen possess are ours.'⁴⁵ Abstract rights could never provide what the British constitution had already delivered to Britons, and Upper Canada in its constitution possessed Britain's constitution. All that was needed was to protect it from its enemies and to guard the crown's prerogative. That sense was never lost. As late as 1840, Robinson, then chief justice, claimed publicly that Upper Canada possessed a 'constitution and laws better calculated than those of any other country to secure the best interests and promote the happiness of the human race.'⁴⁶

In 1822 Mr Justice William Campbell addressed the grand jury of the Home District on the nature of the judicial trust. He noted that 'of all human concerns, the task of administering Justice between man and man, and the power of deciding on the rights, the liberties, the reputation, and even the lives of our fellow subjects, is the most important and at the same time the most honorable trust that can be confided to any man or set of men, &c that the upright and impartial discharge of it, is the greatest benefit that can be conferred on society.' If equality did not exist in nature and could not exist in society, it could, and did, exist before the law.⁴⁷ Four years later, Chief Justice Campbell proclaimed that 'our free constitution does not permit that the life, liberty, or reputation of any subject should be put in jeopardy, on surmise, or on slight or doubtful evidence.'⁴⁸ His utterance on this occasion was a commonplace of judicial charges in Upper Canada. Indeed, these assumptions about the British constitution and the rule of law had deep roots, not only among the Upper Canadian populace but also in Anglo-American political/constitutional thought.

Robert Stanton, publisher of the *U.E. Loyalist*, a paper strongly supportive of the administration in Upper Canada, noted in an 1826 editorial that the 'administration of Justice, under the British Constitution, confers more privileges upon us as a people, than any system of Government the world has ever devised.'⁴⁹ Laudatory echoes of this sentiment were ubiquitous. The following year, in his charge to the grand jury of the Home District, Campbell described trial by jury as the 'Bulwark of British liberty' and the 'Palladium of the British

Constitution.' It was, he thought, 'an Institution admirable in itself, and the best calculated for the preservation of liberty, and the administration of Justice that ever was devised by the wit of man.'[50]

The language of constitutionalism cut across several political traditions, and the judges of the Court of King's Bench had ample opportunity on their circuits to deliver their version with both frequency and force. Through charges to district grand juries, which were often published in local newspapers, the judges had an ideal platform to underscore the salient features of this myth: the superiority of the British constitution and laws above all others, the constitutional enshrinement of civil and religious rights, the basis for those rights in the protection of property, the elevation of the laws and the constitution above arbitrary power, constitutional provision for the right of all to have a voice in the making of the laws, equality before the laws, and, finally, the impartial administration of the law. On these points, the strongest case could be, and was, made from the bench and elsewhere for the preservation of the Constitution of 1791, particularly its provision for appointed councils, and the maintenance of the constitutional *status quo*. That it failed to thwart the criticisms and agitation of the 1820s, or indeed of earlier periods, is testimony to even more compelling elements of the same mythology, such as the concern for the separation of the judicial from the legislative and executive functions of government, the sensitivity to infringements of rights that naturally resulted from the conjunction of those interests, and the destruction of justice's cherished impartiality by systematic abuse.

For men such as John Beverley Robinson and his mentor, John Strachan, the natural order of society was unequal, hierarchical, and aristocratic. That order was protected and sanctified by the British constitution, the rule of law, and the protection of property. Strachan once dismissed the observation of the French political commentator Alexis de Tocqueville concerning the inevitable triumph of democracy over aristocratic states as a fanciful 'theory that there is an irresistible tendency among mankind to Democracy & equality of condition.'[51] He characterized the 'doctrine of primitive equality' as a radical notion that 'never did and never can exist[,] for the distinctions of Society ... are essential portions of the dispensations of Providence.'[52] Equality was possible spiritually but 'not an equality of ability state or condition.'[53]

In 1842 John Strachan told a friend that his former pupil Robinson was 'wiser than I am – to him I give up in most things, but to no other.'[54] Of all of Strachan's students who held office during the Upper Canadian period, Robinson was easily the most important and probably the brightest. By the 1830s – at the very latest – the percipient Robinson was all too aware that Upper Canada lacked, and would never possess, the native aristocracy and landed class which were essential to the hopes for hierarchy expressed in the Constitutional Act. Given the ever-present threats to the colony, both from without – as the experience of the War of 1812 had demonstrated so vividly – and from within – another striking manifestation of the wartime experience – Robinson and others increasingly pinned their hopes not on a nascent social structure but on the Constitutional Act and its provision for an appointed legislative council, and on the rule of law, the security of private property, the magistracy, and the legal profession. These institutions provided the best, and seemingly the only, defence of order in Upper Canada, without which no social blessing could be enjoyed. After becoming chief justice of the Court of King's Bench in 1829, Robinson had ample opportunity to expound on such favourite themes in his charges to district grand juries.

'Order,' he once intoned, 'is heavens first law.' Moreover, there was a direct relationship between order and social structure. 'Among the most powerful securities for the maintenance of order in a community,' he declared, 'is the good conduct of those, to whom the great body of the people naturally look up to, for advice and example.'

It is happy for such persons, & for others, when this influence is beneficially exerted, and ... they are found supporting the best interests of society by showing a ready & implicit obedience to the laws of the land, & by a correct observance of their relative duties – It would be a waste of words, if I were to enlarge upon the advantage ... the necessity of maintaining the authority of the law, in its full force, and upon all occasions – Whatever earthly good we may choose most to value, we can have no satisfactory enjoyment of it, if over life, or over personal freedom, over property or over reputation we held only the arbitrary pleasure of any individual, or of any number of persons – There can exist no liberty – at least no secure rational liberty except under the protection of law – & the liberty of the people in any Country is but a name without the substance, from the moment that the authority of the Law ceases to be supreme – ... Submission to the laws must, where freedom is valued, be prompt & unqualified – That submission need not proceed from the conviction that, the laws in force are absolutely perfect nor does it imply a servility in the slightest degree unbecoming.[55]

'Order, stability, peace [and] security' constituted 'the great blessings of social existence.'[56] If Wise is right about the degree to which the loyalist ethos was imbued with the concern for order and stability, then the myth of the rule of law and British constitutionalism could serve as the primary means of attaching loyalists to that order.

Disorder had its roots in human nature. This was the visible 'meaning' of the moral world. Human beings were tainted by the corruption of original sin and the subsequent fall from grace. Early religious and moral instruction and the union of church and state provided the first great supports of society against the natural tendencies of human nature. Society was further buttressed against disorder by the inequality of the natural social order which limited power to those fit to rule. In a society such as Upper Canada where the wealthy and well born were few in number, the rule and force of law was critical, at times, to deter or to restrain human nature.[57] As the colony became more populous and complex, the problem of social structure would be exacerbated. Then, more direct and drastic forms of social control such as police forces would become necessary to ensure order.[58]

In the meantime, however, provision for the maintenance of order within the colony fell upon a middle ground of custom, habit, and tradition which lay between aristocracy and hierarchy on the one hand and police forces on the other. Without the 'Counteracting influence of an ancient Aristocracy, of a great landed interest or even of a wealthy agricultural class,' there was, Robinson thought, 'little in short but the presumed good sense, and good feeling of an uneducated multitude, (which may be too much tempted) to stand between almost universal suffrage and those institutions, which proudly and happily distinguish Britons from the subjects of other monarchies, and no less so, from the Citizens of that Great Republic [the United States].'[59]

The appeal to the good sense of the uneducated multitude depended not upon its rationality but rather upon impressions formed by customs and traditions which inculcated order through example and influence. Here (after religious instruction) the leadership provided by gentlemen, society's social superiors, was vital.[60] As Robinson put it:

xxxviii 'All the privileges which Englishmen possess'

Among the most powerful securities for the maintenance of order in a Community, is the good conduct of those, to whom the great body of the people naturally look up, for advice and example ... it will always be found that a very considerable influence attaches itself to those who possess the advantages of education, and of superior natural intelligence, and of wealth, and of respectable stations in society, whether arising from public employment, or, from the exercise of the liberal professions.[61]

The 'less reasonable & respecting will be improved,' Robinson argued, 'by their [gentlemen's] example.' Gentlemen, or the *'regularly bred'* as he once called them,[62] were those 'possessed of that degree of intelligence, respectability, & property which naturally confers upon them a salutary influence in Society.'[63] Order depended upon their role in society and their rule over it.

By and large, it was assumed that the unequal possession of property conferred upon its owners influence, standing, independence, and a stake in society. During a discussion in the legislature about the selection of grand jurors, Christopher Hagerman argued that they should be 'taken from the number of persons of the greatest figure and standing in the country ... such are more likely to be obtained ... from among those persons possessed of the greater amount of property.'[64] Thus, the rule of gentlemen was at one with the possession of property.

If property was essential to the order of society, it was secured by the British constitution and, in Upper Canada, by the imperial connection and the Constitutional Act. Robinson declared with satisfaction in 1834 that Upper Canadians 'live in the enjoyment of a system of Criminal law, of Jurisprudence of what we may say with truth that none more just or rational has yet been produced by the wisdom of mankind – the general principles and the leading [illegible word] which govern its administration have become venerable from antiquity, having received the sanction & approbation of ages.' The chief justice further remarked that the 1833 reform of the criminal laws of the province had 'relieved' 'this system ... from the reproach of an apparently indiscriminate severity in awarding Capital punishments.' 'It is most satisfactory,' he reported, 'to find that the security of life & property does not appear to be diminished by withdrawing the terror of an ignominious death.'[65] Robinson noted further that, 'in respect' to capital punishment, few 'were ... so punished.' As for the Constitutional Act, 'That statute was framed in a wise spirit of adherence to the well established principles of British government. It discovers no distrust of the sufficiency of British institutions for protecting the liberties and promoting the happiness of the people. I know not what deviation from it is likely to be found an improvement.'[66]

If, for these reasons – the protection of liberty and happiness – the constitution was inviolable, then property was the bulwark of constitutional liberty. Strachan was explicit on the point:

Does any person doubt whether the British be the freest nation on earth, let him tell me where property and its rights are so well protected. This is the life and soul of liberty. What shall oppression seize when property is secure? Even a tyrant will not be wicked for nothing; but the motives and objects are removed, and the seed of oppression destroyed, when property is safe. By this, life and liberty are rendered sacred.[67]

The British constitution enshrined the rule of law as paramount over the will of men. To be governed by laws, not by men, and to have a voice in the making of those laws were recurrent themes in Robinson's charges: 'To be governed by Laws, and not by the arbitrary will of any man or number of men, & to have the privilege of choosing those who are to have a voice in making the laws are the distinctions of a free people.'[68] The glory of the constitution and the laws lay not only in the security afforded property, life, and liberty. Equality of rank, station, and condition may have been radical will-o'-the-wisps, but equality before the law was not. It was a feature of the constitution and a central aspect of its mythology.

In one of his earliest charges, Robinson emphasized that 'we have ... laws which know no distinction either in principle, or practice, between the rich & the poor – laws to which no man can be afraid to appeal, and which in regard to the protection of the person ... are accessible to the most indigent, as they are indeed to all without cost.'[69] The only distinction before the law, he once commented, was 'between those who observe the laws of the land & those who violate them.'[70] There was simply 'no Country, where the laws are more *just* in principle, or more *mild* in their *actual administration*, none in which the innocent are more effectually & certainly protected, in which the distinction between the rich & the poor, the powerful & the humble has less weight in the scale of Justice – I need not have said *less* weight, for I should not be warranted in conceding that it *has any*.'[71]

xl 'All the privileges which Englishmen possess'

The administration of justice was the foundation of the 'security' of both individuals and society. Moreover, it depended 'wholly upon the supremacy of the Laws; upon maintenance of the social system in such a state that no man ... be afraid to claim the protection of the law of the land, or shall fail to find it honestly & fearlessly enforced to maintain his rights.'[72] No power 'above the law' could be tolerated. Such a constitutional arrangement could be ensured only by taking 'scrupulous care that the whole population shall be brought up in the constant & habitual submission to the civil authority.'[73] The guarantee of that submission was the commonly held belief that all stand before the law 'upon an equal footing.' And the 'permanent tranquility of the Country ... can hardly be seriously endangered so long as a general confidence exists in the unprejudiced and impartial dispensation of Justice.'[74]

The Rise of Lawyers

'Lawyers must ... become the most powerful profession'
John Strachan

'The gentlemen who composed the bar ... were men of learning, honour, and inviolable integrity'
W.W. Baldwin

Irish-born and trained in medicine at the University of Edinburgh, William Warren Baldwin arrived in Upper Canada in 1799 ready to make his way in the new world. He settled on a farm in Clarke Township with his father, but life in the backwoods was not all that he wished, either professionally or socially. He moved to York in 1802; medicine, however, was not a path to preferment. That same year, he advertised the opening of a classical school. The real change in his fortunes came the following year when he became an attorney and was admitted to the bar. This self-taught young man – he had borrowed a set of Sir William Blackstone's *Commentaries on the laws of England* – had found a profession worthy of his ambition and had gained special entrance to it. Within three years, he garnered the first of several government legal positions. His practice grew steadily, even spectacularly. By 1819 he was clearing £600 per annum from his practice alone. The following year, he had a partner and three articling clerks, and was beginning the second of his four terms as treasurer of the Law Society of Upper Canada. William Warren Baldwin the lawyer had most definitely arrived.[75]

Baldwin had chosen wisely. In a colony whose population was growing steadily, York was, and would remain, the largest town. Moreover, as J.K. Johnson has demonstrated in his study of the members of the House of Assembly, law provided the 'best possible background for a wide range of jobs.' Johnson found that, of the forty-seven lawyers who sat in the assembly during the Upper Canadian period, more than 74 per cent held one or more government offices. Law offered, by far, the highest overlap with government preferment of any profession.[76]

When the first district courts of common pleas were established in 1788, there were only two lawyers with legal training in the province. Others practised but without the benefit of training.[77] There were certain advantages to the courts of common pleas located in each district. They offered suitors a comfortable mixture of tolerance for both English and French civil law; they were decentralized and able to meet many local needs, particularly close proximity; and certain judges such as Richard Cartwright exhibited a preference for the interests of justice over the prerequisites of procedure (at least insofar as justice served the interests of large merchants). None the less, there were complaints. For one, the judges were too closely identified with the emerging mercantile class of men. After the establishment of the new province in 1791, officials such as Lieutenant Governor Simcoe and Chief Justice Osgoode were determined to reorganize the colony's legal structure on English models.[78]

Between 1792 and 1794, Simcoe and Osgoode (through executive and legislative initiative – Osgoode, as chief justice, was president of the Executive Council and speaker of the Legislative Council) overhauled the administration of justice in Upper Canada. The essentials of the new order were the reception of English law in matters of property and civil rights (with the exception of the poor and ecclesiastical laws), the introduction of trial by jury, and the establishment of courts of request (organized on a district basis) to handle debt in matters not exceeding 40s. Other acts set up district courts to handle sums above 40s. but less than £15, as well as a court of probate and district surrogate courts.

The centrepiece of judicial reform was Osgoode's so-called Judicature Act of 1794 instituting the Court of King's Bench, which consisted of a chief justice and two puisne justices. The old district courts of common pleas were replaced by King's Bench as the single superior court of both criminal and civil jurisdiction for the whole province. There was no provision for a court of chancery until late in the Upper Canadian period (1837); before then, chancery cases were administered by the master in chancery. Justices of King's Bench travelled on several circuits a year hearing cases in the districts under commissions of assize and nisi prius (for civil cases), and of oyer and terminer and general gaol delivery (for criminal cases).[79]

Within the space of two years, the administration of justice was reorganized upon English models using, for the most part, English forms and procedures. Moreover, its management had been centralized at the capital, York, in the hands of crown officials consisting of the attorney general, the solicitor general, and their tiny administrative staffs, and the justices of King's Bench and their small staff (superintended by the clerk of the crown and the common pleas). These changes erected a significant district legal structure and established an important area for the exercise of the crown's control of patronage in local matters. Just as critical, this patronage was beyond the control or suasion of the assembly. The list of local appointments relating to the administration of justice included: district court judges, surrogate court judges, clerks of the peace (who handled the administration of the district courts of quarter sessions), sheriffs (who were responsible for grand juries, jails, writs of the local courts, and the execution of sentences), and magistrates. The justices of the peace sitting in general courts of quarter sessions of the peace acted as an inferior court of first instance in cases of petty crime (usually drunkenness and minor assault and battery); in addition, they performed an equally important function, that of providing municipal government.[80]

Four short, but crucial, points need to be made about these changes. First, in a manner somewhat similar to that of the Constitutional Act, significant English models were transplanted to a colonial setting.[81] Secondly, there was bitter yet percipient reaction to their imposition, particularly to the Judicature Act, from Richard Cartwright (a loyalist merchant and legislative councillor) and Robert Hamilton (a merchant and legislative councillor). They objected basically to the inherent complexity and centralization of the so-called reforms, their inappropriateness, as it were, to the conditions of a young colony.[82] (It would not be the last time that this charge was voiced; Cartwright and Hamilton were, possibly, slightly more prescient and certainly more self-interested than most.[83]) Thirdly, the new legislation gave rise to a substantial number (by comparison with what had preceded it) of crown appointments within each district. Fourthly, the new edifice could not possibly be managed or maintained without the development of a professional class of lawyers.

The necessity of the latter was recognized in a 1794 act authorizing the lieutenant governor to 'licence practitioners in the law.'[84] The point was to alleviate immediately the paucity of lawyers. Three years later, the legislature passed an act establishing the Law Society of Upper Canada, an act that among other things introduced the distinction between barristers and attorneys, and allowed the new body to draft rules for its own governance.[85] A further act was passed in 1803 to empower the lieutenant governor, once again, to 'licence practitioners in the law.'[86] W.W. Baldwin was licensed under this act, an act which was justified by the belief that 'unless the number [of lawyers] can be speedily increased, justice will in many places be with great difficulty administered.'[87] The colony's population in 1806 was approximately 46,000. The number of attorneys admitted by 1810 was thirty-five, while the number of barristers enrolled was forty-two (almost all attorneys were barristers as well).[88]

The importance of the legal profession, reflected in W.W. Baldwin's stature by 1821, was recognized early in the 1820s by changes to the 1797 act. In 1821 Attorney General John Beverley Robinson and Archibald McLean introduced a bill in the assembly to incorporate the Law Society. The purpose, according to Robinson, 'was principally to prevent persons from Great Britain and Ireland practicing in this Province, without conforming to the rules of the Law Society ... and to enable the Society as a body corporate, to hold a [piece of] land for the erection of a hall, and other buildings for the use of the Society.' The rules deemed that a student-at-law spend five years serving with an attorney, pay £10 on being bound, and £20 on being admitted to the books of the Law Society. W.W. Baldwin was 'favorable to the general provisions,' noting that practitioners from Great Britain and Ireland 'were generally of good education and talents, and could not fail to be an acquisition to the country.' If they met the provisions of the bill, they should be admitted.[89]

Others would not support it. The bill was publicly attacked in John Carey's *York Observer*, and assemblymen of independent and critical mind had difficulty with several aspects of the measure, such as its awarding of potentially exclusionary powers to the Law Society, its giving the society the right to set fees, and its omitting a clause limiting how much the society could raise to buy land and erect a building. Charles Jones,[90] for instance, a Brockville merchant irritated by the imposition of martial law during the War of 1812, was determined to define by statute the Law Society's power to set fees and to determine who should be allowed admittance. What would stop it, he suggested, from charging students-at-law £10,000, thus preventing persons 'from coming forward at all.' As he said, he 'felt suspicious.' Jonas Jones,[91] a lawyer and a friend and classmate of Robinson, deemed his brother Charles's arguments 'ridiculous.' Even were the Law Society to draft 'an improper rule' of that sort, the Court of King's Bench would 'not allow it.'

Charles Jones, however, remained unconvinced. He wanted the Law Society to be 'respectable but he would keep them under the laws,' the justices of King's Bench notwithstanding. 'To give this power to such a society of men was dangerous.' In spite of the reassurances of the attorney general that everything was 'correct and proper,' Jones reiterated the major thrust of his opposition – that the Law Society 'should be governed by law' and that 'this bill did not sufficiently explain their [the society's] privileges.' The assembly, he thought, 'should provide against every contingency, and define the power of the Society so that they should not demand unreasonable terms.' Jones even suggested that, because the present Law Society was so small in numbers and most of its members were friends, it might 'exclude all others' by setting high fees for entry and admission. Christopher Hagerman was simply incredulous at Jones's final statement. Did he think, Hagerman asked, that the 'Law Society could make such rules as to prevent gentlemen from practising?'[92] Even were such rules made, the judges would, as Jonas Jones had stated, set them aside.

John Willson, a populist farmer and Methodist preacher from Winona, was equally critical of what he considered the bill's exclusionary provisions. Willson maintained a lifelong suspicion of lawyers, judges, and the entire administration of justice, basing his attitude on the populist, agrarian position that justice was too centralized, too class-divided, too slow, too expensive, and too complex in its language. He had heard that the real intent of the bill was exclusion and 'wished to watch with a jealous eye any innovations coming from this society.' The bill 'goes to give a monopoly which should not be tolerated.' He had 'a suspicion of the Law Society ... Upper Canada would be ruined at last by the Lawyers' through giving them the power to exclude those already properly qualified for admittance.

Baldwin, as noted, felt no reluctance in supporting the bill. In the first instance, a building was necessary in order that lawyers outside York would have an 'office and a library' when they came to town. As it now stood, although they had 'the most important affairs of the country entrusted to them,' they had 'to enter into public bar-rooms, & in taverns, a most unfit place for gentlemen, who pledged themselves to the interests of their Clients, by the most solemn oath.' The bill would add to the 'importance and respectability' of the Law Society. Baldwin was 'sure that there was no Society for which the country should feel so deep an interest, as for the Law Society. Without it, whose property was safe? Whose life could be ably defended?' For Baldwin, it was essential that the society have the power to exclude those either unqualified or unsuitable for admittance: 'Great Britain abounded with Attorneys, who were described [as] petty foggers, they engaged in low practice, and were looked upon as low ... and if they were admitted to practice in our courts, it would be an injustice to the bar, and to the children of the country. The gentlemen who composed the bar of this country, he was happy to assert[,] were men of learning, honour, and inviolable integrity.'

In the assembly, the bill passed by a margin of nineteen to twelve and became law in 1822. The power of controlling admittance to the legal profession had been turned over more fully to the lawyers themselves. And they now enjoyed the privilege of raising funds, without limit, for the purposes of the Law Society. The leading assemblymen who had spoken in favour of the bill were all lawyers and included such a politically diverse group as Robinson, Baldwin, Jonas Jones, Hagerman, and Barnabas Bidwell. The mercantile and agrarian interests as represented by Charles Jones and John Willson respectively lost the day.

The following year, Robert Nichol, a merchant from Port Dover and one of the leading opposition figures in the assembly, introduced a bill for the relief of John Boswell.[93] Boswell was a recent immigrant who had practised as an attorney in London, England, with the Court of King's Bench and as a commissioner in the Court of Chancery. Upon his arrival, he had applied to the Law Society for admittance as a barrister and was refused. To Nichol's mind, Boswell should have been allowed to practise his profession and 'not be expected to go into the Woods and cut down trees.'[94]

Baldwin defended the Law Society's decision. The act of the previous year had been intended 'to secure to this Province ... [an] honourable Profession, which would protect the rights, liberties, and

xlvi 'All the privileges which Englishmen possess'

persons of the Country.' Boswell's application 'was made in direct opposition [to] that statute.' For the assembly to support him 'would be overturning this Session what they established last.' Nothing, Baldwin asserted, could be 'more dangerous to the honour and respectability of the Society than to open a door for innovation.' Jonas Jones agreed. He had been one of the benchers who had made the decision. There was no objection to admitting Boswell as an attorney if the legislature thought it proper. But it was 'not expedient to call him to the bar to practice as a barrister.'

Nichol took issue with Baldwin and Jones. The history of the Law Society was a history of exceptions such as the acts of 1797 and 1803 appointing barristers by executive fiat. Baldwin replied that when those bills were passed 'there was a scarcity of Lawyers ... and in order to supply the deficiency,' they were enacted. Now, however, circumstances were different; 'lawyers were to be found in every district.' Parents were 'educating their sons at a great expense for the profession of the law' and it would be a 'great injustice' therefore 'to admit gentlemen coming from other Countries.'

David McGregor Rogers, a loyalist assemblyman, raised the old popular concern that 'Counsellors fees were very large' and the Law Society was trying to keep as much for its members as possible. Although Boswell would be entitled to an attorney's fees, 'he should enjoy,' Nichol thought, 'the full benefit' of a barrister's fees as well. James Crooks, another merchant, observed that gentlemen of the bar gladly encouraged immigrants 'to cut down wood, and for other purposes, but they would not admit Lawyers.' A committee, chaired by Nichol, met with the Legislative Council to secure its concurrence. The council made several amendments that were supported by the assembly and the bill ultimately passed.[95] Boswell was admitted as an attorney almost immediately (on 24 April 1823), but the benchers of the Law Society insisted that his name stand on its books for five years before he could be admitted as a barrister. After waiting a suitable period, he was enrolled as a barrister in Trinity Term 1825 along with Robert Baldwin, son of William Warren. In spite of legislative intervention on Boswell's behalf, the Law Society had, as one historian put it, 'saved its face.' More important, the benchers asserted 'their fixed determination to resist all future examinations for admission contrary to the existing Laws of the Province.'[96]

Between 1821 and 1830, 94 barristers were entered on the Law Society's rolls; from 1797 until 1841, a total of 285 men became barristers. In the same period, 322 were admitted as attorneys.[97] As the debates of 1821 made clear, the framers and supporters of the act envisaged a respectable, self-regulating profession of gentlemen. To patricians such as W.W. Baldwin, lawyers had a particular responsibility to uphold what the constitution secured, property and civil rights. Baldwin shared these beliefs with the man who introduced the 1821 bill, Attorney General John Beverley Robinson. From the 1820s on, lawyers, more than any other profession, dominated political leadership in Upper Canada/Ontario. In the minds of Robinson and others, lawyers (and the word, as the 1821 debate demonstrated forcefully, was synonymous with gentlemen) could be counted on to fill the gap in the social structure caused by the absence of an aristocracy. As Strachan put it in 1826: 'Lawyers must, from the very nature of our political institutions – from there being no great landed proprietors – no privileged orders – become the most powerful profession, and must in time possess more influence and authority than any other.'[98]

The Law, the Constitution, and Rights

'Proceedings, heretofore sanctioned by authority, and yet no less derogatory to the prerogative of the Crown than invasive of the privileges of the subject'
Grand jury, London District

'The practice of the Court is unjust, oppressive, and influenced'
J.M. Jackson

'Who would overturn the constitution, and subvert the law'
Joseph Willcocks

British constitutionalism and the mythology of the rule of law was more pervasive than anyone imagined. And its content was more broadly defined than anyone in the colonial administration would have wished. The constitutional and legal structures of Upper Canada had been established, if not in the face of popular opposition, then at least against popular expectations. Loyalists, to the extent that they expressed themselves, had no desire for the constitutional package thrust upon them in 1791. The Judicature Act of 1794 was passed at gubernatorial insistence over significant opposition in the Legislative Council. It is safe to assume that the late loyalists, those non-loyalist

American settlers who flooded into the province after Simcoe's offer of free land to 'such as are desirous to settle on the Lands of the Crown,'[99] could hardly have been enamoured of either development. By 1796 the population had swelled to 25,000 and ten years later reached 46,000; the increase was largely non-loyalist.[100] The late loyalists lacked even an emotional attachment to the crown or Pettit's unspecified commitment to the 'british Constitution.' Typical of the American response to the offer of free land was a petition of 229 Americans who had 'a Wish to embrace the earliest Opportunity ... [to] form a settlement.'[101]

The 1790s witnessed three great popular demonstrations of political opinion that drew their support from loyalist and non-loyalist alike. All were outpourings of hostility to monopoly. The first was a province-wide furore over a contract from the British treasury to supply military garrisons. Agents were appointed in Montreal and Quebec and these merchants, as a result of lobbying in London, subcontracted the supplying of Upper Canadian military posts to four merchants exclusively. Although limited to two years' duration, the monopoly contract aroused almost universal opposition. Concerted pressure at the constituency level was so widespread and sustained that it could not be ignored. Assemblymen were determined to do something and only Simcoe's intervention kept them from acting collectively within the legislature. Instead they petitioned the king in their individual capacities. On 9 July 1793, fifteen of the sixteen members signed a remonstrance protesting 'that all Monopolies in a Young Country are highly injurious' and urged the monarch to action. With Simcoe's blessing the monopoly contract was cancelled the following year.[102]

The second eruption was more local in nature but just as important. It occurred in the Niagara peninsula, one of the first and primary areas of loyalist settlement. There, the leadership provided initially by the officer corps of loyalist military units had been quickly supplanted by a largely Scottish and non-loyalist mercantile élite dominated by Robert Hamilton of Queenston. He had been one of the four merchants connected to the monopoly contract at the centre of the 1793 furore. Six years later, he and two other merchants sought assembly permission to improve the road between Queenston and Lake Erie, and to build a canal linking lakes Erie and Ontario. As recompense for their expenditures, the merchants demanded a monopoly over tolls. An imbroglio ensued. In the election of 1800 the local mercantile candidates, despite their concerted efforts, were defeated by a coalition of aggrieved interests – farmers, petty merchants, and former loyalist officers. After the election, four petitions of varying size – the largest had over 1,000 signatures – were tabled in the assembly. The language of one petition denouncing the merchants' proposal 'as monopolous and oppressive' was typical.[103]

The third outbreak was simultaneous with the campaign against Hamilton's bid for a canal. In this case, the disdain for mercantile monopolies and the friction resulting from a perceived antagonism between farmers and merchants was replayed within the legal realm. At issue was the judgment of the Court of King's Bench on a writ of execution against the lands and tenements of the plaintiff in the case of *Daniel Bliss v. Samuel Street*. Argued before Chief Justice John Elmsley and puisne justices Henry Allcock and William Dummer Powell, the case had aroused intense interest among farmers and merchants alike. The crux of the matter was a process that had, according to Powell, been normal procedure for twenty years.[104] The controversy might even have sputtered and died had the court's decision been unanimous. Elmsley and Powell upheld what the latter alleged was established practice; Allcock, however, recorded his dissent that the 'plaintiff ... cannot take out execution against the defendant's lands.'[105]

Allcock was only defending the landed basis of an aristocratic society,[106] but his dissent provided farmers with a possible legal barrier against the seizure of landed property for debt and the effect rippled through the agrarian community.[107] In the columns of the *Canada Constellation* 'Acres' observed that, 'if lands are taken by execution, it will ruin this country.' 'A Friend to Justice' replied in the *Gazette*, denying any moral difference between landed and movable property. Britain was a commercial country with great wealth and only a few landed proprietors, whereas, 'Canada ... is merely an agricultural country; the wealth of the generality of its inhabitants consists solely in their lands.' He admitted that the property of a farmer and a merchant were 'nominally different,' yet 'in effect' they were 'the same, and should consequently be liable to attachment for their bona fide debts.' The rule of law must apply, he declared, to 'every species of property.' The stake of merchants in the decision was fundamental in a colony such as Upper Canada: 'Where landed property is so general, where so much is transacted on the credit of lands, they may be considered as its immoveable staple, or a species of currency; and on one part the guarantee in all cases of debt, or considerable transactions of the general internal commerce.'[108]

1 'All the privileges which Englishmen possess'

Politics, law, and the structure of the social order overlapped as heretofore largely inchoate undercurrents of popular opinion began to find a political voice, albeit at times in odd places. At this juncture, Allcock's decision made him an unlikely tribune in the election of 1800; he was elected in a campaign that witnessed 'Cato' defending 'eminence of station' as a proper attribute for political candidates, and 'Farmer' extolling the merits of an 'honest, upright and just man.'[109] Allcock's election was contested and he was ultimately unseated. His successor, Angus Macdonell (Collachie) – a lawyer, one of the counsel in *Bliss v. Street*, and a self-styled 'Friend of the People' – saw at work in society a struggle for the rights of the people, farmers and mechanics, against a coalition of officeholders, placemen, and large merchants. Here was something new: the old and common antipathy to higher orders, a thread that seems to have cut across religious denominations and ethnic groups, married to the political language of rights.

Collachie was one of the unfortunates drowned in the sinking of the *Speedy* in 1804.[110] A significant figure in the political landscape of early Upper Canada, he helped to articulate the political language of opposition around which a fluctuating coalition of opposition assemblymen coalesced between 1805 and 1812. Interestingly, his ideas were shared even by a political rival. William Weekes, a quixotic Irish lawyer and client of Allcock, was one of Macdonell's unsuccessful opponents in the election of 1804. In his election broadside, Weekes drew upon the language of rights as well as the constitution, claiming himself to be 'unconnected with any party, unsupported by any influence, and unambitious of any patronage, other than the Suffrages of those, who consider the impartial enjoyment of their rights.'[111]

Ideas were not only useful to political action, they were expressions of the reasons and motivations for political action. Under the banner of these clusters of ideas, diverse interests within the assembly coalesced. Political opposition within the assembly and the discussion of rights and the constitution were coeval; their emergence was not simply a matter of coincidence. Politics was transformed as individual opposition gave way to collective action and the assembly became a place of political initiative rather than merely political reaction. The politics of personalities was replaced by a politics dominated by opposition, issues, and questions of rights. Most important, the political/constitutional language of opposition developed within the framework of the phrase, the king and the constitution. The opponents of successive Upper Canadian administrations emphasized preservation of the king's prerogatives and the people's privileges. The crucial middle ground mediating between a monarch and his people – the aristocracy – was either ignored or attacked.

Following Collachie, first Weekes and then an Irish judge of the Court of King's Bench, Robert Thorpe, defined the colony's problems within the framework of constitutional rights. For example, in an election broadside of 1805 (a by-election to replace the drowned Macdonell) Weekes elaborated a need for the 'vigilance of the legislator over the rights and privileges of his Constituents' and for an impartial and mild administration of justice. Specifically, Weekes attacked the Sedition Act of 1804 as an infringement upon the ancient liberties of Englishmen. Those who 'maintain the immunities of the people,' he reasoned, 'do more than render a temporary benefit to the Country, inasmuch as that a security against arbitrary or oppressive measures tends not only to preserve the tranquillity, but also to promote the prosperity of the State.'[112] One of the salient features of this language was the assembly's inherent right to custodial care and protection of constitutional rights. This insistence dominated the rhetoric of oppositionists such as the Baldwins in the 1820s and the 1830s.

Language of this kind struck a responsive chord in the experiences of the aggrieved. Three examples will suffice to demonstrate the emerging relationship between the opposition within the assembly and that group's use of the language of British constitutionalism, the prerogatives of the people, the privileges of the people, and the rule of law. The touchstone of grievance was the perception of arbitrariness. What was considered arbitrary? – first, executive initiative on matters of immediate concern to ordinary settlers. Between 1798 and 1804, the successive administrations of Peter Russell and Lieutenant-General Peter Hunter implemented changes designed to facilitate the reform of government departments. Hunter, who as commander-in-chief was often away in Lower Canada, formed a committee to handle routine administration on those occasions. This novelty, combined with his personal aloofness and desire for greater efficiency in government, had the effect of concentrating power in the hands of a few, select advisers. Russell noted that three and occasionally a fourth 'are the only persons of his Cabinet.'[113] Two of the crucial three were Scots; one of them was Attorney General Thomas Scott, another Chief Justice Allcock. The effect was to tie the governor and his intimate aides closer together, both in fact and in public perception. The situation also demonstrated a close connection between the first law officer of the crown, the attorney general, and the first officer of the court, the chief justice. Rightly or wrongly, the perception was that the separation between executive and judiciary had been undermined.

Hunter's attempt at 'bringing into order the Land Granting Department, and ... clearing away the very large arrears of Business,' as Allcock later put it,[114] caused no end of grief. There was a backlog, the natural result of patents costing more than what the officials responsible for issuing them were allowed to charge. Hunter simply raised the fee schedule, to universal howls from a society in which everyone wanted land and as cheaply as possible. He also moved to limit the number of free grants on which fees were not payable. Loyalists and military claimants were his main targets. The free grant was a symbol of the crown's bounty, a reward for faithful service, a mark of the covenant that existed between the crown and its loyal subjects. His inspector general struck 900 names from the UEL list. A time-limit was imposed for the submission of loyalist claims, and Hunter even ordered that only personal submissions to the Executive Council would be considered.[115] The loyalists cried their displeasure at the seeming abrogation of their entitlement. A leading loyalist and major Kingston merchant pointed out to Hunter, with classic understatement, that 'discontents are prevailing on this subject.'[116]

Secondly, large numbers of the population could not tolerate the privileges that accrued to the Church of England as a result of the Constitutional Act and the restrictive laws passed by the legislature in 1793 and 1798. The first limited the right to perform legal marriages to Anglicans; the second extended it to Presbyterians and Lutherans. In 1802 alone three petitions were tabled in the assembly urging redress. A group of Methodists claimed that their churches and congregations 'are numerous and a large number of the principal members are of those people called U.E. Loyalists or their descendants ... your petitioners trust their loyalty in the defence of the rights of the best of Sovereigns would be as conspicuous as it heretofore has been.'[117] They complained that they had the same duties as subjects of other denominations had but were denied similar rights; specifically, they did not enjoy 'an equal participation ... in their religious rights,' particularly in solemnizing the 'religious rites of marriage.'[118] Four years later, as a member of the assembly, Weekes tabled an almost identical petition of some 238 Methodists seeking the right for their preachers to perform legal marriages.[119]

'All the privileges which Englishmen possess' liii

The third example concerns one individual rather than a group or a denomination. Yet it illustrates the transformation of private grievance into public action, action framed by the language of civil liberties and the constitution. Benajah Mallory had prospered in Burford Township, London District, as a merchant, businessman, innkeeper, and land speculator.[120] A man clearly on the rise in local affairs, he had a powerful patron at York in the person of Surveyor General David William Smith. The latter had secured for Mallory a captaincy in the militia and later recommended him for the magistracy. Mallory, however, clashed with the local officeholding élite (an élite established, at least in part, as a result of the legal restructuring of 1792–4) as represented by two exemplars of loyalism, Samuel Ryerse and Thomas Welch.[121]

Like many people in the province, Mallory was disenchanted with the operation of district courts and, particularly, the schedule of fees. His criticism of personal maltreatment suffered at the hands of Ryerse, the judge of the district court, brought him into direct conflict both with Ryerse and with Welch, also a leading local official of the court. The prospect of an open breach displeased Welch, who tried to forestall developments with the hope that the 'Religious, the Humane Capt. Mallory' did not 'mean ... to advance your Popularity by impeaching the Conduct of the Judge of this District, and his Clerk.'[122]

In fact, Mallory headed a challenge to the loyalist officeholders. In 1804 he took his challenge into the political arena, contesting the local riding against Ryerse. Lord Selkirk, observing the campaign, noted that 'electioneering seems here to go on with no small sharpness.'[123] Mallory won a convincing victory, 166 votes to 77, thereby setting the stage for an escalation of the factionalism which was, by now, the defining political characteristic of the London District. His entry into the assembly was a case of personal spite and local politics. The district élite, when challenged, responded with denunciations of the Mallory-led group as seditious Methodists determined to undermine 'good Order.' Welch related a conversation with one of Mallory's adherents, who declared that the province would become 'a very good Country after we have adriven out of it all the old Tories and Half Pay officers, and have a new Constitution like that of the United States.'[124]

Although never a major participant in the assembly, Mallory epitomized the American immigrant castigated by Lieutenant Governor Gore as retaining 'those ideas of equality & insubordination much to

liv 'All the privileges which Englishmen possess'

the prejudice of this Government.' These people, he thought, would become 'internal enemies' and would be 'very much to be dreaded' in the event of war.[125]

Ensconced in opposition from 1804 until his defeat in 1812, Mallory felt the wrath, or so he and others thought, of a vengeful executive supported by a compliant judiciary. In 1803 Richard Cartwright had financed the expansion of Mallory's Burford enterprises with a large loan. On 15 January 1807 Cartwright won a judgment against him for debt of £1,887.17s. and costs. Mallory could not pay. As soon as the question of execution against landed property was settled in mid-1809, writs were issued against his land and two parcels were subsequently seized and sold at auction. Thus, he was one of the first to feel the effect of the resolution of that particular legal controversy. In 1810 he was charged with assault against Sheriff Thomas Merritt of the Niagara District, but was acquitted. Late in 1811, he suffered another judgment against him for debts of £1,000 and costs. He later claimed it had cost him 'near' $2,000 just to defend himself during these years.[126] During the summer election of 1812, Mallory entreated the electorate to 'repell oppression accompanied with tyrenhy' and blasted the 'most blackest and unConstitutional Designs' against him.[127] He lost and it was later asserted that the executive had fixed the election against him.[128]

As the case of Mallory demonstrates, the rise of an opposition in the years prior to the War of 1812 was a reaction to threats, either real or perceived, from an executive considered abusive of its power. The challenge to an irresponsible executive drew upon the popular antipathy to monopolies and the aversion of one nationality for another; it gained strength from groups aggrieved over their seeming lack of rights, and also capitalized on the bitterness of other groups smarting from the recent loss of privileges; and finally, it offered an explanation why individuals felt abused when their civil liberties were infringed upon or jeopardized. In this manner, executive action on loyalist grants, legislative inaction on Methodist rights, judicial upholding of merchants' interests over farmers', and individual injustices were drawn together. Since many key officeholders and executive councillors were Scots, Mr Justice Robert Thorpe, for one, loudly railed against the 'scotch Pedlars, that ... have so long irritated & oppressed the people ... this Shopkeeper Aristocracy.'[129] This language could be easily extended – and was, by both Thorpe and Wil-

'All the privileges which Englishmen possess' lv

liam Weekes – to abuses in the public accounts[130] and within the administration of justice.[131]

Men such as Weekes and Thorpe had a good sense of the real grievances of Upper Canadians; in Weekes's case it came from experience, in Thorpe's it was acquired (probably from Weekes).[132] Weekes, as a lawyer, was concerned largely with civil cases concerning both debt and land. He was also, as indicated earlier, a client of Allcock, the dissenting judge in *Bliss v. Street*. Interestingly, Weekes defended William Willcocks in the celebrated case of *Gray v. Willcocks*, which reopened the social and legal issues thought to have been settled by the judgment in *Bliss*. Willcocks's case came before the Court of King's Bench in 1803 but judgment was not rendered until 10 January 1806. Mr Justice Powell adhered to his original decision that landed property could be seized in cases of debt. Mr Justice Thorpe, who seems to have learned what he knew of the province from Weekes, followed the argument developed by Allcock. The split necessitated an appeal to the king and his council and was not finally resolved until 1809, when the original decision of 1799 was upheld.[133] Like land-granting and the extension of religious rights, this issue touched ordinary lives directly. And Upper Canadians knew it. The *Upper Canada Gazette* commented on the extraordinary interest in the case:

As the question excited much anxiety, as well in the Landed as in the Commercial interest; a number of the most respectable persons in the Town [York] and its vicinity, attended to hear the judgment of the Court, and Mr. Justice Thorpe on delivering his sentiments, entered into the consideration of soccage tenures, and the exposition of the Statutes, in a manner which afforded the highest gratification to every admirer of the English language and the Law.[134]

The interplay of interest, grievance, and constitutional rhetoric was evident in the Home District petition presented by Weekes to Lieutenant Governor Gore in August 1806. The signatories expressed their 'unshaken loyalty and attachment' to the king and his government, and affirmed their 'zealous attachment to the constitution.' They criticized the extent to which 'prerogative and privilege have been indiscriminately sacrificed at the shrine or arbitrary imposition.' Their foremost concern was the restoration of, and adherence to, the constitution. They claimed:

lvi 'All the privileges which Englishmen possess'

The institution of the Government, from which we receive our hereditary protection, has antiquity for its origin and the wisdom of ages for its support – That it has gained celebrity with time and perfection with experience, and that any deviation from its principles must be an abandonment to our ruin; but we trust it may not be deemed irrelevant to suggest, that many among us have supported it at the hazard of their lives, and at the expense of their property – that others have resorted to it from choice and ... that it is the common concern of all to transmit it unimpaired from age to age.[135]

Here was proof, if any was needed, that the mythology of the rule of law and British constitutionalism had a range and a currency unlike any other. On his fall circuit in 1806 through the London, Western, and Niagara districts, Thorpe urged the grand juries to venerate the constitution. In the London District the grand jury's response showed how quickly the language of rights had percolated to the populace. It hoped that the new administration of Lieutenant Governor Gore 'may tend to bury in oblivion, the remembrance of proceedings, heretofore sanctioned by authority, and yet no less derogatory to the prerogative of the Crown than invasive of the privileges of the subject.'[136] Thorpe was encouraged.

At Niagara, while arguing before Thorpe, Weekes indulged himself in a wide-ranging tirade. His most passionate abuse was reserved for the late lieutenant governor, Peter Hunter. So violent were the denunciations that Weekes's opposing counsel, William Dickson, challenged him to a duel which was fought on 10 October 1806 on the American side of the Niagara River. Weekes was mortally wounded. Thorpe was stunned. He moved into Weekes's house at York and even won his assembly seat in a by-election the following year. When the polls opened, Thorpe painted a picture of Weekes 'looking down from Heaven with pleasure on ... exertions in the cause of liberty.'[137]

The significance of the Niagara assizes, however, extends beyond Weekes's untimely death and Thorpe's subsequent election. A case that came before Thorpe at Niagara in October 1806 highlighted the concern over executive abuse of individual rights. Earlier that year Mathias Hawn (Haun) had been arrested by magistrate John Warren on a charge of seizing goods from a wrecked ship. At his trial, defence counsel William Weekes denounced Warren as a petty tyrant, and the presiding judge, Mr Justice Powell, dismissed the case owing to 'the Irregularity of the Crown' (although he later claimed to have been unhappy with his decision since Hawn 'merited a capital punishment more than imprisonment').[138] Hawn then launched a civil suit against Warren for trespass, assault, and false imprisonment, Weekes again acting as his counsel. The suit was heard before Thorpe on 3 October.[139]

Robert Hamilton, a magistrate himself and lieutenant of the county, was outraged. Warren's conduct, he alleged, 'was such as we are all free to say would most probably have been imitated by any of us. We might perhaps be mistaken in the Law, or we might deviate from some of its forms, but we have been always taught that Magistrates erring from want of knowledge when the intentions were pure would be treated with indulgence and would meet the protection of higher Courts.'[140] Hamilton spoke to Mr Justice Thorpe before trial, but to no avail. After the appearance of witnesses such as Ralfe Clench, Isaac Swayze, and Alexander Stewart, Thorpe found in favour of Hawn, who was awarded damages and costs of £137.8s. 6d.[141] According to Hamilton, the magistrates had conducted themselves 'uniformly ... with integrity and moderation' and did not deserve 'the appellation of Petty Tyrants.' 'If the Bonds of respect from the People to the Magistrates are once broken,' Hamilton declared, 'there is an end to all order and to all well doing.'[142]

The forum where contending political visions were most in evidence was the House of Assembly. After 1807 Thorpe not only took Weekes's seat in the assembly, he took up his fight as well. The house led by Thorpe and backed by loyalist assemblymen such as Thomas Dorland, Peter Howard, and Ebenezer Washburn took collective initiative on a variety of issues, always in opposition to the administration.[143] Richard Cartwright thought Thorpe had artfully 'seduced' his followers: 'They were in fact acting merely as dupes ... in his [Thorpe's] attempts to create confusion.'[144] Lieutenant Governor Gore was convinced that 'revolutionary principles' underlay his troubles with the assembly.[145] And the assembly was symptomatic of the province as a whole. Gore complained to his counterpart in Lower Canada that most settlers were from the United States 'and of consequence retain those ideas of equality & insubordination, much to the prejudice of this Government so prevalent in that country.'[146]

As Gore became more frantic and used increasingly harsh language to defame his opponents, they, in turn, were increasingly precise in defining their position. Under the pseudonym of 'A Loyalist,' Thorpe set out his case in the columns of Willcocks's *Upper Canada Guardian*. Opposition, loyalty, and constitutionalism cohered:

lviii   'All the privileges which Englishmen possess'

Loyalty I conceive to consist in a faithful and fervent attachment to our King and his Government ... a proper observance of the Laws, combined with a firm, independent and manly determination to support the Constitutional rights and immunities of the people. If then I understand the true meaning of loyalty and have given a proper definition of it – why are we said to be disloyal and rebellious? when, or where have we shewn any dereliction of those principles?[147]

He was, he wrote, only trying to maintain the 'privileges of the people,' impartial justice, and the constitutional rights of juries. He was, in short, a man of the 'most loyal and patriotic motives.'[148] There was a notion that 'to be loyal, is to support any system the Government may adopt, whether consistent with, or subversive of the Constitution.' But, on the contrary, Thorpe argued:

True loyalty is, to be faithful to your King; to guard his prerogatives ... to protect inviolably the constitution of which he is the head, and to obey and uphold the law which he has sworn to administer and maintain; but surely it would not be loyalty to assist a monarch in rendering himself absolute, who would overturn the constitution, and subvert the law? If that were the case our hardy ancestors who opposed the strides of arbitrary power, and raised the fabricks of our glorious constitution, which they cemented with their blood, must have been REBELS ... The true loyalist will obey and defend to the last moment of existence the prerogatives of the Crown, the rights of the people, the Law and the Constitution.[149]

The battle extended into the literary domain, too. John Mills Jackson, an English immigrant to Upper Canada who had close ties with Weekes and Thorpe, returned to England in 1807 full of a profound sense of grievance. Two years later he published a pamphlet entitled *A view of the political situation of the province of Upper Canada*. It was not the work of an agitator attempting to foment discord. As an English gentleman, well connected politically, Jackson appealed to the fount of all authority, sprinkling his pamphlet with familiar encomiums on 'our inestimable laws and unrivalled constitution.' Like Thorpe, he raised the spectre of republicanism as the alternative to reform (perhaps restoration would be closer to his meaning).[150] One of his specific targets was the administration of justice, which he criticized for its partiality. His catalogue of 'impolitic and tyrannical proceedings' included the Hawn affair of three years previously.[151] First, Jackson claimed, an attempt had been made to set the case aside in King's Bench (probably a reference to Hamilton's conversation with Thorpe). When that ploy failed, the crown lawyer ordered the clerk of the court not to issue a writ of execution.[152] 'The practice of the Court,' he concluded, is 'unjust, oppressive, and influenced.'[153]

There were several attempts to undercut Jackson's argument. The text of Strachan's pamphlet on King George III, mentioned earlier, was an absurd combination of sugary images of royalty and hard-edged declarations of counter-revolutionary politics. His tendency to overkill unchecked, Strachan indulged in excesses not even a crazed monarchist could take seriously. To extol the virtues of the king was one thing; to uphold the characters of the royal princes required the suspension of disbelief. Strachan's favourite pupil, Robinson, dismissed the pamphlet; few would have given it credence. A more considered effort was Richard Cartwright's *Letters, from an American loyalist*, released and put on sale at York, Niagara, Queenston, and Kingston in the fall of 1810.[154] Cartwright's purpose was to reassure loyalists that, 'under an Epitome of the English Constitution, we enjoy the greatest practical political Freedom.' The touchstones of that constitution, property and civil rights, had been secured and the influence of the executive upon the assembly was as 'little ... as the most thorough paced Democrat could wish.'[155]

But the combined efforts of Strachan and Cartwright fell upon deaf ears. Political debate was not stifled, political opposition was not cowed; indeed, it continued to grow even under the shadows of war. The battle raged over language, and that language was of civil rights and liberties, the rule of law, and the British constitution. So strong was it that during the summer of 1813, with the colony at war, Joseph Willcocks and Benajah Mallory crossed the Niagara River and joined the Americans. In the aftermath of the imposition of martial law and the suspension of habeas corpus, Willcocks founded the Company of Canadian Volunteers, whose purpose, he said, was 'to assist in changing the government of this province into a Republic.'[156]

Willcocks and Mallory were among those convicted *in absentia* at the treason trials held at Ancaster in 1814. Robinson, then acting attorney general, prosecuted. The flavour of Strachan's constitutionalism had taken a slightly new emphasis, the gist of which was captured in his advice to his former student just prior to the trial: 'Remind

lx 'All the privileges which Englishmen possess'

the Court that the public have rights as well as the Prisoners, that if frivolous objections are allowed to defeat substantial Justice, Society cannot exist.'[157]

Popular Criticism

'Public Justice ought to be equally administered'
St Thomas Resolutions

'A race of attorneys ... is arising ..., crafty and subtle as regards their own private interests'
W.L. Mackenzie

'The fundamental evil which retards the prosperity of this community, is the want of a regular system of jurisprudence adapted to their condition'
Commonweal

In the period from 1791 to 1813, contending factions waged political war within the framework of arrangements set down by the Constitutional Act of 1791. As an opposition coalesced around issues of common concern, it drew support from a broad range of groups. More important, it took its bearings largely from the political language of an Irish lawyer, William Weekes; an Irish judge, Robert Thorpe; and an Irish sheriff, Joseph Willcocks. No one had exclusive possession of the language of British constitutionalism and the rule of law, and the alliances crafted by these men within the assembly proved it. The administration of government and the judiciary had become ensnared in the very language they themselves promoted.

From the establishment of European settlement in western Quebec in the 1780s through the constitutional and legal developments of the 1790s – indeed, throughout the entire Upper Canadian period – there was another language of opposition. Possibly more popular, it had a range of complaints against the legal system, including the infrequency of the assizes, the inaccessibility of district administrative centres where court-houses were erected, the inscrutability of legal language, and the high-handedness of local court officials and magistrates. Yet another early flashpoint of discontent was high legal fees. They had been the focus of agitation in 1804 and again in 1809 and had been seized upon by two of the leading pre-war oppositionists in the House of Assembly, William Weekes and Joseph Willcocks.

The unusually high degree of agrarian interest in a number of legal issues – the seizure of landed property in cases of debt, Mallory's battles with district court and legal officials, the dislike of high fees and imprisonment for debt,[158] Cartwright's and Hamilton's criticism of the adoption of a complex legal structure, and the attacks by Charles Jones, John Willson, and Robert Nichol on the exclusionary powers of a self-governing, self-regulating legal profession – revealed the depths of displeasure. These grievances were a persistent feature of the colony's legal landscape.

The agrarian populist critique (there was a substantial mercantile critique as well) was nurtured by the popular dislike of monopolies, itself an emerging form of emotional egalitarianism. Peter Howard, a second-generation loyalist living in the Brockville area, typified those who had no use whatsoever for the aristocratic emphasis of the British constitution. During the election of 1808, in a document written either by Howard or one of his supporters, he depicted himself as 'the POOR MANS FRIEND' and warned farmers to 'Guard against the Combinations of the great ... it is natural for them to oppress the Poor.' He was particularly concerned about what he called the predominance of 'Law characters' in the assembly, lawyers who would conspire to 'Enact Such Laws As would best Suit themselves.'[159]

The truth of Howard's (or a Howardite's) allegation had long been known to John Willson, but it touched on only part of the problem. In 1819 Willson memorialized the lieutenant governor for the judgeship of the Gore District Court. He noted that there was another suitable candidate in the person of James Crooks, a major local merchant. That was a problem to Willson's mind:

He is a Mercantile gentleman of very extensive dealings an evil not thought of or felt by the People of the Country with respect to that office until the last year of the Late judge [Richard Hatt, another large merchant] when he the said Judge thought proper to call for his debts and dues which was necessarily done through the Channel of a Superior Court to the great delay in the Collection of small debts and to the great addition of costs to many individuals.

Willson, a small, self-taught farmer, had 'for Several years applyed myself with considerable attention to the study of the Laws and Constitution of England and to the attainment of the Knowledge of the Laws and Constitution of this province.'[160] Farmers could look to neither lawyers nor merchants, since both groups were self-serving in terms of the administration of justice. Willson thus offered himself for the judgeship, unsuccessfully as it turned out – the position went to a lawyer. Several years later, in 1827, Willson again offered a glimpse of his view of the world. During a debate on whether to continue public support for reporting parliamentary debates, he pointed out its advantage to farmers. Without such reporting, the assembly would have been 'composed of government officers, place-men, and pentioners' and the consequence would have been 'OPPRESSION.' Even as it was, there were 'too many lawyers' in the house – there were seven or eight lawyers out of a total membership of forty-four – 'for the good of the farmers.'[161]

By the 1820s, government had been at least partially successful in coping with the demands of increasing population by erecting new districts and building new court-houses.[162] Even so, the subject was still capable in the late 1820s of causing profound irritation. The selection of Hamilton in 1817 as the judicial/administrative capital of the newly erected Gore District met with sustained opposition until 1828 from overlooked communities, especially Dundas and Ancaster.[163]

When London was chosen in 1827 as the site for the new district court-house and jail in Middlesex County, the residents of St Thomas adopted a series of resolutions in favour of their own village. The principle, the petitioners argued, was that 'Public Justice ought to be equally administered, and brought as near the doors of all classes of the King's Subjects, as circumstances can admit.' Since the majority of the population lay east of London, 'such disproportionate distances, to travel in attainment of that end is unreasonable, and in the present instance, without any feasible excuse.' Hence, the selection 'was ... contrary to the interest and expressed wishes of the great mass of the population of the said District.'[164]

The actions of magistrates either singly or in concert within quarter sessions were a perennial, deep-seated, province-wide grievance. Moreover, the overlap of judicial and municipal authority could, when abused, add to the charges of partiality. The instances are numerous; Mallory's problems in the London District are an early example. In 1830 W.L. Daly, editor of the *Spirit of the Times*, noted in his paper that it was 'high time that their *Worships* [the magistrates of the Niagara District] should be taught that a provincial statute is paramount to the prejudices of self-interested individuals and that the Judges of the Court of King's Bench to say the least of them are "*coeval* with the *profundity of their legal research.*"' At issue was a letter from 'Z,' 'a very respectable *source*' according to Daly. 'Z' complained that local magistrates had ignored the decisions of three juries and a mandamus issued by King's Bench ordering them to follow a specific line for a road. Indeed, they specifically instructed the municipal pathmaster not to open the road *'where the Juries formed it.'* 'Z' complained that such flagrant disregard not only of juries but also of King's Bench ought not to be tolerated. The magistrates' actions were 'diametrically opposite to that most glorious principle of our unexampled constitution – that our Judges should administer Justice without *fear, favour,* or *affection.*' He wondered when the justices of the peace would cease suffering 'themselves to be dictated to by a ... chairman, for the purpose of being possessed of a little authority, which he converts into a species of petit tyranny?'[165]

'Z''s letter and Daly's editorial struck a responsive chord within parts of the local community. Subsequent issues of the *Times* and of other local papers advanced additional criticisms of the local magistracy, focusing on such events as the accidental death of a prisoner (Isaac Hoff) in the dungeon of the overcrowded Niagara jail. It was the magistrates' 'DUTY to examine the Gaol, and guard against any catastrophe of the kind.' Other complaints in the Niagara District involved abuses by the local clerk of the peace and the high cost of justice (the table of fees established by the justices of King's Bench).[166] In York, Francis Collins reported Hoff's death in the *Canadian Freeman*; the report was titled 'Melancholy and Tyrannical.'[167]

By the 1820s, the law, the legal profession, and the judiciary were at the epicentre of a host of conflicts, each of which on its own might have been sufficient to hobble the administration of justice. Popular criticism of the legal system drew great strength from these various conflicts, but its thrust was continually blunted. It rarely, if ever, seriously altered the legal institutions or legal culture of Upper Canada/Ontario. Indeed, even when farmers and merchants combined, as in their attack upon Robinson's Law Society Act of 1822, they were defeated.

In the flurry of charges and counter-charges, there was one fact upon which the critics and defenders of the legal system could agree: the supremacy of the legal profession, not only among all other professions within the province, but also over political institutions. The leadership of the political opposition, both parliamentary and extra-parliamentary, was dominated to a man by lawyers – W.W. and Robert Baldwin, Marshall Spring Bidwell, and John Rolph – and they had their own agenda, one that would not threaten the hegemony of their profession in the slightest. There were significant areas of disagreement among these men. W.W. Baldwin, for instance, defended primogeniture – a symbol of aristocracy constantly attacked in the 1820s, especially by M.S. Bidwell. But there was broad agreement on matters such as the repeal of the Sedition Act of 1804 (under which Gourlay was banished) and a bill (not passed until 1836) to provide statutory provision for full defence by counsel in criminal cases. It is significant that W.W. Baldwin, a leading member of the bar and one of the foremost critics of executive government in the 1820s, had strongly supported Robinson's Law Society Act, as had Barnabas Bidwell, Marshall Spring Bidwell's father. Baldwin fully shared Robinson's belief in an aristocratic order and he held that there was no higher calling than the law. Baldwin equated the bar with the rule of gentlemen, as did Robinson, and fiercely defended the prerogatives of the Law Society of Upper Canada on the grounds of its link to political stability. 'Without it,' he argued, 'whose property was safe?'[168]

How little things had changed for the system's popular critics is evinced by William Lyon Mackenzie's fulminations in 1830. The editor of the *Colonial Advocate* and a leading critic of the administration, he inveighed against the 'race of attorneys, and other law practitioners ... arising among us, crafty and subtle as regards their own private interests, and evidently lacking that manly spirit of independence, that disinterested love of country, which would seek first the happiness of their fellow citizens.' Mackenzie decried the inability of good lawyers (his idea, no doubt, of an oxymoron) to 'resist the torrent of legal taxation which seems about to mar the prosperity and corrupt the morals of the province.' He urged legislative remedies to provide better (and by that he meant cheaper and simpler) ways of dispensing justice in the civil courts.[169]

A former employee of Mackenzie and now one of his chief critics, Bartemas Ferguson had no qualms in echoing this denunciation. Indeed, Ferguson had an equally acute sense of the overweening power of the legal/judicial system. In 1819 his first attempt at a career as a printer and publisher in Upper Canada had been hobbled by a successful civil judgment against him, and then crippled by his conviction for seditious libel that same year. Commenting on local petitions to urge the legislative assembly to reduce the number of lawsuits, Ferguson lauded legislative enactment as a remedy for 'reducing the grinding law expenses, by which thousands of our most industrious poor are plundered of their substance, and the best energies of the country paralyzed.'[170]

Three years later, Mackenzie denounced the administration of justice root and branch. The hand of the lieutenant governor through his prerogative (which gave him control of patronage) reached to every part of the legal system: the appointment of sheriffs who, in turn, selected grand and petit jurors; the appointment of the magistracy, which in its capacity as the municipal government had sole control over local revenue and in its legal capacity frequently committed outrages against criminal and civil justice; and the appointment of legislative councillors, who repeatedly rejected bills from the legislative assembly. Mackenzie also pointed to the restrictive libel laws; the lack of defence counsel in criminal trials; the failure to abolish primogeniture; and the favouritism given to the legal profession.[171]

So too, in 1834, one of Mackenzie's correspondents, 'Commonweal,' having made the necessary bows to the British constitution, argued for a legal system in accord with the community that it served. He complained:

The fundamental evil which retards the prosperity of this community, is the want of a regular system of jurisprudence adapted to their condition, and the remedy is to be sought only in a thorough revision of the constitution and laws of the province – a revision which shall secure to us all our rights as British subjects, confirm to us the principles of the British constitution and establish such regulations as are applicable to our condition.[172]

To be sure, revisions had taken place – the criminal law of Upper Canada, for instance, had been significantly revised in 1833. But this sort of change was not what 'Commonweal' had in mind. The *cri de cœur* for a popular system of justice would not be answered.

Justice Blind or Justice Cock-Eyed?

'There are no Laws demanding a more religious Observance than those which limit and define the Power of Individuals forming the Government over their Fellow Creatures'
Robert Baldwin, W.W. Baldwin, and John Rolph

lxvi 'All the privileges which Englishmen possess'

'A colony where the most unprecedented outrages have been
perpetrated without prosecution'
John Rolph

'We had hoped that the appointment of judges from England would
redeem the character of the Provincial Judiciary'
M.S. Bidwell, speaker of the House of Assembly

Early in 1863, Sir John Beverley Robinson, a hereditary baronet, died. More than any other single individual, he had incarnated the hierarchical spirit at the heart of the rule of gentlemen. Francis Collins had, for instance, denounced him in 1827 as 'the organ and representative of the Executive Government.'[173] Robinson himself was privately unrepentant in defence of the order that he embodied. In 1851, in a letter to Strachan, now bishop of Toronto, the chief justice commented at some length on mutability in political affairs. He had nothing but uncompromising aristocratic scorn for the present social, religious, and political structure, but he held out hope for the future:

We shall have some years of coarse vulgar democracy, enough to worry us in our time – our sons, or at least our Grandsons will see the beginnings of a re-construction of the social edifice – more worthy of the human race – after the Church of England shall have obtained an undisputed ascendancy which in the progress of time I take to be inevitable – and after men have seen one fallacy after another in the democratic system exposed & have suffered enough from their mistake ... In the mean time, it is no less the duty of all of us ... to act honestly & fairly in our own convictions – believing that these difficulties & changes are appointed for our own trials – and never relinquish the hope that what is true & right will prevail.[174]

After Robinson's death, an old enemy from the 1820s and 1830s wrote a letter of condolence to Robinson's brother. The closest and most uncritical of friends could hardly have penned a more glowing tribute. Yet Marshall Spring Bidwell was careful to add to his eulogy celebrating Robinson's life the qualification that 'the differences between us on political questions while I was in Parliament precluded intimate or confidential relations.'[175]

Fifteen years earlier, Robert Baldwin had written a similar type of letter. It was to Robinson and had been occasioned by the death of Mr Justice Jonas Jones, possibly the most forthright (and that is saying

'All the privileges which Englishmen possess' lxvii

a good deal) defender of the old regime among Robinson and his circle. Baldwin noted Jones's 'abruptness of manner which occasionally startled even those who knew him well and was often misunderstood by those who had not that advantage,' extended his sympathy, and noted his admiration for the 'vigor and industry with which he [Jones] applied himself to the administration of justice.' Baldwin anticipated Bidwell's caveat with the statement that he and Jones had been separated, not only by age and position, but also 'by difference of political views.'[176] And it was just these 'political views' and 'differences' between lawyers such as Robinson and Jones on the one hand, and Bidwell and Baldwin on the other, that led to the internecine war over the administration of justice in the 1820s.

Agitation had been commonplace in Upper Canadian society from the time of its founding. It had not, of course, occurred at every moment of every day in every part of the province, but it had been frequent enough for the observation to be deserving. 'Vast in extent and split up by great barriers of forests and by Protestants' was how Alexander MacDonell of Scothouse, a Roman Catholic priest in eastern Upper Canada, described the province in 1801.[177] No statement captures more neatly the sense of Upper Canadians that theirs was a deeply divided society. For this was not simply a colony or province of 'two solitudes' – it was a land of many solitudes, of autonomous communities separated by great barriers of politics, religion, ethnicity, sex, and geography. And often, the conflicts generated by the warring traditions within Upper Canadian society came to a head over differing conceptions of politics and religion. At the heart of these conflicts and conceptions, to a large extent, were questions about the British constitution, the civil rights of subjects, the rule of law, and the legal system.

An early generation of Upper Canadian historians such as John Charles Dent and Aileen Dunham took seriously the charges against the administration of justice in the aftermath of the War of 1812; later historians were more inclined to overlook the various incidents and so-called outrages, or to dismiss the allegations as the work of political cranks and misfits. The earlier group, however, were building on the foundations of a tradition that had its genesis in William Lyon Mackenzie's public attempts to weave the province's political past into a discernible pattern.[178] His story began only in the years immediately prior to the war, and he never knew that the complaints about both the structure and the administration of justice were rooted in the fabric

lxviii 'All the privileges which Englishmen possess'

of provincial society and were coeval with the founding of the judicial and political system. Criticism peaked and ebbed, but it did not abate.

The so-called alien question of the 1820s focused public attention on the attorney general and the administration in an especially intense way. It first surfaced in 1821, when certain members of the House of Assembly attempted to expel Barnabas Bidwell. Thereafter, the administration of Lieutenant Governor Sir Peregrine Maitland, led by Attorney General Robinson, tried several times to pass legislation disenfranchising the late loyalists. These attempts caused a storm of protest and steady resistance, which cost the administration greatly.[179]

Apart from the alien question, there was also a series of incidents or outrages, some minor, some major, which caught the public eye, aroused local or provincial furore, and – one after the other – steadily eroded confidence in British constitutionalism and the rule of law among significant sections of the population. The first was the Maitland administration's sustained effort against the Scottish agronomist and political reformer Robert Gourlay. The campaign culminated in Gourlay's expulsion from the province in 1819 under the terms of the Sedition Act of 1804; his publisher, Bartemas Ferguson, was charged with seditious libel and imprisoned for eighteen months after a successful prosecution by Robinson.

There followed a succession of apparent abuses which damaged the credibility of Robinson and his administration: the prolonged persecution of Robert Randal through the civil courts; the pettiness displayed against John Matthews, accused – on evidence provided by one of Robinson's students-at-law – of uttering treasonous statements; the depredations committed against William Lyon Mackenzie's printing office (the so-called types riot); the trial and execution of Charles French; the failure to prosecute the assailants of George Rolph (John's brother); the libel charges against two newspapermen, Francis Collins and Hugh Christopher Thomson; and – in 1828 – the persecution of William Forsyth, the dismissal of Mr Justice Willis, and the execution of Michael Vincent. Here, then, was a stunning array of unjust practices which violated civil liberty and civil law, threatened and even took life in ways considered tantamount to judicial murder, undermined the liberty of the press, usurped the role of the jury, compromised the independent role of the judiciary, ignored due process, and turned a blind eye to the criminal behaviour of the magistracy or other leading subjects.

There was a measurable element of popular support for the allegations of partiality against the administration. Over 1,100 people, for example, signed the petition on behalf of Charles French in 1828. As significant, however, was the growing estrangement between the administration and such leading members of the bar as William Warren Baldwin. He acted unsuccessfully for George Rolph in the 1827 civil suit brought by Rolph against his assailants. In his address to the jury, Baldwin (then in his third term as treasurer of the Law Society) noted with disapproval that Rolph's persecutors included local gentlemen, 'persons holding responsible offices, even occupying the seats of Justice – one of them entrusted ... with the sword of Justice.'[180] When they were finally charged with assault, the cases came forward at the same assizes in 1828 at which Vincent was tried. When no one appeared against them, they were discharged. It was, thought the *Gore Gazette*'s pro-administration editor, 'precisely the result which every one ... always anticipated.'[181]

The events of 1828 definitely made that year a watershed with respect to the administration of justice. In January, William Forsyth, an aggrieved hotelier of dubious reputation from Niagara Falls, petitioned the House of Assembly for redress, complaining of Lieutenant Governor Maitland's decision to use military force as a substitute for legal process in an attempt to resolve a dispute over access to the falls. As chairman of the house's select committee investigating the petition, John Rolph lamented the state of 'a colony where the most unprecedented outrages have been perpetrated without prosecution, and even followed, by the patronage of the local government, upon the wrong doers.'[182] The committee's findings precipitated a clash between Maitland and the assembly which resulted in the prorogation of the legislature on 31 March 1828.

The following month, Francis Collins appeared at the Home District assizes before Mr Justice Willis on four counts of libel. Collins defended himself and was allowed to make a statement before the court in which he levelled accusations against Attorney General Robinson, for failing – while acting attorney general in 1817 – to prefer charges against Henry John Boulton and James Edward Small for serving as seconds in the 1817 duel between Samuel Peters Jarvis and John Ridout, and for failing – as attorney general in 1826 – to prefer charges against the looters of Mackenzie's print shop.[183] Willis directed Collins to lay the information before a grand jury. Charges were laid and in the ensuing trials Robert Baldwin, acting as prosecutor, was complimented by the presiding judge, Willis, for his 'moderation and ability.' The seconds were acquitted and the rioters received a small fine. When Robinson, who had brought libel charges against Collins, attempted to have them held over until the next assizes, Baldwin denounced the attempt, successful as it turned out, as 'an unconstitutional infringement on its [the press's] liberty.'[184] At his fall trial, Collins was defended by Robert Baldwin and John Rolph.

In response to the specific charges of partiality, on 12 May 1828 Robinson issued a letter to leading members of the bar, including W.W. Baldwin, concerning the question of bias within his office. Baldwin replied in a lengthy missive, citing specific instances 'wherein I thought you omitted your duty.' The first was Robinson's failure to discipline his clerks who had been involved in the types riot. Their conduct was, Baldwin reminded him, 'quite unbecoming Gentlemen and still more unbecoming them as Students at Law.' The reaction of the crown's leading legal officers (Attorney General Robinson and Solicitor General Henry John Boulton) to the mob's action at Hamilton in the case of George Rolph was also inexcusable in that they had not 'promptly and vigorously turn[ed] the Law against the perpetrators.' When Boulton, who had defended the culprits during the civil suit, later prosecuted them in the criminal action, Baldwin found the series of events 'so subversive of justice that I fully partook of the public disapprobation of that scene.' The final episode, and the earliest chronologically, involved the 1822–3 case of Singleton Gardiner, who had brought a civil suit against two magistrates as a result of a dispute over his performance of statute labour on roads. Baldwin was counsel for the plaintiff and Robinson (arguing that it was his duty to protect the justices) acted for the defendants. For his part, Baldwin took no exception to the attorney general's principle 'wherein they [the magistrates] are in the right; but my opinion also is that it is your duty to prosecute them wherein they are grossly wrong.'[185]

The wrangling over the legal/judicial system reached a climax on 16 June 1828 in the Court of King's Bench. Chief Justice Campbell was absent; only Willis and Mr Justice Levius Peters Sherwood were on the bench. Willis declared that King's Bench required three sitting justices to function. The next day the Baldwins and Simon Ebenezer Washburn enquired of Willis if he would ask Sherwood to render an opinion on the court's constitutionality. If he declined to do so, they asked Willis to 'withhold his Judgement' in cases involving their clients 'untill as their Counsel we be better advised as to the course to be adopted.' On 23 June, the Baldwins and John Rolph remonstrated to

Sherwood 'against any Proceedings ... until the Court be established according to the Provisions of the Provincial Statutes.' It was not, they argued, merely a question of 'the strictest Principles of Law.' 'There are no Laws,' they wrote, 'demanding a more religious Observance than those which limit and define the Power of Individuals forming the Government over their Fellow Creatures.' On 24 June, Maitland dissolved the ninth parliament and called an election for the following month. Two days later, the administration moved to quell the unrest in King's Bench by removing Willis. It miscalculated badly. William Warren Baldwin and Robert Baldwin now entered the electoral fray trumpeting the cause of constitutional/judicial wrong.[186] Among the other candidates were George Rolph, John Rolph, Marshall Spring Bidwell, Robert Randal, John Mathews, and William Lyon Mackenzie, all of whom, like W.W. Baldwin, were subsequently elected. And Robert Baldwin would win John Beverley Robinson's seat for the town of York upon the latter's elevation to the chief justiceship in 1829.

The resolutions of the committees struck in York in July and August 1828 to protest the dismissal of Willis capture succinctly the language of civil rights and liberties of the subject which informed this position. When W.W. Baldwin addressed the July meeting, he spoke the language (and a masculine language at that) of British constitutionalism and the rule of law. The protesters were motivated not by 'unworthy or womanish fears' but by anxiety of 'men and patriots jealous of their rights and anxious to guard their liberties ... from arbitrary power.' He derided legislative councillors, who 'are placemen and pensioners, depending upon the Executive for a living, instead of being an independent gentry,' and hoped, among other things, that the 'laws [would be] impartially administered.'

A petition to the king, which resulted from the July meeting, complained that 'misrule has at length become so bold, and power so indiscriminate of its victim' that a 'judge, without impeachment and even without a charge, can be so ignominiously amoved from his high office.' 'Notwithstanding defects in the law defining our constitution, we are,' the petitioners wrote, 'nevertheless warmly attached to it, and view with just fear every attempt to amend it, without the intervention of our Provincial Legislature, which is the constituted guardian of our rights and liberties, and which, considering the great distance of the Imperial Legislature, can best understand our necessities, and apply the proper remedies.' Of the petitioners' eleven enumerated grievances, six specifically concerned the administration of justice, from the 'undue influence which the mingled duties of Legislative and Executive advice, have on the judicial function' to 'our present imperfect jury system.' The appointment of judges was, they argued, the 'most conclusive evidence of the health of the great body politic.' Willis, whose presence on the bench had presaged, or so the petitioners had thought, 'a new era in the administration of justice,'[187] was replaced two days after his dismissal by Hagerman; the latter's only qualification, Collins argued in the aftermath of Vincent's execution, was 'sycophancy.'[188] The turmoil surrounding the administration of justice resulted in almost irreparable damage. A political/constitutional wedge had been driven through the heart of the legal profession.

During the spring and summer of 1828, assaults on the administration of justice – symbolized most poignantly, perhaps, by the case of Michael Vincent – reached new heights and were launched within a more comprehensive critique of the origins and nature of 'misrule' in Upper Canada by four of the leading practitioners of the bar: William Warren Baldwin, Robert Baldwin, Marshall Spring Bidwell, and John Rolph.[189] On the day of Michael Vincent's execution, M.S. Bidwell wrote to W.W. Baldwin suggesting a meeting, which would include Rolph, to confer 'on the measures to be adopted to relieve this province from the evils which a family compact have brought upon it ... The whole system and spirit of the present need to be done away.'[190] The cumulative weight of past injustices (now brought together and seen as evidence of systematic abuse) imparted a biting sense of grievance to the various denunciations, which called into question the impartiality of the administration of justice, supposedly one of the most sacrosanct blessings of English political and legal culture, and its relationship to the governance of the province. Just how caustic this sense of executive misrule was may be gleaned from a comment in the recollections of Charles Durand. A renowned barrister (he had been enrolled in 1836), he claimed in his 1897 *Reminiscences* that 'lynch law with these Tories of 1828 was as bad as lynch law now in the wicked Southern States committed on poor black men.'[191]

When the tenth parliament met in January 1829, W.W. Baldwin introduced resolutions aimed at 'separating the administration from its advisors, as they were the persons most to blame.'[192] The problems of the administration of justice could be redressed by such a political solution. A governor could be brought to account at great expense by seeking redress in England; but in Upper Canada, 'it was the practice to refer matters to the Executive Council, that Council was within our reach, they were responsible to us, and we might in his [Baldwin's] opinion be their Constitutional accusers.' Accordingly, he called upon the assembly to place itself 'on the same footing with the House of Commons in England' and declare its right to impeach public officers.[193] After heated exchanges and a lengthy rebuttal by Attorney General Robinson, the house on 16 March 1829 adopted a resolution moved by John Rolph. The address to the king declared that the exercise of the royal prerogative was 'consonant to British justice' yet 'that assurance, while it is grounded upon the continued dependency of our Judges can afford no sufficient and practical remedy against the abuse of Your Majesty's Royal prerogative by the provincial administration. This abuse ... has been flagrantly manifested by the late violent, precipitate and unjustifiable removal of ... Willis from the Court of King's Bench in this province.' The assembly asked the king to heal 'the wound inflicted upon the Justice and Constitution of the Country' by inquiring into 'this overbearing and despotic proceeding' and punishing the transgressors. In the event that the king chose to disregard this plea, Upper Canadians would be 'excluded from sharing its [the British empire's] equal and exalted justice.'[194]

In the attempt to remedy the situation, oppositionists emphasized the role of the assembly as the guardian of the constitution and the liberties that it bestowed. When on 3 September 1841 the famous resolutions on responsible government were introduced in the first parliament of the united assembly of Upper and Lower Canada, Robert Baldwin departed from previously established reform strategy and put his own resolutions on record: 'That the most important, as well as the most undoubted, of the political rights of the people of this Province, is that of having a Provincial Parliament, for the protection of their liberties, for the exercise of a constitutional influence over the Executive Departments of their Government.[195]

Upper Canada was a fractious, brawling society in which the politically engaged, more often than not, depicted each other in rhetorical extremes.[196] Yet even with a due allowance for hyperbole, both the level and the intensity of the criticisms concerning the rule of law by leading members of the bar, by large numbers of the legal profession and by significant portions of the public at large, were

lxxiv 'All the privileges which Englishmen possess'

without precedent. The political crisis of 1828, to that point the most serious in the colony's short history, was at bottom a crisis of confidence in the administration of justice. So thoroughgoing was it that hitherto disparate opposition groups, fearful that the very constitution had been suspended, were welded together in a broad, loosely organized, semi-permanent alliance. Small wonder, then, that in 1834 one anonymous critic reviled the administration of justice as the 'fundamental evil' undermining provincial prosperity.[197]

A Lasting Impression

'An innocent man ... executed unjustly'
Michael Vincent, gallows address

In many respects, Upper Canada was a child of counter-revolution, conceived by the loyalist opposition to the American revolution and shaped by hostility to the French one. The Constitutional Act of 1791, with its provisions for appointed legislative and executive councils, an established church, and a hereditary aristocracy, provided the constitutional and political bastion for successive provincial élites both to rally to and to sally forth from. The absence of an aristocracy, to say nothing of the lesser ranks of English landed society, doomed the Upper Canadian counter-revolutionary experiment to failure. The essentially pluralistic nature of loyalist settlement dashed the possibility from the outset.

Yet the structure of government, in itself, imparted sufficient power to the constitution's non-democratic elements to render them unassailable for decades. In the absence of an English landed social structure, the judicial/legislative/administrative élite pinned its hopes for a quasi-aristocratic, hierarchical society on the myth of the British constitution and the impartial rule of law. The judiciary articulated the myth from the bench; the chief justice, in his capacity as president of the Executive Council (until 1831) and president of the Legislative Council (until 1840), supplied a critical link between the legislative/executive and judicial functions; and, by 1821, the attorney general (and oft-times the solicitor general as well) acted as the provincial administration's leader or manager in the House of Assembly. Finally, the rise of the bar and its increasing wealth, along with the social pre-eminence and the political dominance of the legal profession by the mid-1820s, would secure lawyers in a respectable, and respected, position.

Certain of the blessings of the British constitution and the Constitutional Act, sure of the impartiality of justice and equality before the law, the lower orders of society would emulate the *'regularly bred.'* Thus, a love of order would be instilled throughout society, property would be secured, the rule of gentlemen would be assured, and the Constitutional Act (with its appointed, non-democratic elements) would be maintained.

It was not to be. From the outset of sustained European settlement in the 1790s, all aspects of monopolies of power (commercial, religious, and political) were under attack. The legal profession was not spared. From 1791 until 1840 the judiciary, in the person of the chief justice, was tied, usually intimately, to the executive and legislative councils. This link brought the judiciary within the framework of opposition criticism of executive misrule. Judicial independence thus became a touchstone of opposition rhetoric. These problems were exacerbated by the state of the judiciary itself. It was, more or less, fractious until Thorpe's suspension in 1807. Afterwards, it was regularly diverted by intra-élite rivalries until Powell's retirement in 1825, and then it was sidetracked à la Allcock and Thorpe by Willis in 1828. The ascension of Hagerman that same year did nothing – to put it mildly – to divert the controversy: the continuing link in the person of the chief justice between the judiciary and the legislature and the executive was a continuous object of reform and opposition grievance.

As for the legal profession itself, it was deeply divided on the leading political/constitutional questions. By Hilary Term 1828, the incoming treasurer of the Law Society of Upper Canada, John Beverley Robinson, and the outgoing treasurer, W.W. Baldwin, in their persons symbolized perfectly the extent and nature of those divisions. Moreover, through the 1820s, Robinson, as attorney general and *de facto* government house leader, pursued legal reforms that were often the antithesis of those sponsored by opposition leaders such as M.S. Bidwell and John Rolph. The points of difference were sharpened by the perception, generated by the cumulative weight of specific instances of alleged abuse, that the very administration of justice itself was partial and yet another symptom of colonial irresponsibility and executive misrule.

On a popular level, too, the colony's legal system had been under

lxxvi 'All the privileges which Englishmen possess'

sustained assault and continuous suspicion by farmers since the 1790s. Here the grievances focused on an overly centralized, overly complex, overly remote, overly expensive system of laws and professional administration. With the establishment of new districts and the building of new court-houses, justice became somewhat less remote but the furore continued to rage against a self-regulating, seemingly all-powerful legal profession distinguished – it was argued – in the main by pettifoggery, obfuscatory language, and filthy lucre. None the less, the passage of the 1822 amendments to the Law Society Act and the centrality of lawyers within the legislature assured professional paramountcy. To be sure, there would be future challenges to their professional hegemony later in the century, once again from the province's farm community under the 'watchword' of 'no lawyers, more farmers and machinists.' William Lyon Mackenzie led one such famous, and nearly successful, attack in 1851.[198] But, by the end of the 1820s, there was no longer any possibility of implementing serious alternatives. The legal *causes célèbres* of 1828 may have offered an opening for radical change; nothing, however, came of them.

Yet some of the changes that ultimately ended the bitter controversy over the administration of justice were already in place in the 1820s. Imperial fiat removed the chief justice from the presidency of the Executive Council in 1831, and the Union Act of 1840 ended the chief justice's role as speaker of the Legislative Council. The separation of the judicial from the executive and legislative functions allayed the charges of arbitrariness which had resulted from that connection. The sporadic gestures towards a responsible executive council from 1836 until formal realization in 1848 ended, by definition, the old allegations of misrule, irresponsibility, and maladministration, particularly with respect to executive patronage and executive abuse of civil rights.

It is sometimes asserted that the language of rights disappeared from Canadian political culture following the defeat of the Canadian rebellions in 1837–8. Consigned to the fringes of the political spectrum, the discourse of rights, it is said, did not enter the mainstream again until the 1980s and the debate over the Charter of Rights and Freedoms. This view has been justifiably criticized, and one of its most glaring weaknesses is its blindness to the enduring images left by Upper Canadian conflicts. In the hands of succeeding generations of historians, the stories of legal/judicial abuse were passed down over the years, damning and redamning the perpetrators. So thorough

'All the privileges which Englishmen possess' lxxvii

was the condemnation that it was not until S.F. Wise's efforts in the 1960s that Canadian historians considered the 'church and state' adherents of the Upper Canadian period fit objects for study.[199]

In January 1831 John Rolph (Michael Vincent's counsel in 1828) found himself becoming 'less and less efficient' in 'Law matters.'[200] Disgusted by recent parliamentary proceedings and wary of a fickle electorate, he had 'no ambition' to be a 'political Don Quixote.' Rolph longed for 'a peaceable and quiet life.' Within two months his interest had shifted from law to medicine. His time was now 'wholly occupied in medical practice.' 'I think of no other pursuit,' he wrote, 'I engage in no other.'[201] The following year, Rolph gave up law altogether.

Rolph's two adversaries at the Gore assizes in 1828 lasted much longer in the law. Robinson held the post of chief justice until 1862. He retired from the bench only in January 1863, the month of his death. Hagerman served as a temporary justice on King's Bench until 1829, when he became solicitor general. In 1837 he was promoted attorney general before ascending the bench again in 1840. He died seven years later while planning for his retirement.

When old John Ryckman in 1880 cast a backward glance at Hamilton's past, he did not mention Rolph, Robinson, and Hagerman or their roles in Vincent's trial. In fact, Ryckman thought the execution had occurred in 1810 but he was not sure and qualified the date with 'about.' The precise date of the trial had faded with time but the reason why he remembered the case had not: Vincent – in his mind and that of others – was innocent. Rolph's legal exertions on Vincent's behalf were in the end unable to sway either the jury or, perhaps more important, the judge; he did sway the public, or at least a goodly part of it. By 1831 John Rolph may have thought himself 'less and less efficient' in 'Law matters,' but it might be said that, in a certain sense, on 5 September 1828 no one was more efficient.

NOTES

1 A classic of the genre is *A short account of the life and dying speech of Joseph Bevir, who was executed at Kingston, (Upper Canada) on Monday, the 4th day of September, 1815, for the murder of Mary Bevir, his daughter. Written by himself while in prison* (Kingston 1815). The *Kingston Gazette* of 5 September 1815 noted that he 'addressed the numerous spectators in a very impressive manner, and acknowledged that he

merited all that he was about to suffer. He appeared to die very penitent.' Other examples are discussed in R.L. Fraser, 'Cornelius Albertson Burley,' *Dictionary of Canadian Biography (DCB)*, 12 vols. to date (Toronto 1966–90), 6:92, and Elizabeth Abbott-Gibbs, 'William Kain,' *DCB*, 6:370.

2 *Gore Gazette*, 6 September 1828. Publication was delayed 'in order to give an account of' the trial and execution.

3 In 1814 Sir Gordon Drummond, president of the Upper Canadian administration, expressed this conviction neatly, offering the hope that the 'impression made on the Public mind' by the forthcoming execution of traitors would 'be Strong and lasting' (Archives of Ontario [AO], RG 4, A–I, 1, Drummond to Chief Justice Thomas Scott, 9 July 1814). The executions took place in Hamilton on 20 July near the present-day intersection of York and Locke streets.

4 *Spectator*, 4 October 1880. A brief entry on John Ryckman appears in *Dictionary of Hamilton Biography (DHB)*, 2 vols. to date (Hamilton 1981–91), 1:174–6.

5 The foregoing is based on *Canadian Freeman*, 18 September 1828.

6 Ibid.

7 R.L. Fraser, 'Michael Vincent,' *DHB*, 1:203–6

8 *Canadian Freeman*, 20 January 1831. Hagerman never gave an explanation for his behaviour in this case and, given his temperament, probably never thought one was necessary. Upper Canadian judges regularly reported to the lieutenant governor's office on the calendars at the assizes. They generally referred to all capital cases. Hagerman, like John Beverley Robinson, preferred to extend to judges as much discretionary judgment as possible. Ten years later, as attorney general, Hagerman was pressed by John Macaulay, the lieutenant governor's civil and private secretary, for advice on delaying execution of a particular sentence for murder. Hagerman was reluctant and urged the lieutenant governor's office to leave the question 'to the discretion of the Judge – who in all cases would give opportunity for application for Mercy, where it could properly be granted.' For his part, Hagerman thought 'any departure from long established practice in matters connected with the administration of Criminal Justice dangerous and inexpedient.' National Archives of Canada (NAC), RG 5, A1, 114811–13, Hagerman to Macaulay, 21 October 1838

The lieutenant governor's office, which was usually quite scrupulous in overseeing capital cases and their disposition, seems to have

'All the privileges which Englishmen possess' lxxix

been content with Hagerman's charge to the jury and his subsequent sentence, in spite of the controversy in the press. However, John Strachan, rector of York and one close to the inner machinations of government in the 1820s, was convinced that the administration of Lieutenant Governor Sir Peregrine Maitland and his civil secretary, Major George Hillier, had become decidedly remote from its closest provincial advisers in 1828.

Hagerman was not precipitate in all capital cases. Earlier on the circuit, he had reported to Hillier, 'I have so far had no very pleasant duty to perform, nothing has occurred worthy of particular note' (NAC, RG 5, A1, 49698–701, Hagerman to Hillier, 11 August 1828). A clue to his impetuosity in Vincent's case is gleaned from his comments upon passing sentence: murder was 'a crime dreadful under any circumstances, but in the case rendered still more atrocious by the fact that your unfortunate victim was one whom you had solemnly sworn at the altar to cherish and protect.' *Canadian Freeman*, 18 September 1828

Vincent had shattered the sacred bonds of matrimony, and Hagerman was outraged. He had enjoyed a distinguished record as counsel for women in two recent cases, one involving seduction, the other separation and battery (*Kingston Chronicle*, 15 September 1826). Constance Backhouse provides ground-breaking coverage of both cases in *Petticoats and prejudice: women and law in nineteenth-century Canada* ([The Osgoode Society 1991]). In 1829, at Perth, Hagerman tried a case similar to Vincent's. Thomas Early had murdered his pregnant wife and four children. It was, Hagerman wrote, a murder 'of greater atrocity than any I have ever heard or read of – the annals of crime afford no example of a deed so horrible and inhuman.' He dismissed Early's story as 'improbable,' noting that 'Providence however would not suffer so much wickedness to pass unpunished ... He was left for execution and doubtless suffered [it] yesterday.' NAC, RG 5, A1, 53274–7, 25 August 1829

In Early's case, as in Vincent's, Hagerman saw no legal cause for respiting sentence and referring the case to the lieutenant governor. Hagerman, whether as a lawyer or as a judge, had a particular dislike of men who seduced, battered, or abused women. In violation of their sacred oaths, Vincent and Early had gone even further in their brutality. Hagerman was without sympathy for them. He was a naturally aggressive and forceful man. These traits marked his career as a lawyer, customs official, politician, and crown official. It is hardly surprising that they marked him as a judge as well. In Vincent's case, Hagerman's desire to see him punished impelled the judge to overstep his judicial authority and to lay claim to a shared responsibility with the jury.

9 Fraser, 'Vincent'
10 There is an interesting and varied body of literature on this issue of the partiality/impartiality of the administration of justice in Upper Canada during the 1820s and 1830s. Paul Romney, himself one of the leading participants in the debate, has written a perceptive introduction both to the issue and to the literature on it; see 'Very late loyalist fantasies: nostalgic tory "history" and the rule of law in Upper Canada,' in W. Wesley Pue and Barry Wright, *Canadian perspectives on law & society: issues in legal history* (Ottawa 1988).
11 AO, Robinson papers, diary, 1815–16, 'Tour on the continent,' 82
12 S.F. Wise, 'Upper Canada and the conservative tradition,' in Edith Firth (ed.), *Profiles of a province* (Toronto 1967), 20
13 S.F. Wise, 'Liberal consensus or ideological battleground: some reflections on the Hartz thesis,' Canadian Historical Association (CHA), *Historical Papers* (1974), 1–9, 12–13. Graeme Patterson has expanded on Wise's perceptions. Patterson takes great pains to show how cultural and national customs reinforced older political traditions – traditions that were ultimately forgotten as the political history of Upper Canada came to be written in terms of the struggle for responsible government. To his mind, political/constitutional conflict in the province was a 'struggle between warring conservative traditions that came into contact when transplanted from Europe and other parts of North America to the new colony.' See Graeme Patterson, 'Whiggery, nationality, and the Upper Canadian reform tradition,' *Canadian Historical Review* (CHR), 56, no.1 (March 1975), 44. A refinement of these insights is presented in R.L. Fraser, 'Contexts of loyalty: the king's prerogative, the people's privileges, and Yankee spirits – the politics of Upper Canada, 1792–1814,' unpublished paper (presented to the Ontario Historical Society, 1984); see also Fraser, 'David McGregor Rogers,' *DCB*, 6:655–8. For a recent discussion that summarizes much of the recent literature, see Peter J. Smith, 'Civic humanism vs. liberalism – fitting the loyalists in,' *Journal of Canadian Studies*, 26, no.2 (summer 1991), 25–43.
14 NAC, RG 1, 418:P, misc/95d
15 E.A. Cruikshank (ed.), *The settlement of the United Empire Loyalists on*

the Upper St. Lawrence and Bay of Quinte in 1784: a documentary record (Toronto 1934), 40–2

16 The best introduction to the loyalists in western Quebec/Upper Canada is Bruce [G.] Wilson, As she began: an illustrated introduction to loyalist Ontario (Toronto and Charlottetown 1981).

17 Adam Shortt and A.G. Doughty (eds.), Documents relating to the constitutional history of Canada, 1759–1791, 2 (Ottawa 1918), 773–7

18 Ibid., 949–50

19 Quoted in E.K. Senior, From royal township to industrial city, Cornwall, 1784–1984 (Belleville 1983), 60

20 See, for example, Fraser, 'Rogers'; Neil MacKinnon, This unfriendly soil: the loyalist experience in Nova Scotia, 1783–1791 (Kingston and Montreal [1986]); and D.G. Bell, Early loyalist Saint John: the origin of New Brunswick politics, 1783–1786 (Fredericton 1983).

21 Bruce G. Wilson, 'Robert Hamilton,' DCB, 5:402–6; see also his Enterprises of Robert Hamilton: a study of wealth and influence in early Upper Canada, 1776–1812 (Ottawa 1983).

22 AO, Strachan papers, Macaulay to Robinson, 22 February 1850

23 E.A. Cruikshank (ed.), The correspondence of Lieut. Governor John Graves Simcoe, with allied documents relating to his administration of the government of Upper Canada, 1 (Toronto 1923), 245

24 Ibid.; see also J.K. Johnson, 'Hazelton Spencer,' DCB, 5:771–3, for a terse discussion of the lieutenancies of the counties.

25 Elizabeth M. Morgan, 'Joel Stone,' DCB, 6:738–9

26 E.J. Lajeunesse (ed.), The Windsor border region: Canada's southernmost frontier (Toronto 1960), xcviii, 145–7, 150–3

27 Niagara Herald, 13 May 1801

28 R.L. Fraser, 'Like Eden in her summer dress: gentry, economy, and society: Upper Canada, 1812–1840' (PHD thesis, University of Toronto 1979)

29 The classic formulation of providentialism in Upper Canada is S.F. Wise, 'Sermon literature and Canadian intellectual history,' United Church Archives, Committee on Archives, Bulletin (Toronto), 18 (1965), 3–18. Reservations as to the extent of Wise's claims are found in Fraser, 'Like Eden,' chapter 2, 47–103. See also Fraser, 'John Burns,' DCB, 6:93–5.

30 J.B. Robinson, Canada and the Canada Bill: being an examination of the proposed measure for the future government of Canada (London 1840), 42–3

31 Glengarry County, for instance, may well have had a local social

structure that was imported more or less intact from the Highlands of Scotland. See Marianne McLean, *The people of Glengarry: Highlanders in transition, 1745–1820* (Montreal 1990); see also Allan J. MacDonald, 'John McDonell (Aberchalder),' *DCB*, 5:518.
32 Robinson, *Canada and the Canada Bill*, 122
33 Ibid., 144
34 Ibid., 145
35 Ibid., 143
36 The adjective is Gail Campbell's. Her work on the operation of the franchise and voter participation significantly revises older assumptions about a broad, near universal, male suffrage in the British North American colonies. See, for example, Gail G. Campbell, 'The most restrictive franchise in British North America? a case study,' *CHR*, 71, no.2 (June 1990), 159–88.
37 S.F. Wise, 'Introduction,' in S.F. Wise, D. Carter-Edwards, and J. Witham (eds.), *"None was ever better ...": the loyalist settlement of Ontario* ([Cornwall] 1984), and David Mills, *The idea of loyalty in Upper Canada, 1784–1850* (Kingston and Montreal 1988)
38 [John Strachan], *The John Strachan letter book: 1812–1834*, ed. G.W. Spragge (Toronto 1946), 4–9
39 AO, Macaulay papers, Robinson to Macaulay, 25 November 1810
40 Ibid., Robinson to Macaulay, 15 February 1811
41 Biographies of all these figures are found in volumes 5 to 8 of the *DCB*.
42 NAC, MG 11, 313/2, extracts from the *Upper Canada Guardian*, 353, 24 August 1807; 333–9, 'A Loyalist' to the editor, 6 August 1807
43 John Strachan, *A discourse on the character of King George the Third addressed to the inhabitants of British America* (Montreal 1810), 18–19
44 Ibid., 20–2
45 Ibid., 39–40
46 Robinson, *Canada and the Canada Bill*, 23
47 Charge to the grand jury, Home District, 18 March 1822, printed in the *Kingston Chronicle*, 12 April 1822
48 *U.E. Loyalist*, 21 October 1826; see also Greg Marquis, 'Doing justice to "British Justice": law, ideology and Canadian historiography,' in Pue and Wright, *Canadian perspectives*.
49 *U.E. Loyalist*, 28 October 1826
50 Ibid., 20 October 1827
51 AO, Strachan papers, package #1, no.10, 'Prospects of the United States'
52 Ibid.

'All the privileges which Englishmen possess' lxxxiii

53 Ibid.
54 Private archives, John and Robert Cartwright papers, 1828–81, Strachan to John Solomon Cartwright, 10 January 1842 (microfilm at AO)
55 AO, Robinson papers, Charge to the grand jury, Western District, 1836. When I read Robinson's charges they were still in his manuscript collection; they were subsequently moved.
56 Ibid., Charge to the grand jury, Kingston, 20 September 1841. Fraser, 'Like Eden,' wrongly attributes a long quotation concerning 'a love of Order' to Robinson. In fact, it comes from one of John Strachan's sermons (AO, SP, sermons, 'Now the Lord is that Spirit and Where the Spirit of the Lord is there is liberty,' 4 February 1821 [he preached it again on 29 March 1829 and 5 February 1837]). Patrick Brode repeats this misattribution in *Sir John Beverley Robinson: bone and sinew of the compact* (The Osgoode Society [1984], 175–6, in a chapter titled (unhappily, it would now seem), 'A Love of Order.'
57 Ibid., Charge to the grand jury, Picton, 28 September 1835
58 Ibid., Charge to the grand jury, London District, 12 August 1830. To a large extent, Robinson's politics were rooted in an aristocratic landed order. Yet he was capable of adapting to the exigencies of Upper Canadian circumstances. His struggle to develop the agricultural economy brought him into conflict with wealthy commercial interests as represented by Thomas Clark and William Dickson and with large land speculators such as William Warren Baldwin. The point at issue was a land tax, anathema to large landed interests in England. He was even willing at one point to contemplate an income tax. Likewise, on the issue of police forces, he overcame the customary aristocratic reluctance about such institutions when faced by the utter absence of traditional checks on popular disorder. See Fraser, 'Like Eden,' 238–9.
59 Charles Rupert Sanderson (ed.), *The Arthur papers; being the Canadian papers mainly confidential, private and demi-official of Sir George Arthur, K.C.H., last lieutenant-governor of Upper Canada, in the manuscript collection of the Toronto Public Libraries*, 2 (Toronto 1957), 62, Robinson to Lord Normanby, 23 February 1839
60 Robinson, *Canada and the Canada Bill*, 25 and 146
61 AO, Robinson papers, Charge to the grand jury, Western District, 1836
62 AO, Macaulay papers, Robinson to Macaulay, 12 June 1824
63 AO, Robinson papers, Charge to the grand jury, Picton, 28 September 1835; see also *Canada and the Canada Bill*, 34.
64 *Patriot*, 6 March 1835 (debate of 28 February)

lxxxiv 'All the privileges which Englishmen possess'

65 AO, Robinson papers, Charge to the grand jury, Brockville, 20 August 1834
66 Robinson, *Canada and the Canada Bill*, 156
67 Strachan, *A discourse*, 21
68 AO, Robinson papers, Charge to the grand jury, Toronto, 25 May 1841
69 Ibid., Charge to the grand jury, Brockville, 1831
70 Ibid., Charge to the grand jury, [Bathurst District], 11 August 1834
71 Ibid., Charge to the grand jury, Prince Edward District, 16 September 1834
72 Ibid., Charge to the grand jury, London District, 30 August 1836
73 Ibid., Charge to the grand jury, Toronto, 1836
74 Ibid., Charge to the grand jury, [n.p.], 1837; see also Charge to the grand jury, Cornwall, 25 September 1837.
75 R.L. Fraser, 'William Warren Baldwin,' *DCB*, 7:35–44
76 J.K. Johnson, *Becoming prominent: regional leadership in Upper Canada, 1791–1841* (Kingston and Montreal [1989]), 10, 23
77 Frederick H. Armstrong, *Handbook of Upper Canadian chronology* (Toronto 1985), 120
78 The best work on the early civil courts is William N.T. Wylie's tightly argued and incisive 'Instruments of commerce and authority: the civil courts in Upper Canada, 1789–1812,' in David H. Flaherty (ed.), *Essays in the history of Canadian law*, 2 (The Osgoode Society [1983]), 3–48.
79 For the general structure of the courts, see Margaret A. Banks, 'The evolution of the Ontario courts, 1788–1791,' in Flaherty (ed.), *Essays in the history of Canadian law*, 2:492–572; Wylie, 'Instruments of commerce and authority'; and W.R. Riddell, *The bar and the courts of the province of Upper Canada, or Ontario* (Toronto 1928). S.R. Mealing is without equal on the 1790s; see his biographies of Simcoe and Osgoode in *DCB* 5 and 6. The act 34 GIII c.II is reprinted in A.G. Doughty and D.A. McArthur (eds.), *Documents relating to the constitutional history of Canada, 1791–1818* (Ottawa 1914), 146–57.
80 Armstrong's *Upper Canadian chronology* is indispensable for students of Upper Canadian history. Among its many useful features are the careful outlines and thumbnail descriptions of the various structures of government at all levels. For a discussion of crime at the district level, see John Weaver, 'Crime, public order, and repression: the Gore District in upheaval, 1832–1851,' *Ontario History*, 78, no.3 (September 1986), 175–98. For an exploration of magisterial life in a district, see

'All the privileges which Englishmen possess' lxxxv

David R. Murray, 'The cold hand of charity: the Court of Quarter Session and poor relief in the Niagara District, 1828–1841,' in Pue and Wright, *Canadian perspectives*, 179–206.
81 S.R. Mealing, 'William Osgoode,' *DCB*, 6:557–60
82 Wylie, 'Instruments of commerce and authority,' 16
83 The biographies of both men in *DCB* 5 are as substantial as they are good. See Wilson, 'Hamilton,' 5:402–6, and George Rawlyk, 'Richard Cartwright,' 5:167–72.
84 AO *Report*, 1910, 53
85 The statutory history of the profession is set out in W.R. Riddell, *The legal profession in Upper Canada in its early periods* (Toronto 1916).
86 AO *Report*, 1910, 198
87 Quoted in Riddell, *The legal profession*, 15
88 The figures are compiled from Armstrong, *Upper Canadian chronology*. Not all these individuals, of course, were still alive by 1810.
89 The following discussion is based mainly on the *Kingston Chronicle*, 28 December 1821 (debates of 3 and 4 December).
90 Thomas F. McIlwraith, 'Charles Jones,' *DCB*, 7:452–4
91 R.L. Fraser, 'Jonas Jones,' *DCB*, 7:456–61
92 For a discussion of the idea of gentlemen and its relation to the politics of Robinson, Jonas Jones, Christopher Hagerman, and others, see Fraser, 'Like Eden,' chapters 5 and 6.
93 R.L. Fraser, 'Robert Nichol,' *DCB*, 6:539–46
94 The discussion which follows is based on the *Gleaner*, 22 February 1823.
95 AO *Report*, 1914, 270, 278–82, 291–2, 428
96 Armstrong, *Upper Canadian chronology*, 122, 129; Riddell, *The legal profession*, 29–30
97 The figures were compiled from Armstrong, *Upper Canadian chronology*, 122–32.
98 Reproduced in J.R.W. Gwynne-Timothy, *Western's first century* (London, Ont., 1978), 428, as cited by G. Blaine Baker, 'Legal education in Upper Canada, 1785–1889: the Law Society as educator,' in Flaherty (ed.), *Essays in the history of Canadian law*, 2:55
99 AO *Report*, 1906, 174–5. The proclamation was promulgated on 7 February 1792.
100 Douglas McCalla, 'The loyalist economy of Upper Canada,' *Social History*, 16, no.32 (November 1983), 285
101 NAC, RG 1, L3, 283:L1, 1792–95/73
102 Public Record Office (PRO), CO 42/317, ff.186–9, 191, 193–4, 197–205

lxxxvi 'All the privileges which Englishmen possess'

103 AO *Report*, 1909, 135–6. Douglas McCalla has taken issue with historians who seize upon the complaints against large merchants as a means of describing the economy. The point is well taken; obviously, this sort of evidence has limitations. But the political world of Upper Canada was shaped as much by perception as by reality. And the perception of monopoly and its equation with oppression was heady stuff. Merchant-bashing, or rather monopoly-bashing, was simply good politics. Its language had a calculated appeal and was used to manipulate voters for political ends. As crude a man as Isaac Swayze understood that much.
104 *Upper Canada Gazette*, 30 November, 7 December 1799
105 Ibid.
106 Wylie, 'Instruments of commerce and authority,' 26–7
107 *Upper Canada Gazette*, 30 November, 7 December 1799
108 Ibid., 2 May 1800 ('A Friend to Justice')
109 Edith G. Firth (ed.), *The town of York, 1793–1815: a collection of documents of early Toronto* (Toronto 1962), 157–60
110 The tale of the *Speedy* is eloquently told by Brendan O'Brien in *Speedy justice* (The Osgoode Society 1992).
111 *Upper Canada Gazette*, 17 March 1804
112 Ibid., 25 January 1805
113 AO, Russell papers, Russell to Osgoode, 22 July 1802
114 PRO, CO 42/342, f.167, Allcock to William Windham, 16 May 1806
115 *Upper Canada Gazette*, 27 October 1804 (notice of 25 October). The rule was applied to the sons of loyalists only; daughters and wives were exempted (M.M. Quaife [ed.], *The John Askin papers* (Detroit 1928–31), 2:516–17, Alexander Grant to Askin, 9 May 1806. Hunter's successor, President Alexander Grant, rescinded the order on 16 May 1806 in an attempt to deflect some of the criticism. *Upper Canada Gazette*, 17 May 1806
116 AO, Cartwright papers, typescript letterbook, 1787–1808, 220. Cartwright enclosed a list of some 100 people who were to be charged full fees on grants, although either UELs or children of UELs. He did not 'enter into the merits of these cases but ... I know it is your wish to be made acquainted with everything that can give reasonable cause of public dissatisfaction.'
117 AO *Report*, 1909, 265, 11 June 1802
118 Ibid.
119 Ibid. 1911, 63–4, 10 February 1806

'All the privileges which Englishmen possess' lxxxvii

120 R.L. Fraser, 'Benajah Mallory,' *DCB*, 8:606–10
121 Daniel J. Brock, 'Samuel Ryerse,' *DCB*, 5:732–5, and 'Thomas Welch,' *DCB*, 5:845–7
122 Norfolk Historical Society, 982–93 (draft), Welch to Mallory, 3 January 1803
123 [Thomas Douglas], *Lord Selkirk's diary, 1803–1804; a journal of his travels in British North America and the northeastern United States*, ed., P.C.T. White (Toronto 1958) 305
124 AO, Russell papers, Welch to Russell, 31 January 1805
125 Fraser, 'Mallory,' 607
126 AO, GS 1822, Burford Township, Brant County, abstract of memorials, 1800–52, ff.1, 144, 183, 247; RG 22, series 131, King's Bench docketbook, 2 (M–Z), 1797–1830, ff.7, 13–14; *Upper Canada Gazette*, 27 February 1811, 4 May 1812
127 NAC, RG 5, B25, 3 (election papers): 52, Benajah Mallory to the free and independent electors of the counties of Oxford and Middlesex, 23 May 1812
128 *Liberal*, 29 November 1823 (editorial)
129 Public Archives of Canada (PAC) *Report*, 1892–3, note d, 57, Thorpe to Sir George Shee, 1 December 1806. It was alleged by Lieutenant Governor Francis Gore that the letters from 'A Loyalist' in Willcocks's *Upper Canada Guardian* were written by Thorpe. PRO, CO 42/347, f.242, Gore to George Watson, 4 October 1807
130 It was a loyalist assemblyman, Thomas Dorland, who introduced resolutions on this matter in 1806. Moneys spent by the executive without parliamentary authorization 'violated' the 'rights and privileges of the Commons.' AO *Report*, 1911, 101–2, 28 February 1806
131 PAC *Report*, 1892–3, note d, 105, Thorpe to the secretary of state, 14 August 1807
132 Thorpe himself had a civil suit for debt brought against him successfully. AO, RG 22, King's Bench docketbook, M–Z, 1797–1830, f.218
133 AO, RG 22, series 125 (Court of King's Bench, termbooks), 1:8 November 1803, 6 November 1805, 10 January 1806; 2:147
134 *Upper Canada Gazette*, 18 January 1806
135 PAC *Report*, 1892–3, note d, 52
136 Ibid., 53
137 Ibid., 63
138 PRO, CO 42/350, f.175, Gore to Liverpool, 23 April 1810
139 AO, RG 22, series 3, 153:92–3

140 PRO, CO 42/350, ff.76–7, Hamilton to William Halton, 20 January 1807; ff.78–9, Representation of the magistrates of the District of Niagara, 19 January 1807
141 AO, RG 22, King's Bench, docketbook, M–Z, 1797–1830, f.249
142 PRO, CO 42/350, ff.76–7, Hamilton to Halton, 20 January 1807
143 R.L. Fraser has written biographies of all three men for the *DCB*. Dorland and Washburn appear in volume 6. Howard is in volume 7.
144 AO, Cartwright papers, typescript letterbook, 1787–1808, 264–7, Cartwright to Gore, 2 April 1807
145 PRO, CO 42/341, f.59, Gore to William Windham, 13 March 1807
146 NAC, RG 5, A1, 2802–21, Gore to Sir James Henry Craig, 5 January 1808
147 PRO, CO 42/350, ff.223–6, *Upper Canada Guardian*, 6 August 1807
148 Ibid.
149 Ibid., *Upper Canada Guardian*, 27 August 1807
150 [John Mills Jackson], *A view of the political situation of the province of Upper Canada* (London 1809), xi and 3
151 R.L. Fraser, 'John Mills Jackson,' *DCB*, 7:438–40
152 PRO, CO 42/350, f.12
153 Jackson, *A view of the political situation*, 12
154 [Richard Cartwright], *Letters, from an American loyalist in Upper-Canada, to his friend in England, on a pamphlet published by John Mills Jackson, esquire: entitled, A view of the province of Upper Canada* (Halifax [1810]). Often attributed to Mr Justice Powell, the pamphlet was Cartwright's work; see Rawlyk, 'Cartwright.' Information on the pamphlet's publication can be found in *Upper Canada Gazette*, 14 November 1810.
155 Cartwright, *Letters*, 3–5
156 As quoted in Fraser, 'Mallory,' 609
157 Private archives, Sir John Beverley Robinson papers, 106–7, Strachan to Robinson, 2 June 1814 (microfilm at NAC, MG 24, B9)
158 See the assembly debates on this persistent issue in *Western Mercury*, 26 January 1832 (debate of 3 January), and *Correspondent & Advocate*, 29 May 1834
159 R.L. Fraser, 'Peter Howard,' *DCB*, 7:419
160 NAC, RG 5, A1, 21787–94, Willson to Major George Hillier, 4 October 1819
161 *Canadian Freeman*, 18 January 1827
162 Districts were the basic unit of municipal government in the province until 1850, when they were abolished. Four districts were established

'All the privileges which Englishmen possess' lxxxix

in 1788 and by 1841 there were 20. See Armstrong, *Upper Canadian chronology*, 158–61. Between 1791 and 1841, the province's population grew from approximately 14,000 to 450,000. For the former figure, see Douglas McCalla, 'The loyalist economy of Upper Canada,' 285; for the latter, see J.L. Finlay, *Pre-Confederation Canada: the structure of Canadian history to 1867* (Scarborough [1990]), 265
163 R.L. Fraser, 'Peter Desjardins,' *DCB*, 6:198–200, and 'John Willson,' *DCB*, 8:945–7
164 *U.E. Loyalist*, 6 October 1827
165 *Spirit of the Times*, 26 June 1830
166 Ibid., 25 August 1830. This was not an isolated occurrence. On 17 September 1825, for instance, Henry Hamilton, a murderer awaiting execution on 7 October, succumbed to a fever which had lasted two weeks. He had contracted the illness while in Brockville's jail and, 'although every attention was given,' he expired. The verdict of the inquest was that Hamilton's death came 'by the visitation of God.' Nothing was discovered 'to lead to a suspicion that the deceased had come to his end by any improper means.' From the *Brockville Recorder* as cited in the *Weekly Register*, 29 September 1825. The most notorious jail incident occurred on 31 March 1835 when James Owen McCarthy died after an altercation with the jailer – one day before his conditional pardon (the condition was banishment) was to be granted. See R.L. Fraser, 'James Owen McCarthy,' *DCB*, 6:426.
167 *Canadian Freeman*, 29 July 1830
168 Fraser, 'W.W. Baldwin'
169 *Colonial Advocate*, 13 May 1830
170 *Gore Balance*, 7 January 1830
171 *Colonial Advocate*, 25 April 1833
172 Ibid., 24 April 1834
173 *Canadian Freeman*, 8 November 1827
174 AO, Robinson papers, letterbook, private letters of Sir J.B. Robinson, 1814–62, 164–8, Robinson to Strachan, 8 April 1851. There are different historical positions as to whether the church-and-state tradition represented by Robinson had any continuity with the political culture of mid- and late-nineteenth-century Canada. My own argument in brief is that there was no *essential* continuity. Some of the impulses continued, to be sure, but in altered form, and the public philosophy represented by this tradition did not survive the 1840s. Robinson's epistle is nothing more than wishful thinking and just how wishful is revealed by the insistence that not only the old social and political or-

der would be restored, but also the privileged position of the Church of England.

The arguments necessary to making this case take one beyond the usual territory of historians. It is necessary to grasp the core of Western philosophical developments since the fifteenth century. The relationship between the tradition (embodied at least partially by Robinson) and public conservatism is beautifully captured in George Grant's writing. There are relevant chapters in both *Lament for a nation: the defeat of Canadian nationalism* (Toronto 1970) and *Technology and empire* (Toronto 1969).

175 AO, Robinson papers, part II, private letters from family and friends, 1814–62, 249–56, M.S. Bidwell to W.B. Robinson, 24 February 1863
176 Metropolitan Toronto Reference Library (MTRL), Robert Baldwin papers, R. Baldwin to J.B. Robinson, 3 August 1848
177 Archives de l'Archevêché de Québec, 320 CN III:3–8, MacDonell to the bishop, 20 April 1801. On the enduring quality of regionalism within Ontario, specifically its rural areas, see Chad Gaffield, 'Children, schooling, and family reproduction in nineteenth-century Ontario,' *CHR*, 72, no.2 (June 1991), 167. Gaffield's happy phrase is 'a differentiated collection of regions.'
178 Mackenzie surveyed the province's legislative past in the *Colonial Advocate* in 1828 and again in 1833.
179 Paul Romney, 'Re-inventing Upper Canada: American immigrants, Upper Canadian history, English law, and the alien question,' in Roger Hall, William Westfall, and Laurel Sefton MacDowell (eds.), *Patterns of the past: interpreting Ontario's history* (Toronto and Oxford 1988), 78–107; and Romney's *Mr Attorney: the attorney general for Ontario in court, cabinet, and legislature, 1791–1899* (The Osgoode Society [1986]), 82–104
180 Fraser, 'W.W. Baldwin'
181 *Gore Gazette*, 13 September 1828
182 Report of the select committee on the petition of William Forsyth, in Great Britain, Parliament, *House of Commons paper*, 1833, 26, no.543:7
183 *Canadian Freeman*, 17 April 1828
184 Ibid., 24 April 1828
185 Fraser, 'W.W. Baldwin'
186 Ibid.
187 MTRL, Broadsides, 1828 petition; 1828 meeting
188 *Canadian Freeman*, 18 September 1828. The Constitutional Act makes no mention of the appointment of judges to the councils. Osgoode,

'All the privileges which Englishmen possess' xci

the first chief justice, was appointed president of the Executive Council and speaker of the Legislative Council and that tradition continued. Puisne judges occasionally sat on the councils. The assembly passed a resolution in 1825 urging that the judges become as 'independent of the Crown and people as are the judges of England.' The following year, Lord Bathurst, the colonial secretary, noted that 'it does not appear that there is anything peculiar in the state of the Province ... which should make it advisable that this system should be changed.' See Patrick Brode, 'Of courts and politics: the growth of an independent judiciary in Upper Canada,' Law Society of Upper Canada, *Gazette*, 12, no.3 (September 1978), 265 and 267. The issue was also raised in Lower Canada and there it was decided to exclude the puisne justices from the councils (PAC *Report*, 1930, 193-5). Continuing pressure prompted Lord Goderich to state in 1831 that 'there is no Branch of Our Civil Polity which has been more fully proved to be conducive to these Great Ends [stability of government and welfare of the people], than the Establishment of Judges independent at once on the Royal Authority and on the pleasure of the popular Branch of the Legislature.' He directed Lieutenant Governor Sir John Colborne to declare 'that the Commissions of all the Judges of the Supreme Courts shall be granted to endure during their good behaviour and not during the Royal Pleasure.' No judges would be appointed to the councils, with one exception. The chief justice could remain in the Legislative Council 'in order that they may have the benefit of his assistance in framing Laws of a general and permanent character.' Goderich to Sir John Colborne, 8 February 1831, PAC *Report*, 1935, 257-8. The sole proviso was that the assembly grant a permanent civil list.

189 The starting point for the literature is Paul Romney, 'From the types riot to the rebellion: elite ideology, anti-legal sentiment, political violence, and the rule of law in Upper Canada,' *Ontario History*, 79, no.2 (June 1987), 113-44. The biography of W.W. Baldwin in *DCB* 7 covers some of the ground on the events and the language of opposition in the late 1820s.

190 MTRL, W.W. Baldwin papers, B104, M.S. Bidwell to Baldwin, 8 September 1828

191 Charles Durand, *Reminiscences of Charles Durand of Toronto, barrister* (Toronto 1897), 265

192 *Kingston Chronicle*, 24 January 1829 (debate of 10 January)

193 Ibid. The attempt to define ministerial responsibility and to assert the

legislature's control over irresponsible ministers was made by Robert Nichol in 1820. Careful to exempt the crown from wrongdoing, he had 'no intention of charging the head of Government with malpractices, it was his advisers who were the responsible characters ... The king could do no wrong but wicked ministers lost their heads, and wicked and corrupt Governors were brought to trial.' Fraser, 'Nichol,' 544

194 *Kingston Chronicle*, 28 March 1829 (debate of 16 March)
195 Elizabeth Nish (ed.), *Debates of the Legislative Assembly of United Canada*, 1 (Montreal [1970]), 790
196 W.W. Baldwin, for instance, adopted increasingly harsh and inflexible rhetoric between 1820 and 1840. The experiences of the 1820s transformed and hardened his political language; he never turned back from it. For a discussion of this point, see Fraser, 'W.W. Baldwin.' By 1820 Baldwin no longer held out hope for government preferment or patronage. This may explain, in part, his flowering as a trenchant critic of, and oppositionist to, the administration of Sir Peregrine Maitland during this period.
197 *Colonial Advocate*, 24 April 1834 ('Commonweal')
198 Michael S. Cross and R.L. Fraser, 'Robert Baldwin,' *DCB*, 8:56–7
199 An early example of this writing is Charles Lindsey's handling of the trial and execution of Charles French. See his *Life and times of Wm. Lyon Mackenzie*, 1 (Toronto 1862; reprinted 1971), 117–20.
200 MTRL, Robert Baldwin papers, A67, Rolph to R. Baldwin, 19 January 1831
201 MTRL, W.W. Baldwin papers, B105, Rolph to W.W. Baldwin, 24 March 1831

John Rolph

Christopher Alexander Hagerman

William Warren Baldwin.
Lithograph by F. Davignon, after a painting by Théophile Hamel,
published by Nagel & Weingaertner, N.Y.

Robert Baldwin Sullivan

Marshall Spring Bidwell

Robert Baldwin.
Lithograph drawn by Hoppner Francis Meyer.

Jonas Jones

Sir William Campbell

Levius Peters Sherwood

Sir John Beverley Robinson

William Dummer Powell

Christopher Alexander Hagerman's house and law office, Toronto. His law office is the building to the left. Water-colour by Frederic V. Poole, c. 1912.

John Beverley Robinson's law office, Toronto. Water-colour by Frederic V. Poole, c. 1912.

Gore District court-house and jail, 1830, Hamilton.
Michael Vincent was executed in the near foreground. James Owen McCarthy was incarcerated, was tried, and died here. George Powlis was jailed and tried here.

Home District court-house and jail, 1827–40, York (Toronto).
Detail of water-colour by John George Howard.

Home District jail, 1799–1827, York (Toronto).
Etching by Hans Jensen. Elijah Bentley was incarcerated here.

View north along King Street near St. George's Cathedral by James Cockburn, 1829. Pen-and-ink and water-colour on paper. The Midland District court-house is to the right of the church.

Pavilion Hotel, Niagara Falls.
Water-colour by James Pattison Cockburn. The rear verandah provided a view of the falls.

Mohawk Village, c. 1830.
George Powlis was born here, and Susannah Doxater was murdered near the village.

Execution of William Kain, 1830, Kingston.
This drawing appeared on the cover of a pamphlet detailing Kain's life.

Officialdom:
The Judiciary and Crown Officers

HENRY ALLCOCK
Judge and politician; baptized 26 Jan. 1759 in Birmingham, England, son of Henry Allcock and Mary Askin; m. Hannah ——, and they had a daughter; d. 22 Feb. 1808 at Quebec, Lower Canada.

The Allcock family came from Edgbaston, near Birmingham, and moved to the city in the decade before Henry was born. He began his legal studies at Lincoln's Inn, London, in January 1785, and was admitted to the bar exactly six years later. He then practised in London specializing in equity law, which deals with matters not covered by the common law. In November 1798 Allcock was appointed a puisne judge of the Upper Canada Court of King's Bench on the recommendation of his friend, Chief Justice John Elmsley. By early January 1799 he was at York (Toronto), where he took the oath of office to become one of the three judges of the highest court in a virtual wilderness. His duties included attendance both at the court sessions held in the capital and at the assizes held in the local administrative towns, such as Cornwall, Kingston, Niagara (Niagara-on-the-Lake), and Sandwich (Windsor). Although the question of establishing an equity court with Allcock as judge was raised, no action was taken.

Personally, Allcock was a difficult individual, like so many of the fractious misfits who came to the province, particularly in that era. He was quickly on bad terms with his two colleagues on King's Bench, his former friend Elmsley and William Dummer Powell. Legislative councillor Richard Cartwright remarked that what Elmsley supported, Allcock was bound to oppose. Allcock's disagreements with Powell were partly over his own insistence on the use in Upper Canada of the full pomp and procedures of English courts. The Reverend John Stuart of Kingston at first felt that Allcock was 'not so rough in his manners, as the world is pleased to suppose.' But he changed his mind when his son, the Reverend George Okill Stuart of York, was upbraided by Allcock during a church service for a supposed violation of church law. Allcock then began a sort of persecution of the young cleric which, Stuart Sr asserted, was 'passionately illiberal & vindictive.'

Allcock was barely settled in the province before he decided to run for the House of Assembly in the election of 1800, despite the fact that he was on the bench. He was duly elected for Durham, Simcoe and the East Riding of York. Soon, however, there was a petition from some local inhabitants, including Samuel Heron, to Lieutenant Governor Peter Hunter. They asserted that Allcock's agent, William Weekes, had used unwarranted steps to secure the election. When a hearing was held by the assembly into the legality of the election, Allcock made use of a paper drawn up by Attorney General Thomas Scott to argue that the house was incompetent to decide the issue and refused to leave during the proceedings, declaring that he would have to be thrown out by the *'neck and heels.'* On the grounds of irregularities the house unseated him on 11 June 1801; he had, in Alexander Grant's words, 'tryed every means and did not leave a Stone unturned to keep his Seat but could not.'

Allcock was, naturally, a decisive judge. John Askin described him at a land claims hearing in 1799 as 'a very Impartial good man, but so particular & sticks so close to the law, a very unfitt man to act up to the Spirit of the Act'; he added, moreover, that Allcock 'did as he pleased without asking the Sentiments of the othe[r] Commissioners in hardly any case.' The most famous case over which Allcock presided was the trial of John Small for the murder of Attorney General John White in a duel. Allcock, who claimed to have been friendly with White, lamented that the solicitor general, Robert Isaac Dey Gray, 'failed altogether in adducing positive evidence' of Small's guilt and the 'Jury would presume nothing.' Thus the defendant went free, as was usual in trials arising from duels. In 1803, at the assizes in Sandwich, Allcock sentenced two murderers to be hanged till dead and afterward hanged in chains, evidence that he was not lenient on the bench.

After Hunter arrived as lieutenant governor in 1799, Allcock gradually became one of his chief advisers, supplanting Elmsley, and helped him bring some order and regulation to the land-granting system. By 1803 Hunter was recommending him for an increase in salary as a reward for his efficiency. He also supported him for new offices. When Elmsley was appointed chief justice of Lower Canada in May 1802, Allcock, rather than the senior judge, Powell, succeeded to the Upper Canadian post. Allcock became an executive councillor and in January 1803 he was appointed to the Legislative Council on Hunter's recommendation, becoming speaker of that house.

Whatever his office, Allcock constantly pressed for the creation of a court of chancery. In 1801 he prepared a draft bill and also proposed that he be appointed to the new court while retaining his position on King's Bench, an arrangement that would have given him two salaries. The British government delayed taking action but this did not stop Allcock from bombarding it with letters during 1802. By the end of 1803 he had decided that it would be necessary to go home to obtain action and, with Hunter's blessings, he applied for a six-month leave of absence. It was approved in March 1804 but the government refused either to increase his salary or to grant his request for a court. That fall, armed with a letter of introduction from Hunter, which solicited a salary increase for him, Allcock left for England.

While he was there, opportunity presented itself. Allcock had long been eyeing a more lucrative chief justiceship of Lower Canada. As early as 1800 he had begun studying the Lower Canadian statutes and, when William Osgoode retired from the post in 1801, he had attempted, unsuccessfully, to gain the appointment. As 1804 closed and the hopes for the chancery judgeship faded, another possibility opened up – Elmsley was dying at Quebec and Allcock could see the chance of promotion. The main obstacle to his appointment was the Lower Canadian administrative oligarchy, who were unanimous in not wanting a third chief justice brought in from Upper Canada and who had their own candidate in Attorney General Jonathan Sewell. Unlike Allcock, Sewell was expert in French civil law and spoke French fluently. His case was strongly presented by Lieutenant Governor Sir Robert Shore Milnes who noted that Allcock lacked the proper dignity. Sewell was also supported by Anglican bishop Jacob Mountain and other Lower Canadian leaders. Nevertheless, when Elmsley died in April 1805, Allcock succeeded through the influence of a British patron, the lord high chancellor, Lord Eldon. As Sewell was advised, 'there was no resisting such powerful Interest.'

Despite the unhappiness over his appointment, Allcock deferred arriving at Quebec until August 1806, when he was sworn in as chief justice and member of the Executive Council. He became speaker of the Legislative Council the following January. Under the circumstances, he should have looked for allies, particularly since his patron, Hunter, was now dead. The task would have been relatively easy because there were factions among the province's leaders. Instead,

6 Henry Allcock

Allcock began to assail almost everyone in power. Like judge Robert Thorpe in Upper Canada, by the end of 1806 he was writing to the colonial under-secretary, Sir George Shee, expounding on the evils he had found. His indictment of Lower Canadian society was truly comprehensive; neither the French nor the English members of the administration escaped his censure. Among his many complaints were that Milnes's attitude to him personally was unsatisfactory; Administrator Thomas Dunn was mishandling the renewal of the lease on the Saint-Maurice ironworks; the puisne justices, Dunn and Jenkin Williams, were too old and infirm to perform their duties properly; and there was great confusion in the courts of justice. He recommended that French executive councillors who died should be replaced by English, and he expressed the hope that the new governor would not make appointments without consultation, advising Dunn that he 'expected no appointment would be disposed of without his being first consulted.' Soon he was also writing to the colonial secretary, Viscount Castlereagh, stating that Dunn's memory had failed, an accusation not borne out by Dunn's correspondence. Castlereagh investigated the more substantial claims; 'senile' Dunn, however, acquitted himself well. Despite Allcock's efforts, the new governor, Sir James Henry Craig, who arrived in October 1807, quickly fell under the influence of Sewell and Herman Witsius Ryland, the civil secretary, with whom Allcock was also quarrelling. Thus, though he remained in office, he was excluded from the influence he cherished. Early in 1808 he died of a 'bilious fever.'

There is little information on Allcock's personal life. His wife having died in 1802, he was, apparently, planning remarriage near the end of his life. He had a farm near York and he had applied for 1,200 acres of land in November 1798. He did not, however, petition for his full entitlement as an executive councillor until he had left the province. He was a member of the Church of England and in 1803 he presided over a meeting of subscribers to erect the first St James church.

Evaluating Allcock does not lead to pleasant conclusions. His letters reveal a consideration for his family that did not extend to most of his acquaintances; however, he could ingratiate himself with select patrons. His personality, possibly progressively, caused difficulties wherever he went. Like many office holders, he was incredibly persistent in advancing his own interests. Yet in Upper Canada he had undoubtedly helped Hunter make the administration run more smoothly. In Lower Canada he accomplished little but trouble-making. His avarice, importuning, and quarrelsomeness were still legendary when Henry James Morgan did the research for his first collection of biographies some 50 years after Allcock's death. He was one of the more unattractive of the many eccentrics who plagued the Canadas at the opening of the 19th century.

FREDERICK H. ARMSTRONG

ROBERT BALDWIN

Lawyer and politician; b. 12 May 1804 in York (Toronto), eldest son of William Warren Baldwin and Margaret Phœbe Willcocks; m. 31 May 1827 Augusta Elizabeth Sullivan, and they had two sons and two daughters; d. 9 Dec. 1858 near Toronto.

Robert Baldwin grew up in an extended, and somewhat closed, world of Willcockses, Russells, and Sullivans. Few institutions were as important to Upper Canadian society as the family, and the Baldwins' relationships were especially close and affectionate. Unfortunately, the few documents surviving offer only glimpses into Robert's childhood and adolescence. It is clear, however, from his conduct and utterance as an adult that his character was forged in boyhood under the influence of his urbane and talented father and perhaps more important his mother, whom he once described as 'the master mind of our family' and who was probably responsible for Robert's earliest education.

Robert was formally educated in York by John Strachan. In 1818 William Warren said he was 'as forward in point of education as our school here advances boys of his age. I shall keep him yet two years more at school ... – I intend please God to bring him up to the bar.' It was, however, the expectations and standards of his parents, especially their exhortation to goodness and correct conduct, which remained with Robert. If anything, their hopes increased after the deaths of his younger brothers Henry (d. 1820) and Quetton St George (d. 1829). The legacy of principled life and uncompromised action defined Robert Baldwin in his public life, and it hobbled his spirit even as a young man. For he was, as he later put it, 'a sceptic – may God forgive me though I hope not wholly an unbeliever.' Moreover, he was melancholic, sickly, and intensely emotional.

The defining characteristic of the teenager embarking on a career in his father's legal office in 1820 was his idealization of women and his yearning for perfect love. He had few friends. His closest acquaintance was another young man of delicate and refined spirits,

James Hunter Samson, who had moved from York to Kingston early in 1819 and with whom he corresponded, though irregularly. They began a debate that year on the merits of love and friendship. Baldwin was adamant: love between a man and woman was nobler than the friendship of two men.

Some of Baldwin's leisure time went to poetry. He and Samson exchanged their work and offered criticism. In June 1819 Baldwin dropped a planned epic in favour of an 'Ode to Tecumse,' which Samson admired. For Baldwin, poetry was an important means of expressing the thoughts and emotions that dominated him. One recurring theme was love – much of the poetry was dedicated to women, individually or collectively. Another theme was virtue. He admired Tecumseh as one more 'Resolved to perish than to yield.' In his early correspondence Baldwin also exhibits a frailty in health that would be his companion through life. His mental health was equally vulnerable. Yet the public world, and probably his own family, knew little of the doubts and demons tormenting young Robert.

His greatest yearning – for perfect love – was satiated early in 1825. He fell in love with his first cousin Augusta Elizabeth Sullivan. Robert's recently discovered private correspondence with her reveals a man of unsuspected passions, fervidly romantic. Admittance to the bar in April 1825 was secondary to his new-found love. When the families discovered it that same month, Eliza was shunted off to relatives in New York. For Robert, their love was a bittersweet experience. Eliza was the only one to whom he could reveal his innermost longings. In his letters he unfettered his emotions – his pervasive melancholy, his fear of professional failure, and his sense of the fleetingness of happiness. He was to go through life acutely aware of human mutability and its most extreme form, mortality. At last able through his relationship with Eliza to plunge into his unexpressed emotions, he was almost self-absorbed. Eliza became 'the sweetest source of my future happiness and the kindest soother of my future disappointments.' Love for Baldwin was not fancy; nor was it simply passion. It was more elevated, pure and spiritual. Small wonder he had a predilection for novels extolling the virtues of domestic life. His favourite was Fanny Burney's *Camilla*, a panegyric to domesticity and matrimony.

Baldwin was called to the bar on 20 June 1825; three days later he was presented to the court by his father, treasurer of the Law Society of Upper Canada. The true meaning of the occasion was shared only with Eliza: 'When I reflect how much of our happiness depends on my success in my profession ... I own I almost tremble with anxiety.' Yet, despite his preoccupation with Eliza, during their separation Baldwin gained proficiency in the law. He travelled on circuit, probably throughout the western and central districts of the province, and was 'more successful' than he expected. In the late summer of 1825 John Rolph, who had his own law practice, offered to assist him in his. Robert agreed, presumably to gain experience, and found himself immersed in Rolph's 'causes.' In a case before Judge William Campbell, Rolph, assisted by Baldwin, opposed James Buchanan Macaulay. Rolph unexpectedly ordered Baldwin to address the jury. Baldwin demurred, but finally rose. 'Never was I in a more distressing situation,' he wrote Eliza; all he could think of was 'what passed between us' on a night seven months earlier. Then he proceeded, gaining in confidence as he went along. Macaulay spoke highly of Baldwin in his summary; 'it was a moment of great happiness,' he told Eliza. A capital case came next and Baldwin won an acquittal. Late in 1825 he finished his first tour of the assizes circuit. His friends judged him a success and, he confided to Eliza, thought a certain speech 'affords a prospect of my one day not being altogether undistinguished in my profession – I have a horror of not rising above mediocrity.' Baldwin was 'trembling anxious' since 'without commanding respect from my profession I never would be worthy of you I never could make you happy.' The brief experience of professional life had been profoundly revealing for the introspective young man. It had, for instance, illuminated his obsession with being right and its concomitant effects upon him – mental anguish and procrastination. In May 1826 he wrote to Eliza: 'When a person acts only on their own Judgment they are always fearful of being wrong. ... Not that I admire indecision on the contrary I dislike it much[.] I know however it is one of my own faults & it pervades more or less everything I do.'

By the end of a year of separation from Eliza, Robert was pleased with his professional progress. One of his clients was a former chief justice, William Dummer Powell. In May 1826 John Strachan, about to leave for England, called on Baldwin to ask if he wanted his name entered at Lincoln's Inn. Baldwin declined. Love had overtaken a bachelor's plan for the future. In due course Eliza returned and with a few close friends and many relatives present, she and Robert were married on 31 May 1827. If their correspondence is an accurate indicator, they attained matrimonial bliss. The law practice thrived.

Baldwin often cooperated on cases with his father, with his brother-in-law Robert Baldwin Sullivan and, from 1831, frequently with Rolph. Yet life still had its worries. His health was poor and Eliza suffered from continued sickness during her first pregnancy. He fussed over her incessantly, reminding her that Providence had 'ordered that few of those maladies with which your sex are visited at such a period should be dangers – they are however all troublesome & call for a husbands care & a husbands fondness.'

Eliza had an abiding effect on her husband. She was only 15 when their courtship began, and she died before turning 26. Although she was of gentle birth and educated to her station, her early letters are somewhat kittenish; later correspondence displays a greater measure of maturity. What attracted Baldwin was not her appearance, which was plain, but her character and opinions, of which we know little. Still, his expectations could only be met by a rare woman. They read the Bible together, his scepticism giving way to unshakeable faith. He came to believe that the body was but a temporary dispensation and the Christian horizon was eternity. He wanted to be with her *'never* to part,' even after death. The fear of death was removed, 'for guilt alone need make us fear our hereafter.'

Between 1825 and 1828 the administration of Sir Peregrine Maitland came under increasing attack from opposition critics, including William Warren Baldwin and Rolph. Matters came to a head in 1828 and, with personal and professional ties to two leading players, Robert was drawn in. On 17 June, John Walpole Willis delivered in court an opinion that the Court of King's Bench was illegally constituted. He was dismissed by the governor and the Executive Council on 26 June, by which time the Baldwins had become involved in a collective protest against the court's legality and refused to argue before it. The affair prompted the Baldwins, no doubt in collaboration with Rolph and Marshall Spring Bidwell, to launch the first popular campaign for responsible government in the history of the province.

A general election gave the imbroglio political overtones, especially in York and vicinity. Accepting nomination 'in this important and alarming crisis,' Robert ran in the county of York. Late in July the riding was taken by Jesse Ketchum and William Lyon Mackenzie, Baldwin coming in last in a four-man race. The election did nothing to put out the fire of protest ignited by the Willis affair. At a meeting on 15 August, at which a petition was adopted which included a plea for responsible government, the Baldwins played leading roles, Robert moving key resolutions. It was, as he put it, a time when colonial policy had become important because of 'the misrule of Provincial administrations.' Maitland defended his administration in a dispatch to London; in it he referred to the Baldwins as the only gentlemen associated with the opposition.

On 13 November, Robert was named to the committee to prepare an address to the new lieutenant governor, Sir John Colborne. Through the fall and winter of 1828–29 Baldwin participated in meetings and committees protesting Willis's removal, presenting other grievances, and urging the attention of parliament. In a by-election in December 1829, after John Beverley Robinson had been appointed chief justice and resigned his seat for the town of York, Baldwin defeated James Edward Small. In his victory speech Baldwin pronounced himself 'a whig in principle, and opposed to the present administration.' The writ of election had been improperly issued, however. In a new election Baldwin was opposed, unsuccessfully, by William Botsford Jarvis. On 30 Jan. 1830 he took his seat in the assembly.

Baldwin was a regular participant in its affairs but not a dominant figure. He chaired several committees and gave evidence before others, including one headed by Mackenzie on the currency. A stockholder of the Bank of Upper Canada, Baldwin took exception to its administration, which he linked to the provincial executive. The following June he led a group of stockholders in an attempt to have an independent director elected to the board. Nominated himself he was defeated by an administration supporter, Samuel Peters Jarvis. With the death of George IV in June 1830, parliament was dissolved and a new general election called. Baldwin was defeated by W.B. Jarvis and dropped from the political scene. In September 1835 Colborne suggested the Baldwins for the Legislative Council if the secretary of state considered it 'expedient.' Neither was appointed.

Robert disliked politics. More important, he was preoccupied with his practice and family. He worried about the health of Eliza, increasingly delicate, and the daily routine of his expanding family in their Yonge Street home. The birth of Robert Baldwin Jr on 17 April 1834 by surgical means was a blow to Eliza's health. In May the following year she journeyed to New York with her father-in-law to recuperate. On the eighth anniversary of their marriage, Baldwin longed to join her but refrained: 'it would be inconsistent with *duty* And I know my Eliza too well not to know that she could never wish me to sacrifice it to inclination.' Eliza returned home but never recovered. She died on 11 Jan. 1836. Baldwin was devastated. His brief happiness had ended almost as he had foreseen it. 'I am left to pursue the remainder of my pilgrimage alone – and in the waste that lies before me I can expect to find joy only in the reflected happiness of our darling children, and in looking forward, in humble hope, to that blessed hour which by God's permission shall forever reunite me to my Eliza.'

What soon happened to Baldwin publicly takes on added meaning in the light of what is now known of his personal life. The new lieutenant governor, Sir Francis Bond Head, arrived in Toronto on 23 Jan. 1836. Expectations were high among opposition groups that Head would attempt conciliation and reform, as he had been instructed. Maladministration by the Executive Council had been an opposition target since the days of Joseph Willcocks. By 1828 reform of its administration, by responsible government, had become the issue associated with the Baldwins, father and son. Up to 1836 there were a variety of opinions about the most efficacious means of reform: responsible government was only one. Now the opposition looked to the composition of the council for a sign of Head's intentions.

The three executive councillors (Peter Robinson, George Herchmer Markland, and Joseph Wells) were anxious for new appointments. Head's first choice was Robert Baldwin, whom he considered 'highly respected for his moral character – being moderate in his politics, and possessing the esteem and confidence of all parties.' Robert stated obstacles to Head. First, a council could not support the crown unless it possessed the assembly's confidence; thus, further appointments would have to be made. Secondly, although Baldwin was 'on perfectly good terms' with the present councillors 'in private life,' he had 'formerly ... denounced them ... as politically unworthy of the confidence of the country – and therefore ... felt that [he] could not take office with them.'

Having consulted his father and Rolph, Baldwin declined a seat. At a second interview he asked that his father, Marshall Spring Bidwell, John Henry Dunn, and especially Rolph, be appointed. Head consulted with Bidwell before again offering Baldwin a seat on the understanding that, if he accepted, Rolph and Dunn would be appointed. In spite of support from his father, Rolph, and Bidwell, Robert refused because Head was unwilling to dismiss the old councillors. When Rolph felt it wrong to continue the negotiations without a concession, Robert gave 'a most reluctant consent'; he, Rolph, and

Dunn would take office 'as a mere experiment' without pressing for the retirement of Robinson, Wells, and Markland. Head agreed to write to Robert indicating that 'no preliminary conditions' had been imposed by either side. The new councillors were sworn in on 20 February.

The note, however, was not received until after the ceremony. Head wrote, 'I shall rely on your giving me your unbiassed opinion on all subjects, respecting which I may feel it advisable to require it.' This limitation was, according to Baldwin, not in a draft read to him and was unacceptable. On 3 March the council drew up a representation to Head arguing that only responsible government was consistent with the constitution. It was adopted the following day. Head's reply on 5 March disagreed with the interpretation of the constitution and reminded the councillors they had agreed to avoid important business until familiar with their duties. The councillors convened to consider Head's reply and on the 12th all six resigned. The assembly, led by Peter Perry, reacted forcefully, treating Head's action as a violation of the 'acknowledged principles of the British constitution.' On 15 April it voted to withhold supplies. The dispute escalated within and without parliament until it was dissolved. By resigning, the council set Upper Canada's political underbrush on fire.

How responsible was Baldwin, who had been out of politics for more than half a decade and who had just been devastated by his wife's death? Emotionally and mentally spent, he had accepted office as his duty. Always reluctant to take it lest he be seen as compromising, he was equally ready to resign at the possibility of a taint upon his reputation. A gentleman, a man of propriety, and a political and religious moderate, he constituted an effective symbol for reformers of various political hues, but he was not a gifted organizer. It is impossible now to reconstruct exactly the events between 20 February and 12 March that led to the resignation of the council, but it seems unlikely, as Head and subsequent historians would have it, that Baldwin was the prime mover, capable of winning Robinson, Markland, and Wells to his side. Bidwell, the speaker of the assembly, was undoubtedly one of the two key players in any manœuvres; the other was Rolph, who had been persuasive enough to get Robert Baldwin to enter the council. Without Baldwin, it is unlikely that Head would have accepted the others. Years later Rolph's wife claimed: 'I Know well that it was not Mr. Baldwin who wrote the remonstrance

[3 March] to Sir F.B. Head with respect to Responsible Government'; it was her husband.

Baldwin departed the scene quickly. He left for England on 30 April 1836, bearing letters of introduction from Strachan. He made an unsuccessful attempt to plead for redress at the Colonial Office, then went to Ireland. In England he had mostly been a tourist visiting Windsor, Richmond, and Hampton Court. In Ireland he undertook research into his ancestry. He felt at home in 'this dear land of my parents and of my own Eliza and if it makes me a worse philosopher I shall be satisfied if it makes me a better Irishman.' On 10 Feb. 1837 he returned home. Once again he refrained from politics. He had, as Mackenzie asserted years later, no foreknowledge of the rebellion. Still, however, a major figure, he was called upon by Head to carry a flag of truce to the insurgents on 5 December. In the aftermath Baldwin defended several accused rebels, including Thomas David Morrison. In March 1838 Sir George Arthur succeeded Head and two months later the Earl of Durham [Lambton] became governor-in-chief. The Baldwins had a brief interview with him in 1838 and later submitted detailed comments, principally on responsible government. Despite his resignation and the non-official nature of his report, published early in 1839, Durham's recommendation of responsible government and union carried enormous force in the Canadas. The certainty of union and the weight attached to an altered role for the Executive Council ensured Baldwin would remain important to reform. That status was enhanced by his reputation as a man of principle. Francis Hincks, a neighbour, intimate friend, and banker to Baldwin, was now principal strategist of the Upper Canadian reformers and saw the necessity of Baldwin's leading them and of forming close links with their Lower Canadian counterparts.

Architect of the union was Governor Charles Edward Poulett Thomson, later Lord Sydenham. The importance of a new and pragmatic relationship between governor and Executive Council had been set out in the famous dispatch of Colonial Secretary Lord John Russell to Thomson 10 Oct. 1839. Such was its impact that William Warren Baldwin was initially persuaded that responsible government would be established. Russell, in fact, had urged only conciliation and harmony in relations with the assembly. The focal point of this thrust was a reconstituted Executive Council. Thomson, convinced of the value of Robert Baldwin in the realignment of politics in the Canadas, sought him for the new council. Again with extreme reluctance and want of confidence in his colleagues on council, Baldwin accepted, becoming solicitor general in February 1840 but without a seat on council.

When union was proclaimed in February 1841, at which time Baldwin entered council, he faced a dilemma. Reformers were divided over whether he should remain as solicitor general and he himself was ambivalent. He forced the issue of responsibility that month by declaring to Sydenham his 'entire want of confidence' in most councillors. Yet he retreated when confronted by Sydenham and accepted his vague commitment to the unclear principles of Russell's dispatch. The episode confirmed Sydenham's belief that, as he wrote Arthur, Baldwin was 'such an ass!' Sydenham held the upper hand in the general election of March 1841. Although the French party captured nearly half the Lower Canadian seats, corruption and intimidation assured election of pro-government members in Upper Canada. Only six independent or ultra-reformers, including Baldwin, were returned.

Baldwin had withdrawn as a candidate for Toronto when defeat seemed certain but was elected for Hastings and 4th York, choosing to sit for Hastings. The immediate task was to revitalize the party. With French Canadian liberals dispirited and divided over whether to cooperate with Syndenham's government, Baldwin reconfirmed his commitment. When taking the oaths as an executive councillor in May, he refused the oath of supremacy; denying any foreign prelate had authority in Canada, it denied the rights of the pope and the Roman Catholic Church. An irritated Sydenham agreed to forgo the oath but complained to Russell that Baldwin was 'the most crotchety impracticable enthusiast I have ever had to deal with.'

Sydenham and his solicitor general met on 10 June. Baldwin demanded four cabinet posts for French Canadians and warned that on a vote of confidence he would have to oppose the government. Sydenham had had enough. What is usually treated as Baldwin's resignation was no more than a veiled threat by him during the conversation, but Sydenham used it as an excuse. He wrote on 13 June to accept the resignation Baldwin had not offered. It was a coup which, Sydenham was convinced, would end Baldwin's career. For some weeks, Baldwin wrote his father, he felt he was not 'at all calculated' for politics. But, with the firm support of his family, he determined to fight on for his principles.

Yet there was much to the self-analysis. He was not a natural politician. A poor orator, and a less frequent contributor in parliament than other spokesmen, he even lacked the appearance of a leader. Of above average height, he had a pronounced stoop which made him look shorter, as did the heaviness of his body. His pallid complexion and dull, expressionless eyes gave him a funereal bearing. It was his character which made him outstanding. Baldwin lived the rhetoric of his times: he was a gentleman, morally courageous, utterly genuine in his willingness to sacrifice his interests to those of the institutions he revered – the constitution, the law, the church, property, and the family. His political opinions were essentially Whiggish, which meant a commitment to popular government and individual rights, and an adherence to the values of a landholding class and a social structure rooted in the family and traditional forms of mutual obligation. Other politicians, such as Robert Baldwin Sullivan and Sir Allan Napier MacNab, who talked of honour knew it might have to take second place to other considerations. They paid deference to a man for whom there were rarely other considerations. To contemporaries as disparate as Wolfred Nelson and Malcolm Cameron, Baldwin was known for his honesty, integrity, and disinterested views.

Central to the idea of a gentleman was service. Baldwin's station in life thrust on him the responsibility to serve and he accepted it, despite his discomfort in office, his intensely private personality, and the disruption of his family life. Baldwin readily admitted he wished to exercise power but he disliked the politics of winning it and would sacrifice neither principle nor party to gain it.

When the first parliament of the Canadas met in Kingston on 14 June 1841, Baldwin faced challenges from a friend. Francis Hincks found Sydenham's businesslike government ever more attractive. By July his *Examiner* was sympathetic to the ministry, by August he was voting with it on important measures, by Christmas he was urging the reform party to merge with the administration. Dazzled by dreams of economic progress under Sydenham, Hincks rejected Baldwin's alliance with the 'unprogressive' French Canadians. But throughout the session Baldwin himself opposed the expansionist economic programs of Sydenham and Hincks. He and the French Canadians blocked the scheme for a 'bank of issue,' intended to provide sound paper money for Canada, and even opposed, unsuccessfully, the British loan guarantee of £1,500,000, intended for canal construction, which had done so much to lure Upper Canada into the union.

Baldwin combined British passion for liberty with insistence upon justice for French Canada, although he thereby endangered his popularity in Upper Canada. The most practical expression of concern was his arranging for the election in 4th York of the French party's leader, Louis-Hippolyte La Fontaine. The least practical was pushing biculturalism to an absolute balance. In August he opposed a popular bill to provide municipal government for Upper Canada because it did not create parallel institutions in Lower Canada. However, Baldwin's contribution to French-English cooperation was one of his most important legacies to Canadian politics. It was characteristic that he sent all his children to francophone schools in Lower Canada and that he felt acute embarrassment over his own unilingualism.

Baldwin's major concern, responsible government, was raised several times in the assembly during the session. The most important occasion brought his much mythologized action of 3 Sept. 1841. The standard account says that Baldwin introduced resolutions intended to make the assembly and the ministry define a position on the principle of executive responsibility, and that Samuel Bealey Harrison, on behalf of the ministry, countered with his own resolutions, which had to embody much of Baldwin's text to gain a majority. In reality, events were more confused and Baldwin's ideas less triumphant. He had prepared resolutions as had the ministry. Baldwin was shown the ministerial version and agreed, the cabinet thought, to introduce it in a gesture of constitutional harmony. Through misunderstanding or excessive zeal, however, he broke the agreement. In the house he accepted the thrust of Harrison's resolutions but insisted on presenting his own, convinced that only his formulation was fully acceptable. In the end, his version was defeated and Harrison's adopted, Baldwin voting for every one of its resolutions, against predominantly tory opposition. Baldwin had attempted to establish, beyond argument, the practice of responsibility, particularly by insisting on the assembly's right to hold executive councillors responsible for government action. His precise wording gave way to Harrison's carefully ambiguous text. It probably did not matter. In years to come reformers would seize on the Harrison resolutions as a sanction and the subtleties would be submerged in politics.

For the moment it appeared Sydenham had again dammed up constitutional protest. That dam was breached when he died on 19 September. With him went his so-called régime of harmony, based on his personal political ability and ruthlessness. Baldwin could not take advantage of the removal of the Sydenham yoke because of the continuing public split with Hincks and the business-minded reformers Hincks represented. Despite public attacks in the *Examiner*, Baldwin kept lines open to Hincks, even defending him in May 1842 in a libel suit initiated by Archibald McNab. With Sydenham gone, reformers began to wander back into the fold. By the early summer even the tories were listening to Baldwin's proposals for a temporary alliance to defeat the government.

The new governor, Sir Charles Bagot, had neither the strength nor the inclination for Sydenham's ruthless style. Although Hincks became inspector general of public accounts on 9 June, ministerial drift continued. In July, Attorney General William Henry Draper and Harrison advised Bagot the ministry could not survive: he must bring in the leaders of the French Canadians and that meant inviting Baldwin as well. Draper, who considered Baldwin a traitor for resigning the previous year, was nevertheless prepared to make way for him. Although under instructions from Britain to keep Baldwin and the French out, when the legislature convened in September and it was apparent the reformers had a majority, Bagot had to ignore his instructions and call on La Fontaine. The talks nearly foundered on the governor's refusal to include Baldwin but he finally conceded. On 16 September, La Fontaine agreed to enter the ministry, with Baldwin.

Although Bagot and Baldwin would eulogize the triumph of responsible government in what Bagot dubbed his 'great measure,' the achievement was considerably less. Six previous ministers were joined by five reformers, but there was no prior agreement on policy and no commitment to cabinet solidarity. That they worked as a cabinet, and that Hincks rehabilitated himself as a solid party man, owed more to personalities and politics than principle. In October, Bagot prorogued parliament. Forced to seek re-election with the other new ministers, by virtue of their appointments, Baldwin was defeated by Orange mobs in Hastings and 2nd York. He gratefully accepted a Lower Canadian seat. On 30 Jan. 1843 he was returned by acclamation in Rimouski, forging another link between east and west.

During his first term as attorney general west (September 1842–November 1843), Baldwin showed his strengths and weaknesses. He was liberal in his leniency towards all but the most hardened criminals and his support of individual rights against arbitrary exercise of police and judicial power. His effectiveness as a law officer was not matched in his role as political manager. Attacked by critics for operating a spoils system and by supporters for leaving too many tories in office, faced by quarrels even within cabinet over appointments, he found patronage 'the most painful and disagreeable' of political concerns.

Baldwin valued friendship but found it difficult to reach out to maintain it. Friends, including La Fontaine, commented on his elusiveness and his failure to reply to letters. Most contemporaries ascribed his peculiarities to his 'reserve' or to overwork. But by 1843 he was showing symptoms of a severe depressive illness which would worsen as he grew older. By his second term as attorney general, after 1848, he would be incapacitated for extended periods by depressions, unable to represent the crown on the assizes. He claimed the press of political affairs required his presence in Montreal. However, he did not attend some ten meetings of the Executive Council for the first six weeks of the new government. Similar difficulties in business and absences from council marked the last three years of the government, 1849–51. In 1850 he confined himself to home from early January until mid March. The only known visitors outside the family were La Fontaine and Provincial Secretary James Leslie. The former was shocked by the fluctuations of Baldwin's disorder, especially the headaches torturing him year after year.

When his government was threatened in 1850 by the radical Clear Grit revolt in its ranks, Baldwin's growing incapacity weakened it further. A friend and party organizer, William Buell, wrote to him in June that confidence in him was waning; his critics, Buell related, saw him as a spent force, as 'the finality man.' It was a suspicion Baldwin himself nurtured. His need to isolate himself was expressed in his frequent desire to resign.

Since his wife's death in 1836 Baldwin's obsession with her had deepened into a cult in which she was more real than living people. The anniversaries of her death and their wedding were annual rites. Robert's father died on 8 Jan. 1844, leaving him grief-stricken, contemplating retirement from politics. For the introspective son, left to carry on his father's work of achieving responsible government without his father's flamboyant personality, the heritage was onerous. It heightened Robert's well-developed sense of family and feeling of responsibility for it. Unfortunately, he could more easily express this responsibility than the affection behind it. His granddaughter, Mary-Jane Ross, described Baldwin as the only source of affection his children knew and yet he was more venerated than loved: he was 'a schoolmaster' to them. This man of ancient griefs and loves would have been unrecognizable to the political world, where he was so controlled and reserved. It is a measure of his force of character that he played out his role in politics for so long and so well, carrying the weight of oppression in his own mind. However, the reputation he had won for determination in pursuing responsible government must be balanced by his tendency to retreat through abdication. Duty and his father's mission prevented him from doing so permanently, but for a few months each year depression brought isolation.

Still, he was a dominating figure in parliament. After Bagot fell ill in November 1842, Baldwin and La Fontaine had a free hand – the first real premiers of the province. In March 1843 a new governor, Sir Charles Theophilus Metcalfe, arrived with instructions to check the 'radical' government. He expected confrontation, convinced only the tories were loyal. He saw Baldwin as fanatical and intolerant and, curiously, as one who took pleasure in conflict. Baldwin, in fact, was conciliatory. He allowed Metcalfe an involvement in the working of cabinet and administration that Bagot had never claimed, and urged reformers to avoid criticism of the governor. So unaware was Baldwin of Metcalfe's motives that he did not press on with the government's program before the governor could muster support against it.

In May, Baldwin persuaded Metcalfe to withdraw sanctions against his old friend and leader, Marshall Spring Bidwell. He was disappointed that Bidwell did not choose to return to Canada. While Britain was reluctant to grant a general amnesty to those implicated in the rebellions, Metcalfe was permitted to pardon exiles individually. A threat by La Fontaine and other Lower Canadian ministers to resign forced an amnesty for Louis-Joseph Papineau. Baldwin, in contrast, nursed old grievances and made no direct effort for W.L. Mackenzie.

The reformers began a session on 28 Sept. 1843 which was to be, in many ways, a triumph. Hincks and Baldwin cooperated on legislation strengthening the financial base for Upper Canadian schools and providing for separate schools for religious minorities. A motion was passed demanding control for the assembly over the civil list. And, despite the opposition of some Upper Canadian reformers, the ministry acted to move the capital from Kingston to Montreal. Baldwin, although a landowner, strongly supported Hincks's bill to tax wild land, and himself drafted a bill to create the non-sectarian University of Toronto. Both bills died when the government resigned in November.

Relations with Metcalfe had, however, deteriorated. Baldwin had moved to control violence by the Orange order, proceeding by the method followed in Britain: a parliamentary address to the crown asking for action against Orangeism. Metcalfe insisted on legislation. After a violent debate, bills were passed restraining party processions and banning secret societies. Baldwin's family paid a price: on the night of 8 November an Orange mob burned effigies of Baldwin and Hincks outside the Baldwin home in Toronto. Yet, Metcalfe reserved the very legislation, the Secret Societies Bill, he had insisted Baldwin introduce. The bill disappeared into the Colonial Office, to be disallowed in March 1844.

The government might well have resigned over this reservation, but it was patronage that precipitated the crisis. Metcalfe had instructions to control appointments. His practice of that control, without consulting his ministers, made a mockery of responsible government and forced their hands. Following a stormy interview with Metcalfe, Baldwin and La Fontaine met the executive councillors and all but Dominick Daly resigned on 26 Nov. 1843. There was excited debate in parliament on the 29th, highlighted by Baldwin's lucid defence of the ministry and responsible government. The house adjourned three days later.

Baldwin clearly understood the resignation to be one of principle, necessary to resolve the constitutional issue. La Fontaine, on the other hand, expected it to force Metcalfe's recall and the ministry's return. The following year Hincks was reported as saying 'we did not believe our resignation would have been accepted.' Hincks and La Fontaine, it appears, hoped to use the threat of resignation to gain the upper hand on a recalcitrant governor. The election campaign of September 1844 went badly for Baldwin. Metcalfe cried loyalty to the crown: while the French party won a majority in Lower Canada, Baldwin was returned with only 11 followers in Upper Canada. Even Hincks was defeated in Oxford.

Baldwin soon rose from defeat. In the session of 1844–45, he gave the strongest performance of his career. He used debates, whatever the subject, as opportunities to lecture on responsible government. His other major theme was nationalism. Control of the civil list was only partly a constitutional question, it was also a demand that Canadians manage Canadian affairs. His affection for things British took second place to his Canadian nationalism. In March 1846, during a debate on the militia, he insisted it was capable of defending the province without British help: 'We want no foreign bayonets here. ...

He loved the Mother Country, but he loved the soil on which he lived better.'

The tory government of William Henry Draper and Denis-Benjamin Viger was weak, especially after the dying Metcalfe was replaced by the more neutral Lieutenant-General Charles Murray Cathcart, as administrator in November 1845 and as governor the following April. But the reform alliance was rickety. Many French Canadians listened to overtures from the tories. With even La Fontaine teetering in 1845, Baldwin could do little but remind his colleagues of the tory record on French Canadian rights. In the end, all negotiations foundered and the reform party remained intact.

Baldwin reduced his private involvements to concentrate on politics. A relative, Lawrence Heyden, was hired in 1845 to manage the extensive family property. This was salutary because Baldwin found it difficult to resist pleas for loans and could be extremely lenient with some debtors. He withdrew from active participation in his law practice by 1848, leaving it largely to his partner Adam Wilson. The practice had been made difficult by his other partner, cousin Robert Baldwin Sullivan, who was likeable and clever but drunken and irresponsible.

The reformers' prospects had improved considerably after the arrival of Lord Elgin [Bruce] as governor in January 1847. He carried instructions endorsing ministerial responsibility and strict neutrality for the governor. The weak tory ministry avoided controversial legislation in the session of 1847, and Baldwin's major differences were with his allies. He led the successful opposition to William Hamilton Merritt's bill to permit the formation of general partnerships with only limited liability, 'on the old fashioned principle that men were bound in conscience, and ought to be bound in law to pay all their debts.' He attacked the attempts of modernizers in both parties to reduce the dower rights of women. A bill by Solicitor General John Hillyard Cameron would have permitted a husband to dispose of property without his wife's consent. Baldwin contended that 'the main object of this Bill was THE INJURY OF WOMAN, *and to despoil them of the trivial rights they now held.*' He ignited the house and defeated it. His concern, however, was primarily with rights of property and the traditional economy which was being revolutionized by corporations, mining companies, and railways. On dower, as on other issues of 1847, he sought to prevent what he called, in debates on primogeniture, 'the evil of subdivision of properties.' He was not sympathetic to expansion of women's legal rights, and in 1849 his government took away the virtually unused right of Upper Canadian women who met the property qualification to vote.

Parliament was prorogued on 28 July 1847 with every expectation of an election. Baldwin chose his issues carefully. The university question, an emotional cause in Upper Canada, was kept at the forefront by a broadly based committee which supported Baldwin's University Bill of 1843. Baldwin was forced to attend to his own re-election in York North, formerly 4th York, where his campaign was directed by the leader of the Children of Peace, David Willson, his manager in 1844. His opponent was the editor of the *British Colonist*, Hugh Scobie, whose manager, tory William Henry Boulton, waged a scurrilous campaign. Baldwin's canvass of the riding was successful and he carried the election, which ended in January 1848. The Baldwinites took 23 of Upper Canada's 42 seats while their allies in Lower Canada captured 33 of 42. It was an overwhelming majority and Baldwin worried whether it could be kept together and reform expectations of immediate and sweeping change could be met. In February he warned the eastern Upper Canadian chieftain, John Sandfield Macdonald, that if reformers insisted on extreme changes before a proper reorganization of government, they would have to find another leader and would wander in the wilderness until they learned 'more practical wisdom.' This gloomy prognosis in victory was characteristic of the depressive Baldwin, but it was also an accurate prediction of the troubles of the reform ministry.

When the house met on 25 February the tories clung to office. Baldwin's amendment to the reply to the throne speech constituted an expression of non-confidence in the government. It was passed 3 March: 54 to 20. The ministry resigned the next day. La Fontaine was called by Elgin on 10 March and Baldwin and the other ministers were sworn in on 11 March; they held their first cabinet meeting on the 14th. In negotiating the cabinet's composition with the two leaders, Elgin noted that Baldwin 'seemed desirous to yield the first place' to La Fontaine.

Baldwin began with a short housekeeping session. It was a wise strategy, administratively, for it allowed the new ministers to master their departments and sort out the disorder after four years of weak government. Politically, it was a mistake to disappoint the faithful, especially when many would disapprove of the cabinet's composition.

Robert Baldwin Sullivan and René-Édouard Caron, traitors to many reformers, were included. As bad was the fact that 4 of the 11 new ministers did not secure seats and were thus removed from scrutiny in the house, a curious situation for the first responsible government. Only one member, Malcolm Cameron, came from the radical wing, in a newly invented post with no apparent function, assistant commissioner of public works. Baldwin had done little to meet the party's expectations and taken long strides towards alienating the radicals.

The times were not auspicious for the new government, which came to be known as the 'Great Ministry.' The economic depression dragged on and the provincial accounts were running a deficit. Hincks was again inspector general but despite promises of retrenchment, the deficit grew dramatically in the ministry's first year. Faced with political reality, the reformers pushed expenditures from £474,000 in 1848 to £635,000 in 1851. The fortuitous return of good times in 1850 with an increase in customs revenue produced a surplus of £207,000 in 1851. The surplus did not satisfy many reform partisans who had a powerful ideological commitment to retrenchment and smaller government. Baldwin's administration was bedevilled in the house by back-bench revolts over expenditures and warnings from followers that the increase in the size of government was threatening to rupture the party and as one reformer, Daniel Eugene McIntyre, lamented, create 'a precious mess.'

Hincks's ethics were often in doubt; his financial expertise was not. In England in 1849 he persuaded major financial houses to support provincial debentures and railway projects. The results allowed Baldwin and the government to press on with their reforms. Otherwise, Baldwin, who showed little understanding of economic affairs, was not much interested in the fine points of Hincks's financial dealings. He was also unenthusiastic about the grand financial schemes and retrenchment programs of William Hamilton Merritt who joined the cabinet 15 Sept. 1848. However, one economic issue could unite all reformers – reciprocity with the United States. Some liberals responded to British free trade by becoming doctrinaire free traders and others, notably Robert Baldwin Sullivan, called for Canada to develop a policy of protection, but all could agree on the advantages of freer trade with the United States. Baldwin, essentially pragmatic on tariffs and cool to free trade dogma, could join with the *laissez-faire* men on the interrelated issues of reciprocity and free navigation. On 18 May 1848 the Executive Council had attacked continuance of the

British navigation acts, which limited colonial trade to British ships. In January 1849 Baldwin and Hincks moved an address to the queen for the immediate repeal of the acts. It passed unanimously. The offending acts had by year's end passed into the history of empire.

The La Fontaine–Baldwin government pursued freer trade with the Maritimes in 1849 and 1850, only to founder on Nova Scotian suspicions. Always reciprocity was the major goal. Baldwin told Elgin in 1848 that he feared for the British connection if it meant Canadian farmers had to accept less for their grain than American counterparts. His solution was an agreement offering the Americans free navigation of the St Lawrence River in return for free trade in natural products. It was a perceptive suggestion, for these were the lines of the reciprocity settlement achieved in 1854, after Baldwin's retirement. He played a major role in keeping the issue alive, in part through correspondence with reciprocity's chief protagonist in the American Congress until 1850, Senator John Adams Dix, a relative.

International diplomacy began to be part of Canadian politics as La Fontaine, Sullivan, and Hincks were separately dispatched to Washington between 1848 and 1851 to seek reciprocity, but patronage, closely connected to Baldwin's conception of responsible cabinet government, loomed larger. Baldwin had always recognized its importance in breaking the tory hold. But, as in 1842–43, he found patronage distasteful and difficult to manage, and by mishandling it he stirred reform discontent. Hincks named a tory, Robert Easton Burns, a judge without Baldwin's knowledge. Baldwin himself damaged the party in the Henry John Boulton case. Once a compact tory, Boulton now claimed to be a loyal reformer. When it was revealed in 1849 Baldwin had promised Boulton a judgeship, the Toronto *Globe* angrily attacked the would-be judge. Baldwin retreated in January 1850, claiming he had never guaranteed Boulton the job. Boulton soon joined the Clear Grit radicals as a vigorous and troublesome critic of the government.

A lasting legacy of Baldwin's second term as attorney general was the reform of the Upper Canadian judicial system in 1849. A new Court of Common Pleas and a Court of Error and Appeal were created; the Court of Chancery was reformed and expanded from one to three justices. Hincks later said Baldwin had laid out the basics of the reforms and given them final shape, while Solicitor General William Hume Blake had helped in the drafting. Baldwin himself, not one to take credit for others' work, stated that he and Blake had worked together but Blake had drafted the Chancery Bill. Ironically, it was chancery which stirred controversy and helped drive Baldwin from politics in 1851.

Baldwin had to deal with two other difficult issues, the penitentiary question and amnesty. A commission to investigate charges of corruption and brutality at Kingston Penitentiary was dominated by its secretary, *Globe* publisher George Brown. The report was lost in excitement over the rebellion losses crisis in April 1849, but its cruel rationalism about prison discipline, adapted from American models, would not have appealed to Baldwin. He delayed legislating about the prison until 1851 and then only improved its administration, thus souring his relations with Brown.

On taking office in 1848, Baldwin insisted Britain must grant a general amnesty for the rebels of 1837–38. Britain acceded in 1849. However, Baldwin was unable to satisfy three prominent exiles. With Robert Fleming Gourlay, expelled from Upper Canada in 1819, he could not reach an agreement. Marshall Spring Bidwell, despite Baldwin's promises to establish him in a legal career, seemed unwilling to come back with anything less than a guarantee of political leadership. By 1849 he too was complaining to disaffected reformers of Baldwin's ingratitude. The complaints were more justified with W.L. Mackenzie. He had had to wait for the general amnesty. His demands for compensation for parliamentary salary and committee expenses owed him from 1837 were dismissed contemptuously by Baldwin, who had a special hostility for Mackenzie the smasher. Baldwin effectively drove him from the party and made him a dangerous, indeed a lethal, enemy.

The La Fontaine–Baldwin government took office amid extraordinary unrest. Economic depression, the Irish famine migration, and revolutions in Europe helped stimulate riots by the Orange and the Green, Toronto tories furious over Mackenzie's return, angry sailors at Quebec, discontented railway navvies, and thousands more. From 1846 to 1851 rural French Canada saw arson and rioting against attempts to impose a centralized school system on the parishes. The 'Great Ministry' is often seen by historians as committed to rapid progress, operating in a society sharing the same values. Clearly large numbers did not share a sanguine view of progress and Baldwin himself was racked with doubts. It was a time of transition and the movement from a traditional to a capitalist economy was not accomplished without opposition, often violent.

The most serious threat to the government arose from the rebellion losses crisis of 1849, when tory fury was directed against alleged French domination of the province and especially against La Fontaine. Baldwin took little part in the debate, fuelling opposition speculation that he did not support the government's proposal. Indeed, he seems to have had doubts about compensation for those convicted of treason and only assumed leadership when the legislation was amended to exclude convicted rebels. Taking a hard line with the opposition, he kept the house in session through the night of 22–23 February until the resolution was passed.

During the riots in Montreal after the signing of the bill by Lord Elgin on 25 April, Baldwin's boarding-house was attacked by a mob, but there is no indication he was within. He was a member of the Executive Council committee which took responsibility for policing the city and made the potentially disastrous decision to swear in French Canadians as constables and arm them. Only a promise to withdraw these constables placated the tory mob and prevented a blood-bath. Baldwin moved quickly on the political front, urging reformers in Upper Canada to mount pro-government rallies and petitions, and personally financing petition campaigns in rural Upper Canada. He was instrumental in the cabinet's decision to move the capital from Montreal to Toronto in October 1849.

When the disgruntled tories turned to annexation to the United States as the solution to Canada's problems, Baldwin with ruthless efficiency weeded annexationists out of public offices. He was equally firm with the reform party. Peter Perry, suspected of being an annexationist, was the candidate for the radical reformers in a by-election for York East to take place in December. Baldwin quickly set him straight. On 4 October, in a letter wisely published in the reform press, he warned Perry 'all should know therefore that I can look upon those only who are for the Continuance of that [British] Connexion as political friends, – those who are against it as political opponents.' Perry publicly pledged not to discuss annexation and the party was steadied.

The crisis of 1849 helped obscure the government's continuing accomplishments. Just as surely has the achievement of responsible government, confirmed when Elgin signed the Rebellion Losses Bill, diverted attention. Baldwin was seen, by the *Examiner* and others since, as the man of one idea who had little to offer once responsibility was gained. In fact, the government, and Baldwin in particular, had a lengthy list of important reforms.

The Municipal Corporations Act provided the efficient system of local government reformers had been crying for since Durham had emphasized the need in his report. The act replaced the unwieldy districts with counties and allowed for incorporation of villages, towns, and cities, with each receiving an elected council (as did the townships). The act has been seen by some historians as a grand extension of democracy and as Baldwin's creation. By providing elected councils, it gave the municipalities a measure of independence from provincial control. However, it retained three restrictions: division of financial authority between provincially appointed magistrates and county councils, a property qualification for municipal voters, and appointment by the province of key county officials, including the registrar, sheriff, and coroner. Attacked in the house in 1850 by Peter Perry over these undemocratic remnants, Baldwin, unrepentant, argued the crown's prerogative was of the essence of a monarchical system, and officers in the administration of justice must be appointed by the crown. He also argued qualifications for voters and office holders were necessary. Hincks should share some credit for the act. A memorandum of December 1848 called for stronger municipalities with taxing and borrowing powers, and his concerns were embodied in the act, which permitted councils to issue debentures. When Baldwin and Hincks clashed in 1851 over railway financing by local governments, Hincks pointed to the act for authority. Baldwin seemed unaware of these provisions, which suggests he did not draft the act alone.

The University of Toronto was unarguably Baldwin's creation. His October 1843 bill on the university question died with the government in December. Baldwin was determined to settle the issue, to end the connection of church and state in higher education, and to destroy King's College as a visible symbol of Anglican privilege and class favouritism. Soon after taking office in 1848 he had asserted government control. In July he established a commission of inquiry into the finances of the college, which was supported by public lands. Controlled by reformers, the commission documented financial mismanagement and the need for reform. These findings laid the base for the University Bill of 1849, which Baldwin introduced on 3 April. His measure stripped the Church of England of its power in higher education and eliminated denominationalism at the university. To be called the University of Toronto, it would be secular, centralized, government controlled. The denominational colleges in Upper Canada, Methodist Victoria, Presbyterian Queen's, Roman Catholic Regiopolis and Bytown (University of Ottawa), could affiliate, but would lose the right to confer degrees, except in divinity, and have no share of the endowment. Baldwin did not accomplish all he had hoped. The denominational colleges did not give up their independence and indeed, over Baldwin's opposition, Bishop Strachan obtained a charter for an Anglican college, Trinity. Still, Baldwin had presaged the pattern of development for higher education in Ontario.

Baldwin also contended with his church over the clergy reserves. His efforts were hampered by reluctance among French Canadian liberals, including La Fontaine, who feared that if Upper Canadian radicals were encouraged by abolition of the reserves, they would attack the religious institutions of Lower Canada. Nevertheless, under pressure from his left wing, Baldwin tried a compromise. On 18 June 1850 James Hervey Price introduced 31 resolutions in the assembly, the key one asking Britain to give the Canadian parliament power to dispose of clergy reserves revenue. This compromise, at best a modest advance, was adopted but, with the Anglican hierarchy opposed, the British government took no action.

The pressure to settle the reserves question, like the annexation controversy, pointed to one of the most serious threats to the Baldwin government, the increasing impatience of the radical wing. Buoyed by Perry's election, the Clear Grits adopted a separate platform in March 1850 far in advance of Baldwinite reform in espousal of democracy and voluntarism. The seriousness of the challenge was indicated by the desertion to the Clear Grits of the *Examiner*, now published by James Lesslie. During the 1850 session, they behaved more as members of the opposition than as critics within the party.

Baldwin showed neither sympathy for nor understanding of the new liberalism. Indeed, through his mistakes, he fostered it. The token radical in the cabinet, Malcolm Cameron, was assigned in the spring of 1849 to draft amendments to the Common Schools Act of 1841. It was a typical case of Baldwin's preoccupation with private torments and great public issues while details of political success were forgotten. Baldwin allowed the bill to be introduced without reading it, so he was unaware Cameron was proposing a radical restructuring of the Upper Canadian school system. It passed the assembly in May

1849. Its democratic and decentralizing provisions outraged Egerton Ryerson, superintendent of schools, who threatened to resign. Baldwin capitulated, though it involved the humiliation of suspending his own government's act. The inevitable result was the resignation on 1 December of Cameron, who became another rallying point for left-wing discontent. He soon campaigned vigorously for Caleb Hopkins, a Clear Grit, against John Wetenhall, who had replaced him on the Executive Council. Baldwin, suffering from depression, was disconsolate at Wetenhall's defeat and resulting insanity, and was widely rumoured to be ready to resign.

The last year of the La Fontaine–Baldwin government was an extended retreat under continual harassment by critics to the left. The extremism released by the rebellion losses and annexation crises and Baldwin's loss of authority had weakened moderation in politics. The long commercial depression ending in 1850 had increased the attractiveness of economic success in the United States, not only to the Clear Grits but to the tories as well. To Baldwin's dismay, discussion of such constitutional change as fixed times for meetings of parliament and for elections occurred during the session of 1850. These were, to Baldwin, 'part of a plan to change, bit by bit, our present constitution.' He beat back each initiative, but there were always new ones.

Constitutional change was also winning advocates within Baldwin's cabinet. He had long opposed one panacea, an elected Legislative Council, as an innovation which would destroy the British connection. He was shocked when his cabinet determined it should be given to the radicals as a sop. On 10 April 1850 he wrote to Elgin to tender his resignation: he had no alternative but to leave a government committed to so disastrous a policy. His quiet terrorism worked and there was no more talk of the obnoxious reform from the cabinet. However, he heard a good deal from the house. On 3 June 1850 Henry John Boulton and Louis-Joseph Papineau initiated a debate on constitutional change, including an elected council. With a bizarre twist of opportunism, tories such as Henry Sherwood expressed interest. Baldwin struck back. The innovators were republicans, advocates of independence from a generous mother, guilty of 'black ingratitude.' He prevailed and the Boulton–Papineau motion failed, but he had had to threaten resignation, and his defences of the constitutional *status quo* in the house were becoming shriller.

The opposition also hounded Baldwin on retrenchment, the means favoured by free traders and liberals to achieve smaller government.

Its attacks gained force after 21 Dec. 1850, when the popular William Hamilton Merritt resigned from the cabinet, angry that the government would not adopt his sweeping reductions. The rebels found another cause in anti-Catholicism, stimulated by a wave of religious prejudice in England in 1850–51. The chief reform newspaper, the *Globe*, led the crusade. Its alienation from Baldwin, who was considered too closely allied to French Catholics, was completed in April 1851 when George Brown lost a by-election in Haldimand to W.L. Mackenzie, a defeat Brown ascribed to Catholic votes and lack of support from Baldwin.

An element in Baldwin's decline was continued conflict with Hincks over economic policy, and the increasing influence of his inspector general. The lines of division were as they had been in the 1840s, given greater point by the emergence of the railway. Although in April 1849 Baldwin supported Hincks's Railway Guarantee Act, he was suspicious of over rapid development and the financial probity of some companies. That month he unsuccessfully opposed the incorporation of the Toronto, Simcoe and Huron Union Rail-Road, whose money-raising plans sounded to him like 'a lottery scheme.' The following year he was alarmed by legislation to permit municipalities to acquire stock in the Great Western but failed to convince the house of the dangers. Hincks moved an amendment to permit municipalities to invest in all railways, not just the Great Western. In the vote, Baldwin found himself in a minority of eight, with six French Canadians and an English liberal from Lower Canada. It seemed he was back where he had begun in 1841, a lonely voice in a house of modernizers.

Hincks was never reluctant to express his differences. In October 1849, angered by disagreements over patronage and crown lands, and by what he perceived as softness towards annexationists, he told Baldwin the country was disgusted with the ministry's 'vacillating policy' and with 'you in particular.' Baldwin's slowness in making cabinet changes led Hincks to snarl, 'I could myself complete the administration on a permanent and satisfactory footing in 24 hours.' A clear break did not come until 1851, when Hincks proposed in cabinet an extension of the powers of municipalities to support railways. Baldwin had fought it for months in council. On 30 April, Hincks, certain he had a cabinet majority behind him, wrote to La Fontaine to complain about Baldwin's obstruction and said he was prepared to resign. Baldwin, who also had been threatening resignation, had to back down. Saving face, he insisted to La Fontaine he was not 'concurring' in the proposals, he was simply 'acquiescing' in them.

The traditional economy based on landed property, whose values Baldwin adhered to, was being superceded by a capitalist economy. The constitution, which he thought he had settled by responsible government, was under increasing attack. The reform party, his instrument for achieving constitutional purity and French-English unity, was splintering. Religious tensions were transformed into an Upper Canadian outcry over 'French domination' within the Province of Canada, and anti-French feeling had become a potent force as the clergy reserves question remained unresolved and Brown's *Globe* set itself up as the Protestant critic. The basics of Baldwin liberalism seemed to be losing their constituency.

Robert's mother had died in January 1851. Personal and political disappointment produced the usual response. Baldwin lapsed into depression, and was seriously ill in May and June. Continued radical harassment drove him deeper within himself. His class, landed proprietors and professional men, was being rejected by capitalist modernizers and radical agrarians. The greed of lawyers and the elaborate legal system became the focus of discontent. J. Reed, a reformer from Sharon, in Baldwin's own riding, wrote to W.L. Mackenzie in May 1851: 'The watchword is to be no lawyers, more farmers and machinists.' The assault gained strength in the 1851 session. Baldwin's mood was not lightened when, on 26 June, Mackenzie moved for a special committee to draft a bill for abolishing the Court of Chancery and conferring equity jurisdiction on the courts of common law. Baldwin pleaded with the house to give the judicial reforms a chance to prove their value. The house was not listening. Even the solicitor general west, John Sandfield Macdonald, confessed the courts were too expensive and complicated. Mackenzie's motion was lost 30 to 34. But a majority of Upper Canadians had voted for it, 25 against 8 opposed.

The next day Baldwin wrote to La Fontaine that, after analysing the vote, he had concluded 'the public interests will be best promoted by my retirement.' On 30 June he rose in the house to announce his resignation. He explained the vote had left him no choice. In a house where a major reform was given only two years' trial, he felt himself 'an intruder.' Although he had been urged by his colleagues to reconsider, he felt he could be of more aid to them out of office. His emotionally charged address isolated the main theme of his concern: 'the consequences of that reckless disregard of first principles which if left unchecked can lead but to widespread social disorganization with all its fearful consequences.' Saying a final word of thanks to the Lower Canadian liberals for their support, Baldwin took his seat with tears running down his face.

The same day La Fontaine announced that he, too, would leave. Hincks could now create a new and peculiar alliance, joining his modernizing reformers with the Grits and with the French party under Augustin-Norbert Morin. Baldwin watched with discomfort. As a party man he felt that he owed Hincks help, but in September he urged his son-in-law, John Ross, to avoid taking office in the new ministry if he could. Yet Baldwin himself could not avoid the call of duty. He ran in York North in the ensuing general election. It was a disastrous decision. The Grits nominated Joseph Hartman, who recruited Mackenzie to campaign for him. The old rebel dogged Baldwin's heels, following him from meeting to meeting to refute his every claim. Baldwin received only a third as many votes as Hartman. Never an effective organizer at the constituency level, as R.B. Sullivan had observed as early as 1828, Baldwin now had lost touch altogether with local interests. His failure to recognize that a coalition with traditional agrarian interests had been possible allowed the triumph of their common enemy, the modernizing reformers. Baldwin nevertheless remained an important political symbol, a subject of excited rumour whenever political liberalism was in difficulty. Such a rumour in 1853 had him returning to lead the shaky Hincks–Morin government. In 1854 Baldwin broke his political silence to urge support of Hincks's coalition with Augustin-Norbert Morin, which, he said, although far from perfect, deserved public sympathy. In 1856 Auditor John Langton, viewing the tottering ministry of Sir Allan Napier MacNab and Morin, saw Baldwin as the only alternative to John A. Macdonald in reconstructing the government. As late as the summer of 1858 reformers were appealing to him to save the party. Even after his death some moderate reformers, including those led by John Sandfield Macdonald, used the name Baldwinites to distinguish themselves from Brown's more radical supporters. In 1871, in another twist, Brown resurrected the Baldwin tradition and name in urging Catholics to join the Grits in the 'reunion of the old Reform Party.'

Baldwin's relationship with Hincks was not always friendly. A major issue was the University of Toronto. In September 1852 Hincks proposed the abolition of its convocation, which shared government with its senate, and its medical faculty, leaving medical education to private schools such as that founded by Hincks's ally John Rolph. As well, the senate would include representatives from the unaffiliated colleges, who could obstruct the smooth functioning of the university. It was at this time, on 25 November, that the convocation elected Baldwin chancellor. To accept, he wrote to Professor Henry Holmes Croft, 'would imply less hostility than I entertain to the course adopted by the present Government.' His rejection was also motivated by his need to isolate himself. He refused all offers to remain in public life, rejecting judgeships twice, as well as places on commissions and requests to stand for electoral nominations. He narrowed his life to its basics: home, family, and memories. Only the Law Society of Upper Canada, the law as institution, could draw him out. He served as treasurer of the society from 1850 until his death and as its representative on the senate of the University of Toronto 1853–56. The other partial exception was the Church of England. He had become, he told John Ross in December 1853, 'rather a High Churchman as I understand the distinction between High and Low Churchman, though I trust without bigotry or intolerance.' His concern was with maintaining the traditional internal government of the church, in contrast to his pragmatic views on its separation from the state, a reform he had argued was necessary to prevent it from becoming a political football. He did not approve of any democratization of the church. He worked with both high and low churchmen as president of the Upper Canada Bible Society until 1856.

A few honours came his way. On 3 April 1853 the Canadian Institute at Toronto publicly recognized his role as one of its founders. In 1854 he was made a CB. For the most part, however, his was a private existence. He took an interest in improving the property at Spadina, the family homestead, to which he had moved in 1850 or 1851. In summer the garden was a major preoccupation, in winter his past correspondence and the transcribing of his wife's letters filled the hours as he looked out over the family cemetery. To outsiders he was a ghostly figure, only occasionally venturing out into the streets or receiving friends.

After his retirement his health had grown worse. Debilitating illnesses, real and psychological, tortured him. He had temporary problems with motor control and visual perception, shown by shaky handwriting, misspelling, and repetition of words. Depression remains the most likely diagnosis. His reserve deepened into alienation and self-isolation. The most striking evidence of his deterioration was the letter he wrote to La Fontaine on 21 Sept. 1853, refusing his invitation to join him and his wife on an expedition to Europe. He had been ill since May, 'seldom free for two consecutive days from the disagreeable rumbling noise in my head.' He felt giddy, easily worried, and excited. His fear of travel had been fuelled by the death of Barbara Sullivan, his aunt and mother-in-law, who had expired with no warning in 1853. He had a curious preoccupation with his body. As he told La Fontaine, 'My organs are too powerful ... I manufacture blood and fat too rapidly.' This preoccupation contributed to his obsessive thoughts of death. Its nearness had been with him at least since 1826 and especially after Eliza died. The man who had co-ruled Canada was now reduced to pathos, living, his daughter Eliza said, 'in dread of another attack.' The family gathered round the invalid; taking care of the great man was a shared burden. Since he refused to leave Spadina, Eliza and John Ross had to move from Belleville to Toronto. The greatest weight, however, fell on the elder daughter, Maria – housekeeper, entertainer, and adviser to her father. To ensure she remained at home, he refused his permission when the scion of a compact tory family, Jonas Jones Jr, and an American professor both wished to marry her. Her father's prohibitive demands left Maria an embittered and unhappy spinster.

Baldwin's other daughter had a happier fate. Eliza was married to the much older Ross at Spadina on 4 Feb. 1851. Some of the family were dismayed but Baldwin liked Ross, had sponsored his legal career, and, perhaps, recalled family disapproval of his own romance with another Eliza. Baldwin's boys were less successful. The elder, William Willcocks, married in 1854 Elizabeth MacDougall, to whom Robert was devoted, but she died in 1855. According to his younger daughter, her death 'seems to have broken him down completely ... he says to him it is like a second widowhood.' Willcocks remarried in 1856 but he was unsuccessful in his career and, probably because of his father's memory, in 1864 he was given a sinecure at Osgoode Hall. His fiscal irresponsibility forced him to sell his father's beloved Spadina in 1866. The other son, Robert, a young adventurer who went to sea in 1849, was stricken with polio in 1858 and had to live at home, crippled.

By the summer of 1858 there was little left for Baldwin but his dead Eliza. Headaches had become constant and when he could sleep he was tormented by 'harassing and perplexing dreams.' His memory was so unreliable he could not do his law society business at Osgoode Hall. His agony was increased by a last, ill-considered venture into politics in 1858. On the urging of George Brown, now leader of the party, Baldwin agreed to stand for the York divisional seat in the newly elective Legislative Council. It was a nice irony, given that he once had preferred leaving politics to seeing the council become elective. He soon realized he was unfit, physically and psychologically, for public office and on 12 August withdrew.

The family would trouble his last days. By early December 1858 it was clear he was dying, suffering from what the *Globe* described as 'neuralgia in the chest' which had become 'a severe case of inflammation of the lungs.' He tried for several days to make his will, tormented by his son Willcocks, who believed incorrectly that Lawrence Heyden was conspiring to have Baldwin reduce his share of the estate. The will, completed on 9 December, distributed the proceeds of a prosperous law practice and the inherited family properties, both commercial and agrarian, in Toronto and throughout the province. They had made him one of the wealthiest men in Upper Canada. The same afternoon, Baldwin died at Spadina. One of the largest funeral crowds in the history of the province came to honour the dead statesman on 13 December. Baldwin was laid to rest. Or so the mourners thought.

The obsession of Baldwin's later years was his lost wife. His nostalgic love, grief, and guilt that Eliza had died as a result of childbirth were codified in a bizarre document designed to ensure that he would be reunited with her. The nine requests included that certain of her possessions and her letters be buried with him and their coffins be chained together. Most important, he asked that his body be operated on: 'Let an incision be made into the cavity of the abdomen extending through the two upper thirds of the linea alba.' It was the same Caesarean section as Eliza had suffered.

The instructions were left with the faithful Maria. She saw to most of them but, perhaps in a last act of rebellion, did not have the operation performed and apparently told no one in the family of the request. A month after Robert's death, when Willcocks was sorting his father's clothes, he found in a pocket an abbreviated version, carried there in case Robert died away from home. The old man pleaded with whoever found the note that 'for the love of God, as an act of Christian charity, and by the solemn recollection that they may one day have themselves a dying request to make to others, they will not ... permit my being inclosed in my coffin before the performance of this last solemn injunction.' Willcocks heeded this injunction. One bitter January day in 1859, Dr James Henry Richardson, Lawrence Heyden, William Augustus Baldwin (Robert's brother), and Willcocks entered the vault and obeyed his request. It was a suitably strange end for one whose public persona and private agony were the sum of a man few understood, few loved, but all honoured.

By his own standards he was a failure. Compelled into politics by a profound sense of Christian duty, he had striven to preserve the rule of gentlemen and all it entailed. By the time he was driven out of politics, what he stood for had been eclipsed by the march of progress and the rise of the men of capital and machines. His accomplishments, none the less, were legion, most important among them the genius of responsible government and the centrally important heritage of a bicultural nation. That he did so much, at such personal cost, was the real measure of the man. It was fortunate that Robert Baldwin had his Eliza, in life and in death, the one immutable element in a world of puzzling change.

MICHAEL S. CROSS and ROBERT L. FRASER

D'ARCY BOULTON
(baptized George D'Arcy)
Lawyer, office holder, politician, and judge; b. 20 May 1759 in Moulton, Lincolnshire, England, son of Henry Boulton and Mary Preston; m. 18 Dec. 1782 Elizabeth Forster in Bloomsbury (London), and they had six boys and two girls; d. 21 May 1834 in York (Toronto).

When in 1833 William Lyon Mackenzie drew up his list of the 'family compact,' he began with the name D'Arcy Boulton. Next followed Boulton's four sons, like their father office holders all, then one son's brother-in-law, and finally the brother-in-law's brothers. By underscoring family connections and the monopoly of offices, Mackenzie imparted a literal aspect to the political label he helped popularize. That position in this catalogue of names did not correlate with actual political influence did not matter: a connection had been suggested in a formidable manner. Boulton's place – at the top – seems, at the very least, symbolically apt. In the early history of the province he was surely one of its quintessential placemen.

The second son of an old family of Lincolnshire gentry, D'Arcy Boulton followed the example of his elder brother, Henry, enrolling at the Middle Temple in 1788 to study law. Law, however, took a back seat to a business career and Boulton became a partner in the Woollen Yarn Company. The enterprise encountered difficulties and in 1793 the partners declared bankruptcy. Boulton was unabashed and wrote to his wife: 'Set not your mind on riches lest you should be deceived. They have wings to fly away. ... We can, thank God, be as happy with the necessaries of life as many discontented persons *cannot* be with all the possessions of their imaginations.' Bankruptcy proceedings lasted several years and in the end Boulton's financial problems may have had a bearing on his decision to emigrate.

Boulton with his wife and two sons arrived in the United States about 1797 and seems to have settled in New York's Hudson River valley. The exact nature of Boulton's activity is not certain: one story has him starting up a school in Schenectady, another has him an assistant oarsman on a lumber raft operating on Lake Champlain. By the turn of the century, however, he had set his sights north of the St Lawrence River. He first appears on the assessment roll of Augusta Township in 1802. Several years later, he recounted his sentiments at this change of scene in *Sketch of his majesty's province of Upper Canada*: 'English people, untainted by political speculations, are naturally attached to their own constitution. I confess, for my own part, that when I first ... set my foot on British ground, after residing in the American states, I perceived sensations that were unexpected even to myself. I seemed at once to step home. I need not describe my feelings on this occasion; a true Englishman can well imagine them, and with respect to those that are not so, I am perfectly indifferent.'

If Upper Canada offered Boulton a more congenial social and political climate, there were other, more tangible, advantages as well. In 1802 his petition for a land grant was approved and he received 200 acres for himself and an additional 200 acres for each of his children, then five in number. The following year, in response to a dearth of accredited lawyers, parliament empowered the lieutenant governor to authorize attorneys to practise by licence. Boulton and others were examined by Chief Justice Henry Allcock and admitted to the bar in Easter Term 1803; later critics labelled them 'heaven-descended.' Not long afterwards Boulton began his upward climb on the ladder of official preferment. The initial rung was provided him by the death of Solicitor General Robert Isaac Dey Gray in the wreck of the *Speedy* early in October 1804. The following February Boulton assumed Gray's position. Boulton also succeeded Gray in a by-election as the member for the riding of Stormont and Russell.

His next opportunity resulted from the suspension of judge Robert Thorpe by Lieutenant Governor Francis Gore in July 1807. In Thorpe's stead Boulton carried out the business of the Court of King's Bench on circuit. He did, however, suffer a setback when he was defeated in the general election of 1808 by John Brownell. A sympathetic commentator remarked: 'I really could not have believed there was so much ingratitude in the human frame as his former clients have manifested towards him.' Boulton may have suffered by association with an administration unpopular for its slow handling of land claims; he also may have had disgruntled legal customers.

Boulton, in fact, had his own problems in government circles. Gore had grown disenchanted with the legal acumen of both Boulton and Attorney General William Firth – who differed in their legal opinions

– and had begun instead to place his faith in the counsel of William Dummer Powell, an associate judge of King's Bench. When, in the late summer of 1810, it appeared that Boulton had decided to seek the vacant judgeship (Thorpe had received another posting), Gore and Powell worked in tandem to bar his appointment. The matter, however, became academic after the frigate on which Boulton was bound for England to press for the appointment was captured on 22 Dec. 1810 by a French privateer. Boulton fought vigorously in the short-lived attempt to defend the ship; for his troubles he received a sabre slash across his forehead. He was detained for more than two years at Verdun, France, during which time he wrote letters to authorities in London in an attempt to secure his release. He also acted as the lawyer for the community of British prisoners. In this regard he exasperated his son Henry John Boulton who declared, 'My father's letters are always about business for he has numberless "poor devils" to assist as clients.'

By the spring of 1813 Boulton had obtained his parole and crossed the Channel. He had, however, to put aside his hopes for a judgeship since the post had been filled in 1811 by the appointment of William Campbell. None the less, in August 1813 he obtained a leave of absence from his duties in Upper Canada as solicitor general to transact business 'regarding my family affairs of the first importance to myself and my children.' He was admitted to the English bar in May 1814, his lack of this credential having been cited by Gore and Powell in their campaign to keep him off the bench. That June, Firth, who had been dismissed as attorney general in 1812, advised William Warren Baldwin that Boulton was lobbying for the vacant attorney generalship. In this endeavour Boulton proved successful, although his wish that Henry John succeed him as solicitor general was frustrated by the ascending star of John Beverley Robinson. Boulton was appointed attorney general on 31 Dec. 1814; Robinson became solicitor general less than two months later.

Robinson, the brother-in-law of D'Arcy Boulton's eldest son and namesake, proved pivotal in a further reshuffling of places in the colonial administration which occurred three years later and which stemmed from a desire on the part of Gore and Powell to have a vigorous, young attorney general, namely Robinson. A chain reaction had been set in motion by Chief Justice Thomas Scott's retirement in 1816. He was replaced by Powell and the resulting vacancy on the bench was filled by Boulton, who was appointed on 12 Feb. 1818 and replaced as attorney general by Robinson. What ought to have been a fairly straightforward procedure was complicated by Boulton's attempt to make appointment conditional upon Henry John's succeeding Robinson as solicitor general. The ploy, however, did not work. Henry John was named acting solicitor general in 1818, but his commission as solicitor general, although backdated to 2 December of that year, was not issued until 1 March 1820.

By the mid 1820s the rigours of riding circuit had begun to impose too heavy a strain on Boulton; moreover, he had started to become deaf. In 1827, several months after his retirement, his wife died, and Boulton was expected to follow her shortly. Instead, he lived another seven years, dying one day after his 75th birthday at the Grange, the home of his son D'Arcy. His tenure on the Court of King's Bench coincided with Lieutenant Governor Sir Peregrine Maitland's administration, a period of conservative reaction. Boulton could be said to have expressed the spirit of his time and place, and hence was useful to reformers such as Mackenzie as a symbol of the province's grievances. 'How is Justice Boulton's speeches and addresses like saying Mass?' queried Mackenzie. 'Because nine-tenths of the audience don't understand their meaning.' Henry Scadding provides a more personal description, presenting Boulton as 'an English gentleman of spare Wellington physique; like many of his descendants, a lover of horses and a spirited rider; a man of wit, too, and humour, fond of listening to and narrating anecdotes of the *ben trovato* class.'

JOHN LOWNSBROUGH

HENRY JOHN BOULTON

Lawyer, office-holder, judge, and politician; b. 1790 in Kensington (London), England, second son of D'Arcy Boulton and Elizabeth Forster; m. in 1818 Eliza, daughter of Ephraim Jones of Brockville, Upper Canada; d. 18 June 1870 at Toronto, Ont.

Henry John Boulton was born at Holland House in a fashionable suburb of London, the son of a London barrister and grandson of Sir John Strange, master of the rolls. His family immigrated in the 1790s to Rensselaer County in New York and about 1800 to Canada, seeking, as Boulton later said, 'a wider field for our energies.' Boulton probably attended John Strachan's school at Cornwall, as did his three brothers, before beginning legal studies in 1807 in York (Toronto) where his father was solicitor general. Boulton went to England in 1811 to continue his law studies at Lincoln's Inn. He spent three years in a solicitor's office in London, then two years at Oxford beginning in 1814. He subsequently studied under a special pleader and was called to the English bar from the Middle Temple; he was admitted to the bar of Upper Canada on 5 Nov. 1816.

With a solid foundation in English law and considerable intellectual ability and ambition, Boulton returned to Canada where, despite the quick temper he could display in court, he succeeded John Beverley Robinson as solicitor general in 1818 at age 28; Robinson succeeded Boulton's father as attorney general. In 1829 Henry John Boulton became attorney general himself, again succeeding Robinson. Although the patronage of these legal offices was thus confined, Boulton, like his father and Robinson before him, filled the posts so ably and impartially that even Francis Collins, an outspoken critic of the Family Compact who was editor of the *Canadian Freeman*, testified to his fairness.

Boulton was elected to represent Niagara in 1830, styling himself an independent rather than a ministerial candidate. In his election address, he assured the voters that 'in the house he should fearlessly represent their interests as if he held no ... office under the Crown.'

Thus, from the beginning of his parliamentary career, Boulton was identified with an independent position or even a 'liberal cast,' as the *Niagara Reporter* suggested in 1833. Yet the *Canadian Freeman* in 1830 called Niagara a 'rotten borough' and referred to Boulton as a 'ministerialist'; William Lyon Mackenzie described him and his brother George Strange Boulton 'as bad as bad can be, perhaps the very worst members any country or nation can be afflicted with,' and headed his 'Black List' in the *Colonial Advocate* with Boulton's name.

As attorney general Boulton skirmished with the more radical Reformers who disliked his proposed bills in 1830 and 1832 for the incorporation of York. They also resented his legalistic arguments to Lieutenant Governor Sir John Colborne who in January 1833 refused the request of Reform sympathizer Father William John O'Grady to have Colborne lift the suspension as pastor of York imposed on him by Bishop Alexander Macdonell. Yet in the O'Grady case Boulton's action prompted no swift reaction from Irish Roman Catholics such as he was later to provoke in Newfoundland. In York Boulton had the support of Macdonell who had formed a working alliance with the administration in the interest of his co-religionists.

Boulton also provoked Reformers by supporting the repeated expulsions of Mackenzie from the assembly in 1831 and 1832. With Solicitor General Christopher Hagerman Boulton complained of the cordial reception given Mackenzie by Lord Goderich, the colonial secretary, when he presented grievances to the authorities in 1832. As a result of Mackenzie's mission to London, Goderich sent a dispatch to Colborne in November 1832 advising the administration to drop its attacks on the reformer and to institute several financial and political reforms. The Legislative Council refused to accept the dispatch, and in violent debates in the assembly many Tories showed that they were as opposed as Reformers to imperial commands which clashed with their own interests. Boulton's language was characteristically extravagant, and he was described at a public meeting in Brockville in January 1833 as 'the first man in the Province who ever attempted to agitate the question of separation from the Mother Country.' Early in March 1833 Boulton and Hagerman were dismissed from their offices by the imperial government.

Boulton deeply resented his dismissal. He publicized the correspondence between himself and Colborne's civil secretary, Major William Rowan, 'so as to not leave room for unfounded or injurious rumours as to the cause of our dismissal,' and he asked Rowan to state specifically the breach of public duty for which he was removed from office. Rowan replied that it was Boulton's promotion of the repeated expulsions of Mackenzie from the assembly; the Colonial Office had raised constitutional objections which it had conveyed to Colborne and through him to Boulton. Boulton maintained that he had never been informed by Colborne of the Colonial Office's objection. He journeyed to England to seek redress, and the imperial government acknowledged that his removal had been unwarranted. He was immediately offered the more lucrative post of chief justice of Newfoundland, and arrived in that colony in November 1833.

The Supreme Court had been established in the colony only seven years and Boulton's predecessor, Chief Justice Richard Alexander Tucker, had been removed for what Governor Thomas John Cochrane and others considered a recalcitrant attitude and 'a mixing of political duties with his judicial ones.' It was a charge difficult for any chief justice in Newfoundland to avoid since he was also expected to act as president of the Council, which exercised both executive and legislative functions.

Boulton seemed to answer the wish of the Newfoundland administration for a man well versed in English criminal law, able to frame new laws and to remodel the courts and judicial procedures. He set to work with a will. After consultation with the law officers and assistant judges of the Supreme Court, he first changed the method of empanelling juries. Under his new regulations the sheriff was to summon 48 jurors, rather than the previous 18, from which 12 would be drawn by lot; this was the system then used in Britain. For special juries 40 names would be drawn by lot from the 75 qualified grand jurors to form a list from which the opposing lawyers would alternately strike off names, to a total of 12 for each side; the remaining 16 would comprise the special jury.

Among the eligible grand jurors were the Reform leaders, Patrick Morris, John Kent, Patrick Doyle, and Laurence O'Brien, and five other Roman Catholics; the remainder were leading Protestant merchants of St John's. The Reformers attacked the new rules, which, they claimed, 'allowed conservatives to strike off any person who was supposed to differ from him in interest or opinion' and they alleged 'that the Attorney-General [James Simms] availed himself of [this practice] in all the political trials since the alteration was effected.' Undoubtedly the law officers had felt some anxiety that the Reform leaders might not act with the strictest impartiality in cases involving their partisans. In August 1835 Daniel O'Connell presented a petition from the Reformers to the British House of Commons for the removal of Boulton as chief justice. Boulton journeyed to England and apparently satisfied the Colonial Office of the propriety of his actions, for Under-Secretary Sir George Grey defended him in the house.

Early in 1834 Boulton framed a law to incorporate a law society and to regulate the admission of barristers and attorneys to the bar. The Reform opposition claimed that the new rules disbarred aspiring lawyers who could not afford the fees charged by qualified attorneys with whom they had to apprentice themselves for five years.

The fact that in most of these disputes Boulton was the innovator and the Reformers defended tradition and ancient usages became apparent again in several cases in 1834 and 1835 involving the credit arrangements of the fisheries. For instance, seamen were accustomed to receiving their wages, not from the 'planter' who had hired them for the voyage, but from the merchant who received the proceeds of the voyage. Boulton claimed that the seamen were deprived of all security for the payment of their wages under such arrangements, but the fishermen and Michael Anthony Fleming, the Roman Catholic bishop, pointed out that the planter was simply a 'steward' and usually without sufficient means to guarantee wages. The chief justice also annoyed fishermen by altering the writ of attachment so that a fisherman's boat and tackle could be seized for debt, a harsh measure which took from the fisherman his means of engaging in the fishery on his own. The third custom he overturned, in a case involving Patrick Morris, was the practice of 'current supply'; Boulton said that past creditors, and not the supplying merchant – in this case, Morris – had a superior and prior claim to the proceeds of a voyage. In normal commerce such practices would be unquestioned, but these changes in the prosecution of the fishery in Newfoundland brought charges from the Reformers that Boulton shook 'the confidence which induced merchants to afford to planters the means of carrying on their fishing voyages.' In the tense political situation of the early 1830s political leaders could play on the fears of the fishermen and stigmatize Boulton as the author of injustice and bigotry.

At the opening of the Central Circuit Court in 1835 Robert John Parsons, editor of the liberal *Newfoundland Patriot*, published a caricature of Boulton's address to the grand jury, entitled 'Stick a pin here: the beneficial effects of hanging illustrated.' Boulton then charged

Parsons with contempt of court, fined him £50, and sentenced him to three months in jail, asserting that the article 'strikes at the very independence of the seat of Justice. ...' He would have been wiser perhaps to have ignored the article, for when O'Connell brought the case to the attention of the British government, British law authorities decided that although Boulton's decision was strictly legal, the 'practice for many years ... of this country was against him'; the sentence against Parsons was remitted. A second petition against Boulton prepared by the Reform leaders was printed in the *Patriot* on 2 Feb. 1836. These efforts to vilify Boulton did not go unanswered. Some 900 residents of St John's, including merchants, professional men, 17 captains, six carpenters, and 12 illiterates, sent a memorial to the colonial secretary on Boulton's behalf.

During an assembly inquiry in 1837 into judicial administration, at which John Valentine Nugent was both chairman and a witness against Boulton, direct attacks were made on the chief justice. Morris, who had a genuine concern for the Irish fishermen of Newfoundland and whose suspicion of Protestant ascendancy was shared by Bishop Fleming, repeated his longstanding charges that the chief justice 'has exhibited ... great partiality on the bench; his adjudications have been unjust, arbitrary, and illegal, biassed by strong party prejudices. ... [He] has totally subverted the ancient laws and customs of Newfoundland.' When the house ordered that Morris' lengthy speech be printed, Boulton instituted a libel suit for £2,000 damages against Morris, Kent, and Nugent. Boulton proposed the unusual move of stepping down from the bench and acting as his own counsel while the two assistant judges presided, but the case was never heard.

Acting on the report of its committee, the assembly sent Morris, Nugent, and Dr William Carson to London at the end of 1837 to seek Boulton's removal and to ask that in future the chief justice not be a member of the Council. Boulton also left for London to answer the charges. He was not without defenders. In his brief was a deposition from John Stark, registrar of the Northern Circuit Court of Newfoundland, who asserted that crime and litigation had decreased in late years, 'a clear proof that the laws are now more certainly administered and better understood,' and that Boulton was 'just, impartial, upright and independent in his decisions and decrees.' Expressions of support were also sent from Boulton's assistant justices, the members of the grand jury, 928 residents of St John's, the Chamber of Commerce, 39 merchants and lawyers, and the deputy sheriff of Harbour Grace, all attesting to his integrity, ability, and impartiality.

The assembly delegation to London was joined by Bishop Fleming, who wrote to one of Boulton's most outspoken critics, Father Edward Troy, of the 'truly flattering reception of the delegates at the Colonial Office' and stated that it appeared certain that 'Mr. Boulton is disposed of.' With O'Connell as one of their spokesmen, the Reform leaders were confident of success. A committee of the Privy Council, to which Boulton's case was referred, criticized the vehemence of the Reformers' memorial and found no evidence of 'any corrupt motive or intentional deviation from his [Boulton's] duty as a Judge'; however, the committee noted much 'indiscretion in the conduct of the Chief Justice' in participating in party controversies in Newfoundland, and recommended that he be removed from office. Lord Glenelg, the colonial secretary, had, in January 1838, already decided on Boulton's dismissal, and the latter's request for a new appointment was turned down by the Colonial Office.

Thus at age 48, with a family of eight children and bereft of office for a second time, Boulton returned to private practice in Toronto. His old constituency, Niagara, welcomed him back and returned him as an 'independent' to the newly created assembly of the Province of Canada in 1841, and he was appointed a QC in 1842. In the new house it soon became apparent that Boulton did not support William Henry Draper's moderate Conservative ministry on many questions. Contemptuous as ever of public favour or disdain, Boulton made up his mind in favour of responsible government, and openly supported Robert Baldwin by 1843. As chairman of a meeting called in Toronto on 6 Feb. 1844 to establish the Reform Association of Canada, Boulton stated that, 'after considerable experience of Colonial Office Government ... he was convinced, that to ensure the British connexion and Canadian prosperity, it was absolutely necessary that the people of Canada should have the entire management of their own local affairs.' This association with the Reformers brought the wrath of the Conservative press down upon him. The *Montreal Gazette* spoke of Boulton as 'that lord of Misrule ... an office-seeker and demagogue.' The editor of the newly established Montreal *Pilot*, Francis Hincks, defended Boulton, pointing out that his stake in the country 'is so large as to make him much more interested in promoting its prosperity, than he would be by securing for himself what, people who have never tasted them, imagine to be the sweets of office.'

Boulton's support of the liberals resulted in his losing the Niagara seat in 1844, but in December 1846 he was appointed a member of the Executive Council. In 1847 he was given the safe Reform seat of Norfolk, and was described by the Conservative *Toronto Patriot* as being 'brought forward on the ultra-radical ticket.' One of his chief contributions as a supporter of the administration of Robert Baldwin and Louis-Hippolyte La Fontaine was to move successfully the amendment to the 1849 Rebellion Losses Bill that excluded those convicted in 1837-38 from the financial benefits of the bill, a device which finally persuaded the reluctant rank and file Reformers from Canada West to accept the measure. Yet Boulton was never at home among the Reformers and by 1850 he was again an 'independent' member, advocating, as did his nephew, William Henry Boulton, the elective principle in the Legislative Council. He further asserted his individuality by proposing an amendment to the Reform government's speech from the throne which was essentially a demand for representation in parliament according to population. Boulton did not seek re-election in 1851, but continued to practise law in Toronto until 1860 or 1861 when he retired. In 1855 he had been manager of the Canadian section of the Paris exhibition.

Throughout his lifetime, Boulton remained an individualist and was consequently abused as an office-seeker, bigot, unbending tory, and ultra-radical. He was a man of energy and ability with connections that assured him a place in politics, but his inability or unwillingness to conciliate opposition did not permit him to fit into any party. This temperament was manifest in his frequent outbursts of defiance, which could and often did turn political defeat into personal disaster. Yet Boulton was a colourful personality in the assembly, and his parliamentary career cannot be considered a failure. Although forcefully expressed, his opinions were conventional, supporting Sir John Colborne in the 1830s, responsible government in the 1840s, and, later, elective institutions and 'rep. by pop.'

With regard to his years in Newfoundland, Boulton's severest critics were historians D.W. Prowse and Bishop Michael Howley, both of whom relied largely on the hostile assembly investigation and memorial seeking Boulton's removal. Prowse adds, without evidence, a charge of personal meanness. Yet Boulton's concern for individuals in several cases he heard indicates that he was not always the stern, inflexible judge. Charges of religious bigotry are also difficult to sustain. His wife was a Roman Catholic who once on leaving church spoke out indignantly against Father Troy's denunciation of her husband. Like his Protestant contemporaries, Boulton disliked Roman Catholic clerical involvement in politics, and he privately criticized Father Troy's withholding the services of the church from Roman Catholics for political reasons. A modern historian has concluded, as Prowse did, that Boulton was 'the scapegoat, not only of the popular party, [which was] enraged by his bias in the Council and by his inflexibility on the Bench, but of the Colonial Office which had assigned him to these incompatible offices.'

He was an enigma to his contemporaries. Newspapers confined themselves to the barest death notices. The Toronto *Leader* and *Patriot* simply reprinted the biography, probably written by Boulton himself, which appeared in Henry J. Morgan's *Sketches of celebrated Canadians*, but added that he 'was respected by the whole community and was in every sense a good and worthy citizen,' a direct contradiction of J.C. Dent's comment in his book, *The last forty years*, that Boulton was neither respected nor popular.

HEREWARD and ELINOR SENIOR

Sir WILLIAM CAMPBELL

Lawyer, office holder, JP, militia officer, politician, and judge; b. 2 Aug. 1758 in Caithness, Scotland, son of Alexander Campbell and Susannah Poole; m. 1 June 1785 Hannah Hadley in Guysborough, N.S., and they had two sons and four daughters – two of the latter married Robert Roberts Loring and William Robertson; d. 18 Jan. 1834 in York (Toronto), Upper Canada.

William Campbell was born into a branch of Clan Diarmid that migrated north to Caithness late in the 17th century. His paternal grandfather was a captain in the Royal Navy, and his father owned land at Houstry in the south of Caithness, the possible location of William's birth. He attended a grammar school at Thurso where classical languages were taught, and studied law briefly at Elgin before the death of his instructor ended his formal education. By then the American colonies had rebelled, and against the advice of his friends Campbell decided to enter the army. He became a volunteer in the 76th Foot, a Highland regiment in which one of his relatives was a soldier, and accompanied it to North America. Captured at Yorktown, Va, in 1781, he remained a prisoner for some time. Before the end of the war he was awarded a commission in a provincial regiment so that he could receive half pay.

Midway through 1784 Campbell appeared in Nova Scotia with a group of refugees arriving at Chedabucto Bay to settle. He received a water lot in the new town of Guysborough and other acreage, and married the daughter of a pre-loyalist inhabitant. Local tradition tells that when Campbell became discouraged by his prospects his neighbour Thomas Cutler suggested that he study law with him. Records of admissions to the provincial bar for this period are not extant. Campbell seems to have begun practising as an attorney around 1785. A remote fishing village offered little business, and he had to keep a small shop in order to make ends meet. His training and occupation set him apart from his neighbours, and undoubtedly helped him acquire several township offices such as assessor, surveyor, and overseer of the poor. By the early 1790s he had also obtained the socially significant appointments of justice of the peace and captain of militia. In 1799 Campbell was acclaimed to the House of Assembly as one of the two representatives for Sydney County, and he remained a member until his seat was declared vacant for non-attendance in 1806. Although Campbell was an infrequent visitor to the house, he came to notice during 1803 when he was a vocal supporter of fellow assemblyman William Cottnam Tonge. Lieutenant Governor Sir John Wentworth, the chief critic of Tonge, commented that another figure had joined the 'reprehensible opposition.'

Campbell's parliamentary career occurred while he was a member of the government of the neighbouring colony of Cape Breton. His involvement there began in October 1799. The administrator, John Murray, had fallen out with Attorney General David Mathews, and Mathews's supporter Archibald Charles Dodd refused to be a party to any prosecution of him instigated by Murray. Since Mathews and Dodd were the only lawyers on the island, Murray needed independent legal support, and Campbell was evidently chosen because of his proximity to Sydney and his need for work. Murray appointed Campbell solicitor general and, because there was no provision for such an official, a subscription was raised on Campbell's behalf and Murray took him into his home. The death of James Miller, the superintendent of the coal mines, gave Murray the chance to appoint Campbell to that position, though at first he had to share its attractive salary with Miller's sister, Jane. Campbell was also named to the Executive Council, and after Mathews's dismissal as attorney general in November he began to act in his place. In February 1800 Murray assumed control of the mines from the lessees, Jonathan Tremain and Richard Stout, with the result that Campbell had even more responsibility over the operations there.

Despite Campbell's favoured status, he clashed with Murray when the administrator began to take all responsibility for the mines and ignore his remonstrances. He thus abandoned Murray when Murray was disputing the leadership of the government with John Despard in the late summer of 1800. Despard's victory left Campbell in an influential position, and his advice about the mines was solicited by Despard. Campbell disparaged the system of government control, and his arguments in favour of private management persuaded Despard, who advertised in Halifax for bids. When this effort failed, he leased the mines to Campbell, whose offer was accepted over that of his only rivals, Tremain and Stout, and Campbell took possession on 24 Nov. 1801. He promptly proved lacking in the experience to run the mines alone and by January 1803 claimed that his losses had been so ruinous that he required an increase in prices, a reduction in the government duty payable on each chaldron, or a termination of the lease with suitable reimbursement. Despard refused all three alternatives, but Campbell kept up the pressure and avoided sinking the new pit that Despard requested on the grounds that additional workers would cost too much. The disastrous drop in coal shipments which resulted placed Despard in a difficult position, since the money from the duties was a badly needed source of revenue for Cape Breton. By early 1804 Despard realized his mistake in allowing a relatively unskilled lessee to run a resource of such value to the colony, and on 28 February he took control of the mines on behalf of the crown. Campbell surrendered the mining equipment and other stock only after Despard paid him £477 in compensation.

Campbell had arrived in Cape Breton poor and much in debt, a situation which had been eased by the salaries of superintendent and attorney general. He had taken the lease hoping that the profits would solve his financial worries, and his inexperience did not prepare him for his losses, which were harder to take because he had ceased to be superintendent. While lessee he purchased land extensively and started building the largest house in Sydney, perhaps in anticipation of the revenue from the mines. Thus when Despard proved unwilling to help he turned against the administrator, and by February 1804 the rift between the two men was irreparable. That spring Despard took the advice of the other members of the council and ordered that Campbell not be summoned to further meetings because his behaviour had become 'so violent, so disrespectful and indecorous.' However, Despard did not dismiss Campbell as councillor or attorney general.

In his anger at Despard, Campbell tried to have him replaced as military commander in Cape Breton, and when that attempt failed he aligned himself with Richard Collier Bernard DesBarres Marshall Gibbons. The son of the colony's first chief justice, Gibbons had a keen legal mind and a desire to see the island's non-representative government replaced by an elected house of assembly. To this end, about 1805 he began to attack the tax on imported rum inaugurated by Despard in 1801 as illegal because it had not been approved by an assembly, and he went so far as to declare that the same reason made all the colony's ordinances invalid. It is difficult to tell if Campbell supported Gibbons out of a desire for revenge against Despard or because of his genuine belief in Gibbons's views. He may even have put some of these notions into Gibbons's head. Certainly Campbell accepted the principle of reform and subscribed to Gibbons's ideas, although Chief Justice William Woodfall believed that he did not advance them 'quite so daringly' as Gibbons. Around the beginning of 1806 he declared publicly that he would dispute the legality of ordinances passed by the council and refused to prosecute a ship's captain who had carried coal from Cape Breton without a permit on the grounds that the relevant ordinance was illegal. Only after repeated orders from Despard did he take the case to court.

In July 1807 Despard was replaced as administrator by Brigadier-General Nicholas Nepean. A weak man, Nepean quickly fell under the influence of Campbell, whom he summoned to council meetings and nominated mines superintendent. The previous superintendent, John Corbett Ritchie, who had been appointed by Despard, complained to London, and in April 1808 Lord Castlereagh, the colonial secretary, ordered Nepean to reappoint Ritchie and commented adversely on the selection of Campbell. During that spring Nepean made some sort of family connection with Ritchie, and bolstered by the fear of endangering his own position, he dismissed Campbell as superintendent in June. In a further attempt to stay in Cape Breton Nepean then turned on his erstwhile confidant, describing him as an 'instigator of mischief' who had opposed him at every turn. Before his replacement as superintendent, Campbell had lived at the mines and had rented his Sydney house to Nepean. When in July he reminded Nepean that the lease had almost expired the administrator dismissed him as councillor and attorney general and refused to move. Now homeless as well as jobless, Campbell was forced to leave Cape Breton, which he did some time that year, and sail for England to obtain redress.

In London, Campbell pressed his 'hard case' at the Colonial Office, obtaining in March 1810 the promise 'that something should be done to remunerate me for the injustice I have experienced.' He then spent an anxious 15 months while he awaited news as to what that something would be. Moreover, the certainty that 'uncommon and underhand means' had been taken to impugn his character with colonial officials was cause for further unease. An obvious solution and one which Campbell favoured was his appointment to the vacancy on the

Upper Canadian Court of King's Bench. The judgeship had been empty since Robert Thorpe's removal in 1807.

In Upper Canada Lieutenant Governor Francis Gore was eager to fill the vacancy. He urged the Colonial Office in October 1810 either to send out a judge from England or to permit him to make a provisional appointment. By May 1811 Campbell had been informed that the position was his. Immediately Campbell pressed undersecretary Robert Peel for a document making it official, adding, 'I trust ... you will please to pardon any Seeming impatience in me when I inform you that I have been upwards of two years from my family and business, at a very heavy expence.' Campbell received his official appointment on 31 July and arrived at York (Toronto) in November. 'His intelligence and authority,' President Isaac Brock reported, 'promise every thing that can be desired.' The following March Campbell petitioned the Executive Council for land; he was granted a town lot in York and 1,200 acres.

Campbell joined on the bench Chief Justice Thomas Scott, a worn soul eager for retirement, and Mr Justice William Dummer Powell, an able, experienced judge and skilled, ambitious courtier. He seems to have had little desire to win political distinction in Upper Canada, and as a result his career there was blessedly free of the vexation and rancour that had accompanied it in Cape Breton. His was a judicial life with its own particular seasons. Four times a year the Court of King's Bench sat *en banc* at York to decide on appeal issues of law. The terms had been set by statute in 1797 and amended periodically. The court also heard and decided upon motions. Until 1826 it was accommodated in a 'mean and ruinous ... wooden Cottage' which Campbell said was 'in such a state of irreparable decay and dilapidation, as to be unfit for human residence.'

More taxing for the judges were the assizes held once a year in each administrative district. These assizes were combined and arranged into an eastern and western circuit. Held in the district capital, each of the assizes was presided over by a supreme court justice. Civil cases were argued before the judge alone, whereas in criminal cases he was accompanied on the bench by associate judges chosen from the local magistracy. With the establishment of new districts (three were erected between 1816 and 1821, making a total of 11), there was a corresponding increase in travel and judicial workload. Aside from the Home District assizes, which were usually held in April, the other districts were visited by the judges between the spring and fall.

The judges split the duties of the assizes, often taking turns on the eastern and western circuits. In 1825 Campbell opened the western circuit in Sandwich (Windsor) on 1 August and finished at Niagara (Niagara-on-the-Lake) on 16 September.

Campbell found the criminal calendar more onerous although not usually as full as the civil one. For one thing, the decisions of the criminal court had a more direct bearing upon individual lives. For another, until 1835 there was no statutory provision for defence counsel (except in cases of treason), and the interlocutory role was fulfilled by the judge. In sentencing, the judge's discretion was usually circumscribed by statute, in which case it was necessary for him to advise the lieutenant governor if there was any legal cause for gubernatorial intervention and pardon. For all cases of capital conviction the presiding judge was expected – Lieutenant Governor Sir Peregrine Maitland was particularly adamant on this point – to advise the lieutenant governor's secretary on the circumstances of the case. In these instances the judge's counsel was crucial but, more often than not, Campbell was loath to suggest extenuating legal circumstances. During his career on the bench from 1812 to his last assizes in 1827 Campbell presided over 382 criminal cases. His criminal calendar from 1812 to 1819 (excluding the special assizes at Ancaster in 1814) averaged 17.4 cases, whereas from 1820 to 1827 the average increased to 32.5. Most cases involved larceny (of varying degrees) and assault. Sentences normally combined imprisonment, fines, and corporal punishment (whipping and the pillory). Fewer than 10 per cent of Campbell's criminal cases resulted in capital convictions; most of these prisoners received full or conditional pardons.

In Upper Canada, Campbell was noticed and appreciated from an early date. In April 1814 President Gordon Drummond, the performance of his Executive Council hobbled by the deaths of Prideaux Selby and Alexander Grant, recommended to Colonial Secretary Lord Bathurst that additions be made to both the Legislative and the Executive councils. Anxious for two or three appointments, he lamented that the only 'properly qualified' candidate was Campbell. Drummond nominated him for seats on both councils, believing that he would be 'no small acquisition of Talent and information to these Boards.' Nothing, however, came of the suggestion.

Campbell's first years on the bench were uneventful enough. The special assizes at Ancaster in the spring of 1814, towards the close of the war with the United States, was a judicial highlight in the colony's history, but Campbell's role was undistinguished. Six men appeared before him; five were convicted and one acquitted. Of the former, three were executed and two were pardoned. The purpose of the great show-trial was to overawe disaffection. To this end, the crucial decision was whom to execute and whom to pardon. The pre-eminent figure in this process was the acting attorney general, John Beverley Robinson. Campbell was circumspect in suggesting grounds for clemency, although it is worth noting that both men he cited as possibilities for royal mercy received it.

Occasionally Campbell was baffled by popular reaction to convictions and the role it could play in determining a criminal's ultimate fate. In the case of Edward McSwiney, tried before Campbell at Brockville in 1813 and convicted of murder, there was, he concluded, no legal cause for pardon. But McSwiney was a calculating, articulate fellow whose compelling apologia and declarations of pristine loyalty won him the support of local worthies and President Drummond. The eventual result was McSwiney's pardon. A second instance occurred at Niagara in September 1817 during the trial of Angelique Pilotte for infanticide. Although she was convicted before Campbell on what he considered 'clear and sufficient evidence,' he none the less respited her execution because of overwhelming popular support for mercy. In the end, imperial authorities pardoned her conditionally but not before she had escaped.

Between 1818 and 1828 the administration of justice operated increasingly under the cloud of charges of partiality. A series of incidents from the trials of Robert Gourlay in 1818 and 1819 to the dismissal of Mr Justice John Walpole Willis in 1828 convinced many opponents of the administration that justice was not blind but cock-eyed. Perhaps more by luck than connivance Campbell drew assizes with non-contentious cases. He escaped Gourlay's censure because of his handling of the two acquittals in 1818; Gourlay had defended himself, and one observer, Miles Macdonell, commented that 'Judge Campbell gave him every latitude.' Seven years later the jury's acquittal of Robert Randal on a charge of perjury saved Campbell from the public displeasure – in some quarters at least – that would have accompanied a sentence. Still, Campbell's summation in this case has been considered unfriendly to Randal, and Randal himself had in 1820 claimed that Campbell was implicated in the judicial conspiracy to deprive him of his rights. Yet it would seem that the tar did not stick. Indeed, Campbell's handling of William Lyon Mackenzie's suit for damages against the young toughs who had destroyed his types and press – the so-called type riot of 8 June 1826 – earned him a measure of approval from the Maitland administration's most vituperative critic.

On the bench, Campbell displayed a deep concern for constitutionality. In this respect he was not exceptional among his brother judges, but he certainly gave less cause for anyone to doubt his sentiments. The British constitution had acquired, he thought, 'a state of perfection unrivalled in the annals of the world.' Absolute monarchies depended on the 'mere will' of an individual; republics, 'on the wild caprice of a Mob.' But the British constitution had been 'tried by the only infallible test ... that of the experience of mankind from the earliest ages of the world.' Habeas corpus and trial by jury ('the Bulwark of British liberty') were its principal supports. Grand juries held a particular place in his affection as 'the most Constitutional and effectual means of protection against the efforts of public oppression or private malice.' Their 'inquisitorial capacity' – a power progressively circumscribed in the latter half of the century – was indispensable to protecting the constitution. The 'upright and impartial discharge' of justice under that constitution was 'the greatest benefit that can be conferred on society.'

Campbell was not without his prejudices. In an 1826 note to Major George Hillier, Maitland's secretary, on the efficacy of banishing rather than executing two black men convicted of stealing sheep, Campbell stated his opinion that 'Nine tenths of the Blacks in this place [York], and I believe in all other parts of the Province Subsist principally by theft.' An observation the same year at Kingston that 'men as lords of the creation have a right to inflict a little gentle castigation on our rebellious dames' occasioned both public notice in the press and private twittering among Kingston's female gentlefolk. Yet, if the latter remark was conventional, his views on rape were not. The crime was 'under any circumstances ... of an abhorrent nature.' What concerned him was the tendency to call the character of the victim into disrepute during trials, 'for the most common Prostitute is as much under the protection of the law, as the most virtuous woman, – and the violation of her person by force and against her will, is as much a crime.' Campbell lamented a situation in which 'instead of trying the criminal fact, our time and attention would be occupied to little purpose in ascertaining the exact degree of female chastity.'

It was customary in Upper Canada for the superior court judges to apprise the executive of what had transpired on circuit; Campbell was punctilious in this regard. He took pains, for instance, to inform Hillier of anything that even hinted of contention during the assizes. In 1817 he hesitated forwarding a presentment from a grand jury to the lieutenant governor because it was 'somewhat exceptionable both in matter and expression.' However, lest he be blamed for withholding information of a public nature, he submitted the offending material for Hillier's judgement. His correspondence was almost exclusively routed through Hillier and its tone was scrupulously formal and correct. On one occasion in 1825, having already written more often than was usual and without receiving any replies from Hillier, Campbell began 'to doubt the propriety of continuing to trouble you in this sort of demi official style.'

Only rarely was the subject at hand other than formal reports of what had transpired on the circuits or the official business of the court. One instance concerned Campbell's memorial of 1817 on the insufficient salaries of puisne justices. He deemed £750 (sterling) 'very inadequate to the rank and important duties and to that pecuniary independence so essential to the faithful and impartial discharge of those duties.' The sum was payable in England and thus subject to income tax, agency fees, and other incidental charges as well as 'a most enormous discount on Bills of Exchange, amounting sometimes to 25 p.Cent – making in the whole a loss of considerably more than a third part of their income.' On the other hand, he argued, judges in Lower Canada were paid in the colony, clear of 'all expenses, taxes, discounts, or other loss of deductions whatsoever.' Moreover, in 1817 the lower province had two chief justices and seven puisne justices, whereas the upper province had but one chief justice – Powell having succeeded Scott, who retired in 1816 – and Campbell (the bench was not brought back to full strength until D'Arcy Boulton's accession in 1818). The Upper Canadian justices, Campbell complained, 'have to hold assizes at a greater number of Districts, and to perform Circuits of nearly double the extent ... besides the usual Terms and Sittings.' In short, he averred, the 'personal fatigue privations and expences sustained' by Lower Canadian judges on circuit 'bear no reasonable proportion to that which is unavoidably endured and paid by those of the Upper Province, owing to its' far greater extent, more recent settlement, and consequent less improved state in regard to roads, accommodations, and other local disadvantages.' Forwarded to the Colonial Office with Gore's recommendation, Campbell's appeal was turned down by Bathurst.

More frequent in his official correspondence is discussion arising from a judge's role as intermediary between the executive and the district grand juries. Local matters concerning appointments of district officials and the state of the jail and court-house were the stuff of the grand jury recommendations. It was not unusual for Campbell to initiate inquiries as to the fitness of certain men for public appointment or more generally to cast a net for names to be added to the magistracy. In performing the latter responsibilities, Campbell exhibited his characteristic wariness, diligently probing for possible problems. 'Nothing,' he declared, 'can be more repugnant to my sentiments than to be in any degree instrumental in recommending improper characters.'

His official correspondence was mainly concerned with reports of the assizes, the number of capital convictions, the possibilities for pardon, and the nature of sentencing. There was a strained, almost apologetic, quality to Campbell's letters whenever a convict was beyond the reach of royal mercy. This letter of early 1825 is typical: 'It is always matter of extreme regret to me when ... I am unable to make such report as I know would be most gratifying to His Excellency's benevolent feelings without injury to the administration of public justice, – but in the present case it is out of my power to do so consistently with the trust and duties incident to my Situation.' Usually Campbell would respite execution for a sufficient length of time to allow petitions and gubernatorial review. Often good character or respectable connections would be sufficient to mitigate punishment. In 1821, for instance, he recommended a soldier in the 68th Foot 'as a fit object of mercy on account of the favorable character given of him by several witnesses.' Campbell derived 'much satisfaction' in this case from complying with the jury's recommendation of mercy, whereas in another case five years earlier it had been his 'painful duty' to state that there were no mitigating circumstances. Where statutes allowed judicial discretion in sentencing, Campbell was usually prepared to be lenient. In these instances it was his practice to confer with the local justices chosen to sit with him on the bench for the particular assizes.

Evidence of imbecility or a simple nature was yet another reason for urging some commutation of sentence. Penitence on the part of the offender also induced Campbell to incline towards slighter punishment. He was not above a measure of judicial theatrics to induce repentance where none was apparent. In 1825, at Vittoria, Ebenezer

Allan was convicted of two separate capital offences, but even after the verdicts had been delivered 'he evinced a lamentable degree of audacious turpitude and impenitence, ill suited to his Situation.' Campbell, 'in compassion for his immortal fate,' scheduled the execution to follow a 'short period' after the sentencing – a strategy which had 'the desired effect on him, and indeed on all present.' Afterwards, the sheriff reported that Allan 'employs much time in prayer an act of devotion which I am told and verily believe he never before had recourse to.'

Juries had a tendency to acquit – as Campbell said, 'some justly so, – others perhaps by mistake, – but many more I regret to say from less justifiable causes not unfrequent in all small Communities.' Campbell's concern, however, was the possible conviction of the innocent rather than the acquittal of the guilty. In the 1825 cases of King Hans Hawe and Elizabeth Maxwell, convicted of murdering the child of their illegitimate daughter, Campbell had urged 'the Jury to lean strongly to a Verdict of Acquittal – but the Jury thought otherwise and it being their exclusive province to judge of the fact,' he passed sentence. Yet he availed himself of his discretionary power under the particular statute, respited sentence, consulted his fellow judges, and pressed for royal mercy, which was ultimately granted.

Campbell was advancing in age when he took up his duties in Upper Canada. The fluctuating composition of the King's Bench often added to a burden which his health was increasingly unable to tolerate. Powell's leave of absence in 1822 increased Campbell's responsibilities as senior judge and divided an already onerous workload between two judges. Under the strain Campbell's health faltered. On 23 March 1823 he conveyed to Maitland 'my apprehensions that the increasing infirmities of age and ill health will ere long deprive me of the power of fulfilling the important duties of my situation.' For the past two years he had been 'afflicted with occasional attacks of fever and temporary suspension of the mental faculties to a certain extent.' The condition, although 'alarming,' had been brought under control. The following year, after particularly gruelling assizes and the prospect of equally wearisome ones yet to come, Campbell sighed that, 'if he has not had the three regular warnings by being deaf, lame and blind, [he] has almost daily very broad hints to the same effect.'

Age and overwork were taking their toll. The prospect, however, of the imminent retirement of an increasingly cranky and possibly senile Powell held out the possibility of Campbell's elevation to the chief justiceship. Campbell applied for the position and Maitland, anxious to be rid of Powell, warmly recommended Campbell. Bathurst concurred and on 17 Oct. 1825 Campbell became chief justice. As was customary, he also became president of the Executive Council and speaker of the Legislative Council. The emoluments of the chief justiceship and the councillorships brought a hefty increase in salary which Mackenzie claimed was Campbell's only motivation in accepting the appointments. In doing so, the argument ran, he abandoned his 'whig principles' and became the creature of Robinson and John Strachan. His support, for instance, of Robinson's attempt during the alien issue of 1825-26 to deprive a large number of inhabitants of their 'civil rights' was cited as an example of Campbell's 'apostasy.'

The burden of his new duties quickly proved too much. Although Levius Peters Sherwood had replaced Campbell as puisne justice, Boulton was now failing. During the summer of 1826, reporting 'his faculties irretrievably gone,' Boulton was determined to suspend all duties. Forced to compensate for his incapacity, Campbell all but collapsed under the strain. At Brockville in September 1826, Christopher Alexander Hagerman claimed, the 'poor old Chief Justice did every thing in his power to go through all the suits, but his health was not equal to the undertaking.... he was taken so ill while on the Bench, that he was obliged to leave it, and I really thought he would have expired when he got into one of the Jury rooms, he was seized with a sort of fit, which resembled Cholera Morbus.'

Only an extraordinary effort by Campbell and Sherwood (also suffering illness) prevented the administration of justice from grinding to a halt in 1827. Campbell's first inclination was to press for two additional puisne judges in addition to a replacement for Boulton. His personal choice for a judgeship was James Buchanan Macaulay, whom he considered without equal in the colony 'and less extensively, and perhaps less exceptionably connected than some others, a matter of important consideration in selecting a Colonial Judge.' After him he thought Jonas Jones and Hagerman worthy. Campbell took his last assizes in 1827, sailing for England to recover his health the following year. His absence from the bench, by giving Willis the occasion to deny the constitutionality of the court in the absence of the chief justice, precipitated a major crisis. Campbell, however, was beyond the fray. His health did not recover sufficiently to enable him to resume his duties, and in 1829 he retired on a pension of £1,200. He was knighted on 29 April of the same year.

Historians have paid little attention to Campbell. His career in Nova Scotia practically never progressed beyond the boundaries of his county. Although more is known of his activities in Cape Breton, his role there has not been studied in any detail. His long career as a judge in Upper Canada has received only incidental mention. Thus conclusions appropriate to the whole of his career are difficult. Two tentative suggestions are, however, possible. On the one hand, there is, at least until 1825, an attachment to the 'whig principles' mentioned by Mackenzie. Campbell's early support for Tonge and Gibbons may be of a piece with his legal constitutionalism. On the other hand, there is his persistent concern with the precariousness of his finances. The desire for an increased salary, as Mackenzie suspected, may have been the object which weighed most heavily in his decision first to seek and then to accept the chief justiceship in spite of illness and advanced age.

In Upper Canada his career was almost exclusively judicial, and his historical stature suffers by comparison with his predecessor as chief justice, Powell, and his successor, Robinson. Not the saccharine saint portrayed by David Breakenridge Read, Campbell is equally undeserving of William Renwick Riddell's barbed comment: 'Campbell was not a strong judge; he seldom pressed for a conviction, but when a conviction had been secured, he was generally ruthless and seldom recommended commutation.' He did make one significant contribution to Canadian legal history, in 1822 at the trial in Sandwich of Shawanakiskie. His questioning of an Indian's supposed immunity from prosecution for crimes committed by one Indian against another was upheld by imperial authorities. As a result, although the prisoner had escaped, the legality of his conviction had been confirmed and Indians were brought fully within the compass of the criminal law.

R.J. MORGAN and ROBERT L. FRASER

WILLIAM HENRY DRAPER
Politician, lawyer, and judge; b. near London, Eng., 11 March 1801, son of the Reverend Henry Draper; d. at Yorkville (Toronto), Ont., on 3 Nov. 1877.

Educated by private tuition, William Henry Draper ran away to sea at age 15. He made at least two voyages to India with the East India Company, and in the spring of 1820 emigrated to Upper Canada. Settling in Hamilton Township, he lived with John Covert, a prominent Orangeman of the Cobourg area. He appears to have intended at one point to return to England, but he moved to Port Hope, taught school briefly, then began to study law. After a period in the office of George Strange Boulton, Draper was called to the bar in 1828. He was also for a time assistant registrar for Durham and Northumberland. In 1829 he was given a position in the York (Toronto) office of John Beverley Robinson, who was soon to be chief justice, then entered into a legal partnership with Solicitor General Christopher Hagerman. He was also appointed reporter for the Court of King's Bench and named a bencher of the Law Society of Upper Canada. His reputation as a particularly fluent Tory barrister grew rapidly. He early achieved considerable success in the courtroom, and his eloquence gained him the sobriquet 'Sweet William.'

Good fortune, ability, and a pleasing personality thus brought Draper quickly into the society of the group so influential in governing the colony – the 'Family Compact.' He was soon also acquainted with the most formidable man of them all – John Strachan, later the first Church of England bishop of Toronto. It was Robinson, however, who actively persuaded Draper to enter politics; this course was directly against the young lawyer's wishes, but it was no doubt suggested to him as the quickest route to the judiciary where his ambitions lay.

Draper's political *début* was made in the election of 1836 when he handily defeated the Reform candidate in Toronto, James Edward Small. He took his position among the Tory majority gained in Upper Canada that year through the unprecedented intervention in party politics of the governor, Sir Francis Bond Head. In his first session in the House of Assembly, Draper was active, and his position on such thorny problems as the clergy reserves and the charter of King's College early indicated a man less intransigent than the majority of his Tory colleagues. In matters pertaining to the Upper Canada Academy (later Victoria College) in Cobourg his favourable report gained him the friendship of Egerton Ryerson and the Wesleyan Methodists, which was to be one of the constants of his political career. Yet Draper was by no means alienated from his Family Compact friends, and because of their influence with Head his rise was swift. In December 1836 he was made a member of the Executive Council, and in the following March, solicitor general. Shortly afterwards, Head dispatched him to London to present the governor's position in the acute financial crisis of 1836–37. This, however, was a painful episode: Draper's awkward reception by the Colonial Office officials possibly reflected their dislike of Head.

Shortly after Draper's return, the colony was immersed in the rebellion of 1837. It was to his house, on the night of 4 December, that Head brought his wife and other women and children of the little colonial *élite* to seek refuge from the expected assault of William Lyon Mackenzie's 'army.' After the failure of the rebellion Draper organized many of the prosecutions which took place in the next two years when raids by rebels kept the border in constant turmoil. The internal political situation of Upper and Lower Canada was going through an even more basic upheaval with the arrival of Lord Durham [Lambton] and the British government's decision to implement that part of his Report recommending a union of the two Canadas, the appointment of Charles Poulett Thomson to make that union a reality, and Lord John Russell's dispatch of 16 Oct. 1839 which meant in effect that executive councillors could be removed at the will of the governor.

It was during this period of trouble that Draper first began, consciously or not, to tread the pathway towards what was to be the cherished, though unfulfilled, goal of his political career – the formation of a new political party. A conservative party, it would stand ideologically between the old Family Compact Tories, whose system was failing, and the Reformers under Robert Baldwin, whom Draper believed were endangering the connection with Britain. It was a course that would lead to much vilification. Most of it was undeserved, but Draper soon found himself in an undoubtedly compromising position.

He supported the union of the two Canadas in the Upper Canadian assembly on economic grounds. This action alienated many Tories, but he defended his position by pledging himself to the resolutions introduced by John Solomon Cartwright in March 1839 which would have heavily weighted the union against the French Lower Canadians and assured a loyal and probably Tory majority in the assembly. Draper ultimately gave up his adherence to the resolutions in the face of Thomson's determination to force through the union without any such restrictions. However, the publication soon afterwards of Russell's dispatch of 16 October led most of Draper's enemies, Tory and Reformer, to look upon it as an explanation of his conduct in changing his position – he was now simply a placeman of the governor. Draper's denials were not particularly convincing. Though never politically ambitious, he did hope to preserve his place in the government as a route to the judiciary and there seems little doubt that he bent his principles under Thomson's iron pressure.

Yet Draper, who succeeded Hagerman as attorney general for Upper Canada in February 1840, did not gain real credit with the governor for his performance. Once Thomson had pushed through the union of the Canadas by February 1841 (and been created Baron Sydenham), he was determined to act as his own prime minister and to destroy the old political groupings, forming a 'moderate' party devoted to himself. In the election held in March and April (in which Draper was returned for Russell) Sydenham was successful. The French Canadians stood out against him, but in Canada West (still popularly called Upper Canada) both the old Tories and Baldwin's Reformers were reduced to a handful of seats by the Moderates committed to the governor. Draper continued as attorney general west and, as head of the conservative Moderates, was co-government leader with Samuel Harrison in the assembly. But Draper had only four or five real followers, and Sydenham privately considered him a 'poor creature.' It was in Harrison, provincial secretary and leader of the liberal Moderates, that the governor placed his confidence. Unable to comprehend Sydenham's curious blend of liberalism and autocracy, Draper felt baffled and isolated; he had just written a letter of resignation in the autumn of 1841 when he was informed of the governor's death.

The arrival of Sir Charles Bagot as governor in January 1842 marked a new phase in Draper's career. The two men found both their political views and their personalities compatible, and Draper rapidly replaced Harrison as the governor's chief Canadian adviser. Also, Draper's own political philosophy had clarified, and his appreciation of political realities sharpened.

In September 1841, Baldwin had moved resolutions calling for responsible government. These had been parried by Sydenham when Harrison had moved counter-resolutions, ostensibly promising responsible government, in a much vaguer form. It was the Harrison resolutions that were passed, and Draper had supported them. Though he would not have argued that a governor was ever bound to take the advice of his councillors, he now felt himself committed to the principle that executive councillors must have the confidence of a majority of the assembly. This did not necessarily mean a two-party system in the way that Baldwin foresaw; it could also mean a multi-party or a no-party government, and there is no doubt that Draper favoured the last. Now, however, as he began to realize that party government was inevitable, he hoped for a great, loyal Conservative party embracing both French- and English-speaking Canadians – for by now he believed the French to be naturally conservative. He was becoming more convinced that if government were not to founder completely, the French must be brought quickly into it even if they stood by their alliance with Baldwin and the price was a Reform ministry.

It was Bagot who eventually took responsibility for the generous offer to the French that led to the formation of the first Baldwin–Louis-Hippolyte La Fontaine government in September 1842. Acclaim for the governor from the French and Reformers, and disapproval from the British government and the Canadian Tories, resulted. Draper's role in this upheaval was critical: in July he had begun urging Bagot that La Fontaine's French bloc must be brought into the ministry if the governor were not to be placed in an untenable position by being unable to maintain a council acceptable to the assembly. Other councillors, such as Harrison and Robert Baldwin Sullivan, were urging this course, but Draper's advice was the most persuasive. Draper knew that if the French remained committed to Baldwin their accession to power would necessitate his own resignation. This he magnanimously offered, and advised as well that other Tory councillors be forced out. When Bagot still wavered, Draper and Harrison led the Executive Council in forcing his hand by threatening a mass resignation on 12 September. The following day, to La Fontaine, Bagot made his ultimate offer, to place four French Canadians and Baldwin on the council and to retire councillors in whom they did not have confidence. When Baldwin caused further difficulties, Bagot empowered Draper to read out in the assembly the extent of this offer. Most of the French members had not previously known of the magnitude of the concessions, and La Fontaine's hold on his party was briefly shaken. A compromise was worked out and the new Baldwin–La Fontaine ministry formed in a way least damaging to the governor's prestige. Draper resigned from the Executive Council (on 15 September) and from the assembly, and was promised a seat on the judiciary by Bagot.

Draper retired from active politics altogether, taking no great interest in the Legislative Council, to which Bagot appointed him shortly before he died in 1843. Late the same year, however, a crisis erupted under Bagot's successor, Charles Metcalfe, and, led by Baldwin and La Fontaine, the whole of the Executive Council, except Dominick Daly, resigned. When Metcalfe could not form an administration that had a majority in the assembly he summoned Draper and gave him a seat in the Executive Council. With only Daly and Denis-Benjamin Viger, he carried on the administration for nearly a year though he did not hold any portfolio. The non-responsible government of this 'triumvirate' was loudly condemned as autocratic, yet Draper was working towards a broadly based 'Ministry of Moderates,' like the one that had worked under Sydenham. He failed. In Lower Canada, Viger brought over a few individuals, including Denis-Benjamin Papineau, to his cause, but no mass support. In Upper Canada, Draper's appeals to such prominent moderates as Harrison, William Hamilton Merritt, and Ryerson all foundered, and William Morris, who wielded great influence with the Presbyterians, was the only notable accession to the Executive Council (as receiver general) that Draper was able to secure.

Yet a government was somehow patched together in time for the general election in the autumn of 1844. A number of factors – the removal of the seat of government from Kingston to Montreal, the secret societies bill, which had outraged the Orangemen under Ogle Robert Gowan, and a general feeling that the French Canadians were being pandered to – had turned much public opinion in Upper Canada against the Reformers before their resignation and Metcalfe was able to capitalize on this discontent when he entered the campaign and denounced the Reformers as traitors. The result was that, though defeated in the lower half of the province, the government triumphed in Upper Canada and Draper's ministry had a small majority of four or five.

Draper was now in a curious position for one who had resisted so long the doctrines of Baldwin. From late 1844 until his resignation in May 1847 he was virtually prime minister of Canada, and as he had a majority in the assembly, the Reformers could no longer term his administration irresponsible. At the same time, the rapidly failing health of Metcalfe and the lack of interest in domestic politics shown by Lord Cathcart [Charles Murray Cathcart] who succeeded him, meant that Draper saw hardly any interference from above. Yet this was not the greatest anomaly in his situation. He was also a party leader without a party, a prime minister without a following. His majority in the assembly was made up mainly of Tories who had little love for Draper but had been elected to support the governor, and who were largely excluded from the Executive Council. They endured the attorney general as leader because there was no one else to take his place – he had the support of the governors, and the Tories themselves were split into factions led by Henry Sherwood and Sir Allan MacNab.

Under the circumstances, Draper envisaged a period of retrenchment with few controversial issues. In fact, despite the weakness of his position, the last two sessions of the assembly he faced as attorney general saw several important measures. A schools act for Lower Canada drafted by Augustin-Norbert Morin was passed in 1845. The Upper Canada common school act of 1846, drawn up by Ryerson at Draper's behest, has been termed the first really workable settlement of that troublesome problem. The voting of a permanent civil list firmly established the principle that it was the Canadian legislature only that had the right to tax Canadians. Perhaps more significant were Draper's efforts to lay the spectre of the rebellion of 1837. On 17 Dec. 1844 the house addressed the queen, unanimously asking her to pardon all former rebels; two months later, an amnesty was granted. Early in 1845 D.-B. Papineau moved a successful rebellion losses bill for Upper Canada, although the more controversial subject of indemnifying Lower Canadians was not solved until later. Nevertheless, the French Canadians welcomed the repeal of restrictions on the French language, moved by Papineau on behalf of the government, in February 1845. It proved a coup for Draper who had persuaded Metcalfe to disobey his instructions on the subject in order to forestall an address the Reformers were planning to make on the subject of the French language.

Despite such successes, Draper's government gave an appearance of chronic weakness. It was defeated frequently on minor issues and retreated ignominiously over the university bill. This measure, which

Draper considered important enough to warrant his leaving the Legislative Council and seeking a seat in the assembly (for London), was introduced by him on 4 March 1845. It called for a University of Upper Canada to which Queen's College at Kingston and Victoria College would be affiliated, as well as the Church of England King's College (which later became the University of Toronto). Acceptable to the Methodists and the Church of Scotland, the bill aroused the ire of the Church of England, and Strachan managed to rally many of the Tory assembly members against it. Draper persisted, saying he would stand or fall by the measure, and he forced the resignation of his own recently named inspector general, William Benjamin Robinson, on the floor of the house when the latter supported Strachan. Perhaps Draper was hoping for aid from Baldwin's Reformers who had previously framed a similar bill; it was not forthcoming. In the end, a group of Tories, led by Sherwood, threatened to bring down the government if the bill had a third reading. This was too much for the ailing Metcalfe who felt that he would not be able to form a new ministry. Following a plea from the governor, Draper's measure was withdrawn.

From an administrative or legislative point of view, Draper's ministry could hardly be termed more than a limited success. Politically, it seemed to be a complete failure. Yet the attorney general was working towards something important which would bear fruit after his own political retirement: a modern Victorian conservative party. His plan was twofold – to placate the leading English-speaking Tories while he replaced them with Moderates, and to win the French bloc, or a substantial part of it, away from its alliance with the Reformers.

In this last task Draper came remarkably near to success. There was no longer any hope that Viger or D.-B. Papineau would being in any mass support, so Draper struck shrewdly at the weakest link of La Fontaine's supporters, the Quebec City wing, which felt neglected by their Montreal leaders. Negotiations with René Caron, the mayor of Quebec and speaker in the Legislative Council, broke down when Metcalfe refused to eject Daly from the Executive Council and when the correspondence fell into the hands of La Fontaine who read it in the assembly in April 1846. Further negotiations conducted in the autumn of 1846 again came to nothing, but on this occasion Draper managed to drive a wedge between La Fontaine and his chief lieutenant, Morin. In the spring of 1847 approaches were again made to Caron and the Quebec wing of the party, which in turn applied pressure on Morin; in his last approach Draper came closest to success. A substantial section of the French bypassed La Fontaine and empowered Caron to enter the administration if the 'double majority' principle was offered. Acceptance, however, would have given four out of the seven seats on the council to the French, and it seemed a prohibitive demand. Draper was well content to wait.

The negotiations were never again to be taken up. Draper's failure to break the French bloc was matched by a more disastrous failure to contain rising Tory opposition to himself. The departure in 1845 of Metcalfe, whom the Tories had pledged to support and who had himself fully supported Draper, was a serious blow. Nevertheless, factions led by Sherwood and MacNab kept the Tories disunited and provided Draper with the opportunity to pursue his hope of filling the Upper Canadian section of his Executive Council with moderate Conservatives. William Morris, John Hillyard Cameron, John A. Macdonald – these were the stamp of men Draper wanted and ultimately brought into his ministry. William Badgley became attorney general east. But they were too few. Attempts to placate the Tories with positions failed. Sherwood and W.B. Robinson had been brought into office but both had to be ejected, and dealings with MacNab proved disastrous. Only a few men such as William Cayley were acceptable to both right and left wings of the party. The Tory members of the assembly increasingly chafed under the leadership of men many of them despised.

That Draper, who had always disliked politics, should begin to look towards retirement under such discouraging conditions was natural. A further inducement came with the appointment of Lord Elgin [Bruce] as governor in 1847. Since Draper had answered Metcalfe's desperate summons to office in 1843 he had assumed that British governors would be interested, above all, in avoiding a Baldwin administration. But Elgin and Lord Grey in the Colonial Office were quite willing to accept both responsible government and Baldwin. It was becoming apparent to Draper that he was in the way of everyone – governor, Tory, and Reformer. On 28 May, following the death of Christopher Hagerman, Draper resigned as attorney general and became puisne judge of the Court of Queen's Bench of Upper Canada. His ministry fell into the hands of Sherwood until the subsequent election returned Baldwin and La Fontaine.

Draper's legislative accomplishments were real but modest, his efforts to form a moderate Conservative party in alliance with French

Canadians failed, and he swam clearly, if obliquely, against the historical tide of responsible government and reformism. Yet it was he, along with Baldwin and La Fontaine, who really dominated the 1840s. Moreover, the formation of a Conservative party linked to the French Canadians was to become a reality in 1854. It was the creation of Draper's ablest follower, Macdonald, who clearly had the political gift in which Draper was most lacking – the ability to organize a national party with wide popular support.

There are other important aspects to Draper's political career that have rarely been appreciated. Following the racial conflicts of the 1830s, the 1840s were comparatively quiet, owing partly to a reaction against the rebellion, partly to the Baldwin–La Fontaine alliance. Giving the French Canadians their fair share of political power was a factor and Draper's critical part in that episode is clear. Similarly his efforts to form a coalition with the French Canadians between 1844 and 1847 undoubtedly helped to convince them that their claims for office would eventually be met.

Draper's role in the evolution of responsible government was an unwitting one, but perhaps his most important. After the rebellions and the era of Durham and Sydenham, the tide was moving towards acceptance of responsible government. But between 1841 and 1846, when Sir Robert Peel's Conservative ministry was in power in England, particularly when Stanley held sway in the Colonial Office, a different view prevailed there. An unremitting clash between a Canadian legislature championing responsible government and a British Colonial Office and governor could have had serious consequences in this period, and such a clash appeared about to develop in December 1843 with the resignation of Baldwin and La Fontaine. Draper stepped into the breach, first by supporting Metcalfe with his temporary government, and then from 1844 to 1847 by carrying on a full administration which stood on a majority in the assembly after the election of 1844. Thus he neatly bridged the transition between the era of Metcalfe and Stanley and that of Elgin and Grey. In doing so he helped allow responsible government to evolve peacefully, and was thus one of the many architects in the development of commonwealth from empire.

Following his retirement from politics, Draper was at last given the opportunity to advance in what had always been his chosen field of endeavour – the judiciary. After sitting on the Court of Queen's Bench for nine years, he was created chief justice of the Court of Common Pleas of Upper Canada in 1856, succeeding James Macaulay. In 1863 he was named chief justice of the Court of Queen's Bench for Upper Canada; in 1868 he was appointed presiding judge of the Court of Error and Appeal in Ontario, succeeding Archibald McLean, and the next year became its chief justice.

Though eminently distinguished, Draper's later career saw none of the turbulence, nor indeed of the constructive innovations that had marked his political life. To Draper himself it was the consummation of a personal preference for a tranquil and ordered existence. He did, however, make two brief reappearances in the public eye in the 1850s – in the question of transferring the Hudson's Bay Company territories, and as presiding judge over the 'double shuffle' trials.

The HBC question arose when problems concerning the colony of Vancouver Island prompted Henry Labouchere, colonial secretary in Lord Palmerston's administration, to undertake an investigation in 1857 of the company's charter by a select committee of the British House of Commons. In the Canadas, the Macdonald–George-Étienne Cartier government was weak, and the Clear Grit opposition, led by George Brown, had just hammered 'western expansion' into its platform. Though Macdonald was happy to pre-empt an attractive Grit policy, he knew the difficulties of occupying and defending the lands, and therefore had to pursue a policy combining aggressive expansionism with prudent realism. He chose Draper to represent Canada before the select committee, with no powers to commit the province but with wide latitude of argument. It was a task suited to Draper's broad legal knowledge and persuasive powers of argument. Labouchere claimed that Draper, who favourably impressed the committee, was one of the ablest men he had ever met. Concentrating on the necessity of preserving the west from American encroachments, Draper argued that only settlement could achieve this but that the company's interests were inimical to settlement. He suggested that an appeal to the Judicial Committee of the Privy Council might be the best way to test the company's chartered territorial rights.

The work of the select committee bore no immediate fruit, but Draper's arguments had made their mark and the principle that Canada would likely be the ultimate legatee of the HBC's territorial rights became more and more taken for granted.

Draper's next appearance on the political scene in 1858 was a good deal more controversial. In August the Cartier–Macdonald ministry came back into power after a defeat which had resulted in the famous two-day Brown–Antoine-Aimé Dorion administration. The new ministers did not resign their seats and face by-elections as was normal procedure. Instead they swore the oaths for one office, resigned, and swore again for another office. The manœuvre was soon dubbed the 'double shuffle,' and Brown bitterly attacked both the governor, Sir Edmund Head, who had accepted it, and the government. Another Reformer, Adam Wilson, tested the legality of the issue by starting proceedings against Macdonald and two of his colleagues, and the case was heard before Draper. Despite the fact that all the judges involved in the hearings were Conservatives, the Grits appear to have hoped for victory. However, it was on the letter of the law that Draper stood in giving judgement for the defendants on 18 Dec. 1858. Yet, though disclaiming any right of the judiciary to guess what the legislators intended in framing the original act, Draper did interpret what they had 'meant' in dealing with another, more minor point in the issue. This lent some credence to the charges Brown and his allies soon made that both the governor and the judiciary were in an unholy alliance to subvert the constitution at the behest of the corrupt Macdonald. Draper was singled out for particular contempt, and the *Globe* expounded: 'Mr. Draper has mistaken his place and age. He would have made a very fair Jeffreys and might have served for the Bloody Assize.' The charges by the Grits of a conscious conspiracy were unfounded and unfair, but the whole episode of the 'double shuffle' was hardly edifying. The bias in Macdonald's favour and against Brown must, unconsciously at least, have influenced Head and Draper in making their otherwise unexceptionable decisions.

If the remainder of his years on the bench were quiet, Draper was active in many civic and religious organizations, being at one time president of the St George's Society in Toronto, of the Canadian Institute (from 1856 to 1858), of the Toronto Cricket Club, and of the Philharmonic Society. He was president of the Church Association of the Diocese of Toronto, formed in 1873 and including as members William Hume Blake, Casimir Stanislaus Gzowski, and Daniel Wilson, which led to the founding of Wycliffe College in Toronto. In 1854, he was made a CB. He maintained a lifelong passion for exercise but became increasingly infirm in the last decade of his life, and he died on 3 Nov. 1877. He had married Mary White in 1827. They had several children, one of whom, William George, became well known as a lawyer.

GEORGE METCALF

JOHN ELMSLEY (Elmsly)
Judge and politician; b. 1762 in the parish of Marylebone, London, England, eldest son of Alexander Elmsly (Elmslie) and Anne Elligood; m. 23 July 1796 Mary Hallowell in London, and they had five children including John Elmsley; d. 29 April 1805 in Montreal, Lower Canada.

The Elmslie family came from the parish of Touch, Kincraigie, in Aberdeenshire, Scotland, where they were small farmers and Quakers. In the mid 18th century Alexander and his brother Peter moved to London, changed the spelling of their name to Elmsly, and joined the Church of England. John Elmsley entered Oriel College, University of Oxford, on 3 Dec. 1782, graduating with a BA in 1786 and an MA in 1789. He was called to the bar at the Inner Temple on 7 May 1790. Through connections with the Home secretary, the Duke of Portland, Elmsley secured the chief justiceship of Upper Canada in April 1796, when he was resident at Lincoln's Inn. On 20 Nov. 1796 he arrived at Newark (Niagara-on-the-Lake) with his friend, the Reverend Thomas Raddish (Reddish); his bride and her loyalist father, Benjamin Hallowell, followed later after a lengthy visit in Boston, Mass., their home until March 1776.

Lieutenant Governor John Graves Simcoe had left the province in July, choosing Peter Russell to act as administrator in his absence. The government officials were rather unwillingly preparing to follow Simcoe's orders and move the seat of government from Newark to York (Toronto). Elmsley objected strongly to the move because he thought that there would be great difficulty in finding lodgings and jurors for the Court of King's Bench and the Home District court, both of which automatically held their sessions in the capital. He and Russell quarrelled acrimoniously on this issue throughout most of 1797. In July 1797 a resolute Elmsley paid £1,105 for a house in Newark. Russell insisted that the capital be moved, and in June 1797 met his first parliament in York. A compromise was reached by passing a bill permitting the courts to remain at Newark for a further two years. Elmsley finally moved to York in the spring of 1798, building a large house that later became the lieutenant governor's residence.

Russell and Elmsley continued to disagree about almost everything. In November 1797 Russell had renewed his own temporary appointment as a puisne judge, first made by Simcoe in 1795. Elmsley immediately objected, and his objection was upheld by the Duke of Portland on the principle of separation of judicial and executive authority. Other issues continued to divide the administrator and the chief justice.

In April 1799 Peter Hunter was appointed lieutenant governor of Upper Canada and commander of the forces in the Canadas, and on 16 August he arrived in York. Because his military responsibilities necessitated long absences from the province Hunter left its administration mainly to a committee of the Executive Council consisting of Russell, Æneas Shaw, and Elmsley, who was chairman. During the early years of the Hunter administration Elmsley was the most powerful man in the province, but he later lost much of his influence to his own nominee as judge, Henry Allcock, and to the attorney general, Thomas Scott.

While he was in Upper Canada Elmsley was particularly concerned with land granting problems, the provisional agreement with Lower Canada on tariffs, and the administration of the courts and law. In land and tariff matters he was greatly influenced by his friend Richard Cartwright and generally supported the loyalist and merchant point of view. In legal matters he tried to adapt English law to Canadian circumstances. He objected, for example, to the complicated English machinery by which married women alienated property, and introduced a bill to make such transactions easier. In this attitude he was consistently opposed by Allcock, who believed that there should be absolutely no tampering with English law, procedures, and precedents.

Elmsley wrote reports on many subjects in Upper Canada, especially in the early years of Hunter's administration. They are usually clear and sensible, but as in his private correspondence he revealed a tendency to dramatize events, his own actions, and his deteriorating relations with others. He was one of the few university graduates in the province, and was much given to elegant phrases and Latin quotations, a habit that may not have endeared him to all his colleagues.

At the time of his appointment to Upper Canada, Elmsley was promised promotion to the chief justiceship of Lower Canada, should it become vacant. In 1800, however, he withdrew his claim because he feared that he would lose money with another move. Despite his reluctance he was appointed to the Lower Canadian post in May 1802, following the resignation of William Osgoode. The salary was increased from £1,000 to £1,500 a year, and he was to be called to the Executive and Legislative councils with a 'seat next in Rank to the Lieutenant Governor.'

Elmsley was urged to hurry to Quebec, but he waited for Hunter's return to York and did not take the oaths of office in the lower province until 29 Oct. 1802. Although he was 'perfectly master of the French language' and had studied 'the old norman law' in France, he was at a disadvantage in Lower Canada because he constantly had to depend on others for specialized knowledge and advice on French jurisprudence. It probably did not help that he regarded the French judicial system as inferior to the English. In any event his career in Quebec was brief. From June to November 1803 he was on leave in England, and in November 1804 he became seriously ill. In February 1805 he went to Montreal intending to travel in the United States to recover his health, but he died there on 29 April 1805. His widow and children returned to England; his large houses in York and Quebec were both eventually bought by the government.

In this period the position of chief justice was extremely important in the administration of the province. In both Upper and Lower Canada Elmsley was president of the Executive Council and speaker of the Legislative Council. He was particularly powerful in Upper Canada because there was no resident lieutenant governor throughout his entire career there. His difficulty in working with others, however, combined with occasional impetuousness to prevent his accomplishing all that he wished. Like so many of the early government officials he was obsessed with his own importance and with his precarious personal finances. Although his contemporaries all agreed that he had great ability, his quarrelsomeness, especially with Russell and Allcock, greatly reduced his influence.

EDITH G. FIRTH

WILLIAM FIRTH
Office holder; b. 21 July 1768 in Norwich, England, son of William and Elizabeth Firth; m. Anne Watts, and they had five children; d. 25 Feb. 1838 of influenza in Norwich.

The son of a Norwich merchant, William Firth became a barrister and in 1803 was appointed steward of the city, a post in which he acted as city counsel and presided over the sheriff's court. Probably resident in London while he held the stewardship, he resigned soon after being commissioned (19 March 1807) attorney general of Upper Canada through the influence of William Windham, colonial secretary.

He arrived at York (Toronto) in time to take up his duties in November 1807, with high expectations for what turned out to be a brief and unhappy colonial career. His office had been vacant since the appointment (22 Jan. 1806) of his predecessor, Thomas Scott, to the chief justiceship of the province. He got on well with Scott and also – in spite of a dispute over back salary and fees – with D'Arcy Boulton, the solicitor general, who had been performing his duties. He was, however, soon dissatisfied with most of his colleagues, with his status, his income, his prospects, and with life at York. In April 1808 he asked for a transfer to Lower Canada as chief justice. In what may have been his only exercise of tact, he first ensured that Scott did not want the Quebec post; but his application failed. Thereafter he became one of the malcontent officials who plagued Lieutenant Governor Francis Gore's first administration.

He was entirely without sympathy for any kind of political dissent. It was at his persistent urging that Gore agreed to the unsuccessful prosecution of Joseph Willcocks for seditious libel. On Firth's advice, and against that of judge William Dummer Powell, Gore also dismissed the troublesome assemblyman David McGregor Rogers from his post as registrar of deeds for Northumberland County. When the law officers in London upheld Powell's opinion in spite of Firth's vehement objections, the attorney general's prospects of being Gore's confidant ended.

Firth's stipend was £300 sterling a year – about half the cost of his removal to Upper Canada – plus an indeterminate amount in fees. His attempts to increase his fees made him a nuisance to Gore and a target for Powell's resentment of English appointees to Upper Canadian offices. Firth began with a list of 19 minor claims, submitted for the opinion of the new chief justice of Lower Canada, Jonathan Sewell. Sewell's reply of 22 Sept. 1809 agreed with some of the claims, but allowed no fee higher than £2. Firth next claimed fees on all the standard forms issued through his office, although they required no more than his formal signature. On 9 March 1810 the Executive Council declined to audit this last claim. The House of Assembly also asserted the right to reduce legal fees in the Court of King's Bench, from which Firth drew about three-quarters of his income, and to limit his discretion as attorney general in choosing the level of courts for public prosecutions. His protest, in which Boulton joined, that the resulting fee table was 'incapable of supporting any professional character as a Gentleman,' was ineffective. It was cold comfort for him when on 14 March 1811 a committee of the council did acknowledge that some of the fees of office he had demanded were in accord with Lower Canadian practice, which had been adopted for the upper province in 1802 but never specifically authorized by imperial authority.

By the time of this partial success Firth was virtually without friends in the provincial administration, Scott having decided that as a former attorney general he had a conflict of interest in assessing the fees of that office. Firth proceeded to overreach himself in March 1811 by claiming that all legal instruments under the great seal of the province were invalid without his signature. By doing so he obscured the assembly's challenge to his authority as public prosecutor and revived a dispute among officials over their shares of the fees on land grants, threatening the jurisdiction as well as the income of the provincial secretary, William Jarvis. While maintaining that his presence was necessary for the legality of most acts of government, he asked leave to press his case in London. Gore refused: he was offended by Firth's breaches of administrative harmony, he had already consented to the absence of the solicitor general, and he was about to go on leave himself. When Firth left anyway in September 1811, Gore recommended his dismissal. Firth left his plate, crystal, and library in the care of his business agent, William Warren Baldwin, who also took charge of his debts and his unsatisfied claims for fees.

Firth was at first confident that he would not only win his demands but also prevent the return to Upper Canada of Gore, the man who, as he told Baldwin, had 'clouded my prospects in life.' From his first memorial to the Colonial Office in January 1812 to the testimony that he volunteered against Gore in the libel suits later brought by Charles Burton Wyatt and Robert Thorpe, he identified the lieutenant governor as the deliberate and spiteful agent of his misfortunes. After Gore's departure in October 1811 the Executive Council, which Firth denounced as 'abandoned and inquisitory,' had added to his grievances. It twice refused, 'under the very peculiar Circumstances in which Mr. Firth abandoned his Duties in this Province,' to pay the travel expenses of his last judicial circuit in Upper Canada. It did at length agree on 14 March 1812, following the opinion of the law officers in London, that he should receive the fees of office that Sewell had recommended in 1809. Beyond that, all he obtained was a ruling from the secretary of state, Lord Bathurst, that he was entitled to half his salary and fees from the date he left the province until 13 April 1812, when his removal from office was confirmed.

He went back to his legal practice, being promoted to serjeant at law in 1817, and ended his career where it had begun, on the Norfolk circuit. He may not have prospered at the bar. Apart from frequent expressions of affection for his children, his long correspondence with Baldwin shows an increasingly insistent and querulous concern about money. In 1820 he applied for a land grant in Upper Canada, but was refused on the grounds that he was not a resident. For the last year of his life he may have received an income under the will of his eldest daughter, Lucy Rosalind Proctor Firth. He died intestate with assets of less than £200 sterling.

Firth wrote four political pamphlets, all published in Norwich. The first, *An address to the electors of Norwich* ... (1794), opposed war with France because it would harm trade, but in the rest he gave vent to a rigid and bitter toryism. In *A letter to Edward Rigby* ... (1805) he complained that the mayor of Norwich had not celebrated the victory of Trafalgar enthusiastically enough. *A letter to the Right Rev. Henry Bathurst* ... (1813) condemned the bishop of Norwich for advocating the end of civil disabilities for Roman Catholics and Protestant dissenters. *The case of Ireland set at rest* ... (1825) attacked Robert Peel's intended Irish reforms; it had been Peel, when under-secretary of state for War and the Colonies, who informed him of his dismissal from office. The fullest expression of Firth's enduring hostility to Roman Catholicism was his book, *Remarks on the recent state trials ...* (1818), which also argued for more severe punishment of traitors and more rigorous suppression of public disorder. He had returned to England with 'joy in once more beholding this blessed Country,' as he wrote to Baldwin in 1812, but he found as much there to arouse his disapproval as he had in Upper Canada.

S.R. MEALING

ROBERT ISAAC DEY GRAY (Grey)
Office holder, lawyer, judge, and politician; b. *c.* 1772, probably in New York, son of James Gray and Elizabeth Low; d. unmarried 7 or 8 Oct. 1804 in the wreck of the *Speedy* on Lake Ontario.

At the outbreak of the American revolution the Gray family fled to the province of Quebec where James Gray was appointed major in the 1st battalion of Sir John Johnson's King's Royal Regiment of New York. At the end of the war Gray received land and took up residence just east of the loyalist settlement of New Johnstown (Cornwall, Ont.). Robert Isaac Dey Gray received his early education and acquired an interest in law at Quebec, probably under the tutelage of his godfather Isaac Ogden.

Young Gray benefited from the prominence of his father, who had been appointed lieutenant of the county of Stormont by Lieutenant Governor Simcoe. On 5 Sept. 1793 Gray became surrogate court registrar for the Eastern District, serving until his appointment as district court judge for the Home District on 7 June 1796. Along with 15 others he was called to the bar in October 1794 by an act of the legislature. The following month Simcoe recommended him for the vacant office of solicitor general 'not only on his Father's merits' but to enable him to further his education in England 'and by these means acquire the habits and character of the English Bar.' The Duke of Portland, the Home secretary, approved Simcoe's choice in May 1795 but wondered whether 'the present state of the Province required both an Attorney and Solicitor General.' Gray became a barrister in Trinity term 1797 and served as treasurer of the Law Society of Upper Canada from 1798 to 1801.

It was usual in Upper Canada for both the solicitor and the attorney general to hold seats in the House of Assembly and act as administration spokesmen. Gray was no exception. He was elected for the riding of Stormont in the election of 1796 and to the new riding of Stormont and Russell in 1800 and 1804. No scholarly study has yet been made of the alignments in Upper Canada's parliaments; none the less it is possible to pick out significant events in Gray's participation in the assembly. He was one of the more active members but did not dominate proceedings as did oppositionists such as Angus Macdonell (Collachie) or David McGregor Rogers. Although a slaveholder himself, in 1798 he was among the minority that opposed Christopher Robinson's bill extending slavery within the province. The following year he voted with the majority defeating a bill to allow Methodists the right to solemnize marriage. In 1800 he was among the eastern members who opposed Samuel Street's election as speaker and the next year cast his vote against Surveyor General David William Smith's election to the speakership. Gray led the resistance to Macdonell's contempt proceedings in 1803 against the clerk of the crown and pleas, David Burns, yet during the same session he supported Macdonell's Assessment Bill. In 1804 he favoured the passage of the notorious Sedition Bill. He regularly served as the assembly's liaison with the Legislative Council and consistently resisted the assembly's attempts to curtail or limit the prerogatives of the lieutenant governor. He initiated several pieces of legislation usually concerning the reform of law and its administration and took a particular interest in the regulation of inland trade and designation of ports of entry.

When Attorney General John White was killed in 1800, Gray temporarily assumed the duties of that office until the arrival of Thomas Scott in 1801. As solicitor general Gray often represented the crown in criminal cases across the province. On 7 Oct. 1804 he embarked from York (Toronto) on the schooner *Speedy* to prosecute a murder case. The ship went down with all hands off Presqu'ile Point, Brighton Township, that or the following day. Other victims included Macdonell and the recently appointed judge of the Court of King's Bench, Thomas Cochrane.

At his death Gray owned 12,000 acres of land and had debts of £1,200. By his will he freed the old family slave Dorinda (Dorine) Baker and left a trust of £1,200 to provide for her welfare. Earlier in the year on a trip to Albany, N.Y., he had purchased her mother Lavine for $50 and 'promised her that she may work as much or as little as she pleases, while she lives.' He gave £50 and 200 acres each to Dorinda's sons, John and Simon Baker. The remainder of his estate he divided among his relatives and friends including £20 to former Chief Justice John Elmsley 'in token of my regard and esteem.'

ROBERT J. BURNS

CHRISTOPHER ALEXANDER HAGERMAN

Militia officer, lawyer, office holder, politician, and judge; b. 28 March 1792 in Adolphustown Township, Upper Canada, son of Nicholas Hagerman and Anne Fisher; m. first 26 March 1817, in Kingston, Elizabeth Macaulay, daughter of James Macaulay, and they had three daughters and one son; m. secondly 17 April 1834, in London, England, Elizabeth Emily Merry, and they had one daughter; m. thirdly 1846 Caroline Tysen, and they had no issue; d. 14 May 1847 in Toronto.

Few individuals in Upper Canada's at times turbulent political history provoked such extreme hostility as Christopher Alexander Hagerman. Among the men with whom historians have commonly associated him, he was the most obdurate in his defence of church and state. He evinced – by temperament more than by design – the aggressiveness lacking in a John Macaulay and outwardly less evident in a John Beverley Robinson. William Lyon Mackenzie's biographer Charles Lindsey thought Hagerman showed 'a disposition to carry the abuse of privilege as far as the most despotic sovereign had ever carried the abuse of prerogative.' Charles Morrison Durand, a Hamilton lawyer prosecuted by Hagerman in the aftermath of the rebellion of 1837, depicted him as a 'grim old bulldog.' If Macaulay was the back-room boy of Upper Canadian administrations from Sir Peregrine Maitland's to Sir George Arthur's, Hagerman was the bully-boy.

Unlike contemporaries such as Robinson, John Macaulay, Archibald MacLean, and Jonas Jones, all of whom moved easily, and naturally, into positions of influence and power, Hagerman started down life's path as something of an outsider – lacking what Robinson termed 'interest,' by which he meant a patron. It was not that Hagerman had no advantages; it was just that he did not have as many as others. His background was respectable and loyal. Nicholas Hagerman was a New Yorker of Dutch ancestry who 'took an early and an Active part in favour of the British Government' during the American revolution. In 1783 he emigrated to Quebec, and the following year he settled on the Bay of Quinte in what became Adolphustown Township. He acquired a modest stature in the community as a militia captain and justice of the peace. More important professionally was his appointment in 1797 as one of Upper Canada's first barristers.

Within his closely knit family, young Christopher had an especial fondness for his brother Daniel and his sister Maria. From his father, it seems, he derived his keen sense of the loyalist legacy and an uncompromising adherence to the Church of England; it was perhaps symbolic that he had been baptized by John Langhorn, one of the church's staunchest defenders. A boyhood acquaintance, J. Neilson, recalled to Egerton Ryerson in 1873 that Christopher had 'not ... much early learning,' and certainly, as historian Sydney Francis Wise has convincingly shown, he was never a pupil of John Strachan. Hagerman embarked in 1807 upon a career in the law – one of the surest avenues to preferment and a comfortable life – as a student in his father's Kingston office. He would be admitted to the bar in Hilary term 1815.

His personal qualities tended to set him apart. In November 1810, from York (Toronto), Robinson wrote to John Macaulay in Kingston: 'We have been favored for two or three weeks with the company of the enlightened Christopher Hagerman a Youth whose bashfulness will never stand in his way – and who you may undertake to Say will never be prevented by embarrassments from displaying his natural talents or acquired information to the best advantage – After all, tho', he has a good heart, and not a mean capacity, in short he is not So great a fool as people take him to be.' There was, as Robinson's letter catches, a bravado and also an air of self-satisfaction to Hagerman, and they were as discernible in the young man as they would be characteristic of the older man.

His advance in society was effected through the good graces of outsiders, the military men who came to the province during the war years, stayed briefly, and cared little for local cliques. At the outbreak of the War of 1812 Hagerman enlisted as an officer in his father's militia company. In 1833 he would write that he had 'had the good fortune to attract the notice and obtain the patronage' of Governor Sir George Prevost, who was in Kingston between May and September 1813. Hagerman's rise in local and provincial society dates from that period. He carried dispatches for Major-General Francis de Rottenburg, commander of the troops in Upper Canada, in August 1813. The following November he served with credit as Lieutenant-Colonel

Joseph Wanton Morrison's aide-de-camp at the battle of Crysler's Farm. In December he was appointed provincial aide-de-camp to Lieutenant-General Gordon Drummond, Rottenburg's successor, with the provincial rank of lieutenant-colonel. It was a rather remarkable ascent.

More good fortune was yet to come. The office of collector of customs for Kingston had been vacant since the death in September 1813 of Joseph Forsyth, and on 27 March 1814 Hagerman received the appointment. He was with Drummond during the May attack on Oswego, N.Y., and was acknowledged in Drummond's official dispatch for having 'rendered me every assistance.' Present at the siege of Fort Erie in September, he again carried dispatches the following month. Drummond's high regard for his young aide was shared by his successor, Sir Frederick Philipse Robinson, who appointed Hagerman 'His Majesty's Council in and for the Province of Upper Canada' on 5 Sept. 1815. Hagerman had undoubtedly arrived in Upper Canadian society, but under the unusual circumstances of wartime. When normalcy returned with the reappearance of Lieutenant Governor Francis Gore, absent since 1811, Hagerman's appointment as counsel was undermined. Gore had wondered about it – in fact, he probably wondered who Hagerman was – and consulted the judges of the Court of King's Bench. On 4 Nov. 1815 Chief Justice Thomas Scott reported their unanimous opinion 'that under all the circumstances of the intended appointment ... it is not expedient for the present to carry it into effect.'

At the end of the war Hagerman resumed the practice of law in Kingston. His childhood friend Neilson, who observed him at the bar, remarked upon his 'great powers of persuasion,' and these would bring him to the fore of his profession. He found, however, that the collectorship of customs occupied him more than he had anticipated. He had been obliged to rent a house for an office, 'the expense of which is greatly disproportionate to the allowance and fees attached.' Accordingly, in 1816 he petitioned the Executive Council for the grant of a vacant lot in Kingston on which he could erect a house and office. He received one-fifth of an acre. He was already a landowner, having been granted in 1814 1,000 acres, which he located in Marmora Township, and another 200 as the son of a loyalist. As befitted a rising member of the bar, Hagerman involved himself in many community endeavours. Undoubtedly the 'genial qualities' noted by Neilson made him an effective participant. Among the organizations to which he donated or subscribed by 1821 were the Midland District School Society, the Kingston Auxiliary Bible and Common Prayer Book Society, the Kingston Compassionate Society, the Lancasterian school, the Union Sunday School Society, the National School Society, the Society for Bettering the Condition of the Poor in the Midland District, and the Society for Promoting Christian Knowledge. He was a shareholder of the Kingston hospital, a trustee of the Midland District Grammar School, treasurer of the Midland Agricultural Society, and vice-president of the Frontenac Agricultural Society.

Most aspirants to a genteel life in Upper Canada required a wife of respectable family. Hagerman's marriage in 1817 to Elizabeth Macaulay, whose brother George he knew well, was a fine match: her father was well connected, at both York and Kingston; her brother James Buchanan would become an executive councillor in 1825. Hagerman himself was a good catch, securely positioned on the ladder of success. He had an affinity for women and an ease of manner which doubtless aided him in romantic endeavours; he was, as well, tall, rugged, and handsome. (Although in later life his looks were marred 'by an accident to his nose which gave his face a peculiar appearance,' this 'facial deformity,' John Ross Robertson observed, was not 'a bar to success in love:making.') Few details emerge of his personal life, for there are no family papers. What glimpses remain are incidental, but they suggest that the geniality of the public man was as apparent in the private man. He seems to have been an affectionate father and a loving husband. His first daughter was born in 1820; writing to a friend a year later, he tacked on a playful afterthought to a postscript, 'Our little brat is as usual.' He found amusing Chief Justice William Campbell's remark at an 1826 trial that 'men as lords of the creation have a right to inflict a little gentle castigation on our rebellious dames.' The same year he fretted when his wife was stricken with a brief but 'serious attack of illness.'

It was not long after his marriage that Hagerman became involved in politics. In 1828 he would declare that his chief political impulse had been 'his anxiety ... upon all occasions by supporting the views and measures of Government (emanating as he was well convinced they did from a source eminently disinterested and patriotic) to promote the best interests of the Province.' From the beginning he gave vent to that anxiety in a bruising fashion. In June 1818, in a minor way, he helped set the stage for the charge of seditious libel against the Scottish agitator Robert Gourlay. Later that month he confronted

Gourlay in the streets of Kingston brandishing a whip, which he used to good effect on the unarmed Scot. Arrested and subsequently released, he had given Kingstonians a visible demonstration of where he stood politically. A now prominent local, Hagerman was elected to the House of Assembly for the riding of Kingston on 26 and 27 June 1820. He defeated, by 119 votes to 94, George Herchmer Markland, a pupil of Strachan's, a friend of Robinson and John Macaulay, and the son of leading Kingstonian Thomas Markland.

Hagerman entered the eighth parliament (1821–24) with a reputation outside Kingston at odds with his beliefs. A surprised Robinson at York admitted to Macaulay in February 1821 that he had been 'grievously mistaken' about Hagerman: 'He is any thing but a Democrat. Indeed his conduct is manly, correct & sensible & shews in every thing that kind of independence most rarely met with which determines him to follow the right side of a question tho' it may appear unpopular – his speeches gain him great credit.' Such a misapprehension by Robinson, who had known Hagerman since 1810, worked with him (albeit briefly) during the war, and cooperated with him in the charge against Gourlay, may reflect a more widespread confusion about political stances. Mackenzie, after all, initially believed Jonas Jones to be a member of the opposition in the same parliament. Whatever the nature of the misunderstanding, it was quickly rectified. By mid February Hagerman and Robinson were working together and taking the lead on administration measures. The end of session won Hagerman strong praise from the attorney general, who wrote to John Macaulay: 'Our friend Hagerman is a sterling good fellow, free from prejudices, and with every bias on the right side. ... His talents & information can not well be spared.'

In his political views Hagerman was 'illiberal,' to use the word Robinson would attach to himself in 1828 (the word 'conservative' had not yet entered the political lexicon of Upper Canadians). He was also, to adopt another of Robinson's phrases, a 'wellwisher of *Church & State.*' In 1821 he supported William Warren Baldwin's defence of aristocracy and primogeniture against an intestate estate bill sponsored by Barnabas Bidwell and David McGregor Rogers. To vote for the measure would, Hagerman argued, 'be departing from every thing venerable, noble, and honorable; ... Democracy was, like a serpent, twisting round us by degrees, it should be crushed in the first instance, for if the bill passed, it would not leave them the British Constitution but a mere shadow.' For Hagerman, the essence of the constitution was monarchy and executive prerogative. That same year he opposed a bill repealing the civil list since 'it was necessary that the Executive government should have a fund of this description at their disposal; it is the case in all governments except those that are purely democratical.... Monarchy should be supported, and if you infringe a hair's breadth, you endanger the whole fabric.' He was also a leading participant in the debate over Barnabas and Marshall Spring Bidwell's eligibility to sit as members, the opening shot in the war known as the alien question.

At another level, Hagerman proved a good constituency man, working on and proposing a number of measures of local concern. His major role in this regard was to second John Macaulay's leadership of Kingston's pro-union forces when the question of a union with Lower Canada arose in 1822. The separation of the old province of Quebec in 1791, he maintained, had 'most unnaturally rent asunder ... subjects of the same great and glorious empire, whose interests nature has made inseparable, and whose strength and improvement depends solely and entirely on their being united by concurrence of habits and sentiments, and a right understanding of their common interest.' Macaulay argued the case for union on financial and economic grounds; Hagerman agreed with his views but concentrated on political and constitutional matters, which were the leading concerns of anti-unionists such as Baldwin. Hagerman, an ardent defender of the Constitutional Act of 1791, which had given Upper Canada its constitution, was as concerned as Baldwin not to jeopardize any of its essential parts. He favoured union as a means of overwhelming at an early stage Lower Canadian oppositionists whose advocacy of the assembly's powers at the expense of the Legislative Council's threatened 'that balance between absolute monarchy and democracy, which so beautifully distinguished the British Constitution.' What happened in the lower province would affect Upper Canada sooner or later, Hagerman argued. Thus, Upper Canadians should shun the role of 'indifferent observers' or risk 'losing the constitution under which they live.' Though popular with Kingston's mercantile community, Hagerman's advocacy of union was insufficient to guarantee his re-election in 1824.

In fact, in a two-way race – a third candidate, Thomas Dalton, a local brewer and banker, withdrew – Hagerman was defeated, polling a mere 11 votes short of his opponent's total. Dalton took credit for

Hagerman's loss, but the explanation is more complex. As S.F. Wise has argued, Hagerman may have been hurt by his injudicious remarks in the dispute over the 'pretended' Bank of Upper Canada at Kingston. Hagerman had been an early director and shareholder, as was Dalton; at the time of the bank's collapse in 1822 he was its solicitor and shortly thereafter he became chairman of the board of directors to oversee its dissolution. In March 1823 parliament declared the bank illegal, made the directors liable for its debts, and set up a commission consisting of John Macaulay, George Markland, and John Kirby to handle the institution's affairs. The commissioners' report, tabled the following year, was unfavourable to the bank's administrators. Hagerman attacked the report, defending the directors with the exception of Dalton. Dalton responded with a masterpiece of vitriol condemning as spurious Hagerman's criticism of the commissioners and accusing him of being in league with them to destroy his reputation. Since as early as January 1823 Hagerman's own reputation had been undermined by 'reports and insinuations' that his conduct as chairman was not in the best interests of the bank, Dalton's squib identifying him with the agents of the York élite may well have raised the ire of those who suffered by the bank's failure and thus influenced the outcome of the election.

Hagerman's defeat may also have had to do with his bumptious manner, which carried over into every aspect of his career. At a social gathering in York on 30 Dec. 1823 Hagerman, in the presence of Lieutenant Governor Maitland, Chief Justice William Dummer Powell, and Mr Justice William Campbell, insinuated, as Campbell related the incident to Maitland's secretary, Major George Hillier, that judges were 'in the habit of deciding otherwise than according to the laws we are appointed to administer.' An annoyed Campbell was left with the option of passing over the incident 'in silence as an instance of rudeness and ill manners unworthy of serious notice, or of adopting such measures as I may conceive best adapted to the support of my judicial character, and to the proper notice of personal insult.' Early that year Hillier had been 'very much distressed' by a report of a 'flagrant breach of decorum' on Hagerman's part towards Robert Barrie, commissioner of the Kingston dockyard. Strachan informed Macaulay of the 'many rumours' surrounding this affair and of Hagerman's 'recent argument' with Thomas Markland. Yet there was more. Strachan had been told that Hagerman wished to be solicitor for the bank commissioners who were investigating the bank of which he was already the solicitor – 'an indelicacy,' Strachan sighed, 'which I would have considered incredible.'

If Hagerman could give offence, with such apparent ease, to men of his own rank and station, he could prove unbearable to others. As collector, he enforced customs regulations with exactitude. He had, for instance, invaded Carleton Island, N.Y., in 1821 to seize a depot of tea and tobacco kept there by Anthony Manahan, whom he dismissed as a smuggler and a 'Yankee Merchant.' He even suggested to Hillier that he should be allowed occasional recourse to a military force to assist him. Early in July 1824 one Elijah Lyons was accidentally shot by a student in Hagerman's law office who was aiding him in this instance in his customs duties. Two months later 31 Kingstonians complained to Maitland of Hagerman's 'proceedings and conduct.' When 'in the hands of a passionate, vindictive, ambitious, or speculating person' the enormous powers of the collectorship were, the petitioners wailed, 'dangerous to the rights and property of individuals, the usual course of business, and the public peace.'

Having been forced out of political life temporarily, Hagerman returned to his legal practice and his various endeavours. He bought, sold, and let properties throughout the Midland District and beyond it. He served as an agent for a number of proprietors and sometimes acquired lots in partnership with others. He was vice-president of the Kingston Savings Bank in 1822 and a director of the Cataraqui Bridge Company four years later. The failure of the 'pretended' bank had cost him dearly, £1,200 plus contingencies by his reckoning, and by 1825 he had 'to save money.' He declined the offer of a District Court judgeship in October of that year because 'I cannot afford to give up any portion of my practice in the Kings Bench, which I have reason to think wd. be materially affected by discontinuing my acceptance of suits in the inferior court.' He was, however, willing to take an out-of-district judgeship and on 14 June 1826 Hillier notified him of his appointment to the Johnstown District.

Hagerman was a skilled lawyer who had, with Bartholomew Crannell Beardsley, defended John Norton of the charge of murder in 1823. He won further notoriety for himself in the fall of 1826 by defending the young bucks who had destroyed Mackenzie's printing-office and press. Although his law office was 'lucrative' in the 1820s, Hagerman was tiring of it, and his professional weariness coincided with his reservations about town life. In 1827 he purchased a country property, living with his family in a 'small, but comfortable stone cottage' until a 'more spacious Mansion' was completed. He had 'no intention' of returning to Kingston: 'I have been living long enough in a style of expense, agreeable (to be sure) to my own taste, but which with reference to the claims of my little ones, it is not prudent I should continue.'

In that year he was looking for advancement. He sought, he told Hillier, 'preferment *in my profession*' but not 'in any other department.' He hoped that if an opportunity arose 'during the *present administration*' he would not be disappointed. Early the next year he memorialized Maitland for elevation to the Court of King's Bench – Campbell was in England seeking a pension on which to retire and judge D'Arcy Boulton was ailing and close to retirement. At that time the administration of justice was swirling in a storm of controversy, the result of William Forsyth's petition to the assembly in January 1828 complaining of Maitland's high-handed treatment of him. The political skies darkened further with the dismissal of Mr Justice John Walpole Willis in June 1828 and no doubt became even more threatening with Hagerman's unexpected nomination to the bench as Willis's successor that same month. Hagerman was simply too much the partisan for his appointment to restore to the Maitland administration any of the goodwill it had lost on such issues as political reform, the clergy reserves, the administration of justice, and the alien question. There was one boon for the opposition in Hagerman's nomination: he was unable to contest the general election held that summer.

Having been allowed sufficient time to wind up his affairs in Kingston and move to York to take up his unconfirmed appointment, Hagerman went on circuit in August 1828. He reported to Hillier from Brockville that 'I have so far had no very unpleasant duty to perform, nothing has occurred worthy of particular note.' Matters quickly changed when, in Hamilton on 5 September, he presided at the trial of Michael Vincent, charged with murdering his wife. Casting aside the tradition that a judge should serve as the accused's counsel, not his prosecutor, Hagerman advised the petit jury that 'the deceased had been murdered by the prisoner; and he had no difficulty in saying such was his opinion.' Over the objections of John Rolph, who was acting for the defence, the jury retired and found Vincent guilty. Hagerman sentenced him to execution and dissection, and three days later he was hanged in a badly botched manner. Bartemas Ferguson, editor of the *Niagara Herald*, found Hagerman's charge 'remarkable' and wondered whether it had given 'an undue bias to the jury.' Francis Collins of the *Canadian Freeman* saw in Hagerman's action an extraordinary departure, yet another instance of irregularity in the administration of justice. In his view Hagerman was an incompetent whose only qualification for the bench was sycophancy. Although the feeling was by no means universal, it was shared by many among the administration's opponents. After the ninth parliament opened in January 1829, Hagerman was, as Robert Stanton observed, 'every day called Judge Kit and has every odious invective brought against him.' By July rumours abounded that his appointment would not be confirmed. They proved true. Robinson replaced Campbell on the bench and James Buchanan Macaulay replaced Hagerman. The new lieutenant governor, Sir John Colborne, reported to the colonial secretary that Hagerman thought himself 'ill used.'

But there were compensations. Since his arrival in August 1828 Colborne had shunned Maitland's key advisers, Robinson and Strachan, and Hagerman stepped alone into the limelight of gubernatorial favour, becoming for a time the conduit for privileged information. To make up for the loss of his judgeship he was appointed solicitor general on 13 July 1829. His prestige was enhanced the following year by his election victory over Donald Bethune in Kingston. He was re-elected in 1834, handily beating William John O'Grady. By this time Kingston had become Hagerman's private bastion; he was elected by acclamation in 1836.

With Robinson on the bench government management of the assembly in the eleventh parliament (1831–34) fell to Hagerman and Attorney General Henry John Boulton – with disastrous results. The latter was an inept dandy, the former was unequal to the task. Hagerman's strength was his dogged commitment to the administration and to his own principles of church and state. His talent was a natural eloquence invigorated by the passion of the moment. The *Kingston Chronicle* caught him in full swing during an 1826 trial, and the editor's conclusion was apt: 'We have heard those who could, perhaps, reason more closely than Mr. Hagerman but very few indeed whose eloquence ... is more powerful.' He was, as Thomas David Morrison would characterize him in 1836, 'the Thunderer of Kingston,' a man given to 'violent expressions of opinion.' Yet in debate, discourse, or conversation, once excited or engaged, Hagerman usually did more harm than good to the causes he so forcefully espoused. The most glaring example was his role, with Boulton, in the repeated expulsions of William Lyon Mackenzie from the assembly. When word of their actions reached Lord Goderich, the colonial secretary, both law officers were dismissed in March 1833. Colborne protested, however, and Hagerman, now a widower, set off for England to appeal. He returned the following year with a reinstatement from the new colonial secretary, Lord Stanley.

He also returned with a new wife. According to George Markland, 'The match was not approved of in a certain quarter of the country – *they* said openly that nothing had ever occurred which caused so much annoyance – *The* Miss Merry and Kit Hagerman oh it was horrible they said.' Perhaps it was her attractions that made politics and his official duties irksome to Hagerman. Or perhaps it was a desire for change such as had overtaken him in the mid 1820s. Whatever it was, Robert Stanton noted in 1835 Hagerman's inability to put his imprint on the twelfth parliament and his more frequent absences from the house. He was, however, there, and on the defensive, in 1835 when he unsuccessfully opposed M.S. Bidwell's election as speaker, and when the house reduced his salary as solicitor general from £600 to £375.

That year, moreover, he was embroiled in a defence of the Church of England and the clergy reserves following upon Colborne's endowment of 44 Anglican rectories in December, a political error of enormous proportions. For Hagerman, a self-declared 'High Church & King's man' who had equated dissent with 'infidelity,' the established church was a key bulwark against immorality, equality, and a godless democracy. He was a devout member of his own congregation, St George's in Kingston, and in 1825 had been a member, with John Macaulay and Stanton, of a committee that wrote an arrogant defence of the Anglicans' exclusive jurisdiction over the town's lower burial-ground. When John Barclay penned a claim for the equal rights of the Church of Scotland, Hagerman, as Robinson revealed, was one of the three anonymous authors who replied. In 1821 he had naturally assumed a direct connection between Robert Nichol's remark in the assembly that there was no established church in Upper Canada and the desecration of the Anglican church in York later in the evening. Given his convictions, it is not surprising to find him leaping to Colborne's defence in the matter of the Anglican rectories. The lieutenant governor's blunder was, however, only compounded by Hagerman's thoughtless affronts to virtually every other denomination.

Hagerman's efforts in 1836 to stem the political fury aroused in the assembly by Lieutenant Governor Francis Bond Head's confrontation with the Executive Council were futile. He made up his mind 'to retire into private life.' His parliamentary and official duties kept him from his private office 'longer than is convenient, to say nothing of the great draw back upon my domestic comfort.' There had been rumours in October 1834 of his possible re-elevation to the bench. Change did come but it was not what he wanted. On 22 March 1837 he succeeded Robert Sympson Jameson as attorney general; Hagerman's law partner since 1835, William Henry Draper, took over the solicitor generalship. Colonial Secretary Lord Glenelg, however, refused to approve Hagerman's appointment. He had no reservations about Hagerman's 'private character and public merit' but professed grave doubts about the compatibility of his religious opinions with those of the government. At issue were Hagerman's denigrating remarks about the Church of Scotland in the assembly on 9 February. The congregation of St Andrew's Church in Kingston (Barclay's old church) had forwarded to the Colonial Office a resolution condemning Hagerman's 'grossly incorrect statements and intemperate language.' Head explained to Glenelg in September that Hagerman's speech had been 'purposely and mischievously made as offensive as possible to the Scotch' by Mackenzie in his newspaper. Combined with Hagerman's personal assurances as to what had been said, Head's defence persuaded Glenelg to order Hagerman's warrant in November.

The outbreak of rebellion in December 1837 (Hagerman had noted on 30 November 'the general quiet and contentment that prevails') brought – or necessitated – renewed commitment to public life. He was preoccupied through 1838 and 1839 with administrative details and judicial questions relating to the handling of rebels and Patriots. Although he was the father-in-law of Head's secretary, John Joseph, the connection availed him little more than ready access to the lieutenant governor. Robinson was Head's key adviser, and two recent recruits to the administration, John Macaulay and Robert Baldwin Sullivan, were the rising stars. Hagerman could not match their abilities in administrative work, analysis, or policy. Head's terse notations about the men on his executive capture Hagerman perfectly: 'Able speaker loyal constitutionalist but I have no very high opinion of his judgement. Sound, honest.' Neither Hagerman's standing as a courtier nor the cast of characters in government changed greatly when Sir George Arthur succeeded Head in March 1838. Arthur considered him 'an honest straight forward Person – Sees matters rightly, and will speak with energy – but, then, He is not a hard Worker!' Arthur was aghast at Hagerman's reaction to the arrival of the report of Lord Durham [Lambton]: 'He read the Report, and then went out to a party to Dinner! – Whereas He should have sent an excuse, & at once have set down & commented upon it, & without loss of time brought it under the notice of the House.'

The question of a union of Upper and Lower Canada had been a topic of growing concern through the second half of the 1830s and Hagerman's stand is of interest. In February 1838 he indicated in debate that he would support union only if there were sufficient safeguards to ensure English-Protestant supremacy. Confronted by the union bill of 1839 he damned it as 'republican in its tendency' and urged strengthening the 'Monarchical principle.' But when the bill came to a vote in the assembly on 19 Dec. 1839, Hagerman, brave declarations of opposition to the contrary, supported the union. The swaggering attorney general had in fact wilted under pressure from Governor Charles Edward Poulett Thomson. On 24 November Thomson, in private conversation with Arthur and John Macaulay, had wondered why 'officers appeared to act as if they regarded not the will of the Government in any matter of public policy.' The governor's first impulse was to dismiss his recalcitrant law officer but he decided against it on the advice of Arthur. After a frank discussion with Thomson on 7 December, Hagerman emerged with his bold opposition to union intact. Five days later he declared in the assembly that administrators could not be coerced into supporting it. He was, however, crumbling rapidly. In the assembly on the 19th he explained that since the union resolutions were before the house 'by command of the Sovereign,' 'if the vote in favour ... was persisted in, he would vote for them.' John Macaulay informed a correspondent that he was disturbed to 'see Hagerman's friends set up a comparison between his conduct & mine upon the Union Question – I would be sorry to set up so high as he did & after all break down.' 'You will soon hear,' he added, 'that he has retired ... to a Puisne Judgeship.' And indeed, with Levius Peters Sherwood's retirement, Hagerman joined Robinson, J.B. Macaulay, MacLean, and Jones on the bench, the appointment taking place on 15 Feb. 1840. His former partner Draper succeeded him as attorney general.

Upon his elevation Hagerman turned over his law practice to James McGill Strachan. He had hoped for an immediate leave but was obliged to wait until late August 1840 before sailing to England with his wife;

they returned in July 1841. Compared to the demands of his previous life, the routines of the court must have seemed somewhat dull. Between March 1840 and October 1846 he travelled the circuit to various assizes on ten occasions, holding court almost 50 times. He also had the regular sittings of Queen's Bench *en banc*. His career as a judge awaits further study but one possible contribution should be noted. On 15 April 1840 he presided at the trial in Sandwich (Windsor) of Jacob Briggs, a black man charged with the rape of an eight-year-old white girl. The legal definition of rape required proof of both penetration and emission, and Hagerman so instructed the jury. Despite contradictory evidence – medical testimony for the defence held 'it would have been impossible for a full grown man, particularly a Negro to have entered the body' of a young girl – the jury found Briggs guilty, and Hagerman sentenced him to execution. Reporting on the case to the Executive Council, Hagerman overlooked the necessity of proving emission and concentrated on the question of penetration, coming to the conclusion, 'most consistent with Law and reason,' that to convict for rape it was not necessary to prove that the hymen had been ruptured. After consulting with his colleague J.B. Macaulay, Hagerman decided that there was no legal objection to the jury's verdict. The councillors agreed but commuted the sentence to transportation. The following year the statute on rape was revised and the technicality with respect to emission abandoned, a move hailed by feminist historians as a major turning-point in the law. Although evidence of a direct connection between Hagerman's report and the 1841 law is lacking, it seems reasonable to conclude that it had some impact upon law officers as indicating the views of the judiciary.

Political power was gone for Hagerman in the 1840s. Chastened by his brush with Thomson, he had assured Arthur in August 1840 of his resolve 'not to mix myself with party strife or discussion in any way.' The following year, from London, Arthur reported to Thomson, now Lord Sydenham, that he had seen Hagerman at a party and that he 'talked a great deal as he always does but he was subdued in all his remarks.' In 1842, however, Hagerman did not hesitate to urge John Solomon Cartwright 'on *no account whatever* to associate yourself in the Govt with abettors of treason – or the apologists of traitors.'

In his private life Hagerman was shaken by the death of his second wife in 1842, but his grief was allayed by his faith in the providential origins of all change. In 1823 he had offered his sympathy to John

Macaulay on the death of a younger brother. 'We cannot,' he wrote, 'expect to pass through this life without afflictions, and when Providence dispenses them we may be benefited by reflecting that by being good and virtuous we shall *avert* the *remorse* which attaches to those who are compelled to regard them as the punishments due to vice.' He himself had been fortified by his convictions over the course of many family bereavements. Of his daughter Anne Elizabeth Joseph's death in 1838, he notified an acquaintance that 'it has pleased God to take this Child from me.'

Hagerman was married for a third time in 1846. Caroline Tysen was an English lady like his second wife. That year he was planning to retire to England when he took ill. His will, signed in a barely legible scrawl and noteworthy for the omission of any mention of religion, stipulated various bequests, the most important of which went to his two surviving daughters. He made provision for his son Frank, presumably a feckless youth who had been a disappointment to him, with the caveat that the executors pay the yearly amount only if they 'shall consider that it is right and proper ... having a due regard to the manner in which he shall conduct himself.' On 18 March 1847 Larratt William Violet Smith, a young lawyer, wrote: 'Poor Judge Hagerman is still lingering on, so reduced that he may be said to be dying. His worthless son staggers drunk to his bedside in the daytime, whilst his nights are spent in the most abandoned company.' Hagerman died two months later; shortly afterwards his wife returned to England.

Hagerman had been useful to successive administrators from Maitland to Arthur. He enjoyed his greatest intimacy with Colborne, who would, however, in time seek out Robinson as a confidant. Hagerman was, perhaps, especially in the late 1830s, a convenient symbol of the uncompromising courtier in what was then known as the 'family compact' – certainly Francis Hincks's *Examiner* portrayed him as such – but he lacked the talents and intellect which made Robinson, Strachan, Macaulay, and Jones more important. His forte was sound and fury and more often than not it got him into trouble.

ROBERT L. FRASER

ROBERT SYMPSON JAMESON

Lawyer, judge, politician, and office holder; baptized 5 June 1796 in Harbridge, England, son of Thomas Jameson and Mary Sympson; m. 9 July 1825 Anna Brownell Murphy in London; they had no children; d. 1 Aug. 1854 in Toronto.

Of a modest but aspiring family, Robert Sympson Jameson was born in Hampshire and raised and educated at Ambleside in the Lake District. From childhood he was a close friend of Hartley Coleridge, son of Samuel Taylor Coleridge and himself a poet, who later dedicated three sonnets to him. Jameson was admitted to study law at Middle Temple, London, in 1818 and was called to the bar in 1823. For the next six years he worked in London as an equity draftsman and during this time co-edited two volumes of bankruptcy case reports, but he continued his literary interests through an association with the *London Magazine* and the preparation of an edition of Samuel Johnson's *Dictionary of the English language*.

Jameson first met Anna Murphy in the winter of 1820–21. After a protracted and intermittent courtship, they began an unhappy marriage in 1825. The incompatible pair lived together until 1829 when Robert gained appointment in the West Indies as the chief justice of Dominica; Anna, already launched on a promising literary career, travelled to the Continent. Jameson's four years of 'wearisome banishment' in the tropics brought frustration; he sought unsuccessfully to reform the judicial system which the powerful local slave owners manipulated to their personal advantage. Repelled by the West Indies, categorized by him as a 'dismal, vulgar, sensual, utterly unintellectual place,' he declined an offer of the chief justiceship of Tobago (Trinidad and Tobago) and returned to London in 1833. Possibly through the efforts of influential friends, he was promptly made attorney general of Upper Canada that March in place of Henry John Boulton, who had been dismissed from office. He assumed his duties in York (Toronto) in June 1833, the last Upper Canadian attorney general to be appointed by the British government.

Jameson capably performed the large and varied business of his new office, handing down legal opinions, reporting on petitions, reviewing applications for licences and patents, and dealing with legislative, administrative, and judicial matters. Although an outsider, he soon found himself embroiled in the turbulent provincial politics of the 1830s. During the election of 1834, he and Ogle Robert Gowan, the ever-active leader of the Orange order, ran successfully as 'Constitutional' candidates for the riding of Leeds; however, their reform opponents, William Buell and Mathew Munsel Howard, proved their charges that voters had been intimidated by Gowan's supporters, and the results of the election were controverted. In an 1835 by-election, violence again nullified Jameson's victory, and he was not a candidate when yet another by-election was held the following year.

Anna finally consented to join her husband late in 1835 and set out for Toronto in the fall of 1836. She found provincial society insufferable, however, and left permanently after less than a year, having secured an annuity and a separation agreement from Robert and collected material for another travel book. *Winter studies and summer rambles in Canada* (1838) met with great success but Anna's husband, always anxious about his position, did not welcome her caustic account of the province.

With or without a wife, Jameson had secured a respectable niche in Upper Canada. In 1837 he was appointed vice-chancellor of the newly created and long overdue Court of Chancery, the chancellorship being nominally held by the lieutenant governor of the province. As vice-chancellor, he also became a member of the Court of Appeal. His training in English equity made him one of the few capable local candidates for the demanding post, the jurisdiction of which included cases of fraud, accident, and account; co-partnerships; and matters relating to trusts and mortgages. Although for more than a decade he handled the onerous load of the court alone and with dignity, some solicitors became impatient with his excessive caution and respect for precedent. Jameson's limited practical experience, the cumbersome procedures inherited from English equity, and the presence in the court of several outstanding lawyers such as William Hume Blake, James Christie Palmer Esten, and Robert Baldwin Sullivan, further complicated his task as vice-chancellor. A drinking problem, starting probably in Dominica, also progressively reduced his effectiveness.

During his years in Upper Canada, Jameson's official and social position drew him into many activities, often involving contentious political issues. He served as treasurer of the Law Society of Upper Canada during 1836–41 and 1845–46. He was a member of the Legislative Council for the province of Canada between 1841 and 1853, and its first speaker until 1843. He sat on the council of King's College (University of Toronto) from 1834 and was one of the first councillors of Trinity College when it was founded in 1851. In 1842 he became chief superintendent of education, though the actual work of the department was carried out by his deputy superintendents, Jean-Baptiste Meilleur in Lower Canada and the Reverend Robert Murray in Upper Canada. Jameson also served on a number of important government commissions including those concerned with treason during the rebellion of 1837–38, with the operations of the Indian Department and the Inspector General's Office in 1839, with the establishment of a lunatic asylum in Toronto in 1840 and with its superintendence from 1841, with the review and adjudication of claims to unpatented land grants between 1841 and 1848, and with the practices of the Court of Chancery in 1842 and 1843.

Other activities reflected his personal interests. As Henry Scadding recalled years later, Jameson 'was a man highly educated and possessing great taste, and even skill, in respect of art. He was a connoisseur and collector of fine editions. His conversation was charged with reminiscences and anecdotes of ... the Coleridges, Wordsworths and Southey, with all of whom he had been intimate in his youth.' Jameson helped to organize and served as president of both the Toronto Literary Club (1836) and the St George's Society (1839–41, 1848), and was a founding patron of the Toronto Society of Arts (1847). He also helped found the Anglican Church of St George the Martyr, Toronto, and was president of the British Emigrant Society of Upper Canada (1835) and of Thomas Rolph's Canadian Emigration Association (1840). In 1845 he established a gold medal, which he designed himself, to be awarded for 'proficiency in History and English Composition' at King's College.

By the late 1840s Jameson's position was declining. He had sought to retire from the vice-chancellorship as early as 1847, and in 1849 had to have a leave of absence from the Legislative Council because of his 'shattered health.' George Ridout spoke for many members of the bar when he wrote to Attorney General Robert Baldwin urging Jameson's retirement as vice-chancellor. With the reorganization and expansion of the Court of Chancery in 1849, William Hume Blake, who had piloted the reforms, became chancellor and James Christie Palmer Esten, senior vice-chancellor; Jameson was demoted to junior vice-chancellor. A year later, a broken man, he resigned on a government pension of £750 a year. He had already sold the house he had built for his wife to Frederick Widder and seems to have been speculating heavily in land. In 1854 Jameson died of pulmonary consumption while in the care of the Reverend George Maynard, an eccentric master at Upper Canada College, and his wife Emma. To them and not to Anna, he willed his personal effects and his 'property on Queen Street' in what is now the Parkdale section of Toronto. His burial at St James' Cemetery, Toronto, in the family vault of his late friend Lieutenant-Colonel Joseph Wells, received little notice.

Jameson's life was marred by ruined ambitions and personal unhappiness; however, he served with dignity and self-sacrifice, if not always great distinction, in many important and constructive capacities for more than two decades. His efforts and contributions deserve more attention than they have received. This neglect is probably due in large part to the more renowned and colourful career of Anna Jameson, whose published letters give an all too sketchy and jaundiced view of Robert Sympson Jameson.

JOHN D. BLACKWELL

JONAS JONES

Lawyer, militia officer, politician, judge, office holder, farmer, businessman, and JP; b. 19 May 1791 in Augusta Township (Ont.), third son of Ephraim Jones and Charlotte Coursol (Coursolles); m. 10 Aug. 1817 Mary Elizabeth Ford in York (Toronto), and they had 11 sons (3 of whom died in infancy) and 3 daughters; d. 30 July 1848 in Toronto.

Jonas Jones was raised in an atmosphere of privilege. His father was a loyalist who had risen in wealth and influence after settling in Augusta Township. Young Jonas was educated, as were many children of the province's early élite, at John Strachan's grammar school in Cornwall. There he formed friendships with other pupils such as John Beverley Robinson, John Macaulay, George Herchmer Markland, and Archibald McLean. In 1808 Jonas embarked on a career in law as a student in Levius Peters Sherwood's office at Elizabethtown (Brockville).

After their school days in Cornwall, the coterie of friends corresponded regularly for a time. But gradually the glow of those years faded as differences in personality and deportment became more apparent. In Robinson's opinion Markland was too effeminate, McLean's personal appearance left much to be desired, and Jones's single-minded sexual interests were (though Robinson himself was no prig) inappropriate to a gentleman. In May 1809 Robinson wrote to Macaulay that Jones's frequent letters 'often ... to be sure do not afford much mental food for he talks of nothing but what he calls *"pieces."*' The randy young squire from Elizabethtown pursued this topic to a point that made Robinson terminate their correspondence the following year.

The death of his father in 1812 did not affect Jones's career. He was left approximately 900 acres of land, £200 to purchase law books, and a sum for 'reasonable expences, till he shall be admitted to the bar.' The War of 1812 intervened in his career but did not deter his professional advancement. Jones enlisted as a lieutenant in the 1st

Leeds Militia and saw action under George Richard John Macdonell at Ogdensburg, N.Y., on 22 Feb. 1813. By the conclusion of hostilities Jones was a captain commanding a flank company. He was admitted to the bar in 1815 and set up a practice in Brockville.

Jones took easily to politics. His family, along with the Sherwoods and the Buells, dominated Brockville, the district town. With his strong regional base he was elected in 1816 in the riding of Grenville to the seventh parliament (1817–20), and was re-elected in 1820 to the eighth (1821–24) and in 1824 to the ninth (1825–28). From the political standpoint of the late 1820s and early 1830s, it was easy for oppositionists such as William Lyon Mackenzie to lump Jones with Robinson, Macaulay, and Christopher Alexander Hagerman as if their political opinions were identical. In 1824, however, Mackenzie believed Jones to be an opponent of the administration of Lieutenant Governor Sir Peregrine Maitland. Jones was certainly never as unabashed a supporter of the executive as Robinson and Hagerman, and, in fact, moved closer to a ministerialist position only during the turmoil of the ninth parliament. In the previous two parliaments he was an independent. Yet disagreement with the pre-eminent courtiers was a matter of emphasis rather than fundamentals. Jones had, for instance, played a part in the opposition to Robert Gourlay in 1818. At a meeting held by Gourlay in Augusta Township on 27 May Jones attempted to dissuade 'the people ... from falling into his delusive schemes.' Moreover, at Gourlay's trial for libel on 31 August Jones acted as the prosecutor. To him, Gourlay's activity was illegitimate for it seemed to call the nature of government into question.

Jones's criticisms in the seventh and eighth parliaments concerned measures which would, he thought, threaten the balance of the British constitution. In 1817 he questioned Robert Nichol's legislation of the previous year which had provided the executive with a perpetual annual grant of £2,500. During the parliamentary session of 1821–22 he initiated a bill to repeal this grant against the opposition of Attorney General Robinson and Hagerman. In his view, it was a matter of constitutional principle that 'all grants to his Majesty's government should be annual, and not permanent.' It was, he thought, 'an injustice to the country at large to put the privilege of disposing of the public money out of their [the assembly's] own hands' and he read from Sir William Blackstone to support his point. Jones, in a speech which later caused Mackenzie to suppose him a radical, was astonished that Hagerman appeared willing to surrender not only the 'privileges of the house, but the liberties of his constituents, and of the whole country' to the executive. He supported royalty, he exclaimed to applause which 'shook the building to its very base,' 'but not by *slavish* obsequiousness.' The assembly's power was 'the constitutional check of the democratic upon the other branches of the Legislature,' and Jones wanted it 'inviolable.' The same constitutional concern led to his opposition to the proposed union of the Canadas in 1822. At a Brockville meeting chaired by Sherwood on 19 November, Jonas and his brother Charles were among those objecting to various clauses of the imperial bill for union. Most objectionable were provisions calculated to reduce the prerogatives of the assembly and increase those of the executive. Jones had already written to Macaulay, the chief advocate of the union in Upper Canada: 'You are a Staunch Gov't man. I am as much disposed to support the Govt in what I consider right as you or any other man can be; but I will never consent to yield the privileges of the people and sacrifice all to the Influence of the Crown.'

Jones showed his independence on other issues. Although an Anglican, he was a moderate with respect to the Church of England's privileges. On several occasions he supported bills which would have liberalized the province's restrictive marriage law. In 1821 he seconded William Warren Baldwin's bill to repeal the Sedition Act of 1804, which had made possible Gourlay's banishment. The act had few defenders, among them Robinson and Hagerman. Jones supported his profession in defending the Law Society Bill of 1821, which his brother, then MHA for Leeds, attacked on the grounds that 'to give this power to such a society was dangerous.' Furthermore, Jonas was capable of supporting initiatives on non-political issues made by political opponents. In 1825 he supported Marshall Spring Bidwell's bill to abolish the statutory provision for punishing women by whipping.

In his early parliamentary career Jones approached the 18th-century English tradition of a country opposition on such matters as executive power, protection of individual liberty, and the rights of the assembly. Here there was little difference between him and Baldwin or, after 1816, Nichol. But on a range of issues crucial to provincial economic development, Jones moved close to the court tradition best articulated by Robinson and Hagerman. They emphasized a strong government (albeit, in contrast to Jones, one dominated by the executive) and a positive role for the state in matters such as finance and economic development, particularly the building of large public works. Improvements to navigation had been a favourite and early topic of Nichol's, but the first substantive attempt to direct the house's attention to it was by Jones. On 23 Feb. 1818 he moved that the house take 'into consideration the expediency of improving the Navigation of the River St. Lawrence.' The occasion marked the public beginning of his longstanding interest in canals and economic improvement. He was named chairman for the assembly's representation on a joint parliamentary committee. Its report, tabled on 26 February, claimed improvement of the St Lawrence to be of the 'very first importance' to Upper and Lower Canada. By 11 March the assembly and Legislative Council had agreed to a joint address urging President Samuel Smith to raise navigation with the governor-in-chief, Sir John Coape Sherbrooke. The address led to the appointment of commissioners from both provinces, who adopted, in August 1818, six resolutions favouring improvement. In October Jones brought the commissioners' report before another joint parliamentary committee, which supported its thrust but concluded that provincial financial resources were inadequate to the task.

The assembly slowly adopted an expanded role in the planning of large public works, especially canals, through the 1820s. The principals in determining strategy were Nichol, Macaulay, and Robinson. Jones, whose family had firm roots in the Laurentian trading system (Charles owned mills and a store), played an important role as an assemblyman in assisting Robinson's initiatives. In January 1826, for example, he seconded a bill introduced by the attorney general authorizing the government to borrow £50,000 on debenture to be loaned to the privately owned Welland Canal Company. Such loans were anathema to oppositionists such as Bidwell and John Rolph. Jones's support, however, was not unqualified. During a debate early in 1827 he flatly opposed another loan to the company 'unless ... the resources of the Country would authorise it, independent of the necessary sums for other public works.' Jones feared undue concentration of resources upon the Welland Canal at the expense of canals along the St Lawrence, which he considered to have priority. With Charles Jones, Robinson, and McLean, among others, he was a member of the joint parliamentary committee struck in January 1827 to study improvement of the St Lawrence. It reported, later in the month, that the proposed canal should be undertaken as a 'public measure' and be able to accommodate navigation by schooners, the largest lake-travelling vessels, but no action was taken.

Jones's early reputation for political independence had crumbled by the late 1820s. More important, and perhaps related, the base of his political success was weakening. In 1827 Mackenzie described the two Jones brothers as ministerialists, supporters of the tainted Maitland administration. To the diminutive Scot, they were 'the bullies of parliament: Noisy, ill-bred, and quarrelsome from disposition, they are rendered much more so by the indulgence of the assembly.' As the general election of 1828 approached, the rumour was, Mackenzie reported, that they would maintain their political hegemony 'chiefly thro' IRISH influence.' But it was not to be. Charles was appointed to the Legislative Council and, running in Leeds, Jonas finished a poor third behind John Kilborn and William Buell Jr. Three years later a return to the assembly was thwarted by Hiram Norton in a by-election in Grenville.

Several circumstances contributed to Jones's defeats. Factionalism was rife within the local élite and, though suited to the rough-and-tumble of politics, Jones suffered the consequence of those divisions. Moreover, his appearance of independence had suffered. During the Maitland administration he had acquired a plurality of offices: notary for the Johnstown District (1818), trustee of the district board of education, judge of the Bathurst District Court and Surrogate Court (both 1822), judge of the Surrogate Court for the Johnstown District (1824), and judge of the Johnstown District Court (1828). He had also been appointed colonel of the 3rd Regiment of Leeds militia in 1822. He had become, to a growing opposition, a symbol of the favouritism which seemed to mark Maitland's governorship. Thirdly, the old loyalist townships fronting on the St Lawrence, whose interests were represented by men such as Jones, faced a challenge from the back townships and the Irish who settled there. And, on one particular issue, the alien question, Jones was vulnerable. He had played a leading role during the seventh parliament (1821–24) in unseating Barnabas Bidwell and then in the attempt to expel his son Marshall Spring. But the alien question, as it unfolded during the 1820s, had potential repercussions for Irish immigrants as well as Americans. Jones introduced in 1826 the petition of Joseph K. Hartwell, a local Orangeman, and others of the Johnstown District to be naturalized under a private member's bill if a public act was not forthcoming. Jones supported their petition and, according to Robert Stanton, 'this staggered a good many.' Jones expended much time in the spring of 1827 clarifying his support for the government-sponsored Naturalization Bill. In characteristic fashion he quoted from Blackstone as an authority validating his stand. Mackenzie certainly thought the Irish would support Jones in the election of 1828 and perhaps they did. Their presence had made an impact by 1826, and within a few years, under the leadership of Ogle Robert Gowan, they became a force to be reckoned with by Jones and others.

On the domestic front Jones enjoyed a growing family – between 1818 and 1840 his wife gave birth to 14 children – and affluence. His legal practice flourished. He had become a bencher of the Law Society of Upper Canada in 1820 and was recognized as a leading member of the bar. He enjoyed the benefits of his judgeships. Major George Hillier, Maitland's secretary, conferred with him on patronage within the district, and on occasion Jones undertook legal work for the government at various assizes. He sought other offices. In 1828 he applied, unsuccessfully, for the collectorship of customs at Kingston, which Hagerman had vacated upon his temporary elevation to the Court of King's Bench. Jones, in fact, had been Maitland's first choice for this judgeship but he had been dissuaded by Strachan, who argued 'that the Province would not bear two Brothers in Law on the Bench.' (Judge L.P. Sherwood had married Jones's sister.) It was Jones's 'misfortune,' Strachan wrote to Macaulay, 'to be one of a connexion which engrosses so many offices he suffers from it.' Any suffering was mitigated by Jones's prosperity. In addition to the land he had inherited, he himself received several grants from the crown as the son of a loyalist and as a militia officer during the war. To these lots he added many acquired by purchase, thus becoming one of the leading landowners in the Johnstown District. When the construction of the Rideau Canal opened up new areas for settlement, Jones could offer for sale in 1829 more than 60 lots scattered across four districts.

A gentleman farmer well known as a 'spirited Agriculturalist,' Jones oversaw a thriving farm near Brockville. He specialized in breeding livestock, particularly sheep. In 1830 he purchased pure-bred animals from Commodore Robert Barrie of the Kingston dockyard. Five years later his sheep won prizes in competition at local fairs; in 1837 he was offering brood-mares, colts, draught-horses, oxen, and sheep for sale. As well, Jones had business interests. With his brother Charles he owned mills at Furnace Falls (Lyndhurst). In January 1837 they offered to sell their site there as well as the Beverly Copper Mine to two Americans. In the 1830s Jonas had badgered the president of the Bank of Upper Canada, William Allan, to open a branch in Brockville but Allan was, he wrote to Macaulay in June 1830, 'not in favour ... *at Present.*' Undeterred, Jones chaired a meeting at Brockville in August calling upon the legislature to charter a local bank. In 1833 a branch of the Bank of Upper Canada was established and Jones was appointed a director of it. That same year he became a director of the Saint Lawrence Inland Marine Assurance Company and in 1834 he was made its president.

Jones's continued interest in navigation on the St Lawrence became a preoccupation during the 1830s. At the opening of the second session of the tenth parliament in 1830 Lieutenant Governor Sir John Colborne drew the notice of the legislature to the great river. Within a short time an act was passed providing for three commissioners to determine the best mode of improving navigation. Chaired by Jones, the commission estimated costs for the appropriate canals. An act establishing another commission for the improvement of the St Lawrence was passed in 1833. Jones was appointed its president, and John Macaulay and Philip VanKoughnet were among its members. The commission first met on 19 Feb. 1833, whereupon Jones and two other commissioners travelled to New York, Pennsylvania, and New Jersey to gather information and confer with American engineers. Jones tabled the commission's report in December. On the basis of a survey by Benjamin Wright, the dean of American canal-builders, it 'safely' estimated that £350,000 would provide obstacle-free navigation for steamboats from Lake Ontario to Montreal. The commissioners urged borrowing the entire sum even without the co-operation of Lower Canada since Upper Canada 'could not possibly incur any risk of financial embarrassment.' Jones had attempted to raise a loan of £70,000 while in the United States but failed. As a result of the commission's recommendations the 1833 act was repealed and a new one was passed in 1834. The following year parliament approved a bill to appropriate £400,000 for building the St Lawrence canals and refinancing the public debt. No single piece of legislation in provincial history furnishes such tangible evidence of the Upper Canadian faith in canals and economic development, and Jones had been one of the faith's first prophets. In 1834, under his presidency, work had begun on the first project, the Cornwall Canal, and within two years plans were under way to extend work to other sections of the St Lawrence.

Politically, developments in the early 1830s had been less edifying. The bruising and at times violent entry of Gowan and his Orangemen into politics brought about a major realignment of political power in the Johnstown District. In 1833 Jones and Henry Sherwood were elected to represent the East Ward on Brockville's Board of Police, and Jones became its president. The contest had been a bitter struggle with the Orangemen. Further acrimony resulted from the disruption of a board meeting presided over by Jones in October. The culprit was James Gray, a disgruntled political rival of Jones's and a friend of Gowan's. On 9 Jan. 1834 the barn, stables, and sheds of Jones's farm were burnt. Gray was charged, convicted of arson, and imprisoned without benefit of bail. His wife and friends, including Gowan, petitioned on his behalf, complaining of Jones's 'unbounded influence ... over the Sheriff, and the great Majority of the Magistrates.' The following month Gowan found even more reason to complain. He had arrived back in Brockville from a trip to find his nephew in jail. Unable to secure his release, Gowan was on the verge of going to York when, he wrote, Jones procured a 'Warrant against me, for a conspiracy to injure his character, founded upon the Affadavit of a Girl of ill fame, and the inmate ... of a Bagnio in this town.' He was astounded that his bail was set at £400 and that he would be tried before Jones and other magistrates, 'the majority highly excited against me, and having Mr Jonas Jones, as my Judge and Accuser.' Tension between the camps of Jones and Gowan heightened during the election of 1834, in which Jones supported reformers William Buell Jr and Matthew Munsel Howard. Jones and his followers were apparently duped by Gowan, who topped the polls in Leeds with a fellow tory, Attorney General Robert Sympson Jameson. In one fracas of an election marred by Orange violence Jones was roughed up while trying to restore order. His last electoral triumph – he failed to win the tory nomination over Richard Duncan Fraser for the spring by-election in Leeds in April 1836 – came in Grenville in the general election later that year. By an uneasy anti-reform truce with the Orangemen, Jones and Gowan defeated Buell and Howard.

Jones was nevertheless tiring of politics. In the first session of the thirteenth parliament (1836–40) he showed little of the relish of his early days as a parliamentarian. He was, with Archibald McLean and Allan Napier MacNab, a candidate for the speakership. McLean would win but the prospect of Jones as speaker dismayed W.W. Baldwin, who thought he would 'probably offend half his side of the house – his rough and confident manner is often provoking.' On one notable occasion in February 1837 Jones supported Hagerman's unrepentant defence of the Anglican rectories recently established by Colborne.

His most important contribution came as chairman of the house committee on finance. It was examining the provincial debt, which had reached almost £600,000, most of it for public works and especially St Lawrence navigation and the Welland Canal. Yet, with financial crisis looming, Jones remained convinced that the works would be 'a productive source of revenue.' Moreover, they were essential to the prosperity of 'a new Country like Canada, with a limited revenue,' and could 'only be constructed upon the credit of the Province.'

When the opportunity arose to leave politics, his law practice, and Brockville, Jones seized it. On 23 March 1837 Lieutenant Governor Sir Francis Bond Head appointed him and McLean to fill two openings on the Court of King's Bench. Jones quickly resigned his other judgeships. He attempted to give up the presidency of the St Lawrence commission but Head prevailed upon him to wait and Jones did not relinquish it until the following year. He was succeeded by John McDonald amidst financial difficulties resulting from the depression of 1837 and disruptions caused by the rebellion. Jones suggested to Head that he and McLean should receive registrarships of counties as a means of vacating their seats in the assembly; otherwise, he wrote on 29 May 1837, 'I am apprehensive that some embarrassment and difficulty may be produced.' Head agreed and Jones was appointed registrar for Dundas County, from which office he resigned on 14 June.

Jones had barely settled into the routine of his judicial activities when rebellion broke out in December. He was immediately appointed one of Head's aides-de-camp and commanded a small picquet; he was the first man to enter Montgomery's Tavern after the rebels had been routed. The aftermath of the rebellion and the subsequent border raids increased the work of the judges for a short period. Jones with Robinson recommended in May 1838 that executions be kept to a minimum and banishment, 'an appalling punishment,' be reserved for but a few. He repeated this advice to Lieutenant Governor Sir George Arthur in December after the capture of numerous prisoners at the battle of Windmill Point. The object of the death penalty was 'to hold out an example of terror and by that means to prevent as far as possible' repetition of the offence. Thus, 'judicious selection' rather than 'the great number of executions' was desirable as 'frequent exhibitions of the last pangs of expiring nature have a tendency to counteract the end of punishment.' Jones handled several treason cases with little of the sympathy he often evinced for criminals. The jury's verdict of guilt for Jacob R. Beamer he considered 'fully warranted.' At Benjamin Wait's trial, the jury recommended mercy, prompting Jones to demand it produce the grounds on which the recommendation was based, but it could not.

Like most Upper Canadian superior court judges, Jones had little use for men who abused women. When John Solomon Cartwright forwarded a petition in favour of the convicted rapist William Brass, Jones reported to John Joseph, Head's secretary: 'I consider the case a very aggravated one and unattended with a single palliating circumstance.' In October 1839 he took no notice of petitions from the chiefs of the Six Nations attacking the credibility and character of a young Indian woman who had been raped by Noah Powlis, a Mohawk. Between November 1839 and July 1840, Jones used every judicial means possible to obtain a free pardon for Grace Smith, a young black girl convicted of arson. When his own recommendation failed to convince an Executive Council anxious to make an example, he consulted his brother judges and delivered their opinion that 'the Judgment of death ... in this case is erroneous.' This time the council concurred. In October 1840 he urged Arthur not to consider a pardon for Eliza Mott who had been convicted with her ten-year-old daughter of stealing. He had sentenced the girl, 'apparently very intelligent and ... an interesting child,' to a mere week in jail in the hope that, 'if she is provided for, away from her mother she may yet become a good Member of Society, with her, it is not to be expected.'

Politically, Jones got on well with Head, who later described him as 'the most calm fearless man it had ever been my fortune to be acquainted with,' but his influence on the administration was negligible, even though reform-oriented men such as James Buchanan, the British consul in New York, considered him one of the major figures in the 'family compact.' Jones did replace Robinson as temporary speaker of the Legislative Council in 1839 after Robinson went on leave, but he resigned the position in June 1840 upon the chief justice's return. Arthur had apparently expected much of Jones as speaker and was disappointed. When MacNab sought the position early in 1841, Arthur wrote to Governor Sydenham [Thomson]: 'His connexion Mr Justice Jones with five times the natural Talent, and with rather superior *legal* acquirements, was quite unequal to it.'

From his appointment in 1837 almost to his death in 1848, Jones sat on the King's Bench with some of his oldest friends (Robinson, McLean, and Hagerman). His death was unexpected. He left his chambers feeling drowsy and at Robinson's suggestion decided to take a walk before dinner. He collapsed in a building he owned and was found hours later (a child had reported that judge Jones was lying there drunk), completely paralysed on the right side and unable to talk. He died on 30 July and was buried before many of his family had arrived. His will was unusual – he left everything to his wife. An obituary noted that his 'keen talents ... as a debater, together with his sterling consistency, did much to stem the torrent of republicanism in the stormy days of Mackenzie's career.' Robert Baldwin wrote to Robinson: 'I ever admired the vigor and industry with which he applied himself to the administration of justice And the real kindness of heart which notwithstanding an abruptness of manner which occasionally startled even those who knew him well and was often misunderstood by those who had not that advantage, I think eminently distinguished him.'

Hagerman had died the previous year. It seemed as if an age was passing. Worn out by decades of political battle, the youthful friends had left the fray one by one. By the time of the declaration of union on 10 Feb. 1841, the political views which they represented were in eclipse. A generation of native-born political leaders was quickly, and for the most part quietly, passing from the scene. John Macaulay was disturbed by these deaths and wrote to Robinson in a long lament for the age of gentlemen: 'Poor Christopher & Jonas! the former, liked by me, notwithstanding some feelings of which the world sometimes spoke too severely – more distinguished as a barrister than as judge – the other, an old & valued friend whose sudden loss I can hardly get over.'

ROBERT L. FRASER

Sir JAMES BUCHANAN MACAULAY

Army and militia officer, lawyer, politician, and judge; b. 3 Dec. 1793 in Newark (Niagara-on-the-Lake), Upper Canada, second son of James Macaulay and Elizabeth Tuck Hayter; m. 1 Dec. 1821 Rachel Crookshank Gamble in York (Toronto), and they had one son and four daughters; d. 26 Nov. 1859 in Toronto.

James Buchanan Macaulay was born in the fledgling loyalist settlement of Newark to parents recently arrived from England. His father, a British army surgeon, and his mother enjoyed the personal friendship of the province's first lieutenant governor, John Graves Simcoe, to which the given names of James's older brother, John Simcoe Macaulay, bear eloquent witness. In 1795 or 1796 the Macaulays followed the seat of government to York near which the doctor had been granted a park lot. This land, stretching north into the edges of uncleared forest, rapidly attained the tag of Macaulay Town and as York grew it became a considerable financial asset for the Macaulay family.

In 1805 James was sent off to join other sons of Upper Canadian professional men in the privileged coterie of the Reverend John Strachan's school at Cornwall; there he undoubtedly rubbed shoulders with a fair number of his colleagues in later public life, including three future judges: John Beverley Robinson, Archibald McLean, and Jonas Jones. On 14 Dec. 1809, a few days after his 16th birthday, Macaulay was commissioned an ensign with the 98th Foot, then stationed at Quebec. Appointed lieutenant in the Canadian Fencibles during the winter of 1812, that June, as rumours of war with the United States grew stronger, he became a lieutenant and acted as adjutant in the provincially raised Glengarry Light Infantry Fencibles. Almost immediately he was thrown into battle, first on 19 July at Sackets Harbor, N.Y., where he was wounded in the left hip, and then in February 1813 at the battle of Ogdensburg, N.Y., where he led a gallant, if not entirely sensible, charge across the frozen St Lawrence into American artillery fire. For this action he received the commendation of his commanding officer, Lieutenant-Colonel George Richard John Macdonell, and of Lieutenant-Colonel John Harvey, deputy adjutant general of the Upper Canadian forces. Briefly in command of the garrison at York in June 1814, Macaulay again fought courageously at Lundy's Lane and Fort Erie later that summer. His military career had little future at the end of the war, however, and when his regiment was disbanded in the summer of 1816, he appears curiously enough even to have flirted with the notion of joining the new military settlement at Perth, Upper Canada, as a pioneer farmer. Instead he turned to that eminently attractive profession in the young province – law.

Macaulay entered his name on the books of the Law Society of Upper Canada in 1816, when he was 22, and began studying in the law office of Attorney General D'Arcy Boulton. He was soon involved in the litigation following the incident at Seven Oaks (Winnipeg) in June 1816 and prepared charges for the trials of 1817–18, which were held, coincidentally, before Boulton, who had recently been appointed one of the assize judges. Continuing his studies with Boulton's son Henry John Boulton, Macaulay became an attorney-at-law in 1819 and served briefly in the office of John Beverley Robinson, who had succeeded the elder Boulton as attorney general. By the beginning of 1822 Macaulay had been called to the bar and had married a daughter of the late John Gamble, one of his father's medical-military colleagues. Three years later he was admitted to the professionally desirable ranks of the Law Society benchers.

Macaulay's industrious advocacy at the bar, revealed in the official law reports, and his impeccable social standing brought him to Sir Peregrine Maitland's attention as an obviously desirable addition to the province's ruling élite. On 5 May 1825 he was appointed to the Executive Council, an undoubted bastion of the 'family compact,' where he joined James Baby and John Strachan. His executive role was to be short-lived for his last appearance in council was on 2 July 1829. The intervening years were not exactly smooth for Macaulay but he weathered them with expected ease. As an executive councillor he had inevitably to suffer William Lyon Mackenzie's attacks in the *Colonial Advocate*, culminating in one on 18 May 1826 which described him as 'a *stink-trap* of government.' That attack had not been entirely unprovoked for earlier in the month Macaulay had issued a pamphlet (of which no copies survive) uncharacteristically replying in kind to Mackenzie's sniping. The next month, just prior to his official swearing-in as an executive councillor on 27 June 1826, Macaulay acted for Samuel Peters Jarvis, Henry Sherwood, and other young bloods from local society families whom he had seen toss Mackenzie's type into the harbour on the evening of 8 June. At their trial that October a jury found in favour of Mackenzie and shortly thereafter Macaulay paid to Mackenzie's lawyer the costs and damages assessed against his clients.

Macaulay was also party to the celebrated decision which removed Judge John Walpole Willis from the Court of King's Bench in 1828. During the long acrimonious dispute over his dismissal, Willis characterized Macaulay as 'a Lieutenant on half pay, who ceased to be a Judge in consequence of my appointment.' In fact, when Judge Boulton had retired in 1827 prior to Willis's arrival in Upper Canada, Macaulay had been temporarily appointed puisne judge to officiate during the summer assizes and had returned to his law practice that September when his commission had ended. This experience made him 'a most eligible' candidate to replace Willis the following year, but since Macaulay had recommended in council 'the measure which had occasioned the vacancy,' the appointment went instead to his brother-in-law, Christopher Alexander Hagerman. Hagerman's appointment was not confirmed, however, and in July 1829 Macaulay was elevated to Willis's seat on the bench. That August he withdrew from the Executive Council in order to confine himself as much as possible 'to duties exclusively Judicial.'

During the previous three years, Macaulay had collected several of the commissions necessary for the discharge of justice. As one of the three King's Bench judges, he became enveloped in the sheer quantity of work both at sittings at York and on circuit when travelling conditions and weather permitted. Along with Chief Justice John Beverley Robinson, he presided over a welter of cases dealing principally, in the absence of a court of equity, with matters of civil litigation. Macaulay's judgements on the many cases before him in the 1830s cannot be easily categorized but the law reports reveal the majority to be fair if cautious and rather more sensitive to social considerations than those of his fellow judges. He tended to clemency in cases of murder, though he rarely advised it directly. Most apparent from extant reports is his painstaking analysis of a case and the almost extreme lengths he would go to in order to be seen to be fair. His rulings and later recommendations on Orange rioters in the Johnstown District in 1833 and on the murder trial of John Rooney and James Owen McCarthy at Hamilton in 1834 nicely demonstrate Macaulay's good sense and his understanding of human failings. A deep-seated concern for the orderly regulation of justice and for prison conditions is evident in his advocacy of provincial supervision of district jails during a charge to the grand jury at the Gore District Assizes on 17 Aug. 1835. With liberal sensibility Macaulay advised that 'the Law is neither in a sealed book nor a dead letter' – a statement that might easily be hung as a label upon his legal career.

In 1838 Lieutenant Governor Sir Francis Bond Head, writing to his successor, Sir George Arthur, highly recommended Macaulay as 'most excellent – man & lawyer.' More than 20 years later the writer of his obituary would note that 'whether ... as a soldier, a lawyer, a judge, or ... a Christian, ... in all his actions' can be traced 'the same entire devotion to the calls of duty.' As a devout Anglican and a warden of St James' Church for most of his adult life, Macaulay dealt with all sorts of parochial affairs including provision for poor relief. As a former army officer and militia colonel, he had directed the militia in the defence of Toronto during William Lyon Mackenzie's uprising in December 1837. As a provincial judge with a capacity for hard work and a reputation for clear thinking, he was asked by Lieutenant Governor Arthur in 1839 to complete an investigation of the Indian Department begun by the provincial secretary, Richard Alexander Tucker.

During March and April of that year Macaulay, though professing uncertain health and overwork, rushed off a lengthy report on the economic and social plight of what he termed 'the degenerate races.' This long-winded survey (some 446 manuscript pages) reveals concern and indicts some past practices, but it offered very little for future improvements in handling Indian problems and appears to rely on an extension of 'Christian charity' to cope with the 'far greater numbers of destitute tribes' that 'inhabit the remote regions of the North,' beyond lakes Huron and Superior and certainly beyond the experience or knowledge of James Buchanan Macaulay. The hurried examination was well enough received, however, for he was appointed with Robert Sympson Jameson and William Hepburn to a more formal examination of the Indian Department as part of the general investigation of provincial administration in 1839–40. Simultaneously he served as chairman of the committee investigating the workings of the Executive Council. Though Macaulay's insight into public affairs is not revealed in these departmental reports, Governor Lord Sydenham [Thomson], who had known him only for a short time, had no compunction in recording early in 1841 that 'in political matters I know of no one whose opinions I would rather consult for I esteem him highly.'

Nevertheless, it was to judicial matters that Macaulay turned for the remainder of his life. Along with commissioners John Beverley Robinson, William Henry Draper, and John Hillyard Cameron, he embarked on the first revision of Upper Canadian statute law in 1840 and served on the commissions of 1842 and 1843 inquiring into the Court of Chancery. In 1843 he was appointed to the Court of Appeal and in 1849 he was clearly the most logical and desirable choice for the position of chief justice in the reconstituted Court of Common Pleas. Macaulay held this post until the pressure of unremitting daily work on and for the bench, together with a self-admitted hearing loss, forced him to retire in 1856. That April he received the title of Queen's Counsel and the following January he agreed to supervise yet another statute revision committee, this time for both Upper and Lower Canada. Fellow commissioner David Breakenridge Read lauded Macaulay for his amazing attention to details of law and of language and for his refusal to accept any remuneration over and above his pension though he served as chairman for nearly two years. Despite Macaulay's failing health, another judgeship followed in the summer of 1857, a seat in the Court of Error and Appeal. The next year he was made a CB and on 13 Jan. 1859 he was knighted. That February the Law Society of Upper Canada, which Macaulay had shepherded and served for more than 35 years, conferred on him the office of treasurer, succeeding the late Robert Baldwin. Quite fittingly, perhaps, in retrospect, it was at Osgoode Hall on the morning of his re-election to this position that his heart failed.

James Buchanan Macaulay ended his days in what the young attorney general, John A. Macdonald, paying tribute to him at a retirement dinner in 1856, had called 'an untiring assiduity.' The *Upper Canada Law Journal* that year noted the 'ample monuments' represented by Macaulay's judgements in the law reports and observed quite accurately that he was the sort of figure whom 'men of all parties looked up to as a pattern of judicial purity.' He had, in short, as that journal recorded at his death, quite simply 'grown with the country.' A shy, retiring man, hesitant in speech but fluent and eminently rational in his reports, charges, and judgements, Macaulay had developed vast experience in watching over and guiding the new society.

His opinions and recommendations were sought on a wide range of issues affecting the machinery of government, his citizenship and private life were exemplary, and his military youth suitably dashing. To his equally reticent wife, who survived him until 1883 when she died in England at the home of a married daughter, Macaulay left the family home in Toronto, Wykeham Lodge, and an estate worth $40,000. To the province he left a legacy of quiet public service and principled professionalism.

GORDON DODDS

JOHN MACDONELL (Greenfield),
Lawyer, office holder, militia officer, and politician; b. 19 April 1785 in Greenfield, Scotland, the fourth son of Alexander Macdonell of Greenfield and Janet Macdonell (Aberchalder), sister of John McDonell (Aberchalder); d. 14 Oct. 1812 in Queenston, Upper Canada.

Little is known of John Macdonell's early life. In 1792 his family immigrated to Glengarry County, Upper Canada, and under his father's leadership it enjoyed a measure of prominence in the military and political affairs of the county. Some sources suggest that John, like his younger brother Alexander Greenfield, attended John Strachan's grammar school at Cornwall. This seems improbable. Strachan's school was established in the summer of 1803 and on 6 April of that year Macdonell became a law student. In 1862 Chief Justice John Beverley Robinson recalled that Macdonell served in the law office of William Dickson at Niagara (Niagara-on-the-Lake). Several historians have speculated that he was persuaded to take up law by his uncle Alexander McDonell (Collachie), sheriff of the Home District and member of the House of Assembly for the riding of Glengarry and Prescott. In 1808, having articled for the requisite five years, Macdonell was called to the bar in Trinity term. Thereafter, according to Robinson, he 'established himself very successfully in business' at York (Toronto).

Macdonell's legal career was brief but meteoric. Through Collachie he became acquainted with judge William Dummer Powell, gaining both his friendship and his patronage. At the height of his political power during the administration of Lieutenant Governor Francis Gore, Powell on 19 Aug. 1808 solicited an appointment for the young barrister as clerk to several court commissions for the Newcastle, Midland, Johnstown, and Eastern districts. By 1811 Macdonell was firmly established in his profession. A combination of personal ability and Powell's patronage brought recognition of his legal prominence when on 16 July he was appointed to conduct the criminal prosecutions on the western circuit in the absence of Solicitor General D'Arcy Boulton.

Powell's wife, Anne Murray, wrote enthusiastically that 'our young Friend J McDonnel goes as king's counsel.' He had also begun to attract law students and that year Robinson and Archibald McLean joined his practice. The following year the astute Ebenezer Washburn, ever alert for suitable prospects for his family, arranged for his son Simon Ebenezer to article with Macdonell but the War of 1812 disrupted these plans. Macdonell's professional stature had been complemented by an increasing social prominence. In December 1811 he was secretary to the subscribers to the library in York and in 1812 esquire was added to his name on the town census.

Early in his career Macdonell established a reputation for a quick temper. In 1808 he reacted strongly to a statement about his practice made in court by Attorney General William Firth and on 16 September sent his close friend Duncan Cameron to demand a retraction. Firth refused and Cameron challenged him to a duel on Macdonell's behalf. Firth seems to have had little use for the code so dear to the gentlemen of Upper Canada and faint-heartedly dismissed the challenge as contrary to law. Macdonell could give offence as easily as he took it. In April 1812 William Warren Baldwin objected in court to his 'wanton & ungentlemanly' expressions. Chief Justice Thomas Scott reprimanded Macdonell but Baldwin remained dissatisfied. He demanded an apology and when Macdonell refused challenged him to a duel. They met on 3 April but Macdonell would not raise his pistol, having decided to admit his fault by receiving Baldwin's fire. Baldwin 'took this as an acknowledgement of his error – we joined hands and thus this affair ended.' Baldwin's initial objection seems to have been prompted by Macdonell's arrogance and success. Several weeks after the incident he wrote to his friend Firth describing Macdonell as 'such a paragon of excellence that he leaves no virtue no commendable qualification for others to found pretensions on ... the field, the cabinet and the Forum are all to be the scenes of his Renown – his honors rain not upon him, they come in tempests.'

The mark of Macdonell's rapid ascent was his assumption of the duties of attorney general on 28 Sept. 1811. Firth had returned to England to defend his accounts and Boulton had been imprisoned by the French in Verdun. Gore was less than enthusiastic about the appointment and two days later urged Lord Liverpool, the Colonial secretary, 'to lose no time in procuring a fit subject for that high and confidential situation' because 'there is no Person at the Bar in this Province, whom I consider qualified for the office.' Gore returned to

England in October and Macdonell made a more favourable impression on the administrator of the province, Isaac Brock. Macdonell's appointment was confirmed on 14 April 1812 and a warrant issued on 18 June. His nomination was a testament to Powell's influence: Brock, 'who appeared to repose as much on my Judgement & Counsel as his predecessor ... afforded Strong proof of this in naming ... the youngest Practitioner at the Bar merely on my recommendation.' Powell, an able judge of men, saw in young Macdonell 'a fair proportion of legal acquirement ... Sound Discretion and highly honorable spirit.' The appointment was the first for a native-trained barrister, thus suiting Powell's 'object to retain the Honors of the profession amongst ourselves without risque of receiving from Europe Subjects often less suitable & no credit to the good wishes of the Minister, and to the good Service to the Colony.'

The fourth and fifth parliaments of Upper Canada had witnessed the rise of opposition in the House of Assembly; war with the United States seemed imminent. In this atmosphere of early 1812 Macdonell decided to contest the riding of Glengarry for the sixth parliament. His decision was probably influenced by his political friends, mindful of the need for a loyal assembly, and by the decision of his uncle Collachie, who had held one of the Glengarry seats since 1800, not to stand for a fourth term. Macdonells from various branches of the family had virtually monopolized the Glengarry seats since 1792 and in his election broadside John Macdonell reiterated the traditional social bonds of extended family and clan loyalty which characterized the Highland settlements of Glengarry, describing himself as 'connected with many of you by the ties of blood, and possessing one common interest with you all.' In May, on a leave of absence from official duties, he travelled to the Eastern District with John Beikie, the first clerk of the Executive Council, who had been encouraged by Father Alexander McDonell to contest the riding of Stormont and Russell. Archibald McLean, one of the priest's political contacts in York and a friend of John Macdonell, wrote of their candidacy, 'At this time it is particularly to be desired that the House of Assembly should be composed of well informed Men who are *well affected* to the Government.' Both were elected, Macdonell in conjunction with Alexander McMartin. Whether Macdonell attended the first session of the sixth parliament called by Brock to pass emergency legislation occasioned by the war is unknown. After his death he was succeeded in the assembly by his uncle Collachie.

Macdonell's abilities were not apparently restricted to politics and law. Brock found him 'so useful' as a soldier that on 15 April 1812 he appointed him provincial aide-de-camp with the rank of lieutenant-colonel in the militia. In his memoir of the war William Hamilton Merritt was to comment on Brock's staff appointments as 'most judicious.' On 18 June the Americans declared war. Macdonell accompanied Brock to Sandwich (Windsor) in August and was at the council of war called on the 15th. Only Macdonell and Robert Nichol approved Brock's plan to attack the American army commanded by William Hull at Detroit. That same day Macdonell and Major John Baskerville Glegg, Brock's military aide-de-camp, were deputed by Brock 'to conclude any arrangement that may lead to prevent the unnecessary effusion of blood.' Within an hour they returned with the conditions of the American capitulation. On 30 August Brock wrote to Lord Liverpool that Macdonell had 'afforded me the most important assistance' at Detroit, and he asked Liverpool to confirm his appointment as attorney general because of 'the very important Services which I have derived ... both in his Civil and Military Capacity.'

After the victory at Detroit Brock and Macdonell returned to the Niagara frontier, alternating between their political duties at York and preparations for the next military crisis. When word reached Brock on 13 October that the Americans had attacked at Queenston he hastened there, followed by Macdonell and Glegg. After Brock met his death on the heights in an effort to retake a battery, a detachment of York militia, including Macdonell's closest friends, Cameron and McLean, and his student Robinson, joined with the 49th Foot in a new attack led by Macdonell. In Robinson's words, 'McDonell was there mounted, and animating the men to charge.' He was wounded in three or four places as well as trampled by his horse, and was aided to safety by McLean and Cameron. He died the next day after 20 hours of 'excruciating suffering, his words and thoughts appeared ever occupied with lamentations for his lost friend [Brock].' Brock and Macdonell were buried on 16 October in what George Ridout described as 'the grandest & most solemn [burial] ever I witnessed.' In 1824 and again in 1853 they were re-interred in the successive monuments to Brock.

Macdonell's gallant death, like that of Brock, became part of the lore of the War of 1812 which flourished in the 19th century. The monuments at Queenston enshrined their heroic moment. Yet the ultimate victory at Queenston belonged to Brock's successor Roger Hale Sheaffe, and the charge led by Macdonell, although valiant, was perhaps foolhardy. Robinson observed the following day that 'the attempt was unsuccessful and must have been dictated rather by a fond hope of regaining what had been lost by a desperate effort than by a conviction of it's practicability. ...' Less than two weeks after the battle Glegg wrote that Macdonell had 'appeared determined to accompany him [Brock] to the regions of eternal bliss.' Possessed of a poetic sensibility and keen intelligence yet headstrong and violent, Macdonell was a man whose abilities marked him off from the generality of society. He was the epitome of a Highland gentleman. The bravery and impetuosity of his last act were entirely characteristic of such a man. His brief life was the stuff of legend. To Robinson's mind he was 'as noble a youth as ever inherited his name, which is saying much.'

Two stories have persisted about Macdonell: that at the time of his death he was engaged to Mary Boyles Powell, daughter of William Dummer; and that he had been converted to the Church of England from Roman Catholicism. There is no doubt that Macdonell was Mary Boyles's ardent suitor. Books of poetry he gave her, dated 1805, are still in the possession of the Macdonell family. It has often been assumed that the 500 guineas Macdonell left Mary in his will proved their relationship, if not their engagement, but this is not the case. On 22 Feb. 1812 Anne Powell wrote that her daughter Mary 'assiduously avoids every mark of [Macdonell's] attention, as any other would court it. ... Except herself no young Woman in the Province would reject a Man of 25; of Talents integrity & exemplary goodness & who at this early period is at the head of his profession.' In 1815 Anne described the tragic effect of Macdonell's death: 'Mary is changed beyond description ... more to unceasing regret for her unkindness to one who merited and ... possessed her best affection ... the generous bequest of our ever lamented Friend was a proof of his regard, which she could not but feel a reproach for her capricious conduct.' For Macdonell's religion the evidence is less conclusive. According to a still persistent family tradition Macdonell made the change at York, but the only supporting evidence is the payment of pew rent in St James' Church by Macdonell on at least one occasion for his uncle Collachie's family, with whom he had lived as a student; this does not seem significant since St James' was then the only church in York and Collachie's wife belonged to the Church of England. Collachie himself was a Catholic, as was Macdonell's brother Donald, and the first conversion within the family seems to have been that of one of Donald's sons to Presbyterianism.

In his will Macdonell left his two lots in York to his cousin James Macdonell (Collachie), another lot in Whitby Township to William Powell, grandson of William Dummer Powell, several pieces of property in Scarborough and Saltfleet townships to his niece Ann, the daughter of Miles Macdonell, various personal bequests, and the remainder to his father.

CAROL WHITFIELD and ROBERT L. FRASER

ARCHIBALD McLEAN
Lawyer, politician, and judge; b. 5 April 1791 at St Andrews, Luneburg District, Province of Quebec, second son of Neil McLean and Isabella Macdonell; m. Joan McPherson, and they had seven children; d. 24 Oct. 1865 at Toronto, Canada West.

Archibald McLean's father was prominent in the Eastern District, serving at various times as sheriff, militia colonel, and judge. Archibald attended John Strachan's school in Cornwall and developed a lifelong friendship with its master. In 1809 McLean articled in law at York (Toronto) under William Firth, then attorney general. The War of 1812 interrupted his legal studies and he became a subaltern in the 3rd Regiment of York militia. At the battle of Queenston Heights on 13 Oct. 1812, McLean was seriously wounded, but he crawled from the battlefield to a nearby village where his wounds were hurriedly dressed. His recuperation, prolonged because of an infection resulting from the late removal of a bullet, was not yet complete when the Americans attacked York on 27 April 1813. Still unfit for combat because of his illness, McLean buried the York militia's colours in the woods and escaped to Kingston. He was back in action on 25 July 1814 at Lundy's Lane, where he was captured by the Americans and held prisoner for the duration of the war.

In 1815, after declining a commission in the British regulars, McLean was called to the Upper Canadian bar and entered the firm of William Warren Baldwin. The following year McLean established his own lucrative practice in Cornwall. The McLean family were members of the Church of Scotland, leaders in the Cornwall area, and related through marriage to prominent local Scottish Catholics. It was to be expected, therefore, that as a rising member of the Family Compact, McLean should be elected to the assembly for the county of Stormont in 1820. In the assembly he gradually became a leading Tory member and an advocate of recognizing the rights of the Presbyterian Church as equal to those of the Church of England. McLean held the Stormont seat until 1834 when Cornwall was incorporated as a town and received its own seat. That year he won election as member for Cornwall and he became speaker of the assembly in 1836. He again represented Stormont in the 13th parliament which opened 8 Nov. 1836.

Promoted colonel in the militia during the Rebellion of 1837, McLean was involved in routing the rebels in Toronto, commanding the left flank of the loyalist forces under Colonel James FitzGibbon in the attack on Montgomery's Tavern. McLean initially opposed the union of 1841 out of fear that Upper Canadians would be dominated by French Canadians. He saw responsible government as a danger to the British connection and to the ordered freedom and the recognition of class and property of the British tradition, but he quickly adjusted to the new reality.

Archibald McLean began his long judicial career with an appointment to the Court of King's Bench for the western circuit in March 1837; he was replaced as member for Stormont by his brother Alexander in December of that year. In 1850 he was transferred to the newly created Court of Common Pleas where he served with James Buchanan Macaulay and Robert Baldwin Sullivan. In 1856, when he was passed over as this court's chief justice in favour of William Henry Draper, he returned to the Queen's Bench as a senior judge. In December 1860 McLean dissented in the case of John Anderson, a fugitive slave, and argued that he should be discharged: 'in administering the laws of a British province, I can never feel bound to recognize as law any enactment which can convert into chattels a very large number of the human race.' On 15 March 1862 he was appointed chief justice of the Court of Queen's Bench for Upper Canada. McLean was a Conservative from a prominent old Tory family. Nevertheless, in July 1863 Reform Premier John Sandfield Macdonald, who had articled with McLean and served under him on the western circuit, had him appointed to the less onerous post of presiding judge of the Court of Error and Appeal when Sir John Beverley Robinson died. McLean, now 72, was replaced as chief justice by Draper.

For many years McLean was president of the St Andrew's Society of Toronto. When he died in 1865 he was honoured by an impressive public funeral. The *Upper Canada Law Journal* commented that McLean 'upon the bench was dignified and courteous; unsuspicious and utterly devoid of anything mean or petty in his own character, his conduct to others was always what he expected from them.'

BRUCE W. HODGINS

WILLIAM OSGOODE
Judge and politician; b. March 1754 in London, only son of William Osgood; d. there 17 Jan. 1824.

The elder Osgood (his son added the 'e' after 1781) was a Leeds hosier who moved to London and left an estate of about £20,000 when he died in 1767. A friend and patron of John Wesley, he sent William to the Methodist school at Kingswood, near Bath, for a classical education. Osgoode then attended Christ Church College, Oxford (BA 1772, MA 1777), entered Lincoln's Inn in 1773 and, after a year in France, was called to the English bar on 11 Nov. 1779. In that year he published *Remarks on the law of descent*, a critique of Sir William Blackstone's *Commentaries on the laws of England*. He did not practise in the circuit courts, either because a hesitation in his speech made him an ineffective barrister or because he was not dependent on his fees as a lawyer. He appears to have accepted no common-law briefs, but gained a reputation as a draftsman in the courts of equity. There is no evidence to support the family tradition that he was an intimate of William Pitt; and the story that he was a natural son of George II is without foundation or plausibility.

He had enough influence in Whitehall to be appointed first chief justice of Upper Canada (31 Dec. 1791), with an undertaking that he could expect to succeed the ailing William Smith in the same post at Quebec. It was as his nominee that John White became attorney general for the upper province. Although Osgoode failed in an attempt to nominate his own replacement in Upper Canada in 1794 when he moved to Quebec, he retained the good opinion of successive secretaries of state for the colonies until 1801; and he was to keep up a frankly partisan commentary on his fellow officials at Quebec in private correspondence with the under-secretary, John King.

In Upper Canada, too, Osgoode won friends. Richard Cartwright's first impression of him as 'a very worthy and respectable man' appears to have survived their differences over the law of marriage and the formation of the courts. Osgoode's disapproval of William Dummer Powell, because he was not an English lawyer, was merely part of his generally condescending attitude towards colonials. His good manners, good looks, and kindliness – at Quebec he took in White's two sons for a time after their father's death – made him popular. He got on especially well with the new lieutenant governor, John Graves Simcoe, whom he joined at Quebec (2 June 1792) on his way to Upper Canada. He lived with the Simcoes at Newark (Niagara-on-the-Lake) until almost the end of the year. He wrote periodically to Mrs Simcoe [Elizabeth Posthuma Gwillim] long after leaving the province, just as he continued to advise Peter Russell when the latter became administrator. Two years after Osgoode's departure for Lower Canada in 1794, Simcoe still found his absence 'most severely oppressive.'

The two agreed on most questions, including their mistrust of merchants as monopolists; but Osgoode never had Simcoe's commitment to the province, and his toryism was more rigid. His hostility to Americans was unqualified: he thought New York 'the very Nest & Hotbed of Turbulence and Disaffection.' In spite of his Methodist upbringing, he was ambitious for the effective establishment of the Church of England in both provinces and with Bishop Jacob Mountain was to regret that it had no legal claim to the tithe in Lower Canada. Notwithstanding his own origins (about which in later life he was secretive), he was sometimes more an aristocrat than a lawyer: he sympathized with duelling if it was conducted with proper restraint and he secured the acquittal of a duellist at Kingston who had been obliged to kill a persistent opponent. Passing through Montreal in July 1792 he was surprised to find that women could vote and that 'the Returning Officer was an Englishman which makes it more Extraordinary.'

In his application of English legal models to Upper Canada, Osgoode was in some ways discriminating. He gave attention before leaving England to 'the different Arrangements it may be needful to make in attempting to simplify and adapt the Artificial practice & proceedings of English Jurisprudence to the circumstances of an infant Colony.' It was, however, from English lawyers that he sought advice. His concern was not with frontier conditions but with the unreformed procedure of the English common-law courts. He was an accomplished equity lawyer in a period when the Court of Chancery and the equity jurisdiction of the Court of Exchequer had done far more than parliament to reform the law; he thought those courts of equity more just in their law and more reasonable in their procedure than the common law courts of common pleas and king's bench; and he did not mean to introduce into Upper Canada what he regarded as anachronisms in England. In drafting his first provincial statute, therefore, an act in 1792 to adopt English civil law, he retained the simple writ of summons and the proceedings already in use in Quebec after 1763. The act did not adopt the English bankruptcy or poor laws, nor the law relating to ecclesiastical rights and duties. He may have been in favour of limiting imprisonment for debt to cases of fraudulent evasion, although the change was not included in the act.

Never a finicky lawyer, he did not think it necessary to legislate the adoption of English criminal law, the proclamation of 7 Oct. 1763 having done so in general terms. He considered it enough to adopt recent English extensions of the right of trial by jury. His successor, John Elmsley, would think differently in 1800. Similarly, he was of the opinion that simple letters of declaration issued with title deeds were enough to ensure the legality of land grants made before 1791. Although he had set three as a quorum for the Executive Council, he and Russell sometimes conducted its business alone. The greatest compromise that he accepted in Upper Canada, however, was forced upon him by the House of Assembly on the initiative of Cartwright. Osgoode's marriage bill of 1793, intended merely to validate existing marriages, was amended to allow justices of the peace to perform marriages whenever there were fewer than five Anglican clergymen in a district, none of them within 18 miles. Illiberal as those terms were for a province with a minority of Anglicans, a barrage of complaints against them did not force a change until 1831. In practice they allowed what amounted to civil marriage so long as the Anglican form of service was followed.

The Judicature Act of 1794 was the legislation by which Osgoode most hoped to set his mark on the province. It abolished the district courts of common pleas set up in 1788, replacing them with a single court of king's bench as the superior court for the whole province. An accompanying bill set up new district courts to settle contract disputes, not involving land titles, of from 40s. to £15. An earlier act had on the assembly's initiative empowered any two justices of the peace to hear cases involving less than 5s. A court of probate with district branches (surrogate courts) had also been introduced to settle the inheritance of estates. There was no provincial court of common pleas and no court of chancery.

The Judicature Act had a difficult passage through the Legislative Council, where it was attacked as too elaborate, centralized, and expensive for a province still thinly settled, and also because it put the chief justice in the position of hearing appeals from his own decisions. It was, however, as simple an arrangement as Osgoode and Simcoe would consent to. Its excessive centralization was mitigated from 1797, when the writs necessary to begin an action in king's bench could be obtained from a district rather than the provincial capital. In the short run at least it was a visionary scheme: even its central establishment – the chief justice, two puisne judges, an attorney general, a solicitor general, two sheriffs, and a clerk of the crown and pleas – could not be staffed by trained lawyers. Besides Osgoode and White, Powell and Walter Roe of Detroit were the only lawyers in the province. Nevertheless, Osgoode's measures did regularize and extend the jurisdiction of the untrained justices of the peace and district magistrates who settled most of the legal disputes in the province.

These were Osgoode's main pieces of legislation during his two years in Upper Canada, the acts to abolish slavery and organize the legal profession being the work of White. But Osgoode was also a member of both the Executive Council (sworn in 9 July 1792) and the Legislative Council (sworn in 12 July 1792 and speaker from 10 September). He was the only member to attend all the meetings of both bodies over the next two years. In the Legislative Council he was in effect manager of government business, its chief defender against the opposition of Cartwright and Robert Hamilton. Although his commission as chief justice at Quebec was issued on 24 Feb. 1794, he remained in the upper province for the next summer's meeting of the legislature.

He arrived at Quebec on 27 July, barely three weeks after his last meeting of the Executive Council at Newark. He was again a member of both councils (sworn in 19 Sept. 1794), and again speaker of the Legislative Council. He began his unhappy career at Quebec by chairing the Executive Council's committee on land grants. He had the misfortune to deal with two governors, Lord Dorchester [Guy Carleton] and Robert Prescott, who had grown old and irascible, but he himself became a prickly and vindictive character. Simcoe did not help matters with Dorchester by offering Osgoode as his spokesman on two disputed questions, the lease of the Six Nations' lands and the provisioning of troops. It was, however, with Prescott that Osgoode came to an open and bitter quarrel.

The land grants of Lower Canada were in confusion from lax administration, lack of surveys, and the prevalence of unauthorized settlement. The Executive Council's solution was merely to rescind township grants not already confirmed and to regrant the land. Prescott thought this too favourable to land speculators, among whom he included members of the council; his new regulations recognized actual settlement and even pending applications if they had been properly recorded; the rest of the lands were to be put up for sale. These regulations had been approved by the secretary of state, the Duke of Portland, when Prescott asked the Executive Council to advise him on their publication. The council's report of 20 June 1798, drafted by Osgoode, objected both to publication and to the regulations. Prescott then published them with the council's objections and with a foreword, highly critical of the council, by the disappointed land applicant William Berczy. Osgoode was outraged by the publication, with its attack on his character by the 'miserable Alien' Berczy, and perhaps most of all by the resulting personal incivilities. 'How it will be relished at Home,' he wrote prophetically, 'remains to be seen.' Prescott, at odds with most of his subordinates, was recalled to explain his conduct and never returned.

Robert Shore Milnes, who came out in June 1799 as lieutenant governor, found Osgoode little easier to deal with. In May 1800 the chief justice demanded the dismissal of Pierre-Amable De Bonne from the bench for adultery, absenteeism, and faulty court procedure. Unwilling to stir up further bitterness by a public inquiry, Milnes refused. When in 1801 the assembly passed an act to remit arrears of *lods et ventes* on crown lands, Osgoode objected: it was, he wrote, 'an established rule as well of decency as of policy' that such concessions ought to be made by the crown, not the legislature. The assembly's request for a return of crown property held *en roture* seemed to him an unwarrantable interference with the royal prerogative; and he made it a grievance that the Executive Council was not forced by the secretary of state to record his protest in its minutes. He had already offered to resign on condition of receiving an £800 pension. When that was confirmed, he left Quebec in the summer of 1801, his resignation taking effect on 1 May 1802.

At Quebec Osgoode seems never to have been the charming and indefatigably industrious public servant that he was in the upper province. Prescott never accused him of being a land speculator, only of being vain and idle enough to act as the speculators' stalking-horse on the Executive Council. Since Osgoode received grants totalling nearly 12,000 acres, the governor might have gone farther in his accusations. Osgoode's disapproval extended beyond his colleagues on the bench and in the councils. He did maintain good relations to the end with Bishop Mountain, but almost the only other living things to win his approval in Lower Canada were the horses, 'the best little Creatures in the Universe.' Although he had shrunk from the first sight of the black cap among his judicial robes, he even became a harsh judge. He had no choice in July 1797 about condemning David McLane to death, nor about decreeing life imprisonment for McLane's merely foolish accomplice, Charles Frichet; but he did not recommend mercy for either of them, and poor Frichet's sentence was remitted without his advice. Milnes wrote that Osgoode would not be content except as 'the sole adviser to government.' Certainly Osgoode never again enjoyed so large a share of confidence as Simcoe had given him, and never worked as well without it.

Back in London Osgoode lived fashionably in apartments formerly occupied by the Duke of York, but he did not receive another judicial appointment. He was able to return to his interest in procedural reform as a member of the royal commissions on the courts of law which eventually led in 1832 to the Uniformity of Process Act. Osgoode Hall, first built in 1829–32 as the headquarters of the Law Society of Upper Canada, was named after him. His portrait by George Theodore Berthon hangs there.

S.R. MEALING

WILLIAM DUMMER POWELL
Lawyer, judge, office holder, politician, and author; b. 5 Nov. 1755 in Boston, eldest son of John Powell and Janet Grant; m. 3 Oct. 1775 Anne Murray, and they had nine children; d. 6 Sept. 1834 in Toronto.

William Dummer Powell was descended on both sides of his family from 17th-century emigrants to Massachusetts from England. His maternal grandfather, William Dummer, had been lieutenant governor of the colony; his paternal grandfather, John Powell, had come out as Dummer's secretary. His father, also named John Powell, was a prosperous Boston merchant, the holder for three decades before the American revolution of a naval victualling contract. The Powells had been Anglicans and royalists, the Dummers Presbyterians and parliamentarians. By an agreement between his parents, the second John Powell was brought up in the Church of England, but his two younger brothers were raised as Congregationalists. Even before the declaration of American independence the family was also politically divided, John being a declared loyalist and his brothers rebels.

By that time William Dummer Powell had completed his formal education and was trying to decide on a career. After three years at the Boston Free Grammar School he had been sent to an Anglican school in Tunbridge (Royal Tunbridge Wells), Kent, for four years and then to Rotterdam, where for two years he studied French and Dutch. At the age of 16 he had then returned to England for a year, where he 'cultivated the good graces of the ladies more than any other pursuit,' until concern for his father's health recalled him to Boston in 1772. By his own later admission he had been a far from assiduous student: fluency in French, an enthusiasm for cricket, and a continuing taste for the Latin classics seem to have been the main results of his schooling. The Powell view of what constituted frivolity was, however, severe; his letters to his parents reveal a rather priggish young man, serious if not especially studious. He already showed the intense concern for social position that was to characterize him all his life, reacting vehemently to an inaccurate report circulated at the Tunbridge school of his father's insolvency.

Back in Boston, his father's bout of rheumatic fever over, Powell set about looking for commercial opportunities. His father proved unwilling to give him a share of the naval victualling contract. A plan to go into business with his mother's relatives in London having come to nothing, he visited Montreal in the summer of 1773 and Pennsylvania and New York in the next year. In the winters he studied law under the attorney general of Massachusetts, Jonathan Sewell (Sewall), but his object was to prepare himself for public life, not for a legal career. In 1774 Powell hoped to go into business in New York, where anti-imperial sentiment was less widespread than in Boston; but his journey there was interrupted by the death from smallpox of his mother, to whom his attachment was very strong. Returning to Boston, he threw himself into politics as one of the organizers of a declaration of loyal citizens against the revolutionary party (19 April 1775). He served in arms, although apparently not in action, as a volunteer with the British garrison. With open rebellion approaching and his opposition to it established beyond any chance of compromise, he decided to leave North America. He also met Anne Murray, the daughter of a Scottish physician, who had come to live with relatives in Boston. They were married just before leaving for England in October 1775 and settled near her family at Norwich.

His father followed within a year, taking up residence at Ludlow in Shropshire, the country from which his family had come. He continued to support his son, but his ability to do so was now diminished, mostly because a West Indian plantation in which he had invested heavily went bankrupt. A part of his Boston estates was confiscated on 30 April 1779 under an act of that year classifying him as an absentee rather than a traitor; but the confiscated part, inventoried at £902 1s. 2d., went to his rebel brother William, who had advanced him £1,000 when he left Boston. Under a later Massachusetts act of 1784 absentees were allowed to reclaim their property. It was to be a lifelong grievance of William Dummer Powell that he was never able to recover all his father's estate under the terms of that act, but it seems that most of the elder Powell's real property in America was retained in spite of his loyalism. It was nevertheless clear that the son would have to find a career to support his growing family.

He was unsuccessful in his competition with other loyalists for a government appointment, and a second scheme for going into business with a relative of his mother's (this time in Jamaica) failed. He therefore decided upon the practice of law. By May 1779 he had kept the necessary terms at the Middle Temple. Unable then to afford the fees, he did not arrange his formal call to the English bar until 2 Feb. 1784. Yet another of his mother's relatives, William Grant, the former attorney general of Quebec, recommended that province; and Powell arrived at Quebec in August 1779.

He obtained a licence to practise, but was disappointed in his hopes of patronage from the governor, Frederick Haldimand. On the advice of the attorney general, James Monk, and the deputy commissary general, Isaac Winslow Clarke (a fellow Bostonian loyalist who later married his sister Anne), he went into private practice in Montreal. It proved a happy decision. Montreal was a growing commercial centre of some 15,000 people where there were not yet half a dozen lawyers. Powell did well enough to bring out his family, to acquire a house on Mount Royal, to command the highest fees at the Montreal bar, and perhaps even to dispense with his father's assistance.

Yet he was soon dissatisfied in Montreal. Paradoxically, part of the reason was his success at the bar. His first client was Pierre Du Calvet, charged with a libel against the judges of the Court of Common Pleas in Montreal. Du Calvet, displeased at an earlier judgement by the court, had published a letter critical of the judges and had beaten one of them, John Fraser, who had attacked him. Although warned by Monk that any lawyer who took the libel case would earn the resentment of the whole bench and of the governor as well, Powell defended Du Calvet and persuaded the jury to acquit him. In January 1780 he scored another triumph, this time before a court of quarter sessions without a jury. He was able to show that an old English statute on which Haldimand had relied to prosecute grain merchants for price-fixing had been repealed. Powell was willing to defy popular as well as official disapproval – he undertook prosecutions for refusals to transport military stores under the law of corvée – but his successes branded him as an opponent of the administration. That did not prevent his being retained on government as well as on commercial cases, but it was a role which his toryism made uncomfortable.

He was, however, convinced that government and the administration of justice under the Quebec Act of 1774 were arbitrary, in particular that English law relating to juries and the writ of habeas corpus must be introduced. He claimed later to have been silent himself and to have 'inculcated silence and subordination in others,' but his views were well enough known to make him one of the delegates who sailed from Quebec on 25 Oct. 1783 with a petition against the Quebec Act. Nothing immediate came of the petition, but on his way back from England Powell spent almost a year in Boston. He attempted to recover the confiscated part of his father's property. He agreed to manage the estates of his rebel uncle Jeremiah Powell for a time and he even hoped that, with the American war over, he could return to Boston without renouncing his British allegiance. The failure of his attempt, the disappointment of his hope, and the death of his uncle sent him back to Montreal early in 1785.

There he not only recovered his position at the bar, he found that most of the sources of his earlier discontent had been removed. An ordinance of 29 April 1784 had introduced habeas corpus, and another of 21 April 1785 soon adopted the general common law right to jury trials in civil cases. Perhaps best of all, Haldimand had gone. Sir Guy Carleton, now Lord Dorchester, arrived in October 1786 for his second term as governor of Quebec; and under him Powell at last found official favour. He must be said to have earned it. In 1787 he served without remuneration as one of two commissioners sent to report on the dissatisfaction of loyalists settled on the upper St Lawrence, who were worried about the tenure of their lands. This commission recommended the 200-acre bonus for settlers who had made improvements to their land that became known as 'Lord Dorchester's bounty.' Powell wrote the commission's report for a similar investigation of the seigneury of Sorel. He was on a commission to settle claims for freight charges against up-country traders who had used government vessels during the war. Finally, he led the board of inquiry into claims against the Quebec merchant John Cochrane, who had supplied specie to the army during the war and was accused of profiteering on bills of exchange. The board recommended dismissing the claims and found the court proceedings that had been taken against Cochrane improper. Powell therefore encountered the renewed hostility of the judges involved, Adam Mabane and John Fraser. Mabane accused Powell of having taken an oath of allegiance to the American government, but he was not believed. Powell was granted the 'few Acres of land' (in fact 3,000 acres) that Mabane was trying to deny him. Successful though his return to Montreal was, he could hardly look for a judicial appointment there.

The whole upper part of the province, which was to become Upper Canada in 1791, was still included in the district of Montreal. Except for justices of the peace, any two of whom could hear actions for debt up to £5, its only civil jurisdiction was the Montreal Court of Common Pleas. The St Lawrence loyalist settlers had petitioned for a separate province in 1785, and Montreal merchants in the next year made concerted complaints about the lack of courts in the interior. Dorchester opposed a separate province, but on 24 July 1788 he did create four new districts, each with a court of common pleas. The most westerly of them was Hesse (renamed the Western District from 15 Oct. 1792). Three judges were appointed for it, all residents of Detroit; Jacques Baby, *dit* Dupéront, and William Robertson were merchants, and Alexander McKee was an officer in the Indian Department. All three joined in the inhabitants' petition for a trained lawyer, following no other profession and not connected with trade. Powell, with his experience of up-country cases in Montreal, was an obvious choice. On 2 Feb. 1789 he was appointed first judge, and as it turned out the sole judge, of common pleas at Detroit. The stipend of £500 (sterling) probably exceeded his Montreal income. In retrospect, Powell claimed to have accepted the position 'with the latent but confident expectation' of getting the chief legal appointment when a new province was created. At the time, it may have been enough that the court of Hesse, because the fur trade required it to have jurisdiction over acts outside its district (ordinance of 30 April 1789), was from a lawyer's perspective the most important of the new courts.

Detroit was a rough town of about 4,000 people, the smallest and most remote place in which Powell had ever lived. He was to spend nearly all the rest of his life in smaller towns; York (Toronto) had not yet reached half that size when he retired there in 1825. Detroit was picturesque, and the officers of the garrison provided a society that Powell's wife and sister Anne found agreeable, but the Powells were not happy there for long. He made no particular enemies through his court, which sat at L'Assomption (Sandwich) because Detroit itself was on American soil. He instituted simple procedure and dispensed quick justice, perhaps aided by the fact that he never called a jury. But he was also on the land board (7 Aug. 1789 to October 1792), where his refusal to recognize irregular purchases from the Indians and his faithful attendance – he missed only 5 of 53 meetings – made him a threat to the military and Indian Department officers who were unused to interference, especially from a newcomer. Powell's life was threatened, his wife and children frightened by mock Indian ambushes, and his loyalty questioned. In October 1791 his wife took the family to England to keep them safe and to put the two eldest boys in school. Finally two officers, in what may have been intended as a cruel joke, forged a treasonable letter from Powell to the American secretary of war, Henry Knox.

By then Powell had other reasons for alarm. Upper Canada had been made a separate province, but Dorchester's advice had been ignored in choosing the officials of its government. His choice for lieutenant governor, the loyalist Sir John Johnson, had been passed over. Their combined support for Powell did not get him the post of chief justice which he coveted, nor even a place on the Legislative and Executive councils. His authority as a judge of common pleas was extended beyond the Hesse District to cover the whole province (31 Dec. 1791), but his new masters were strangers with whom he had no influence. In February he went to Quebec to meet the new lieutenant governor, John Graves Simcoe, and to disavow the forged letter. Their first acquaintance was reassuring to both of them, and he returned to his duties at Detroit. In the fall he went on leave to England, carrying Simcoe's guarded endorsement that 'the behaviour and conduct of Mr. Powell, as far as lies within my knowledge, has been in every respect such as becomes the station He holds.' He got similar assurance from the home secretary, Henry Dundas.

He remained an outsider under the new administration. The chief justice, William Osgoode, who had none of Powell's experience of legal practice, of the bench, or of the province, did not consult him in reorganizing the courts. The new scheme replaced the district courts by a central court of king's bench having criminal as well as civil jurisdiction. Before this judges like Powell had only limited criminal jurisdiction, supplied by temporary commissions of oyer and terminer and of general jail delivery. Powell was commissioned puisne judge of king's bench on 9 July 1794. He first presided on the following 6 October at Newark (Niagara-on-the-Lake), his wider jurisdiction having released him from Detroit. Since the only other regular judge of the court was the often absent chief justice, Powell bore the brunt of its work from the beginning, as he did for the rest of his career.

Except for the location of the capital at York, Powell did not object to the policies of Simcoe's administration: his criticism of district land boards had already foreshadowed the grounds on which Simcoe abolished them, and he was an enthusiast for the plan of endowing the Church of England by leasing the clergy reserves. Yet he resented the young Englishmen set over him, was ostentatiously patient about the disappointment of his ambitions, and referred rather too often to 'the long and unimpeached discharge of my Duty as the first Magistrate of this new Colony before its Seperation from Lower Canada.' He was right in questioning the legality of land grants made before 1791, but he did so in conjunction with the malcontent Niagara magnate Robert Hamilton, leaving the provincial attorney general, John White, to find out about it after the law officers in Westminster had given their opinion. Without the substance of opposition, he deliberately gave the appearance of it: knowing of Simcoe's antipathy towards the governor at Quebec, he named his home at Newark 'Mount Dorchester.' When Osgoode left the province, Powell was again passed over, Simcoe urging a chief justice who was 'an *English* Lawyer.' There were private grounds for bitterness, too: the sale of Powell's house in Montreal to Monk led to a long squabble, and Mrs Powell's attempts to collect a Boston inheritance got her little except a quarrel with her brother, George Murray.

Powell's patience was to be tried further. His friend Peter Russell, who administered the government after Simcoe's departure, lacked the influence to be his patron; Powell acted as chief justice for over two years, only to see the appointment go to John Elmsley. His claims were not entirely unrecognized: another lobbying trip to England, obtained by a threat of resignation, won him half the chief justice's salary, if that post was vacant, in addition to an increase in his own. This increase more than doubled his income whenever he was alone on the bench to £1,300 (sterling), although nearly half of that was taken up by the expense of making six district circuits a year. He had considerable political sense, as he showed in attempting to compose the quarrels of William Jarvis, provincial secretary, with his colleagues. He advised David William Smith, elected to the first assembly for the riding of Suffolk and Essex, that he could not expect French Canadian votes but could win without them. His advice against prosecuting the son of Joseph Brant [Thayendanegea] for murder (3 Jan. 1797) was based on political considerations, although he did at that time think that Indians in their own villages were independent of the courts. On the first Heir and Devisee Commission from 1797 he showed the assiduity, grasp of detail, and concern for fairness that made him a good if unimaginative administrator.

He thought of himself as a man of principle, willing for its sake to risk the displeasure of authority, but his principles were apt to be most in evidence when his own interests or his partisan feelings were involved. When he called attention to the justice of loyalists' claims to special importance in Upper Canada, he added his own claims to advancement. He pointed out, in the long wrangle among officials over land fees, that Jarvis's share did not cover his costs; Jarvis was a friend, whose eldest son Samuel Peters was to be Powell's business agent and to marry his youngest daughter, Mary Boyles. When Lieutenant Governor Peter Hunter put government during his frequent absences in the hands of a committee of the Executive Council, Powell insisted on the possible illegality of the arrangement; he had just been ignored again for a seat on the council, and offended by Hunter's supersession of Russell. He felt himself to be 'without Patronage in Europe,' as he wrote Dorchester, 'in a species of disgrace here, where my local Information and Zeal for the Service were an unpardonable libel on the new Government.'

He continued to memorialize Whitehall on his merits and on the improvements to provincial legislation that he would have advised if asked. Before his ambition could be fulfilled, he had still to outlast two more immigrant chief justices: Henry Allcock and Thomas Scott. He got along well enough with the latter to borrow $400 from him in July 1806 during the most melodramatic of his personal crises. His fourth son, Jeremiah, having joined a quixotic and farcical attempt to assist rebellion in the Spanish colony of Venezuela, lay in the notoriously fever-ridden prison of Omoa, near Cartagena (Colombia), sentenced to ten years' hard labour. Powell took six months' leave of absence to lobby in Boston, New York, Philadelphia, London, and Madrid for his son's release. Jeremiah was set free in 1807, only to die at sea the following year. Powell's success reveals that his connections outside Upper Canada were more extensive and effective than he admitted – they ranged from the Duke of Kent [Edward Augustus] to the godmother of the son of the Spanish minister to the United States – and his grief did not prevent him from pressing his own case while in London. The deaths of his favourite sister Anne in childbirth at Montreal in 1792, of his infant daughter Anne in 1783, of his second son William Dummer in 1803, and of his youngest child Thomas William at school in Kingston in 1804 had been more tragic, but they had not drained his energies and finances as had Jeremiah's escapade. He returned to York, worn out, in October 1807. He and his wife were now touchier and more status-conscious than ever, jealous of their claims to precedence in York society and ready to feel slighted at the formal manners of a new lieutenant governor, Francis

Gore. Mrs Powell was insulted in September 1807 at the prospect of having a wealthy York merchant, Laurent Quetton St George, as a son-in-law. She ignored her husband's requests and risked Gore's displeasure in refusing to cooperate in his attempt to rehabilitate Mrs John Small in York society.

In fact Gore's arrival marked a turn in Powell's fortunes. He declined the lieutenant governor's first offer of a seat on the executive council, because it would have been unpaid; but a regular salaried place came open and he was sworn in on 8 March 1808. He remained stiffly independent, offending Gore by his decision on 15 July 1809, upheld on appeal to the imperial law officers, that David McGregor Rogers could not be dismissed as registrar of deeds because of his opposition in the House of Assembly. Gore however returned to the opinion he had expressed in the preceding March, that Powell was 'a Gentleman who has discharged the duties of his important office with probity and honour for upwards of twenty years and whose local knowledge particularly fits him' to be an executive councillor. The council, with two assiduous and competent members in Powell and John McGill, now made progress with its backlog of business, Powell undertaking a simplification of the confused process by which land patents were issued. His credit rose steadily, and he soon had the satisfaction of being petitioned by such magnates as Richard Cartwright and such prominent immigrants as John Strachan to use his influence with the lieutenant governor.

That influence was exaggerated in popular conception at the time, as it was by the later reform critics Robert Gourlay, Francis Collins, and William Lyon Mackenzie. It also appears greater and more personal in retrospect than it really was, because the later correspondence between Gore and Powell reached a level of cordiality exceptional in Powell's life. The two agreed that the subordinate officers of government should be men with experience of the province, but whereas that was a matter of practical common sense for Gore, for Powell it was a desire to 'retain the Honors of the [legal] profession amongst ourselves.' Powell could obtain the appointment of his eldest son John as clerk of the Legislative Council (19 Feb. 1807) in succession to James Clark, but not that of his protégé John Macdonell (Greenfield) as attorney general. It was Isaac Brock, administrator of the province during Gore's absence, who agreed to Macdonell's appointment and who recommended that Powell's third son, Grant, be made principal of the Court of Probate (April 1813). Powell drafted Brock's celebrated reply of 22 July 1812 in response to Brigadier-General William Hull's proclamation issued at Detroit. In Powell's view at the time, Brock and later Sir George Murray (administrator from 25 April to 30 June 1815) relied on his advice as much as Gore had done.

The decade up to 1818 saw the height of Powell's career. Although in 1797 he had sworn never to settle his family at York, he now had an impressive house, Caer Howell, with another 100 acres in York Township and 5,000 more throughout the province. He assumed the obligations marking the status of which he, and still more his wife, were jealously proud; always complaining of the expense, he duly subscribed to building funds for a fire hall (1802) and for St James' Church (1803), and was director of the subscription library (1814), the Loyal and Patriotic Society of Upper Canada (1812), and the Society for the Relief of Strangers in Distress (1817). As his wife was to write in 1819, 'in an aristocratical Government, expences must be incurred according to the station held.' York was for him no longer, as he had called it in 1797, the seat of 'the little policy of a remote Colony,' it was his home. His family ties to Boston had been cut well before the War of 1812 and he was committed to York, where most of his success and all of his prospects lay.

After the war came, he resolutely stayed at York during its occupation by American troops. He ran no military risk – 'Our principal distress,' he wrote in 1815, 'arose from the incredible Expense of living enhanced by the demands for the Army' – but he did keep British commanders informed of enemy movements and he sent regular reports on the state of the occupied town to the commander-in-chief, Sir George Prevost. Less flamboyantly but just as firmly as Strachan, he insisted that the American commander maintain order and protect property against looting, whether by his own troops or by the civilians whom Powell thought chiefly responsible. The old charges of American sympathies, last raised briefly in 1807, were now totally implausible. By the end of the war, with Chief Justice Scott gravely ill and Gore returned from leave, Powell's ascendancy on the bench and his influence in council were unquestioned. He was appointed to commissions to hear charges of treason (11 April 1814) and claims for wartime losses (21 Dec. 1815). The assembly granted him £1,000 for his continued work on the Heir and Devisee Commission. When Scott became unable to chair the Legislative Council, Powell felt strong enough to drive a mean bargain. He accepted a seat on the council and its speakership on condition that Scott resign them at once, giving up the salary. When commissioned (21 March 1816) Powell took no salary, but he recovered the arrears two years later. And at last he received the post to which he had felt himself entitled 25 years before and in which he had so often acted: on 1 Oct. 1816 he was commissioned chief justice of Upper Canada.

The war and his own success resolved some complications in his toryism. He no longer had reason to be jealous of appointees from England, and his self-consciousness as an American loyalist was no longer defensive. His old sense of grievance and of colonial inferiority persisted only in the retention of personal animosities: memories of Haldimand, Simcoe, Osgoode, Elmsley, Hunter, and Allcock were an irritant all his life. He was incurably, perhaps deliberately, provincial in dress, manners, and speech – he bought his clothes in Boston, when at home gobbled food with his fingers, and his voice never lost its Yankee twang – but these had become assertions of his independent character, not obstacles to his success. He remained convinced that Upper Canada was by right destined to be a special loyalist province and that most of the refugees from New York in 1784 would have come to it if imperial delays in arranging their reception had not left their establishment in New Brunswick 'too far effected to think of removal.'

Upper Canada had become his country, with the imperial connection its essential support. The dangers that he saw to it arose not from imperial neglect or American aggression but from a spirit of democratic opposition and the pretensions of the legislative assembly. Much as he had disapproved of Robert Thorpe's combining his judgeship with political opposition in 1807, he had seen the main danger of Gore's early critics as lying in the popularity of Joseph Willcocks's newspaper, the *Upper Canada Guardian; or, Freeman's Journal*. He was worried enough by the radicalism of John Mills Jackson's *A view of the political situation of the province of Upper Canada* ... (London, 1809) to annotate his copy for a reply. The reply actually published, however, *Letters, from an American loyalist* (Halifax, 1810), was written not by Powell, as Robert Thorpe supposed, but by Cartwright. The assembly's claim to the sole initiative in introducing money bills had seemed to him a threat to the Legislative Council long before he took a seat on the latter, and he had denied the lower house's right to examine administrative expenditures even when it was asserted against the lieutenant governor he most actively disliked, Hunter. The assembly's final clash with Gore in April 1817, although it was led by

Robert Nichol, a land speculator whose interests coincided with his own, was for him evidence that the province was facing the same danger of democratic subversion that had driven him from Boston.

Perhaps he had simply been a malcontent for so long that he needed an object of disapproval. At any rate, from early in 1817 the references in his correspondence to the society of Upper Canada were increasingly gloomy. Having undertaken to raise his granddaughter Anne Murray Powell at York, he shared his wife's concern that 'there can in this place be no distinction of classes,' and that the young lady might therefore acquire plebian manners. It was probably as much a source of comfort as of concern for the Powells to find after the election of 1828 that 'the majority of the lower House are too *low* to render association pleasant,' but he had a growing sense that the province was departing from its original loyalist design. In 1822, by a passionate appeal to the 'true British and Loyal' origins of the province, he secured the rejection of an assembly motion to restore the original name of Toronto to the town of York. When the town was at last incorporated as the city of Toronto in 1834, he recorded his objections to 'the wild and Terrific Sound of TORONTO entailing upon its miserable Inhabitants the annual Curse of a popular Election to power to call forth all the bad passions of human nature.' His disapproval of popular elections might have been mitigated if he had lived to see his grandson John chosen alderman in Toronto in 1837 and mayor of the city, 1838–40.

His appointment as chief justice and his reputation as the most experienced member of the provincial administration did not end his capacity for making enemies. His neighbour in York, John Strachan, conceded in 1816 that Powell's 'knowledge of this Province (and perhaps of the Lower) exceeds that of any man living,' but he was offended that Powell's displacement of Scott was 'not conducted with delicacy.' The two soon disagreed over plans to endow the Church of England in the province. It was Powell's early view that the term 'Protestant clergy' in the Constitutional Act of 1791 did not confine the clergy reserves to the Church of England. He changed his mind some time before February 1828, when he sent to the secretary of state, William Huskisson, a pamphlet *On clergy reserves* objecting to Presbyterian claims to a share of the revenue from them. He held to the opinion that the reserves had been intended as a substitute for tithes, which Strachan hoped to introduce. Apart from any question of their legality, Powell thought that it would be impractical to attempt the collection of tithes. It was hard enough to find tenants for the clergy reserves, because settlers with so much land open to them required 'very strong baits to spend their labour on another's soil.' By May 1817 Strachan had relegated Powell to being only 'Perhaps' an adherent to the Church of England, although Powell's daughters were teaching in his Sunday school, and was regretting that Powell would be 'a little indifferent or inclined towards opposition but would be afraid to come forward boldly' in the Legislative Council against Strachan's plans for the clergy reserves.

Apart from disagreements on policy, they were both jealously ambitious men; if Strachan resented Powell's greater influence, Powell resented Strachan's pretensions. They were also rivals over which of them could claim to be the patron of John Beverley Robinson, Strachan's pupil who with Powell's support had risen to be acting attorney general (1812–14) and solicitor general (13 Feb. 1815). Powell helped Robinson to get two and a half years' leave to study law in England, but Robinson returned with London connections of his own that secured his appointment as attorney general (11 Feb. 1818) and left him little need of either Strachan's or Powell's favour. He also returned with an English wife, dashing the hopes of Powell's daughter Anne. As attorney general he soon found that Powell was not an easily managed judge. A new lieutenant governor, Sir Peregrine Maitland, found the same. The two parted company over a plan to tax unimproved lands. Maitland wanted legislation to make an existing tax effective. Powell objected to bringing the assembly into a matter that belonged to the courts and the administration. Maitland thought him pedantic, opinionated, and self-interested, while he thought Maitland neglectful of the royal prerogative and indifferent to local experience. In 1821 Powell was humiliated in the Legislative Council, which replaced him with Robinson as a commissioner to seek imperial help in settling the division of customs duties with Lower Canada. Powell, bitter at being displaced by his own protégé, believed that Robinson and Strachan had conspired against him; but it is more likely that his irascibility had simply offended too many people and would have made him a bad commissioner. There was worse to come: his daughter Anne, still enamoured of Robinson, defied her parents to follow him when he went to England as commissioner and was drowned in the wreck of the ship *Albion* (22 April 1822).

Powell's primary loyalty was always to the principles of English common law, not to the provincial administration of Upper Canada.

The pettiness, the ungenerous spirit of calculation, and the tendency to store up resentment which characterized his pursuit of office contrasted with his joviality and concern for defendants on the bench. His judicial humour was merely conventional: to a divided jury in a murder trial he explained that he could neither half hang the defendant nor hang half of him, so that the verdict amounted to acquittal. His faith in jury trials did not involve a high opinion of jurors' ability to understand the law or even to distinguish the relevant facts in a case. His instructions to juries left little doubt as to which witnesses he himself found credible or what verdict he expected. When the slave Jack York was tried for burglary in September 1800, Powell cautioned the jury emphatically against the self-interest of York's owner, James Girty, as a defence witness. York was convicted, and Powell sentenced him to death. A month earlier, he had pronounced the same sentence on William Newberry, the son of a loyalist, after his conviction on the same charge. If the two cases were parallel in law, however, Powell did not think that the practical results ought to be the same. He expected the letter of the law to be tempered with mercy; but mercy was properly a matter of prerogative discretion, not for the sympathy of juries. York, whose owner was connected with the Indian Department officers with whom Powell had clashed at Detroit, would have hanged if he had not managed to escape from jail; but Powell recommended to the lieutenant governor that Newberry's sentence be reduced. In a less dramatic case in August 1810, having charged the jury to convict a Methodist minister of illegally solemnizing marriages, he recommended a pardon.

Powell opposed the suspension of habeas corpus and the declaration of martial law during the War of 1812 and disliked the resort to special commissions on treason charges, because he thought that the regular course of the common law should not be interrupted for the sake of administrative expediency. In June 1814 he took turns with Chief Justice Scott and Mr Justice William Campbell in presiding over treason trials at the Ancaster assizes. He charged the jury to convict only 7 of the 50 defendants whose cases came before him *in absentia*, despite his personal belief that they all deserved punishment. He presided over 6 of the 18 trials at which prisoners appeared to plead not guilty. His harsh view of what constituted a treasonable act, uncompromisingly conveyed to the jury, resulted in the conviction of the luckless Jacob Overholser. Three others, against whom there was an abundance of evidence, were also convicted. Yet, of the four prisoners acquitted at Ancaster, two, Robert Troup and Jesse Holly, were tried when Powell was presiding; and his summaries of the evidence clearly anticipated their acquittal. He was, however, unwilling to extend anything beyond strict justice to traitors: unlike the other two judges, he made no recommendations for mercy.

In the years after he attained the post of chief justice, Powell's crankiness began to show itself on the bench. He had long felt that the rules of his court were inconveniently restricted by statute; his original procedures, after having been changed to a more elaborate English model by Elmsley, had been partly restored by the assembly in 1797, in an act 'ill comprehended by the Law makers ... almost compelling the Court to evade by Shifts, Anomalies and Inconsistencies which could not be reconciled.' He responded by an increasing, and to many it seemed an increasingly partisan, tendency to raise technicalities in the law, some of them of doubtful application. In August 1819, charging the jurors in an action for damages (*Randal* v. *Phelps*), he was said by the plaintiff Robert Randal to have threatened them with a writ of attaint – a writ unused for more than 100 years – if they did not follow his own preference for the defendant. He told the grand jury at Sandwich (Windsor) in 1821 that Indians, although subject by common law to the regular courts, might be exempt from their jurisdiction by treaty. The next year this remark became the basis for the defence in the murder trial of Shawanakiskie, whose conviction was therefore not confirmed until after reference to the imperial law officers four years later. In October 1823 the trial for infanticide of a servant girl, Mary Thompson, showed how far Powell had retreated into technicalities. The jury in convicting her recommended clemency, and Powell himself felt sympathy for her, but her pathetic circumstances were not enough to make him recommend a pardon. It was only after finding that some of the evidence he had allowed against her would not have been admissible in contemporary English practice that he changed his mind. Growing finicky about the letter of the law did not prevent him, near the end of his career, from becoming a little vague about the limits of his authority. In 1823 he refused to support the nomination as commissioner for war claims of Alexander Wood, to whose morals he objected. When Wood was appointed anyway on Strachan's recommendation, Powell as chief justice refused to swear him in. Wood successfully sued him for £120 damages. Powell tried to set aside the judgement by a bill of exceptions, which would have required Maitland to have acted as a judge in equity. Even when this dubious and obscure device failed, he refused to pay; and the debt was forgiven after his death.

His descent with advancing age into pedantic crankiness was not surprising in one who had always been so self-consciously insistent on the independence of the bench. Perhaps the only concession to administrative expediency that he ever made as a judge was to refrain in the winter of 1791–92 from questioning the continued legality of his Quebec commission after Upper Canada was proclaimed a separate province. In 1818 he caused inconvenience to the provincial administration in a series of decisions arising from the quarrels of the Earl of Selkirk [Douglas] in the Red River colony, some of which produced law suits in the courts of Upper Canada. To the chagrin of Robinson, he rejected charges of conspiracy against Selkirk; and to the outrage of Strachan he threw out most of the charges that Selkirk had brought against his opponents. In the most spectacular of his trials, however, Powell found himself trapped by the law into unwilling cooperation in a course of action that he thought unnecessary at best. He thoroughly disapproved of Robert Gourlay and recommended that land grants should be withheld from those who attended Gourlay's convention at York in July 1818, but he repeatedly advised that there were no legal grounds for prosecuting Gourlay's attacks on the administration of the province. When such grounds were found under the Sedition Act of 1804 and persisted in by Robinson in spite of Gourlay's obviously incapacitating illness, Powell had no choice but to pronounce a sentence of banishment.

Most of his cases, however, were mundane. He was uncompromising in the belief not only that convicted debtors should be imprisoned but that those accused of debt should be held in jail for trial. A survey of the province's 11 district jails in 1827 showed them to have a capacity of 298 cells, 264 of them occupied. Of the prisoners, 159 were being held for debt, and only 29 for felonies. In his last years on the bench he defied both the assembly and the councils by insisting that even legislators were not immune from arrest for debt. By 1824 his judicial duties had become as wearisome to Powell as his administrative work, and he planned to retire from the bench when he reached the age of 70 in November 1825.

He had made too many enemies to be left to a peaceful retirement. On 24 Oct. 1824 Mackenzie published a letter in the *Colonial Advocate* signed A Spanish Freeholder, which in the course of attacking the York élite lampooned Powell as 'Cardinal Alberoni, Lord Chief Justice of His Imperial Majesty of Spain.' It revived the old charges of his American sympathies at Detroit, alleged that he had obtained the chief justiceship in return for the harshness of his sentences at the Ancaster assizes, and condemned his behaviour on the bench in a case not named, but clearly that of Singleton Gardiner in 1822–23. Gardiner, a Middlesex farmer politically at odds with two local tory magistrates, Mahlon Burwell and Leslie Patterson, had brought a suit against them. Powell doubted that he had a good legal case, but by referring it to a jury he publicized the magistrates' abuse of their authority. He had acted correctly, but probably also with malice: Burwell in the assembly had promoted Robinson's appointment as commissioner in 1821, and he was the lieutenant of Thomas Talbot, towards whom Powell's enmity went back to Gore's administration. The Spanish freeholder was probably Burwell's younger brother, Adam Hood Burwell. Before it was printed in Mackenzie's paper, his letter received an approving notice, hinting broadly that it referred to Powell, in Charles Fothergill's *Weekly Register*. The letter soon received an equally intemperate reply in a pamphlet, *The answer to the awful libel of the Spanish freeholder, against the Cardinal Alberoni*, published under the pseudonym Diego ([York, 1824]).

Although Diego's pamphlet has been attributed to Powell and to his son-in-law Samuel Peters Jarvis, it is far more likely to have been the work of John Rolph, Jarvis's law partner and the recent victor over Mahlon Burwell in the election of 1824. Even before the pamphlet appeared, however, Powell's temper had led him into indiscretions that neither Maitland nor the councils had the slightest disposition to forgive. Refusing to be content with the grudging apology that Maitland had exacted from Fothergill, the angry old judge prepared two pamphlets of his own: *Correspondence and remarks, elicited by a malignant libel, signed 'a Spanish freeholder'* and *Spanish freeholder, app.A*. They had little to do with the recent libel: the first rehearsed his grievances against Maitland and his secretary, George Hillier; the second was addressed to his quarrel with Robinson in 1821; and both printed correspondence meant to be private. Beginning as the victim in the affair, he had turned himself in the eyes of the York administration into the chief offender. On 28 Jan. 1825 the Executive Council reported that he had laid himself open to the legal charge of repeating a libel, had abused the lieutenant governor's confidence, and had exposed 'measures of Government to public contempt and reprehension.' This rebuke was the more bitter because its author was John Strachan, the other two councillors present being the quiescent James Baby and the aged Samuel Smith. And although Strachan was by this time more an instrument of the lieutenant governor than an influence upon him, he felt secure enough to add that the chief justice had been sulking ever since Robinson's appointment as attorney general. Maitland refused to speak to Powell again except in the presence of a witness.

Powell was obliged to resign from the Executive Council in September 1825. He remained a legislative councillor until his death, but had to yield the speakership to William Campbell, who also succeeded him as chief justice (17 Oct. 1825). The secretary of state, Lord Bathurst, allowed Powell a pension of £1,000 (sterling) a year, in spite of the Executive Council's advice that he was 'unworthy of such a favour.' After almost three years in England, securing his pension and justifying his conduct, he returned in 1829 to spend his last years at York. He took no further part in public affairs, except to publish his correspondence with Maitland over the Wood affair.

No one else had put such sustained effort and such shrewd intelligence into the government of Upper Canada. In the history of the province, only Allcock in Hunter's administration and Robinson in Maitland's had greater influence than Powell. Strachan and Christopher Alexander Hagerman may have approached it, but only briefly. Powell had achieved prosperity and seen his surviving children comfortably established. Yet he was pessimistic about the state of the province, with reform politics rising in the House of Assembly, and he had been without real friends in the administration ever since Gore's departure. Gourlay had well nicknamed him 'Pawkie,' for his awkwardness in personal relationships never left him. As his health declined, so did his mental powers, obviously enough to give malicious satisfaction to his erstwhile allies, Robinson and Strachan. He reviewed the quarrels of his life, writing self-justifying memoranda on them, and publishing a rather maudlin outline of his life, *Story of a refugee* (York, 1833). In the end, all his formal successes brought him little pleasure and little faith in the future of his adopted province.

S.R. MEALING

Sir JOHN BEVERLEY ROBINSON
Lawyer, politician, and judge; b. 26 July 1791 at Berthier, Lower Canada, second son of Christopher Robinson and Esther Sayre; d. 31 Jan. 1863 in Toronto, Canada West.

John Beverley Robinson's father, a Virginia-born loyalist, had served in the Queen's Rangers in the closing stages of the Revolutionary War. The regiment was evacuated to New Brunswick and then disbanded in 1783. Christopher Robinson the following year married Esther Sayre, the daughter of a well-known loyalist clergyman, and in 1788 the family moved to Quebec, where John Beverley was born three years later. In 1792 they went to Kingston, Upper Canada, where Christopher was appointed surveyor general of the woods and reserves of Upper Canada; in 1794 he was called to be bar. Then, suddenly, on 2 Nov. 1798 he died. The Robinsons and their children, the eldest of whom was Peter, age 13, had moved from Kingston to York (Toronto) only a short time before.

The seven-year-old John Beverley was sent to Kingston to live with and be educated by his father's friend, the Reverend John Stuart, with whom he remained for four years. In 1799 the boy was enrolled in the school opened by the recently arrived John Strachan. Four years later Strachan was ordained a priest of the Church of England and given the charge at Cornwall, where he also re-established his school. Until 1807 Robinson lived in the Strachan household at Cornwall, his fees paid by Stuart and the executor of his father's estate, although Strachan had offered to take him free of charge. In the relationship of pupil and teacher was formed Robinson's life-long admiration for and friendship with Strachan.

At age 16 he left Strachan's tutelage to article in law with D'Arcy Boulton Sr, the solicitor general of Upper Canada. He mixed easily with the young people of York's society, worked hard, read avidly, and when the assembly was in session, watched many of its debates. As a former pupil of Strachan and a bright, personable young man, he was drawn into Chief Justice William Dummer Powell's circle, a connection which helped him in his early career. In 1811, after Boulton had been captured by a French privateer on his way to England, Robinson had to move into the office of John Macdonell (Greenfield), the newly appointed attorney general, to finish the last year of his articling.

During the spring of 1812, as war clouds blew north from the United States, Robinson volunteered to serve in one of the flank companies – special militia companies designed for regular service. When war was formally declared on 18 June 1812, these companies were called to train for active service. As one of those best qualified by education and family, Robinson was given an officer's commission. His role in the fighting was brief and glorious. He went with Isaac Brock to the southwestern area of the province in August to repel General William Hull's invasion, and commanded the volunteers who accompanied the regulars to take formal possession of Detroit. The volunteers then took parties of prisoners back to York. In September the York flank companies were sent to reinforce the Niagara frontier. Robinson was temporarily in command of one of these companies when the invaders crossed at Queenston. Arriving there just moments after Brock's death, Robinson's company was ordered on another charge like that in which Brock had been killed. John Macdonell, commanding the militia flank companies, was mortally wounded, and the companies fell back. They were then sent on the long flanking march which led to victory in late afternoon.

When he returned to York with prisoners, Robinson was congratulated on his new appointment. Only after asking was he told that he had been made acting attorney general of the province. Powell's recommendation had secured him the post, although he was just 21 years old and not yet even a member of the bar. It was subsequently rumoured that Robinson's friendship with Powell's daughter, Anne, had won him the appointment, but in his later life, when he was displaced from power, Powell would still insist that Robinson had been chosen for his abilities. From 1812 to 1814 the young Robinson performed the functions of attorney general, giving legal opinions to the provincial government and handling crown prosecutions of criminals.

His most serious problem in the context of the war was the potential disloyalty of many recent immigrants to the province; most of these were Americans who, in moving westward to obtain land, had crossed into Upper Canada, and their loyalty, whether to the United States or to Upper Canada, was not strong. In retrospect, it is clear that relatively few settlers actually deserted to the Americans during the war, but there was evidently sufficient disaffected talk to upset the government and its leaders. The American invasion intensified the disaffection, and some prominent critics of the government prior to the war, such as Joseph Willcocks, did desert. When a party of settlers from Norfolk County obtained arms from the Americans and returned to that area to terrorize their neighbours, a group of militia officers and volunteers acted to stop them and 18 of the renegades were taken in arms. The arrests gave government authorities the chance to make a deterrent example; the 18 were charged with treason and Robinson was made responsible for their prosecution. General Francis Rottenburg, the provincial administrator, urged haste in holding the trial, suggesting that some of the accused, as militiamen, might be court-martialled. Robinson resisted Rottenburg's pressure and proceeded methodically to assemble evidence to hold civil trials for treason. Three of the 18 prisoners from Norfolk agreed to turn crown's evidence. Nineteen persons were finally tried: 15 from Norfolk, two indicted at York, and two who had surrendered voluntarily. The grand jury also indicted another 50 persons who had fled to the United States. The trials began at Ancaster on 7 June 1814 and lasted two weeks. Fourteen were found guilty, one pleaded guilty, and four were acquitted. Robinson subsequently recommended to Sir Gordon Drummond, commander of the forces, that seven of the convicted should be executed, but Chief Justice Thomas Scott added another, and on 20 July eight men were hanged. It is doubtful whether the name 'Bloody Assize,' used subsequently to describe the trials, was really deserved. Those executed had committed treason in wartime.

Robinson had also to prosecute normal criminal offences and to appear at the assizes in each district of the province. He was expected to provide names of people suitable to act as justices of the peace, and many administrative procedures required the attorney general to act on behalf of the governor. In addition, he had his own private practice. When D'Arcy Boulton returned to Canada in the autumn of 1814 he was appointed attorney general because of his seniority in years of service. Robinson was given the post of solicitor general on 13 Feb. 1815.

The war's end and relief from its responsibilities gave Robinson, encouraged by Strachan, the opportunity to go to England for further legal studies and be called to the bar there. With Powell's aid, he was granted a leave of absence by the new provincial administrator, Sir George Murray, and on 1 Sept. 1815 left York. By late October he was settled in London, where he was received graciously by Lord Bathurst, the secretary of state for war and the colonies. Among his sponsors at Lincoln's Inn was the solicitor general of the United Kingdom. Between terms of study he travelled to the Continent and to Scotland and northern England. His leave of absence was twice extended at full pay and a third time on half salary.

One of Robinson's letters of introduction had been to William Merry, the under-secretary for war. On his first call at the Merrys he met 'an exceedingly fine, pretty little girl – a Miss Walker – there; very pleasant and engaging in her manner and appearance.' On 5 June 1817 he and Emma Walker were married, and in early July they left England for Upper Canada. Robinson continued as solicitor general for a few months, but the promotion of Boulton to the bench led to his appointment as attorney general on 11 Feb. 1818.

As attorney general, Robinson received a salary which seems to have been regarded as a retainer, as well as fees for his work for the crown. He still pursued his private practice, and on his return from England in 1817 he had been retained by the North West Company to represent them in litigation against Lord Selkirk [Douglas], an affair which would give him much notoriety. Following the destruction of his colony on the Red River by the Nor'Westers, Selkirk had hired a band of Swiss mercenaries, come to Canada, armed himself with a magistracy from Lower Canada, and headed west. He had seized Fort William (Thunder Bay) and its contents, expelling the NWC's people. The company, which had first contemplated civil action for damages, decided to press criminal charges of theft and assault against Selkirk in the Western District of Upper Canada. Robinson as attorney general was expected to prosecute. He returned his retainer to the company, but naturally was open to suspicion of a conflict of interest. His attempt to have an indictment preferred against Selkirk at Sandwich (Windsor) in September 1818 failed, as did a second bill, for conspiracy, which went to a jury. Shortly after, Robinson brought charges against the Nor-Westers for felonies against Selkirk and his people, but all the accused were acquitted.

The bitterness evident in the Selkirk affair was symptomatic of Upper Canada following the war. The collapse of the NWC's business in the American west simply exacerbated the already difficult economic situation in Upper Canada. The end of the war had brought a drop in farm prices. The war had also ended immigration from the United States so that land development had slowed and land prices had fallen. Damage to property, particularly in the Niagara peninsula, had been extensive and compensation was not yet being paid. The discontented soon found spokesmen.

Shortly after Robinson's return to Upper Canada in 1818, a Scot named Robert Gourlay had appeared to scout a piece of land his wife owned in the western part of the province. Unduly influenced by his wife's relatives, Thomas Clark and William Dickson, who were large-scale land developers and speculators in the Niagara area, Gourlay blamed the government for its restrictive development policies and its discouragement of immigration by Americans. In order to get information for a proposed book Gourlay composed a questionnaire, to be printed in the *Upper Canada Gazette*, which invited information, complaints, and suggestions for improvements from landowners. Both Powell and Samuel Smith, who was administering the government, approved the questionnaire and its intent, but Strachan, more suspicious, saw that it provided a vehicle for many Upper Canadians to express grievances.

Robinson, deeply involved in the Selkirk litigation, seems to have paid little attention to Gourlay until Smith, who had become alarmed by the spring of 1818, ordered him 'to watch the progress of' Gourlay for an 'occasion to check [him] by a criminal prosecution.' In June Robinson rendered an opinion that Gourlay's third printed address was 'grossly libellous' and 'entirely subversive,' but told Smith that prosecution should be considered carefully before any court action which might give importance to what would otherwise be an insignificant affair. Gourlay's meetings across the province Robinson considered 'dangerous,' however, because they pointed out 'the mode by which popular movements on pretences less specious than the present can be effected.'

Smith decided to act, giving the prosecution to Henry John Boulton, the solicitor general. Gourlay was acquitted of a charge of seditious libel. However, the new lieutenant governor, Sir Peregrine Maitland, at Strachan's urging, decided to silence the agitation, and the assembly, so recently critical of government, passed with only one dissenter an act 'to prohibit certain meetings within this province.' Under a statute of 1804 Gourlay was ordered to leave the province. He did not, and was arrested and jailed in mid January 1819. Robinson represented the crown at Gourlay's trial in Niagara the following August.

Convicted of ignoring the order to leave the province, Gourlay was banished from Upper Canada.

The government, alarmed by the discontent voiced by Gourlay, decided that a spokesman was needed in the assembly for the lieutenant governor and his advisers in the Executive and Legislative councils. At the general election held in midsummer 1820 Robinson was returned for the town of York, and the labour of preparing, presenting, and defending government measures in the assembly thereafter fell mostly on his shoulders. Although he told his friend John Macaulay that he was not fond of politics, Robinson continued in his leading role until 1828. The goals which Maitland and his chief advisers, Robinson and Strachan, set out to achieve in the 1820s were to promote economic development through the encouragement especially of British immigration and the construction of public works; the creation of a centrally controlled banking system like that advocated earlier by Hamiltonian federalists in the United States; the maintenance of the constitutional connection with Britain and of British political institutions; support for the Church of England, tolerance of some religious sects, and friendliness to Presbyterians and conservative Methodists; public support for elementary education; and avoidance of some aspects of the American experience, such as a wide electoral franchise and the separation of church and state.

When the assembly met in November 1821, Barnabas Bidwell, the member for Lennox and Addington, took his seat. Bidwell, a former member of the United States Congress and state official in Massachusetts, had come to Canada in 1810 fleeing a charge of malversation of government funds in that state. Robinson thought him a 'rascal' and was only too happy to promote any measure to get him out of the assembly. Like many other Upper Canadian Tories, Robinson saw Bidwell as the product of an American political system which, based on republicanism and reform, encouraged corruption and disloyalty in its adherents. The attorney general presented a petition to the house from some electors in Lennox and Addington who wanted Bidwell's election declared 'null and void,' thereby preserving the 'pure and unsullied ... dignity' of the assembly. After long debate in which Robinson played a prominent role, and a close decision, Bidwell was expelled and a bill was passed barring persons who had held office in the United States from standing for election. Yet Marshall Spring Bidwell, after two disputed by-elections, was returned in his father's place in the general election of 1824. The episode was the beginning of the alien question which was to divide the province after 1824.

Robinson was also personally concerned with the government's desperate need for revenue. The legislatures of Upper and Lower Canada had failed to agree since 1819 on the division of customs duties between them. Both houses of the Upper Canadian legislature decided that the attorney general should go to England to persuade the imperial government to intervene in the deadlock. Robinson, his wife, and brother Peter set off for London via New York in February 1822. Two days after their departure Anne Powell followed, against her family's wishes. She joined the Robinsons at Albany, but Robinson refused to allow her to sail from New York with them. She crossed in another packet which broke up in heavy weather on the rocky coast of southern Ireland. Anne's body was cast ashore. Her father, whose influence had waned with the coming of Maitland and who was in England seeking preferment, was crushed. Much against his wishes his daughter had pressed her attentions on Robinson for five years; the infatuation had now ended in tragedy.

Robinson's principal task in England was persuading the imperial government to enable Upper Canada to obtain some of the arrears in customs revenue due since 1819 and guarantee the province a share of future revenue. When he arrived he found, however, that the Colonial Office was considering a political union of the Canadas. A group of officials from Lower Canada, including Solicitor General Charles Marshall and Receiver General John Caldwell, were pressing for such a union to create a predominantly anglophone province whose legislature would be dominated by English-speaking members. The colonial secretary and his senior officials, anxious to solve the political impasse in Lower Canada, seemed receptive to the plan. Robinson joined in the talks, but soon realized the discussions were unlikely to assist Upper Canada and pressed to have provision dealing with the financial problem inserted in the union bill. He won his point, but when the bill was introduced in the British parliament, it met unexpected opposition. The government withdrew it and Robinson was asked to redraft the financial and trade provisions into a new bill, which became law as the Canada Trade Act in August 1822. The act established a comprehensive scale of import duties on goods from the United States entering Upper Canadian ports of entry on the Great Lakes. Shipping tolls on the St Lawrence were eliminated, and Upper

Canada was paid one-fifth of the duties collected from 1 Jan. 1819 to 1 July 1824, with its share to be revised every three years thereafter.

Robinson was now ready to return home, but Lord Bathurst held him back as an adviser. Meanwhile he was completing his terms at Lincoln's Inn. He also began negotiations with the under-secretary for the colonies, Robert Wilmot-Horton, with whom he had dealt on the proposed union and trade bills, for a proper post office in York. He pressed Wilmot-Horton and the crown law officers for an opinion on whether persons who had been resident in Upper Canada for seven years but had not taken the oath of allegiance and become naturalized British subjects were legally able to hold land. Both Robinson and Maitland felt that immigrants should be legally secure in their lands but they were also fearful of the potential disloyalty of unnaturalized Americans and sought legislation to exclude aliens from the assembly. The imperial government was not, however, ready to make a hard ruling at this time.

Robinson also raised the question of war damages. Two boards of inquiry had assessed the value of the damages at £230,000 and £182,130 respectively, but no money had been paid. An unofficial committee in England, consisting of Edward Ellice, Alexander Gillespie, and John Galt, had been pressing for payment to some Canadian claimants since the summer of 1821. In the fall of 1823 the British government authorized Maitland to make an initial payment from imperial funds of one quarter of the second award, if the provincial government would pay another quarter. The rest of the claim was also to be shared equally. The result was disappointing to Robinson because the province was already in severe financial difficulties. Galt recommended that payment of the imperial funds should be handled through Gillespie's company, a Montreal and London mercantile and forwarding house; the money would thus be channelled through a company which was a creditor of many Upper Canadian businessmen. Henceforth Robinson had little use for Galt.

During the summer and autumn of 1822, Robinson and Wilmot-Horton saw each other constantly, becoming close friends. In discussing colonial policy they developed a project to encourage British immigration to Upper Canada, believing it to be the way to offset the influence of predominantly American immigration, increase the anglophone population in Canada, and maintain the British connection with the colonies. To Wilmot-Horton the plan, which received government approval in January 1823, would make 'the redundant labour and the curse of the mother country, the active labour and blessing of the colonies.' As they considered potential immigrants, their attention turned to Ireland as a source and they received encouragement and help from the Irish administration. Robinson's brother, Peter, was asked by the colonial secretary to supervise the migration to Upper Canada.

Discussion of the union of the two provinces had continued through the summer and into the autumn. Although he personally disliked the idea, Robinson had not spoken against it until signs of adverse public opinion in the Canadas began to arrive. He disliked the enlarged and strengthened elective assembly, and felt that English-speaking Montreal merchants were merely trying to drag in Upper Canada to help with their own political and economic problems. When a new union bill was introduced to the British house early in 1823, it died in the face of vigorous opposition by the reformers who pointed out that French Canadians rejected the measure. Robinson in the meantime had been thinking of an alternative. His pamphlet on the plan, published in London in 1824, contained two papers by himself, one by Strachan, and one by James Stuart of Quebec. Robinson proposed a union of all the British provinces in North America as a more effective deterrent to United States encroachment, and he argued that government officials would be more secure, for a civil salary list would be easier to pass in a single legislature. The union would be federal in nature with provincial governments, constituted as they now were, looking after local matters. The union parliament would consist of an upper house with members summoned from the provincial legislative councils by the governor general, and a lower house elected by the provincial assemblies or by electors meeting a fairly high property-requirement franchise. This parliament would 'enact laws for the general welfare and good government of the United British Provinces.' It could deal with religious matters, subject to the restrictions in the Canada Act of 1791, with commerce, and with defence. It could levy tariffs, whereas the provincial governments would depend on excise and land taxes. Such a proposal would strengthen the British hold in North America, for the anglophone majority it would establish in the united legislature would be able to prevail over the French Canadians, whom Robinson considered conservative, agrarian, and opposed to commercial development. This concept of union, though rejected by the imperial government at the time, remained in Robinson's mind throughout his life.

In February 1823 he completed his terms at Lincoln's Inn and was called to the English bar. Strachan had urged him to attempt public life in England and was willing to provide a forgivable loan of £1,500 for the purpose. More tempting was Lord Bathurst's offer of the chief justiceship of Mauritius at £3,500 per year, a salary greater than Robinson would ever earn on the bench, plus a housing allowance. But he preferred to stay in Canada: 'One day or other we shall become a great people – that's certain – our boys may live to see it,' he wrote Macaulay. He returned to York in early July 1823.

Robinson came back to York as one of the two most influential men in the province. The friendship which he and Strachan shared with Lieutenant Governor Maitland and the supporters they had in the Legislative Council and House of Assembly gave them much influence. As chief officer of the government during the 1820s Robinson was not the leader of a cohesive political party based on a constituency of support for policies across the province, but he was at the centre of a group of administrative officers and government supporters in the legislature who were bound together by friendships and common interests. This group, called the Family Compact by its Reform opponents, had fought together in the War of 1812 and was distinguished by support of the British connection, opposition to the United States, a desire to assimilate French Canadians into a 'British' culture, and support of commercial development and the construction of public works. Strachan was the Compact spokesman on religious and educational matters, while Robinson led the group in the assembly. The Reformers nevertheless attributed more unity of purpose to the Compact than in fact existed; on banking, land, education, and religious policy the group was not always in agreement.

Robinson was once more returned for York in the 1824 elections, after a bitter campaign. William Lyon Mackenzie, in the newly founded *Colonial Advocate*, remarked: 'His abilities are greatly overrated; his flippancy has been mistaken by some for wit; but not by us. ... We account him to be a vain, ignorant man.' Robinson commented to the governor's secretary: 'Another reptile of the Gourlay species has sprung up in a Mr. Mackenzie. ... What vermin!' The narrowness of Robinson's victory signalled a change in the political temper of the assembly: in the coming sessions the house would be evenly divided between government supporters and opponents. The opposition was even more diffuse in character than the Compact group. Opposition members coalesced around a series of issues, primarily the alien question, but they were as often motivated by personal axes as by high ideals and ideology. There was a coterie of friends and supporters centred around Marshall Spring Bidwell, a few radicals influenced by the British Reform movement, a group who opposed the Church of England and its claims to church establishment, individuals some of whom disliked the government's land and development policies, or, like Robert Randal, had personal grievances against the government.

The first session of the 9th parliament opened in January 1825 with much talk and little legislation. But behind the scenes the great issue of the 1820s was developing. The British courts had ruled that persons who had remained in the United States after 1783 and their descendants could not continue to be considered British subjects. Lord Bathurst in passing on the decision to Maitland late in 1824 advised him that neither Bidwell could sit in the assembly. But because so many people in Upper Canada would be adversely affected, in both their right to hold land and their civil rights, the dispatch was not acted on. Instead, Robinson and the colonial secretary discussed the matter when the former went to England in the summer of 1825. Since the imperial parliament would not act at that time, it was agreed that a bill of limited scope should be passed by the Upper Canadian legislature to confer the civil rights and privileges of British subjects upon those who had resided in Upper Canada for seven years and who would renounce their American citizenship.

There had been spirited public discussion of the issue for months prior to the meeting of the assembly in November 1825. Robinson's draft bills passed through the council but when he presented them to the house, explaining how the legislation would solve the problem, a storm of protest erupted. Robinson felt that the opposition deliberately misrepresented the government's position in arguing that the bills were a gratuitous insult to people born or long resident in Upper Canada. The opposition also questioned the right of a colonial government to act in this matter and the house passed an address asking the imperial parliament to intervene.

This parliament then gave the Upper Canadian legislature the power to naturalize persons resident in Upper Canada who met the qualifications of British naturalization laws, but instructions for modified legislation had not been received when the Upper Canadian legislature reconvened in December 1826. Robinson, knowing what the instructions from England would be, found himself fighting a politically popular bill introduced by John Rolph, which provided that all resident settlers were to become British subjects unless they registered their dissent. When the imperial government's instructions finally arrived, Rolph's bill was amended by the attorney general to conform with them. Once more the opposition took exception to the Colonial Office's requirement that persons register their naturalization and again take an oath of allegiance. Robinson felt that they were arguing against the judgement of the courts and against a measure which would relieve people of disabilities arising from that judgement. After angry debate and the defection of members from the opposition, the amended bill was passed.

The enraged opposition sent Robert Randal to England to protest. Randal consulted both the colonial secretary and the radical parliamentary opposition; fear of raising the issue in parliament forced the new colonial secretary, Lord Goderich, to agree to instructions for a new bill which passed the Upper Canadian legislature in May 1827. All who had received land grants, held office, taken the oath of allegiance, or been resident in the province before 1820 were to be admitted to the rights of British subjects. No provision for renunciation of allegiance to foreign countries was made. This new bill was acutely embarrassing to Robinson and the government party in Upper Canada. After they had patiently accepted Colonial Office dictation and defended the unpopular decisions made, a new colonial secretary had bowed to pressure by the Upper Canadian opposition and undermined the colonial administration.

While the alien question was still at full heat in 1827, D'Arcy Boulton's replacement on the bench arrived in York. He was John Walpole Willis, an equity lawyer, who was expected to serve only briefly on the Court of King's Bench until the provincial legislature created a court of equity in Upper Canada. He developed a dislike of Robinson, perhaps because by now so many in the province deferred to his legal abilities. The conflict came into the open when Willis presided over the trial of Francis Collins, the fiery newspaper editor, whom Robinson was prosecuting on three charges of libel. Previously, and in the course of his trial, Collins charged that Robinson had been remiss in not laying criminal charges against some of those involved in the Samuel Peters Jarvis–John Ridout duel ten years before, and in not prosecuting those who had destroyed William Lyon Mackenzie's press in 1826. From the bench, Willis agreed with Collins. Over Robinson's objections Willis ordered prosecution in both cases. The seconds in the duel, Solicitor General H.J. Boulton and James Edward Small, were acquitted of murder charges, and Mackenzie's tormenters were fined five shillings. Robinson deeply resented the criticisms of him implicit in these prosecutions. Willis urged him to drop the libel charges against Collins, who had precipitated the furore, but Robinson merely held them over until the fall assizes. Shortly after, Willis argued that the Court of King's Bench could not act without all its three members present, as it had done in the past. He withdrew from the bench, and thereby not only stopped the functioning of the provincial courts but brought into question the validity of all the court's previous decisions. Maitland, after seeking the advice of Robinson and Boulton, removed Willis from the bench.

The alien question, Willis' removal, and criticism of the clergy reserves were province-wide issues in the election of 1828. Robinson again won his seat narrowly, but his work was made more difficult by the fact that the new house was overwhelmingly anti-government and anti-Anglican. When Chief Justice William Campbell retired in the spring of 1829, Robinson was appointed to replace him and resigned his seat in the assembly. He had refused the appointment in 1824 because he could not afford to give up his law practice for the salary of the chief justice. Robinson's elevation to the bench removed him in large part from political struggles, although his appointment carried with it the speakership of the Legislative Council and the presidency of the Executive Council.

As government leader in the assembly throughout the 1820s Robinson had demonstrated a legalistic and constitutional approach to the solution of problems which the opposition had handled in a more openly 'political' fashion. He had shown a consistent concern for sponsoring a controlled, commercially based development of the province through the encouragement of immigration, the construction of public works, and the discouragement of land speculation. Although much interested in the welfare of the Church of England, he at times disagreed with John Strachan's passionate advocacy of its rights. Robinson seemed to have taken for granted the Anglican dominance of education and had been instrumental in preventing the sale of the clergy reserves to the Canada Company in 1826. Nevertheless, his critics in the assembly saw him grow in tact and caution, and he had been successful in pushing much basic housekeeping legislation through a sharply divided assembly.

Robinson lost his real influence with the appointment of the new governor, Sir John Colborne, in August 1828. Colborne did not lean on the advice of a few Compact councillors as had his predecessor. He was a conservative, but many of the leading men in the Compact party distrusted him. However, when the Reform-dominated assembly demanded that Robinson be removed from his political posts in the councils in accordance with the 1828 Canada Committee report which had recommended political independence for the judiciary, Colborne was quick to defend Robinson's worth. Although Robinson might not have objected to losing the posts 'to save him from the drudgery of colonial politics,' Colborne felt that he should continue at least in the speakership because his legal experience would be helpful in drafting legislation. The colonial secretary accepted the substance of the assembly's demand and ruled that no judges were to serve in the executive or legislative councils in future. Robinson remained a legislative councillor but was advised to confine his contributions to giving legal advice. He and Colborne became friends and Colborne consulted him on occasion over provincial affairs. Robinson remained the senior Tory in the province, a kind of figurehead. No one emerged in the assembly with his knowledge or effectiveness in debate. Only once, in 1832, did he break his cautious abstention from politics: to pen the reply of the Legislative Council to a dispatch from Lord Goderich which seemed to pay too much attention to Mackenzie and his grievances.

Robinson's relations with Colborne's successor, Sir Francis Bond Head, were closer, and more cordial, though in personality they differed. Certainly many radicals saw them as working too closely together. Both agreed that an outward show of calm was necessary as rumours of rebellion began circulating in Toronto in the summer and fall of 1837. The chief justice willingly stood in the ranks of militia called out to resist Mackenzie. On 7 December, when the militia marched north to Montgomery's Tavern to defeat the rebels, Robinson sat in his study writing a history of the rebellion. Because of his advice and support during the crisis, Head recommended that Robinson be knighted, but Robinson declined the honour.

As chief justice, Robinson presided over the trials of those charged with insurrection or treason in connection with the rebellion and the Patriot invasions from the United States in 1838. Over 900 had been arrested, but most were released without trial and bound to keep the peace. Robinson presided daily over the actual hearings and passed sentence on those convicted. Thirty-seven men were sentenced to transportation or had death penalties commuted to that punishment, but on Robinson's recommendation only 25 were actually transported. Others were given prison sentences of a few years. However, it was Robinson's view that 'some examples should be made in the way of capital punishment,' and Samuel Lount and Peter Matthews, both leaders in the rebel movement who had pleaded guilty to high treason, were hanged.

Through discussions of the treatment of insurgents, Robinson came into contact with Sir George Arthur, who had relieved Head in early 1838. Although the two were carefully formal to begin with, Arthur too succumbed to the knowledge and experience of his chief justice and relied upon his 'friendly advice.' When Governor General Lord Durham [Lambton] visited Upper Canada for a few days in July 1838 he too took the opportunity to seek Robinson's views on a proposal to federate the British North American provinces in an elaborate political system of local and general governments with ill-defined areas of jurisdictional competence. Robinson made a number of comments on the scheme, objecting most strongly to suggestions that the legislative councils be abolished and that the elected assemblies control the entire provincial revenues. He had few illusions that his discreet advice would be heeded because 'nothing but a notorious, factious opposition to government in the adviser is acknowledged as giving any value to Colonial opinions.'

Ill health forced Robinson to ask for a leave of absence in the summer of 1838 so that he could seek medical advice in England. He and his family stayed with his wife's friends at Cheltenham. In December Colonial Secretary Lord Glenelg asked him to come to London to discuss Canadian affairs. It was the first of many interviews with influential British politicians, including Sir Robert Peel, the Conservative leader, who, in a period of unstable Whig governments, were reluctant to move decisively in formulating Canadian policy. At this time Robinson visited Durham, and found him still undecided about what to recommend in his report, trying to please both 'the ballot and short parliament people' (radicals in England) and the British in the Canadas.

Durham's report was tabled in the House of Commons in February 1839. To his wife Robinson described it as 'horrid,' and he saw the sections on Upper Canada, which criticized the Family Compact, as 'disgraceful and mischievous.' He gave his opinion to Peel and the Duke of Wellington without delay. Once more, as in 1823, Robinson pointed out to colonial office officials that the union of the Canadas

Durham recommended would only drag Upper Canada into the difficulties in Lower Canada. He foresaw that the assembly proposed would be closely divided between French and English and would give 'no assurance of anything but bitter and hateful conflict.' To attempt to submerge the French Canadians in the legislature would be to force them into a 'close phalanx against the British portion of the Legislature,' without any guarantee that the anglophones would remain 'faithful to British supremacy.' To give the governor power temporarily to suspend elections was unfair to all the colonies. Reinvestment of control of colonial lands in the British government to encourage immigration was unwise since the colonial governments would be unwilling to give it up. The abolition of the clergy reserves he rejected, for the Protestants of the province would be left 'destitute of any public provision to support the public worship of God, and to ensure the maintenance of religious instruction.' The proposal that the governor carry out his responsibilities through heads of departments in whom the legislature placed its confidence was absurd. 'The Assemblies of the Provinces ... displayed a degree of selfishness (if not corruption), a prodigality, a negligence, a recklessness beyond what one can think credible ... it is happy indeed that they have not had higher and greater interests at their mercy.' Such a form of government would lead to 'a servile and corrupting dependence upon Party'; it would be without parallel in the British empire and 'in comparison with it the Republican Government of the United States would be strongly conservative.'

In the following weeks Robinson made a number of his own confidential recommendations to deal with Canada's problems. What was needed were guarantees against American aggression, the restoration of order so that investment might once more flow into the Canadas, governmental forms to prevent the recurrence of disturbances, and financial assistance to Upper Canada to offset the effects of suspended immigration and a decline in commerce and revenue. Robinson's alternatives to Durham's plans for union included the annexation of Montreal to Upper Canada and the maintenance of separate provincial governments, with Lower Canada to be governed for up to 15 years by an appointed executive and a partly elected, partly appointed legislative council. To better control the rebellious Lower Canadian population he suggested various measures to assimilate French Canadians into the English language culture, including the use of English in government and the courts and the substitution of English for French civil law in Lower Canada.

In April Robinson came up to London. He saw Peel regularly and conferred with many leading Whigs and Tories in an effort to discredit Durham's report. The weakness of Lord Melbourne's ministry gave him some hope and the abandonment of a union bill offered in parliament in June 1839 seemed to augur well. Throughout the summer while he consulted physicians and tried to rest Robinson continued writing to Tory leaders and to supporters of the Anglican establishment and the clergy reserves.

During the summer the government placed the Canadian issue at the top of its list of priorities: Lord John Russell was appointed colonial secretary in August and shortly afterwards Charles Poulett Thomson was appointed governor general of British North America. Robinson, who had had his leave extended to 1 March 1840, now anticipated for himself even more effort to fight the union. In the autumn of 1839 he began a short book criticizing the proposal. After a long introductory chapter on the geography and economy of the British North American provinces, it gave a detailed argument against the union bill as presented in June 1839. With the publication of *Canada, and the Canada Bill* in February 1840, Robinson had shot his bolt against the union project.

His efforts in the winter and spring of 1840 were turned to the clergy reserves. He met with leaders of the high church party in parliament such as Sir Robert Inglis and Henry Phillpotts, bishop of Exeter, to present his views. Early in 1839 the Tory majority in the Upper Canadian legislature had passed a bill providing that the income from the clergy reserves be applied to 'religious purposes' in a manner to be determined by the British parliament, rather than by the Upper Canadian legislature. This reinvestment of the reserves in the crown was rejected by the British government on the grounds that the drafting of the bill had constitutional defects. Robinson was not unhappy at the rejection because he felt that this reinvestment merely opened use of the reserves' income to future political pressures. An act passed in August 1840 by the imperial parliament was something of an improvement, built on the principle of dividing the reserves among denominations, but giving a bigger share to the Church of England. Robinson's cultivation of pro-Anglican British politicians had proved effective. Most Anglicans in Upper Canada were aware that the imperial act was better than they could have obtained in Upper Canada, though few in 1840 could have been happy that this legislation provided support for other denominations as well.

The winds of change over the winter of 1839–40 were blowing hard. The Upper Canadian assembly voted to support the proposed union, and, in consequence, the English Tories, who had been neutral although sympathetic to Robinson and his arguments, decided to support the union measure. But Robinson's consorting with the Tories in England and his absence from the bench began to excite comment. In mid March Russell told Robinson that his presence in England was no longer required or welcome. After a few weeks of visiting and farewells, the Robinsons embarked from London.

The new union bill was introduced in the spring of 1840 just as they left. The Canadas were to be reunited for legislative and executive purposes. Equal representation in the assembly was accorded to each of the former provinces in order to ensure anglophone domination. Other recommendations made by Durham were ignored or dealt with in different ways. The new governor general of the Canadas engineered an Upper Canadian solution to the clergy reserves by which one-half of the revenues were to be divided between the Anglicans and the Presbyterians, the other half, when funds permitted, among all denominations. He also introduced many of the administrative reforms advocated by Durham. But many of the points Robinson had argued had been accepted and incorporated in the bill. Legislative councillors were to hold office for life, executive responsibility to the legislature was not specified, and the courts were clearly established; indeed, his only objection would probably have been to the union itself and the basis of representation with its potential for political deadlock between French and English.

When Robinson and his family returned to Toronto the political climate of Upper Canada had completely changed. As a judge, he was effectively divorced from political life, and as an old Compact Tory he was excluded from political power. He made some effort to maintain the unity of the high Tories in Upper Canada, but their exclusion from office made this a difficult task. He no longer had personal contact with the governors, although Sir Charles Metcalfe, after reading *Canada, and the Canada Bill*, corresponded with him.

Much of his time outside his legal duties in the next 20 years was devoted to the Church of England. He served on the executive of the Church Society, the body charged with managing the temporal affairs of the Toronto diocese as well as carrying out good works. He became a vice-president of the Society for the Propagation of the Gospel and was active in the Society for Promoting Christian Knowledge. He believed firmly in the union of church and state and the need for an established church because he felt the only secure basis for civil authority was religion. Hence he defended the clergy reserves, although his views about how to do so were more liberal than Strachan's. He was friendly with the leaders of the high church party in England and associated with them in Canada, but was never attracted by the Oxford Movement or the Tractarians or their followers in Canada. Whether or not he ever accepted a separation of church and state as did Strachan is uncertain. He was always hesitant to make religion a subject of political contention.

Robinson was not narrow in his religious views. He gave land and support to the Methodists because he felt their preachers had brought the Christian message to the frontier when no one else had. He appeared publicly several times in the 1840s and 1850s at meetings of the British and Foreign Bible Society, an organization to which normally only evangelical Anglicans belonged. He had played an active role in establishing King's College, an Anglican university in Toronto, and strongly defended its denominational character. 'A college or university which professes to take the range of the sciences – and to send forth a youth in the world qualified to act his part in it – and yet carefully abstains from including any religious doctrine must be an abortion,' he told Strachan in 1844. Following Robert Baldwin's act to secularize King's College in 1849, he advised Strachan that he should not be satisfied with merely a theological seminary, but that the Anglicans, like the other major denominations, should have their own college. Strachan and his supporters obtained a charter for the University of Trinity College in 1852; Robinson became its first chancellor, serving until his death.

In 1849 Governor General Lord Elgin [Bruce] recommended Robinson for a knighthood as one means of placating the ultra Tories. Robinson told Elgin's secretary rather cynically that he would accept but that he hoped responsible government would not lead to a too generous creation of knighthoods. He was made instead a Companion of the Bath in 1850, but in 1854 was created a baronet of the United Kingdom.

His work as chief justice of the Court of Queen's Bench naturally occupied most of his time. He worked hard; there was seldom an arrears of business in the court. In fact, Robinson had specifically asked for legislation to allow the court to convene and render judgements after the regular terms as a means of speeding up procedure. The *Upper Canada Law Journal* noted in its obituary: 'Few opinions will ever command more respect or carry more weight than those delivered by Sir John Robinson. They are remarkable for their lucid argument, deep learning, strict impartiality and pure justice.' D.B. Read observes that he tended towards severity in criminal matters. As a judge he was courteous and careful, if anything rather conservative. No man has served longer as chief justice than did Robinson, and his judgements are among those which merit a full examination by a legal historian of Canada.

His judgements seldom excited controversy. Two did, however: one in 1859 in which he gave a light sentence to an Orangeman charged with attempted murder following a public brawl, and the John Anderson extradition case which aroused intense public interest in both Canada and Britain. Anderson, a slave from Missouri, had, it was alleged, murdered a man in making good his escape to Canada. In 1860 the Court of Queen's Bench presided over by Robinson granted Anderson's extradition to the United States, but the Court of Common Pleas overturned the ruling on a technicality.

Robinson's years on the bench were financially comfortable, but his income was less than it might have been if he had remained at the bar. Indeed, with the help of his prosperous private practice in the 1820s he had built one of Toronto's best homes in Beverley House. He also accumulated a good deal of land, some of which he inherited from his brother Peter in 1838. In 1852 he owned 300 acres in Simcoe County, over 1,000 acres in York, some land in Ontario and Peel counties, and some 29 parcels elsewhere. Nevertheless he was by no means wealthy. He and his wife had four sons and three daughters. Three sons became lawyers; the youngest entered the British army and attained the rank of major-general. His second son, John Beverley, entered politics, serving briefly in the cabinet before confederation and as lieutenant governor of Ontario in the 1880s.

Robinson had never really liked the notoriety of political life; his career on the bench was probably most satisfying because it removed him from politics. He never seems to have thought of power as such; rather he accepted responsibility to govern and to be a public servant. He saw himself as part of the governing class, the 'regularly bred,' who must take up his duty. He thought that he acted in a liberal or benevolent way on principles which would preserve and strengthen an essentially good Upper Canadian society. His loyalist background, his education by Strachan, and his experience during the War of 1812 shaped his attitudes fundamentally. Looking back from the 1840s, he argued that the war had given Upper Canadians a sense of identity, a sense of anti-Americanism and of pro-British sentiment. He would long remember that many Upper Canadians had been lukewarm in defence against the United States, and remained suspicious of American-born settlers and those whose politics were 'republican.' Indeed, maintenance of the British connection was his major goal, a goal which could be attained only by encouraging immigration from Britain and by establishing British political institutions in Canada. That British political institutions changed during his lifetime made it difficult for him to adjust his thinking.

He saw what he described as 'ancient and venerable institutions,' 'respect for rank and family,' 'the power of wealth,' and 'the control of numerous landlords over a grateful tenantry' as part of the essential fabric of a stable society. That these did not exist in Canada meant that government depended on 'the presumed good sense, and good feeling of an uneducated multitude' which periodically could be led astray. Even late in life, when he had begun to feel that he had often been mistaken in his understanding of public wants, he still distrusted democracy. He believed always in a balanced constitution – an elected assembly, an independent upper house to act as a check on the assembly, and an independent executive which could be checked by both houses of the legislature and check them in turn. A society governed in this way could prosper through the work of its people.

Robinson was always a supporter of British immigration and of development. He subscribed to the stock of the Welland Canal Company and the Desjardins Canal Company because of the assistance they would give to the Upper Canadian economy. Nevertheless, as his comments on the United States in the 1830s indicate, he did not favour extravagant development and widespread credit to encourage it.

He was also an early advocate of British North American union. From 1823 onwards he saw such a union as preferable to the union of the two Canadas. The control of Canada by its anglophone majority could only be ensured by bringing the Atlantic provinces into the union. By the 1840s many Upper Canadian Tories shared his views. His loyalism, his Anglicanism, and his distrust of democracy did not make him into a colonial, however. He would visit England often, be friendly with that country's leading men, and be offered attractive opportunities outside Canada, either in England or in other colonies, but his sense of duty and his love of Upper Canada kept him a Canadian. Indeed, in the last years of his life, he reconciled himself to the concept of responsible government as he saw it working and realized that it was the means by which the British connection could be maintained.

In the spring of 1861 Robinson suffered such a severe attack of gout that his work on the bench had to be curtailed. He was able to resign from the Queen's Bench on 15 March 1862, at which time he was appointed presiding judge of the Court of Error and Appeal. That fall he was again seized cruelly by gout but continued to serve until pain forced him to retire to his home in January 1863. On 28 January the aged Bishop Strachan gave him communion, and three days later he died.

ROBERT E. SAUNDERS

PETER RUSSELL

Office holder, politician, and judge; b. 11 June 1733 in Cork (Republic of Ireland), only son of Richard Russell and his first wife, Elizabeth Warnar; d. 30 Sept. 1808 in York (Toronto), Upper Canada.

Peter Russell was the son of an improvident Irish army officer who claimed without much evidence to be related to the Duke of Bedford. His formal education consisted of boarding for four years with the Reverend Barton Parkinson, first at Cork and then at Kinsale, where he shared studies and a bed with his first cousin William Willcocks and where he became 'a very pretty Schollar' according to Parkinson. For six months in 1751 he attended St John's College, Cambridge, but his university career ended abruptly because of his extravagance. He considered entering the army, navy, or trade; he chose the army because he thought he was too weak for the navy and too old for his first choice, trade. Unfortunately there was neither enough money to buy his commission nor enough influence to get one without purchase; Russell had to wait for the Seven Years' War to enter the army.

In 1754 Major-General Edward Braddock, commanding officer of Russell's father's regiment, the 14th Foot, and newly appointed commander-in-chief in North America, advised Russell to go there as a volunteer because chances of a commission were good. Russell arrived in South Carolina on 21 May 1755, but delayed joining Braddock's army because of sickness, difficulties in communication, and high living. In July he heard of Braddock's defeat and death, and of his own appointment as an ensign in the 14th, still at Gibraltar. Russell stayed in North America until November, finally arriving in Gibraltar the following May. From July to October 1756 he took part in the second abortive attempt to relieve the garrison on Minorca. After becoming a lieutenant on 8 May 1758, Russell returned to England, became dissatisfied, and 'quitted his commission in a pet.' Realizing, however, that he was too old to begin a new career he accepted Lieutenant-Colonel John Vaughan's offer of a lieutenancy in a new regiment, the 94th Foot, raised for service in North America. Commissioned on 12 Jan. 1760, Russell sailed for North America on 26

August, serving as adjutant and paymaster mostly in the West Indies until the reduction of the regiment on 24 Oct. 1763.

In August 1763 Russell arrived in New York owing more than £1,000 after a disastrous final week of gambling in Martinique. Successful gambling in New York enabled him to settle his army accounts; even greater success in Virginia brought him a 462-acre tobacco plantation 42 miles west of Williamsburg. Here Russell lived on half pay for almost eight years, hiding from his creditors and longing for capital to enter the lucrative slave trade. To raise funds he once more tried gambling, but again he lost; to pay his Virginia debts he had to sell his estate and return to England. Arriving home on 14 Oct. 1771, he was beset with demands for payment of his Martinique debts, and in November 1773 he was forced to fly to the Netherlands where he stayed for ten months before returning. After a humiliating residence within the bounds of Fleet prison he was discharged on 7 Oct. 1774 under the Insolvent Debtors Relief Act.

War in America once more gave him an occupation. On 15 Aug. 1775 Russell was commissioned lieutenant in an additional company of the 64th Foot raised for the war. For several years he recruited in Ireland; finally on 25 Feb. 1778 he sailed for America because promotions were given only to officers there. He succeeded to the captain-lieutenancy of the 64th on 18 August and in October became an assistant secretary to the commander-in-chief, Sir Henry Clinton. After taking part in the capture of Charleston, Russell was appointed judge of the Vice-Admiralty Court of South Carolina on 19 May 1780 by Clinton, but this appointment was disallowed and given to a lawyer with prior claim. On 19 December Russell finally received his captaincy in the 64th. He sold it nine months later at an inflationary price of £2,000 just before leaving with Clinton on his unsuccessful attempt to relieve Lieutenant-General Charles Cornwallis at Yorktown, Va. On 1 Jan. 1782 Clinton appointed him superintendent of the port of Charleston and on 15 April captain in the Royal Garrison Battalion, but Clinton's career in America was over, and on 13 May 1782 he and Russell sailed for England.

Because of the sale of his commission Russell for the first time in his life had money, which he showered on his father, his half-sister Elizabeth, and even the mendicant Willcocks family. By 1786, when his father died leaving him only debt and the responsibility for Elizabeth, Russell was once more a poor man begging unsuccessfully for insignificant posts. Since his return to England he had helped Clinton in his controversy with Cornwallis and had written a monumental history of the American campaigns attacking Cornwallis. To protect Russell it was decided to publish it under Clinton's name, although as Clinton wrote, 'You have already uttered too many galling truths to be forgiven.' Russell's book was too controversial to be published, and it finally appeared under Clinton's name in 1954.

In 1790, then, when Upper Canada was about to come into existence, Russell was struggling to support himself and Elizabeth on a captain's half pay, his patron having lost all influence through his quarrel with Cornwallis. Clinton and other fellow officers, including Simcoe whom Russell had met in America, still tried to help, and in the summer of 1790, when Simcoe was promised the lieutenant governorship of Upper Canada, it seemed as if Russell too was to be fortunate. In October he accepted the position of secretary to Andrew Elliott, who was going as British minister to the United States, but Elliott eventually declined the posting, destroying Russell's prospects. Simcoe then recommended Russell to Home Secretary Henry Dundas on 12 Aug. 1791 for appointment as Upper Canadian receiver and auditor general with seats on the Executive and Legislative councils. The appointments were approved in September, although Russell's commission was not issued until 31 Dec. 1791 and not received until a year later. He still hoped for something better since he would have to give up his half pay in return for only £300 a year, but when nothing materialized he left England in the spring with his half-sister, Chief Justice William Osgoode, and Attorney General John White, arriving at Quebec on 2 June 1792.

When Russell arrived in Upper Canada he was 59, much older than most of his colleagues. His closest friends were probably the ablest members of Simcoe's government – Osgoode, White, and Surveyor General David William Smith – but he disagreed with White and Smith in their criticism of Simcoe's autocratic methods. With Simcoe himself he was on good if not cordial terms. He was a faithful member of the councils and did his share in establishing the working machinery of government. Because all senior government officers were ill-paid, bickering over their relative portion of fees began early and continued for many years; in this squabbling Russell also did his share.

In the beginning there were only four executive councillors, with Russell's name the last on the list. In 1794, however, after Chief Justice Osgoode was transferred to Lower Canada and only one judge was left on the Court of King's Bench in Upper Canada, it was Russell whom Simcoe appointed a temporary puisne judge, with a salary of £500 a year. On 6 July 1795 Russell took over Osgoode's former position as speaker of the Legislative Council. On 1 Dec. 1795 Simcoe requested leave of absence, and recommended that Russell, 'the senior Executive Counsellor, (not a Roman Catholick) and ... in all respects the proper person,' be chosen to administer the government. Russell was appointed administrator on 20 July 1796, and on the following day Simcoe left York. At 63, Russell was in a position of authority for the first time in his life.

Russell's administration began auspiciously with the peaceful transfer of six border posts from the British to the Americans under the terms of Jay's Treaty. Even the American occupation of Fort Niagara (near Youngstown), N.Y., within firing range of Fort George (Niagara-on-the-Lake), went off smoothly without the repercussions that were feared. It was a good beginning but Russell's early days in office were marred by the discovery that Simcoe had left him only 12 official documents, taking with him all his other papers including his correspondence with London and Quebec. Throughout his administration, the unfortunate Russell was ignorant of the intentions of both Simcoe and the British authorities on every aspect of government.

At this period the granting of land was the most important responsibility of government. By 1796 the machinery for handling it was grinding slowly and capriciously, not keeping up with the demand for crown grants or for the transfer of property. There was justifiable fear that speculators were acquiring too much land. Russell had always been interested in the problem: 25 years earlier, on his return from Virginia, he had tried to interest the government in his program of reform for land-granting abuses there. In Upper Canada he tightened up the system, closing loopholes and making it more efficient. The loyalist lists were revised; claims for privilege through family relationships were restricted; the surveyor general's office was to keep a list of undesirables; every petitioner was to state clearly what land he had already been granted and this declaration was to be checked; every petition was to be approved by the lieutenant governor or the administrator; no land was to be transferred until the deed had been issued; the system for the collection of fees was revised.

Because of previous irregular land transfers an act was passed in June 1797 to secure land titles, establishing a land commission to settle individual cases. The Heir and Devisee Commission reported the following month on the grants of townships to proprietors who had agreed to settle and improve them. Simcoe had already rescinded township grants to several proprietors including Russell's cousin, William Willcocks, who had accomplished nothing. Russell went even further and rescinded all township grants, giving compensation for actual settlement only. The most famous instance involved William Berczy, who lost Markham Township. His vehement protest was in vain for 'all the Branches of this Government,' according to Russell, 'have but one opinion' and thus settlement by township proprietors ended. During Russell's administration there was one other attempt at mass settlement, wished on him by the British government. In the autumn of 1798, 40 French *émigrés* led by Joseph-Geneviève de Puisaye, Comte de Puisaye, arrived and were settled up Yonge Street. Russell obediently followed instructions to assist this scheme, but it was doomed to failure from the outset.

Another vexing problem concerning land was the anomalous status of the large tract on the Grand River belonging to the Six Nations Indians. Joseph Brant [Thayendanegea], the Indian leader, asserted the Indians' right to sell their land; however, Simcoe and Russell maintained that it had been given in perpetuity and could not be alienated. After Simcoe's departure Brant became more insistent; Russell temporized, writing desperately to London for instructions when Brant sold 381,480 acres and demanded that deeds be issued to the purchasers. During the winter of 1796–97 there were rumours of unrest among the Indians on the Mississippi River, so that the continued loyalty of the Upper Canadian Indians was vital. On 29 June 1797 the Executive Council recommended that Russell come to an immediate decision without waiting any longer for instructions from London. Accordingly Russell agreed to issue the deeds. On 15 July, before the details had been settled with Brant, the dispatch from London finally arrived instructing Russell not to accede to Brant's request; the British government would give the Indians an annuity in lieu of permission to sell their land. Brant refused this offer, forcing Russell to disobey his instructions and to issue the deeds on condition that no more land be alienated. In the midst of this controversy Russell learned that responsibility for Indian affairs in Upper Canada had been transferred to him from Quebec on 15 Dec. 1796.

Until the arrival of the new chief justice, John Elmsley, on 20 Nov. 1796 Russell's Executive Council was weak. Unfortunately Elmsley, although strong, opposed Russell almost continually. Their first major battle was over the seat of government. Before Simcoe left he had moved his capital from Newark (Niagara-on-the-Lake) to York, despite the lack of enthusiasm of most government officials, including Russell. Elmsley objected vigorously, but Russell doggedly followed Simcoe's directions, and met his first parliament in York in June 1797. He spent much effort in improving the capital: the New Town was surveyed and opened west of Simcoe's original site; a primitive zoning plan was established; work on public buildings was accelerated; plans were made for adequate defence; some local self-government was granted; police-force regulations were proposed (but blocked by Elmsley); better transportation links with other parts of the province were provided by extending Simcoe's Dundas and Yonge streets into the town and by building the Danforth Road east to Kingston.

Russell's reappointment of himself to the Court of King's Bench was also sharply criticized by Elmsley. Though the reason for his holding the judgeship was no longer valid, Russell kept reissuing his own commission, the last time being on 17 March 1798. He probably did it for the salary; as administrator he received no additional remuneration. With no legal training Russell was vulnerable to ridicule on the bench while at the same time he was breaching the principle of separation of executive and judicial powers. Finally he was ordered to give up the judgeship in return for half Simcoe's salary and fees.

Until the spring of 1798 Russell had expected Simcoe's return to Upper Canada. Thereafter he hoped, without much expectation, to become governor, but in June 1799 he heard of Peter Hunter's appointment and that August Hunter arrived in Upper Canada. The new lieutenant governor was much impressed by Elmsley, so that Russell's influence as well as his position was greatly diminished. He remained receiver general and was a member of the small committee that governed the province during Hunter's absences, but he had little power. Simcoe had asked that some provision be made for him because he was very old, but nothing was done. After Hunter's death in 1805 Alexander Grant was appointed administrator because his name preceded Russell's on the official list; Russell protested in vain. Although he owned thousands of acres of land in Upper Canada (as an executive councillor he was given 6,000 acres) he could not find purchasers and could not therefore afford to return to England. He remained in York, tired, sick, and old, still interested in scientific experiments which he had begun long ago in Virginia, still conscientiously doing his duty as receiver general. At his death his estate, which was rapidly increasing in value, passed to Elizabeth, who left it to William Willcocks's daughters in 1822.

Russell has never been considered one of the great men of Ontario. Although later criticism has rather unjustly charged him with greed for land, his contemporaries objected to his greed for fees and offices. As administrator he was cautious, practical, capable, and painstaking. Unlike Simcoe he had little imagination, sometimes had difficulty making decisions, and was willing to devote much thought and effort to detail. Russell, however, was administrator, not lieutenant governor, and he had neither the authority nor the security of governorship. Yet the record of legislation during his administration is impressive, not for great statutes but for those which corrected abuses, improved conditions, or made the machinery of government work more smoothly. Russell was not a great man and his abilities may have been pedestrian, but his accomplishments were very real.

EDITH G. FIRTH

THOMAS SCOTT
Office holder, judge, and politician; baptized 18 Oct. 1746 in the parish of Kingoldrum, Scotland, son of the Reverend Thomas Scott; d. 29 July 1824 in York (Toronto), Upper Canada.

Aspiring to a position in the British gentry, Thomas Scott first sought to follow in his father's footsteps by training for the ministry of the established Church of Scotland. When he failed to obtain a posting, he became a tutor in the house of Sir John Riddell in the south of Scotland; in later years he became the Riddells' benefactor. From an early age he also assumed responsibility for the support of his younger brother, William. These commitments were to intensify his career-long quest for financial security.

In 1788 he journeyed south to Lincoln's Inn in London to study law and was called to the bar in 1793. Unable to establish himself comfortably in Britain, in 1800 he accepted the appointment of attorney general of Upper Canada, which came with a promise of eventual preferment for the chief justiceship. He was already in his 55th year. In Upper Canada Scott sought to make himself indispensable to Lieutenant Governor Peter Hunter, who had supported his appointment. Besides attending to his legal duties, Scott plunged into an exhausting round of political activities, becoming second in influence only to Henry Allcock, the chief justice after 1802. Both men supported Hunter's policy of rushing the preparation of land patents to remove the confusion regarding land title in the province. The program increased their income from fees, but antagonized many settlers struggling to meet the costs of establishing new farms. The strain of Scott's duties probably contributed to the ill health which plagued his later career.

In 1805 the attorney general was appointed to the Executive Council and reached the height of his political influence. With Hunter dead and a figurehead – Alexander Grant – in control of the government, Scott and John McGill, the inspector general, blocked the aspirations of rival officials and briefly became the colony's most powerful politicians. Scott was now expected to exercise political skills which he did not possess in abundance. Opposition to the government's land policy was growing in the assembly. Yet acting on Scott's advice, Grant attempted to usurp financial appropriations which were rightly within the control of the elected body, thus furnishing an opening to the opposition. The situation was exacerbated by the rivalry of Scott and Robert Thorpe, a judge of the Court of King's Bench, for the position of chief justice, now vacant with the transfer of Allcock to Lower Canada. Thorpe sought to attract attention by joining the critics of the administration, but this move only led to his dismissal.

In 1806 Scott was made a member of the Legislative Council and finally received the appointment of chief justice. Almost immediately he attempted to minimize further responsibilities. He refused to be considered for promotion to chief justice of Lower Canada on the grounds that 'at my time of life, it is too arduous an undertaking for me to attempt.' Although expected to serve as the lieutenant governor's major adviser, he declined further involvement in provincial politics. Describing Scott's contributions on matters of state as 'water gruel,' the new head of government, Francis Gore, turned to William Dummer Powell, another judge of the King's Bench, as his chief adviser. In 1811 Scott applied for a pension to enable him to retire in dignity. Unsuccessful in obtaining it, he was forced to remain the leading judicial officer of the province during its years of greatest turmoil.

The War of 1812 marked a crisis of authority for the ruling gentry. They doubted the loyalty of the colony's largely American-born population. In vain the leading officials advocated the selective suspension of civil liberties and the imposition of martial law; they were blocked until 1814 by members of the assembly such as Abraham Markle who were reluctant to antagonize their constituents. As a distinguished resident of York, Scott played a modest role in encouraging order, but was easily outshone by more energetic men such as Powell and the Reverend John Strachan. Scott filled a similar function during the trials of 1814 which were intended to reassert the authority of the state. The strategy of the government was to manipulate the provisions of the law to strike a balance of terror and mercy. Consequently, while the courts convicted 15 persons, including Jacob Overholser, of treason, only 8 were executed, the sentences of the remainder being commuted to banishment. Scott supported these decisions, but the initiative came from others, especially Attorney General John Beverley Robinson.

In 1816 the chief justice finally received the pension he needed for retirement. He spent his last years quietly in York where he died in 1824. Ever loyal to his personal commitments, he left an estate sufficient to support his brother in Scotland for the rest of his life. In his public career, however, Scott had been less successful. While his judicial opinions had been competent, he showed little liking for the wider responsibilities expected of legal officers in this period. His failings were partly the product of old age and uncertain health. Yet, his record was similar to that of many administrators who were drawn to this remote colony during its first generations of existence.

WILLIAM N.T. WYLIE

LEVIUS PETERS SHERWOOD

Lawyer, office holder, militia officer, politician, and judge; b. 12 Dec. 1777 in St Johns (Saint-Jean-sur-Richelieu), Que., second son of Justus Sherwood, a loyalist, and Sarah Bottum; m. 1804 Charlotte Jones, daughter of Ephraim Jones, and they had four sons and three daughters; d. 19 May 1850 in Toronto.

Levius Peters Sherwood was educated in the law and called to the bar of Upper Canada in 1803. The following year he was appointed registrar for the counties of Grenville, Leeds, and Carleton and collector of customs, as well as inspector of flour, potash, and pearl ashes. On 16 March 1812 he was appointed surrogate treasurer of the Johnstown District. The coming of the War of 1812 served to increase his influence, both in the Johnstown District and beyond it. In March 1814 he was involved in the naming of magistrates for the district. On 24 May 1816, with the rank of lieutenant-colonel in the militia, he was appointed to examine applications for military pensions in the district.

Sherwood's public prominence continued to develop in post-war Upper Canada. In July 1818 he took part in the general conservative attack against Robert Gourlay, who was gathering information about the province's condition. In October Sherwood was in York (Toronto) where he successfully defended two of Cuthbert Grant's party of Métis, Paul Brown and François-Firmin Boucher, against charges in connection with the murder of Robert Semple during the troubles at Red River in 1816. Sherwood argued persuasively that the settlement there was little more than a camp of traders, by definition a rather wild group. His legal career continued to advance and in November 1820 William Dummer Powell recommended successfully that he become a judge in the Johnstown District Court.

As his importance rose provincially, Sherwood maintained a strong influence in the district and in Brockville, where he had settled. In July 1822 he applied for membership on the district land board. He was active on the local board of education, and in April 1825 he was one of three churchwardens entrusted with land for the construction of St Peter's (Anglican) Church.

Sherwood entered provincial politics in the general election of 1812 when he defeated Peter Howard in the riding of Leeds. Sherwood took the riding again in 1820, leading the poll with 515 votes. By September 1821 he was serving as speaker of the House of Assembly, and the demands on his time were considerable, especially after the house was plunged into an extended controversy about Barnabas Bidwell's right to hold a seat. On at least two occasions Sherwood was compelled to ask for leaves of absence from his judicial duties in order to fulfill his political responsibilities.

The apogee of Sherwood's judicial career was his appointment to the Court of King's Bench in 1825. His priorities now shifted away from politics. In the years which followed, he found himself dealing with such varied cases as those of Dennis Russell, found guilty of rape in 1828, and Francis Collins, a newspaper editor convicted of libel in the same year. A squabble with a fellow judge, John Walpole Willis, in 1828 led to a strong defence of Sherwood by John Strachan, who described him as 'a most upright and religious man anxious to perform his duty.'

Sherwood became increasingly unpopular in reform circles. In 1835 a rumour developed that he would shortly be retiring. Reluctant to see him on the civil list, the Canadian Alliance Society, a reform group, passed a series of resolutions condemning the suggestion that he should be pensioned off when he was clearly young enough to serve another 20 years. Nothing came of the rumour and Sherwood remained on the bench. Indeed his stature as a pillar of the establishment grew sufficiently that, on 17 Feb. 1838, a Kingston newspaper, the *British Whig*, specifically labelled him as a member of the 'family compact.'

In the immediate aftermath of the rebellion of 1837, Sherwood was prominent in the trials for treason which began at Toronto in March 1838. Late that year Lieutenant Governor Sir George Arthur asked him what should be done with the prisoners taken during the failed invasion at Prescott in November. Sherwood recommended that only the ringleaders should be hanged and that the others be committed to a penal colony for life. Execution, he argued, often excited pity in those who witnessed it, and thus undermined the lesson it was intended to teach.

Sherwood always kept an eye open for opportunities to deal in land. In 1820, in cooperation with Captain John Le Breton, he had obtained a valuable lot near the Chaudière Falls on the Ottawa River; he later acquired more land there. By 1832 he was living in York near the foot of Yonge Street and had bought a lot adjacent to his residence which he was prepared to sell, at a high price. In 1840 he sought a lease for part of an island in the Ottawa River in order to erect a mill at the nearby falls.

Sherwood retired from the bench in 1840 although he continued to be vocal in conservative circles. In November 1842 he was a founding member of the Toronto Constitutional Society which had been formed in reaction to the policies of Governor Sir Charles Bagot. In October 1843 Sherwood made it known that he supported a resolution William Henry Draper had introduced in the assembly opposing the transfer of the seat of government from Kingston to Lower Canada. During this same period, he was appointed to the Legislative Council on 19 Aug. 1842 and the Executive Council on 1 Nov. 1843.

During the final years of his life he remained active both in his profession and in the religious and educational life of the community. In 1842 he had served as treasurer of the Law Society of Upper Canada. Two years later he expressed his willingness to return to the bench by sitting on the Court of Appeal. His devotion to the Church of England moved him in May 1842 to volunteer his services as a vice-president of the Church Society. Four years later, he was appointed, along with John Beverley Robinson, to be treasurer of the Society for the Propagation of the Gospel. His contribution to education was as a member of the council of King's College in Toronto to which he was named on 27 Dec. 1841. For nearly half a century before his death in 1850 Levius Peters Sherwood, a man of devout conservative conscience, had served his community in many capacities.

IAN PEMBERTON

ROBERT THORPE

Judge and politician; b. 11 July 1765 in Dublin, second son of Robert T. Thorp, a barrister, and Magdalen Bonna Debrisay; m. 29 July 1791 Sarah Featherston, and they had seven children; d. 11 May 1836 in London.

Robert Thorpe graduated with a BA in 1788 and an LLB in 1789 from Trinity College, Dublin. He received an LLD in 1801. Admitted to the Irish bar in 1790, he entered the colonial service in 1801 when he was nominated chief justice of Prince Edward Island.

This colony was governed by the able, if somewhat venal, Edmund Fanning who, through geniality, deft duplicity, and judicious inaction, had successfully steered his way between the demands of local factions and unpopular policies of the Colonial Office since 1786. Fanning was in collusion with the Island's landed proprietors, as Thorpe was not; moreover, the lieutenant governor's *laissez-faire* rule was antipathetic to the judge's rigidity of mind and probably stood as an obstacle to his ambition to make a name for himself in London. Something might be made of the colony, he once thought, 'but the government must acquire vigour and respectability, the middle orders more sense and less sufficiency, and the lower classes must be less drunken and Idle before any good can be effected.' Thorpe soon stirred up the attorney general, Peter Magowan, to launch a number of prosecutions which seem to have been minor but irritating, and perhaps unjustified. Living on a salary in arrears, in a small house with a leaking roof, having a complaining wife and seven sickly children whom he despaired of educating, Thorpe was meanwhile 'obliged at different times to quarrel with all orders through finding virtue in none.' He came to loathe the colony. In hope of securing his salary, he sailed to England in 1804, carrying with him an unsolicited plan for uniting Prince Edward Island, Cape Breton, and Newfoundland to impress the colonial secretary. Off the coast of Ireland he was captured by the French and carried into Spain, from whence he contrived to escape.

In 1805 he was appointed puisne judge of the Court of King's Bench in Upper Canada. Arriving in York (Toronto) by 1 October, he found the reins of government in the hands of Alexander Grant, the temporary replacement for Lieutenant Governor Peter Hunter, who had died that August. Thorpe almost immediately fell in with a fellow Irishman, Executive Councillor Peter Russell, who had expected to be made lieutenant governor himself, but never even regained the power and influence he had enjoyed before Hunter's arrival. Thorpe's opinions about Hunter, whom he never knew, almost certainly derived from the Russell circle, as did his hostility to Grant. 'I expected that the avarice and imbecility of our [Upper Canadian] government would be highly injurious, but it has far surpassed my fears,' Thorpe reported to the Colonial Office, and began to manœuvre to take the interim management of affairs into his own hands. Reasonably enough, he argued for establishing a court of chancery; and, harmlessly enough, he founded agricultural societies and tried to promote the building of roads by means of a lottery. But more important, he attempted to manage a political opposition of which he had a limited and distorted understanding. Grant held office until August 1806 when he was succeeded by the new lieutenant governor, Francis Gore.

Political divisions in Upper Canada were essentially local in nature, having emerged within the districts either between justices of the peace representative of opposed sectional interests or, more commonly, between these appointed officials and their disappointed rivals for place who were beginning to oppose them from the hustings. Such divisions were often reinforced by further oppositions between long settled loyalists and newcomers from the American republic who were swamping them. At the ideological level politics were therefore characterized by the noisy opposition of a rhetoric of republicanism and one of loyalty to government established by law, a conflict made the more intense by threat of war with the United States. By 1806 a few spokesmen for the disaffected were being returned to the House of Assembly. But also at the capital were a number of persons who were at once alarmed by the threat of republicanism yet disaffected themselves from the Hunter government by reason of the 'maladministration' and 'unconstitutional' practices which they tended to assign as the causes of popular unrest. Among them were some Anglo-Irishmen – notably Russell's friends and Thorpe's crony the demagogic barrister William Weekes – who, tending to understand local politics in terms of Irish analogies, became the judge's friends and advisers.

Thorpe's ideas derived from these people, from rhetoric and constitutional theory related to the paper independence enjoyed by Ireland prior to the union of 1800 and, more especially, from the ancient English law upon which that independence was theoretically based and upon which the judge was taken to be an authority. Loyalty to the crown would be maintained in Upper Canada, he argued, only if British subjects enjoyed certain rights to which they were entitled by law but which had been ignored during the Hunter régime. This enjoyment, it appeared, involved holding the executive responsible to the elected representatives of the people. Indeed, it is likely that Thorpe was the author of a tract in which it was contended that the 'British Connection' might best be maintained if, after the model of the parliament at Westminster, executive authority were vested in a cabinet responsible, not to the governor, but to the local legislature. He expounded related doctrine both before the bar of the assembly and from the bench; and, during his victorious election campaign in 1807 to succeed Weekes in the assembly, these ideas informed his slogan: 'The King, the People, the Law, Thorpe and the Constitution.'

As a practical politician, Thorpe was foolish to a degree; but as a link between English and Irish constitutional concepts of the 17th and 18th centuries and certain notions later associated with the slogans 'Responsible Government' and 'Home Rule,' he is a figure of some consequence in the history of ideas. His views and actions were incompatible, however, with what was then accepted imperial doctrine; and he was suspended from office by Gore in July 1807.

Despite his record as a trouble-maker, in 1808 Thorpe was appointed chief justice and judge of the Vice-Admiralty Court in Sierra Leone. He did not sail from England, however, until 1811 and he returned on leave in 1813. He then became involved in a dispute with the Colonial Office over £630 he was said to have owed to a surrogate who had acted for him in Sierra Leone during his absence. In March 1814 this sum was ordered paid out of his salary. In January 1815 he transmitted to the colonial secretary a number of charges against Charles William Maxwell, one-time governor of Sierra Leone, which also involved the probity of the African Institution, an organization set up by evangelical philanthropists to aid freed slaves. Lord Bathurst, the colonial secretary, was requested either to deal with these charges himself or to lay them before the prince regent in council. At the same time, Thorpe presented a memorial on his own behalf, praying for the return of the £630. Apparently scenting blackmail, Bathurst ordered him dismissed on the ground that, even if his charges were true, he had been derelict in his duty in not having brought them forward at an earlier date.

Up until 1828 Thorpe wrote many pamphlets in which he sought to bring his cause, and that of Sierra Leone, before parliament. In 1827 Joseph Hume appealed to Lord Goderich 'as an act of humanity if not of justice' to do something for Dr Thorpe 'to prevent him and his family from absolute starvation.' At his death in 1836, however, former surveyor general Charles Burton Wyatt reported to William Warren Baldwin that Thorpe had left 'an amiable family comfortably provided for.'

G.H. PATTERSON

JOHN WHITE

Lawyer and office-holder; b. c. 1761, only son of John White of Hicks's Hall, parish of St Sepulchre, Middlesex, England; m. 1784 to Marrianne Lynne of Horkesley, Essex, and they had two sons and a daughter; d. 4 Jan. 1800 in York (Toronto).

John White was admitted as a student at the Inner Temple, London, on 17 Oct. 1777. In 1783 his only sister Elizabeth married his fellow student, Samuel Shepherd, who became a distinguished British jurist and throughout his life remained White's staunch friend and patron. White was called to the bar in 1785 and the following year went to Jamaica, where he practised law without success. In 1791 he was living with his family in Wales, intending to become a clergyman. Shepherd recommended him as a suitable attorney general of Upper Canada to William Osgoode, who had been selected as chief justice of the new colony. Osgoode passed on the recommendation to Evan Nepean, a commissioner of the Privy Seal, and White was appointed on 31 Dec. 1791.

White sailed for Canada in the spring of 1792 with Osgoode and with Peter and his half-sister Elizabeth Russell, the three of whom remained his closest friends in Canada. After a brief period in Kingston, the government moved in September 1792 to Newark (Niagara-on-the-Lake); White and Osgoode lived together there until White acquired a house the following year. In 1797 he moved to York where Mrs White, from whom he had been estranged, joined him with their children. Their reconciliation was unsuccessful; in 1799 Mrs White returned to England with their daughter.

As the first attorney general of Upper Canada, White was concerned with the adaptation of the laws of Britain to the vastly different conditions of the new colony. There were many problems concerning the ownership of land, especially of land granted before the passage of the Constitutional Act of 1791 and of land transferred by the original grantee before the issuance of his deed. Prosecuting for the crown, White had difficulty getting convictions for murder, even with strong evidence. Because of the absence of jails, petty offenders were punished by fines rather than imprisonment; according to White, these fines were rarely paid.

Like other early attorneys general White carried on a private law practice to supplement his income. Irregularities occasionally resulted. In 1793 Lieutenant Governor Simcoe was told that White, as attorney general, had prosecuted on an assault and battery charge and had then put up the bail for the defendant, lodged him in his own tent when the sheriff was looking for him, and defended him in the ensuing civil action. Simcoe ignored the complaint, possibly because the defendant was an officer in the Queen's Rangers.

White was active in the founding of the Law Society of Upper Canada in 1797; as its first treasurer he was also its first president. Alone among the lawyers attending its early meetings he supported the distinction between attorneys and barristers. His objection to combining them was overruled 12 days after his death.

During his stay in Kingston in 1792 White had been elected to the House of Assembly as the member for Leeds and Frontenac. He and the surveyor general, David William Smith, led the support of government-sponsored legislation in the assembly, including the 1793 bill which provided for the eventual abolition of slavery in the province. White was most concerned personally with the bill establishing the Court of King's Bench and the district courts in 1794. He was not a member of the second parliament, but in 1799 he contested a by-election in Addington and Ontario. After his defeat his election expenses were paid by the government. In November 1799 he agreed to contest a seat in Lincoln, but he died before the election.

White's salary as attorney general was £300 a year, supplemented by fees for particular duties, the most important of which was drawing up land deeds. He was seriously in debt to Shepherd when he came to Canada, where he continued to live beyond his means. He constantly sought more highly paid positions and was fiercely resentful of any threatened reduction of his income. A running battle developed among White, the provincial secretary, the surveyor general, the receiver general, the clerk of the Executive Council, and the lieutenant governor, who all shared the fees from the issuance of land deeds. This quarrel deeply divided the officers of government, reduced their efficiency, and caused much bitterness.

White's first impressions of Upper Canada and Simcoe had been favourable, but he rapidly became disillusioned with the country,

Simcoe, many of his colleagues, and his own prospects. As his health deteriorated he grew depressed and irascible. He had apparently had a brief affair with the wife of the clerk of the Executive Council, John Small. Mrs Small slighted Mrs White at an assembly in York; White made a scurrilous comment about Mrs Small's virtue to D.W. Smith. Eventually this remark reached Mrs Small, whose husband challenged White to a duel. White was shot, and died 36 hours later. Mrs Small was ostracized, Smith's appointment to the Legislative Council was postponed indefinitely, and scandal and ill-feeling permeated the insular society of York.

White died heavily in debt. His executor, Peter Russell, sent White's sons to Shepherd and tried to disentangle his estate. In response to White's requests, the Duke of Portland, secretary of state for the Home Department, had approved a land grant equivalent to that of an executive councillor; news of his decision reached York after White's death, and the land was given to his wife and children. White had attempted to make provision for his mistress in York, Mrs Susanna Page, and their two daughters, but nothing was done for them. His estate was not settled until a private bill was passed in 1837.

White was deeply involved in establishing the legal and judicial system of Upper Canada. He had difficulty, however, working with others and is now chiefly remembered for the circumstances of his death.

EDITH G. FIRTH

JOHN WALPOLE WILLIS

Judge; b. in England, 4 Jan. 1793, son of William Willis and Mary Smith; d. 10 Sept. 1877 at Wick House, Wick-Episcopi, Worcestershire, Eng.

William Willis died in 1809 leaving little estate and John Walpole rose by a combination of ambition, legal talents, and charm. He published his first legal work in 1816 and was called to the bar the following year. Willis' interest in equity led to the publication in 1820 of a book that long remained an authority, and of a third work in 1827. His increasingly successful practice of the law was matched by a profitable advance into established society. These interests converged in 1823–24 when Willis was retained by the 11th Earl of Strathmore. In August 1824 their association led to his marriage to the earl's elder daughter, Mary Isabella Bowes-Lyon, aged 22.

As a successful barrister and an authority on equity, Willis might have thrived indefinitely amid the efforts of Sir Robert Peel, as home secretary, to encourage the codification and moderation of English civil law and commercial law. But marriage to Lady Mary did not guarantee solvency or harmony. She brought no great dowry. Her life with Willis in Hendon, a quiet London suburb, offered little excitement; his limited means meant that his mother and sister were forced to share their home. Lady Mary's consciousness of her rank appears to have grown, rather than diminished, following her marriage; her ambitions and the other financial and professional demands of Willis' career were propelling him forward at a forced pace.

In 1827 the Colonial Office played briefly with the idea of pressing upon Upper Canada some of the current British legal reforms and of establishing a court of chancery through which remedies could be sought in equity. The Earl of Strathmore suggested that his son-in-law could grace that new bench with authority during the period of necessary adjustment. The reform was not yet finally settled, but on some loose understanding Willis accepted an interim appointment as junior puisne judge on the province's Court of King's Bench. Willis, with the entire Hendon *ménage*, arrived in York (Toronto) on 18 Sept. 1827. He was to be in Canada only nine months – less than half of

Robert F. Gourlay's stay – but he would cause nearly as much alarm in official circles and stir the reform-minded at a decisive moment in their organization.

Willis discovered immediately that the governor, Sir Peregrine Maitland, and his Executive Council questioned the Colonial Office's flirtation with chancery. The attorney general, John Beverley Robinson, and other Family Compact lawyers, including the solicitor general, Henry John Boulton, differed over important details of the plan; Maitland's strong will, thus reinforced, gave way only slowly to Whitehall's proposals for a provincial enabling act. Robinson was prepared to accede to the proposal and even entrusted the drafting to an opposition lawyer, Dr John Rolph, but Willis over-reached himself in attempting to force the pace of negotiations. The Reformers were anxious to bargain with the government by log-rolling – an equity court in return for a more independent judiciary. Willis abandoned his natural alliance with Robinson to consort with four lawyers who were then chief opposition spokesmen – Rolph, William Warren Baldwin, Robert Baldwin, and Marshall Spring Bidwell. Despite such advocates, Willis' bill was emasculated and finally abandoned in the Tory assembly. Meantime, the imperial law officers had advised Whitehall not to press the matter further. Thus, the junior puisne judge was forced to reassess his prospects in the less familiar field of common law and in a provincial society.

At the outset Willis and his wife had been warmly accepted into York's small circle. If Lady Mary thought her charms wasted, Willis quickly joined the round of parties and fashionable charities with the confidence that had served him at home. This goodwill, however, was soon squandered. Willis' appointment had been deeply resented by aspirants such as Robinson, Boulton, and Christopher Hagerman, who had prepared themselves through years of service in the common law and in Upper Canada's legal system. Willis' contempt for their abilities was expressed plainly, as was his poor opinion of his two superiors on the King's Bench, Chief Justice William Campbell and Levius Peters Sherwood. In part Willis' cause was sound: he argued, for example, that punishment in criminal cases was inhumane by contemporary English standards. But, by flaunting his own lack of factional spirit, he made the case for equity seem like a call for purity. Neither a demagogue like the earlier Judge Robert Thorpe, nor a firebrand like Gourlay, he, with his charm and plausibility, seemed a more formidable opponent. Moreover, Governor Maitland's wife, daughter of a duke, saw a threat to her social position from an earl's daughter. These social and professional conflicts had developed so quickly that an open conflict must arise when Willis, after being resident only a few weeks, applied, in rivalry with Robinson, for succession to the chief justice's seat.

On 11 April 1828, taking advantage of the absence of his two colleagues, Willis behaved extraordinarily while presiding over the libel trial of Francis Collins, editor of the *Canadian Freeman*. Collins had sought the latitude customarily accorded those appearing without counsel, but Willis permitted and even encouraged him in a prolonged, irrelevant attack upon the law officers, Robinson and Boulton. On Robinson's interjection, Willis presumed to question from the bench Robinson's entire record of public office, threatening to make 'a representation ... to His Majesty's Government.' As John Charles Dent concludes, 'Judge Willis seems to have been wrong in his law, wrong in his etiquette, wrong in his temper, and wrong in his construction of judicial amenities.'

By now, however, an impending general election invited hyperbole and postures of convenience. Maitland hastily assured Whitehall that because no one had before protested against 'the laws, or the manner in which they have been administered, I must conclude that the people are content with both.' On the other hand, 'the people' – including the most notable Reform lawyers – had already decided for Willis. Memory of the application of the sedition act to Robert Gourlay and Barnabas Bidwell was fresh. Willis' legitimate concern for the laws, however, threatened to give way to demagogy – an easy trap for a man of his vanity.

On 16 June Willis displayed a sensitivity for legal technicalities that would not have served him on 11 April by declaring that the act establishing King's Bench required the presence of the 'Chief Justice, together with two puisne justices.' Campbell was still absent on leave, as legal and administrative officers had frequently been of necessity in the past. Willis now presumed to cast doubt upon the entire legal foundation and record of the court for the past generation. The technicality needed to be met: the Baldwins refused to pursue justice further in King's Bench. But Willis had really sought to indict a society, not a court. Public alarm and confusion might gain him much.

On 26 June, advised by the threatened law officers, Maitland and his council agreed to the 'amoval' of Judge Willis; a week later, Hagerman was named to fill the post. Public meetings and messages of condolence encouraged Willis to press his case in London. Trustees, including the Baldwins, John Galt, and their wives, offered to care for Lady Mary and the family, and Robert Baldwin undertook to act as her solicitor. But committees can only do so much, and when Lady Mary was to rejoin her husband in England, she quietly chose instead to take up residence in Montreal with an officer in the 38th Foot, Lieutenant Bernard, and subsequently to elope to England, leaving her son in a maid's care.

John Willis' career and Upper Canada's fortunes might have improved from that moment. Willis, as a cause, had helped to knit together the Reformers, who in the election of 1828 won their first assembly majority and elected Bidwell as speaker. Willis appealed his removal, lost an initial round, but was rehabilitated by the Privy Council, which overruled his amoval without chance of defence; he was given a new judicial appointment in Demerara (now part of Guyana). His marriage was dissolved, and in 1836 he married Ann Susanna Kent of Wick-Episcopi, Worcestershire, by whom he had three children. In 1841 he received another judicial appointment, in New South Wales, but again he clashed with a strong-minded governor, Sir George Gipps, and was amoved without notice; again, the Privy Council sustained his appeal on the same technicality. This time he received no new appointment. He retired to Wick House and lived privately for another 30 years.

In retirement Willis composed a summary of his colonial experiences, *On the government of the British colonies*. In it he displayed all that lack of faith in the colonies that had been implicit in his public career. Colonies, he argued like John Graves Simcoe, only deserved recognition equivalent to English counties; as their highest political ambition they might be represented in the British parliament, but they should be administered by lords lieutenant. Whatever the convenience of the Willis incident to the Reformers of 1828, those future advocates of responsible government could not have lived with Willis for long – nor could most people.

ALAN WILSON

The Legal Profession

WILLIAM WARREN BALDWIN

Doctor, militia officer, JP, lawyer, office holder, judge, businessman, and politician; b. 25 April 1775 at Knockmore, the family estate south of Cork (Republic of Ireland), fifth of the 16 children of Robert Baldwin and Barbara Spread; m. 26 July 1803 Margaret Phœbe Willcocks, daughter of William Willcocks, in York (Toronto), and they had five sons, including Robert; d. 8 Jan. 1844 in Toronto.

Robert Baldwin Sr was a Protestant gentleman farmer who had, by the time of William Warren Baldwin's birth, acquired both office and prestige. For a time in the 1780s he published, with his brother, the *Volunteer Journal; or, Independent Gazetteer*, which William Warren later claimed had been 'favorably spoken of' by Charles James Fox. In spite of continuous attention to his estates during his political involvement with the volunteer movement and despite the financial support of his patron, Sir Robert Warren, Robert slid into bankruptcy about 1788 None the less, young William received a proper education. In his will he was to leave a small sum to an heir of the Reverend Thomas Cooke, 'my careful and good schoolmaster, whose attention and kindness to me demands this small acknowledgement.' About 1794 he entered medical school at the University of Edinburgh, from which he graduated in 1797.

That same year, enticed by descriptions sent back by a former neighbour, Robert Baldwin resolved, contrary to his patron's advice, to emigrate to Upper Canada. He sailed in 1798 with William, one other son, and four daughters. Forced to winter in England, the family set forth again the following spring. Although family accounts give 13 July 1799 as the date of their arrival at York, Robert's first petition for land is dated 6 July. In it he expressed his desire for a grant, having heard 'of the fertility of the soil & the mildness & good Government' of the province. There was, however, more to his emigration: Baldwin had been, according to the reminiscences of his youngest daughter, deeply alarmed by the persistent rumours of impending

French landings in Ireland, in anticipation of which he had barricaded his house and armed his servants. The unrest preceding the uprising of the Society of United Irishmen in 1798 had also played a part in convincing him of the need to leave. William noted in 1801 that the 'horrors of domestic war [had] conspired to drive us from our native country.'

Robert's entry into Upper Canadian society had been well prepared. On 20 Aug. 1798 his friend Hugh Hovell Farmar wrote a letter introducing him to President Peter Russell, another Irishman, which described him as a 'Gentleman of excellent Family, of Honor & excessively clever in the farming Line, with great Industry.' For his part, Russell strongly recommended Baldwin's petition to the Executive Council and he received 1,200 acres. He settled, however, on land he had purchased near an acquaintance in Clarke Township. With excellent connections, he soon acquired offices, among them the lieutenancy of Durham County, and influence.

William found his new life in the Upper Canadian wilds unprepossessing. There, he wrote to his brother in 1801, he was 'banished from all that is engaging in life, flattering to our hopes, or grateful to our industry.' Although his father's appointments from Lieutenant Governor Peter Hunter were 'all honour but not profit,' he found them 'agreeable,' assisting 'in some measure to soothe the mind.' He himself was appointed lieutenant-colonel of the Durham militia, a group he considered 'a lawless ... damned set of villains'; he also became a justice of the peace on 1 Feb. 1800. William was concerned about unrest in the province, which he attributed to 'unprincipled wretches' from the United States who 'would, had they the least prospect of success, tomorrow attempt to overturn the order of things in this country.'

Finding little scope for his professional ambition in the backwoods of Clarke and preferring the allures of York's small society, Baldwin moved in 1802 to the capital, where he entered the somewhat closed family world of the Russell and Willcocks households. His connections to them were established in Upper Canada but the ties wen back to Cork and Hugh Farmar, who was 'nearly allied' to both families. Peter Russell's 'friendship' was of particular consolation to Baldwin, and Peter was a first cousin of William Willcocks, soon to be Baldwin's father-in-law. Another close friend was Joseph Willcocks, a distant relation of William. In June 1802 Baldwin acted as Russell's intermediary with Joseph Willcocks, whose advances to Elizabeth

Russell had caused a breach in their relations. But even York offered little scope for an aspiring young doctor and in December he advertised the opening of a classical school for young gentlemen. What became of it is not known. Baldwin's career now took a new direction. The young man who had borrowed Sir William Blackstone's *Commentaries on the laws of England* from Russell became an attorney on 22 Jan. 1803 and was admitted to the bar in Easter term of the same year.

Baldwin was a visible member of York's social circle and was one of the town's most eligible bachelors, a state ended by his marriage to Phœbe Willcocks in 1803. The young couple lived briefly with the Willcockses until they moved into their own home shortly before the birth of their first child, Robert, in May 1804. In spite of the death of their second son in 1806 and the frailness of the third, William Willcocks reported in 1807 that his daughter was 'happily Married.' With the birth of sons in 1808 and in 1810, Baldwin's family would be complete. He was a doting father, often glimpsed in the diaries of early York making his rounds of the town with one or more children in tow.

The society of York was a cliquish world in which competition for the few profitable offices was fierce. Conventional wisdom attributes William Warren Baldwin's rise to Russell, but he was in fact in eclipse when the Baldwins arrived and they garnered most of their early rewards from Hunter. In 1806, while the vultures of official York were awaiting the fall of James Clark, clerk of the Legislative Council, Russell was unsuccessful in persuading President Alexander Grant that Baldwin should succeed him. For several weeks early in 1806 Baldwin had served as acting clerk of the crown and pleas. In spite of judge Robert Thorpe's recommendation that he was 'the only educated and qualified person in the Province' for this position, it went to John Small. None the less, Baldwin picked up his share of plums. On 5 Feb. 1806 he followed David Burns as master in chancery, on 19 Nov. 1808 he became registrar of the Court of Probate, and on 22 July 1809 he was appointed a district court judge.

During Lieutenant Governor Francis Gore's first administration (1806–11), many of Baldwin's friends – Joseph Willcocks, William Firth, Thorpe, and Charles Burton Wyatt – were either suspended or dismissed from office. Despite Baldwin's association with them and despite Gore's suspicion of him as an 'Irishman, ready to join any party to make confusion,' he survived. His political legerdemain was remarkable and deliberate: although it was clear who his friends were – and although he supported Thorpe during his trial for libel in 1807 – he avoided any overt demonstrations of his political sympathies. Indeed, in October 1809 he wrote to Wyatt of Gore's 'disposition to befriend' him. But if William did well during this period, as his appointments to office in 1808 and 1809 evidence, others were doing better. Baldwin was not the only able and ambitious lawyer in town and he resented, although he professed not to, the meteoric ascent of John Macdonell (Greenfield). When Greenfield made some 'wanton & ungentlemanly' references about him in court, Baldwin demanded an apology and ultimately challenged him to a duel. In a note he enjoined his wife, whom he had described in a hastily made will as 'unparalleled in all the excellent qualifications of her sex,' 'not to indulge a rash or resentful spirit, but to protect me from insults, which as a gentleman I cannot submit to.' On 3 April 1812 the two men met on Toronto Island. Macdonell did not raise his pistol, which Baldwin interpreted 'as an acknowledgement of his error – we joined hands thus this affair ended.'

Baldwin gloried in domesticity. By the end of the War of 1812 his household included his wife, four sons, father, three sisters, sister-in-law, Elizabeth Russell, and a few servants. The extended family, usually with more relations living in close proximity, became a pattern found in several generations of Baldwins. William believed that 'nature has placed the Father in the situation of absolute Governor in his own House.' The centre of the household was Phœbe, whom her son Robert later described as 'the master mind of our family.' A sister of William's extolled Phœbe's 'excellent understanding and mental attainments,' which 'were of the greatest consequence and assistance to him.' Phœbe herself caught what marriage meant to the Baldwin men in a letter to Laurent Quetton St George in 1815: 'No real domestic comfort is to be enjoyed without a *good Wife.*' She rarely emerges from the shadows (few letters from her have survived) but what gleanings there are point to a dominant figure. William himself was an urbane, polished gentleman, tough-minded and possessed of a high self-regard. Yet he harboured a vulnerability which, if trifling in comparison to his son Robert's, was more real than has often been supposed. Elizabeth Russell described him in her diary as 'a poor dead hearted creature and always fears the worst.' Phœbe's illness in the fall of 1809 occasioned 'a gloomy mood'; as he later explained to St George, 'I am an Irishman and my wife was ill.' To be sure, in such a large extended family illness and death were frequent. Peter Russell died in 1808 and William Willcocks in 1813. Robert Sr, a man subject to 'low spirits,' died in November 1816. William himself suffered 'an attack which ... nearly carried me off' in the spring of 1817 and he was a long time recuperating. About this time his sister Alice (Ally) slipped into a sometimes violent and 'unhappy insanity.' After two suicide attempts, she was sent in 1819 to the Hôpital Général of Quebec (where she remained until her death in 1832). Elizabeth Russell's death in 1822 was another blow, although long expected. Most distressing were the deaths of Baldwin's children, 'the greatest blessing of human life.' 'Sweet' Henry's death in 1820 left William grief-stricken, as did his youngest son's in 1829. In his will William would direct that his 'mortal remains' be placed as close as possible to the latter 'dear child.'

By contrast with his family life, William's professional life was largely free of woe. It was not, however, necessarily easy. He travelled on the assize circuit, picking up business where he could and carrying out actions on behalf of various clients. In June 1814 he spent a few days at Ancaster, where the treason trials were in progress, but 'I was not applied to in behalf of any of them.' Life on circuit was hard if not on occasion harrowing. A story is told of Baldwin's becoming lost in the woods in 1815 and having to swim a swollen Credit River in the morning. Still, his practice was growing. He reckoned in 1819 that he cleared about £600 per annum, a sum sufficient – when combined with his emoluments of office and income from property – for him to have built the previous year a country house, which he called Spadina ('the Indian word for Hill – or Mont'), about three miles from York on land received as a gift from his father-in-law. Baldwin 'cut an avenue through the woods all the way so that we can see the vessels passing up and down the bay.' When finished, with a stable and gardens, the house cost about £1,500. By 1819 he had three clerks in his law office: James Edward Small, his nephew Daniel Sullivan, and Simon Ebenezer Washburn. The following year his son Robert joined the firm as a student-at-law and in 1823 his nephew Robert Baldwin Sullivan began his articling period. Washburn was a partner from 1820, the year he was admitted to the bar, until 1825, when Robert was admitted to the bar and became a partner.

Commerce was the basis of any Upper Canadian legal practice and William's was no exception. From 1815 he had, for instance, the principal responsibility for superintending the Upper Canadian enterprises of St George, who had returned to France. The following year he gave up the registrarship in the Court of Probate when he was appointed judge of the Surrogate Court, succeeding his father in this lucrative position. Estates inherited by the family and William's astute management of them not only added to his office's business but laid the basis for considerable wealth in the next generation. His wife and sister-in-law had inherited William Willcocks's properties, and when Maria Willcocks died in 1834 her estate went to the Baldwin family. Maria and Phœbe also inherited the vast Russell tracts after Elizabeth Russell's death. William himself was the heir to his father's property. Land acquisition and estate management were vital to Baldwin's prosperity and he amassed choice lots of both cultivated and uncultivated land. In the post-war years York was undergoing development and the value of property there was increasing. Baldwin benefited. He had acquired valuable land in town, some lots through purchase, others from his father-in-law's estate. By the 1820s he had become a large landowner and a wealthy man. His practice was now worth £700 a year while his wild (uncultivated) lands yielded an annual income of £1,400 (no figure is available for his rented farms or buildings but it was doubtless considerable). Although he lacked a single, large landed estate, he none the less closely approximated the English landed gentry in his ability to derive income from his holdings. He had all the trappings and attainments of gentility: education, refinement, a country home, and independent wealth. He was, as well, the doyen of his profession, holding the esteemed treasurership of the Law Society of Upper Canada for four separate terms (1811–15, 1820–21, 1824–28, and 1832–36).

But Baldwin's stature in Canadian history has little to do with these accomplishments. Rather his eminence lies in his contribution to the development of the best known, and least understood, principle of Canadian political life, responsible government. Generations of Canadian historians have accorded the Baldwins, father and son, pride of place in the elaboration of the central doctrine of colonial evolution to nationhood, and of the transformation of empire into commonwealth.

For someone considered so essential to this process of political development, Baldwin became publicly involved with it rather late in his career, probably deliberately so. Before 1820 he was not without political opinions – his association with the pre-war opposition is evidence of that – but his views are difficult to discern. One notes, for instance, his agreement with Firth in 1812 that 'a change of the Governor can effect but little change in the measures or deportment of the administration.' He undoubtedly shared Wyatt's disappointment in Joseph Willcocks's treason, but he applauded his castigation of 'those who persecuted him.' He also shared in the dissatisfaction with the administration's favouritism. Of Gore's departure in 1817 one of Baldwin's correspondents remarked, 'It's of very little consequence as the Scotch Party are at the Head yet and have it all among themselves.' This complaint – it had been a tenet of the pre-war opposition that Scots monopolized both offices and executive influence – was one with which Baldwin agreed. In 1813 he had related to Wyatt a pertinent incident. An altercation between officers of the Royal Newfoundland Regiment and a brother of Alexander Wood had resulted in criminal charges against the officers, and Baldwin defended them. When they were convicted of assault, he moved for an arrest of judgement but Chief Justice Thomas Scott overruled him, levying 'most unmeasured fines' on the officers. 'Such,' Baldwin reasoned, 'is the consequence of touching a Scottsman.'

His entry into politics came in the general election of 1820. Running in the riding of York and Simcoe and confident of success, or so Robert claimed, he was returned with Peter Robinson. Politically, the election came hard on the heels of Robert Gourlay's banishment, the prosecution of Gourlayite printer Bartemas Ferguson, the dismissal from office of the president of the Gourlayite convention, Richard Beasley, and Robert Nichol's formidable leadership of the opposition within the House of Assembly. Baldwin considered that electors had solicited his candidacy 'on the expectation of [his] rigid integrity towards the Constitution.' In a broadside he professed 'an affectionate regard' for British liberty and the British constitution, and 'to preserve the latter ever pure,' he declared, 'the first must be preserved unwounded.' He promised to avoid factious opposition to 'legitimate objects of the Administration' while maintaining 'that the purest Administration requires a vigilant activity on the part of all its constitutional checks.' Thus William thought his victory had given 'great public satisfaction to the independent part of the community & mortification to others.' Yet one historian who has analysed his conduct in this contest has depicted him as the eloquent defender of the administration, deeply grateful to it for office. The interpretation is exaggerated. Baldwin was 'thankful' to the administration that 'gave it, and the Government that has continued it to me' – nothing more. Two things are clear:

first, Baldwin was sufficiently prosperous to risk estrangement from government; secondly, he was not yet of a mind that such estrangement was warranted.

Baldwin was neither a manager, nor an organizer, nor a leader in the day-to-day affairs of the eighth parliament (1821–24). Nichol resumed his leadership of the opposition, although Barnabas Bidwell was a commanding presence for the one session he was in the house. Leadership for the administration was in the hands of Attorney General John Beverley Robinson and his principal supporters, Christopher Alexander Hagerman and Jonas Jones. Compared to Baldwin, assemblymen such as John Willson or Charles Jones spoke more often in debate and produced more legislation. Baldwin's initiatives were usually confined to debate on topics that reflected his own priorities.

His privately expressed concern for the state of the economy took public shape as a motion proposing the formation of a committee to examine the agricultural depression and the collapse of British markets. The resulting committee on internal resources (which included Baldwin and was chaired by Nichol) tabled its report – the first attempt to devise a comprehensive provincial strategy for economic development – on 31 March 1821. Eight months later Baldwin supported Hagerman's resolution for encouraging hemp production, a favourite policy of the executive since Hunter's administration. Later still, in a manner calculated to advance the interests of a large landowner, he lamented 'those restrictions, fees, and regulations, which operated equally against the poor as the Capitalist' in the administration of land grants, and he championed the principle that 'capital ought to be blended with labour' to ensure prosperity. In 1824, and again in 1828, he was one of the most percipient critics of Robinson's acts taxing the uncultivated lands of speculators such as Baldwin himself. On both occasions, he joined forces with the Niagara area merchants Thomas Clark and William Dickson, who opposed the measures in the Legislative Council.

A gentleman who advocated a hierarchical society, Baldwin delivered in December 1821 the clearest enunciation of his aristocratic beliefs. The occasion was his attack on a bill sponsored by Bidwell and David McGregor Rogers which would have eliminated the operation of primogeniture on intestate estates. This 'visionary scheme,' more appropriate to a republic, 'aimed at a total Revolution in the laws.' 'Aristocracy, upon which the *happy, happy* Constitution of Great Britain rested, would be destroyed,' and he wished to see aristocracy 'supported in this Colony to preserve the constitution ... and not [to] run into a scheme of Democracy by establishing new fangled laws.' Robinson, the avatar of the *ancien régime*, was left with nothing to say but that he 'agreed with every word.'

Baldwin was a whig constitutionalist whose ideas on law and politics were similar to those of the pre-war opposition led by Thorpe and Willcocks and the post-war opposition initiated by Nichol. His emphasis on limited government, retrenchment of expenditures, the independence of the constitution's respective parts, and the civil rights and liberties of subjects was consistent with the country tradition in English politics. His first substantial speech in 1821 was on an attempt to repeal the Sedition Act of 1804, which – although it had been used only to banish Gourlay – had been a frequent target of Nichol's since 1817. So long as it remained law, Upper Canadians were 'without a constitution; at least a *free one*.' The act 'remained in force, not only in the face of Magna Charta, but directly in the face of all the statutes made for the liberty and protection of the subject.' He then read to the house long passages from Blackstone on the liberties of subjects. Used against British subjects, he argued, the act was 'arbitrary and tyrannical.' It undermined trial by jury, 'the great land-mark in our constitution,' and was more cruel than 'the Inquisition or Star Chamber.'

These utterances were commonplace and they serve only to locate Baldwin within the whig tradition. More important were his thoughts on Upper Canada's constitution. He freely invoked the solemn authority of Blackstone on liberty but preferred Irish models for the question of the sovereignty of colonial legislatures. His remarks on this subject were prompted by the report of a joint committee of the assembly and the council on commercial intercourse with Lower Canada. Chaired by William Dickson and Robinson, the committee tabled its report (written by the attorney general) in December 1821. Baldwin had specific objections to it but his salient points were matters of principle: 'it admitted as a principle that ... this legislature cannot impose duties on imports'; 'it acknowledges an incapacity in ourselves to govern ... ourselves – & in effect gives our consent to surrender our Constitution [the Constitutional Act of 1791] back to British Parliament'; and 'it does not in distinct terms present what we would wish – but leaves it to the discretion of the Imperial Parliament to do with us as it may please.' These principles were 'subversive of every thing Valuable in our constitution. ... The B. Parliament could not repeal that Law – the British Parlt can make and repeal the Laws of England because the parties to the making of the Law are the parties to the repealing of it, but not so here – that act gives legislative power to the inhabitants of this province – and the Law cannot be repealed without those inhabitants are parties to the repeal.' 'But alas,' he added, 'here is the point of dread.'

That point became clearer, as Baldwin had anticipated, during the debate in 1823 over a proposed union of the Canadas. In his view the Constitutional Act of 1791 conferred on the province's inhabitants 'the right to make laws for their peace, welfare and good government, reserving certain powers to the King and Parliament ... to legislate in particular cases.' The imperial parliament, he argued, 'could not constitutionally alter *this* law without our consent; for if so, we had no constitution at all.' The proposal for union had originated with a 'commercial faction' in Lower Canada willing to trade 'some speculative objects of imaginary advantages ... in exchange for our Constitution.' Denouncing many of the clauses of the imperial union bill as 'ruinous innovations,' he found 'neither wisdom, good sense, nor justice evinced by the framers of that monstrous bill.' The most intriguing contribution to the debate was Baldwin's statement that what the Canadas had received was not, as Lieutenant Governor John Graves Simcoe had often averred, 'the image and transcript' of the British constitution, but rather the spirit of the constitution. Why, Baldwin wondered, would restless spirits abandon the Constitutional Act just as it was about 'to change the French-man into the Englishman; or rather, as it was about to change the Frenchman into the Canadian; (for there might be, and there *was*, a Canadian Character distinct from the French, and though not English was yet properly reconcilable to and perfectly consistent with English feelings, English connection, and English Constitution;).'

Baldwin stood again for York and Simcoe in the election of 1824, placing a close third in a ten-man race and thus losing his seat. Unfortunately, that defeat eliminated his participation in assembly debates, the reporting of which provides historians with a valuable source for the study of Upper Canadian political thought during the tumultuous ninth parliament (1825–28). During this period, Baldwin turned his attention to what he began to see as partiality in the provincial administration of justice; in the process he became a partisan opponent of Sir Peregrine Maitland's government and of his chief advisers.

In 1818 William had written of Robert's future, 'I intend please God to bring him up to the bar.' There was no higher calling. When stepping down as treasurer of the Law Society in 1836, William detailed in his letter of resignation the special relationship of the constitution, parliament, and the law. As embodied in the 1791 act, the constitution was decidedly aristocratic, and Baldwin was not only one of its greatest admirers but also one of its greatest defenders. His willingness to duel for the sake of his honour and his ardent defence of primogeniture were tied to the natural, political, and social inequality he wished to preserve. He had defended in 1821 a bill enabling the Law Society to raise money for offices and a library to eliminate the necessity of new lawyers conducting their business in places 'unfit ... for gentlemen.' 'There was,' he reasoned, 'no Society for which the country should feel so deep an interest. ... Without it, whose property was safe?' As he wrote in 1836, the society 'has ever appeared to me of most importance to the preservation and due administration of our Constitution.' In a province lacking an aristocracy, the rule of gentlemen and the presence of a legal profession were indispensable. Crucial to gentility were rectitude, disinterested behaviour, and decorum; crucial to the legal profession was defence of the constitution and the rights which it entailed.

Baldwin's address to the jury in 1827 during George Rolph's civil suit against his assailants in a celebrated tar-and-feather incident is a specific example of Baldwin's convictions. He was disturbed that Rolph's tormentors, who were successfully defended by Allan Napier MacNab, included several gentlemen prominent in the Gore District, 'persons holding responsible offices, even occupying the seats of Justice – one of them entrusted ... with the sword of Justice.' Subsequent events served to concentrate his attention on the administration of justice. Rolph's case was followed by hotelier William Forsyth's petition to the assembly in January 1828 complaining of Maitland's substitution of military force for legal process 'to decide the question of right' in a dispute that became renowned in opposition lore as the outrage at Niagara Falls. A select committee's investigation led to a full-scale constitutional confrontation between Maitland and the assembly, which the lieutenant governor prorogued on 31 March. Then, in April at the York Assizes before John Walpole Willis, the opposition journalist Francis Collins reprimanded Attorney General Robinson for his partiality in the administration of justice.

In response to this charge Robinson, on 12 May 1828, sent out a letter to members of the bar raising the question of bias in his department. Baldwin replied on the 31st in a lengthy note. Although he had thus far 'preserved a public silence,' Robinson's circular compelled him 'candidly' to state 'wherein I thought you omitted your duty.' The first instance he cited was the attorney general's failure 'in some public and impressive manner [to] reprove your Clerks who were parties in' the riot which resulted in the destruction of William Lyon Mackenzie's press in 1826. Their conduct was 'quite unbecoming Gentlemen and still more unbecoming them as Students at Law.' The printer's conduct was 'very bad' but Baldwin averred that his punishment should have been 'reproof or prosecution,' not 'outrage.' The assault on Rolph was another instance of dereliction of duty, Baldwin continued, and neither Robinson nor Solicitor General Henry John Boulton could escape public censure for not 'promptly and vigorously turning the Law against the perpetrators.' It was unconscionable in his view that Boulton might later act as the public prosecutor in a criminal action against the culprits, having already defended them against Rolph's civil suit. He found the whole episode 'so subversive of justice that I fully partook of the public disapprobation of that scene.' The last instance he cited was the 1822–23 case of Singleton Gardiner, who had confronted two magistrates over the performance of statute labour. Abused by them, Gardiner, with Baldwin as his counsel, had launched a civil action against them. Robinson, acting as their attorney, insisted it was his duty to protect the justices. Baldwin agreed 'wherein they are in the right; but my opinion also is that it is your duty to prosecute them wherein they are grossly wrong.'

Matters came to a head in June 1828. On the 16th Willis declared that, to function, the Court of King's Bench required the presence of the chief justice and the two puisne justices. With Chief Justice William Campbell on leave, only Willis and Levius Peters Sherwood were sitting. With the constitutionality of the bench in doubt, the Baldwins and Washburn wrote to Willis the following day enquiring if he would invite Sherwood's consideration of the question and asking, in the event Sherwood's opinion was not immediately forthcoming, if Willis would 'withhold his Judgement' in any cases involving their clients, 'untill as their Counsel we be better advised as to the course to be adopted.' On 23 June the Baldwins, in conjunction with John Rolph, protested to Sherwood 'against any Proceedings ... until the Court be established according to the Provisions of the Provincial Statutes.' The issue was not merely a debate about 'the strictest Principles of

Law.' 'There are no Laws,' they wrote, 'demanding a more religious Observance than those which limit and define the Power of Individuals forming the Government over their Fellow Creatures.' The administration's decision to remove Willis in late June precipitated a political reaction unlike anything the province had known, and the sense of crisis was fuelled by the impending general election in July. The Baldwins entered the fray, William in Norfolk and Robert in the riding of York. The elder Baldwin had been *'required, and not invited'* to run by John Rolph, who considered him 'the only person ... combining all that is desirable in a representative of a free people.' Although Robert lost, William was elected along with incumbent Duncan McCall. Provincially the opposition gained a clear majority of members.

In York William was at the centre of a whirlwind of activity. During the campaign he had become, according to the pro-administration journalist Robert Stanton, 'a regular travelling Stump *Orator*.' Stanton thought him 'mad' but Baldwin's commitment to opposition was principled, and total. The legacy of the Willis agitation over the summer and fall of 1828 was multifold: formal reform organizations at York which would endure until the rebellion of 1837, sustained cooperation among pre-eminent reform leaders, and tactical planning by the opposition for the legislative session of 1829. William Baldwin loomed large in these developments as the elder statesman of the opposition coalition, and Robert was also prominent. It was not so much that the Baldwins needed other reformers; rather the reformers needed the Baldwins. The period was, after all, still the age of gentlemen, and the Baldwins were nothing if not gentlemen. And, as gentlemen, they were symbols of legitimacy for the broad reform alliance. Maitland put the point neatly in September 1828, describing Baldwin as 'the only person throughout the Province, in the character of a gentleman, who has associated himself with the promoters of Mr. Hume's projects,' his allusion being to the British radical Joseph Hume. The most perceptive opposition leaders, John Rolph and Marshall Spring Bidwell, realized the importance of the Baldwins in this regard and used their organizational and manipulative talents to manœuvre the father and son into the positions to which their duty, as lawyers, Christians, and gentlemen, pointed.

Dr Baldwin addressed a constitutional meeting convened on 5 July 1828 to 'complain of the arbitrary, oppressive, and high-handed conduct of the Colonial Executive' in removing Willis. The purpose of the meeting was, he said, to consider petitioning the king for redress of grievances. The alarm of those assembled sprang not from 'unworthy or womanish fears' but from the concern of 'men and patriots jealous of their rights and anxious to guard their liberties ... from arbitrary power.' To acquiesce in the administration's conduct would be tantamount to surrendering the constitution. He urged his listeners to be 'watchful at election,' for the power was in their hands to return men independent of the executive. In language faintly reminiscent of his attack on the union, he suggested that the 'legislatures of these Provinces have never been formed agreeable to the spirit of our constitution.' In Upper Canada, for instance, legislative councillors 'are placemen and pensioners, depending upon the Executive for a living, instead of being an independent gentry.' He hoped the council would be remodelled, 'odious' statutes repealed, and the 'laws impartially administered.' Of his seven proposals for redressing the colony's grievances, his sixth is of particular interest. He called for a provincial act 'to facilitate the Mode in which the present constitutional Responsibility of the Advisers of the Local Government may be carried practically into Effect, not only by the Removal of these Advisers from Office when they lose the Confidence of the People, but also by Impeachment for the heavier Offences chargeable against them.'

It having been decided to memorialize the king, Baldwin presided at a meeting called on 15 August to draw up the petition. A number of resolutions were proposed and accepted. The critical 13th, moved by Robert, was an unequivocal summation of William's position on the sovereignty of the Upper Canadian legislature: 'That our constitutional act ... is a treaty between the Mother Country and us ... pointing out and regulating the mode in which we shall exercise those rights which, independent of that act, belonged to us as British subjects, and ... that that act, being in fact, a treaty, can only be abrogated or altered by the consent of both the parties to it.'

William's outstanding contribution to Canadian and imperial history is assumed by many historians to have been the idea of responsible government. Others have stressed his role in the transition from the idea of ministerial responsibility (that is, the legal responsibility of the king's ministers to the legislature enforced by impeachment) to the idea of responsible government (which meant the political responsibility of individual ministers or the cabinet to the elected house), a change which supposedly took place in the thinking of Canadian reformers between 1822 and 1828. The former concept was commonplace in England by the 1760s, had been used by Thorpe and Pierre-Stanislas Bédard before the War of 1812, and had been articulated by Nichol in 1820. So far as can be determined by the newspaper accounts of the debates of the eighth parliament (1821–24), Baldwin did not express himself on the matter, confining his remarks to the sovereignty of the colonial parliament as derived from its constitution; however, it would be fair to assume, given his statements on these questions, that he was familiar with the notion of ministerial responsibility. Both notions are present in his speech of 5 July 1828.

In a memorandum he penned in his copy of Charles Buller's *Responsible government for colonies* (London, 1840), Baldwin gave an account of responsible government in Upper Canada, a 'subject [that] well deserves complex elucidation in the way of an historical exposition of the evils, which early accruing and becoming inveterate led to its regeneration [there].' As the public documents for the early history of the province had, he thought, largely been lost, he began his history with a petition against union that he had drafted in 1822. He did so not because it touched on responsible government but because it presented evidence of the 'constitutional rights then entertained by the people, in Contra distinction to the sentiments of the executive authorities ... and of their dependents & partizans.' He moved to the resolutions of 15 Aug. 1828 as the next bench-mark in the development of the great principle. He then proceeded to his own letters to colonial authorities which 'contain the development of the nature of the responsibility required and of the means of affecting it, after the example of the British Constitution; The suggestion in its distinct shape was made by Robert Baldwin ... in private conversation with me on the occasion of penning those letters.'

William Baldwin had realized as early as 1812 that merely changing a governor did not necessarily change an administration. For a whig of an aristocratic bent, the Legislative Council was the means by which the mixed constitution was kept in balance and liberty preserved, and as late as July 1828 Baldwin seemed to be thinking of the constitution from that perspective. The new tack he adopted, whether originating with his son or not, necessitated acceptance of the executive's political responsibility to the assembly, and from it to the electorate. The electorate at issue was not the British one limited to the world of gentlemen, however, but the Upper Canadian electorate based on close to universal manhood suffrage. The great question is, why did the Baldwins think such a principle would preserve a deferential and aristocratic society? The answer, if there is one, is not clear.

Behind the scenes, Rolph and Bidwell were exerting their influence on the elder statesman of reform. On 8 Sept. 1828 Bidwell suggested to William a conference to include Rolph 'on the measures to be adopted to relieve this province from the evils which a family compact have brought upon it. ... The whole system and spirit of the present administration need to be done away.' Baldwin relayed the message to Rolph who, 'as one of His Majesty's faithful opposition,' urged a concerted effort to choose the speaker for the forthcoming session of parliament as 'a serious part of our cabinet arrangements.' He also hoped that the assembly under Baldwin's 'wise and prudent counsel ... shall be enabled to carry the strongest measures and the most vital improvements.'

Copies of the August petition were circulated widely for signatures through the fall and early winter of 1828. On 3 Jan. 1829 Baldwin forwarded the accumulated petitions to the British prime minister, the Duke of Wellington, inviting his 'thoughts to that principle of the British Constitution, in the actual use of which the Colonists alone hope for *peace Good Government and Prosperity*' as pledged by the Constitutional Act. The principle alluded to was the 'presence of a Provincial Ministry (if I may be allowed to use the term) responsible to the Provincial Parliament, and removable from Office by his Majesty's representative at his pleasure and especially when they lose the confidence of the people as expressed by the voice of their representatives in the Assembly; and that all acts of the Kings representative should have the character of local responsibility, by the signature of some member of this Ministry.' Once he had adopted this language and principle, Baldwin's rhetoric became less moderate and more censorious. Bidwell had written to William on 28 May 1828 that 'Power, unaccompanied with any real responsibility, any practical accountability, can never be confided safely to any man.' It seems reasonable to assume that the influence of Rolph and Bidwell, whose language was much sharper, much earlier, had had an effect in showing Baldwin how executive power could be made practically accountable.

Baldwin's remarks in the house in early January 1829 on the speech from the throne highlight his new approach. Conveniently forgetting some of his own favourable statements, both private and public, about the Maitland administration, he now lumped together successive administrations from Simcoe's onward and lashed them for their pursuit of 'the same injurious course.' He also described as 'evil' the advisers who had tried to foist union on the province. The assembly should, he thought, 'be considered the great Council of the country.' In a private letter to Robert on 25 January he listed the evil advisers, some of whom were on the Executive Council: Robinson and his brother Peter, John Strachan, Henry John Boulton, and James Buchanan Macaulay. They should be 'dismissed from office and from the *Cabinet Council* – this term might be adopted with advantage.' Terms such as this one he was picking up from Rolph and Bidwell. In the debate on the speech from the throne he had urged Rolph's appointment 'at the top of the Treasury Bench as it had been called.' It had been called that minutes earlier by Rolph himself. On the abstract level, Baldwin noted in the house that the assembly 'should be placed on the same footing as the House of Commons ... otherwise those who sat in it could not properly be called the Representatives of the people.' Responsible government made the executive accountable to the assembly – suggesting parties even in an inchoate state – and the electorate. In 1836 he was to write to Robert, 'It was no matter what the parties were called, whig or tory – parties will be, and must be ... therefore it becomes important [for the executive] to have the concurrence of the Assembly.' A year after the throne debate, Baldwin suggested to Joseph Hume four means for remedying the evils of Upper Canada: control of revenues by the assembly, exclusion of the judiciary from the councils, reorganization of the Legislative Council (but not on an elective principle), and the 'formation of a new executive or Cabinet Council, responsible and removable as the public interest may demand – which it is anticipated would of itself indirectly lead to the removal of all our present grievances & prevent the recurrence of any such for the future.'

William and Robert both contested their seats in the election of October 1830 and lost. Bitter, William withdrew from political life. In 1831 he seems to have retired from his law practice, or at least let Robert and his new partner, Robert Baldwin Sullivan, assume the greater part of the burden. That same year he and Phœbe moved back into York to live with Robert and his family. The 'extreme fickleness of popular opinion' at elections weighed on his mind and in 1834, when offered an opportunity to participate in a political meeting, he declined. His public role was not in eclipse, however. The gentlemanly Baldwins were attractive to conciliatory administrators as the right sort of oppositionists. Both were considered for the Legislative Council in 1835, but neither was appointed. In that year Spadina was razed by fire. A smaller house would be erected on the site; William was also to design and build a large Georgian-style mansion in town.

The arrival of a new lieutenant governor in Toronto on 23 Jan. 1836 stirred reform hopes. Sir Francis Bond Head made overtures to the opposition by reconstructing the Executive Council. After numerous negotiations, Head brought Robert Baldwin, Rolph, and John Henry Dunn into the council. William, whose name had come up, was not interested. He was convinced that the answer to the colony's problems was 'a responsible Government through the medium of the Executive Council ... discharging its duties in the way analogous to the Cabinet Council of the King in England.' The council's subsequent resignation in March hurled the province into its most serious political-constitutional crisis since the Willis affair. Robert, whose wife had died on 11 January, headed off to England and Ireland to be alone with his grief while William superintended family matters at home and witnessed the political desertion in March of his brother Augustus Warren and of his nephew Robert Baldwin Sullivan to Head's council, into the arms of the 'Tory junto' as he put it.

Meanwhile, no doubt at the urging of a neighbour, Francis Hincks, Baldwin joined the executive committee of the Constitutional Reform Society of Upper Canada, where he consorted with William John O'Grady, Rolph, and others. He was given the most distinguished positions: he became president of the society and was also made chairman of the Toronto Political Union. That July Head dismissed him as district and surrogate court judge, citing as reason his signature as president on a reform society document upholding the basic doctrines of reformers. William denounced the election of July 1836 as Head's 'vicious triumph over the people.' Head believed Baldwin knew of the preparations for the rebellion of 1837, but Baldwin denied it and Mackenzie later corroborated his statement. On 1 Jan. 1838 Baldwin published a letter indicating his position. 'Great reform' was still required but it must be 'lawful and constitutional.' His political activity after the election of 1836 had been 'solely directed to the means of discovering the facts of unconstitutional interference in behalf of Government.' When the discussions of reform groups proved 'unproductive,' he no longer went to meetings and could not recollect having attended any since Robert's return from England in February

1837. He deplored the 'rash insurrection' which had the effect of 'silencing for many years to come, the voice of Reform, even the most rational and temperate.' As for the Patriot incursions, he considered them foreign invasions and was willing to take up arms against them.

Many remedies were put forward in the 1830s by various reformers to eliminate the evil rule of what most considered a corrupt oligarchy. Responsible government, the favourite of the Baldwins, was but one, albeit the least threatening – or so the Baldwins thought – to the constitution, the social order, and the British connection. William understood oligarchy in terms of classical political philosophy: it was the degenerate, or unconstitutional, form of aristocracy. He believed, even in mid 1836, that the political contention within the upper province was related 'to the mere administration of affairs'; in Lower Canada, it concerned the actual 'form of government.' The failed rebellion eliminated more radical proposals while elevating the status of the Baldwins' moderate principle. In fact, a gesture in their direction was considered in 1835 and proffered in 1836. The Baldwins had a brief interview with Governor Lord Durham [Lambton] during his July tour of Upper Canada in 1838. By this time responsible government and the voluntary principle with respect to church and state had become the key articles of reform canon. The reformers' chief desire, articulated by Hincks in the *Examiner* of 18 July, was that the lieutenant governor 'administer the internal affairs of the Province with the advice of a RESPONSIBLE PROVINCIAL CABINET, and not under the influence of a *Family Compact*, as at present.' On 1 August William sent Durham, as did Robert, a long letter 'on the subject of public discontent.' Among the 20 causes he listed were the crown and clergy reserves, the land-granting department, the monopoly of the Canada Company, interference by the executive in elections, revenues of the executive independent of the assembly, parliamentary obstruction by the Legislative Council, the encouragement of Orange societies, and the 'extravagant waste' on projects such as the Welland Canal. His chief recommendation was the application of 'English principles of responsibility ... to our local Executive Council.' Implementation of those principles came bit by bit.

William was now too old to participate actively in politics and was content to advise the chief standard-bearer of responsible government, Robert. William's understanding of the idea had been certain for some time, and it would not change. He thought it was 'conceded' by Colonial Secretary Lord John Russell's dispatch of 10 Oct. 1839.

And he held out high hopes initially for Governor Charles Edward Poulett Thomson's plans for a reconstituted Executive Council of the soon-to-be united province. In the late 1830s his descriptions of politics evolved, as they had in 1828, into increasingly harsh portraits. Head's interference in the election of 1836 was without parallel: 'There could not be devised ... by the most despotic Government a more wicked scheme of oppressing us.' By June 1841 he saw politics as an 'important struggle between good Govt. and evil govt.' Several months later the contest had acquired Manichean tones: 'I really believe the fight is with the powers of darkness.' And he meant it. The 'horrible violence from the Tories' which had so astonished him during the Yonge Street riot of November 1839 seemed to have acquired a permanency which was, as late as 1843, still upholding the 'old vile Tory system.'

William was an Anglican of deep personal faith, intolerant of the Orange order – he had tried to legislate its suppression in 1823 – and the clergy reserves, but tolerant of dissenters and Roman Catholics. He shared with most of his contemporaries a providential faith which focused increasingly by the late 1830s on Robert's appointed role in the divine plan. 'God will direct you,' he wrote to him in 1841, 'therefore you cannot err.' Robert believed him and agonized even more over every decision. In his will of 1842 William, who still believed firmly in primogeniture, left almost everything to Robert, explaining his decision to Phœbe in this way: 'One child only can be born first – and this in all time and societies ... has been received as the appointment of Providence. ... It tends to preserve a reverence for the institutions of our ancestors, which though always tending to change, for by nature all human affairs must change, yet resist innovations but those only which are gradual and temperate.' Perhaps William's greatest legacy was the deep personal impression he made upon his eldest son. After his father's death in 1844 Robert wrote: 'Those only who knew him intimately can appreciate the loss which we have sustained in the death of such a parent – All that is left us is to honour his memory by endeavouring to imitate his example.' And honour it Robert did.

William Warren Baldwin had had a variety of social and cultural concerns. A wealthy man, he subscribed to most philanthropic bodies, and he was a director of the Bank of Upper Canada, manager of the Home District Savings Bank, and a member of both the Medical Board of Upper Canada and the York Board of Health. He was also an early president of the Toronto Mechanics' Institute, a member of St James' Church, and an advocate of missionary work among the Indians. Charles Morrison Durand, a Hamilton lawyer, remembered him as a 'haughty, prejudiced, Protestant Irish gentleman ... very rough and aristocratic in his ways.' Although warm to his family, he had an aloofness that reflected a tough inner core. He knew this quality in himself. 'I seem to myself quite hard – when I witness the distress of those around me – what a strange comportment is Mine – I really know nothing of myself – I wish a friend could tell me – and yet I would shrink from his candour.'

ROBERT L. FRASER

DONALD BETHUNE
Shipowner, lawyer, and politician; b. 11 July 1802 in Williamstown, Charlottenburg Township, Upper Canada, youngest of nine children of the Reverend John Bethune and Véronique Waddens; d. 19 June 1869 at Toronto, Ont.

Donald Bethune's early education was obtained at the grammar school of his brother John in Augusta Township and at John Strachan's school in Cornwall. Another of Donald's brothers, Alexander Neil Bethune, was Strachan's protégé. At age 14 Donald began articling in law under the prominent Brockville lawyer and politician, Jonas Jones, and in 1823 was called to the bar of Upper Canada. In 1826 he was appointed commissioner of customs for the Midland District and between 1826 and 1835 he was twice appointed judge of the Bathurst District Court and once of the Prince Edward District Court. In Kingston, where he had settled in 1824, competition between lawyers was rigorous. Of necessity Bethune began to diversify his interests. He became involved in local banking politics and ran as an independent conservative in the 1828 House of Assembly elections, defeating the influential incumbent Christopher Hagerman. His two years in the assembly were undistinguished and he in turn was defeated by Hagerman in 1830.

While continuing his association with the Kingston branch of the Bank of Upper Canada, as both a local director and solicitor, Bethune began to dabble in the shipping and forwarding business. Business contacts for these activities were provided by his brothers, and by his father-in-law, Peter Smith, an early settler and notable businessman of Kingston, whose daughter Janet (Jennet) Bethune had married in 1826. Bethune launched his first steamboat in 1833. The pattern of his initial experience was to be repeated throughout his career as an owner of steamboats on Lake Ontario. He quickly ran out of cash as did his brothers, James Gray and Norman, with whom he had close financial dealings. Their conduct aroused the ire of the cautious William Allan, president of the Bank of Upper Canada, who wrote to

John Macaulay in 1833: 'I am perfectly sick of ... hearing of the many traffics and speculations entered into as long as they can draw Dft. [drafts] or get Notes discounted at the *Bank.*' It was beyond his comprehension that Donald Bethune could 'ask for *time* and indulgence' and that he was involved 'in business as much out of the way of what he ought to be ... is [as this]. ... ' If Allan ever confronted Bethune with this advice, it was ignored.

Bethune's headquarters were at Cobourg between 1840 and 1843. Attempting to capitalize on his prestige as lieutenant-colonel of militia in the Cobourg area during the rebellion and border problems of 1837-40, Bethune ran as an independent conservative in Northumberland South in the election of 1841. Branded a 'troublesome person' by Sir George Arthur because of his challenge to Hagerman and his business dealings, and because he was considered a follower of Sir Allan MacNab, Bethune did not receive the backing of influential Toronto Tories and was defeated by George Morss Boswell.

He then devoted himself to his shipping interests. Awarded the government contract for mail delivery in 1840, he quickly arranged route and rate agreements with potential competitors such as John Hamilton, Hugh Richardson, Thomas Dick, and Andrew Heron, and between 1840 and 1842 purchased five steamers from the Niagara Harbour and Dock Company. Liberal credit was extended to Bethune by William Cayley, then president of the dock company, by the Bank of Upper Canada of which Cayley was a director, and by the Commercial Bank of the Midland District. In 1842, Bethune had an interest in, if not sole ownership of, at least ten Lake Ontario steamboats.

Bethune moved his operations to Toronto after 1843. Aspiring to monopoly, he was faced with only one major competitor by 1846 – Hugh Richardson of Toronto, owner of three vessels. Price-cutting ensued and as a shrewd observer, John Elmsley, put it, 'Bethune and Richardson I look upon as gone loons ... they are now running against each other to their mutual destruction.' When Richardson declared bankruptcy in the summer of 1846, Bethune probably anticipated no financial difficulties. But by 1845 he had already severely overextended his credit, and the purchase of one or more of Richardson's boats in 1847 sealed his fate. Desperate, he mortgaged boats in favour of his major creditor, the Bank of Upper Canada. His wife's uncle, John David Smith, endorsed for him a note for £16,000 which both he and Bethune ultimately failed to meet. Bethune raised rates for the transport of goods and passengers, and even ran unsuccessfully for the assembly in Toronto in 1847 on a platform decrying the lack of protection for the merchants of Canada's inland seas. All his measures failed. Beset by the recession of 1848, new competition, decaying equipment, and a debt to the Bank of Upper Canada exceeding £30,000, as well as innumerable debts to merchants along the shores of Lake Ontario, Bethune's business collapsed late in 1848. Sued for non-payment of debts, he was forced to hand over his boats to the sheriff of York for public auction. The bank, however, could not afford to let Bethune go under and therefore leased the mortgaged boats to him. By 1851, despite rate agreements with competitors, Bethune was again bankrupt. In 1853 he left for England with £4,000 of company funds, and by 1855 all of his boats had been sold.

Bethune returned to Canada in 1858 after what he probably hoped would be the last suit concerning his bankruptcy. To his chagrin he was forced by the master in chancery to assume liability for part of his debts. He settled in Port Hope and resumed the practice of law. Two pieces of evidence indicate that he had attained some degree of prosperity by 1864: he was being bothered by old creditors for repayment of debts and his prowess as a lawyer was recognized by his being named QC.

Donald Bethune's business activities had no permanent results for Upper Canada. Yet his career is important as a significant example of the reckless promotion characteristic of both water and rail transportation. Banking methods were loose and credit was easy; owners and operators were often prepared to seek profits at the expense of customers and creditors. Bethune's career accurately reflects the expansive tempo of the times.

PETER BASKERVILLE

MARSHALL SPRING BIDWELL

Lawyer and politician; b. 16 Feb. 1799 in Stockbridge, Mass., son of Barnabas Bidwell and Mary Gray; m. Clara Willcox of Bath, near Kingston, U.C., and they had four children; d. 24 Oct. 1872 in New York City, N.Y.

Marshall Spring's father, Barnabas Bidwell, who had been attorney general of Massachusetts, a member of Congress, and an ardent Jeffersonian, was forced to leave his home state in 1810 after he had been accused of malversation of funds. The family settled in Upper Canada at Bath just before the War of 1812. The young Bidwell was educated in the local schools and at home by his father who laid the foundation of his profound legal learning. When he was about 17 Marshall Spring was articled as a student to Daniel Washburn and Daniel Hagerman, barristers and attorneys-at-law in Kingston, where the Bidwell family soon moved, and in 1821 he was called to the bar. From the beginning he had outstanding and continuous success as a courtroom lawyer.

Marshall Spring Bidwell and his father first came into public prominence in Upper Canada in the early 1820s in connection with the 'alien question': whether Americans who had come into the colony in the previous quarter century must undergo a complicated naturalization procedure before they could enjoy political and civil rights as British subjects. In 1821 the House of Assembly voted to expel Barnabas from the seat he had won a few weeks earlier, on the grounds that the charges earlier made against him in Massachusetts rendered him unfit to hold his seat. A law was subsequently passed obviously intended to exclude the elder Bidwell from membership. Thereupon Marshall Spring offered himself as a candidate at the ensuing by-election, but the returning officer declared him ineligible to be a candidate. Again in 1823 the matter came before the assembly, which now declared that the younger Bidwell was eligible for membership so far as allegiance was concerned. In a second by-election in 1823, however, he was again excluded by the returning officer, and again the assembly declared the election void. Finally, in the general elections of 1824, the returning officer allowed votes to be counted for him; he was elected and took his seat, despite a ruling by the British law officers that he as well as his father was not qualified for membership. He represented Lennox and Addington until defeated in 1836.

The assembly of 1824, for the first time in Upper Canada's history, contained a majority of members highly critical of the executive branch of government – that is, of the group soon to be known as the 'Family Compact' – and determined to seek reform through new legislation. At the outset, the young Bidwell, still in his mid-twenties, took front rank as a leader of the assembly, working closely with his colleague from Lennox and Addington, Peter Perry, and with Dr John Rolph. Bidwell in the years 1825–28 moved the adoption of bills on such subjects as allowing benefit of defence counsel for persons tried for felony, providing for more equal distribution of the property of persons dying intestate, the abolition of imprisonment for debt and of punishment by whipping and the pillory, wider control by the assembly over the revenue and the post office, and the broadening of the law governing the solemnization of marriage. He also supported bills for the sale of the clergy reserves, with the proceeds to be used for erecting schools, and for the regulation of juries. These bills passed the assembly session after session but were as regularly thrown out by the Legislative Council. Bidwell also played a leading role in the protracted alien controversy, which resulted, in 1828, in the passage of a naturalization act acceptable to the American-born element in the province.

Party feelings and alignments were further inflamed and sharpened in 1827 by the Reverend John Strachan's 'Ecclesiastical Chart,' which inflated the strength of the Church of England in the province and accused Methodist clergymen of being agents of Americanization, and by the university charter, secured in England by Strachan, which reserved seats on the council of King's College to Anglicans. In response, the assembly set up a select committee, chaired by Marshall Spring Bidwell, to look into the danger of 'ecclesiastical domination.' Its report of 1828 is probably an accurate reflection of Bidwell's political outlook. It stated that the people of Upper Canada had a 'strong aversion' to an established church and to 'artificial distinctions between men of the same rank,' that they demanded an educational system free of distinction based on 'religious profession or belief,' and that the university should not be 'a school of politics or of sectarian views.' On 28 May 1828 Bidwell wrote to his fellow Reformer, William Warren Baldwin, that the affairs of the province were in a state of crisis because the government held 'power, unaccompanied by any real responsibility, any practical accountability' and that 'power, under such circumstances, will always be abused and its possessors corrupted.' On the following 8 September, he assured Baldwin: 'I shall be happy to consult with yourself and Mr. Rolph on the measures to be adopted to relieve the province from the evils which a family compact have brought upon it. ... The whole system and spirit of the present administration need to be done away with.' He also wrote on 7 Jan. 1829 to John Neilson, the Quebec newspaperman and moderate Reformer, that changes would come about, not by making appeals to the British government, but by the people of Canada acting 'with union and concert and tak[ing] such ground only as can be maintained by reason and truth.'

In the elections of 1828 the Upper Canadian Reformers strengthened their majority in the assembly and proceeded to elect Bidwell speaker. At this time, before the advent of cabinet or responsible government, the speaker was not an impartial presiding officer; instead, he was an active, partisan politician. Bidwell's election, like that of Louis-Joseph Papineau as speaker of the Lower Canadian assembly, marks him as the leader of his party. As speaker, however, he did not make motions or vote, and it is not possible to identify him directly with the work of the short parliament of 1829–30. It can be assumed, however, that he was a strong supporter of such bills as those to abolish imprisonment for debt, to sell the clergy reserves, and to broaden the law governing solemnization of marriage, as well as of numerous resolutions sharply critical of Lieutenant Governor Sir John Colborne and the executive government.

In the 1830 elections enough seats changed hands to place the Reformers in a minority, and Bidwell resumed his role as Reform floor leader. Although outnumbered, he and his followers were often able to carry their measures, such as the intestate estates bill, through the house. A Tory newspaper explained the situation as follows: 'Mr. Bidwell, notwithstanding the inferiority of his party both in talent and numbers, has acquired an influence in the present House, beyond any other member in it. ... The ministerial party ... have no acknowledged leader – no mutual understanding – and no common or uniform system of action ... while the party of which Mr. Bidwell is the head ... is a well-drilled and compact little body – always at their post, and always ready to follow their leader.' Nevertheless, the Reformers were often outvoted, particularly in the matter of the several expulsions of William Lyon Mackenzie, when Bidwell argued that 'the utmost latitude [should be] given to the freedom of the Press' in a province where the executive had such 'great influence.' At the time of the last expulsion he accused the conservative majority of 'making Mr. Mackenzie a man of the greatest importance in the eyes of the freeholders, who look on him as a martyr in the cause of their civil rights. In doing this what a spectacle you make of this House! You are injuring its character, preventing those enquiries to which its attention ought to be directed, conducting the most important matters in the most careless and hasty manner, and trifling with the important duties you were sent to fulfil.' Bidwell's greatest coup in this parliament was his moving, early in 1834, an address to the king protesting against the British government's disallowance of banking bills passed by the legislature of Upper Canada; the address, which Mackenzie called 'The Latest Declaration of Independence,' passed with only one negative vote.

In the elections of 1834 the Reformers were again victorious and again Bidwell was elected speaker, despite Christopher Hagerman's charge that he was 'a disloyal man ... politically connected with persons desirous of separating this Province from the Mother country.' As in the 1820s the assembly passed the usual bills on the reform programme, and added to them one to legalize voting by ballot, all of them being again thrown out by the Legislative Council. But as the province moved in to the boom years of the mid-1830s there were signs of a growing split between the Reform majority led by Bidwell and Perry and a small group of agrarian radicals, led by Mackenzie. The majority supported bills to build canals and to charter banks and insurance companies which Mackenzie vehemently opposed. After Mackenzie had brought in his bulky and indiscriminate *Seventh report on grievances* in 1835, Perry sought to dissociate himself from it, and it is probable that he was also speaking for Bidwell. The year before, at a political meeting, Perry had said that 'no two persons disapproved more at times of Mr. Mackenzie's occasional violence, than Mr. Bidwell and himself.'

At the beginning of 1836 the provincial political scene was quickened by the arrival of a new lieutenant governor, Sir Francis Bond Head, sent out by the Colonial Office to deal with the grievances listed in Mackenzie's *Seventh report*. Inexperienced in politics, of a volatile temperament, and totally ignorant of Upper Canada, Head was astounded when, in a personal interview, he was informed by Bidwell that the people had grievances not mentioned in Mackenzie's 553-page *Report*. From that time forward Head was suspicious of Bidwell, not understanding the growing rift between the latter and Mackenzie and the different approaches to reform of the two men.

Finding it necessary to enlarge the Executive Council, Head, in February 1836, appointed three new members: J.H. Dunn and two well-known Reformers, Robert Baldwin and John Rolph. Reform hopes were soon dashed, however, when in less than a month the entire Executive Council resigned on the ground that they were not being adequately consulted by the lieutenant governor. There then followed a bitter quarrel between Head and the Reform-dominated assembly. The latter adopted addresses to the king and to the British House of Commons, each signed by Mr Speaker Bidwell and each denouncing the lieutenant governor as despotic and deceitful. The assembly then voted to stop the supplies and shortly afterward Bidwell entered on the *Journals* of the house a letter from Mr Speaker Papineau, asserting that 'The state of society all over continental America requires that the forms of its Government should approximate nearer to that selected ... by the wise statesmen of the neighbouring Union.' For his part, Head dissolved the legislature and plunged the province into one of the hottest election campaigns in its history. He was convinced that he 'was sentenced to contend on the soil of America with Democracy,' and that the leader of his 'republican' opponents was Marshall Spring Bidwell.

The Reformers were routed in the 1836 elections, and among those not returned was Bidwell. In addition to the general swing against his party, there were probably some personal reasons for the speaker's defeat in Lennox and Addington. He had recently moved to Toronto as a better site for his growing law practice, and Canadian voters have often resisted non-resident candidacies. And Bidwell apparently did not campaign very hard in a heated political atmosphere that was not to his liking. At any rate he wrote to Robert Baldwin that 'twelve years hard labour have exhausted my hopes, my strength ... and I was unwilling to incur expence or trouble.' Also, like other Reformers, Bidwell attributed his downfall to unfair tactics used by the other side. He now resolved to retire from politics, and he played no part in the events of the next year and a half culminating in the rebellion of December 1837.

While he was in political retirement, Bidwell, unknown to himself, was a central figure in a clash between Head and the Colonial Office that eventually led to the governor's resignation. In a dispatch of 5 April 1837, Head refused to restore George Ridout to offices from which he had been dismissed, and he also refused to appoint Bidwell to a judgeship. He stated that Bidwell's 'legal acquirements are ... superior to at least one of the individuals whom I have elevated. His moral character is irreproachable. ... But, anxious as I am to give talent its due, yet I cannot but feel that the welfare and honour of this province depend *on his Majesty never promoting a disloyal man.*' On 14 July Lord Glenelg insisted that Bidwell be offered the next vacancy on the Court of King's Bench, and on 10 September Head 'determined to take upon myself the serious responsibility of positively *refusing* to place Mr. Bidwell on the Bench, or to restore Mr. George Ridout to the Judgeship from which I have removed him.' On 24 November Glenelg informed Head that his resignation had been accepted. The colonial secretary regarded Head's disobedience in the Ridout affair as the more serious, but clearly Bidwell had, unwittingly, played a part in the recall of the lieutenant governor.

But Head was to have his revenge. Before Glenelg's dispatch reached Toronto, Mackenzie's attempt at armed rebellion had been made and easily put down. Among the items left by the rebels as they scattered was a flag bearing the inscription 'BIDWELL, AND THE GLORIOUS MINORITY! 1837, AND A GOOD BEGINNING.' This was, in fact, an election banner dating back to 1831, with the date altered. A day or two later Head confronted Bidwell with the flag, stated that he could not guarantee him security of person or property in the existing excited state of feeling, and that he would give him a letter of protection if he would leave the province. Bidwell, later described by Egerton Ryerson as having a 'retiring, timid and even nervous' temperament, denied that he had had any part in the rebellion but nevertheless agreed to the governor's proposal that he leave Upper Canada forever. On 9 Dec. 1837 he crossed Lake Ontario to New York State. He carried with him a hastily written note from his old antagonist Christopher Hagerman which stated: 'I have known you long and in some respects intimately and my respect for your private character as a neighbour and a friend arising from a knowledge of your amiable disposition in those relations of life which do not involve political controversy has impressed me so strong with feelings of friendship and esteem that I cannot now part with you perhaps forever without emotion.'

This personal note did not prevent Hagerman, some weeks later, from stating in the Toronto *Patriot* that Bidwell had left Upper Canada after Head had offered him a choice between having letters addressed to him in the Toronto post office opened and read or having them returned to him unopened and leaving the province. The accusation brought Ryerson, the province's most powerful controversialist, into the lists on Bidwell's behalf. Ryerson had been Bidwell's political opponent from 1833 to 1836, but he was now convinced that the former speaker had 'been banished for his talents and opinions,' not his actions, and that whenever a people allowed their rulers to attach 'pains and penalties ... to opinions ... that very moment they sign the death warrant of their own liberties, and become slaves.' Ryerson's condemnation of Head has become the verdict of history.

Although most of the leading exiles of 1837 eventually returned to live in Canada, Bidwell never did. On at least two occasions in the 1840s attempts were made to secure his return but they came to nothing. He kept in touch with many Canadians and his later New York associates always regarded him as an authority on Canadian affairs. In 1872, shortly before his death, he paid a brief visit to Toronto, sharing a pew one Sunday morning with Ryerson.

Not long after he left the province Bidwell had two final contacts with its governors. In March 1838, when he was in Albany applying for admission to the New York bar, he accidentally met Sir George Arthur, Head's successor, who had stopped to pay his respects to Governor William L. Marcy before continuing to Toronto. His finding Bidwell in the governor's residence immediately convinced Arthur that the former speaker must be an untrustworthy character, while his conversation with Arthur convinced Bidwell 'that there will be no liberality under him.' Shortly afterward, as he was passing through New York City on his return to England, Head invited Bidwell to call on him. At first their conversation was politely formal, but when Head informed him of the exchanges with Lord Glenelg about a judgeship, the usually mild Bidwell exclaimed that his banishment had been 'exceedingly arbitrary, unjust and cruel.' He probably now believed that Head had forced him to leave in order to score a point against the Colonial Office.

When Bidwell left Upper Canada more than two-thirds of his career still lay before him. At first he was despondent and pessimistic, writing to friends that he was too old 'to get into business ... in a strange land' where he had never practised his profession. Nevertheless, he was soon admitted to practise by both the state Supreme Court and the Court of Chancery, and after moving to New York City he was taken into partnership in George W. Strong's law firm. After Strong's death Bidwell continued as its senior figure in partnership with Strong's son, George Templeton, later joined by the latter's cousin, Charles Edward. The firm of Strong, Bidwell and Strong became one of the most eminent in the metropolis, and Bidwell was soon known as one of the most learned lawyers practising before the American courts, with an unrivalled knowledge of the law of real estate. In his diary, George Templeton Strong states that 'we all leaned on him, too much for our own good. Instead of studying up a question, I usually went to Bidwell and received from him an off-hand abstract of all the cases bearing on it and of all the considerations on either side. He loved law as a pure science.' Another associate remarked that Bidwell had 'often said that he found far more entertainment in tracing some legal principle back through the Reports of the seventeenth century, than in perusing the most attractive work of fiction.' He lectured frequently at the Columbia Law School, and in 1858 Yale University conferred on him the degree of Doctor of Laws.

According to William M. Evarts, Bidwell decided that 'the circumstances which withdrew him' from Upper Canada must cause him 'to abstain from any participation in active political affairs' in the United States. G.T. Strong also noted at Bidwell's death that it was 'strange that this family, after so many years in New York, should have formed no positive friendships or alliances, especially considering poor, dear old Bidwell's warm-heartedness, geniality and strong social instincts. ... I suppose poor Bidwell's Puritanic convictions led him to look on "calls", tea parties, and all the little two-penny machinery of "social" life as of the nature of evil, in spite of his own natural impulses.' Throughout his life Bidwell was a devout Presbyterian and a temperance advocate, and in his New York years a faithful supporter of the American Bible Society and of other religious and charitable organizations and institutions.

Of his career in Upper Canada, Bidwell himself wrote the best evaluation in a letter dated 29 April 1838: 'All my offence consisted in a faithful, honest, disinterested attempt by constitutional means, in the discharge of public duties, to improve the conditions and support the rights of the people of Upper Canada. If my views had prevailed, there would have been no rebellion.'

G.M. CRAIG

ROBERT EASTON BURNS
Lawyer and judge; b. 26 Dec. 1805 in Niagara (Niagara-on-the-Lake), Upper Canada, eldest of the five children of the Reverend John Burns and his wife Jane; d. 12 Jan. 1863 at Toronto, Canada West.

Robert Easton Burns (named after the Reverend Robert Easton of Montreal) was the son of a Presbyterian minister of the Associate Synod of Scotland who emigrated to Upper Canada from Pennsylvania in 1804 and settled first in Stamford, then in 1806 at Niagara. Burns was educated at home and later at the Niagara District Grammar School where his father served as master. In 1822, at age 16, he was admitted as a student-at-law with John Breakenridge in Niagara. Burns completed his legal training in 1827 and was admitted to the bar of Upper Canada in that year. He established an office in St Catharines, and for the next nine years practised successfully in the Niagara, St Catharines, and Hamilton areas.

His ability led to his appointment as judge of the Niagara District on 16 July 1836. Burns, however, was not happy with the routine duties of a district court, and he resigned his post in the spring of 1838. He moved to Toronto and entered into a partnership with Christopher Alexander Hagerman, then attorney general of Upper Canada. Hagerman had an extensive practice and needed a partner to relieve him of some of its work. Burns practised extensively in the Court of Chancery, and followed that court when it moved with the seat of government to Kingston in 1841. In 1844 the court moved back to Toronto, and, upon his return, Burns entered into a partnership with Oliver Mowat and Philip M.M.S. VanKoughnet, two recently admitted lawyers. The firm of Burns, Mowat, and VanKoughnet was one of the largest in Toronto at that time. On 19 Aug. 1844 Burns was appointed judge of the Home District; he gave up his partnership with Mowat and VanKoughnet the next year when an act was passed forbidding district court judges from engaging in private practice. He served the court for four years, during which time he wrote *A letter on the subject of division courts* (1847), his only published work. Addressed to the attorney general of Canada West, it suggested improvements in the system of division courts, especially in the area of jurisdiction over small claims, based on legislative changes in Great Britain in 1846.

Burns resigned from the bench in 1848 and entered again into private practice, this time with John Duggan of Toronto. However, in late 1849 he and Henry John Boulton were nominated to fill the vacancy on the Court of Queen's Bench left by the death of Hagerman. Through the influence of Francis Hincks, Burns received the appointment as puisne judge of this court on 21 Jan. 1850. He sat on the court until his death. During his career, Burns was an active bencher of the Law Society of Upper Canada, serving on several committees and as treasurer of the society in 1849–50. He was popular with the law students and was for many years elected president of the Osgoode Club, a student organization.

He was also active in the affairs of the University of Toronto. On 20 July 1848, he, and John Wetenhall and Joseph Workman, were appointed by the government of Louis-Hippolyte La Fontaine and Robert Baldwin commissioners to investigate the financial affairs of the University of King's College and of Upper Canada College. Their report, presented in 1852, was severely critical of the financial management of both institutions. On 11 Dec. 1857 Burns was appointed chancellor of the University of Toronto, succeeding William Hume Blake, and he retained this post until the end of 1861.

Burns was married first, on 10 Feb. 1835, to Anne Flora Taylor of St Catharines by whom he had four sons. She died in September 1850, and Burns married in 1856 Britannia Warton of Toronto; she died in 1858. Burns himself died at his Toronto home in 1863.

His legal career was not brilliant but he applied himself diligently to his work as lawyer and judge, and his decisions were well considered and well delivered. He was noted for his integrity and liberal views. 'He was,' writes David B. Read, 'eminently a self-made man, of plodding habits and honesty of purpose, which obtained favourable recognition from all who knew him.'

BRIAN H. MORRISON

JAMES CLARK (Clarke)
Merchant, lawyer, and office holder; b. in Quebec, probably at Trois-Rivières, son of James Clark and Jemima Mason; m. 29 Aug. 1795 Elizabeth Hare in Newark (Niagara-on-the-Lake), Upper Canada, and they had four children, three of whom survived infancy; fl. 1790–1807 in Upper Canada.

James Clark's father, a native of Somerset, England, came to Quebec in May 1768 with the 8th Foot. He was posted to Trois-Rivières and served there until 1777, when he was appointed naval storekeeper at Carleton Island (N.Y.). Several of his children, including James, were educated 'at a French and English Seminary' and were, as their younger brother John recalled many years later, 'good scholars for that period.' According to John's memoir, James and his elder brother Peter became merchants at Montreal, and Peter appears on the lists of Indian trade passes for 1782 and 1785. In 1785 Clark Sr was sent to Napanee (Ont.) to run the government grist-mill that Robert Clark (no relation) was building there. When in 1788 western Quebec was divided into the four administrative districts that later became Upper Canada, James Clark Sr was appointed to the Mecklenburg District land board and Court of Common Pleas, and made a justice of the peace. That same year he was appointed naval storekeeper at Kingston and took up residence there, becoming a leader of the new community. This relocation may have had some effect on his sons; John Clark wrote that in 1790 James and Peter moved to Kingston where they engaged in the Indian trade.

The division of Quebec and the establishment of a separate government for Upper Canada in 1791 opened up new possibilities for patronage, and the elder Clark may have influenced Lieutenant Governor Simcoe's appointment of Peter Clark as clerk of the Legislative Council on 29 Sept. 1792. Peter died in 1793 as a result of a duel and on 27 May of that year was succeeded by his brother James, who then moved to the provincial capital at Newark. Clark's duties included administering oaths, supervising the copying of the council's minutes, transmitting messages from the speaker of the council, and sending out copies of statutes to local clerks of the peace. He was the chief administrative officer of the council and in conjunction with his counterpart in the House of Assembly, for many years Angus Macdonell (Collachie), coordinated the work of successive parliaments. In 1796 the responsibility for superintending the printing of acts by the king's printer seems to have unexpectedly devolved upon him. The following year he petitioned the Executive Council for additional remuneration since this new burden was, he believed, 'distinct' from the duties of his office. But a committee of the council, headed by Chief Justice John Elmsley, refused his petition on the grounds that his salary of £125 per annum was 'very ample compensation' for all the activities associated with his position.

It is possible that Clark had received some legal training. As early as 1790 he acted as his father's attorney in civil suits before the Court of Common Pleas. In 1794 he was one of the original 16 men called to the bar by act of parliament. He was also one of the founding members of the Law Society of Upper Canada, which was established in 1797. Between 1799 and 1802 judgements against him in the Court of King's Bench usually identified him as 'one of the attorneys' but it is not known whether he was a practising member of the bar.

Like most Upper Canadians, Clark petitioned the government for land, and he received 1,200 acres which he located in Murray, Pittsburgh, and Marysburgh (North and South Marysburgh) townships. In 1797, the year he moved with the government to the province's new capital at York (Toronto), he was granted a town lot there, and also a 200-acre farm lot in the vicinity, with the stipulation that no warrant be issued for the latter parcel of land until he had actually settled on it.

Clark was a minor office holder who did his job competently and conscientiously but, unlike Macdonell for instance, made little impact either socially or politically upon York society. By 1799 debt had become a constant feature of his life. Between that year and 1804 he had five judgements against him in civil court for varying sums. His situation thereafter became increasingly desperate and by 1805 he was issuing drafts against his salary as clerk, hoping that Receiver General Peter Russell would honour them. Merchants such as George Forsyth and William and James Crooks promptly forwarded their claims to Russell. In late 1805 Clark owed the Crooks brothers £100; they noted in applying to Russell about his draft, 'We have made some sacrifice in the way of assistance to his family to obtain it.' On one occasion Clark even denied, to no avail apparently, that the signature on a particular draft was his own.

The last years of Clark's life were characterized by insolvency, dissipation, and woe. In January 1806 Russell's half-sister, Elizabeth, noted in her diary the possibility that Clark's position might become vacant because of 'his ill state of health or death.' Already the official families of York were scrambling to secure his office for one of their number. The clerk's salary and contingent account were a generous reward for working only six weeks a year. In the midst of the turmoil surrounding the clerkship, Clark's infant daughter died in March 1806; seven months later his wife died as well. Yet Clark held on to his position. He served during the legislative session of February–March 1806 and as late as November was still acting in his official capacity.

The combination of stresses, however, proved too much for Clark to bear and he turned to alcohol. Completely without influence, he became an even more tempting target for the York élite. According to Mrs Anne Powell [Murray], early in 1806 government officials had agreed to remove him but Administrator Alexander Grant had been unwilling to initiate the change. The new lieutenant governor, Francis Gore, however, felt that Clark 'should no longer hold a responsible situation to which his vices render'd him inequal.' On 13 Feb. 1807 Mrs Powell wrote to her husband that, according to Legislative Councillor Richard Cartwright, Gore had decided to give the clerkship to the Powells' son, John. The only problem was that 'James Clarke was upon the spot, & it was painful to dispossess him entirely.' So it was agreed that John Powell should offer to share the salary with Clark. The offer was put to Clark some time on 13 or 14 February; he refused. Mrs Powell dismissed him as 'long devoted to the most confirmed habits of intoxication, & for some time ... advancing with hasty strides to that grave, which can alone cover his disgrace.' The government acted quickly. Clark's brother later recalled that he had had to relinquish his position 'from habits of indulgence, to the great regret of his family.' A regular of the law society, Clark attended his last meeting on 18 Feb. 1807. The following day, John Powell became clerk of the council. The disgraced Clark then disappeared from sight; there is no record of his subsequent whereabouts. His health, however, was very poor and it is likely that he died shortly thereafter.

In collaboration with RICHARD A. PRESTON

GEORGE MACKENZIE

Lawyer; b. 1795, probably in Dingwall, Scotland; m. 19 May 1829 Sarah Mackenzie in Ernestown (Bath), Upper Canada, the ceremony being performed by the Reverend John Machar; they had no children; d. 4 Aug. 1834 in Kingston, Upper Canada.

George Mackenzie immigrated to British North America from Scotland before 1823. He settled at Kingston in the mid 1820s after a brief stay in Lower Canada and Ernestown. In 1828 he was called to the bar of the province and immediately went into private practice. Within a couple of years his practice was flourishing and he had staked out a prominent place for himself in Kingston society.

Along with other leading figures in the town, Mackenzie decried the monopoly of the Bank of Upper Canada and asserted the need for an independent bank in Kingston. At a public meeting there in January 1830, a committee was formed to draft rules and regulations for a Kingston bank and to petition the government for a charter; Mackenzie was secretary. A bill to charter the Kingston bank was soon after brought before the legislature, but it was defeated by the Legislative Council, most of whose members were directors and stockholders of the Bank of Upper Canada. Mackenzie persevered during the next year, speaking at public meetings on the advantages that would accrue to eastern Upper Canada from a Kingston bank, articulating the complaints of the growing non-tory commercial interest group to which he belonged, and galvanizing popular support behind a bank independent of the tory compact's control.

In February 1831 a second bill chartering the proposed bank passed the House of Assembly and was lost in the council, but the growing discontent over the Bank of Upper Canada's monopoly, combined with the assembly's refusal to pass a bill authorizing an increase in its stock, caused the supporters of the bank in council to relent. In the fall session of 1831 a bill to charter the Commercial Bank of the Midland District was passed by the assembly and the council. Only the extreme radicals – who objected that the new bank would be fashioned too much in the image of the hated Bank of Upper Canada – and the extreme tories – who warned that the establishment of another bank would impair the credit of the Bank of Upper Canada – voted against it. The first president of the new bank was John Solomon Cartwright; its first solicitor was Mackenzie.

Although obviously not a tory, Mackenzie did not sympathize with the reformers. In February 1832 he attended a reform meeting held in Fredericksburgh by assembly representatives Peter Perry and Marshall Spring Bidwell. He expressed his opposition to a resolution denouncing the Legislative Council and, chiding the reform members of the assembly, spoke long and effectively on the need for moderate reform without disloyalty to the crown. He then moved support for the government. Mackenzie later claimed that his motion had carried and that the meeting had been dissolved, but others, including the meeting's chairman and secretary, disputed his version of events.

Whatever happened, the fate of Mackenzie's resolution is not as important as the political ideas expressed in his two-and-a-half-hour speech. He disagreed with the expulsion of William Lyon Mackenzie from the assembly and entered into a detailed account of the privileges of the legislature which did not follow the hard line of the tory party. Yet in phrases redolent of the tory spirit he dismissed Mackenzie as ill mannered and ill fitted to be a representative of his constituency. His moderate position regarding the clergy reserves steered directly and reasonably between the tory and reform camps. Most reformers by this time advocated the sale of the reserves, the endowment to be used to support secular education. John Strachan and the high tories would have preferred little change in the existing situation. Mackenzie argued, as William Henry Draper would advocate four years later, that the reserves should be used to support clergymen of all 'respectable denominations.' He disagreed with the more conservative elements in denying that the Church of England was or had ever been the established church in Upper Canada. The administration of Sir Peregrine Maitland, he added, had done much that was injurious to various religious denominations, but he felt that Sir John Colborne's government 'was on a conciliatory, moderate path.'

As a lawyer Mackenzie was known to accept liberal causes, perhaps the most controversial of which was his defence of George Gurnett, the editor of the *Courier of Upper Canada* (Toronto), who was alleged to have libelled tory John Elmsley over the latter's conversion to Roman Catholicism. The case came before the Court of King's Bench in April 1834. Elmsley was able to retain five of the most renowned lawyers in Upper Canada – Draper, Marshall Spring Bidwell, Robert Baldwin Sullivan, Allan Napier MacNab, and Robert Baldwin. Mackenzie, assisted by three other lawyers, represented the defendant and he alone spoke for the defence. After his four-and-a-half-hour speech, which was lauded throughout the Upper Canadian press as one of the most eloquent defences of freedom of the press ever voiced in the province, the jury returned a verdict for Gurnett. Mackenzie was the real victor, since his firm was now known throughout the province.

Mackenzie was a leader of the Scots community in Kingston: he was a member of the temperance society, the Emigration Society of the Midland District, and the bible society; he had been a lay commissioner at the Kingston convention of June 1831 which established the synod of the Presbyterian Church of Canada in connection with the Church of Scotland, and he often served as legal adviser to the church. He was actively associated with various committees important to the administration of town affairs, such as the committee to reform municipal government and another established in 1832 to alleviate the effects of the cholera epidemic. His name was put forward in 1834 as the Frontenac County candidate for election to the legislature, and he was widely supported throughout the campaign that summer as a moderate non-tory candidate. It seemed as though he would be elected, but his political career was cut off by his sudden death of cholera on 4 Aug. 1834.

In the early spring of 1830, 15-year-old John A. Macdonald had been articled to Mackenzie as a student-at-law. For the next three formative years of his life he studied under Mackenzie and for most of that period boarded at the Mackenzie home. He gained his earliest understanding of the law and commerce under Mackenzie; he developed his first clientele and business contacts through him. In 1839 Macdonald became solicitor to the Commercial Bank of the Midland District, as Mackenzie had been, and on the verge of the public career denied to Mackenzie, Macdonald would also be a corporate lawyer and businessman, a moderate conservative whose fortunes and interests were tied to Kingston and to the commercial development of Upper Canada. At the time when Macdonald was articled to Mackenzie's law firm, the increasingly populous, clannish Scots community was infiltrating the positions of tory authority, was beginning to control commerce, and was laying the basis of a liberal-conservative faction whose stress on economic expansion would present an alternative to William Lyon Mackenzie's hope of establishing a rather traditional agrarian order. It was largely this same social and political group which would coalesce and gain prominence as an emerging capitalist class in the late 1830s and 1840s. Then, it would be largely led politically by Macdonald, Mackenzie's former student.

WILLIAM TEATERO

WILLIAM BIRDSEYE PETERS

Office holder, army officer, lawyer, and journalist; b. 5 June 1774 in Hebron (Marlborough), Conn., only child of the Reverend Samuel Andrew Peters and his third wife, Mary Birdseye; m. 4 May 1796 Polly (Patty) Marvin Jarvis of Stamford, Conn., and they had nine children, seven surviving infancy; d. 4 June 1822 in Mobile, Ala.

William Birdseye Peters was descended on both sides from Puritans who settled in New England in the 1630s. His mother died a few days after his birth; his father was the Church of England minister in Hebron. In September 1774 Samuel Peters's strong tory views forced him to flee, first to Boston and then to England, leaving his baby son with the boy's maternal grandparents in Stratford, Conn. William lived with the Birdseyes until he was 14, studying under nearby Congregational and Episcopal ministers. He then joined his father in London, and in 1789 went to school in Arras, France, where he remained for three terms. He matriculated into Trinity College, Oxford, on 12 Oct. 1792; in that year also he was a law student at the Inner Temple. Growing concern was felt for his health, and in the summer of 1793 he was sent to North America to recuperate.

Although his half-sister, Hannah Peters, had married William Jarvis, secretary and registrar of Upper Canada, and was living in Newark (Niagara-on-the-Lake), Peters's first visit to the province was a brief one in 1794. Instead of returning to England to complete his education, he stayed in the United States, mainly in Connecticut, renewing acquaintance with relatives and friends. Hannah urged him to settle in Upper Canada, and in 1796 he married an American niece of William Jarvis, and moved to Newark.

In the beginning Peters had many advantages. Lieutenant Governor John Graves Simcoe, who had tried unsuccessfully to have Peters's father become the first bishop of Upper Canada, appointed him assistant secretary and registrar of the province on 3 May 1796, and on 26 May licensed him to practise law. A grant of 1,200 acres was recommended on 25 July, and on 26 December he was commissioned an ensign in the Queen's Rangers. In addition, both he and his father were on the United Empire Loyalist list, and the Jarvises believed that other government appointments would be forthcoming.

Peters thus began his career in Upper Canada with a sound footing in three professions – the civil service, the law, and the army. Although multiple appointments were not uncommon in 18th-century Upper Canada, Peters encountered problems after Simcoe's departure. Chief Justice John Elmsley refused to permit him to practise law because he was an army officer, and Major David Shank of the Queen's Rangers thought that he could not hold his government position while on active service, despite the precedent of David William Smith. Peters, however, was not ordered to join his regiment until the secretary's office was moved to York (Toronto) in 1798. In Newark he worked under Jarvis, who complained that he was lazy and uncooperative; Peters wrote that the Jarvises expected him to be '*their Slave*' and that he was paid too little and too irregularly. Peters was unsuccessful in obtaining other government appointments, in his opinion because the Jarvises had no political influence, and also because he himself was a 'Yankee.' In 1799 Peters and his father were struck off the United Empire Loyalist list, because Samuel Peters had never come to Upper Canada.

While in Newark, Peters spent much time with the American officers at Fort Niagara (near Youngstown, N.Y.). From them he learned of opportunities for advancement in the American army, and in 1798 he applied for a commission to the American secretary of war. Shortly afterwards he moved to York and reported for duty to Lieutenant-Colonel Shank, who told him that promotion was likely within the British army. Peters therefore cancelled his American application, but Jarvis discovered it and sent a copy to Shank, according to Peters because he thought he had to sacrifice Peters to save himself. To the loyalist Jarvis, Peters was guilty of treason, but Peters claimed that he had merely breached military etiquette in not informing his commanding officer of his intentions. His explanation satisfied Shank, who did nothing further.

After this episode, Peters's relations with the Jarvises were strained. In York he served with the rangers until the regiment was disbanded on 25 Oct. 1802, when he retired on half pay. No longer an active army officer, he applied for admission to the Law Society of Upper Canada in Easter Term, 1803, and was called to the bar. On 16 June

1803, however, he moved to New York, where he established a dry goods store under the name William B. Peters and Company, with money borrowed from relatives and $2,000 won by his wife in a lottery. In two years he had lost everything and was $11,000 in debt. By 1808 he was a discharged bankrupt in Connecticut, living on the Birdseye estate with no means of support.

In 1807 Hannah Jarvis had advised against his return to Upper Canada, since 'he is supposed to be in the opposition, he becoming a subject to the United States.' In 1810, however, Peters settled in Niagara (Niagara-on-the-Lake) to practise law. Hannah hoped that he would 'have the discretion to be Nutral,' but he had no discretion and was soon writing for Joseph Willcocks's radical newspaper, the *Upper Canada Guardian; or, Freeman's Journal*. Through his friend the Reverend Robert Addison, he applied for the position of clerk in the projected Gore District in February 1812, but the new district was not established until after the War of 1812.

When war was declared, Peters immediately moved his law office to York and his household to John Mills Jackson's home three miles up Yonge Street. From the beginning his loyalty was suspect. After the capture of York by the Americans in April 1813, the acting attorney general, John Beverley Robinson, was instructed to lay charges against him for providing information to the enemy, but sufficient evidence could not be found.

Peters was in serious trouble again after the second occupation of York. When the Americans marched in on 31 July 1813 'he met them with Expressions of Joy and shook hands with a number of the enemys officers and men.' According to a second witness, Peters often said that the Americans would conquer the country, and was pleased at the prospect. The committee of information, consisting of five prominent York citizens, believed that suspicions of Peters were justified, and that 'from his Information and talents he is capable of doing much mischief.' Although he was possibly guilty of sedition, there was no evidence of actual aid to the enemy, and so no charges were laid. Preparations were being made for a great show trial of traitors – the 'Bloody Assize' held at Ancaster in May–June 1814. Peters was defence lawyer for at least five of those accused of high treason; of these, two were acquitted, the sentence of one was commuted, and two were executed.

After the war Peters returned to Niagara to practise law. In 1816 he moved to Thorold and then to Hamilton, where he was the first lawyer in the new Gore District. By November 1819 he was back in Niagara, where he maintained a legal practice and succeeded Bartemas Ferguson as publisher of the *Niagara Spectator*. Ferguson, a critic of the government, had been convicted of libel the previous August; Peters changed the newspaper's name to the *Canadian Argus, and Niagara Spectator* and published it until some time in 1820 when Ferguson, having been released, resumed his connection with the paper. That autumn Peters went to New York and briefly practised law. On 27 December he sailed for Mobile, Ala, where he died of yellow fever. His son, Samuel Jarvis Peters, became a prominent merchant, developer, banker, and politician in New Orleans.

Peters was one of the few gentlemen in Upper Canada popularly accused of treason. He never understood that Upper Canada was not part of the United States, and obviously felt no particular allegiance to either government. Basically an unsuccessful opportunist, he moved back and forth across a border he did not perceive. Despite his advantages, he was a failure in both countries.

EDITH G. FIRTH

THOMAS MABON RADENHURST

Lawyer, politician, and office holder; b. 6 April 1803 in Fort St Johns (Saint-Jean-sur-Richelieu), Lower Canada, son of Thomas Radenhurst and Ann Campbell; m. 9 Nov. 1834 his cousin Lucy Edith Ridout, daughter of Thomas Ridout, in Toronto, and they had four sons and six daughters; d. 7 Aug. 1854 in Perth, Upper Canada.

Thomas Mabon Radenhurst's father came from Cheshire, England, to Lower Canada in February 1776 as storekeeper to the hospital at Trois-Rivières and ten years later married the daughter of a loyalist in Montreal. His death in 1805 left Thomas and his seven brothers and sisters under the sole care of their strong-willed mother. She managed to get commissions in the army for two of her older sons and later to have Thomas accepted at John Strachan's Home District Grammar School at York (Toronto). From there he went on to study law in the office of his cousin George Ridout. Called to the bar in the spring of 1824, Radenhurst left York for Kingston and then moved to the new community of Perth, which in 1823 had become the judicial seat of the Bathurst District. There he built a prosperous legal practice out of the usual material: trespasses, debts, petitions, and assaults. Typical were his cases on behalf of the settlers of McNab Township against Archibald McNab, his role as solicitor for William Morris's Tay Navigation Company, and his defence of the Reverend William Bell in a libel suit instituted by John Stewart of the *Bathurst Independent Examiner*. Also typical of his class and age were the land speculation and the various private commercial transactions with which he augmented his professional income.

Radenhurst moved in the upper ranks of Perth society among the half-pay officers, merchants, and lawyers who composed the town élite. In 1832 he bought the Reverend Michael Harris's magnificent stone residence (now known as the Inderwick House), a visible crown to his successful career. Radenhurst's hatred, however, of fellow lawyer James Boulton (brother of Attorney General Henry John Boulton) climaxed in a duel they fought in 1830. Fortunately 'the matter ended without injury to either party.' More serious consequences attended the duel fought in 1833 by their law students John Wilson and Robert Lyon. Robert, the brother of Radenhurst's old friend and brother-in-law George Lyon, was killed and was buried in the Radenhurst family plot.

The 'Father and Champion of Reform' in Lanark County, Radenhurst dated his 'adhesion ... to Reform principles' to the general election of 1828 when he ran successfully for the Carleton seat in the House of Assembly, which he represented until 1830 when the house was dissolved after the death of George IV. Deeply affected by the dismissal of Judge John Walpole Willis, he served in 1829 on the select parliamentary committee chaired by William Warren Baldwin inquiring into the case. In February 1840 when Robert Baldwin was offered the position of solicitor general by Governor Charles Edward Poulett Thomson, he wrote to Radenhurst for advice. Radenhurst warned Baldwin of the perils of compromising his principles and accepting office under 'what [Sir Francis Bond Head] would say is the *bread and butter* system.' None the less the bread and butter system did not hurt Radenhurst. Treasurer of the Bathurst District since 1840, he was appointed judge of the district court in December 1841, a position he declined on the grounds that it was not remunerative enough, and frequently served as crown prosecutor for the Eastern and Midland circuits. Criticized by Baldwin when a verdict went against him in 1851, Radenhurst could remind Baldwin of his impeccable handling of 'all the public business you have entrusted to me since 1842.' He could also ask Baldwin to 'use your influence' to affect local appointments.

Radenhurst's local political influence, however, was overshadowed by that of Malcolm Cameron, who in the election of 1836 emerged as the power of the reform party in the Bathurst District. When Cameron decided to run for the riding of Kent in 1847, Radenhurst, who had repeatedly withdrawn his candidacy in Lanark at the party's request, fully expected to win the reform nomination there. Instead, William Bell's son Robert was selected at a sparsely attended reform convention. Ignoring his promise to support the convention's candidate and his own earlier warnings against splitting the party, Radenhurst threw his hat into the ring, but despite the split Bell was able to carry Lanark for reform. In 1851 Radenhurst ran again and this time emerged as the sole reform candidate but, having 'injured himself beyond recovery' because he 'broke faith last election,' he was defeated by tory James Shaw.

Despite his lack of political success Radenhurst was admired by contemporaries 'for his strict integrity in his professional pursuits.' In 1847 an observer describing Radenhurst's courtroom manner commented that he 'lounges in his chair with an easy familiarity.' Yet despite his 'seeming abstraction ... nothing has escaped his notice. ... The witness finds that he is in the hands of a master.' Above all, Radenhurst could convince a jury that he believed 'there is such a thing as truth' and that 'whatever may be the merits of the suit the advocate is an honest man.' He was made a queen's counsel in December 1850, but did not live long to enjoy the honour. Ill for several months, on 4 Aug. 1854 he suffered 'a return of his disorder – (paralysis)' and died three days later. The mighty of Lanark County formed part of his funeral procession to the Perth Episcopal cemetery. At his death Radenhurst left behind a large family, an estate valued at more than £5,000, and a reputation as 'a leading member of the Bar in Canada.'

WILLIAM COX

GEORGE RIDOUT
Lawyer and judge; b. Quebec, 1791, second son of Thomas Ridout, surveyor general of Upper Canada, and of Mary Campbell; d. at Clinton, Ont., 24 Feb. 1871.

George Ridout attended John Strachan's school at Cornwall from 1805 to at least 1807, in company with the sons of many other families prominent in early York (Toronto). He subsequently studied law in the office of John Macdonell, who was appointed attorney general in 1812, and was admitted to the bar 4 Jan. 1813. The next year he attended the court at Ancaster as acting solicitor general. In 1820 he became a bencher of the Law Society of Upper Canada and continued to serve in this capacity for the next 50 years until his death. He succeeded Dr William Warren Baldwin as treasurer of the law society in 1829 and served in this position until 1832, during this time presiding over the planning and construction of the original building of Osgoode Hall, perhaps the most important of the early buildings still surviving in Ontario. He also took a lead in establishing the library of the law society. Ridout was appointed judge of the Niagara District Court in April 1828, and reappointed to this office in April 1832.

Ridout served with the York volunteers during the War of 1812–14, and took part in the battle of Queenston Heights as 3rd lieutenant in the grenadier company of the York militia. He was taken prisoner of war on 27 April 1813 when the Americans occupied York. He maintained his interest in military matters in subsequent years and served as colonel of the East York militia.

Ridout took an active part in the social life of York. Dorset House, the substantial home he built about 1820, was long a landmark of the community. However, although the Ridouts were one of the oldest families in York, their frequently independent views were suspect to some of the other early established families. This rivalry and tension, in particular between the Ridouts and the families of William Dummer Powell and William Jarvis, found expression in the duel between John Ridout, George's brother, and Samuel Peters Jarvis, son of William, in 1817, in which John was killed, and it was a factor throughout the social and political career of George Ridout.

In politics Ridout was a moderate, in general supporting constitutional reform and the position of W.W. Baldwin and his son Robert; his family was connected with the Baldwins by marriage. He was defeated in his own attempts at office: in the elections for the legislature in 1816 when he sought to succeed his father as the representative of Simcoe and the East Riding of York and was beaten by Peter Robinson who had the support of Strachan; and in the elections for city council in Toronto in 1837 at the time of his dispute with the lieutenant governor. However, he often gave active and effective support to the candidacy of others: for example, to Robert Baldwin in his successful attempt to unseat Sheriff William Botsford Jarvis in the elections for the House of Assembly in 1830, and to Robert Baldwin Sullivan in 1835 in his successful campaign to replace William Lyon Mackenzie as mayor in Toronto's second municipal election.

Ridout was dismissed on 12 July 1836 from the offices of judge of the Niagara District Court, colonel of the East York militia, and justice of the peace by Sir Francis Bond Head, who 'as Lieutenant-Governor, by the advice of my Council, deliberately selected him for punishment, as the most intemperate of my opponents.' The charges, which Ridout denied, were insult to the person and office of the lieutenant governor and disloyalty to the policies of the crown. The dismissal became a *cause célèbre* in the colony and at the Colonial Office, and it was one of the major political issues in Upper Canada during the subsequent 18 months leading up to the outbreak of rebellion in December 1837. Responding to a petition from Ridout, the colonial secretary, Lord Glenelg, ordered his reinstatement. Head declined and submitted his resignation rather than comply with this instruction, 'it being utterly impossible for me to obey this order, and retain my authority in the province.' The resignation of the lieutenant governor, primarily on this issue, and on the related issue of his refusal to name Marshall Spring Bidwell a judge as Glenelg wished, was in fact accepted in a dispatch from London, dated 24 Nov. 1837, a week before the rebellion broke out in Upper Canada, where people were still unaware of this development. The dispute over Ridout's appointments, rather than the rebellion, was thus the main cause of Head's resignation, and, as such, a significant episode in Canadian history.

Ridout also played an active part in municipal affairs. He was a prominent member of the York Board of Health, proposing the establishment of a receiving house for cholera patients during the epidemic of 1832, and presenting a report in the same year which focussed public attention on the weakness of the board because of its lack of funds and insufficient legal authority. He was a strong advocate of the merits of retaining York as the capital of the province and helped to draft legislation to incorporate and enlarge York as a city under the name of Toronto. The choice of the name Toronto in 1834, in preference to the name of York, reflected the long-standing preference of the Ridouts for the original Indian name and was one of the bones of contention between them and some of the more Tory pioneer families.

Ridout's varied business interests included participation in 1822 in the founding of the Bank of Upper Canada, of which he became a director. He was elected a member of the board of the City of Toronto and Lake Huron Railway in 1845.

George Ridout married twice: first, Dorothy McCuaig of Boston; secondly, Belle Nelson. He had one daughter by his first marriage and four daughters and four sons by his second. His older brother Samuel was sheriff of the county of York and his younger brother Thomas Gibbs was for many years cashier of the Bank of Upper Canada.

THOMAS H.B. SYMONS

WALTER ROE (Row)
Lawyer and office holder; b. *c.* 1760 in London, England; m. 1 March 1790 Ann Laughton of Detroit, Mich., and they had four children; d. 7 Aug. 1801 in Upper Canada.

Walter Roe was one of the first lawyers to practise in Upper Canada. Apparently an only child, he left home after the death of his father, 'a man of some means,' and the subsequent remarriage of his mother. Joining the Royal Navy in 1779, he served for the duration of the American Revolutionary War and attained the rank of warrant officer before taking up residence in Montreal in the mid 1780s. Evidently well educated, he had greatly impressed his commanding officer during the war, and upon leaving the navy he had been persuaded by the same officer to begin the study of law. After receiving his early legal training in Montreal, he was admitted to the practice of law in the province of Quebec on 13 April 1789.

During his stay in Montreal, Roe undoubtedly came into contact with William Dummer Powell, then one of the most prominent lawyers in the city, and Powell's patronage and influence may have been useful in launching Roe's legal career. Certainly, it was not long before the careers of the two men became intertwined. In 1788 Governor Lord Dorchester [Guy Carleton] had appointed Alexander McKee, Jacques Baby, *dit* Dupéront, and William Robertson judges of the Court of Common Pleas in the newly formed District of Hesse, the most westerly section of what was soon to become the colony of Upper Canada. Baby and Robertson resigned almost immediately, however, claiming that their business activities would prevent them from exercising judicial impartiality. At this point all three appointments were revoked and Powell was made the sole judge of the district. The position of court clerk went to the young Roe.

Roe's arrival on the western frontier coincided with the establishment of civil authority in the region. Following the British conquest, the 1,500 inhabitants residing along both sides of the Detroit River had been under military rule. This situation seemed about to change with the passage of the Quebec Act of 1774, but the American revolution postponed the creation of the civil and legal institutions planned for the interior. Only in 1788 was the territory west of the Ottawa River organized into four governmental districts, with the Detroit frontier included in the District of Hesse. Under the proclamation of 1788, the boundaries of Hesse were purposefully left vague so as to encompass the area south of the Great Lakes, an area officially ceded to the United States in 1783 but still occupied by British troops. Given its tenuous claim to the American side of the boundary, Britain was reluctant to include it too formally within an administrative district. Even so, colonial officials were aware that since Detroit was the centre of the fur trade south of the lakes, some institutional authority was required. As a result, although the Court of Common Pleas created in 1788 held its sessions on the Canadian shore, it also had jurisdiction at both Detroit and Michilimackinac (Mackinac Island, Mich.).

As for Roe, he may have been in the west earlier, perhaps while still in military service, for his name appears on a list of loyalists and disbanded troops granted land on the north shore of Lake Erie in 1787. However, he never occupied his Lake Erie grant, residing instead at Detroit, the most important settlement in the region. Within a short time after his arrival there in 1789, Roe found his legal services in constant demand. Besides his official duties as court clerk, he built up a thriving legal practice, including among his clients such prominent people as William Hands, Sarah Ainse, John Askin, and Angus Mackintosh. A large part of his business involved collecting debts, certifying land transfers, and attending to the estates of deceased or absentee merchants. During the early 1790s the Montreal merchants Isaac Todd and James McGill gave Roe the job of watching over their land and other interests in western Upper Canada, and also recommended him to William Robertson, then absent in England, as the best person to handle his substantial property holdings. Unfortunately, there soon developed considerable criticism of Roe's lack of diligence in meeting his responsibilities, and it is clear that by the mid 1790s his career had begun to decline.

Roe's professional difficulties, however, were not entirely the result of personal failings; they were also due partly to the fact that he was no longer the only lawyer in the area, and partly to changes in the administration of justice. Having been trained in French law, Roe was at a distinct disadvantage after the passage of the Constitutional Act of 1791, which provided for the introduction of English law and the creation of a new court system. Always interested in real estate, he now renewed his efforts to accumulate land, no doubt to compensate for his dwindling professional income. Claiming 2,000 acres from the government, he was eventually allotted more than 1,400 acres near York (Toronto), but several years elapsed before the titles were secured and he never cultivated the land.

In 1794 Roe was made a clerk of the peace for the Western District, having been recommended by Attorney General John White and James Baby, a member of the Executive and Legislative councils. He was given the rather dubious distinction of surrendering the keys to the fort at Detroit when in 1796 the British evacuated the posts held south of the Great Lakes, and afterwards he and his family joined a number of British subjects who moved across the river to the recently established town of Sandwich (Windsor). In 1797 he was selected as one of the original six benchers, or governors, of the Law Society of Upper Canada, but there is no evidence that he attended any of the meetings. As deputy registrar of the Western District, a post to which he was appointed by Lieutenant Governor Simcoe in 1796, Roe was required to travel quite regularly the 17 miles from his home in Sandwich to Amherstburg, Britain's new military entrepôt for the Detroit frontier. These trips were both irksome and difficult, and in 1800 Roe, acting in his capacity as clerk of the peace, forwarded to the Executive Council a petition from the grand jury of Sandwich stressing the need for better transportation facilities along the route. Roe was to drown on one of these same trips to Amherstburg. According to John Askin, on 7 August 'poor Mr. Rowe was found suffocated where there was very little water.' There was some suggestion that Roe had become an alcoholic and had fallen off his horse while intoxicated.

D.R. FARRELL

JOHN ROLPH
Physician, lawyer, and politician; b. 4 March 1793 at Thornbury, Gloucestershire, England, son of Dr Thomas Rolph and Frances Petty; d. 19 Oct. 1870 at Mitchell, Ont.

John Rolph was the second of 18 children. His father, a surgeon, emigrated about 1808, staying briefly at Les Cèdres, Lower Canada, and then settling near Vittoria in Norfolk County, Upper Canada, where he died in 1814. The family was soon respected in the area, and noted for its hospitality. Two of the sons became Church of England clergymen: Romaine studied divinity under John Strachan and served in several parishes in Upper Canada; Thomas lived in England. Another son, George, became a well-known lawyer. A daughter married George Ryerson.

John Rolph did not accompany his family to Canada, but continued his education in England. In 1809 he was admitted as a student of law at the Inner Temple (London). Immigrating to Upper Canada in 1812, he served during the war as paymaster of the London District militia. He also took up land near Port Talbot and in these years he and members of his family were on excellent terms with the archtory, Colonel Thomas Talbot. In 1817 Rolph took the initiative in inaugurating the 'Talbot Anniversary,' honouring the founding of the settlement by the colonel in 1803. Soon afterward Rolph returned to England to resume his education. From 1818 to 1821 he studied both law and medicine at St John's College, Cambridge, and medicine at Guy's and St Thomas' hospitals in London. He also undertook studies leading to a divinity degree. He was called to the bar of the Inner Temple in 1821, and in the same year, soon after his return, to the bar of Upper Canada. In 1826, on a subsequent visit to England, he was admitted by examination to membership in the Royal College of Surgeons. He practised medicine in the province during the 1820s, although he did not apply for and receive his licence until 1829. In 1824 he wrote to Colonel Talbot, asking him to be the patron of the Talbot Dispensatory, which he and Dr Charles Duncombe proposed to establish for the dual purpose of offering free medical advice and instructing students. The dispensatory soon disappeared from sight; it may have been projected mainly to establish good relations with Talbot.

Rolph's active pursuit of two professions made him widely known in the London District. On 2 Sept. 1824 William Lyon Mackenzie in the *Colonial Advocate* stated that 'there are thousands in the district, whom he has been the means of restoring to health and strength.' He was soon drawn into politics and was elected in Middlesex County for the House of Assembly in 1824. Rolph now sacrificed whatever friendly ties he had with Talbot and quickly assumed the leadership of those members (soon to be called Reformers) who were opposing the official party (soon to be called the Family Compact); indeed, the assembly sessions from 1825 through 1828 were to a considerable extent dominated by a continuing political duel between Rolph and the attorney general, John Beverley Robinson. In an assembly not noted for learning, a man with Rolph's thorough and varied education, his good social background, and his powerful (if somewhat florid) eloquence, was best equipped to stand up to the highly competent and masterful attorney general.

Of all the issues before the legislature elected in 1824, the most controversial was the 'Alien Question' – whether American-born settlers who had come into Upper Canada since 1783 were aliens and, if so, how they were to be naturalized. The question affected the political status, and possibly the property titles, of over half the province's population. Despite his English birth, Rolph embraced the cause of the American-born settlers, who were numerous in his own constituency; he saw it as a 'popular' cause being attacked by the executive branch and the Legislative Council. More specifically, he denounced the habitual attacks of conservative loyalist members, many of them from the eastern part of the province, on everything American. He called upon Upper Canadians 'to give over indulging in worthless slander of our neighbours and friends.' Upper Canada had nothing to fear from American settlers; they had not fled from 'a bad government and a barren soil' but had come willingly and were quickly developing a 'deep personal interest' in the province and its institutions. After the assembly had passed resolutions demanding that resident American-born settlers be recognized as having all the rights of British subjects, Rolph went to England in the spring of 1826 as a spokesman of the Reform majority in the assembly to try to influence the Colonial Office to respond to the resolutions. In London he was courteously received and consulted and appeared to be satisfied with an act of parliament empowering the provincial legislature to pass a naturalization bill of limited scope; it would have to contain provisions such as a renunciation of allegiance to the United States and a public registry of naturalized Americans which many found repugnant. However, after Rolph returned to Upper Canada he introduced in December 1826 a bill which differed from imperial instructions and made the naturalization process much easier and more palatable to American-born settlers. (There is a certain air of mystery in the whole transaction – as in so many episodes in Rolph's career.)

The alien controversy reached new heights of bitterness in 1827. After some complicated legislative manœuvring, in which Rolph and Robinson both took leading parts, the assembly reluctantly and somewhat surprisingly passed a bill conforming to the Colonial Office's instructions, presumably on the assumption that no better measure was obtainable. Reformers opposed to the measure were determined on a further appeal to England and once again hoped that Rolph would represent them. He apparently decided that his professional obligations made another lengthy trip impossible and, instead, Robert Randall was sent. The latter's mission was completely successful: the act, largely shaped by Robinson, was disallowed, and the assembly was invited to pass a measure to its own liking; it did so in 1828. Because of the leading part he had taken in the assembly Rolph could claim a large share of the credit for this outcome.

From 1825 to 1828 Rolph was also prominent in questions and controversies that were defining and sharpening political alignments in Upper Canada. He harked back to the wrongs done to 'the martyred' Robert Fleming Gourlay. He deplored the harsh treatment meted out to his colleague from Middlesex, Captain John Matthews, whose army pension was suspended for remarks considered sympathetic to the United States. He defended Francis Collins, editor of the *Canadian Freeman*, in his quarrels with the administration and, especially, with Robinson. Along with other Reform lawyers he criticized the 'persecution' of Judge John Walpole Willis. In the assembly he spoke against the 'exclusive' claims of the Church of England (even though he was a member), attacked all connection between church and state, and defended the Methodists from John Strachan's criticisms. He sponsored a number of reform measures, most notably in an eloquent speech on a bill to abolish imprisonment for debt. In many of these activities he was closely associated with Marshall Spring Bidwell and with Dr William Warren Baldwin and his son Robert. After the convincing Reform victory in the elections of 1828, and his own easy return in Middlesex, Rolph might have been chosen speaker; in any case in the short, Reform-dominated assembly of 1829-30 an unfriendly Tory observer noted that he led 'the house like a flock of sheep.'

Following this intense political activity, however, Rolph was not a candidate in the 1830 elections. One can only guess at his motives: perhaps he had concluded that political action in the assembly was futile as long as it had no control or influence over the lieutenant governor, the Family Compact, and the Legislative Council. Perhaps he had lost touch with his constituency, since he had moved eastward to Dundas some years earlier and had spent much time in York (Toronto), the provincial capital, as well as in England in 1826. Perhaps he had found it impossible to do justice to his two professions and at the same time perform the time-consuming and often thankless duties of a political leader. In fact he was having to choose between law and medicine. Early in 1831 he wrote to Robert Baldwin: 'Every day I become less and less efficient in these Law matters' and a few months later to W.W. Baldwin: 'My time is wholly occupied in medical practice – I think of no other pursuit, I engage in no other: but it is laborious. Country practice must be so. ...' He was accepting no new suits at law, and about 1832 he transferred the remainder of his practice to his brother George. (He might have been amused if he had known that, shortly afterward, the colonial secretary wrote confidentially to Lieutenant Governor Sir John Colborne that Rolph would be a suitable person for the vacant post of solicitor general.) By early 1832 he had moved to York, where he not only built up his practice but accepted students in what was apparently the only 'medical school' in the province at that time. He was also active in establishing the mechanics' institute in York, where he gave popular lectures on a variety of subjects. Like other doctors in the town, he sought to relieve the sufferings of cholera victims in the epidemics of 1832 and 1834. In the latter year he was married to Grace Haines, of Kingston, a woman of strong character who shared fully in his career, particularly in the administration of his various medical schools. They were to have four children.

Early in 1834 York was incorporated as the city of Toronto, and in the elections for aldermen and councilmen Rolph's name headed the poll in St Patrick's Ward. There was general expectation that the Reform majority on council would elect him the city's first mayor. But the councillors apparently felt the honour should go to Mackenzie in recognition of the 'persecutions' he had recently been suffering. When he learned of this plan, Rolph promptly resigned his seat and took no further part in municipal politics, leaving everyone to guess at his motives. Nor was he a candidate in the elections for the assembly in 1834, which resulted in a resounding Reform victory. Rolph's life now appeared to be devoted almost entirely to the practice and teaching of medicine, although he also served as a director and first president of the People's Bank, founded in 1835, with many leading Reformers, including Francis Hincks, active in it.

Nevertheless, it was soon clear that Rolph was still a political force, all the more, perhaps, because he had recently been somewhat out of the public eye. At the end of January 1836 Sir Francis Bond Head arrived in Toronto to replace Colborne as lieutenant governor. He found that the Executive Council had only three members, and that there was an immediate need to enlarge it. Although he felt instinctively antagonistic to Mackenzie and to the American-born Bidwell, Head was prepared to see the Executive Council broadened by the appointment of suitable men from outside the Tory ranks. Robert Baldwin and Rolph were obvious possibilities. Despite misgivings on Baldwin's part, he and Rolph, along with John Henry Dunn, the receiver general, were sworn as members of the Executive Council on 20 Feb. 1836. Rolph and Baldwin were determined to be more than mere ciphers: they wished to be consulted regularly by the lieutenant governor, to have an influential voice in the dispensing of patronage, and to see 'the Affairs of the Province ... distributed into Departments, to the Heads of which shall be referred such matters as obviously appertain to them respectively.' They succeeded in convincing the entire council to prepare a memorandum supporting this stand, which Head later stated had been taken at Rolph's initiative. The lieutenant governor at once rejected the memorandum, stating that in Upper Canada he alone could be the 'responsible Minister,' and inviting the council to resign if they felt that their 'Principles' were being compromised. This they did on 12 March, thereby precipitating a political crisis which poisoned the political air of Upper Canada for many months.

Rolph, however, did not take any prominent part in the debate between Head and the 'Constitutionalists' on the one side and the

Reform and radical leaders of the assembly on the other. He was clearly identified with the Reform side, but with the moderate, 'responsible' brand associated with the Baldwins, and not at all with Mackenzie or even with the actions and statements of the assembly majority. Thus he was not especially vulnerable when provincial opinion veered sufficiently to defeat the Reformers in the elections of 1836. It is curious – but unexplained – that Rolph chose this somewhat inauspicious time to return to politics. Although now a resident of Toronto, he stood as a candidate in Norfolk County, where he had long associations and where he was easily elected.

Reformers were outnumbered in the new assembly by more than three to one; with Mackenzie, Bidwell, and Peter Perry all defeated and with Robert Baldwin still withdrawn from politics, Rolph once again found himself the leader of the party. He appears to have shared to the full the Reformers' indignation at the methods that, they felt, had been used to defeat them. 'Orange violence, bribery and corruption, manufactured deeds, false evidence ... and malicious official misrepresentation, and ultra tory returning officers, and the like abuses together with the aid of a state paid priesthood, turned the elections against us ... there is not a baser or more unprincipled government in the world than the one we are now enduring here,' Rolph wrote Baldwin in July 1836. The tone of this letter points to Rolph's role in the assembly in 1836 and 1837 and it may even help to explain why he was willing to flirt, in his own way, to be sure, with involvement in the rebellion.

In the assembly Rolph could of course achieve no legislative goals against the overwhelming Tory majority, but he could hearten Reformers by his oratory and by his persistent attacks on the Tories and their allies. The hostile Toronto *Patriot* on 20 Dec. 1836 paid him grudging tribute as 'the great leader of the minority, and the only one worth listening to,' while denouncing his 'wily sophistry.' His main interventions were two speeches on the clergy reserves in December 1836 and in the following month during the 'inquiry into the charges of high misdemeanors at the late elections preferred against Sir Francis Bond Head.' In the first, which was widely reprinted and was in part a debate with Christopher Hagerman, he asserted that a connection between church and state was always harmful to religion, as was the state endowment of any denomination, and he denied that the Church of England was established in Upper Canada; he ended by moving that the clergy reserves be sold and 'the proceeds [be applied] to the purposes of General Education.' It is probable that much of Rolph's popularity as a Reform leader throughout his long career derived from his eloquent and consistent support for the voluntary principle in religion. The second speech contained a slashing attack upon Head, accusing him of having used 'the language of an agitator,' of having treated 'the friends of reform ... as enemies,' and, in appealing 'from the throne to the passions of the people as "Englishmen, Irishmen, Scotchmen and U.E. Loyalists," [of having] forgot, yes sir, forgot the CANADIANS! ...' Rolph wondered whether Upper Canada would 'ever again have a free Election.' It is impossible to know whether this remark was merely a rhetorical flourish or whether it indicated real despair over the prospects for peaceful change.

But, whatever despair Rolph may have felt, he took no visible part in the mobilizing of radical opinion and in the preparations for the armed uprising of December 1837. He and Mackenzie had never been intimates, or even working associates, and like his neighbour in Toronto, M.S. Bidwell, and his friends the Baldwins, he did not associate himself with the little editor's increasingly frenetic course in the latter months of 1837. How much he knew about Mackenzie's plans by November and how much he was consulted by Mackenzie are other, and perhaps unanswerable, questions. In the event of success Mackenzie would obviously need men of respectability and standing to assume leading roles and no one was better fitted for such a task than Rolph. Mackenzie later claimed, and went on claiming all his life, that shortly before the outbreak of the rebellion Rolph had agreed to become 'the Executive' who would direct operations in secret until the time came to reveal his identity. Rolph denied this claim, and there is no evidence to support Mackenzie's assertion. But it is clear that Rolph was consulted by Mackenzie and it appears Rolph agreed that Mackenzie should continue to investigate the state of opinion north of the city at the end of October and in November. Later in November he also learned that Mackenzie had fixed on Thursday, 7 December, for the insurgents to assemble north of Toronto and advance on the capital. Rolph apparently had no part in this decision, but he did not report the information to the authorities. His complicity apparently went considerably further: as far as can be gathered, he agreed that in the event of success he would, in John Charles Dent's words, 'assume the direction of the Civil Government.'

From his vantage point within Toronto and his access to information and rumour, Rolph learned late on 2 December that the government intended to arrest Mackenzie and to take other precautionary measures. Rolph could see the uprising being nipped in the bud and he sent word to Samuel Lount advising him to move on the city at once with 300 men in order to maintain the advantage of surprise. Lount received the message the next day and the men did begin to assemble at Montgomery's Tavern on Monday, 4 December. Mackenzie was furious at this turn of events, for there was still much to do before an effective operation could be mounted. On this same day, he conferred with Rolph outside the city, when the latter apparently advised abandoning the uprising. But it was now too late, and the men were moving down Yonge Street.

On Tuesday, 5 December, occurred the single most controversial episode in Rolph's long career. In the morning Head decided to send a message to the rebels, under a flag of truce, advising them to return peacefully to their homes. After one or two other names had been canvassed, Robert Baldwin and Rolph were selected and agreed to undertake the mission. They met with the rebel leaders, who insisted on having the lieutenant governor's message in writing. Baldwin and Rolph returned to the city, only to find that Head had determined not to parley further with the rebels. They delivered this message to the rebels, again under a flag of truce, and the mission was at an end. The controversy surrounding this affair started a little more than a month later when Lount was captured and made a statement, prior to his execution, that on the first trip, Rolph 'gave me a wink to walk on one side, when he requested me not to hear the message but to go on with our proceedings.' If this account was correct, Rolph had obviously played a double, indeed a traitorous, role, posing as the trusted envoy of the lieutenant governor while counselling the rebels to attack the city. Rolph's version was that he had given this advice to Lount on the second trip, after he had delivered Head's message and when the truce mission was at an end.

Upon his return to the city in the middle of Tuesday afternoon Rolph apparently busied himself in urging radicals to arm themselves to join with Mackenzie's men, who were expected imminently. But hours passed and in the evening it was learned that the rebels, after an exchange of fire with an outpost guard, had precipitately retreated. As midnight approached and the loyal forces were clearly gaining strength and confidence, Rolph realized the insurgents' cause was hopeless and he sent out a messenger advising them to disperse. So far, his implication in the movement had not come to the attention of the authorities, but when on the morning of 6 December Dr Thomas David Morrison was arrested and officials began to search Mackenzie's house and office, Rolph perceived that evidence of his complicity would probably come to light. With his accustomed self-control he casually walked westward from the centre of town to a spot where one of his medical students had a saddled horse waiting. He was stopped once by loyalist volunteers but allowed to pass after a doctor (a former student of his) vouched for him, and after riding all night he reached the Niagara River and exile in the United States. On 11 December the lieutenant governor issued a proclamation stating that facts had come to his knowledge indicating that Rolph 'had been concerned in the traitorous attempt ... to subvert the Government of this Province' and offering a reward of £500 for his apprehension. Head later stated to Lord Glenelg that 'Dr Rolph has been proved to have been the ... most crafty, the most bloodythirsty, the most treacherous, the most cowardly, and ... the most infamous of the traitors who lately assailed us.' He further noted that on 20 Jan. 1838 Rolph, accused of having 'combined, conspired and confederated, with the rebels,' had been expelled from the assembly.

Rolph lived for more than five years in the United States, mainly in Rochester. At first he showed some interest in the Patriot activities along the border, and he occasionally corresponded with exiles from both Upper and Lower Canada. But he soon dissociated himself from such activities and began to re-establish himself as a doctor and medical teacher. Some Canadian students came to study under him. He managed to get a good deal of his property out of Toronto and he was presently joined by his wife. No doubt exile was bitter, but his was a good deal more comfortable than that of many who had been implicated in the rebellion, including Mackenzie, who later insisted that Rolph had failed to befriend him when he had been jailed in Rochester. Such aloofness on Rolph's part was not only characteristic but also not surprising in view of the accusations Mackenzie had been publishing. Mackenzie asserted that he had been the mere agent of the 'Executive,' John Rolph, that Rolph had ruined any chances of success by changing the date of the rebellion, and that his appearance with the flag of truce had discouraged the rank and file of the insurgents. Rolph prepared but did not publish a 'Review of Mackenzie's publications ...,' in which he accused Mackenzie of endangering the lives and liberty of Reformers by leaving evidence of the rebels' plans in Toronto and by publicizing the names of those associated with the movement. He laid the failure of the rebellion to Mackenzie's own mismanagement, especially the tardiness in moving on the city after the end of the flag of truce mission. The review, found later among his papers, was in the third person and, as usual, volunteered no information about Rolph's own actions or motives.

A grant of amnesty in 1843 permitted Rolph to return to Toronto that August. The event was greeted on a strictly party basis: the *Examiner* welcomed the return 'of a man whose profound talents are calculated to ornament any department of life'; in the legislature Dr William Dunlop remarked that Rolph and others 'kept back and pushed better men than themselves forward to bear the brunt of the contest. If the sleek and wily traitor, Rolph, was to be pardoned ... why not Mackenzie?' Rolph resumed his old residence and soon re-established his medical school and practice. At this time King's College was just getting under way, and Rolph's school was aimed at 'medical students who do not intend to enter the University.... They would be conducted through the usual course of medical studies ... and prepared for their diploma from the Medical Board.' He assembled a competent staff, and for a time the school – incorporated in 1851 as the Toronto School of Medicine – flourished.

Meanwhile, Rolph had reappeared as a controversial figure in the public prints. In April 1848 the government of Robert Baldwin and Louis-Hippolyte La Fontaine dismissed Dr Walter Telfer, the medical superintendent of the Provincial Lunatic Asylum in Toronto, and replaced him with Dr George Hamilton Park, a brother-in-law of Rolph. There were adequate reasons for the dismissal and Park appears to have been suitably qualified for the post, but in a small community intensely interested in patronage and riddled with personal animosities, the incident became the centre of bitter partisan recriminations in the newspapers. Matters were intensified when Rolph, serving as acting superintendent in Park's absence, clashed with the asylum's board of commissioners. Personal relations between Baldwin and Rolph had never been fully restored after the flag of truce incident, and supporters of Baldwin saw Rolph's actions in a sinister light. James Hervey Price called him 'a black hearted rascal,' determined 'either to destroy the Baldwin ministry or to compel that ministry to alter the Bill for the Lunatic Asylum giving all power to Park that Rolph and his medical School might rule it for the School's benefit.' The rift was widened when the Baldwin government dismissed Park in January 1849.

This incident coincided with a deepening split in the Reform party, as its radical or 'democratic' wing (coming to be called the Clear Grits) became increasingly impatient with the Baldwin government's moderate and cautious policies. By-elections from 1849 to 1851 marked the growing strength of this group and in the fall of the latter year the tired and discouraged Baldwin resigned. It fell to Francis Hincks to reconstruct the Upper Canadian portion of the government and he decided that party harmony dictated the inclusion of two Clear Grits in the cabinet. The man above all others whom the Grits wanted included was Rolph.

Why they wanted him is less clear. As so often it is uncertain what part Rolph had played in the rise of the Clear Grits, although he was accused of writing anonymous anti-Baldwin articles in the *Examiner*. Perhaps the Clear Grits simply wanted a spokesman in the cabinet who was a powerful orator and who had been identified with Reform principles for more than a quarter-century. The *Examiner* asserted, 'There is not a man in the entire ranks of our party whom the tories dread half as much as Dr. Rolph.' In fact, however, as the *Globe* noted in November, Hincks had made a master stroke. Once two of their number (Malcolm Cameron was the other) had accepted the responsibilities of office, the Clear Grits were bottled up and rendered ineffective.

Rolph was appointed commissioner of crown lands when the government of Hincks and Augustin-Norbert Morin took office on 28 Oct. 1851. Governor General Lord Elgin [Bruce], perhaps worried that the colonial secretary might query the inclusion in the government of one 'whose conduct in 1837 was not above reproach,' noted that 'He is an Englishman, educated at one of the Universities and has a brother a Rector.' Besides, the cry of 'rebel' had lost much of its force since the Tory violence of 1849. In the general elections some weeks later, Rolph was a candidate in Norfolk County and was easily elected. In fact, his popularity with Clear Grits was so great that his name was mentioned as a possible candidate in several other constituencies.

The Hincks-Morin government, which held power until September 1854, was not especially distinguished, and Rolph did little to make it more so. He carried on a personal quarrel with his Clear Grit colleague Malcolm Cameron, and he further weakened the morale of the Grits by failing to press within the government for measures to which Grits were committed, including the secularization of the clergy reserves. Rolph developed a considerable talent for disappearing when critical votes were to be taken. He was apparently rather ineffective in the Crown Lands Department and was shifted to the presidency of the council and the Bureau of Agriculture in 1853. One observer felt that as a minister Rolph 'showed how little talent he really possessed.' By 1853 many Reformers were turning against him because of his continued association with Hincks despite the fact that the latter's railway deals were coming to light. The *Globe* denounced Rolph as 'a sleek visaged man ... deep, dark, designing, cruel, malignant, traitorous ... [whose] manners are civil and insinuating. ... It is thought that he is an agile man – he is certainly a slippery one.' Hincks, who himself had often enough been the target of the *Globe's* attacks, came to share this harsh assessment when Rolph, dissatisfied with Hincks' policies and wishing to re-establish his standing with independent Reformers, deserted the government in September 1854. The ministry collapsed, and the two men parted amid mutual recriminations.

Three incidents in Rolph's life during the years of the Hincks-Morin government are worth noting. The first was the revival of the flag of truce controversy by a Conservative member from Toronto, William Henry Boulton. Rolph had apparently been expecting an attack for he had taken the trouble, two months earlier, of securing an affidavit from Hugh Carmichael, who had been the bearer of the flag and was now in Rolph's employ, which completely corroborated Rolph's version: it stated that during the actual mission Rolph did not communicate separately with Lount or say 'anything irrelevant to the Flag of Truce or against its good faith.' Boulton accepted Rolph's explanations, but another member of the assembly, none other than Mackenzie, felt called upon to defend Lount's memory, and to go back over the whole story, in speeches, editorials, and, finally, a pamphlet. On Rolph's behalf, David Gibson prepared a reply to Mackenzie, but Rolph did not use it; he wrote to Gibson that 'the time has not yet arrived' to 'repel' Mackenzie's charges.

The second incident involved that old source of controversy, the lunatic asylum. In 1853 the government, at Rolph's behest, secured the passage of a bill reorganizing the asylum; subsequently Dr Joseph Workman, an associate of Rolph's, was appointed medical superintendent and another member of Rolph's school was made consulting physician. The reorganization improved the administration of the asylum, but to his critics the whole episode was but another example of Rolph's labyrinthine ways.

The third incident also raised the suspicion that Rolph used his influence in government to serve the interests of his medical school. In these years the legislature was sitting in Quebec, and Rolph was perforce removed from his school. Letters from his staff indicated that it was in a state of decline, unable to meet the competition of the medical faculty of the University of Toronto, and also probably suffering the competition of the recently formed Upper Canada School of Medicine, affiliated with Trinity College. In 1852–53 a bill passed through the legislature reorganizing the university by making it an examining and not a teaching body and thus abolishing instruction in the faculties of medicine and law. Rolph's school was no longer faced with competition from the university.

In the 1854 election following the break-up of the Hincks-Morin ministry, Rolph was re-elected in Norfolk, but he was now in opposition. He remained in the legislature until 1857 but attended infrequently, now more than ever a relic from a former age.

In his last 15 years Rolph resumed his career as a medical administrator, but with limited success. In 1854 the Toronto School of Medicine became affiliated with Victoria College, thus enabling its graduates to secure degrees from that institution, even though the latter was still located in Cobourg. Two years later, however, Rolph's entire staff resigned on the same day to remove themselves from his ineffective and autocratic leadership. They established a rival institution under the old name, and by legal action prevented Rolph from further using that name. Nevertheless, Rolph's students remained loyal to him; he secured new staff and continued as dean of the medical faculty of Victoria College, which conferred an honorary LLD on him in 1859. For the next decade Rolph was still highly regarded as a teacher, and still practised his profession, despite failing powers following a stroke in 1861. He no longer had the capacity to function effectively as dean, but refused to relinquish control. Finally, early in 1870, he was, in effect, forced to retire, and he went to live with his daughter and son-in-law in Perth County, where he died a few months later.

At the time of his death the controversies associated with Rolph's political career had receded into the distant past; there was a general willingness to pay tribute to him as a Reform leader, a medical teacher, and an orator, and to gloss over his weaknesses. But 15 years later dispute again erupted with the publication of the first volume of Dent's *The story of the Upper Canadian rebellion*, which disparaged

Mackenzie and praised Rolph. Old Reformers sprang to the defence of Mackenzie, revived all the earlier charges against Rolph as devious, cunning, and self-seeking, and probably helped establish the picture of him that has widely prevailed. Rolph's own habitual secretiveness and the absence of adequate personal papers make it difficult now to draw a full and sympathetic portrait. But his contributions to the emerging reform movement in the 1820s and to medical education over a longer period will continue to be remembered, and the intricacies of his personality will continue to fascinate.

G.M. CRAIG

JAMES HUNTER SAMSON

Lawyer, politician, and office holder; b. 14 June 1802 in Ireland, son of James Samson, who later became an officer in the British army, and Susanne Connell; m. 4 March 1828 Alicia Fenton Russell, niece and ward of Sir John Harvey, in London, and they had no issue; d. 26 March 1836 in Belleville, Upper Canada.

James Hunter Samson probably came to the Canadas in 1813, when his father's regiment, the 70th Foot, began its tour of duty there. At the age of 16 he sought, unsuccessfully, an ensigncy in the 70th. Studying at York (Toronto) in 1818, he became the close friend of Robert Baldwin. In 1819, as a law student in Christopher Alexander Hagerman's Kingston office, he began a regular correspondence with Baldwin. His letters show Samson as articulate, sensitive, fond of poetry, hard-working, and ambitious, but also insecure, subject to fits of depression, and extremely jealous of anyone who threatened to come between himself and Baldwin.

After Samson was called to the bar in November 1823, he became the first resident lawyer at Belleville. Life was not easy in this lumbering, farming, trading community of fewer than 500 people. He claimed 'many battles and storms' with one judge and he was financially embarrassed on occasion. He came, however, to enjoy a reputation as a 'Barrister of no ordinary talent' and was recognized by the Law Society of Upper Canada, which elected him a bencher in 1835. Samson championed the cause of the fledgling Church of Scotland congregation at Belleville, serving as a trustee, writing letters to the press and various officials, and putting up the first minister after his arrival from Scotland. When cholera threatened in 1832, he donated funds to help build Belleville's first hospital, personally supervising its hasty construction within a fortnight. He also served as a member of the local board of health and was a member of the village council.

From 1828 until his death he represented the riding of Hastings in the House of Assembly. Initially, he claimed to be a moderate, supporting the 'principles of Whiggism'; however, in 1829 during the assembly's first session Samson revealed his true colours. After attempting, unsuccessfully, to delete comments that were highly critical of the executive branch of government from the reply to the speech from the throne, he was the lone member to vote against the reply. His military background, allegiance to Hagerman (regarded by historians as a pillar of the 'family compact'), aristocratic connections through marriage, and basic distrust of republicanism probably explain this vote.

Samson's subsequent voting pattern led William Lyon Mackenzie to call him 'a selfish illiberal creature' and place him prominently on his 'Black List' for 1830. Stung by this attack, Samson played a leading role in the libel and breach of privilege charges against Mackenzie in December 1831. He described articles in the *Colonial Advocate* as 'gross, scandalous, and malicious libels – intended and calculated to bring this House and the Government of this Province into contempt.' The assembly declared Mackenzie guilty of the libel and also approved Samson's resolution that Mackenzie's defence tactics made him 'guilty of a high breach of the privilege of this house.' Samson then won support for his motions expelling Mackenzie from the house and calling for a new election.

When Mackenzie's supporters touched off a series of protest rallies, Samson appeared at the Belleville meeting to expose the 'falsehood, absurdity and inconsistency' of Mackenzie's position. His own resolution of loyalty recognized that Upper Canada's institutions were imperfect, but it maintained 'we have less cause of complaint, than any people on earth; and the means of redress are in our own power.'

From 1832 to 1835 Samson played a modest role in the assembly. He chaired several committees, including the 1832 select committee on grievances that dealt with civil rights and favoured the creation of additional banks in the province. He also spoke out on the need for improving navigation of the St Lawrence. In 1836 his health and state of mind became topics for local editorial comment when he was unable to attend the house. His father's death in 1832 had been a serious blow and political differences with Baldwin had diminished this once vital friendship he had clung to. Samson sought solace in alcohol, which contributed to his death in March 1836, aged 36.

GERALD E. BOYCE

ROBERT BALDWIN SULLIVAN

Lawyer, office holder, politician, and judge; b. 24 May 1802 in Bandon (Republic of Ireland), son of Daniel Sullivan and Barbara Baldwin; m. first 20 Jan. 1829 Cecilia Eliza Matthews, and they had a daughter; m. secondly 26 Dec. 1833 Emily Louisa Delatre, and they had four sons and seven daughters; d. 14 April 1853 in Toronto.

Robert Baldwin Sullivan's father was an Irish merchant, and his mother was a sister of William Warren Baldwin. The first member of Robert's family to come to York (Toronto), Upper Canada, was Daniel, his eldest brother, who became a law student under Baldwin and lived with another uncle, John Spread Baldwin. The rest of the family immigrated in 1819 and the ambitious Daniel Sr established himself as a merchant in York, dealing in soap and tobacco. After a promising beginning, the Sullivans' aspirations were dashed. In 1821 Daniel Jr died; the following year his father's death left Robert as the head of the family. Once again the extended family lent its support; in 1823 William Warren Baldwin placed his nephew on the books of the Law Society of Upper Canada and secured for him a position as librarian to the House of Assembly. Having received a solid education in private schools in Ireland, Robert excelled in his law studies and was called to the bar in Michaelmas term 1828.

Sullivan first took an active role in politics during the exciting provincial election of 1828, as a campaigner for his uncle. Symptomatic of the increasing organization of the reform movement, John Rolph had arranged W.W. Baldwin's candidacy in his home riding of Norfolk, though Baldwin remained in York to aid in the campaign of Thomas David Morrison. Sullivan went to Vittoria to represent his uncle, who was elected, he noted, largely because of Rolph's influence. Sullivan subsequently returned to the capital and took part with Baldwin and his son Robert in Morrison's challenge to the return in York of their arch-foe, tory John Beverley Robinson. He then gave counsel and support to Rolph in his legal defence of Francis Collins, a supporter of his cousin Robert. Despite the fact that Morrison was defeated and Collins found guilty of libel, Sullivan's considerable legal talents did not go unnoticed.

His future looked bright indeed, but not in the provincial capital. He returned to Vittoria, apparently determined to settle there and take over the law practice vacated by Rolph as a result of his move to Dundas. Shortly afterwards, in early 1829, he married a daughter of John Matthews, a reform colleague of Rolph's. But once again, after a promising beginning, successive tragedies unravelled Sullivan's personal life: on 20 Dec. 1830, six months after the birth of their daughter, Sullivan's wife died; three months later the baby died. Sullivan quit Vittoria and returned to York to seek the support of his family once more.

Upon his return, he again entered the law offices of W.W. Baldwin and Son, and later, in 1831, he established a partnership with Robert, who had married his sister. The firm, with such talented young lawyers, was soon prospering. On his birthday in 1833, the obviously bright and sensitive Sullivan reported to his brother Henry, then studying medicine in Ireland, that things were going well: 'Augustus [another brother] ... is now a Student of the Learned Society of Osgoode Hall – we have six clerks with plenty to do.' The partners were preparing 'to go into parliament with the honorable body of Colonial Whigs. next election.' Sullivan and Baldwin had advanced their careers enough to consider themselves eligible to replace the recently dismissed attorney general, Henry John Boulton, and solicitor general, Christopher Alexander Hagerman. But, Sullivan said, because of their rumoured replacement by law officers from England, neither he nor Baldwin stood a good chance of getting 'a silk gown.' By the end of 1833 Sullivan was once again thriving and on Boxing Day, in Stamford (Niagara Falls), Upper Canada, he married Emily Louisa, daughter of Lieutenant-Colonel Philip Chesneau Delatre.

His contemplations aside, Sullivan did not seek a seat in the election of 1834. The following year, however, he stood successfully as an alderman for St David's Ward, Toronto, no doubt with the mayoralty in mind. A gentleman of Sullivan's social standing and proven ability would have had little interest in aldermanic duties on a council just one year old. The mayoralty was another matter, however, as John Rolph's actions the previous year had indicated. At the first meeting of council in 1835, Sullivan was confirmed mayor by tory and radical alike. As Toronto's second mayor, he proved himself a competent administrator, approaching the problems of council from a practical rather than partisan perspective. Contested ward elections were the first problem; under Sullivan's guidance, council adopted a set of regulations for hearing these grievances before proceeding with individual cases. Plagued with the same financial problems that had faced the first council, Sullivan turned his attention to amending the assessment laws. He was, as well, able to arrange financing for the city's first major works project, a trunk sewer.

Public interest in municipal affairs was, however, sporadic at best. During 1835 council frequently could not convene for want of a quorum and there was discussion about compelling aldermen to attend. Sullivan's last council meeting, lacking a quorum, was adjourned, and he declined to run again. There was, however, no lack of public interest in provincial politics, especially with the arrival of the new lieutenant governor, Sir Francis Bond Head, in January 1836. And it was Sullivan, the erudite lawyer, who, as mayor of the provincial capital, delivered an address of welcome from the outgoing council.

The resignation on 12 March 1836 of Head's Executive Council, of which Robert Baldwin had been a member, plunged the colony into its greatest political and constitutional crisis up to that point. With a haste that was indecent if nothing else, Sullivan accepted appointment to council and on the 14th was sworn in along with Augustus Warren Baldwin (another uncle), John Elmsley, and William Allan. Upper Canadian history provides other possible examples of political turncoats: Henry John Boulton deserved the epithet, John Willson probably did not. But Sullivan's volte-face is without parallel. At the time of the reform brouhaha in 1828 over the dismissal of Judge John Walpole Willis, Sullivan had declared, 'It was against my principles to shew any respect to the present judges,' and, like his cousin, refused to plead before the 'Pretended' Court of King's Bench. A few years later he professed his eagerness to join the 'Colonial Whigs' in the House of Assembly. Yet, without warning, he bedded down in 1836 with a group denounced by William Warren Baldwin as the 'Tory junto.'

Sullivan has, unfortunately, left no explanation, or even rationalization, of his flip-flop. Reward was not long in coming: on 13 July he accepted the commissionership of crown lands, a plum worth £1,000 per annum. The patriarch of the Baldwin–Sullivan family was scathing. 'R.S.,' W.W. Baldwin wrote to his son Robert, 'is in the midst of enemies but he has thrown himself into their arms, & when they shake him over the precepice, he will not have a friend to console him.' A pariah among acquaintances and an object of rebuke by the whig press, Sullivan was isolated, almost. Robert Baldwin reminded his irate father that 'family love' was 'heavens best gift ... let us not let political differences interfere with the cultivation of it – but on the contrary where such unhappily exist always forget the politician in the relation.' Despite Baldwin's support for Sullivan, their legal partnership appears to have ended some time between 1836 and 1838.

Lord Durham [Lambton] later derided Head's appointments as ciphers. Sullivan proved an administration man, but he was no one's tool. And what cannot be questioned is his ability. Head defended his choice, describing Sullivan as well-educated, a leading lawyer, and 'a man of very superior talents ... and of irreproachable character.' He quickly became the dominant figure in an increasingly active council. In a memorandum on the councillors prepared by Head, probably for his successor, Sir George Arthur, Sullivan was lauded as possessing 'great legal talent [and] sound judgement particularly on financial questions,' whereas Allan, although honest and honourable, had 'not much talent or education' and Elmsley was a 'wrong headed man but brave.' Arthur relied heavily on forceful men with incisive analytical minds, such as Chief Justice John Beverley Robinson, John Macaulay, and Sullivan. In June 1838 Sullivan assumed the additional office of surveyor general. During Robinson's long absence in England from 1838 to 1840, Arthur tended to ignore his law officers and other councillors in preference to Sullivan, who 'takes a more enlarged view of the subjects, or, at all events, his sentiments fall more in with my motives of dealing with political questions in the present day; and, therefore, I have generally conferred with him in his office as presiding member of the Executive Council.' In February 1839 Sullivan was appointed to the Legislative Council. So crucial was he to the business of council and to the lieutenant governor as a policy adviser, that Arthur appointed Kenneth Cameron to serve as surveyor general pro tem, between October 1840 and February 1841, so that more important business need not be neglected by Sullivan.

In 1838, in the aftermath of the rebellion, Arthur had relied on him increasingly. That year Sullivan prepared, for instance, a mammoth report on the state of the province. The degree to which his analysis fell in line with that of his old enemies can be measured by Robinson's enthusiastic approval. The report was 'natural & forcible' and its tone 'liberally conservative.' Sullivan took for granted that without natural or cultural barriers separating Upper Canada from the United States, the colony 'must be materially affected by the state of Politics and of the popular mind in the neighbouring republic.' He uttered, albeit eloquently, the usual bromides that depicted American political culture in terms of 'tyranny of a majority' and mob rule. He repeated, in short, current tory denunciations of responsible government and an elective legislative council as mere half-way houses to full-blown democratic institutions and chaos. In a manner worthy of Robinson at his best, he defended the Constitutional Act of 1791, the integrity of office holders, and the absolute need, if not the right, of an executive claim to revenues independent of control by the assembly.

Sullivan's foray, in the same report, into policies on immigration, finance, and land matters marked his point of departure from tory nostrums. To his mind, tranquillity was a corollary of prosperity, which could only be achieved through large-scale immigration, a rise in the value of land, and productive public works. These measures would make people much happier 'than any abstract political measures' could, and would have the effect of restoring public confidence and the colony's trade. An enormous public debt sucked up available revenues and was responsible for leaving the province a largely inaccessible wilderness. The lack of superintendence of crown land produced a decline in revenue and immigration. Upper Canada, Sullivan maintained, must gain control of its major source of revenue, customs duties raised at Montreal and Quebec. To this end he gave full voice to a favourite tory war cry – annex Montreal, Trois-Rivières, and the Eastern Townships to Upper Canada, thus leaving the French Canadians to enjoy their own 'bad laws, bad roads bad sleighs, bad food ... in peace and quietness injuring no others and not being interfered with themselves.' The resurrection of union as a panacea for the Upper Canadian crisis would therefore be dangerous, since it would bring together and make supreme the democratic elements in Upper and Lower Canada. Over a year later, in 1839, Sullivan reiterated his hostility to union and his attachment to British institutions in a memorandum sent under Arthur's name to the Colonial Office. He was at pains to distinguish two elements among the 'conservatives': those 'who are so from principle, or attachment from sentiment to British institutions,' and the 'Commercial party' which supported 'prosperity, public credit and public improvements' but was conservative out of self-interest and only in prosperous times.

Sullivan's lucid analysis of the province's problems was matched by his equally deft set of practical prescriptions. He favoured the centralization of power, having urged Arthur in April 1838 to retain the power of patronage over the militia and not relinquish it to local colonels. That same year he recommended suspending work on the St Lawrence canals, lest the work become a 'perpetual monument of Legislative folly & extravagance,' and he cautioned Arthur to rein in the commissioners responsible for the work. Although he supported the legitimacy of the constitutional privileges of the Church of England, the clergy reserves issue had to be settled in the interests of internal harmony. To this end he favoured dividing the reserves among the Anglicans, Presbyterians, and Wesleyan Methodists, with the proceeds from the reserves used 'to secure religious instruction according to the protestant faith.'

In 1839 Arthur directed the Executive Council to prepare a report on how best to adapt land policy to the anticipated increase in immigration. The council split. Minority reports were submitted in 1840 by Sullivan and Augustus Warren Baldwin on one side, and William Allan and Richard Alexander Tucker on the other. In fact, the reports were the efforts of Sullivan and Allan. Sullivan's represents an eloquent and closely reasoned defence of an agrarian society, composed largely of independent farmers, as the basis for social and political stability and economic prosperity. Allan argued that the province's economic backwardness could only be overcome by capitalist undertakings. Possessed of a shrewd, intuitive grasp of Upper Canada's situation and its potential, Allan urged seizing the opportunity to establish 'what we have been taught to consider a great desideratum, viz, a class of labourers, separate and distinct from Land owners.' Although Governor Charles Edward Poulett Thomson (later Lord Sydenham) noted agreement with Allan's position 'as applied to a country under ordinary circumstances,' he saw the province's present situation as different and he dismissed Allan's opinion as biased and his arguments as 'trashy in the extreme.'

Thomson, the architect of union, soon realized how useful Sullivan could be. He abandoned his previous hostility to union, a position which, as Attorney General Hagerman found out, Thomson would not tolerate. Sullivan was prominent in shepherding the measure through the Legislative Council, and appeared a solid 'Governor's man' at its inception. He was one of the four executive councillors, along with William Henry Draper, Charles Richard Ogden, and Charles Dewey Day, in whom Robert Baldwin expressed want of confidence in February 1841. Sullivan retained the commissionership of crown lands until June of that year, in which month he was appointed to the new Legislative Council.

John Charles Dent's description of Sullivan, as a brilliant orator who charmed with his 'Irish provincial accent' but who lacked conviction and steadiness of purpose, is accurate. He seems to have dozed through his duties as president of the Executive Council in 1841–42. He performed another wonderful turn-around in September 1842. When the new governor, Sir Charles Bagot, was struggling to avoid a reform-dominated ministry, Sullivan supported him in the Legislative Council, asking, 'Are we to carry on the government fairly and upon liberal principles or *by dint of miserable majorities*?' Yet he happily remained as president of council when the miserable majority prevailed, holding that position until November 1843.

Indeed, he rapidly became a partisan of the new order, presumably an indication of his love of intrigue, his respect for power, and his weakness for flamboyant oratory. In October 1842 he was involved in the obdurate politics of the newly formed ministry of Baldwin and Louis-Hippolyte La Fontaine, chairing the committee of the Executive Council which recommended withdrawing government advertising from newspapers 'found to join in active opposition to the Government.' Sir Charles Theophilus Metcalfe, Bagot's successor in March 1843, was relatively complimentary to Sullivan as a minister, given that Metcalfe thought most of the executive councillors were fanatics, villains, or incompetents. According to his biographer, John William Kaye, the governor saw Sullivan as talented but dismissed him as inconsistent and lacking the 'weight of personal character.' If a lightweight, Sullivan was prominent enough to be a target of the Orange order. After passage of the Party Processions and Secret Societies bills, there was a huge, furious Orange demonstration in Toronto on 8 Nov. 1843. Sullivan's name was joined with those of the 'traitors Baldwin and [Francis Hincks]' on the mob's banners.

During the ten-month crisis which followed the resignation of the Baldwin–La Fontaine ministry in November, Sullivan was in his element. His talents as an orator and pamphleteer gave him a prominent role in the reform campaign to justify the actions of the late ministry and win the election of 1844. His excessive zeal, however, at times injured the reform cause. He took part in the early meetings of the party's new provincial organization, the Reform Association of Canada. At its first public meeting, in Toronto on 25 March 1844, Sullivan

– ironically, given his 'miserable majorities' speech – moved the resolution insisting that provincial ministries required the support of parliamentary majorities. He campaigned in 4th York with Baldwin and advised him on tactics. In September Baldwin reported consulting with Sullivan, James Edward Small, and John Henry Dunn about whether to resign his militia commission and relinquish his appointment as queen's counsel, in protest against Metcalfe's autocracy. On their advice Baldwin retained his militia commission.

Sullivan's most important role continued to be that of public controversialist. In May 1844 Egerton Ryerson had begun a series of newspaper articles which supported the governor, and later published them as a pamphlet. He claimed to have been sympathetic to the councillors until their 'real motives' were revealed by Sullivan and Francis Hincks, when he came to see Metcalfe as 'a misrepresented and injured man.' Under the transparent *nom de plume* of Legion, Sullivan answered in 13 letters in the *Examiner* and the *Globe*. The letters, which also appeared as a pamphlet, contained no new insights but were an effective summary of the Baldwinite arguments for responsible government and provided a puncturing lampoon of Ryerson's pomposity. They show, at places, Sullivan's tendency to get carried away with his rhetoric. Later in the year the tories made good use of his indiscretion at an election meeting in Sharon, where, in ridiculing the governor as 'Charles the Simple,' he seriously overstepped even the limits of that day. His excesses, however, were only one small factor in the reform defeat in the election of 1844. Sullivan ascribed it in large measure to the influence of the Orange order. 'Ireland in its worst time,' he told Baldwin in January 1845, 'was not more completely under the feet of an orange ascendancy than is Canada at present.'

With the party in opposition, Sullivan was not very active in the Legislative Council. He continued to be a close adviser to Baldwin on political matters, presumably more because of Baldwin's stout family loyalty than because of his chequered record as a political tactician. He had a good deal to say about the worst crisis facing the party between 1845 and 1847: the tories' wooing of French Canadians disenchanted with the reformers after the 1844 defeat. William Henry Draper came close to forging an alliance with René-Édouard Caron and others in 1845–46. To Sullivan, writing to Baldwin in August 1846, Caron was 'a false sneaking knave'; Hincks, who toadied to the French to maintain support, was nearly as bad. This outburst suggested that Sullivan had a conveniently short memory. La Fontaine did not. During the Draper–Caron flirtation, La Fontaine reminded Baldwin that Sullivan had made a similar attempt, in July 1842, to split the French from the reform party. He had approached both La Fontaine and Caron to enter the Bagot–Draper ministry and leave Baldwin behind.

There were issues on which the cousins differed. During the winter of 1844–45 Sullivan, who joined William Hume Blake in a campaign to reform the Upper Canadian judicial system, expressed his deep disappointment that Baldwin would not give leadership on that effort in the assembly. More significant was their disagreement over tariff policy. After Britain's adoption of free trade, Baldwin urged Canada, in a speech in November 1846, to follow that lead. Sullivan, however, was an early advocate of a different approach. Speaking to the Hamilton Mechanics' Institute on 17 Nov. 1847, he championed the emerging capitalist interests of Canada, in sharp contrast to his position in 1840. Rapid industrial development was the solution to Canada's economic problems, and he suggested the adoption of protective duties as a means to foster the needed industry. Published the following year, Sullivan's Hamilton appeal was frequently cited when the protectionist movement began to gain strength after 1849.

Despite his political success in the 1840s Sullivan's heavy drinking and fecklessness in business matters nearly destroyed his career. In 1843 he lamented his difficulty in collecting accounts, suggesting that his hand was all too often limp. In this he stood in marked contrast to his cousin. Baldwin was especially fierce in pursuing payment from the wealthy, who, he believed, had a moral duty to meet their debts. In 1844, however, things looked up. Oliver Mowat, then a gossipy young lawyer, reported that Sullivan had joined the 'total abstinence society.' It was a necessary step, in Mowat's view, for no one in Toronto's legal community had confidence in the drunken Sullivan. The reformation did not last. In the spring of 1848 Baldwin's property manager, Lawrence Heyden, told Baldwin that Sullivan was in serious difficulty: 'It is very generally reported here that he is broken out again.'

Dry or wet, Sullivan remained an intimate adviser to the party chief. His views were sought on delicate matters, such as the manœuvres in 1847 to find a seat for the recent convert from high toryism, Henry

John Boulton, who remained anathema to many local reformers. When the party swept the election of January 1848, Baldwin suggested to La Fontaine 24 names, including Sullivan's, as possibilities for the 11 cabinet positions. According to Baldwin, Sullivan preferred a judgeship, but his experience would be useful in cabinet. Presumably La Fontaine was not as generous about the missteps of Baldwin's errant cousin, for Sullivan's name did not appear on the cabinet list presented to Governor Lord Elgin [Bruce] on 7 March 1848. La Fontaine and Baldwin told him they needed the seat to conciliate a faction in the party. On Elgin's urging, however, they reconsidered and the next day Sullivan was included as provincial secretary, becoming the most senior of the ministers in terms of service. The governor was delighted for he considered Sullivan both able and 'more British' than any other Canadian politician. In July he described Sullivan to Colonial Secretary Lord Grey as the member of council 'who has the strongest feeling in favor of settling the lands of the Province and has most influence with his colleagues on questions of this nature.' Sullivan, for example, favoured free land grants and the construction of colonization roads – programs for these would be initiated in the 1850s.

Sullivan nevertheless played no major role in the 'Great Ministry' and on 15 Sept. 1848, after resigning from council, he received his desired reward, a puisne justiceship on the Court of Queen's Bench. He did not, however, entirely give up a political interest. While in cabinet, in April 1848, he had dismissed the medical superintendent of the Provincial Lunatic Asylum, Walter Telfer, and replaced him with the apparently more politically sound George Hamilton Park. Park proceeded to feud with the staff and to fire employees without authorization. Sullivan followed the case closely and gave his assessment of it to Baldwin in January 1849; Park was dismissed that month and the radical newspaper, the *Examiner*, took his side against the 'tyrannous' government. Sullivan guessed correctly that Park's brother-in-law, John Rolph, was behind the crisis and warned Baldwin that the case was being used by such dissident reformers to embarrass the ministry.

Sullivan held his seat on the Legislative Council until May 1851. In January 1850 he had moved from Queen's Bench to the newly formed Court of Common Pleas, where he sat until his death three years later. A superb orator and incisive analyst when sober, Sullivan nevertheless remained known as a flawed figure, devoid, in the opinion of Dent and others, of 'genuine earnestness of purpose' and 'strong political convictions.'

VICTOR L. RUSSELL, ROBERT L. FRASER, and MICHAEL S. CROSS

SIMON EBENEZER WASHBURN

Militia officer, lawyer, officer holder, and politician; b. probably 1794 in Fredericksburgh Township, Upper Canada, son of Ebenezer Washburn and Sarah De Forest; m. 12 April 1821 Margaret FitzGibbon; d. 29 Sept. 1837 in Toronto.

The sixth of nine children in a prominent loyalist family, Simon Ebenezer Washburn attended the Kingston grammar school and then served in the militia in the War of 1812. He studied law under Dr William Warren Baldwin in York (Toronto), was called to the bar of Upper Canada in January 1820, and practised in partnership with Baldwin until he established his own office in May 1825. He became a successful and highly respected lawyer. Among those who studied with him were William Hume Blake, George Duggan, and Joseph Curran Morrison.

Washburn was clerk of the peace for the Home District from October 1828 until his death. As such, he administered the Court of Quarter Sessions and kept the court records; the fees he received averaged about £290 a year. He was also commissioned to administer oaths of various kinds, including the oath of allegiance. On 4 May 1829 Washburn became reporter to the Court of Kings' Bench, but he resigned six months later pleading the pressure of other business. He was a bencher of the Law Society of Upper Canada from 3 Nov. 1829 until his death. During the 1832 cholera epidemic he served on the York Board of Health.

Simon Washburn's name is connected with two Upper Canadian controversies. When, in June 1828, justice John Walpole Willis cast doubt on the legality of the operations of the Court of King's Bench, Washburn joined William Warren Baldwin and his son Robert in writing to request the opinion of justice Levius Peters Sherwood. Washburn pursued the matter no further and was not involved in the ensuing dispute. In a customs scandal of 1830 Washburn was criticized for delivering £75 to a customs officer for the release of some pork, allegedly smuggled by York merchant William Bergin. The payment had been arranged by Washburn's brother-in-law James FitzGibbon, clerk of the House of Assembly, who was accused of bribery. Washburn, whose role was that of agent for FitzGibbon, emerged with his career undamaged.

In politics, Washburn had only minor success. He failed twice, in 1830 and 1832, to unseat William Lyon Mackenzie as member of the assembly for York County, but he succeeded in 1837 in being elected alderman for St David's Ward in Toronto. He was active in the militia and in 1835 rose to be colonel of the 2nd Regiment of West York. As churchwarden of St James' Church, he assisted Archdeacon John Strachan in the financial campaign to have a new stone church built in 1833.

Although Washburn was a conservative, Mackenzie observed in an obituary that 'in some measure' he 'took the liberal side in politics,' a reference, presumably, to his association with the Baldwins in the Willis affair. Mackenzie noted also that as a lawyer Washburn had done some 'very kind and generous' things, referring to his actions on behalf of blacks and others sentenced to flogging, execution, or lengthy imprisonment for relatively minor crimes. In such cases, he almost certainly provided free legal aid.

Simon Washburn was a generous and public-spirited man. He had a zest for life, exemplified by his love of skating, and was considered slightly eccentric for wearing a monocle.

RUTH McKENZIE

WILLIAM WEEKES
Lawyer and politician; b. in Ireland; married; d. 11 Oct. 1806, probably in Niagara (Niagara-on-the-Lake), Upper Canada.

In 1798 William Weekes settled at York (Toronto), Upper Canada, where, having been admitted to the bar, he soon became embroiled in factional politics. Because he was Irish, because he had lived for a time in the United States, and because he became a fierce critic of the provincial government, it has sometimes been suggested that he sympathized with the cause of Irish independence, admired the republican and democratic institutions of the United States, and was predisposed to the pursuit of radical politics in Upper Canada. This was not the case. The 'blessings' of the United States, he wrote privately in 1801, were 'evinced in the broil of faction, the spirit of enmity, and the practices of fraud'; its independence was 'a savage licentiousness, uncontrolled by authority and undignified by Sovereignty.' Were the 'inflammatory Innovators in Ireland' but to travel in that country, he declared, they would lose 'all rage for democracy, all furor for reform.'

For a time Weekes supported the administration of Lieutenant Governor Peter Hunter, whom he initially discovered to be 'rigorous in his mandates, and deliberate and judicious in his measures,' and from whom he had hopes of advancement. It is possible that he hoped to win official favour when he attempted to secure the election of judge Henry Allcock to the House of Assembly in 1800. As the agent of Allcock, but apparently upon his own initiative, Weekes contrived to have the poll closed, by reason of riot, when his candidate was in the lead. This election was voided, however, upon appeal to the assembly.

In 1804 Weekes himself stood for election at Durham, Simcoe, and the East Riding of York. Defeated by the incumbent, Angus Macdonell (Collachie), Weekes blamed government influence. The following year, having campaigned against the Sedition Act passed during the previous session, and against the removal of moneys from the treasury by the executive without approval of the assembly, he was returned in a by-election for the same riding. Immediately upon taking his seat he gave notice of motion to consider 'the disquietude which prevails in this Province by reason of the administration of Public Offices.' The money issue was settled when the administration restored the amount to the treasury; Weekes's motion was defeated by a vote of ten to four.

In 1806, when arguing at the Niagara assizes before judge Robert Thorpe, Weekes referred to the late Lieutenant Governor Hunter as a 'Gothic Barbarian whom the providence of God ... removed from this world for his tyranny and Iniquity.' His fellow counsel, William Dickson, took issue with the propriety of the remark. Two days later Weekes challenged him to a duel that was fought on 10 October in the vicinity of Fort Niagara (near Youngstown), N.Y. Weekes was mortally wounded and died the following day. The funeral was held at the home of the Niagara merchant John MacKay; Ralfe Clench, Robert Nelles, and Isaac Swayze were among the special mourners, most probably because they were fellow assemblymen.

Weekes's career was distinguished by the extravagance of his rhetoric, which perhaps truly reflected an unbalanced political judgement. He is chiefly important by reason of his influence upon Thorpe, a fellow Irishman who, having arrived in the province only in 1805, knew little of local politics and came to entertain the views of his friend Weekes. He was apparently stunned by Weekes's death, writing that 'this sudden and shocking catastrophe has shaken me much ... my heart is wrung.' He moved into Weekes's house and succeeded him as the focus for opposition in the assembly to the administration now headed by Lieutenant Governor Francis Gore. At the opening of the poll that resulted in his election to the assembly, Thorpe invoked the image of Weekes 'looking down from Heaven with pleasure on ... [the electors'] exertions in the cause of liberty.'

G.H. PATTERSON

The Accused

ELIJAH BENTLEY
Farmer, Baptist minister, and office holder; son of Samuel Bently, 'a steady Loyalist during the american war'; m. with three children; fl. 1799–1814.

Elijah Bentley's life in Upper Canada is little more than a series of fragments highlighted by his trial for sedition during the War of 1812. In 1799 Samuel Bently, a blacksmith and scythe-maker, probably from Rhode Island or Massachusetts, led his sons Reuben, Elijah, and Ira and two sons-in-law into Upper Canada. Reuben and Elijah brought their families; the others planned to return for theirs upon obtaining land. Elijah farmed briefly on a rented lot in Clinton Township and in 1801 received a grant, which he patented, in Markham Township, also the choice of the rest of his family. When Elijah sold his lot in 1805, he had cleared more than eight acres, fenced seven, and built a house. Whether he subsequently purchased or rented another lot is not known, but, by his own account, he continued to reside and farm in the area until 1814.

The Bentleys had probably been Baptists in the United States, and following their arrival in Upper Canada Elijah became increasingly involved in the province's rapidly expanding Baptist community. The church advanced steadily before the War of 1812: in 1802 missionaries of American Baptist associations commenced regular tours in the colony, and Michael Smith, the Baptist preacher and author, reported in 1813 that there were 15 churches and 11 resident preachers. Bentley himself had established a church at Markham in 1803. Two years later he was ordained by elders Reuben Crandall, Joseph Winn, and Abel Stevens. He hoped to take advantage of the wording of the Marriage Act of 1798, which extended the authority to perform legal marriages, hitherto the privilege of the Church of England, to 'members of the Church of Scotland, or Lutherans, or Calvinists.' The act was intended to defuse opposition to the Church of England's favoured position, but it was clearly limited to Lutherans and Presbyterians. Although one Baptist minister, Crandall, had gained the right to solemnize marriages, Bentley's own hopes were quickly dashed. After setting aside his initial application because it lacked 'sufficient proof' of his ordination, on 8 April 1806 the Court of Quarter Sessions for the Home District, which included William Jarvis and William Willcocks, rejected it as 'being under the signature of one, who states himself a Baptist.' Bentley next appears in records in 1809, when at a church conference in Townsend (Nanticoke) he urged the Baptists there to break with the Vermont-based Shaftsbury Association and join the Thurlow Association, which had been formed in 1802 in Thurlow Township. The next year, as an agent of the Thurlow Association, he visited Baptist churches throughout the province.

Bentley's activities were not limited to the church. On 10 April 1805 he was appointed one of three constables for Markham. More important was the notice taken of the Bentley family's espousal of Robert Thorpe's candidacy in the election of 1807. Lieutenant Governor Francis Gore believed the political inclinations of the opposition associated with Thorpe to be democratic. Moreover, he considered American emigrants, such as the Bentleys, to have 'brought the very worst principles of their own constitution with them.' The papers of the Executive Council contain an alphabetical list of 346 signatories, including the Bentleys, to an 1807 petition supporting Thorpe. It is worth noting that 12, and possibly 13, of the 32 men charged in 1813 with treason in the Home District had signed the 1807 petition.

Just a month before the outbreak of war in June 1812, Bentley was assisting Surveyor General Thomas Ridout with a project of some sort in Markham. The war upset the equipoise of his life. The dubious allegiance of non-loyalist American settlers, whom Smith estimated at 60 per cent of the population, now became one of the foremost concerns of military and civil officials. Even after the victories at Detroit and Queenston Heights in 1812, disaffection and treason plagued the colony's military administrators. The occupations of York (Toronto) in 1813 revealed to élites throughout the province a sub-political seam of discontent and republican sentiment within the Home District. Public declarations of sympathy for the enemy, incautiously uttered tavern oaths denouncing monarchy, crude egalitarian declamations, and fraternization with the enemy spurred civil authorities such as William Allan and William Dummer Powell to urge coercive measures 'to suppress the disloyal and confirm the wavering.' The administrator of the province, Francis Rottenburg, was duly alarmed and on 13 Aug. 1813 he ordered the acting attorney general, John Beverley Robinson, to report on 'dangerous and treasonable inclinations.' The next day Robinson met with Allan, Ridout, Alexander

Wood, Duncan Cameron, and John Strachan. On the 16th they submitted a cursory analysis which caught the prevailing spirit of official anxiety by pressing the need for 'the influence of some present example.' Robinson suggested the formation of a committee to prepare an official report. Rottenburg agreed; the aforementioned group, with Robinson replaced by his brother Peter, began work immediately.

The committee reported on 29 September; 64 depositions had been taken and 32 men were subsequently charged. Although anxious to make examples, the members of the committee were not the dupes of their own prejudices. Of the depositions, they astutely commented: 'Some are mixed with prejudice, some with malice, others are clear and pointed.' The greatest number for one person, 11 in all, concerned Bentley. One deponent, Samuel Heron, had heard Bentley deliver a sermon in which he 'thanked God there was never such freedom for poor people in York as there was since General [Henry] Dearborn set foot in it.' Others claimed that Bentley had publicly described himself as a 'great friend to the United States And no friend to the King' and that he had directed American troops to government stores, 'endeavoured to alienate the minds of His Majesty's Subjects from the Government,' and sought a parole for his son Benjamin. One even commented, perhaps justly, that Bentley was 'more dangerous from his great opportunities as a Preacher.'

Bentley was charged with seditious utterance, spreading false intelligence, and inviting the militia to accept Dearborn's offer of parole. He appeared before the Home District Assizes on 26 Oct. 1813 but on Robinson's motion was released on bail for trial on 31 March 1814. On this occasion the trial judges were the chief justice, Thomas Scott, and the associate justice, Ridout. Bentley pleaded not guilty, but after hearing the testimony of four witnesses the petit jury found him guilty. The following day Scott sentenced him to serve six months in jail and to give bonds to keep the peace for five years. On 18 July a chastened Bentley petitioned Gordon Drummond, Rottenburg's successor, to commute the remainder of his sentence on the grounds that 'a larger confinement threatens the ruin of his health & property.' Whether he was released is not known. Presumably he survived his incarceration and immediately returned to the United States with his family. Members of the extended family continued to reside in Markham, but Samuel and Ira, who were indicted at the great treason trial held at Ancaster in 1814, also left. Although the war proved only a temporary set-back to the Baptists in Upper Canada, without Bentley the church in Markham took 25 years to recover.

Bentley's arrest and imprisonment highlight a basic feature of Upper Canadian politics in the years prior to the war – the association, by many government officials, of American settlers with democratic politics. This perception was undoubtedly true. The most notorious traitors, the men of Joseph Willcocks's Company of Canadian Volunteers, were (with the exception of Willcocks himself) American-born. At a less active level of involvement, a man such as Bentley illustrates perfectly the meaning of 'dubious allegiance.' Although his political impulses were always suspect, he was willing to avow openly his sympathy for a more democratic and egalitarian society only when it seemed that the province had been lost to the Americans. In the end the British prevailed, but the actions of men like Bentley undermined the traditional civilian opposition to military demands for martial law or the suspension of habeas corpus. Sedition and treason during the war hardened the anti-American, anti-democratic strain in the colony's political culture and resulted in attitudes that shaped political battles years later, such as the alien issue of the 1820s.

ROBERT L. FRASER

WILLIAM BRASS
Fur trader, merchant, and convicted rapist; baptized 8 May 1796 in Kingston, Upper Canada, son of David Brass and Mary Magdalen Mattice; m. Elizabeth —— ; they had no children; d. 1 Dec. 1837 in Kingston.

Born about 1792, William Brass was the son of a respectable and wealthy loyalist settler at Kingston. In 1821 William received a grant of land north of the town, in Loughborough Township, where he carried on business as a merchant and fur trader. Little is known about his life except that he spent considerable time trading among the Indians. After one such expedition, in 1834, he was reported to have been devoured by wolves – part of a skull and some bones were found 12 miles from Kingston and identified as his. The rumour proved false, but is illustrative of his nomadic, rather wild existence.

As a result of the settlement of Loughborough in the 1820s and 1830s and the diminishing economic importance of the fur trade in the province, Brass's business began to falter. He attended the occasional reform meeting, but he seemed to care little for the social and moral conventions of most of the Upper Canadian community. He began to drink heavily, and his wife left him. In June 1835 he hired lawyer Henry Smith to straighten out his financial problems. Instead, Smith obtained the patent for Brass's property in his own name by taking advantage of his client's excessive drinking. During one of these terrible bouts, in June 1837, he was arrested on a charge of raping eight-year-old Mary Ann Dempsey of Loughborough, who had been left in his care.

After eight days of delirium tremens Brass sobered up to what was going on around him. In September he launched three separate legal actions against Smith: one on the alleged land fraud, one for damages, and another of forcible entry into Brass's house. To defend him against the charge of rape he employed lawyers Henry Cassady and John A. Macdonald. The Kingston *British Whig* reported that Brass had 'fallen victim to an infamous conspiracy commenced by a rascally individual in whom he placed confidence, and carried into execution by wretches as worthless as himself.'

The trial, which took place on 7 October before judge Jonas Jones, was a major sensation. Solicitor General William Henry Draper prosecuted. He called the alleged victim to the stand and she described the incident. Two medical practitioners and a midwife gave evidence which established the probability of the child's having been violated. John Caswell, the last witness for the crown, claimed to have seen the rape but not to have interfered, because, he said, the defendant was armed. The 'very able defence' was led by the 22-year old Macdonald, who impressed the *British Whig* as a rapidly rising young lawyer. He and Cassady tried to prove that Smith, Caswell, Stephen Acroid, and other neighbours of Brass were conspiring against him in order to deprive him of his lands. The defence attempted to show further that he was drunk at the time of the alleged rape and incapable of intercourse. Even if he had committed the crime, they argued, he was unquestionably insane at the time and therefore not accountable in law. After a little more than an hour's deliberation the jury found Brass guilty. Jones sentenced him to be hanged on 1 December.

Many people felt Brass did not deserve to hang. Lieutenant Governor Sir Francis Bond Head was petitioned by 135 inhabitants of the Midland District, among them 18 justices of the peace, to grant Brass his life, but without success. By stressing his father's military service to the crown in Butler's Rangers the petition made clear the tension that existed in Loughborough between loyalist families and more recently arrived groups of immigrants. John Solomon Cartwright's preface to the petition reveals the preference loyalists expected from colonial administrators in matters where judicial discretion could be exercised. Meanwhile the defence tried to get a new trial, and depositions, many from loyalist descendants, were taken which discredited Caswell's testimony. Three individuals swore that he was somewhere other than Brass's house when the alleged rape took place; one deponent, Filinda Chadwick, swore to having overheard a conversation a few days before the trial in which Caswell told Mrs Brass that he could either save her husband or hang him. The controversy raged in Kingston until 1 December.

On that day Brass and his executioner, both clad in white gowns, appeared upon the temporary gallows built out of a window in the court-house. Brass, who had been vilified and feared by his neighbours, was now a public spectacle. In a resolute, calm voice he declared his innocence and repeatedly accused Smith, Acroid, and Caswell of conspiring against him. He asked if these men were present, for he hoped to look down upon them for the last time. When he finished speaking, part of the platform gave way and he dangled, suspended by it for a moment. He was then kicked from the platform and fell, not into eternity, but all the way to his coffin, waiting below. The crowd began to shout murder and a rescue was attempted, but soldiers prevented a riot. The bumbling sheriff, Richard Bullock, cut the noose from Brass's neck and dragged him up the court-house stairs. Brass shouted triumphantly to the crowd: 'You see I am innocent; this gallows was not built for me – 'tis for Young Henry Smith.' He was thrown from the window a second time, with a shorter rope around his neck, and he plunged to his death with Smith's name on his lips. Brass was buried the following day, not in the family plot in Kingston but on his farm in Loughborough.

Reaction to Brass's conviction and death was hotly mixed. To many farmers in Loughborough, struggling against the wilderness, Brass had seemed almost supernatural because of the ease with which he slipped in and out of that hostile environment. Reduced finally to a near animal state, he was hated as a symbol of the wilderness and this enmity possibly made the farmers more willing to believe in Brass's guilt and less receptive to evidence suggesting his innocence. Elsewhere, however, others were shocked by the uncertainties surrounding the case and by the botched execution. A letter to the *British Whig*, written from Adolphustown and requesting more information on the hanging, stated that the 'intense feeling produced by the account of his m——r' surpassed any response to a crime the writer had ever witnessed in that area. It was rumoured there, he continued, that through surgical aid Brass had been resuscitated and was still alive.

WILLIAM TEATERO

CORNELIUS ALBERTSON BURLEY
(Burleigh)

Blacksmith; b. c. 1804 in Upper Canada, son of William Burley; m. c. 1825 Sally King; m. secondly June 1829, while his first wife was still alive, Margaret Beamer (Beemer) of Dumfries Township; hanged 19 Aug. 1830 in London, Upper Canada.

Although executions in Upper Canada were infrequent, those that did occur provided an extraordinary entertainment for pioneer society. From the standpoint of the law, moreover, the spectacle of the gallows produced a salutary impression on the public and, especially important, on the potential criminal. Yet the lesson could be reinforced. Upper Canada being an essentially religious society, it was felt to be necessary that the offender atone for his misdeeds, explain his immoral behaviour, and acknowledge his faith in Jesus Christ. Thus the gallows address usually took the form of a confession whereby all concerned could be assured that justice had been done. One of the best examples is the trial and execution of Cornelius Albertson Burley.

Burley's family settled in Beverley Township in 1827; Burley himself claimed to have been a blacksmith. His story begins in the late summer of 1829, when he killed a yoke of steers belonging to a Mr Lamb, presumably Henry Lamb, and a warrant was issued for his arrest. Burley claimed that Lamb had defrauded him and, unable to get legal redress, he had exacted his own form of vengeance. He was arrested by a Gore District constable, Timothy Conklin Pomeroy, but escaped and fled to the farm of his uncle Henry Ribble (Ribbel) in Bayham Township. Accompanied by his wife, he arrived there late in August. He worked on the farm until Pomeroy arrived on the scene on 13 September. About 3 o'clock on the morning of 16 September Pomeroy was shot, and he died shortly thereafter.

Murder was not uncommon but the killing of a constable in execution of his duty was sensational and unsettling news. The *Gore Emporium* claimed that 'a more foul, cold-blooded murder scarcely ever disgraced the annals of civilization.' Residents of both the Gore and the London districts petitioned Lieutenant Governor Sir John Colborne, complaining of the magistrates' 'gross neglect of duty' in failing to apprehend the constable's murderer(s). After consulting with judge James Buchanan Macaulay, who stressed the necessity of 'the most prompt and diligent exertions' in order to satisfy the concern for 'Public Justice,' Colborne on 23 September mildly chided Mahlon Burwell, a local magistrate, and the sheriff for not making an immediate report. In fact, Burwell was not to blame; the problem was dated information, the natural result of slow communication.

On 19 September a man fitting Burley's description but claiming to be William Ribble had been captured by settlers in Dunwich Township; he was taken to St Thomas. The same day Burwell and two other magistrates examined the prisoner, who then identified himself as Burley. He recounted his flight from justice in Gore, claiming his innocence. He also gave his version of events leading up to Pomeroy's death, saying that when the constable and another man had appeared at Henry Ribble's farm on 14 September he had hidden in a field and then in the barn. Believing Pomeroy had spotted him, he fled the following night, taking with him his wife and a rifle that he obtained from the home of his cousin, Anthony Ribble. Burley stated that he knew nothing of the murder and did not hear a gunshot on the night in question. He had travelled about 50 miles before being arrested.

On 20 September the JPs arrived from Bayham with three witnesses in tow: Isaac D. White, Henry Ribble, and his son David. The information of the Ribbles cohered neatly. When Pomeroy's party appeared, Henry Ribble urged Burley to give himself up but he refused, saying that 'if they got him they should take him dead.' On the morning of Pomeroy's killing, Henry had been wakened by a shot. He claimed that about a half-hour after sunrise, Burley appeared with a rifle and claimed to have shot Pomeroy in the leg. White, a member of Pomeroy's group, followed the same sequence of events sketched by the Ribbles, but put them in a different context. The Ribbles had been uncooperative. Anthony Ribble told Pomeroy to leave his house quickly, 'or he would have his blood spilt and that Damned quick.' While searching Henry Ribble's house about 45 minutes before his death, Pomeroy had unsheathed his sword to guard himself. He was shot returning from Henry Ribble's and in close proximity to Anthony Ribble's, where White saw a light burning. White did not know who shot Pomeroy. On 21 September the JPs committed Burley to jail charged on the oaths of the three witnesses. He was 'put in Irons' and sent to London to await trial. The following month an indictment was issued against Anthony Ribble as well and he, too, was held over for trial. In the spring of 1830 a number of prisoners – Ribble among them – escaped. Burley remained behind; he may have been chained to the floor. Ribble was soon recaptured.

The assizes opened on 12 Aug. 1830 with Chief Justice John Beverley Robinson presiding. His associates from the local magistracy were Burwell and James Mitchell. The grand jury found a true bill against Burley on 16 August and his trial, separate from that of Ribble's, commenced the following day. Only three witnesses were called for the crown by Solicitor General Christopher Alexander Hagerman. Burley was found guilty and Robinson sentenced him to be executed on the morning of the 19th. In his subsequent report Robinson noted that the 'evidence was such as to place the guilt of the convict beyond doubt. ... He fully confessed his guilt.' The confession, however, had come after sentencing and not during the trial. The Reverend James Jackson noted that it was made 'about forty-one hours before his execution.' Presumably, then, it had some impact upon Anthony Ribble's trial on the 18th; he was acquitted. Burley's was the only capital conviction on the Western Circuit in which Robinson did not order a respite of execution, probably because of the confession.

Burley had been the object of the attention of local clergy during the assizes. Jackson saw him 'every day but one' and claimed, 'Never have I witnessed so great an instance of obduracy and insensibility.' Eventually, however, the clergy's discussions with the prisoner 'wrought a victory over his unfeeling heart; he burst into a flood of tears' and confessed. Prior to going to the scaffold he received the sacrament of baptism and the Eucharist from the local Anglican clergymen. Jackson copied down the confession and read it from the scaffold before a crowd of some 3,000. Another minister addressed the throng and concluded with a prayer, whereupon the trapdoor dropped. But, as often happened, the execution was botched. The rope broke and Burley fell to the ground. It was some time before another attempt could be made because the sheriff had to buy a new rope. Throughout Jackson claimed that Burley was composed and 'seemed as if the world was lost from his view, and his whole mind was devotion, prayer, praise, singing, and thanksgiving.' When all was again ready he walked to the scaffold 'without any appearance of hesitation; but with the utmost composure, submitted to his fate.'

Some historians have questioned how much Jackson's efforts influenced the act of confession and several have concluded that Burley was probably innocent and Anthony Ribble guilty of Pomeroy's murder. On the first matter, there was nothing unusual about clergy and magistrates urging a convict to confess for the good of his soul and for the benefit of society. With regard to the confession itself, Jackson says, simply, that he copied down Burley's statement; however, he no doubt added a literate quality that otherwise would have been absent. Whether Burley was guilty must remain, in the absence of further evidence, a moot point. It seems that the evidence was stacked against him. The source of the accusation was Henry Ribble who, Burwell noted, 'candidly believes that Cornelius Burley was the man who shot Pomeroy.' But as White declared, it was the Ribbles who had threatened Pomeroy. Moreover, the *Gore Emporium*'s report of the magistrates' investigation stated that the Ribbles' evidence 'betrayed strong symptoms of guilt.' In the end Burley's confession probably saved Anthony Ribble. 'I am constrained to say,' the confession read, 'that he had no hand in the crime whatever. Neither had any other person.'

Burley's confession was published in Bartemas Ferguson's *Gore Balance*; Ferguson also printed 1,000 copies as handbills. As an example of its type, the confession is a model. Burley hoped it would 'have a tendency to check the progress of evil, and prevent others from doing as I have done.' He had been 'wicked and thoughtless from my youth.' He was raised without the benefits of education or religion and was unable to read or write. He wandered through the world 'under the influence of depravity. ... I was often found in the merry dance, & lost no opportunity of inducing thoughtless & unguarded females to leave the paths of innocence and virtue.' He took upon himself all guilt for the act, noting, 'I only suffer the penalty that is justly due to my crimes.' He thanked the ministers who saved him and claimed, 'In my great extremity I have gained a confidence that through the merits of Christ alone I will be saved, although the chief of sinners. ... I now leave this world with the fullest confidence that my sins are washed away in the Blood of the Lamb.'

But it was not quite the end. As the sentence stipulated, Burley's body was given to surgeons for dissection. According to one account, Orson Squire Fowler, later a noted American phrenologist, had visited Burley in his cell and reported on his phrenological character. After the dissection on 19 August, Fowler received the head and the following day used it for a public lecture. Before leaving London he sawed it in two and took the top part with him. He subsequently used it on his extensive American and European tours. The bottom portion was discovered in London in 1960 and is now on display in Eldon House, a local museum.

ROBERT L. FRASER

JOSHUA GWILLEN (Gillam) DOAN (Done)
Farmer, tanner, and Patriot; b. 1811 in Sugar Loaf,
Upper Canada, youngest son of Jonathan Doan; m.
29 Sept. 1836 Fanny Milard in St Thomas, and they
had one son; executed 6 Feb. 1839 in London,
Upper Canada.

Before the War of 1812 Jonathan Doan and his family emigrated from Pennsylvania to the Niagara District, where Joshua Gwillen was born. In 1813 the Doans moved to Yarmouth Township, near the future site of Sparta. Jonathan, an agent for the Baby family's lands in the township, settled a number of Pennsylvania residents on them. He became a 'respectable farmer' as well as a miller and a tanner. A prominent Quaker, he had the local meeting-house on his farm.

Joshua also took up farming; then, when his brother Joel P. opened a new tannery in 1832, he joined the enterprise. In 1836 he married; the next year the young couple had a son. All in all, Joshua was very much a part of his community and that community was heavily reform, or 'Republican,' as an unfriendly source had it, in politics. He played his part in the reform agitation of the fall of 1837, attending at least one meeting designed to further the creation of the political unions advocated by William Lyon Mackenzie.

In November and early December Mackenzie hurriedly organized a revolt at Toronto, and, though the uprising was quickly crushed, report had it otherwise. In the west Charles Duncombe, reform MLA for Oxford County, decided to capitalize on the situation supposedly created by Mackenzie and to forestall reprisals on local reformers by mustering a second rebel force near Brantford. His call for men reached Yarmouth. At a recruiting meeting in Sparta on 9 December Joshua and Joel Doan 'were very forward,' and Joshua was elected lieutenant of those raised. In the next few days he joined Streetsville resident Martin Switzer and others in persuading men to enlist and to round up arms. He also gathered ammunition, which he distributed to the approximately 50 rebels under David Anderson who set out for Scotland, near Brantford, on the 12th. Brother Joel supplied the provision wagons. Shortly after the arrival of the party at Scotland, Duncombe's forces scattered as loyalists under Allan Napier MacNab poured in upon them. Joshua succeeded in reaching the United States, despite a government reward of £100 for his capture. Both he and Joel, who had also escaped, were indicted for their parts in the rebellion, and both were exempted from the partial amnesty issued in October 1838.

In the United States Joshua became involved with the Patriots, those Upper Canadian refugees and their American sympathizers who hoped to produce by invasion what Mackenzie and Duncombe had failed to achieve by revolt. He was at Detroit in December 1838 with the group that planned to cross over to Windsor. He and others were told that 600 residents of the Windsor area intended joining them and that settlers about London were already in revolt. Led by 'generals' L.V. Bierce and William Putnam, the Patriots launched their raid on 4 December, burning the steamer *Thames* and killing a handful of inhabitants. (Later, some eyewitnesses insisted Doan had been implicated in at least one death, a charge he rejected.)

When the Patriots were finally dispersed by Colonel John Prince, 25 of the invaders had lost their lives, and a number, including Doan, their freedom. Forty-four of the latter were taken to London for trial before a court martial under Henry Sherwood. Doan was tried for treason in early January, and, though he protested his innocence, was found guilty and sentenced to death. Vainly, he petitioned Lieutenant Governor Sir George Arthur for mercy, claiming that two witnesses had perjured themselves, and that he had been obliged to join the Patriots and had fled them at the earliest opportunity. Later, he admitted his involvement in the raid and issued a statement intended to dissuade others from invading the colony. He enjoined his wife to 'think as little of my unhappy fate as you can' and bade her 'meet that coming event with ... Christian grace and fortitude.'

On 6 February he and Amos Perley, another of the six raiders whose sentences were not commuted, mounted the scaffold and, according to a newspaper account, sprang 'into eternity, without a struggle.' Both were taken to the Quakers' burying-ground in Sparta. Joshua left a widow, eventually married by brother Joel, and a reputation as 'a brave, true-hearted man.'

COLIN READ

WILLIAM KAIN
Labourer and convicted murderer; b. 24 Nov. 1809 on the island of St Vincent; d. 6 Sept. 1830 in Kingston, Upper Canada.

The details of William Kain's life can be found in a short biography published just after his execution for murder. When he was three years old, he emigrated from St Vincent to Kingston with his hard-drinking father, who was serving in the 70th Foot; his mother, reportedly either French or West Indian, did not accompany them. In Kingston, William was educated at the regimental school until the age of 14, when his father was discharged. Of necessity, he went to work and was soon in constant demand for his great strength and skill at hunting, fishing, farming, and lumbering; he performed 'miraculous feats, in chopping and clearing.' Intelligent and articulate, he was also an ardent reader of the Bible and was instrumental in the building and running of his neighbourhood's Sunday school. Yet he sparked fear and dislike as well as respect in his community, for he suffered a fundamental ambivalence of character. He had unsteady work habits, moving restlessly from job to job. An excessive drinker, he formed the anti-temperance Buck Skin Society. He also earned a reputation for 'unbridled passion' and for his close association with Kingston's criminals.

Towards the end of his adolescence Kain seemed to stabilize, labouring two years in Camden Township for John Rodolph Couche, a 40-year-old army pensioner. He even encouraged Couche to marry so as to free both men from domestic chores. Couche complied and wed 19-year-old Rebecca Smith of Richmond Township. Trouble began; Couche discovered that Rebecca had seduced Kain and he threatened to end the marriage. But Rebecca persisted in her adultery until June 1830 when Kain voluntarily left, returning briefly in August only to depart again after Couche refused to pay his wages and vowed to 'take out his guts.' On 15 August, infuriated by Couche's attitude and warning that he should never 'enjoy the crop, or reap one sheaf,' Kain returned and shot Couche five times.

Alerted by Rebecca, neighbours John and Samuel Foster apprehended Kain. His celebrated quarrel with Couche made him the obvious suspect. He was made to sit beside the corpse for several hours before being taken to the coroner in Kingston, William J. McKay. Kain freely confessed to the murder but pleaded self-defence, even castigating his neighbours for not having forced Couche to pay his wages.

At his trial on 3 September, Kain, defending himself, pleaded not guilty. The crown, represented by Attorney General Henry John Boulton, called six witnesses, the defendant none. The jury required only five minutes to condemn Kain, despite his claims of being goaded by Couche's threats and refusal to pay him. He was then sentenced to hang three days later with his body to be given over to medical dissection. 'The laws ought to punish and will punish,' declared Judge James Buchanan Macaulay, 'as long as necessary, until the arm of violence shall be restrained.' He characterized Kain's action as 'heedless, malicious, vindictive, and blood thirsty,' and referred sarcastically to Kain's renowned strength: 'One would almost suppose that some people believed their strength given to them, for no other purpose than to abuse it.'

Kain heard Macaulay's address with outward indifference, even the admonition that he devote his final earthly days to achieving 'a joyful immortality' by 'weeping, by fasting and by prayer, by penitence and contrition.' Yet the judge's advice or personal revelation revived Kain's latent religiosity, for he remained sleepless, praying, reading the Bible, and performing spiritual exercises with two ministers and his former Sunday school teachers. The evening before his death he was visited by Archdeacon George Okill Stuart, and that same night he composed a scaffold address blaming alcohol, neglect of the Sabbath, and bad company for ruining his life 'just in the prime.' He died reciting the Lord's Prayer, apparently reconciled to his fate, repentant for the murder, confident of salvation. He was unswerving in his right to the wages he was owed by Couche, earmarking the money 'to establish or support any school that may require it.' Any other funds were to be used to erect a fence around his father's grave.

William Kain's life was brief, beginning and ending in bitterness. He died in profound disgrace, in front of 'a large concourse' of curious spectators. Kain was equal to this occasion as to most others, couching his personal tragedy in terms of sin and erroneous judgement. Yet even his contemporaries sensed the hollowness of these explanations, and today it is difficult to penetrate the essence of the young man who was special and disturbing even to his obituary writers, and whose life embodies the age-old mysteries of the roots of criminality and violence.

ELIZABETH ABBOTT GIBBS

JAMES OWEN McCARTHY (McCarty)
(often known as James Owen or Owens)
Tailor and convicted murderer; b. *c.* 1794 in Ireland; m. Ann (Hannah) —— , and they had several children; d. 31 March 1835 in Hamilton, Upper Canada.

The emigration boom of the early 1830s added a new dimension to the social structure of the villages of Hamilton and Dundas – a large population of Irish Roman Catholics. Mired in poverty in what the local priest, John Cassidy, described as a 'rude and toilsome mission,' the Irish seemed particularly prone to the petty violence that characterized frontier towns. Indeed, from the 1830s to the 1850s, the face of such crime in the Gore District was Irish. For Cassidy, the 'poverty and the vices' of his flock were a burden. In 1834 he was anxious about the forthcoming St Patrick's Day celebrations and spent 'all the Lent' preaching 'against their past drinking their riots and their ignorance.' His efforts were to no avail. On 17 March 1834 a brawl erupted at a Dundas tavern in which 'none were concerned but Irish Catholics.' One man died of wounds suffered in the mayhem. Charged with wilful murder were John Rooney, a local innkeeper, and James Owen McCarthy.

McCarthy was a tailor who about 1821 was employed by R. Law and Company of London. Subsequently, he joined another establishment (reputedly tailors to George IV) as foreman. He then opened his own shop in Dublin, which he described as a 'large and respectable' business with a select clientele. McCarthy left Ireland about 1832 and opened a store in New York City. Having 'lost the whole of his effects by Fire,' he moved with his family to Dundas in the fall of 1833. In jail awaiting trial, he wasted little time before seeking intercession on his behalf. On 26 March he wrote to Frederick Shaw, a former customer and one of the foremost Irish legislators, acquainting him with his situation, asserting his innocence, and begging Shaw to 'use your influence with Mr Stanley [the Colonial Secretary] ... that he might Intercede Immediately.' Shaw forwarded the letter to Stanley, commending McCarthy as a 'respectable well-Conducted Man.'

Stanley could hardly intervene in the manner suggested but he did forward the documents to Lieutenant Governor Sir John Colborne, indicating his interest in the case.

Imperial interest was sufficient to ensure the keen attention of local authorities when McCarthy appeared before judge James Buchanan Macaulay on 4 August, two days after Rooney had been found guilty in spite of the work of his defence counsel, Robert Baldwin Sullivan and William Henry Draper. Once testimony was concluded McCarthy addressed the jury with, as Macaulay noted, 'great vehemence and gesticulation ... and instead of manifesting any feelings of remorse or regret, rather exulted in his conduct as amply excusable.' He was pronounced guilty, and Macaulay sentenced both men to be hanged. The judge, however, was a prudent man who was careful to act in accord with the 'policy' of the legislature and the 'Sense' of the bench with respect to capital convictions. Accordingly, he respited the sentences to allow opportunity for appeal and gubernatorial review.

The usually mute Irish Roman Catholics responded almost immediately to the plight of their countrymen, as did the local community at large. Cassidy, who had earlier dismissed McCarthy as a 'loose character,' forwarded a petition bearing 154 names, mainly Irish, which argued that both men were deserving of royal mercy since neither had acted with malice aforethought. The crime had been committed in the heat of temporary passions, 'on a day when Irishmen are apt to indulge too freely in the intoxicating cup.' John Law, a local worthy and representative of R. Law and Company, also came to McCarthy's defence. McCarthy's own petition for clemency cast his plight in the usual manner. A 'stranger in the Country' whose wife and children would be left 'destitute and friendless' upon his execution, he sought a pardon 'that he may Strive to retain the good opinion of his fellow men, And have time to make his peace with his offended Maker.' In spite of provocation, he maintained, nothing could have induced him 'designedly to Shed the blood of his fellow man.' His petition was supported by 307 men, including many of the prominent such as Allan Napier MacNab.

Uppermost in the minds of McCarthy and his petitioners was the question of intent, for without premeditated design the appropriate charge was manslaughter. Macaulay had touched on this issue in his address to the jury and both his remarks and the jury's verdict were upheld by Chief Justice John Beverley Robinson. Colborne, however, was not satisfied and he urged Macaulay to reflect further on the case.

The judge, feeling 'much repugnance to capital punishments in cases not tainted with deliberate aforethought,' none the less held to his original conclusions and considered the question to be now one for the 'Executive Govt.' Colbourne referred the matter to the Executive Council, chaired by John Strachan. On its recommendation, which included respites for both executions, the question was referred in late August to the imperial government. In spite of Macaulay's repeated confirmation of the justness of the sentence, Colborne correctly ascribed to him 'some doubts' as to whether manslaughter might not have been the more proper verdict. Imperial reservations about the inadequacy of the submitted documents notwithstanding, approval was given for conditional pardons. Before word of the pardons had reached the Gore District – it was sent from Toronto on 23 Jan. 1835 – Cassidy forwarded another petition from the Irish asking for commutation of the sentence. Dreading the personal consequences of attending the doomed men at their execution, he revealed a political awareness hitherto not evident in his community. He alluded to the burning of a Roman Catholic convent in the United States by an 'American Mob,' an incident that had occasioned a 'Strong Sensation' among his parishioners. What had struck them was the acquittal of American incendiaries and the conviction of McCarthy and Rooney. Irish Roman Catholics were learning, Cassidy stated, the 'Strict meaning of *Malice pretense*.'

Before their pardon (including banishment) was due to take effect on 1 April, McCarthy and Rooney began complaining of the conditions of their confinement in what they described as an overcrowded, poorly ventilated, and unheated jail. McCarthy denounced the jailer's 'Tyranical conduct ... Such I think as Never disgraced the pages of history.' Sheriff William Munson Jarvis tried to blunt the prisoner's charges by denigrating his character, noting that McCarthy's supposed wife (he claimed they had never been married) 'has had Causes more than once to regret the Difference between his strength and hers' and that McCarthy himself was 'very much addicted to Liquor.' Jarvis hinted at the possibility of a plot to free McCarthy, who had himself vowed 'to break Gaol or die in the attempt.' He concluded that there had never been in the jail a 'worse Character than Owen the Language he makes use of is enough to make any person shudder.'

On 31 March 1835, one day before his release, McCarthy died 'after a dispute with the Gaoler in which much violence took place.' The official conclusion, by a coroner's jury, that he died of 'an enlargement of the heart' touched off a further controversy. In late April McCarthy's wife presented a petition signed by some 1,200 people questioning the cause of her husband's 'sudden and mysterious death' and wondering why 'no action has been taken against the gaoler and his assistants.' In an editorial in the *Correspondent and Advocate*, William John O'Grady juxtaposed the inquest, 'the verdict of only twelve men,' and the petition of 1,200. 'To which should credence be given?' The jailer and his deputy were later absolved of criminal conduct by a grand jury. However, the state of the jails was a matter of both provincial and imperial concern, and McCarthy's death, probably by reason of the unusual imperial interest in his case and his demise, brought many of the problems to the fore. Two investigations concluded that the jails were greatly overcrowded and inadequately regulated. The second investigation, conducted by a committee of judges including Robinson and Macaulay, was the more important of the two; its report, tabled in the legislature on 22 Dec. 1835, urged the establishment of 'more precise and satisfactory regulations than are at present provided.' The result was a statute enacted in 1838 which attempted, with limited success, to bring district jails under a comprehensive system of provincial regulations.

ROBERT L. FRASER

EDWARD McSWINEY
Clerk and militiaman; m. with four children;
fl. 1812–15.

One of the significant aspects of the 19th-century loyalist account of Canada's origins is the role of Upper Canadians and the militia in successfully repelling American invaders during the War of 1812. In fact, however, this loyalist myth (long since discredited) was in part generated by contemporaries such as John Strachan who feared that the province would be lost by the actions of the disloyal. Since at times the foremost problem of civil government and military command was disaffection, it is not surprising that an outstanding demonstration of loyalty, no matter how suspect, could be its own reward in a society anxious for examples of zealous adherence to the crown. The hitherto untold tale of Sergeant Edward McSwiney is a case in point.

A 'British European' by birth, McSwiney came to Upper Canada from the lower province to clerk for surveyor Reuben Sherwood. Soon after the outbreak of war in June 1812 McSwiney enlisted for service, becoming a sergeant in his employer's company of 1st Leeds Militia. On 10 October he stood guard at the arms depot of the Elizabethtown (Brockville) garrison. When a fellow militiaman, Andrew Fuller, attempted to take several items without authorization, McSwiney challenged him. After exchanging abusive language, the two men scuffled. A friend of Fuller's, Daniel Cloud, encouraged him to whip 'the damned Rascal.' Now threatened by two men, McSwiney discharged his musket, mortally wounding Fuller. McSwiney was arrested and turned over to the district sheriff.

After a lengthy incarceration he was indicted by the grand jury at the Johnstown District assizes on 7 Sept. 1813 and was tried three days later before William Campbell. The petit jury, after hearing the evidence of eight witnesses for the crown and one for the prisoner, found McSwiney guilty. Campbell sentenced him to be hanged on 18 October, thereby allowing sufficient time for the usual petitions for pardon to be made on the prisoner's behalf. Campbell himself reported to the administrator that there was no legal cause 'to induce a Mitigation of his fate,' but he mentioned McSwiney's 'having declined to avail himself of the opportunity to escape afforded him by the Enemy on the 6th February last.' On 17 September, 'in his own hand writing,' McSwiney penned the first of several eloquent petitions seeking royal mercy.

The petitions reveal a shrewd mind. Here was a man who knew how to make a case for himself. He drew on the commonplace elements of such documents: personal suffering, disgrace, and the plight of his family. But his genius was to emphasize aspects of his case which on a larger scale were provincial concerns raised by the exigencies of the war. In a district that was later called the most disaffected within the province, he was a man who sought 'to retain life, only that he may devote it to his Country in defending it from the grasp of a malignant and inveterate foe.' Taking for himself the cloak of loyalty, he tarred both his victim and the jury with the brush of treason. Fuller was 'a man recently from the United States, a mercenary, or hired Substitute for one of the Militiamen, of base dissolute reputation, and strongly suspected as being inimical to His Majesty and Government.' Seizing upon the desertions which had been rife among the colony's militia since the beginning of the war, McSwiney tied Fuller's action to the 'daily occurrences of Mens deserting to the Enemy.' Fuller's accomplice, Cloud, whom McSwiney noted in a later petition had deserted to the enemy, was hostile to him because of his 'strict enquiries' about Cloud's brother, also a deserter. As a man of only pure and patriotic impulses, McSwiney disavowed any malice on his part in the fatal shooting. It had occurred 'in the heat of momentary passion [and was occasioned by] his Zeal for the service, his Loyalty and the most affectionate attachment to his ever beloved Sovereign and Country.'

The heroic deeds of the war were not confined to the battlefield. The unquestionable proof of McSwiney's ardent loyalty was the incident mentioned by Campbell that occurred on the night of 6 Feb. 1813, when American troops raided Elizabethtown, taking several captives and, according to McSwiney, 'liberating the Prisoners from the Gaol.' All, that is, but one. Animated by an abiding patriotism, McSwiney remained in an empty jail. He wrote that he had 'spurned the thought of becoming a Fugitive in the land of, and amongst the Enemies of his King and Country.' But his refusal to leave the jail had been ignored by a jury 'prejudiced against him. ... Had [he] been a Yankee, or [been] possessed of Yankee principles ... the Testimony would have been less criminating, and the Verdict less severe.'

But McSwiney's sterling example of loyalty had made a deep impact upon local militia officers and the leading members of society in the Johnstown District. Each of his petitions bore the support of members of the local élite, including Archibald McLean and Jonas Jones. McSwiney's craft in framing his petition had its calculated effect. Upon receipt of the first petition, the provincial administrator, Francis Rottenburg, 'felt inclined to pardon him.' Acting Attorney General John Beverley Robinson apprised him that pardon fell within the royal prerogative and that the appropriate course of action was to postpone the execution and recommend McSwiney to 'His Majesty's mercy.' Campbell was shocked. He was unable to 'report any thing favorable' of McSwiney and regarded even the mere application for clemency as 'totally unmerited.' None the less, the execution was respited 'until His Majestys pleasure shall be known.' At issue was not legal cause – neither Campbell nor Robinson thought much of McSwiney's claims in this regard – but his manifest loyalty on the night of 6 February. Not all, however, were as impressed by this act as the provincial administrators were. The jailer on that fateful evening noted tersely that McSwiney, in spite of his assertion to the contrary, was the 'only one [in jail] at the time the Americans passed this place; it was impossible for him to make his escape unless rescued as he is kept in Irons and chained.'

At this juncture the case became complicated by the change of administrations (Rottenburg was succeeded by Gordon Drummond in December 1813), by the rudimentary state of the attorney general's office, and by legal technicalities. McSwiney insisted that the reprieve constituted a pardon, but there was no copy of it at York (Toronto) and matters rested until January 1814, when Robinson, after receiving a copy from the Johnstown District sheriff, apprised Drummond that the convict was mistaken. McSwiney continued to languish in jail, 'kept in Irons – hands as well as legs, and chained to the floor,' while Robinson attempted to sort out matters. The sentence was continually respited until on 25 Oct. 1814 Governor Sir George Prevost's secretary notified Drummond that the case was entirely within Upper Canadian jurisdiction.

Finally, on 2 Jan. 1815, Drummond forwarded to the Colonial Office McSwiney's plea for mercy, supported by petitions and his own recommendation. The local petitions urging clemency were of critical importance. Drummond described them as coming from 'gentlemen ... of the most respectable Standing ... and they bear strong testimony of the Loyalty and Zeal for the Service of his King and Country which he [McSwiney] had evinced.' Drummond added that the jury was 'prejudiced against McSwiney, not only on account of his Loyalty and Activity in bringing the Seditious to justice but because the man who had ... provoked the occasion ... was one like themselves.' The appeal was forwarded immediately to the Home Department where it was passed to the Prince Regent and Privy Council for their consideration. Once again McSwiney's deft handiwork proved utterly convincing; a pardon was drawn up on 29 June. After passing back down the successive stages of authority, Attorney General D'Arcy Boulton issued a fiat for McSwiney's release on 30 October. McSwiney thereafter disappeared from sight and likely left the province.

The case of Edward McSwiney is a marvellous illustration of individual cunning. Gaining a pardon was no mean feat. A lowly sergeant, he had to overcome the legal opinion of Campbell that there was not a shred of evidence to support his extravagant claims. Moreover, Robinson was totally unsympathetic for reasons probably similar to Campbell's. But men of a less legal bent were easily won. The ultimate success of McSwiney's petitions without judicial recommendation reflected the mentality of a harrowed administration; men such as Drummond were as anxious to reward loyalty as they were to suppress disaffection. Had allegiance been more certain it is possible that the beguiling productions of that most artful of dodgers, Edward McSwiney, would have received short shrift from all concerned.

ROBERT L. FRASER

PETER MATTHEWS
Militiaman, farmer, and rebel; b. 1789 or, more likely, 1790 in the Bay of Quinte region (Ont.), son of Thomas Elmes Matthews and Mary Ruttan (Rutan, Rattan); m. c. 1812 Hannah Major, and they had five children; m. secondly 26 Oct. 1831 Hannah Major (Smith), and they had three children; hanged 12 April 1838 in Toronto.

The early years of Peter Matthews's life are obscure. His mother was from a loyalist family and his father was probably a loyalist. It is difficult to determine where his family lived because records are incomplete and Peter's father was rather careless about patenting his lands. Thomas Matthews apparently was granted land in Marysburgh Township and then in Sidney Township. By 1799 he also had been granted 350 acres in Pickering Township, and Mary 200 acres.

In Pickering the Matthews family was quite public-spirited, contributing to the building of a school and working to improve the major road in the area, the Brock Road. Thomas was active as a local official, and he and two or three sons served in the militia during the War of 1812, Peter being a sergeant. Peter pledged a donation to the Methodist college to be built at Cobourg, but died before it could be honoured.

It was this desire to serve others that apparently caused Peter's death. The family was unhappy with the services provided to the rural inhabitants by the government at Toronto. Although not as prominent a public figure as his father had been, Matthews was involved in local reform politics in a small way and was drawn into the events preceding the rebellion of 1837. He was active in the political union movement of the summer and fall of that year, which was designed to pressure the British government to grant reforms, and he was evidently persuaded by some of his neighbours, most notably the Baptist minister George Barclay, to take part in the uprising planned by William Lyon Mackenzie. A much liked and a prosperous man who had a successful farm and the proceeds from the sale of his father's land in Sidney, Matthews was a logical choice to lead the men from Pickering and nearby townships who joined the rebellion.

Matthews's party of about 50 left Pickering on 5 December and arrived at Montgomery's Tavern on Yonge Street north of Toronto the next day. On the morning of the 7th, Matthews and about 60 men were sent by Mackenzie to the bridge across the Don River east of the city. There they were to create a diversion which Mackenzie hoped would prevent government forces from attacking Montgomery's until the reinforcements he was expecting had arrived there. Matthews's party killed one man and set the bridge and some houses on fire before being driven off by loyalist forces. The rebellion failed that day and Matthews fled, but he was captured in a farmhouse in York Township. He pleaded guilty to a charge of treason and petitioned for mercy. Although evidence about his role was contradictory, the Executive Council decided that he had been a leading figure in the uprising and held him responsible for the fires and the death at the bridge. Despite appeals for clemency signed by thousands, Matthews was executed with Samuel Lount on 12 April 1838. His property was seized by the crown, but in 1848, after pardons had been extended to most of the rebels, it was returned to the family.

RONALD J. STAGG

MARY OSBORN (London)
Convicted murderer; b. *c.* 1773 in Bedford, Pa; m. Bartholomew London, and they may have had one child; d. 17 Aug. 1801 in Niagara (Niagara-on-the-Lake), Upper Canada.

In the early years of Upper Canadian settlement major crimes were infrequent and cases resulting in capital convictions rare. Attorney General John White complained in 1795 to the French traveller La Rochefoucauld-Liancourt that, although one or two people had been tried for murder in every district of the province, 'they were all acquitted by the jury, though the evidence was strongly against them.' Convictions were indeed difficult to obtain. But the sparing ways of the juries aside, between August 1792 and September 1800 there were six cases ending in capital convictions: four for burglary, one for forgery, and one for murder. Three of these trials were of black slaves, among them Jack York; the first execution in the province's history was of the black slave Josiah Cuttan (Cutten) in 1792. The first execution for murder and the first execution of a woman occurred in 1801.

In the late summer of that year the attention of the Niagara peninsula was riveted on the trial of Mary London and George Nemiers (Nemire) for the murder of her husband. The trial was sensational in appeal, exposing the adultery of young lovers, the betrayal of an old husband, the role of unnamed accomplices and confidants, and clandestine trips to obtain poison. Moreover, the local appetite for scandal was whetted by the first newspaper coverage of a criminal trial held in the province. For reasons that are not entirely clear, the printer and editor of the *Niagara Herald*, Silvester Tiffany, covered the trial and execution in detail extraordinary for a period in which local and provincial news rarely received more than short shrift. For the most part, the following account is based on his reports.

The basic outline of events leading to the trial seems clear. In 1789 Bartholomew London, a small farmer from New Jersey who claimed to have been imprisoned during the American revolution because of his loyalty to the British, entered the province with four children and four grandchildren. Drawing on the support of a fellow New Jerseyman and local office holder, Nathaniel Pettit, he obtained a grant of 200 acres in Saltfleet Township. An older man, he appears to have been unmarried upon his arrival in the colony. At some point he married the young Mary Osborn, an emigrant from Pennsylvania whose family still resided there in 1801. How they met is unknown, but whatever the scenario it was complicated by the appearance of George Nemiers. About 28 years of age and from Carlisle, Pa, Nemiers likely worked as a labourer on the London farm. By December 1800 Mary London and Nemiers were lovers. When Bartholomew London died on 17 Feb. 1801, Mary, then four months pregnant, and Nemiers were arrested and charged with felony and murder.

The trial began on the morning of 14 August before judge Henry Allcock and his local associate justices, Robert Hamilton and William Dickson. The petit jury included the Niagara merchants James Crooks and John Dun. Among the 14 witnesses were Tiffany, his brother Oliver, Dr Robert Kerr, and Robert Nelles. Attorney General Thomas Scott opened the proceedings with an address to the jury which, according to Tiffany, 'moistened many eyes, and captivated many hearts.' Eight hours were then spent in examining the witnesses. The coroner and medical men established that London's death was a result of poisoning and not a fractured skull. The rest of the testimony was apparently circumstantial, but Tiffany, himself a witness, reported that, although there was a lack of 'positive proof as to the person or persons who administered the poison,' 'the facts and the numerous circumstances left no room for doubt.' After the jury delivered its verdict of guilty, Allcock, 'who had all along "judged with mercy,"' pronounced the 'dreadful sentence.' On the morning of 17 August, the lovers were to be hanged 'until they be dead, dead, and afterwards their bodies to be Dissected.'

The interlude of two days gave Tiffany time to interview the two convicts. Nemiers, 'penitent and perfectly resigned,' absolved his 'honest parents ... who discharged their duty in instructing him in the strict observance of the Sabbath and his duty to God and man ... and blamed none but the guilty copartner in the crime ... who lured him to unlawful intimacy and connection about 9 months ago, and from the sin of adultery to that of murder.' She had first suggested 'shooting the old man' and later raised the possibility of poison. Nemiers attempted to obtain poison at Ancaster, but 'he there felt some remorse of conscience.' Later, his moral qualms resolved, he secured two ounces of arsenic and one ounce of opium from a 'medical gentleman' in Canadaigua, N.Y. (Tiffany's home after leaving the province in 1803). Insisting that 'it was not the estate, but the woman he wanted,' and that a third party was involved in the crime, he confessed to causing London's skull fracture with a shoe-hammer.

But it was Mary London's seeming indifference 'to a sense of her true standing' that intrigued Tiffany. Possibly because she was a female, Tiffany had expected a full confession. Instead all she had offered during the trial was 'a partial confession ... framed to her own innocency and the guilt of Nemiers.' When Nemiers spoke to Tiffany of a guilty third party, she 'checked' him, saying 'two of us to die for this is enough.' But afterwards she confirmed that another had suggested murdering London to get 'the old rascal out of the way.' She denied administering anything more than opium to her husband, indicating that the unnamed accomplice was the culprit. But the contradictions in her story and her tendency to lie led Tiffany to disregard her statements and conceal the names of those implicated. Only once did her steely reserve falter: returning to her cell after sentencing she had cried aloud, 'I am guilty, I gave the poison and knew it.' To Tiffany, she later confided that she did not know who was the father of her child, Catherine, then but a few days old and baptized by Robert Addison the day before the execution. Like Nemiers, she did not blame her parents 'for any neglect.' Tiffany believed that Mary first realized her fate in the preparation room on the morning of the 17th: 'When she came out to her place, she said, 'May this be a warning to you all,' and prayed to God to have mercy on her soul.'

The execution was attended by a 'large concourse of people' and was marred when 'a female (it is to be regretted it was one of that sex)' mocked the cries and gestures of Mary London. Following English practice, the bodies were turned over to medical men for dissection, the first instance in Upper Canada of a procedure that continued at least until the execution of William Kain in 1830. As was often the case with criminal trials during this period, the convicted passed quickly from the written record and possibly from memory. Tiffany saw in the case a moral lesson: 'Visible in the whole of this business, [is] the hand of Providence pursuing with vengeance offenders even in this life; for in it we see punished adultery, disregard of marriage vows, and murder: and to those who indulge themselves in the two former, it may be a lesson of instruction, that from them to the last is but a step.'

ROBERT L. FRASER

JACOB OVERHOLSER (Oberholser)

Settler and convicted traitor; b. *c.* 1774 in the American colonies; m. Barbara ——, and they had four children; d. 14 March 1815 in Kingston, Upper Canada.

Jacob Overholser led a life that in most respects was singularly unexceptional. A simple man, probably illiterate, he immigrated to Upper Canada with his wife and children about 1810 and settled in Bertie Township, where in 1811 he bought a farm. From all accounts he appears to have worked hard, made friends with his neighbours, and enjoyed a moderate degree of prosperity. Unlike officials at York (Toronto), the mercantile élite of the Niagara peninsula was not over concerned by the presence of American settlers, and Overholser seems to have met with the approval of John Warren of Fort Erie, the pre-eminent man of the township, and his family.

The War of 1812 shattered Overholser's life. The peninsula was the scene of heavy fighting throughout the war and, as opposing armies moved back and forth, civilian life was altered in their wake. Without a strong and lasting military presence by either army, order often quickly broke down. A regrettable, but probably a natural enough, consequence was that some seized on this instability to settle private grudges or further personal ends. A recent American immigrant such as Overholser was a likely target for the vengeful.

Although the exact time frame is not clear, Overholser had problems with a set of louts – principally members of the Anger family – whose actions towards him were tinctured with malice. After the retreating American army burned Niagara (Niagara-on-the-Lake) on 10 Dec. 1813, these men threatened to take his land and set fire to his buildings, and on one occasion several of them stole four horses from his barn. About 20 December Overholser, together with Thomas Moore, a Quaker neighbour, approached Major-General Phineas Riall to seek redress. The general referred the case to the Queenston merchant and magistrate Thomas Dickson, who ordered the animals returned. The Angers then charged that during the American occupation Overholser had accompanied the enemy when members of their family were taken prisoner. The charge was serious and Dickson had no choice but to refer the matter back to Riall and ask John Warren Jr, also a magistrate, to investigate.

Extant documents relating to Overholser's actions from about the 1st of December 1813 to 26 Jan. 1814 are so fragmentary and elliptical as to render impossible a full reconstruction of events. Before Dickson, Overholser's accusers had charged that on or about 1 Dec. 1813 he had been seen 'in Company with the Americans' when Benjamin Clark and two members of the Anger family were captured. The prisoners were removed to Black Rock (Buffalo), N.Y., and the following day Overholser testified against them for having broken the conditions of a previous parole granted them by the American forces. Warren's inquiry established that the basic outline of events was true but that Overholser had been compelled by the Americans to accompany them and carry a rifle. Warren concluded that there was no substance to the charge and that the whole episode amounted to 'Nothing more than an ill Disposition' by the Angers towards Overholser. Moore interjected that even if the charges were true, the Angers' crime in stealing Overholser's horses was the greater. Obviously alarmed by the possibility of charges against them, the Angers then suggested that they would return Overholser's property if the matter was dropped. Warren agreed 'and there it was supposed to end.' However, the Angers, a thuggish lot, took the first opportunity – the absence of Dickson and Riall – to revive their charges against Overholser, and another magistrate, apparently unfamiliar with the case, ordered him jailed. Towards the end of January 1814, through the intercession of Riall, Moore secured bail for Overholser, an extraordinary departure in circumstances involving possible charges of high treason. Later, when ordered to appear in court, Overholser voluntarily surrendered himself to the sheriff.

Overholser's situation was serious but his prospects were hopeful. The charges seemed to lack substance, his accusers were a disreputable set, and Dickson, Warren, and Riall supported him. But Overholser's fate did not turn on legal niceties; his story became intertwined with, and inseparable from, the grim determination of military and civil authorities to overawe dissaffection by exemplary punishment. The genesis of this resolve deserves an explanation.

The experience of the American revolution and the examples of the French revolution and the Irish rebellion of 1798 had made the Upper Canadian élite highly suspicious of non-loyalist American settlers, anxious about political opposition, and inflexible on the meaning of loyalty. The rise of a parliamentary and extra-parliamentary opposition associated with William Weekes, Robert Thorpe, and Joseph Willcocks exacerbated these anxieties. Although, in large part, the parliamentary opposition drew its strength from matters of local concern, it took its political language from a transatlantic whig tradition rooted in the 18th century which emphasized constitutional liberty, civil rights, and the prerogatives of elected assemblies. The heyday of the opposition, the legislative sessions of 1812, brought these ideals into conflict with the exigencies of war. Administrator Isaac Brock had grave doubts about the effect of a largely American population upon Upper Canada's security. He feared that the war might be lost not from 'any thing the enemy can do, but from the disposition of the people.' In an address to the House of Assembly in which he recalled the experience of Great Britain between 1792 and 1795, a period sometimes known as the 'White Terror,' Brock sought sanction for emergency measures such as a suspension of habeas corpus to secure the province 'from private Treachery as well as from open dissaffection.' These proposals violated sacred whig principles and the assembly under the leadership of men such as Willcocks and Abraham Markle rejected them.

Brock's suspicions about the popular mood were further confirmed by the reaction in the western areas of the province to American brigadier-general William Hull's proclamation of 12 July 1812. The problem of disaffection was kept in abeyance by the military victories at Detroit and Queenston Heights, but throughout 1813 the situation steadily deteriorated. Following the American capture of York on 27 April 1813, an event that led to an outbreak of disorder and the voicing, albeit in a coarse manner, of explicit egalitarian and democratic sentiments, the concern for constitutionalism on the part of the élite all but collapsed. Little more than a week later prominent men of the Niagara peninsula such as James Crooks and Robert Nichol petitioned Major-General John Vincent to take measures sufficiently severe to quell the traitorously inclined, and on 28 June judge William Dummer Powell opined that in the event of a military disaster it would be difficult for the loyal to 'keep down the Turbulence of the disaffected who are numerous.' In July Governor Prevost authorized the formation of general courts martial in cases requiring 'an immediate example.' When on 3 August the influential York merchant William Allan charged certain people with seditious behaviour during the occupation, Administrator Francis de Rottenburg instructed the acting attorney general, John Beverley Robinson, to investigate the instances of 'dangerous and treasonable inclinations.' Several days later the Executive Council recommended increased military surveillance and the detention of suspects, and the report of the committee appointed by Robinson to inquire into the situation at York urged the need to make examples of the disaffected. It was probably just this change in the constitutional climate of the province that prompted the treason of Willcocks and Markle in the summer of 1813.

As the military situation west of York deteriorated, the civil situation became even more acute. On 13 November 18 marauders were captured in Norfolk County. Rottenburg ordered Robinson to take prompt measures to bring the renegades to trial and advised him that a special commission – the instrument used in extraordinary circumstances to summon the full majesty of the law – would be appointed. Gordon Drummond, Rottenburg's successor, issued the commission on 14 December for the trial of all persons accused of treason, with special concern for the London and Home districts. Uppermost in Drummond's mind was the need 'to make examples' immediately. Robinson, however, proceeded slowly. The peculiarities of the law regarding high treason required him to take great care to avoid errors. Moreover, he hoped to avoid departing from normal civil procedures because executions 'by military power would have comparatively little influence – the people would consider them as arbitrary acts of punishment.'

When Robinson reported to Drummond on 4 April 1814 Jacob Overholser was among the men to be charged. Drawn into a web of events beyond his own making, he was now to be lumped together with men who were avowed traitors and who had actually taken up arms. The site of the great show trial of Upper Canadian history was Ancaster. The court opened on 23 May with the three justices of the Court of King's Bench, Thomas Scott, William Campbell, and Powell, presiding. Three of the associate judges, Richard and Samuel Hatt and Thomas Dickson, were drawn from the local magistrates, and the 17-man grand jury included some of the area's leading merchants and office holders, notably James Crooks, Robert Nelles, and Samuel Street. In all the jury found true bills against 21 prisoners and 50 others. Overholser was indicted on 24 May and two days later decided on John Ten Broeck and Bartholomew Crannell Beardsley as his counsel. His trial took place on 8 June before Powell, the Hatts, and Dickson. He pleaded not guilty, a petit jury of 12 was picked, and the witnesses appeared – four for the crown (three Angers and Clark) and five for the defence, including Dickson and Warren. Unfortunately for Overholser, his Quaker friend Thomas Moore refused to take the required oath and could not be sworn.

Overholser was charged with a branch of high treason known as adherence to the enemy; his specific act was alleged to have been carrying arms and assisting the enemy in making prisoners of the king's subjects. According to Robinson's summary of the case and Powell's bench notes on the trial, the evidence against him was as follows. On or about 1 Dec. 1813 Overholser had accompanied an 'armed party of the Enemy' to the homes of his neighbours, Clark and the Angers, who were then made prisoners. Overholser stood armed guard over them before they were taken to Black Rock. The following day he 'voluntarily' appeared at Buffalo claiming that at some point before their capture Clark and the Angers had broken the terms of their parole with the American army by making him a prisoner. The ensuing day at Black Rock he attended the examination of the prisoners, who were then sent to Fort Niagara (near Youngstown), N.Y. Overholser's defence was developed along two lines. First (and this was undoubtedly the work of his counsel), he argued that since he was an American citizen the withdrawal of the protection of British forces had absolved him of the allegiance he owed the king. Thus, his action constituted only 'a Trespass against the Individuals and not Treason,' according to this act's definition by statute. Secondly, he repeated his testimony before Warren to the effect that he had been 'impelled to join the Enemy by Apprehension of Danger to himself.' But Powell noted that his defence 'was not sustained by Evidence' and that the charge of treason 'was fully and satisfactorily proved by the Testimony.' From the bare outline of the trial in the minute-book it seems that the jury had some difficulty reaching a verdict. No doubt the testimony of John Warren Jr that the prisoner was a 'quiet, inoffensive Man, always obedient to the requisitions of the Magistrates' had something to do with its discussion. The deliberations lasted for an hour and a half before Overholser was pronounced guilty.

Overholser was not alone in his misfortune: of the 21 men tried, 17 were convicted. The penalty for high treason was harsh and calculated to have a 'strong and lasting' impact upon the 'Public Mind.' On 21 June Scott read the sentence to the convicted men: 'You are to be drawn on Hurdles to the place of execution where you are to be hanged by the neck, but not until you are dead, for you must be cut down while alive and your entrails taken out and burnt before your faces, Your Heads then to be cut off, and your bodies divided into four quarters, and your Heads and quarters to be at the Kings disposal.' Since Drummond and others believed that 'many examples were not necessary to convince the Province that Treason will meet with its due reward,' the thorny question was whom to pardon. Robinson provided him with detailed recommendations on each of the cases. As far as Overholser was concerned, Robinson termed him an 'ignorant man ... of considerable property – a good farmer ... not a man of influence or enterprise, and it is thought acted as he did from motives of personal enmity to the persons [the Angers and Clark] ... who are not of themselves men of good characters.' The proper objects of punishment, he noted, were not unfortunates such as Overholser, but notorious offenders. A petition for clemency signed by 95 residents of Bertie Township claimed that Overholser was 'an honest peaceable Sober and Industrious Inhabitant.' John Warren Jr's name headed the list of signatories and he forwarded the petition observing that Overholser was 'worthy of every indulgence.'

On 9 July Drummond approved Robinson's recommendations and respited the executions of nine men, one of whom was Overholser; the eight selected for execution were hanged, until dead, at Burlington Heights (Hamilton) on 20 July. Overholser was sent immediately to York and then forwarded to Kingston where he languished in a military jail awaiting confirmation of a royal pardon and transportation to Quebec and banishment. On 14 March 1815 he died of typhus fever. At the time of his death his farm was not fully paid for. A dispute over ownership ensued but his wife continued to reside there at least until January 1818. Ultimately his 196 acres were vested in the crown and sold in 1821.

The trial at Ancaster has been dubbed the 'Bloody Assizes,' perhaps from too great an emphasis on the executions on the heights and not enough on the trial itself and the deliberations that preceded it. From the War of 1812 until almost the present day Canadian political culture has shown little of the 18th-century whig concern with civil liberties. It is not, perhaps, unreasonable to discern in the wartime climate of opinion – the preoccupation with maintaining order and the demand by those in civil and military authority for immediate examples – an early manifestation of this tradition. Yet the wonder is that the result was not more bloody. In the end, young Robinson's insistence upon adhering 'as much as possible' to the 'common course of Justice' avoided the gory consequences which surely would have attended the summary treatment of traitors by the military under martial law. But, as events turned out, there were victims and Jacob Overholser was surely one. Although spared the horror of 20 July 1814, he was convicted of an overt act of treason. Correct according to statutory definition, the charge of treason against him was lacking altogether in substance. Overholser was an enemy of Clark and the Angers but he bore no treasonous intent towards Upper Canada. The magistrates knew it, his neighbours knew it, and, indeed, Robinson admitted it. This knowledge, however, was sufficient only to respite Overholser's execution, not to prevent his prosecution. The press of events – beleaguered authorities, a perilous military situation, and the perception of widespread disaffection and active treason – was his undoing.

ROBERT L. FRASER

ANGELIQUE PILOTTE
Servant; b. c. 1797 near Michilimackinac (Mackinac Island, Mich.), in her own words 'the natural daughter of a Squaw, and a native of the Indian Country'; fl. 1815–18.

About 1815, because of her 'good natural qualities,' Angelique Pilotte was engaged as a servant to a woman on Drummond Island (Mich.). She accompanied her mistress on a trip to France but when the latter died suddenly, Pilotte returned, landing at Quebec on 4 June 1817 and making her way back to Drummond Island. With 'strong recommendations in her favour,' she was hired as a 'waiting woman' to Elizabeth Ann Hamilton, also of Drummond Island, and they left almost immediately on a three-week voyage to the home of John Ussher (Usher) of Chippawa, Upper Canada, arriving on 29 July 1817.

Pilotte attended to her routine household duties until about 8 August when the body of a dead baby boy was discovered in a very shallow grave near the Ussher home. When questioned by her mistress the following day, Pilotte confessed to being the baby's mother, 'and was for the first time apprised, that she had committed a crime in the Eye of English Law.' Later that day, while 'in a state of extreme convulsion,' she made the same admission before justices of the peace Samuel Street and Thomas Clark, whereupon she was held over for trial under a bill of indictment for infanticide; the act invoked was that of 1624 (21 Jac.I, c.27), which had been passed 'to prevent the destroying and murthering of Bastard Children.'

The assizes began at Niagara (Niagara-on-the-Lake) on 8 Sept. 1817. A grand jury was summoned and found a true bill against Pilotte. At the outset of the trial the next day justice William Campbell appointed lawyer Bartholomew Crannell Beardsley as Pilotte's counsel; she pleaded not guilty. The attorney for the crown, Henry John Boulton, prosecuted the case to a quick conclusion after the introduction of Pilotte's confession and the examination of seven witnesses. The petit jury found her guilty but 'strongly' urged mercy. On 11 September Campbell, who later claimed that the defendant had been convicted on 'clear and sufficient evidence,' sentenced her to be hanged. His confident assertion to the contrary, however, the case was not clear-cut. Pilotte's own petition for mercy, written on 15 September and maintaining her innocence, was supported by the grand jury; its members were 'strongly inclined *to give* credit to its assertions' and, like the petit jurymen, they recommended that she be pardoned. Moreover, several other petitions championed her cause. Campbell soon decided to respite the execution and refer the case to the administrator of the province, Samuel Smith, to determine whether Pilotte was a 'fit object for the exercise of the Royal Mercy.' On 18 September he sent Smith copies of the pertinent documents, along with Pilotte's petition, in which she pleaded her innocence. A few weeks later, Smith, noting 'the very uncommon Interest the case seems to have excited in all Ranks' and the 'unusual demonstrations' on the part of the juries in particular, transmitted these documents to Colonial Secretary Lord Bathurst to forward for royal consideration.

The reaction of the 'respectable' to Pilotte's plight – a reaction that was not to be duplicated at the trial of Mary Thompson in 1823 – was possibly the most notable aspect of the case. On the grand jury that supported Pilotte's petition, 11 of 20 members were justices of the peace and included such worthies as Robert Nelles, William Johnson Kerr, and William Hamilton Merritt. A number of the magistrates and 'principal Inhabitants' of the Niagara area, among whom were Thomas Clark, an associate judge at the trial and one of the JPs who originally examined Pilotte, William Claus, and James Crooks, also recommended mercy. Even the officers of the 70th Foot stationed at Fort George (Niagara-on-the-Lake), although admitting that 'it may perhaps be out of our line of duty,' petitioned for mercy through their spokesman, Henry William Vavasour of the Royal Engineers. This popular clamour is difficult to explain, but it may be significant that many of those who came to Pilotte's defence had connections with the Indian community through the American revolution and War of 1812, the fur trade, the Indian Department, and intermarriage.

By the terms of the act of 1624 Pilotte was guilty on her own admission. The act was of unusual construction. One of the few statutes in English law that presumed the guilt of the accused, it made the very fact of concealment of the birth of a bastard child, later found dead, sufficient presumption that the mother had committed murder. Although Pilotte did not deny that the child was a bastard, her statements about its birth were contradictory. In her petition she maintained that the child had been stillborn en route to Chippawa, but her confession established that the child had been born on the Ussher property, that he had been born alive, and that his birth had been concealed. Claiming to have given birth in a field adjoining the Ussher home at about 2 a.m. on the morning of 30 July, Pilotte stated that the child 'moved its little legs, but did not move its arms.' After staying with him for an hour or so, she left him 'upon the grass then moving his legs but not crying.' She went back to the house for about two hours, 'being sick,' and returned to the field to find the baby 'which was still moving its legs.' After wrapping a 'cloth very tight about the child,' she left him behind a stable until about 2 a.m. on 31 July. When asked by the magistrates why she had wrapped the infant tightly, she replied that 'it was for the purpose of choaking it.' Then, if her confession was true, she buried the child, possibly while he was still alive.

The confession was sufficiently damning and the statements of the witnesses supported it to the extent that they established that the child had been born on the Ussher property. Thomas Clark stated that the confession 'was freely made, neither threats nor promises being used to induce or influence her.' Mary McQueen, the Usshers' servant who had shared her bed with Pilotte, testified that Angelique had got up two or three times during the night of 29–30 July and appeared sickly. Mary Margaret Clark, one of three women who had 'privately examined' Pilotte, concluded that 'she had lately been delivered of a Child.' Elizabeth Hamilton also reached the same conclusion. Mary Ussher (née Street), John's wife, had gone through Pilotte's linen and found with her clothing 'an Infant's Shift.' She had not suspected her to be pregnant but recalled that she had heard a 'Strange Noise' on the night in question, 'which instantly occurred to her was like the crying of an Infant – but having no idea of any Infant being there, she imagined it must have been a Cat.'

As to whether the baby had been alive or dead at birth, the evidence of the witnesses was less conclusive. Miss Hamilton and Mrs Clark reiterated Pilotte's assertion to them that the baby had been stillborn; however, Pilotte's own confession made that possibility seem highly unlikely. Moreover, a local surgeon's testimony that the body 'was perfect in form, and had every appearance of mature birth' was coupled with the statement that a live child so 'tightly pinned up ... must necessarily soon be smothered.' Under cross-examination by Beardsley he added that death might have been caused by 'the want of proper assistance at time of delivery.'

Another point that either was established by the testimony or, if not made in the first instance, emerged under cross-examination was the fact that, as Thomas Clark noted, Pilotte 'appeared Simple and Stupid.' No one disagreed and indeed Elizabeth Hamilton said that Pilotte 'boarders on Idiotism' and was 'so Simple and ignorant as not to know right from Wrong, nor that she thought it a crime to Kill her own child.' Later, when faced by the pressure of the combined petitions, Campbell used Hamilton's testimony on this matter as grounds for ordering a respite of execution and referring the case for further consideration.

Pilotte's petition was carefully framed, no doubt by her counsel, and emphasized the extraordinary circumstances of the case. She was a 'poor girl,' with 'no education whatever, nor the slightest instruction in the Principles of Christian Religion.' Utterly helpless, she was depicted as a victim of the judicial process. She had been unaware of her right to counsel and thus the lawyer appointed by the court to defend her had had insufficient time to prepare her case adequately. Moreover, some of the statements in her confession were flatly contradicted by her petition. Here she claimed that while in France she had had 'an unhappy connection' with a friend of her employer, a British officer whom she identified as a Lieutenant Lutman of the 81st Foot, and became pregnant. During the latter days of her voyage to Chippawa she went into labour. The child was stillborn and, fearing the wrath of her mistress, she wrapped the body, brought it ashore, and on the night of 29–30 July buried the baby in a shallow grave in an open field. The petition pointed out that the presence of infant's clothing, by proving the mother's intention to care for the child, was sufficient evidence according to English legal practice to remove a case from the purview of the 1624 act. More important, it drew particular attention to the different cultural customs of Indian women in childbirth. All Pilotte knew was the 'customs and maxims of her own nation'; thus, she was guilty only of 'the invariable custom of Indian women to retire and bring forth their children alone, and in secret.'

Pilotte had to spend many months in prison before learning of the crown's response to her plea for mercy. Transatlantic appeal was, naturally enough, a lengthy process and the delay eventually led Robert Fleming Gourlay to claim that the government had not acted with proper dispatch, a charge that was completely unfounded. On 27 March 1818 Lord Sidmouth, acting on behalf of the Prince Regent, changed her sentence to one year's imprisonment. On 13 May Bathurst notified Smith of the royal decision.

It is extremely difficult for an historian to judge on the basis of incomplete records whether Pilotte was guilty or innocent of infanticide. Certainly, according to the act under which she was charged, the grand jury (in the first instance, the petit jury) and the judge agreed that there was sufficient evidence to proceed with a trial and ultimately to convict her. The peculiarities of that act aside, it cannot be known for certain whether the baby boy was stillborn or murdered. However, Pilotte's assertions on the former count are not very convincing. What moved the juries and local inhabitants was probably sympathy for her helplessness and simplicity before a law which, in a sense, put the Indian tradition of childbirth on trial. As for Pilotte herself, little is known of what became of her. On 15 Oct. 1818, the *Gleaner* noted that a Peter Wheller had been sentenced to one month in jail 'for the escape of Angelique Pelotte.'

ROBERT L. FRASER

GEORGE POWLIS (Powles)
Convicted murderer; b. 1812 in the Mohawk Village (Brantford), Upper Canada, son of Paul Powlis (Paulus Paulus) and Margaret Brant; m. Susannah Davis, and they had six children; d. in or after 1852 in Upper Canada.

The presence of Indians in Upper Canada posed special problems at times in the application of the law. Until 1825 the judiciary considered them to have – by virtue of their treaty rights and unceded lands – a legal immunity from prosecution for crimes committed by one of their number against another. Even when the law could be applied, there was an appreciable cultural problem and the case of Angelique Pilotte in 1817 illustrated the intrinsic difficulties in judging the customs of one society by the laws of another. The judicial basis for the Indians' immunity was reinforced by the military threat they posed collectively and by the possibility of retaliation against sheriffs, constables, or magistrates acting against them.

After the War of 1812 white settlers increasingly deplored the behaviour of the Indians. In 1817 a Gore District grand jury condemned the Grand River settlement of the Six Nations as a 'frequent scene of riot and tumult ... out of the reach of the law.' Its pressing concern was the effect of such activity on settlement and progress. A year later Peter Lossing and others petitioned the Legislative Council about the 'frequent depradations' of the Six Nations Indians against each other and neighbouring whites, and the 'repeated instances of horrid murder ... among themselves.' The petitioners called 'loudly' for 'some further legislative interference ... to establish civil authority,' blaming 'a laxity in [the Indians'] former modes of regulating and punishing offenders' on 'the baneful effects of intoxication' and prolonged acquaintance with 'white people.' In 1822 Judge William Campbell questioned the legal immunity of Indians in the case of Shawanakiskie, who had killed an Indian woman in Amherstburg. Three years later it was finally determined that the criminal law could be fully extended to Indians.

George Powlis grew up on the Six Nations' lands. His lineage was distinguished: on his father's side he was a grandson of Sahonwagy, a Mohawk sachem; on his mother's side, a grandson of Joseph Brant [Thayendanegea]. Powlis, who was a member of the Church of England, was 5 feet 9¾ inches tall with black hair and hazel eyes. On 22 Feb. 1839 George, his brother Joseph, and their father were arrested for murdering Susannah Doxater, a Mohawk, and were incarcerated in the district jail at Hamilton. By this time there was no longer any judicial trepidation over prosecuting Indians.

The Powlises were tried on 6 June before Levius Peters Sherwood and two local associate judges, John Willson and Richard Beasley. The case was prosecuted by Hamilton's leading citizen, Sir Allan Napier MacNab. The Powlises were defended by two local lawyers, Miles O'Reilly and George Sylvester Tiffany. Murder cases in Upper Canada were usually decided upon circumstantial evidence; this trial was no different. Some facts were beyond doubt. The victim had been seen walking home towards the Mohawk Village about sunset on the evening of 16 February. Two days later, her naked body was found on the side of Vinegar Hill, which was known locally as a 'place of resort for dissolute people.' The examining surgeon thought she might have died by strangulation. Evidence indicated that the murder had not occurred where the body was found but at one of two nearby sites littered with chestnut shells and food. The tracks of four men and one woman led from one site to the other. At one a ring was found. Sleigh tracks led to these locations. Witnesses established that Doxater, an old woman who 'occasionally got drunk,' had been sober and one witness thought she had been 'ravished.'

The Powlises were connected to the murder by slender evidence. They had been seen in Brantford on the day of the murder. They left for the Mohawk Village 'about sunset'; George was dropped off at Vinegar Hill while Paul and Joseph went on to the village. Sleigh tracks were found leading from Joseph's log cabin to the murder site. His sleigh had distinctive tracks and he was not in the habit of lending it. George had bought chestnuts and had some with him on his way home; there were shells at the murder site and between it and Joseph's cabin. The ring was identified as one that had been sold to George in Brantford that day. Finally, he was not seen after being left at Vinegar Hill. That night someone called several times at Joseph's cabin. No one saw the visitor, but one witness, who had been sleeping there, thought he spoke Mohawk. These visits agitated Joseph and

Paul (then living with his son), who left the cabin each time for prolonged periods.

In his charge to the petit jury Sherwood concluded that most of the evidence was circumstantial and that the 'real difficulty' was establishing whether the Powlises had killed Doxater or were present as accomplices. The testimony concerning George's ring constituted 'strong presumptive evidence against the owner' because no explanation for it was given. Sherwood instructed the jury that the whole testimony was not conclusive of the guilt of any of the prisoners and that they should be acquitted if there was any doubt. After little more than an hour, the jury acquitted Paul and Joseph. George, however, was found guilty and sentenced, two days later, to be executed on 18 June.

Powlis immediately petitioned for royal clemency, claiming his innocence and arguing that the evidence was so palpably insufficient that the jury's decision was unwarranted. His plea was supported by 14 chiefs and others of the Six Nations. On 11 June, Sherwood tendered his report of the trial for the consideration of Lieutenant Governor Sir George Arthur. The judge admitted his own doubt of Powlis's guilt but did not wish to intimate an error by the jury. The Executive Council, the provincial body which usually reviewed capital cases, met on 13 June. Sherwood appeared before it and reiterated his conclusion: there was sufficient evidence to find Powlis guilty but it was 'wholly circumstantial.' Moreover, several facts were wanting to make the case 'so conclusive as would be satisfactory in a case of capital punishment.' The council followed Sherwood's lead. Solicitor General William Henry Draper, however, urged that a murder committed by a Indian 'should be visited with a punishment calculated to produce a deep impression on the minds of those of his own race.' He recommended that the sentence be commuted to transportation for 14 years, but the council, with Arthur's concurrence, decided upon 7 years of hard labour in Kingston Penitentiary. William Allan reasoned that 'protracted imprisonment ... would be more Salutary, and even felt to be more severe by the Indians.'

Uncertainties about Powlis's conviction lingered. Andrew Drew, who had known Powlis for seven years, sought clemency for him in February 1840. Aided by Miles O'Reilly and William Johnson Kerr, a son-in-law of Joseph Brant, Drew had investigated the case and was convinced that Powlis had not 'acted a principal part in the murder.' O'Reilly felt there was 'a possibility' of guilt but 'the evidence did not show even a probability of it.' Again, Arthur referred the case to the Executive Council and on 2 March 1840 Robert Baldwin Sullivan reported that no new facts had been disclosed to warrant a further commutation of punishment.

The case was reopened for the last time on the petition in May 1841 of Powlis's wife and his mother, supported by chiefs and warriors of the Six Nations. Emphasizing Powlis's 'good character,' his conviction upon 'slight grounds,' and his relationship to Brant, the women urged Governor Lord Sydenham [Thomson] to pardon him. The matter was referred to Sherwood, who wrote on 6 July that although he still had some doubt of Powlis's guilt, he was not sure the verdict was wrong. Since the jury was better acquainted with the witnesses and the locale, he had reasoned that it was 'more capable' of drawing a correct conclusion. Asked to comment on the judge's response, Samuel Peters Jarvis, chief superintendent of Indian Affairs, urged 'favorable consideration' of the petition. Civil Secretary Thomas William Clinton Murdoch disagreed on the grounds that 'it is with these people [Indians], more than others, that it is necessary to discourage the ideas that such crimes may be committed with impunity or atoned for by light punishment.' Sherwood, however, had been troubled by the case. He reread his notes and discussed the case with Chief Justice John Beverley Robinson. The chief justice was a much more decisive and self-assured man than Sherwood and undoubtedly his influence can be seen in Sherwood's letter of 13 July declaring, 'I now think there is sufficient doubt of his guilt to warrant his discharge.' The following day Powlis was pardoned and released from penitentiary.

The decision was, undoubtedly, the correct one. Although Powlis had never explained his whereabouts on the night of the murder or why his ring had been found at the murder site, the evidence could not sustain the jury's verdict. From the outset Sherwood had legal grounds for recommending a pardon; it was his failings as a judge that had imprisoned Powlis. The convict, on the other hand, was not the paragon depicted by his family, friends, and Drew. Kerr had alluded to the 'bad Company' he kept and the beneficial effect likely to result from his imprisonment. A Mohawk woman, Sarah Ruggles, complained in June 1841 that Powlis was a 'wretch' who, with others, had cheated her of her lands. Subsequently, the only surviving mentions of Powlis are on an 1849 census list for the Six Nations and on the provincial census of 1852.

ROBERT L. FRASER

NILS VON SCHOULTZ
(baptized Nils Gustaf Ulric)
Patriot; b. 6 or 7 Oct. 1807 in Kuopio (Finland), second surviving child of Nils Fredrik von Schoultz and Johanna Henrica Gripenberg; m. 20 March 1834 Ann Cordelia Campbell in Florence (Italy), and they had two daughters; hanged 8 Dec. 1838 in Fort Henry, near Kingston, Upper Canada.

Surely no more delightful or respected scoundrel ever set foot in Canada or left as much of an impression there in such a short time as Nils von Schoultz. The son of a middle-rank official, Nils was taken to Sweden with the rest of the family when the Russians overran the province of Finland in 1808. After his father's death in 1816, his mother took all but one child back to Finland, where her brother ran a school. Schoultz was educated there and, when the family returned to Sweden in 1821, at the military academy in Karlberg. The same year he entered the Royal Svea Artillery Regiment, and by 1825 he had become a warrant officer second class. He resigned his commission in November 1830, quite possibly after being asked to do so because of gambling debts, and worked for the army for a while.

In 1831 Schoultz began the semi-nomadic existence which was to characterize the remainder of his life. He went to Poland to fight against the Russians for Polish freedom. Captured, he escaped and made his way to France, where he joined the Foreign Legion, and he served in north Africa. The type of warfare was repugnant to him, and in 1832 he managed to leave the Legion. The next year he arrived in Florence to visit some members of his family. There he met and courted Ann Campbell, a young Scottish tourist. The newlyweds moved to Sweden in 1834, accompanied by Ann's mother and sister, and with the small part of his mother-in-law's estate that was immediately available to her Schoultz paid some of his debts and purchased a mill. However, he was without a continuing livelihood, and in addition to a wife, in-laws, and servants he soon had two young daughters to support. As a result he established a laboratory and began experimenting in the hope of discovering potentially valuable manufacturing processes.

In June 1836 Schoultz journeyed to England, both to find a buyer for a red dye he had invented and to obtain more of his mother-in-law's estate. The dye proved unstable and Schoultz, who had much energy and enthusiasm but less patience, apparently became discouraged. He accepted a fellow Swede's offer of passage to the United States in the hopes of becoming a success there. When he left England he told neither his wife nor his wife's relatives in London, who had been entertaining him.

It was as Nils Scholtewskii von Schoultz, a 39-year-old Pole, that Schoultz introduced himself in the United States. Upon his arrival at New York in August 1836, his entrepreneurial instincts directed him to the salt works at Salina (Syracuse) and Syracuse in upstate New York, where considerable profits were to be made by extracting salt from brine. Schoultz soon devised an improved process for obtaining the salt, had it tested, and travelled to the American salt-producing areas interesting manufacturers in his process before applying to have it patented. Everywhere his courtly and charming manner won him new friends and even financial supporters. He acquired property in Virginia, applied for American citizenship, and settled temporarily in Salina with a new friend, Warren Green, to await the granting of his patent. Some contemporary accounts suggest that he was courting a local woman, possibly Emeline Field, Green's niece. He wrote to his wife in June 1837 promising to send a large amount of money in the near future, but he had no further correspondence with Europe. These actions suggest that Schoultz was building a new life; however, his sudden death makes it impossible to establish his ultimate intentions.

Just as the Polish cause and life in the Foreign Legion had seemed romantic and heroic to Schoultz, so did the cause of the Canadian people in 1838. He was drawn into one of the Hunters' Lodges, secret societies formed in the northern states following the rebellions of 1837 for the purpose of freeing the Canadas from British rule. After recruiting in New York City in the fall of 1838, Schoultz agreed to take part in an attack planned against Prescott, Upper Canada. On 11 Nov. 1838 the steamboat *United States* left Sackets Harbor, N.Y., and then towed two schooners full of men down the St Lawrence towards Prescott. One of the schooners, carrying Schoultz and between 150 and 200 men, landed a short distance east of Prescott. However, mishaps and the fire of a British war steamer prevented the other vessels from reaching the Upper Canadian side. Schoultz had only a minor rank, but with the senior officers on American soil he was elected leader. Using a stone windmill and several stone houses, he organized a defence which held for five days against a large British force of militia and regulars commanded in succession by colonels Plomer Young and Henry Dundas, and supported by three armed steamers under Captain Williams Sandom. Contact with the American side brought word of reinforcements and later of rescue, but neither was forthcoming. On the 16th the invaders, who by then were reduced to firing bolts, door hinges, and nails, succumbed to a mass attack.

Schoultz and his surviving men were taken to Fort Henry, where a court martial began on 26 November. At the suggestion of some British officers, who were impressed by his manner and his military background, he employed a young Kingston lawyer, John A. Macdonald, as his counsel. However, Schoultz's gallant nature worked against him. Despite Macdonald's advice, he insisted that although he had invaded Upper Canada in a complete misunderstanding of the inhabitants' desires he was still guilty of an attack and should pay for his crimes. Accordingly, he was condemned to hang, but since he was believed to have been a Polish officer it was decided to execute him at Fort Henry instead of at the district jail with the other nine condemned men from the Prescott invasion force. Sentence was carried out on 8 December.

To the end Schoultz remained a gallant romantic. His will divided the bulk of his estate, most of which was to come from the sale of the patent to his salt process. Some of the proceeds were to be used to support the widows of the four men killed on the British side during the battle and to assist the Roman Catholic Regiopolis College being built in Kingston. The remainder of his money was to be divided equally between his wife and his mother, Warren Green, and Green's sister. Of Green's share, $1,000 was to go to his niece. There is no evidence that money was ever received for the patent. In letters published after his death Schoultz asked the American people not to think of avenging him and acknowledged that the Canadians were not discontented. At the end of his hectic life he was 31 years old.

RONALD J. STAGG

JOSEPH SEELY (Seeley, Seelye)
Militiaman; b. 1786, probably in western Quebec, son of Augustus Seelye (Sealey); m. with children; last known to be living in 1814.

Details concerning the Seely family are scarce. Seelys from Connecticut were common in New Brunswick and in the Johnstown District of Upper Canada, and it is likely that the various families were related. According to Joseph Seely, his father had served under Jeffery Amherst during the Seven Years' War and in a corps commanded by Captain James Campbell during the American revolution. The elder Seelye was on the United Empire Loyalist list for Lancaster Township, Upper Canada, but the family probably never resided there. By 1801 they were in Elizabethtown (Brockville), where Joseph took the oath of allegiance the same year. Six years later he petitioned for 200 acres of land as the son of a loyalist and received a patent for a lot on Lake Gananoque in Leeds and Lansdowne Township on 24 March 1812.

Here Seely might have spent a life toiling in happy obscurity but for the intervention of the War of 1812. 'As became a good subject,' he volunteered for duty and served nine months with Captain Charles Jones's dragoons. He then enlisted in the 1st Leeds Militia, enticed by Captain Adiel Sherwood's 'promise of a Sergeants situation and rations for my small family.' The higher pay must have seemed a boon to a prospective young farmer and the supply of provisions essential to a family dependent upon the male to clear, sow, and harvest the land. In April 1813 the newly enlisted men were ordered to Prescott, where they were divided into companies the following month.

Seely's hopes were quickly scotched. Since Sherwood had failed to recruit the required quota for his unit, Seely was assigned to Captain Archibald McLean's company as a private. The promotion to sergeant was not forthcoming and the rations for his family were never issued. After serving briefly under McLean, Seely was transferred to the 'Engineer Employ.' Aggrieved, dispirited, and no doubt anxious about his family, the young soldier deserted in late August. About 20 November he was captured 'in the Enemy's Camp' on the

American shore by a party of Leeds and Grenville militia led by Captain Herman Landen.

It had been a critical year for the civil and military administration of the province. The problems that had confronted Isaac Brock worsened under his successors Roger Hale Sheaffe and Francis Rottenburg: disaffection was widespread and desertion endemic among the militia; the House of Assembly was reluctant to allow the administration to use arbitrary powers to meet the civil problem; and initial military successes at Ogdensburg, N.Y., and at Frenchtown (Monroe, Mich.) had been offset by the capture of York (Toronto) in April, the defeat of Robert Heriot Barclay on Lake Erie, and the rout of Tecumseh and Henry Procter at the battle of Moraviantown on 5 October. The outbreak of disorder during the occupation of York had been particularly unsettling. In an atmosphere charged with fear and suspicion even judges such as William Dummer Powell urged dispensing with the due process of civil law to overawe the disaffected. In July Governor Prevost, possibly acting upon information supplied by Powell, empowered Rottenburg to convene courts martial to make examples. The pervasive belief that such action would quell the disloyal culminated in the execution of eight men at the Ancaster 'Bloody Assize' in 1814.

Charged with desertion to the enemy and with aiding 'in piloting one of the Enemy's boat's,' Seely was tried before a court martial at Kingston on 9 and 10 Dec. 1813. The court was composed of 13 of the leading militia officers of the Johnstown, Midland, and Eastern districts. The prosecution was handled by the acting judge advocate general, Edward Walker. Seely was left to conduct his own defence – a daunting task for a mere private; he pleaded not guilty. Walker called four witnesses: Landen, Archibald McLean, and two privates from Landen's party. Walker's aim was simple: to establish that Seely had served with the militia until late August and that at his capture he was in an enemy camp within the United States. An unabashed Seely handled his defence with marked aplomb. He did not deny the charges but rather emphasized a family and personal history of loyalty, a laudable record of military service, and a reasonable motive for desertion – the breaking of the promise that had occasioned his enlistment.

Seely's previous military record was not disputed. In testifying to his loyalty, Landen, who had known the prisoner for 16 or 18 years, stated, 'No one would I have ventured my life with sooner. ...' He also mentioned that Seely had fought with 'some Americans ... on account of their celebrating the Independence.' After his capture Seely's behaviour was extraordinary. Landen related how he 'cried very much and said although you were a prisoner, you were going to a Country you loved, and that you had not been contented since you left it.'

Seely's speech in his own defence did not attempt to prove his innocence but rather addressed the circumstances of the case. His loyalty was instinctive, inspired by the attachments of family and by traditions learned from a loyalist father: 'I reluctantly left the Country In which I have been brought up from my childhood and to which I was attached by all the ties of Loyalty, Friends and Kindred not with smallest or most distant ideas of *aiding* or *assisting* in the service of an Enemy that I have always been taught to detest. ... With such a parent to instil the Principles of Loyalty into his Family, it is almost impossible for any member of it, to have any attachment to any other Government than that to which he belongs. ...' His motivation was simply a sense of injustice – 'I considered my promise to serve as void.' All the conditions of his enlistment had been broken. Although he had been an acting sergeant for a few days, Seely's application for permanent rank was rejected when McLean called attention to his lack of education. The extra rations, which Landen stated were 'the reason that many men with large families engaged,' were not delivered. Although Seely was on the ration list, his family was not 'in consequence of their being such a number.'

The court found Seely guilty of desertion but acquitted him of the second charge. He was sentenced to be transported for seven years but in spite of Rottenburg's approval of the court's judgement he did not meet his fate. Rottenburg had intended to pardon Seely on condition that he enlist in the New Brunswick Fencibles. On 29 Jan. 1814 Rottenburg wrote to his successor, Gordon Drummond, on this and other related matters. Drummond acted accordingly and on 18 April 1814 issued a 'full, and unlimited Pardon' with the suggested proviso attached. It does not seem that Seely complied with the terms. Neither did he return to his land on Lake Gananoque; it was sold in two instalments many years later.

Seely might have fared worse. Another militia private tried for desertion at the same court martial was promptly shot. What distinguished the two cases was Seely's adroit defence. His ability to combine a sense of just cause and personal loyalty no doubt resulted in the milder sentence and later the pardon. It is commonplace, and perhaps sensible, to see in instances of disaffection and treason the American political sympathies of an Elijah Bentley or an Abraham Markle. It is also prudent to bear in mind the frustrated self-interest of an Ebenezer Allan and an Andrew Westbrook. And as a reminder that personal lives sometimes do not fit any mode of interpretation, it is instructive to remember the case of Joseph Seely.

ROBERT L. FRASER

SHAWANAKISKIE
Ottawa and convicted murderer; m. with at least one child; fl. 1813–26 in Upper Canada.

In 1813 Shawanakiskie fled from Amherstburg, Upper Canada, with Major-General Henry Procter's army when it retreated to the head of Lake Ontario. In the fall of 1821 he killed an Indian woman in the streets of Amherstburg. No details of the case survive, except for a reference to an 'atrocious' and 'heinous' crime. On 27 October he was lodged in jail at Sandwich (Windsor), pending his trial, which took place in August 1822 before Mr Justice William Campbell. The case was prosecuted by Christopher Alexander Hagerman, acting counsel for the crown on the Western circuit. The proceedings, according to Shawanakiskie in a later petition, were conducted solely in English, with no attempt to translate them into his native tongue. George Ironside, Indian Department superintendent at Amherstburg, testified, despite threats from the accused against his family. Widely known as a violent individual, Shawanakiskie, according to a statement by Ironside, had 'half scalped' a marine stationed at Amherstburg, allegedly murdered an old woman of his tribe, and killed his sister by cutting her throat. Shawanakiskie's counsel, probably William Horton, argued that in the matter at hand the accused had only avenged the murder of a parent, a custom sanctioned by native law. He further stated that the exercise of native laws and customs was guaranteed by treaty, thus rendering Indians immune from legal proceedings in such circumstances. None the less, Shawanakiskie was found guilty – the case, according to Campbell, having been 'fully proved' – and sentenced to death.

Campbell, however, was uncertain about the terms of the supposed treaty and delayed the execution to permit time for Lieutenant Governor Sir Peregrine Maitland to 'ascertain upon what authority such opinion is founded.' Maitland referred the question to Chief Justice William Dummer Powell, whose reply was inconclusive. He then submitted the whole matter to the colonial secretary, Lord Bathurst, who in turn passed it on to the Home Department. Before acting, the home secretary, Robert Peel, requested any information in the colony regarding the existence of such a treaty. Thus in August 1823 Bathurst wrote to Maitland informing him that the contentious legal question was back on his desk. At stake was an important legal issue for both the Indian and the white communities, namely the applicability of English criminal law in cases involving Indians only. Of more immediate concern to local residents living in unsettled areas near the reserve, however, was the question of protecting themselves and their families.

It took over two years to check through the Indian Department's records. Finally, in November 1825 Maitland reported that 'after the most diligent Search ... there appears to exist no treaty that can give color to the idea that an Indian is not to be considered as amenable to the law for offences committed against another Indian within His Majesty's Dominions.' Armed with this information, officials at the Home Department quickly concluded that there was nothing to prevent the law from taking its course. Yet because of the possibility of extenuating circumstances of which Maitland alone would be aware, the warrant issued for Shawanakiskie's execution included a proviso that the lieutenant governor could commute the sentence to transportation for life.

There is no evidence that Shawanakiskie received such a conditional pardon. Given his character and the threats to Ironside, it seems likely that he was executed at the Sandwich jail, probably in 1826. The legacy of his case was the resolution of a vexing legal question. Thereafter, as in the case of George Powlis, an Indian could gain a pardon only on the grounds of legal cause and not by right of immunity.

DENNIS CARTER-EDWARDS

HENRY SOVEREENE
(Souvereene, Sovereign)
Farmer, shingle weaver, and convicted murderer; b. c. 1788, probably in the vicinity of Schooley's Mountain, Morris County, N.J., eldest son of David Sovereen and Anne (Nancy) Culver; m. Mary (Polly) Beemer (Beamer); hanged 13 Aug. 1832 in London, Upper Canada.

Young Henry Sovereene was among a large party of Sovereen and Culver relatives who immigrated to Upper Canada in 1799. Travelling in some 20 wagons, together with 40 yoke of oxen, 300 sheep, and a large number of horses and cows, the group arrived about July at Long Point, where Jabez Collver had settled a few years earlier. By 1802 David Sovereen's family was living at Round Plains in Townsend Township. Henry was a farmer in Windham Township and probably married, when in 1812 he purchased a 200-acre lot in that township from his uncle. Four years later he sold part of this lot.

In August 1819 he was tried and found guilty of 'knowingly, wilfully, and maliciously shooting a horse' and was sentenced by Mr Justice William Campbell to be hanged. Lieutenant Governor Sir Peregrine Maitland, however, commuted the sentence and by 1821 Sovereene had resumed farming in Windham. Having sold the remainder of his land, he took up residence on the north part of lot 1, concession 5, owned by Ephraim Serles, his uncle by marriage, who lived close by. Although later described as industrious and a good provider – he made shingles as well as farmed – he had long been addicted to alcohol. Generally he got along well with his neighbours, many of whom were relatives. When sober he was 'rather affectionate to his wife and children' but when drinking he could be abusive and had at times even threatened their lives.

Before sunrise on the morning of 23 Jan. 1832, Sovereene informed the Serles household that two men with blackened faces had broken into his house. He feared for the safety of his family as the men had stabbed him in the arm and on the chest. In his house neighbours found the bodies of two children; a third was fatally wounded, and a fourth was sleeping unharmed. Outside were discovered the bodies of four more children and the 'perfectly cold' corpse of Sovereene's wife. When one of the murder weapons – a son's knife – was found by a constable, suspicion immediately turned to Henry. A bloodstained jackknife, believed to have been used by Sovereene to inflict wounds on himself, was found in his vest pocket; another weapon, a beetle or maul used to split wood in the making of shingles, was discovered, gory and almost covered with human hair of different colours, concealed between the straw and feathers of a bed in the house. Following his arrest and an inquest, Sovereene was transported to the London jail.

Prior to the assizes, London had been ravaged by cholera and most of its residents had fled. Only nine grand jurors were present for the opening of the court and bystanders were recruited to fill out the jury. Sovereene was tried on 8 Aug. 1832. After retiring for less than an hour, the jury found him guilty. Mr Justice James Buchanan Macaulay sentenced him, on the basis of extremely strong circumstantial evidence, to be hanged two days later. This date was subsequently postponed until 13 August.

Sovereene, who had always been extremely obstinate and self-willed, had shown no emotion during the trial, steadfastly and calmly maintaining his innocence. On the day of his execution he firmly and resolutely ascended the scaffold. After his death, witnessed by a crowd held to some 300 by fear of cholera, his body was handed over to surgeons for dissection. According to legend he was later interred in the Oakland Pioneer Cemetery. He was survived by three older children, away on the night of the murders, and by Anna, aged three, who had been found unharmed. No motive for the murders was ever established. When Sovereene called at the door of the Serles household that early January morning, he had 'exhibited no signs of insanity' and 'was perfectly sober.'

DANIEL J. BROCK

DANIEL SULLIVAN
(also known as Daniel Tim-Daniel O'Sullivan)
Blacksmith, innkeeper, and farmer; b. *c.* 1808 in Ireland;
d. on or about 5 Jan. 1887 at Norway
(now part of Toronto), Ont.

Daniel Sullivan achieved notoriety in the mid 1830s as a storm-centre of Toronto 'street politics.' Between 1832 and 1837 he was prosecuted for at least 13 offences involving individual or collective violence (assault and battery, riot, and affray), and appeared as prosecutor in at least four cases of a similar nature. In nearly every instance, Sullivan's adversaries were Tory partisans or Orangemen and the violence was connected with parliamentary elections or Orange demonstrations.

Although the frequency of Sullivan's court appearances attest to his pre-eminence as a practitioner of partisan rowdyism, his brothers, Jeremiah and Patrick, and a brother-in-law, Patrick Cassady, were also no mean performers. The Toronto *Recorder and General Advertiser*, an Orange organ, complained in July 1835: 'The character of the Sullivan's is well known in this city, and not a row of any consequence takes place but the name of Sullivan is connected with it. ... This name carries terror along with it, to every peaceable and well-minded citizen.' William Lyon Mackenzie, however, in a slighting reference to Robert Baldwin Sullivan's political tergiversations and upward social striving, asked: 'Has not this same Mr. Sullivan ... a few relatives in town, known as "the Sullivans," who have neither turned their coats, SOLD THEIR RELIGION, nor got ashamed of the hammer and anvil by which they earn their bread?' On another occasion Mackenzie referred to Daniel as R.B. Sullivan's 'Cousin Dan,' but there is no other evidence that they were related.

The nature of Sullivan's relations with Mackenzie is obscure but interesting. One might expect the puritanical Scot to have disliked the riotous Irish blacksmith and his hard-drinking Catholic lower-class associates, but apparently their support in Toronto was vital to a politician as dependent on popular favour as Mackenzie. Two incidents which occurred during the provincial election of 1834 suggest this. One night in early October, after a brawl on the hustings in which Sullivan had figured prominently, a pro-Tory mob attacked his house, endangering those within. Mackenzie, as mayor of Toronto, later imposed on two participants in the riot sentences so severe that a petition signed by many leading citizens was mounted on behalf of one of the convicted men, while milder sentences awarded by Mackenzie to Sullivan at the same time provoked accusations of favouritism. The night after the attack on Sullivan's house, a party of constables led by Toronto's chief constable, or high bailiff, William Higgins, clashed with a gang of anti-Tory rioters, one of whom was Sullivan, and a rioter, Patrick Burns, was killed. Mackenzie, spurred by complaints from the victim's friends, held a police court investigation of the incident and committed Higgins to stand trial for murder at the next assizes. The grand jury exonerated Higgins in April 1835 and returned a bill for riot against Sullivan and other companions of the dead man. Tory newspapers accused Mackenzie of collusion with the witnesses to create the case against Higgins, and stressed his friendly relations with Sullivan.

Mackenzie was not, however, the only prominent Reformer with whom Sullivan's name is associated in contemporary records. In November 1834, Toronto's Constitutional Reform Society named him to the St George's Ward committee which was to prepare for the municipal elections of 1835; his fellow-members included Judge George Ridout and two aldermen, Dr John E. Tims and Edward Wright. What part Sullivan may have taken in other elections is unknown, but a newspaper account of a brawl during the provincial election of 1836 reported that he visited the home of the Reform candidate, James Edward Small, and left in the company of Ridout and a prominent Toronto radical, Charles Baker. Two of Sullivan's petitions for remission of sentence, dating from 1837 and 1848 respectively, bear the supporting signatures of a number of leading Reformers (some of them Protestant), including several merchants, city councilmen, and justices of the peace. On the later petition, Charles Morrison Durand calls Sullivan 'a good citizen and worthy man.' These petitions also contain Tory signatures, such as that of the former MLA and ex-mayor of Toronto, George Monro, and two city councilmen, James Trotter and James Browne.

Sullivan's brief career as *primus inter pares* of the lower-class, anti-Tory Catholics of Toronto seems virtually to have ended in November

1837, when he was sentenced to three years in the Kingston Penitentiary for assault with intent to kill. The details of this case are unknown. Sullivan fared well in prison, labouring at his trade and avoiding disciplinary sanctions, and was released in March 1839. For the next ten years his whereabouts is unknown, but by September 1848 he was living in York Township. Here, but for a spell across the township line in Scarborough, he spent the rest of his life.

That Sullivan had not entirely abandoned his old ways as late as 1848 is shown by his trial for riot after he, his brother Patrick, and a third man attacked 14 armed Orangemen in a tavern. But he was becoming, in a small way, a man of property. Even in 1837 he had been tilling a small plot and employing men in stone-hauling. He now became both innkeeper and farmer, producing chiefly hay, potatoes, apples, and wool. The 1871 census shows him owning 157 acres and occupying 249 in all, although he possessed less at his death. In the 1870s he began to adopt the style of 'yeoman.' City directories of 1884 and 1885 call him 'labourer,' but his will styled him: 'Daniel Tim-Daniel O'Sullivan, gentleman.'

Sullivan, a sort of petty tribal leader of the Irish Catholic labouring element, was an equivalent of such petty Orange chieftains of mid-19th-century Toronto as John 'Tory' Earls, an innkeeper and carter, called 'Prince of Loafers,' and William Davis, an innkeeper, minor civic official, and city councilman. His will, with its pious bequests (he left $50 each to Archbishop John Joseph Lynch, the Toronto House of Providence, and Father Michael McCartin O'Reilly of St Joseph's Parish, Leslieville) and ban against his two nephews selling the land he left them outside the family, evinces the traditionalism of his outlook. If Sullivan was Irish and Catholic first and foremost, he did not, however, adhere to Bishop Alexander McDonell's anti-Reform entente with the Orange order in 1836 or shrink from marrying an Anglican Irishwoman in 1870. Nor did he conform to the stereotype of the 19th-century Irish Catholic manual labourer. Even in the 1830s he had rented quite a substantial house and always had the money to pay his fines and court costs. At his death he had risen modestly but significantly in the social scale.

PAUL ROMNEY

MARY THOMPSON
Servant and convicted criminal; b. 1801 in Upper Canada, daughter of Alexander Thomson; fl. 1823–24 in Upper Canada.

The veil of obscurity that cloaked Mary Thompson's life was lifted on 15 Aug. 1823 when she was charged with murdering her newborn infant. An illiterate young woman, Thompson was a member of a poor, landless family resident in the York (Toronto) area. At the time of her arrest she was single and had been a domestic servant for but a few months. The evidence for Thompson's trial is scanty, and so a detailed reconstruction of the crime or much insight into her personal life is precluded. Although her case has therefore less inherent interest than that of Angelique Pilotte in 1817, it is of greater importance because of its impact upon Upper Canadian legal history.

For a time after her arrest Thompson 'steadily denied' knowledge of the crime with which she was charged. At length, however, a confession was obtained and she led the authorities to the child's grave. Her incarceration was noted in Charles Fothergill's *Weekly Register* under the heading 'Horrid Murder.' He commented that she had 'evinced but little concern' during the investigation. Indicted under a statute of 1624 (21 Jac.I, c.27), she was tried before Chief Justice William Dummer Powell on 17 Oct. 1823. Attorney General John Beverley Robinson prosecuted; the defence counsel was probably George Ridout. After considering the testimony of seven witnesses, a petit jury, including John Doel, found her guilty but recommended mercy. Powell, however, in spite of his obvious sympathy for Thompson, lacked legal cause to refer the case to Lieutenant Governor Sir Peregrine Maitland. He sentenced her to be hanged on 20 October but he wrote to Maitland's secretary, Major George Hillier, offering an opportunity for gubernatorial intervention. For his part, Maitland would not absolve the judge from signifying legal cause for review.

On 18 October Thompson petitioned Maitland for clemency. Unlike Pilotte, she did not plead innocence. She admitted that she had been 'fairly and patiently tried with every Opportunity of Defence.' However, she claimed that she had failed to present the 'real situation' to the jury. She now declared that her labour had been 'unexpected' and that 'in the pains and anguish of child-birth ... her unfortunate Offspring met it's untimely end, and that it's death was not the consequence of any premeditated design to conceal her shame, any predisposition to commit a Deed so foul, any felonious violence by the arm of an unnatural Mother.' She appealed to Maitland's 'known clemency' to 'save her from that pending death she is so little prepared to meet.' Two days later her father, who had spoken to Powell personally on the night of the conviction, uttered a plea for his 'wretched Child ... so lately the hope of an affectionate parents future happiness, [who] by one false step productive of Shame is doomed to die an ignominious death.' Making no claim for her innocence, he simply urged that 'the spirit of holy feeling and charity' be extended to his daughter as it had been to others.

By now Powell had decided to respite the execution because of new information. Under the statute of 1624 three key areas of evidence had to be established: that the pregnancy and birth were concealed, that the child was a bastard, and that it was born alive. After the trial, a 'medical Person' had informed him that evidence admitted which had been taken as conclusive proof that the child was born alive had been 'for many years disallowed' by English judges. This information threw doubt upon Powell's ruling in the last area, and by respiting the sentence, he was able to confer with justices William Campbell and D'Arcy Boulton. They agreed that he had erred in accepting the medical evidence as conclusive, but they added that the jury had convicted on the whole body of evidence and thus there were no grounds for overturning the verdict. On 25 October Powell reported their conclusions to Maitland, but he was still personally convinced that 'the verdict might have been other wise had the Evidence been stated as hypothetical.' He urged a further respite and royal review. Maitland concurred and directed him to prepare a report on the case to be forwarded to Colonial Secretary Lord Bathurst.

On 28 November the report was ready. In it Powell reviewed the statute and outlined the evidence bearing upon the verdict. He expressed the view that a major weakness in the crown case had been the failure to produce conclusive evidence consistent with English judicial precedents that the child was born alive. During the trial Powell had admitted the evidence of 'two medical witnesses' who had immersed the child's lungs in water 'and found them to float.' At the time he had believed that there was 'no question' but that the child was born alive and the compelling and gruesome circumstantial evidence of 'a fracture of the skull, braine and extravagate blood,' which the defendant had attributed to her falling with the baby while 'crossing astride, a rail fence,' had convinced both judge and jury of the prisoner's guilt. In his report, however, Powell indicated that English judges now regarded such evidence as either inadmissible or hypothetical, and that it was a principle of English law to require tangible and positive proof and to 'admit no Inference from Circumstances.' He also noted the disparity between the reformed English statute of 1803, which had reduced concealment to a misdemeanour, and the unreformed Canadian law.

On 30 July 1824 Powell granted his last respite. Finally, on 6 August, 'in consideration of some favorable circumstances,' Thompson was granted an unconditional pardon. Her name appears, for the last time, on the jail return of 30 Sept. 1824. After her release she returned to the obscurity from which she had come. But her disappearance from official notice in no way detracted from the parliamentary and legal ramifications of her case.

The most striking effect of Thompson's case was the nine years of parliamentary effort to repeal the unusual act by which she had been convicted. Interestingly, the initiative came from, and was sustained by, some of the most powerful political figures in the province: John Strachan, John Beverley Robinson, George Herchmer Markland, and Jonas Jones. The difficult and chequered course of their efforts began shortly after Thompson's trial when, on 27 Nov. 1823, Markland gave notice in the Legislative Council of a repeal bill. It passed quickly through the council, but died in a House of Assembly committee. In 1825 the bill reappeared as part of Robinson's wider attempt at reform of criminal law; it was introduced in council by Strachan and steered through the assembly by Jones and Robinson. However, it was disallowed by the imperial government in 1827 for reasons which are not clear. For the next few years no action was taken but the bill was not forgotten. In 1830 Robinson introduced it in the council, but it died on the assembly's order paper. Finally, the next year, again on Robinson's initiative, it was passed by the assembly and council and received royal assent. The act, 2 Wm.IV, c.1, voided the authority of the old act because of 'doubts ... respecting the true meaning' and specified that trials for the murder of bastard children were to proceed like other murder trials. Concealment was reduced to a misdemeanour punishable by a maximum prison term of two years. Juries were empowered upon acquittal of child murder to find concealment and the court would then sentence on that ground.

Judicial handling of the Thompson and Pilotte cases suggests, as the court records bear out, that cases of infanticide rarely reached the court. On 18 Aug. 1825 Fothergill commented on yet another young servant 'who, after repeatedly denying her state of pregnancy, was privately delivered of a fine male child, which was discovered in a Privy, on the following morning.' In this instance the woman escaped custody and fled. Fothergill feared that it was 'not an uncommon offence' and noted that it was usually restricted to the 'lower classes.' Harsh winters and periods of economic distress, to say nothing of the shame of having a child out of wedlock, contributed to the incidence of infanticide.

Dead babies, whether found in shallow graves, privies, or under the ice of a frozen bay, were, and are, grim reminders of a brutal side of Upper Canadian life. So disturbing and contemptible a crime as infanticide elicited pity for, rather than outrage against, its perpetrators. In Mary Thompson's case, however, it was not her pathetic circumstances which occasioned the intermittent efforts of some of the most powerful men in the province, especially Robinson, to repeal the statute. It was rather the determination, in spite of uncooperative assemblies, indifference, and imperial disallowance, to rid the law of an act unusual in its presumption of guilt and difficult to enforce because of doubts as to its true meaning.

ROBERT L. FRASER

JACK YORK
Black slave; fl. 1800.

The life of Jack York is known only through a single criminal act. In 1800 he was one of several black slaves living on the farm of James Girty of Gosfield Township in the Western District of Upper Canada. Girty had served during the American revolution as a 'partizan' in the Indian department with his brother Simon and his fellow Pennsylvania loyalists and friends Matthew Elliott and Alexander McKee. In this period all of these men became slave-holders by treating captured slaves as personal booty rather than prisoners of war. It is possible that Jack York was acquired in this manner and in 1788 was brought to the District of Hesse. Slavery had been common in that area as early as 1782. By 1807 it was becoming increasingly unpopular, but the renowned anti-slavery statute of 1793 had not changed the lot of slaves such as York; rather it had secured them as the legal property of their owners. Indeed, as late as 1798 Christopher Robinson had sponsored a bill in the House of Assembly which would have extended slavery within the province, although the efforts of Richard Cartwright and Robert Hamilton in the Legislative Council prevented it from passing. York's life seems to have been spent in relative ease, tending to his master's animals, possibly fathering children by a female slave Hannah, and devoting his idle hours to hunting. His relationship with his master seems to have been one neither of deference nor strict discipline.

In late August 1800 York's life changed abruptly when he was charged with burglary with intent to commit a felony. He was tried on 12 September before Justice William Dummer Powell and an associate judge, Alexander Grant. After a short trial a petit jury of 12 men deliberated only momentarily before finding York guilty. But the charge masked the real nature of his supposed crime, the rape of a white woman, Ruth Tufflemier. The burglary charge was sufficient to support the indictment, and spared the crown the difficulty of establishing the 'usual technical Evidence of the rape being perpetrated.'

The only record of the testimonies of the seven witnesses is in

Powell's bench notes. Ruth Tufflemier testified that on a 'star light night' about 20 August she was awakened and discovered York peering into her cabin. Being alone she took her husband's rifle and waited. Some 15 minutes later she heard a noise and noticed that the device fastening the door had been removed. Fearful of letting York know she had recognized him, she threatened to shoot if he breached the door, whereupon he burst in, hit her with a large stick, 'treated her with great violence, entered her body, and did not leave until he had completed his purpose.' The removal of the door fastener was crucial to the burglary charge. Powell questioned her in order to make sure that the door had been locked in the usual manner and that she could positively identify the accused. Under cross-examination she said that 'she could distinguish between a white man and a black man' and that 'no private Picque or resentment' had motivated the accusation.

The sole supporting evidence was circumstantial, from a friend, Hannah Boyles, who recounted that Mrs Tufflemier had visited her home on 20 August, claiming that 'she had been abused by Mr Girty's black man Jack' and had recovered from unconsciousness to find 'he had ravished her,' and who described injuries to Mrs Tufflemier's body suggesting that 'the woman was forced' – 'Her breast [was] scratched, her loins [were] bruised, and her left thigh just above the Knee was much bruised.'

The testimony of Jacob Tufflemier was surprisingly ambivalent. He stated that when York was arraigned his wife had 'not sworn positively to the Prisoner, but to the best of her belief.' Moreover he introduced the possibility that resentment had motivated the charge by recounting a dispute he had had with York 'a long time ago' over Girty's hogs which had culminated with an exchange of violent threats. Tufflemier was absent on the night of the alleged rape but he too contended it was a 'Star light night.'

The remaining witnesses were York's fellow slaves and master whose testimony suggested that he could not have committed the rape at the time in question. A black woman Hannah testified that she had been 'in bed with him that night, untill about 10 or 11 oClock.' Another slave, James, said he had seen York 'strip to go to bed' and had later awakened with him to shoot an owl, after which they returned to their huts. When questioned by the prosecution, James said that he did not 'know the Prisoner is attracted to white women, or that he ever expressed a desire to have connection with Stofflemire's wife.' The testimony of James Girty, 'a black man,' who may have been

Girty's illegitimate son, added to the impression that York's only activity that night had been shooting an owl. Girty's own testimony substantiated this incident; moreover he asserted that the night was overcast and that York could not have left his hut without Girty's noticing. Girty told the prosecution he evaluated York at £121 and said his only complaint about York's character was his tendency of 'being free of his Tongue and that only to such as made free with him.' When York himself took the stand he described a long-standing association with Ruth Tufflemier. They had met 'alone in the woods and other places frequently, and [he] had never offended her.' He confirmed the quarrel with Jacob Tufflemier which resulted in his own banishment from the Tufflemier abode and he proclaimed his innocence stating that he had been 'in his bed at Mr Girty's all night.'

During the trial Powell received personal attestations to York's 'good Character from long acquaintance' from Thomas McKee, the son of Alexander, George Ironside, and William Hands, all three prominent in the local community. McKee had succeeded his father as deputy superintendent of Indian affairs and was a member of the assembly for Kent. He was also the son-in-law of one of the most powerful men in the district, John Askin. McKee tried to impugn Ruth Tufflemier's character, claiming that she 'had been an Indian Prisoner, redeemed by his father, and had lived in his Kitchen, and He did not think her credit good.' Ostensibly because this information was not given under oath, Powell chose to ignore it.

Powell's address to the jury was the critical juncture in the trial. Reiterating that the charge was burglary, he declared that the evidence was clear and consistent, and only the visibility possible on the night in doubt. He admonished the jury about Girty's 'avowed Interest ... in saving the Prisoner' and said 'all depended upon the Credit due to the witness Ruth which was unimpeached by anything on the Trial.' After the jury's speedy verdict Powell sentenced York to death.

Powell's reasoning is a matter of conjecture. In two earlier burglary cases involving black slaves prejudice does not seem to have affected his judgements, and there is no evidence it played a role in the York case. The trial of William Newberry invites comparison. Powell had sentenced him to death a month earlier after conviction on a charge of burglary, but convinced that the charge was bogus (the 'real crime' was attempted rape) and the penalty of execution unjust, although he admitted the conviction was legal, he had written to Lieutenant Governor Peter Hunter to get the sentence reduced. Newberry's father had been a loyalist spy executed 'for bearing arms in the Royal Cause' and this background may have influenced Powell. In contrast, Powell's long acquaintance with Indian department frontiersmen such as Simon Girty may have had something to do with his distrust and outright dismissal of the evidence of Girty and his slaves which was in York's favour. Powell had acted on Haldimand's behalf against Girty, Alexander McKee, and James Baby earlier when they were involved in 1780 in seizing slaves on a raid into Kentucky, and he had come into conflict with certain of them again on the land board of the District of Hesse between 1789 and 1791. In a note written in 1809 on the prospect of his son joining the department, Powell expressed 'my personal aversion to the Indian Department ... it holds out too many Temptations to Honesty & if persevered in has no Credit with the World.'

But regardless of Powell's opinion of them, these men, and McKee in particular, were powers to be reckoned with. McKee had financed York's defence and had made it known that he intended to apply for mercy on York's behalf. Powell had no reason or wish to defer the execution of a criminal 'convicted of the most atrocious offence, without any circumstances of doubt or Alleviation.' But in a move calculated to preclude political repercussions, he withheld signing the warrant for execution until Hunter could be consulted. Hunter upheld Powell's decision rejecting McKee's plea for mercy, but York was not executed. On 1 November the sheriff of the Western District, Richard Pollard, had notified Powell of York's escape. When after several weeks York had not been recaptured, an enraged Powell informed Hunter on 24 November. Clearly Powell suspected collusion and urged Hunter to order a 'serious Enquiry,' but it is not known whether any action was taken.

Jack York disappeared after his escape. James Girty died in 1817 and his will of 1804 leaves a clue which may pertain to York's fate after 1800. Among his property Girty listed six slaves, aside from his 'negro wench Sall,' including James, Hannah, and one named Jack!

ROBERT L. FRASER

The Critics and the
Causes Célèbres

BARNABAS BIDWELL
Author, teacher, and politician; b. 23 Aug. 1763 in Tyringham, Mass., son of Adonijah Bidwell and Jemima Devotion; m. 21 Feb. 1793 Mary Gray (d. 1808), and they had a son and a daughter; d. 27 July 1833 in Kingston, Upper Canada.

Descended from Puritan divines on both sides of his family, Barnabas Bidwell attended Yale College, from which he was graduated in 1785. As an undergraduate he was a prize essayist and the author of two plays: 'The modern mistake' and *The mercenary match: a tragedy*. The latter is distinguished, according to one biographer, 'by the general smoothness of the blank verse and the occasional felicity of the phrasing – qualities seldom found in eighteenth-century American plays.' Indeed, the play is considered by that biographer to be Bidwell's chief claim to fame. In any event, this serio-comic burlesque is of interest to the student of the author's later career as a party politician. The long speeches with which it is filled reveal something of Bidwell's early interest in polemics, and the play itself reveals a hostility to the idea of party he would later depart from.

Upon graduation Bidwell taught in a school for young ladies at New Haven until 1787, when he was appointed to a tutorship at Yale. In 1790 he unexpectedly resigned from this position to study law under judge Theodore Sedgwick of Stockbridge, Mass. Sedgwick, a prominent member of the House of Representatives and later a senator, was an important spokesman for the Federalist party. Bidwell, disappointed, according to historian Paul Goodman, at failing to secure a postmastership, joined the emerging Democratic-Republican party to become an arch-enemy of Sedgwick.

Admitted to the bar in 1791, Bidwell established a practice at Stockbridge. The same year he was appointed treasurer of Berkshire County, which the Republicans had just captured from the Federalists. From 1801 to 1805 he was a member of the Massachusetts Senate and from 1805 to 1807 he sat as a state representative in Congress. Re-elected in 1807, he resigned without taking his seat to become attorney general of Massachusetts. Honorary degrees of AM were conferred on him by Williams and Yale colleges, and in 1805 he was granted an LLD by Brown University. Then, in 1810, when he was being considered by President James Madison for appointment to the Supreme Court, discrepancies were found in his accounts as Berkshire treasurer. He fled in disgrace to Upper Canada.

In the House of Representatives, Bidwell had displaced John Randolph of Roanoke as administration leader and become the leading spokesman of President Thomas Jefferson. In this capacity, he successfully defended the president's policy of imposing economic sanctions in response to British violations of neutral rights at sea. He also directed the campaign to purchase Florida and was deeply involved in the movement to abolish the slave trade. Experience gained within the house, however, was less relevant to Bidwell's later career than that gained as a party organizer and a manipulator of public opinion at the grass roots.

Notable in this regard was the attention he paid to the partisan press. 'The people must judge from impressions, communicated through Newspapers principally,' he wrote to Aaron Burr. 'The true explanations of controverted measures should be communicated and circulated. They should be uniform in all parts of the United States. ... For this purpose there ought to be an authentic paper, from which Republican editors can take their texts.' Notable too were his views, which he expounded as a pamphleteer, on the necessity of the War of American Independence, on the excellence of the written American constitution, and on history in general. His own party was identified with a native, patriotic, non-European republican tradition, that of his opponents with an alien, decadent, monarchical, British tradition. The unwritten British constitution and the political thought of Edmund Burke, which were admired in certain Federalist circles, were objects of determined attack. Also of interest is Bidwell's early use of the term 'family compact.' In Canada this expression later took on a strange life of its own to shape political and historical thinking for many decades. Bidwell's views, however, are perhaps chiefly noteworthy as genuine expressions of an early form of American nationalism. This nationalism was to be quite at odds with sentiment which yet prevailed in George III's remaining North American colonies.

In Upper Canada, to which Bidwell fled in 1810, the American revolution, at least at a rhetorical level, long continued to be fought. First settled by American tory refugees committed to the idea of a continuing united British empire, it had later filled up with other settlers from the United States. When differences developed between these two groups, or when opposition to government opened within either group, so too emerged the rhetoric of revolution and republicanism. In part, this language was perhaps due to prior ideological commitment, and certainly opposition to established institutions often gave birth to republican commitment. More largely, however, the rhetoric of republicanism was the only language of opposition with which most of these folk were at all familiar. None the less, when understood within the context of then very strained British-American relations and against the threat of invasion by American armies, this language gave rise to intense concern on the part of those who supported the established government. Thus when Bidwell, who settled near Kingston, involved himself in controversy, he became an object of suspicion. And, by reason of his acknowledged political and intellectual ability, he became much feared.

The occasion of his first involvement sprang from the publication of *A discourse on the character of King George the Third*. Written in 1810 by John Strachan, a then obscure Cornwall schoolmaster, this pamphlet was primarily a refutation of George's republican traducers and a defence of British institutions against republican critics. Strachan also assailed philosophical assumptions which underlay the Declaration of Independence and contended that the practice of government in the United States fell far short of the republican ideal. Bidwell, writing under the pseudonym 'A Friend of Peace,' replied to Strachan in the *Kingston Gazette* of 9 Oct. 1810. Touching not at all upon the question of British institutions, he concurred with Strachan's 'encomium upon those conjugal and domestic virtues ... so justly ascribed to His Majesty.' Then he took issue with certain 'uncandid and ill-timed' reflections upon the people and government of the United States, focusing upon a remark to the effect that, although Britain had lost the revolutionary war, she might be in a position to avenge herself against a hostile United States at the end of the current war in Europe. 'From such an unprofitable, ruinous contest, without a prospect of gain,' replied Bidwell, 'good Lord deliver us! should be the prayer of our teachers and rulers, and all the people should say Amen.' Strachan's clumsy attempt at instilling loyalty in the populace was thus represented as provocative of war.

In contrast to much of Bidwell's other polemic, the tone of this letter, although condescending, was moderate. But he soon became an object of fierce controversy in the columns of the *Gazette*, when his pseudonym was pierced. Then, on 11 March 1811, a committee announced the opening of an 'Academical School' at Ernestown (Bath). This school was to offer a more practical education than the classically oriented, government-sponsored grammar school at Kingston. It was with horror that conservative circles in the latter town learned that the 'experienced preceptor' of this new school was to be Barnabas Bidwell. That he was more than well qualified academically was unquestioned, but he stood indicted before the courts of Massachusetts for embezzlement and forgery. Moreover, he was, as one contemporary has noted, 'a distinguished partizan of democracy in the most unqualified sense of the word' and he was therefore deemed quite unfit to shape tender Canadian minds. This latter consideration, however, may well have been his chief attraction for prominent radical leaders in Ernestown such as the Perrys who had long been at odds with leading Kingstonians. Certainly the Ernestown Academy was more important as a political symbol than as an institution of learning.

During the War of 1812 Bidwell, suspected of acting as an American agent, was compelled by local authorities to swear an oath of allegiance. How much truth lay behind these suspicions, it is now almost impossible to determine. It is perhaps significant, however, that they were shared by certain American opponents of the war. Soon after Brigadier-General William Hull's abortive campaign of 1812 a satire, *The wars of the gulls*, was published at New York. In this pamphlet 'the Gulls,' Madison and his friends, having decided that Upper Canada could be captured by proclamation alone, dispatch 'Hull-gull,' enjoining him in the event of failure to 'call for advice upon their trusty ci-devant cabinateer Barnabas Bidwell, and other confidential friends of the great Mo-gull [Madison] resident in that country.' Bidwell, it appeared, had 'made a generous sacrifice of his reputation at home' that he might reside with a better grace in an enemy country, there to make 'gradual preparations for the reception of the victorious Proclamation, by teaching the illiterate natives how to read it when it should arrive.' Although it would be absurd to suppose that Bidwell took up residence in the colony with any such purpose in mind, he may well have advised the American administration about the nature of Upper Canadian public opinion having regard to the probable reception of Hull's army and proclamation. The authors knew about Bidwell's teaching activities in Ernestown; they may have known more.

Little is known, however, of Bidwell's activities either during or immediately after the war. At some point he became a law clerk in the office of Daniel Washburn, a radical elected in 1818 to Robert Gourlay's Upper Canadian Convention of Friends to Enquiry. Bidwell himself seems to have taken little or no part in the Gourlay agitations, although he did give Gourlay his unpublished manuscript 'Sketches of Upper Canada,' which was later published as part of Gourlay's account of the province. In 1820 Washburn was disbarred for theft and Bidwell took over the management of his affairs.

This same year he stood for election to the assembly in the riding of Lennox and Addington where, it seems likely, the now-disgraced Washburn had intended to stand as a Gourlayite. Bidwell was not very successful. Heading the poll was Daniel Hagerman, who had led the opposition to Gourlay, with 521 votes. He was followed by two other conservatives, Samuel Casey and Isaac Fraser, with 309 and 192 votes. At the bottom of the poll were Bidwell with 162 votes and a Mr Detlor with 43. Then, in the summer of 1821, Hagerman died. In the ensuing November by-election two candidates divided the conservative vote and Bidwell was returned with a majority of 49.

At this point, the attorney general, John Beverley Robinson, suggested to Bidwell's opponents that, if a certificate could be secured from the United States establishing that, as an American official, Bidwell had forever renounced allegiance to the king, he could be unseated. But, perhaps because of the complicating factor of the oath Bidwell had been compelled to swear during the war, his antagonists also obtained certificates pertaining to his alleged malversations in Massachusetts. Thus, within two weeks of his election the outcome was protested on *moral*, as well as *legal*, grounds.

This stratagem completely backfired. Bidwell had paid the moneys he owed to the county of Berkshire and he now counter-petitioned that, all criminal charges having been laid before the electors and explained to them, he be confirmed in his seat. His petition opened up a debate in the House of Assembly as to the proper judge of moral fitness of assemblymen – the house or the electors. At stake were not only the privileges of the electors but also the vexed question of setting a precedent which would open the way to a host of petitions against the alleged moral failings of other members. To the embarrassment of those members, all such petitions would have to be tried. These issues, however, were avoided when the assembly resolved that it could not enter into consideration of crimes alleged to have been committed in the United States.

Legal arguments were also produced, but these proved more perplexing than the moral ones. Bidwell's opponents sought to establish that the oath he had taken in 1812 had been sworn reluctantly; that first having attempted to take novel oaths of his own devising, he had indeed sworn according to the proper form but had afterwards declared this oath invalid since it was taken under duress. Bidwell's friends then sought to establish that the magistrate before whom this oath had been made, and upon whose affidavit the case against Bidwell rested, was a notorious liar. The evidence produced by both parties was more bewildering than germane to the matter at hand; for the law seems to have been on the side of Bidwell. He, after all, had taken the oath, and his motives in doing so were scarcely relevant.

There was other law, however, arising from the Constitutional Act of 1791, which was not on Bidwell's side. This imperial statute provided that 'no Person shall be capable of voting at any Election of a Member to serve in ... an Assembly ... or of being elected at any such election who shall not be ... a natural born Subject of His Majesty or a Subject of His Majesty having become such by the Conquest and cession of the Province of Canada.' This provision had never been amended, and Bidwell fell into neither category. But neither did other members of the assembly and neither did vast numbers of voters who, having entered the province as post-loyalist American emigrants, had hitherto been deemed subjects erroneously. The law was quite clear, but to fall back upon it was to invite a political convulsion such as the province had never seen. Hence, when on 30 Nov. 1821 Jonas Jones and Mahlon Burwell moved that Bidwell, 'not being naturalized by any British Act of Parliament, is an Alien, and is therefore incapable of being elected to serve in the Parliament of this Province,' they were supported only by legal purists and blind tories. Their motion was defeated 12 to 20. But then, having declined either to enter into a consideration of Bidwell's American past or to declare him an alien, the assembly proceeded to find on 4 Jan. 1822 by a majority of one that 'sufficient of the allegations' made by the petitioners had been proved in such a manner as to render his election void. What these allegations were, or just how they had been proved in view of the house's own resolutions, it was most difficult to discover. And although the assembly later passed a bill disqualifying from membership all persons who had taken an oath of abjuration against His Majesty's government, or had held office in the United States, or had committed serious felonies, the impression lingered that Bidwell's expulsion had resulted more from opportunism than from any dispassionate consideration of law and evidence.

By itself this notion would have had little impact outside of the region around Lennox and Addington. But another, entirely false impression, zealously propagated by Bidwell, also lingered. This was that he had been expelled as an alien by ruthless tory opponents bent upon depriving all other unnaturalized persons of their civil rights. This alien question, the influence of which lasted for years, was of key importance in winning popular support for an emerging provincial reform party.

Bidwell himself never again stood for public office. He brought forward his son, Marshall Spring, as a candidate in his place, acted as his close political adviser, and busied himself orchestrating the press. In due course Marshall became a most able member of the assembly and a leader of the reform party. But tory opponents long remained persuaded that the tactical mind behind both him and the section of the reformers he led was that of Barnabas.

Up until 1828 there was much truth in this belief; thereafter, however, rather less. In 1828 the alien question was politically resolved and Marshall began to cooperate closely with William Warren Baldwin. A leading reformer but not a republican, Baldwin proposed to reform government by making it conform more closely with that practised at Westminster. Barnabas was undoubtedly angered and dismayed. This reaction was strongly conveyed by a letter printed in Hugh Christopher Thomson's *Upper Canada Herald* of 14 Oct. 1829 and almost certainly written by the elder Bidwell under the pseudonym X.

The letter was a bitterly sarcastic commentary upon another document, likely written *circa* 1806–7 by one Canadiensis, who was most probably judge Robert Thorpe. As such, X's letter was an attack upon William Warren Baldwin who, in 1828, had advanced again Thorpe's mostly forgotten proposal of ministerial responsibility within the colony as a solution to Upper Canada's political difficulties and as a means of maintaining the connection with the mother country. Reminiscent of Bidwell's early pamphlets in which he assailed Edmund Burke's views, X's letter clearly emanated from the pen of an American-oriented, republican separatist. It was probably elicited from Bidwell when he discovered his own son was being drawn into a system he abominated.

When Bidwell died in 1833, he was remembered by an American friend, judge William P. Walker, as one who in 'his intercourse with his neighbours ... was peculiarly mild and conciliating, and *no man had fewer personal enemies, except from political considerations.*' The emphasis is Walker's and his exception is a most important one; for the politics of conciliation were anathema to Bidwell. Partly for this reason, no reform politician in Upper Canada ever inspired as much political hatred as did he. Even his friends sometimes had reservations about the political means he employed. In a curious sermon preached at his funeral, for example, the Reverend J. Smith felt obliged to observe that, 'whatever may be said of his mode of accomplishing his intentions, none will say that these were not of a most liberal description, and designed for the general good.' Bidwell having departed this world of party conflict, Smith added, perhaps he 'may have already viewed many transactions in a different light, and weighed his own and others conduct and motives in a different balance than he formerly did.'

In assessing Bidwell's methods, the 19th-century American historian Richard Hildreth wrote of him as 'timid indeed, but cunning, supple and sly.' The more perceptive of his tory enemies in Upper Canada would not have agreed that he was timid, and they would have pointed to a rigidity of mind which they ascribed as much to his Puritan background as to his uncompromising republicanism. The views of most tories, however, were coloured by their belief that they were dealing with a thief and a traitor.

In both instances, they were mistaken. In 1810 Bidwell's estate had been attached for $10,000 as the amount of his indebtedness; but the final judgement of the Berkshire court against him, which he paid in 1817, amounted to only $330.64 damages and $63.18 costs. Since Bidwell seems to have been able to pay both amounts, he did not flee on that account. There is little reason, moreover, to doubt his assertion that, because his public offices required his presence elsewhere in the United States, he employed clerks to handle his duties in Berkshire, one of whom, dead at the time of financial exposure, had been responsible. He fled, he claimed, from fear of his political enemies who were exaggerating his personal responsibility and indebtedness. As for the charge that he was a traitor, it is clear that he remained an American patriot until the day of his death.

G.H. PATTERSON

FRANCIS COLLINS
Journalist, printer, publisher, and office holder; b. *c.* 1799 in Newry (Northern Ireland); m. 1824 Ann Moore of Newry, and they had four children; d. 29 Aug. 1834 in Toronto.

After receiving what he said was a 'tolerable' classical education in Newry, Francis Collins served an apprenticeship in Dublin as a printer and also learned to write shorthand. For a brief period he ran a whig opposition newspaper known as the *Ulster Recorder*, which, he claimed, was forced to shut down because of pressure exerted by Lord Castlereagh. He emigrated to Upper Canada in 1818 and obtained a grant of 100 acres near York (Toronto). Soon after his arrival he found employment with Robert Charles Horne, the king's printer, as compositor on the *Upper Canada Gazette*. As well, in early 1821 he began reporting House of Assembly debates for the *Gazette*, as John Carey was doing for the *Observer*. His stenographic reports were fuller and in general more accurate than any that had previously appeared in print. Yet he gave more extensive coverage to reform members than to tories, and on one occasion Attorney General John Beverley Robinson protested in the house that Collins's report of a debate could not have been 'more false, absurd, even ludicrous.' Horne was reprimanded at the bar of the house and he apologized for the report in the *Gazette*, but he retained Collins, cautioning him to report impartially. 'Trifling inaccuracies' Horne later blamed on the cramped quarters assigned to reporters in the gallery – what Collins called 'the fiddlers' box in the cock-loft.'

When Horne resigned as king's printer in 1821, Collins hoped to succeed him but was told that the office would be given to 'no one but a gentleman,' an affront he resented since he traced his ancestry to the ancient kings of Ireland. General satisfaction with his reportorial skill, however, led to his appointment for the 1821–22 session as official reporter to the legislature and also, at about this time, as court stenographer; the position as house reporter he seems to have held for five years. In July 1825 he established his own newspaper, the *Canadian Freeman,* and at once began attacking the administration of Lieutenant Governor Sir Peregrine Maitland and his 'reptile band' of tory advisers. He protested against the government's policy in the alien controversy and published a pamphlet on the subject. He also took a firm stand for freedom of the press when a group of young tories raided William Lyon Mackenzie's printing-house in 1826, but he held no brief for Mackenzie himself as a man or as a politician. Indeed he expended an arsenal of insulting epithets on most of his fellow editors, whether reformers or tories.

In 1826, following the dismissal of Charles Fothergill as king's printer, the chairman of the assembly's printing committee, Hugh Christopher Thomson, had solicited tenders for printing the journal of the house. Mackenzie got the contract by submitting a bid below the going rates, much to Collins's annoyance. 'We shall have cheap journals this session!' commented Thomson. But when Mackenzie's press was destroyed by the rioters, he had to turn over the printing to Collins, though he retained his own imprint on the journal's title page. Collins lost the contract to Mackenzie again in 1827, partly because he could not resist heading his tender 'Proposals for Printing "Cheap Journals,"' a gibe at Thomson which did not amuse members of the assembly. Collins was cited for contempt of parliament and summoned to apologize at the bar of the house. In January 1828 a motion carried in the assembly to divide the printing of the house among Collins, Carey, and Mackenzie. The following year, while Collins was incarcerated for libel in the York jail, his press published the journals from 9 January to 20 March 'by order of the House of Assembly.'

Because of his attacks on the administration in the *Canadian Freeman,* the executive in 1826 had withheld payment of the stipend voted to him by the assembly for reporting the debates. But instead of restraining him, this action gave him another stick with which to beat the government. Maitland reacted by having Collins indicted on four counts of libel in the spring of 1828. When the editor appeared in court without counsel, he was allowed by judge John Walpole Willis to make a preliminary statement and took the opportunity to attack Attorney General Robinson, who was prosecuting the case for the crown, for dereliction of duty. Robinson, said Collins, had failed to bring criminal charges against Henry John Boulton and James Edward Small, Samuel Peters Jarvis's seconds in the fatal duel he fought with John Ridout in 1817; he had also failed to prosecute the rioters who had destroyed Mackenzie's press. Against Robinson's protest, Willis instructed Collins to lay this information before the grand jury. True bills were found. In the subsequent trials the seconds were acquitted and the rioters let off with a nominal fine. Willis then recommended that the libel charges against Collins be dropped 'in order to quiet the public mind,' but Robinson held them over until the fall assizes.

On Collins's second appearance in court in October 1828, he was defended by John Rolph and Robert Baldwin. Three charges were withdrawn and on the fourth he was acquitted. Robinson then laid two new charges, one for a libel on himself, Collins having accused him of 'native malignancy,' the other for the journalist's disrespectful reference to judge Christopher Alexander Hagerman. The presiding judge in the trial, Levius Peters Sherwood, was temporarily absent from the bench when the jury brought in a verdict of guilty on the first count only. Hagerman, acting for Sherwood, instructed them to bring in a general verdict, which would cover his own case as well. The jury complied and Sherwood sentenced Collins to one year in jail, a fine of £50, and sureties of £600 for good behaviour for three years – a sentence widely condemned as out of all proportion to the offence.

At public meetings in York and in Hamilton on Collins's behalf, subscriptions were taken up and protests sent to Lieutenant Governor Sir John Colborne. On 26 Nov. 1828 and again on 4 December Collins himself petitioned Colborne, who declined to take any action. The assembly then took up his cause and, with only three dissenting votes, passed a resolution asking that his sentence be remitted. When this appeal, too, failed to move Colborne, the assembly drew up a much stronger address to the king praying for royal clemency. The crown's response was positive and Collins was released in September 1829 after serving 45 weeks in jail, his fine and sureties remitted.

If his persecutors had sought to silence Collins by incarceration they had badly misjudged their man. From his jail cell he had continued to edit the *Freeman*, denouncing his opponents with scathing sarcasm in a series of 'open letters.' After his release he concentrated his editorial attacks mainly on Egerton Ryerson and the Methodists, and on Mackenzie, whom he accused of republicanism. As a self-professed independent whig, he believed in reform on the British rather than the American model. When in 1831 Mackenzie was expelled from the assembly for libelling the house in the *Colonial Advocate*, many reformers counted on Collins once again to lead a crusade for liberty of the press. Instead, he branded the *Advocate* a seditious publication and commended the assembly for ousting a 'despicable demagogue.' When Mackenzie set about collecting 'grievances,' Collins retorted that there was no grievance a good assembly could not remedy. In Maitland's administration, Collins contended, 'there was much to blame and little to praise,' in Sir John Colborne's 'much to praise and little to censure.' Accused of turning tory, Collins replied that he had joined with 'the rankest Tories' to prostrate Mackenzie and his faction, but having accomplished this purpose he would continue to state his political opinions 'without regard to sect or party.' By 1833 Collins was in a benevolent mood towards his former tory antagonists, declaring in the *Freeman*: 'It is very well known that "the highest law officers of the crown" prosecuted the Freeman, at one time. ... Well all that has been forgotten, we believe, on both sides, by the parties concerned, and mutual forgiveness extended.'

During the last three years of his life, Collins became embroiled in a bitter public dispute with the Reverend William John O'Grady, the Roman Catholic priest in York. Trouble first began when in July 1831 Collins's brother John had to sue O'Grady for recovery of debt. Reports of this case in the *Freeman* angered O'Grady, who then refused baptism to Collins's son. The feud might have subsided had not O'Grady, smarting under a reprimand from Bishop Alexander McDonell, disputed McDonell's authority, claiming that he held his commission directly from Rome. Collins was the chief lay supporter of the bishop, and James King the principal ally of O'Grady. When Rome intervened in support of McDonell, O'Grady capitulated and, with King, established a radical reform journal, the *Canadian Correspondent*, which carried on a weekly vendetta with the *Freeman*.

But for Collins, time was running out. During the cholera epidemic of 1834 he visited Irish victims in the hospital. Late in August he himself contracted the disease and died soon afterwards. His wife and eldest daughter also succumbed, as did his brother and sister-in-law.

John Charles Dent wrote of Collins that 'his nationality was clearly indicated by his personal appearance, his features being rough-hewn and unmistakably Celtic; while his red hair and beard, usually not very well cared for, gave him an aspect of uncouth wildness.' A complex and paradoxical character, he could be generous, humane, and forgiving, but too often indulged in crude polemics and personal abuse. Opposed to arbitrary power whether of the right or the left, he believed in constitutional reform within the framework of loyalty to the king and the British connection. In an obituary tribute that appeared in the *Patriot* on 29 Aug. 1834, Thomas Dalton described him as a true liberal who cared 'alike for the honor and dignity of the Crown and rights and welfare of the subject. ... It is [questionable] if the Press of Upper Canada can now boast so robust an Advocate of Principle as was departed Francis Collins.'

H.P. GUNDY

REUBEN CRANDALL

Baptist clergyman; b. 24 March 1767 in Northeast Township, Dutchess County, N.Y., believed to be the son of Laban Crandall and Molly Seein; m. first c. 1786 Lida (Lydia) Mace, and they had seven children; m. secondly December 1813 Julia Smith, widow of Joseph Beemer, and they had two children; d. 28 Sept. 1853 near Aylmer, Upper Canada, and was buried east of Aylmer in the Burdick Cemetery.

Reuben Crandall was converted to the Baptist faith at the age of 16 and shortly thereafter was licensed to preach by the Baptist church in his native township or by some other congregation located nearby. In June 1794 he immigrated to Hallowell Township, Prince Edward County, Upper Canada, and immediately began to conduct religious services around West Lake. Unable to support himself entirely through preaching, he obtained a grant in 1796 of lot 28, concession 2, Cramahe Township, Northumberland County, where he farmed. Upon his arrival there he began travelling extensively throughout the district as a missionary preacher while working to build a congregation near his home. In 1798 he was instrumental in organizing a church with branches in Cramahe and Haldimand townships. Formally ordained at the church in Hallowell by a council of fellow Baptists on 27 Oct. 1799, Crandall appears to have enjoyed considerable success. In 1804 a visiting American missionary wrote that 'Elder Crandall had had a comfortable season in the year past. The church is increasing in members, and we thought in graces likewise.'

Ordination permitted Crandall to apply for the right to perform marriages in his district. That privilege had been restricted to clergy of the Church of England until a statute of 1798 extended it to clergy of certain other denominations. On 9 April 1805 the Court of Quarter Sessions, meeting in Haldimand Township, granted Crandall the authority to perform marriages in the Newcastle District.

The following August he joined Joseph Winn and Abel Stevens in ordaining another Baptist preacher, Elijah Bentley. For the next seven years Crandall continued to serve the church in the central part of the province. In 1812 he relinquished his oversight of the Cramahe and Haldimand congregations and moved to the area west of Lake Ontario where he and his wife became members of the church at Boston in Townsend Township. While there, Crandall took frequent missionary tours through the newly opened districts along the Lake Erie shore. It was shortly after his move to Townsend that Crandall's first wife died. His subsequent remarriage within a year was viewed as a scandalous act by the conservative members of his church. Crandall, however, refused to acknowledge that the church had any right to question him on the matter and the issue was quietly dropped. He then apparently settled for a brief time in Oakland; by 1816, however, he had made his permanent residence in Malahide Township near the present town of Aylmer. Here he led in the organization of a Baptist church which was established in October of that year with a charter membership of 12. Aylmer was to remain the focus of his future activities.

In 1820 Crandall was arrested and tried at the spring assizes of the London District for illegally performing marriages. He had been granted permission to conduct such services in the Newcastle District, but that authorization was not valid in other areas. Following Crandall's conviction Attorney General John Beverley Robinson noted in a letter to the lieutenant governor's secretary, Major George Hillier, that Crandall had not only performed marriages without permission but, unlike the Methodist clergyman Henry Ryan, had 'solemnized matrimony in a manner that could not have been legal whatever his authority.' Robinson further stated that the judge was obliged by the statute to impose the full punishment – banishment for 14 years. Crandall, however, was contrite. According to Robinson he 'urged' in his own defence that 'Preacher tho' he was, he could scarcely read and could not write,' and claimed that he had broken the law in ignorance. Given the situation and evidence of Crandall's good character, Judge D'Arcy Boulton decided to recommend clemency. The decision was supported by the grand jury and a full pardon was ultimately granted by Lieutenant Governor Sir Peregrine Maitland.

In the early 1820s Crandall gave up his pastorate at Aylmer but retained a permanent home in Malahide. He returned for a brief while to minister at Cramahe, and then moved to Southwold Township in the southwestern part of the province where he stayed approximately three years. By 1832 he was ministering to the church in Dumfries

Township, and his address was given as Galt (Cambridge). He is also said to have worked in nearby Blenheim and Zorra townships. Some time in the late 1830s Crandall retired to Malahide and there lived frugally until his death.

Sources clearly show Crandall to have been a sincerely devout, humble yet determined minister of the Christian gospel. A notation in the minute-book of the Aylmer church dated 28 Sept. 1853 shows the loving respect in which he was held: 'Elder Reuban Crandall, who has been a member of this church from its commencement, died today at the age of 86. Mark the perfect man and behold the upright, for the end of that man is peace.' By his life and work, Crandall is a superlative example of the evangelistic Protestant clergymen who did so much to develop church and community life in the rural environs of early Ontario.

DOUGLAS L. FLANDERS

BARTEMAS (Bartimus) FERGUSON
Newspaperman and printer; b. *c.* 1792 in Vermont; m. with at least five children; d. 19 Jan. 1832 in York (Toronto), Upper Canada.

Bartemas Ferguson first appeared on the Upper Canadian scene in 1817 working as a job printer in St Catharines. From this modest position he quickly became involved in politics. In February of that year he printed for James Durand an election bill attacking Durand's opponent John Willson; the bill also appeared in the *Niagara Spectator*, published by Amos McKenney and edited by Richard Cockrell. Years later Ferguson noted acidly that Durand had refused to pay him for his three days and nights of 'indefatigable labour.'

In 1818 Ferguson moved to Niagara (Niagara-on-the-Lake), where by 6 August he was printer and publisher of the *Spectator*. Under McKenney, the *Spectator* had supported the agitation of Robert Gourlay. Nothing changed under Ferguson; he, too, obviously sympathized with Gourlay's efforts, for he continued the policy of printing the Scot's blasts against the government. This action was fraught with peril. Gourlay was already awaiting trial on two separate counts of seditious libel; moreover, his 'Upper Canadian Convention of Friends to Enquiry' of early July had deeply alarmed the administration of Lieutenant Governor Sir Peregrine Maitland. When on 3 Dec. 1818 the *Spectator* (by then published jointly with Benjamin Pawling) printed Gourlay's article 'Gagg'd-Gagg'd, by Jingo!,' the stage was set for confrontation. Gourlay was ordered from the province and upon his refusal arrested. Ferguson was jailed overnight on 16 December and released the next day on a technicality.

Pawling, who had been charged with Ferguson, died on the very day his colleague was arrested. Ferguson now again assumed sole control of the *Spectator*. A committed Gourlayite, he continued unabashed in his support of the imprisoned Scot. On 1 July 1819 the paper carried Gourlay's 'Address to the parliamentary representatives.' A short time later the House of Assembly unanimously passed a motion calling upon Maitland to order the prosecution of the author and publisher. Ferguson was arrested on the night of 13 July. Undaunted by the experience of several days' imprisonment, he was confident of acquittal and depicted himself as the champion of a free press. Just before his trial he suffered a setback on another front: Amos McKenney obtained a judgement of £1,000 against him in civil court.

Ferguson appeared at the Niagara assizes on 19 August before Chief Justice William Dummer Powell on a charge of seditious libel. A special jury was picked and the case was prosecuted to a rapid conclusion by Attorney General John Beverley Robinson. In spite of what was, in Robinson's opinion, 'an able defence' by Ferguson's counsel, Ferguson was found guilty by what Gourlay called a 'weak jury' and held over for sentencing until 8 November at York. There has been some confusion as to the identity of Ferguson's counsel. What seems most likely is that Bartholomew Crannell Beardsley defended him at the trial and Thomas Taylor acted as his counsel at sentencing. In any case, the defence was unsuccessful and Ferguson was sentenced to a fine of £50 provincial currency, imprisonment for 18 months, and the pillory for one hour daily during the first month of incarceration. Moreover, at the expiration of his jail term, he would not be released until he had given £500 in sureties for his good behaviour over the next seven years. Through the intervention of Maitland, however, Ferguson escaped the pillory.

Ferguson's conviction was the turning-point in his life. He lost his paper; his family suffered; his health failed; and his spirit was broken. The stress proved too much to bear and, on 4 March 1820, he petitioned the assembly in chastened tones to urge royal clemency for the remainder of his sentence, claiming that his punishment would 'operate as an example to all others who may violate the laws of public decency.' Satisfied of his contrition, the assembly, despite the opposition of Robert Nichol, recommended a pardon and the administration concurred. Upon release, he was quick to take up his calling again and by 2 November, in partnership with one Davidson, was printer and publisher of the *Canadian Argus, and Niagara Spectator*, which soon failed.

Ferguson moved to Lewiston, N.Y., where by 6 July 1821 he was publishing the *Niagara Democrat*. Although no copies are extant, Ferguson's prospectus was reprinted in several Upper Canadian newspapers. Its politics, he declared, 'will be purely democratic.' Thomas Dickson reported to the government that the paper was 'circulated here ... and libels some of the first characters in the province.' Dickson wondered whether Ferguson should be arrested if he entered the province. In an 1822 report to the Colonial Office on Gourlay, Robinson damned the paper for traducing 'every respectable person in the Province.' How long Ferguson continued to publish the *Democrat* is not known.

In 1826 he appears at York, first on 2 February as one of the subscribers to a fund in support of Robert Randal, later managing the *Colonial Advocate* in William Lyon Mackenzie's absence. The following year he surfaces in York again as the unsuccessful defendant in a civil action for debt amounting to £412. Ferguson's love was newspapers and on 24 Jan. 1828, with Edward William McBride as co-publisher, he put out the first issue of the *Niagara Herald*. Again the venture proved short-lived. A dispute with the paper's proprietor, John Crooks, led to Ferguson's ejection in late October 1829. As was usual when the Ferguson family found themselves in dire financial straits, Mrs Ferguson promptly opened a millinery and mantua shop.

This time, however, Ferguson's prospects looked more promising. The Hamilton region had lacked a paper since George Gurnett moved to York in 1829. Encouraged by offers of financial support from several 'patriotic individuals,' Ferguson had moved to Hamilton by early November. The publication of the first issue of his *Gore Balance* on 12 Dec. 1829 heralded an era of vigorous newspaper publishing in Hamilton that was to last about 15 years. Like Ferguson's other efforts, however, the *Balance* did not last long. In spite of Ferguson's success in expanding the number of subscribers from fewer than 100 to more than 400, the paper ceased publication on 2 Dec. 1830 and was sold soon afterwards. The press and type were sold to the *Western Mercury*. In spite of its short duration and the problems that plagued its brief life, the *Balance* is notable because it captured the spirit of the emerging political culture of the boisterous entrepôt at the Head of the Lake (the vicinity of present-day Hamilton Harbour). The defining characteristic of local politics in Hamilton from the 1820s to the present has been an unbridled enthusiasm for economic development combined with only a passing concern for political reform. Ferguson was the first to give voice to this attitude, which later received classic expression in Robert Reid Smiley's *Hamilton Spectator*. At a time in the province's political history when an editor of a whiggish bent had any number of issues on which to lash the government, Ferguson all but abandoned the concerns of his youth. In part, this transformation can be explained by changes in the colony's political life. It also seems likely, however, that his brush with authority had made him extremely reluctant to tilt at government windmills. He now applauded the measures initiated by his old antagonist, John Beverley Robinson, to implement a provincial strategy for economic development. He also supported Willson and Allan Napier MacNab and spared nothing in his mordant attacks on Egerton Ryerson and Mackenzie.

Throughout 1831 Ferguson tried to collect the *Balance's* outstanding accounts. Finally, in August, he published notice that unless debts were immediately paid he would resort to the courts. But he died on 19 Jan. 1832 in the hospital at York. Francis Collins, the editor of the *Canadian Freeman*, attributed Ferguson's death to disease that had its origins in his imprisonment. Rather than dwell on his later career, Collins chose to hallow the memory of the young Ferguson, the supporter of the Gourlayite convention, the champion of the liberty of the press, and the victim (like Collins himself) of the harsh laws of libel. Mackenzie concurred, depicting Ferguson as one who was crushed 'when the iron hand of power fell upon him ... ruined his prospects, and aided in injuring his constitution.'

ROBERT L. FRASER

WILLIAM FORSYTH

Farmer, businessman, and militiaman; b. 1771, probably in Tryon County, N.Y., son of James Forsyth and Mary —— ; m. first *c.* 1795 Mary Ackler, and they had ten children; m. secondly Jane —— , and they had nine children; d. 27 Feb. 1841 in Bertie Township, Upper Canada.

In the late 18th and early 19th centuries few natural scenes then known could equal the spectacle of the great falls at Niagara. Renowned for its power and magnificence, the falls lured visitors of every sort: tourists, eccentrics, would-be poets and artists, and others less taken with the falls' majesty than with reaping a profit from nature's sublimity. These hucksters-cum-entrepreneurs have been an enduring presence at the falls and a carnival-like atmosphere and an often slatternly appearance have been their legacy. William Forsyth was such an entrepreneur, the first on the Canadian side of the Niagara River.

Forsyth's father was a loyalist farmer who in 1783 or 1784 moved his wife and five children to the west side of the Niagara River. The family made its home in Stamford Township, where William was living in 1796 when he first petitioned for land. Three years later, then described as a yeoman, he stood trial for a felony. He was acquitted but on 7 March was jailed for a capital offence. Escaping the next day, he was foiled in his attempt to reach the United States and, back in prison, he petitioned Administrator Peter Russell for release conditional upon 'his banishing himself.' Despite the support of Robert Hamilton, the most powerful man in the district and an important figure in the portaging trade around the falls, Russell hesitated since Forsyth's offence involved 'so many Questions of Prudence – Policy – & Law.' By mid May he had still not made a decision, after which date nothing further is known of the incident.

Forsyth next appears as a farmer living close to the Horseshoe Falls. In his reply to an 1824 query about Forsyth's claim for losses in the War of 1812, Thomas Clark, a neighbour and commanding officer of the 2nd Lincoln Militia (Forsyth's unit), reported him 'a man of uncouth behaviour.' Clark remembered that he had given 'some displeasure and trouble to my Officers by leaving his duty and going home at nights.' On the other hand, Clark believed that at the battle of Beaver Dams in 1813 'he behaved very well in harassing the Enemy before taken prisoners.' That fall American forces plundered Forsyth's home and farm. More damage was done to his house by Indians during a council convened by Major-General Phineas Riall. Clark noted that in 1814, when Major-General Louis de Watteville was quartered there, he used Forsyth as a spy 'to go across the river ... but report says that he took over as much if not more than he brought back.' Clark was not in the province at the time, however, and was unsure how true the allegation was: 'Forsyth is a man not generally liked, and perhaps malice may have instigated the report – his neighbours ... have no doubts about his loyalty – and further say that when the Enemy were in possession here, he did, and did naturally shape his Conduct as well as he could to save his property.' Although Forsyth's claim of more than £425 for losses was initially rejected, upon appeal, and after Clark's review of his wartime record, he was allowed £90 in 1824.

Rumour and innuendo hung over Forsyth like the ever-present mist over the falls. The wartime stories did not impugn his character but they detracted from it, suggesting a man with a sense of what was best for himself. One popular historian, Gordon Donaldson, has hinted that Forsyth used his knowledge of the river to smuggle goods to and from the United States. There is no corroboration but Forsyth's early brushes with authority, mad escape from jail, and self-serving character suggest that there may be room for doubt.

Some time after the war Forsyth built an inn on his property. Charles Fothergill stayed there in early April 1817. Two years later botanist John Goldie described it as the 'nearest' to the falls of several inns along the river. In 1818 Forsyth had erected a covered stairway into the gorge for a different view at 1s. per person. These stairs were, he admitted, 'upon the chain reserved for Military purposes, in front of ... [his] Land between it and the River.' The falls was Upper Canada's greatest scenic attraction and Forsyth's inn was the place to stay. The Duke of Richmond [Lennox] stayed there in 1818 as did Lord Dalhousie [Ramsay] a year later. The duke's party were less than pleased by the innkeeper's ability to accommodate them, in spite of his professed exertions, and there was a problem over the account. When

Dalhousie arrived Forsyth's reputation was suspect; none the less, he found the 'tavern & accommodation ... were very good indeed, and the man himself, tho' a Yankee & reputed to be uncivil, was quite the reverse to us, obliging & attentive in every way.' Visitors often seized upon other traits: Adam Fergusson pronounced Forsyth a 'personage sufficiently shrewd and well informed' whereas Samuel De Veaux found him 'a man of enterprising character.'

Forsyth was an aggressive entrepreneur anxious to cater to the public and expand his business as the tourist influx increased. In his situation, he needed to court the government, not run foul of it. In October 1820, through Robert Randal (a self-styled victim of judicial partiality and executive persecution), Forsyth petitioned the Executive Council for a lease of occupation of the 66-foot-wide allowance reserved for military purposes, which fronted his property. He also wanted to secure the privilege of operating a ferry below the falls. The government, however, had no intention of leasing the military reserve, and ferry rights had already been awarded. Randal had been told that Forsyth was the 'last man to look for indulgence of any Kind whatever' on account of his behaviour to Richmond. Forsyth's hurried explanation of May 1821 noted that 'much has been said and that greatly misrepresented in respect to my conduct on that occasion.' But his account, reasonable as it seems, availed him nothing.

Forsyth's intentions were twofold: to enlarge his accommodation for tourists and to ensure his control over the pre-eminent view of the great cataract. His own lands (inherited from his father) were just downriver from the falls, and he purchased from William Dickson the farm adjoining his own. Forsyth's combined acreage gave him a monopoly of the best views, especially that from Table Rock, the famed outcrop near the edge of Horseshoe Falls which offered the finest prospect of it. On his newly acquired property Forsyth had built by 1822 the Pavilion Hotel, also known as the Niagara Falls Pavilion. It was described ten years later by Thomas Fowler as a 'handsome frame building, ... three stories high, with piazzas on both sides.' In 1826 Forsyth added wings which were 'chiefly filled with bed rooms.' No expense was spared. It was, he thought, 'perhaps the most splendid establishment of the kind,' 'unequalled in this new country' and 'a place worthy of fashionable resort – whereat visitors of rank and distinction may always have suitable accomodations.' An 1827 advertisement emphasized its claim as a luxury establishment 'for noblemen and gentlemen of highest rank with their families, & for pleasure parties.' It had 'ample' rooms and one of the main rooms allowed 100 people to 'dine with ease.' The larder was stocked with 'viands from every land,' the cellars offered 'the best flavoured and most costly wines and liquors,' and good stabling was available across the road. As late as 1832 the approach to the falls from the Pavilion was through a forest which, as Fowler put it, 'conceals the prospect till close at the place, when the scene instantaneously bursts forth with astonishing grandeur! The place at which the visitor arrives by this route is Table Rock.' At the hotel, the falls was visible only from the rear balconies.

Among Forsyth's services were daily stages to Buffalo, Niagara (Niagara-on-the-Lake), Queenston, and Lewiston (he had successfully petitioned the House of Assembly, with the assistance of Robert Nichol, to prohibit Americans from operating stages 'along the Niagara Frontier'), the rental of carriages and post-horses, the stairway, and a ferry service to the United States. Table Rock was the site of the entrance to Forsyth's stairway, at the bottom of which he eventually added a tour behind the Horseshoe Falls. For 50 cents the visitor was outfitted with waxed pantaloons, frock coat, Dunstable hat, and shoes. Forsyth did everything in his power to lure tourists and to make them comfortable. 'I have ever had,' he said in 1826, 'a great desire to add to the unrivalled natural beauties of the wild and romantic scenery in the midst of which I dwell.' Accordingly, he claimed in 1829 to have spent 'perhaps not less than Fifty thousand Dollars' on his operation.

By 1827 he was 'reaping,' as one account put it, 'a fair reward from a generous public.' But his dominance had been challenged: a rival, John Brown, had built a hotel upriver, although his Ontario House could not equal Forsyth's establishment, or so it was said. In 1826 it was burnt under mysterious circumstances while one of Forsyth's sons was resident. Brown rebuilt the following year. A note published in William Lyon Mackenzie's *Colonial Advocate* hinted that Brown was the instigator of 'infamous reports' that William Forsyth had been 'privy to the burning.' Brown's purpose in venting the rumour, the note continued, was to deprive Forsyth – 'an enterprizing individual who had done more to accommodate the public, than any other stage proprietor or tavern keeper in Canada' – of his fair share of business. To increase that share the imaginative Forsyth was planning the first in a long history of spectacles, an event calculated to draw an extraordinary number of visitors and produce an extraordinary profit.

Carnival days were dawning at the falls and Forsyth would be the ring-master.

In August 1827 Forsyth, Brown, and Parkhurst Whitney, owner of a hotel on the American side, advertised that a 'condemned' schooner, the *Michigan*, with a 'cargo of Living Animals' would be sent 'through the white tossing, and the deep rolling rapids of the Niagara and down its grand precipice, into the basin *"below."* ' When in early September the great day arrived, Mackenzie was there. The roads were jammed, the hotels and galleries 'were crowded with people dressed in the pink of fashion,' 'every place and every corner and nook was filled.' Bands played, a lion roared, and 'show-men with wild beasts, gingerbread people, cake and beer stalls, wheel of fortune men' hawked their wares or plied their trades to a throng estimated by Mackenzie to have been at midday about 8,000 to 10,000. Finally, about 3:00 P.M., the ship made its appearance with its unwitting cargo: two bears, a buffalo, two foxes, a raccoon, an eagle, a dog, and 15 geese. The crew departed at Chippawa above the falls and the *Michigan* was towed closer to the rapids before being cut adrift. When it hit the first set, 'there was a simultaneous shout of applause' from the appreciative crowd. In the second the ship lost its masts and several of the cargo, including a bear and the buffalo. It reached the falls rent in half and was smashed on the rocks below. One goose survived. The bear had swum to an island above the falls where it was recaptured; it was later sold to a hotel on the American side for display. Not long after, spectacular stunts by daredevils such as Sam Patch and Jean-François Gravelet (Charles Blondin) became a regular attraction at Niagara Falls.

Forsyth's interest derives from his accomplishments in turning the sublime (the word most often used by visitors to convey the falls' majesty) into the ridiculous. But there is more to his historical reputation than his being the founder of the first tourist trap in Upper Canada. He was the central figure in the so-called Niagara Falls outrage, an event first drawn to public notice by Mackenzie in 1828 and since recounted by several historians. For John Charles Dent writing in 1885, as for Mackenzie, the outrage was a 'violent and utterly unjustifiable exercise of brute force' sanctioned and ordered by Lieutenant Governor Sir Peregrine Maitland. And, like Mackenzie, Dent considered the outrage part of a pattern of events leading back to the attack on Mackenzie's printing-shop, the type riot of 1826. This sort of interpretation, 'a simple case of Might *versus* Right,' has been out of historical fashion for some time. Most recently Paul Romney has returned to this incident and others like it which 'created the impression of a province ruled by men who were ready to punish any sort of opposition by violence and coercion.' Indeed, it was the Forsyth affair which led to an investigation by a parliamentary committee into the administration of justice.

Fought on several fronts, the war which culminated in the outrage had its origins in a contest over tourist dollars. The major dispute focused on control of the military reserve fronting Forsyth's property, particularly the land which he had purchased from Dickson. In 1826 he applied to Dalhousie, with whom he enjoyed good relations, for a licence of occupation which would give him legal control of the reserve. He had heard rumours that 'many applications' had been made for it and, 'as it is the only bar between my lands and the Cascade I feel the utmost anxiety to ascertain whether it is yet indisposed of.' Its loss would jeopardize his stairway (and another which he planned to build, with free use by the public, in 1827), his road from the hotel to Table Rock, and, most important, his control over the view from the latter. Dalhousie was reassuring. He did not think Maitland would grant to others a licence to a strip 'so immediately convenient' to Forsyth's buildings. And, in any event, he believed there was no 'intention of granting it because [it was] reserved expressly for public purposes – free from the exclusive control of any person.'

Of immediate concern to Forsyth was his dispute with John Brown, who had built a plank-road to the falls from the Ontario House and constructed a stairway which, Forsyth alleged, was on his property. The stakes were high and Forsyth was not reluctant to take matters into his own hands. Brown had not only been burnt out in 1826 but had also had his road blocked by Forsyth, who fenced his property from the hotel to the falls so as to deny Brown's patrons access except across Forsyth's property. Into the fray stepped Clark, who, he later testified, had told Brown that Forsyth 'had no right to put the fence where he did.' Clark had his own interests in this fight. First, he was Forsyth's rival in a bitter struggle over the ferry rights below the falls which had been awarded to Clark and his partner, Samuel Street, in 1825. Clark later complained to Attorney General John Beverley Robinson that they had been unable to occupy the site because of Forsyth's harassment. Although he lacked direct proof, Clark blamed the Pavilion's owner for the loss of three boats in 1826 and for a broken stairway in 1827. Secondly, as was also revealed in later testimony, he had 'a claim upon' Brown's hotel. It was not long after Clark's suggestion about the fence that some residents of the area complained to Maitland 'of being ... shut out from the river by the illegal act of an individual.'

Thus in May 1827 Captain George Phillpotts, the commanding Royal Engineer in Upper Canada, appeared at the falls to resolve the matter. Crucial to his decision was a determination as to the exact location of the reserve. Forsyth, for instance, contended that the 66-foot allowance ran from the river's edge, thus minimizing the effect of the reserve below the falls, where some of it would be in the gorge. There were two other possible interpretations: first, that the reserve extended back from the edge of the gorge, known to contemporaries as the lower bank; secondly, that it extended back from the edge of the escarpment (both the Pavilion and the Ontario House were near that edge), known as the upper bank. Phillpotts decided that the reserve was taken from the upper bank, and thus extended almost to Forsyth's inn and, in fact, included on it some of his out-buildings as well as his fences.

Rather than press the matter in court, in May 1827 Maitland ordered Phillpotts's party to tear down the fence 'to prevent any Monopoly' – and thereby perpetrated the outrage. Forsyth put it up again, and later that month this second fence was torn down. On the second occasion a blacksmith's hut belonging to Forsyth was dumped over the escarpment. Now the various disputes went to court. On 30 Aug. 1827 Brown won a civil action against Forsyth, who was convicted of tearing up Brown's road. Then, on 3 September, Clark and Street won their suit against Forsyth for obstructing their ferry. Robinson successfully upheld the crown's claim to what it considered reserve property in a trial before James Buchanan Macaulay (the presiding judge in the two previous cases) and associate judges Clark and William Dickson. Forsyth lost but the jury had taken 24 hours to reach a decision. He filed counter-suits against Phillpotts and sheriff Richard Leonard for trespass, but lost both actions.

The affair took a political turn when a petition from Forsyth to the House of Assembly was presented by John Matthews on 28 Jan. 1828. It led to a major confrontation between the crown and the assembly. The gist of Forsyth's complaint was 'the substitution of a military force to decide the question of right ... in a country not under martial law.' He asked the house for redress and requested it 'to watch over and protect the rights of the people from the encroachment of military power.' His petition went to a select committee composed of John Rolph in the chair, Robert Randal, Matthews, and John Johnston Lefferty. When the committee demanded the appearance of the adjutant general of militia, Nathaniel Coffin, and the acting superintendent of Indian affairs, James Givins, Maitland refused to give his permission. On 22 March the two men were jailed for contempt of the house and three days later the lieutenant governor prorogued the session. Given that Rolph had acted as Forsyth's counsel in the 1827 suits and chaired the committee, it is not surprising that Forsyth won its support. James Stephen, the colonial under-secretary, upheld the committee while the colonial secretary, Sir George Murray, notified Maitland's successor, Sir John Colborne, on 20 Oct. 1828 that Maitland 'would have exercised a sounder discretion had he permitted the officers to appear before the Assembly; and I regret that he did not accomplish the object he had in view in preventing Forsyth's encroachments by means of the civil power ... rather than by calling in military aid.'

There were complications still to come. On 31 Aug. 1827 the wily Clark had obtained with Samuel Street a licence of occupation on 'that part of the reserve near the ferry, up and down the river.' The object, according to Solicitor General Henry John Boulton, who granted the licence, was 'to protect the lessees in the proper enjoyment of their right of ferry, and to keep the shore open and free of access to the public who had been shut out by Forsyth.' The licence had been suggested by Clark in a letter to George Hillier, Maitland's secretary, in May, not long after the outrage. Clark wanted to end Forsyth's obstruction of his ferry rights and to end Forsyth's unauthorized ferry service. The licence would allow him to take legal action against his rival although he expressed some disingenuous concern that it might have a 'grasping or Monopolising appearance.' Licence in hand, the partners warned Forsyth on 14 September that any subsequent incursions would render him liable to prosecution. With Forsyth at their advantage, Clark and Street did not hesitate to press their position and in December 1828 they brought, and won, two suits of trespass against him. Forsyth was badly shaken and on 16 Jan. 1829 he petitioned the Executive Council asking that the reserve 'instead of being converted into a Monopoly for the benefit of speculating individuals be thrown open to the public.' He thought 'it hard to have his front taken from him and given to another whose lands are not adjoining.' Even his stairs had been taken away by this decision and part of his meadows and buildings lost as well. The council found no irregularity in the lease of the ferry rights to Clark and Street but recommended against the continuation of the license of occupation for the reserve. Colborne himself noted that a 'certain extent' near the ferry should be granted to the partners but that a one-chain strip on the top of the bank 'should be thrown open to the public for a road.' Council concurred.

Mackenzie was an old acquaintance of Forsyth and had the outrage raised by Joseph Hume in parliament in 1832. In the mean time, Forsyth, 'harrassed by Law – injured by the Government – persecuted for the sake of his property and embarrassed in his business,' sold his hotel and property to a group of investors that included Clark, Street, and William Allan, who planned to subdivide the land for the proposed 'City of the Falls.' Forsyth was to remain as proprietor of his hotel (the group had also acquired the Ontario House) until December 1833. In total, he sold 407 acres plus the buildings for £10,250 which was, by his estimate, $15,000 less than what the property was worth. When Clark and Street erected a museum and baths on the reserve, Colborne took action. Phillpotts had been succeeded by Richard Henry Bonnycastle, who took 'care not to employ the military in any shape' in ordering them to desist. The partners 'now turned, full of grievance, against the government,' as Bonnycastle put it, and won damages in 1833, a verdict which astounded Forsyth, not unreasonably.

Forsyth was by no means destitute. He had bought land in Bertie Township near Fort Erie in 1832. Despite the years of litigation and petitioning, he lived in comfort and elegance in Bertie Hall, his fashionable, pillared home. Yet he lived in hopes of receiving the compensation he felt was owing over the outrage. In 1835 Mackenzie raised the issue in the house, with predictable results. The select committee, which he chaired, considered that Forsyth had 'sustained great injury at the hand of Sir Peregrine Maitland ... and is entitled to compensation.' On 2 April 1835 he wrote to Forsyth, 'You may think that I have been neglectful in your cause, but it is not so – I have done all I could.' Months later, having heard the ferry rights of Clark and Street had reverted to the crown, Forsyth applied for them but was informed that the lease had not expired. That fall he sought a licence of occupation for the portion of his lands in Bertie fronting the Niagara River; however, executive councillor Robert Baldwin Sullivan later explained that council could not allocate 'any part of the chain of reserve ... originally made for public purpose.' Squabbling over the reserve continued unabated through the 19th century, the crown contending against entrepreneurs. It was finally ended in December 1892 by a decision by John Alexander Boyd in the High Court of Justice. With great understatement, he wrote that the 'matter presented for determination has, in various forms, occasioned doubt and perplexity for some hundred years.' Phillpotts's survey of 1827 was upheld.

Forsyth had fought tooth-and-nail to monopolize the tourist trade at the falls. When he failed to obtain what he wanted by lawful means, he did not hesitate to use coercion. He built a tourist empire and lost it to his most serious competitor, Clark. Unable to get redress in the courts and out-manœuvered by Clark, who was able to make his own deal for the vexed strip of military reserve, Forsyth sold out. But the river never lost its lure and Forsyth never left it. When he died in 1841 he bequeathed more than 800 acres and £1,000 to his children and wife. To one son he allowed whatever 'Money as my Executors may recover or receive from Her Majesty's Government for Claims for Damages.' In June 1850 Nelson Forsyth approached Mackenzie about raising the claim yet one more time but nothing came of it.

ROBERT L. FRASER

CHARLES FRENCH
Printer's assistant and convicted murderer; b. *c.* 1807 in Ireland, son of John French and his wife Jane; hanged 23 Oct. 1828 in York (Toronto), Upper Canada.

The son of a former corporal in an Irish fencible regiment, Charles French spent about four years learning the printing trade in York, first with Robert Charles Horne and then with Charles Fothergill. After working as a journeyman in William Lyon Mackenzie's office, he went to the United States before returning to York and serving as a surgeon's helper and later with Mackenzie again. In 1828 he was dismissed because of what Mackenzie regarded as his dissolute habits; afterwards he worked on the House of Assembly journals. A young man of respectable, if humble, parents, his only brush with notoriety occurred when he witnessed, while in Mackenzie's employ, the so-called type riot of 1826 in which Mackenzie's press was destroyed by a gang of young tories led by Samuel Peters Jarvis.

Two years later French won a broader measure of notice when towards midnight on 4 June two small bands of youths collided violently in the streets of York; Edward Nowlan died at the hands of French, who gave himself up to the authorities. The incident provided a platform for journalist Francis Collins to bewail the increase of 'vice and immorality' and point to possible remedies: more police, better street lighting, and a reformed House of Assembly. Mackenzie, with puritan gusto, expressed similar concerns. In 1828 muddy York had, by Mackenzie's reckoning, some 60 taverns or the like for a population of about 2,000. Along with theatres, these spots were the popular rendezvous points for many young people, including French. Here he enjoyed with his companions the town's limited pleasures, indifferent to, or unmindful of, his parents' displeasure. To them, these establishments were the haunts of 'the gay and the dissolute – the idle and the profligate – the ruffian and woman of lost fame.' Mackenzie damned them as 'hotbeds of vice and infamy.'

French was charged with murder, his companions James Pratt Goslin and William D. Forest with abetting. On 17 Oct. 1828 French was tried before judge Levius Peters Sherwood. On the request of his counsel, Simon Ebenezer Washburn, French's accomplices were to be tried separately the following week. After French's plea of innocence, Attorney General John Beverley Robinson opened the case with a 'simple history of the facts.' On the fateful night, French was at the theatre, one of his favourite pastimes (on occasion he had even appeared in minor roles). Later, having borrowed a pistol, he shot Nowlan in the streets. The central question in the trial concerned French's motivation. Was the murder done in self-defence or with malic aforethought? Robinson tried to establish that French wanted revenge on Nowlan for a past indignity and that Nowlan's actions on the evening in question had not provoked French's violent action. In his cross-examination Washburn hinted at his line of defence: French was drunk and did not know what he was doing; Nowlan was a hot-tempered, swaggering ruffian.

Defence witnesses amplified Washburn's argument. Concerning Nowlan's reputation, which Robinson did not challenge, there was no doubt: Nowlan was a hard-drinking, 'stout powerful man,' 'a noted bully' whose character was bad. On the other hand, French was a small, 'very inoffensive young man,' antagonized by a quarrelsome lout who had threatened him. Pre-trial publicity had underscored French's mental problems. Washburn's witnesses depicted him as simple-minded, given to fits of insanity, and at times suicidal. Robinson countered by drawing from Mackenzie the more qualified statement that French was not 'entirely insane'; rather he was 'not of as sound mind as others.' Weak of intellect he may have been, Robinson observed, but he knew right from wrong: his testimony, for instance, in the type riot trial had been accepted in court. Finally, French himself addressed the jury – rather inadvisedly, Collins thought, for the effect was to raise doubt about his supposed insanity.

The jury deliberated about an hour before finding French guilty. Sherwood then addressed the prisoner, noting that vice had led to his downfall and imploring him to seek mercy in the hereafter. 'The blood of your victim,' Sherwood emphasized, 'demands retribution.' French was sentenced to be hanged and then dissected on the 20th, but the judge respited execution until the 23rd in the event that the trials of Goslin and Forest had any bearing on French's case.

The trial had caused much excitement and generated a good deal of sympathy for French. Indeed, within hours of his conviction, some 1,100 men signed a petition urging royal clemency. After the acquittals of Goslin and Forest, Lieutenant Governor Sir Peregrine Maitland, always punctilious about capital cases, required Sherwood to report on the possibility of clemency for French. The judge indicated that, although the accomplices' trials did not affect French, affidavits which had been sworn by them after their acquittals might. In particular, the new information challenged the crucial crown argument that Nowlan had not made a threatening gesture to French before he was shot. Sherwood concluded that 'the Jury might have found French guilty of Manslaughter only.' An emergency meeting of the Executive Council was convened at 5 A.M. on the 23rd: present were Maitland, James Baby, Peter Robinson, and James Buchanan Macaulay. Sherwood was questioned about the importance of the new evidence. He responded equivocally and attempted to shift the burden of the decision to the council. Prodded further about whether the affidavits warranted another respite and a recommendation for mercy, Sherwood replied affirmatively, reiterating, however, that it was not his decision. The council adjourned, directing him to compare Goslin's original deposition to the coroner with his later affidavit and to confer with judge Christopher Alexander Hagerman. Sherwood found contradictions between the two documents and, for reasons known only to himself, considered the deposition to have 'more credit.' He thus sealed French's fate. Lacking legal cause for mercy, the council 'felt it their painful but incumbent duty to advise His Excellency that the Law should be allowed to take its course.' Maitland concurred.

At 2:30 P.M. on the same day, attended by clergymen Thomas Phillips and William Ryerson, French was led to the gallows and executed. In the days previous he had spent much time with these men and the Reverend John Saltkill Carroll preparing for his end with an equanimity that Carroll felt bordered on eagerness. He had prepared a gallows address which was read by Ryerson and later published by Mackenzie. In it he upheld the justness of his conviction and sentence, blaming 'bad company and drinking' for his unhappy fate. Urging the young to avoid vice and ruin, he enjoined them to accept the 'wholesome restraints' of parental discipline 'for their present as well as eternal good.' After his death, a few perfunctory incisions were made upon his body in accordance with the sentence. He was then sewn up and given a 'decent private funeral' in the Presbyterian burial ground.

On the cultural level, the effect of French's case was the suspension of popular theatre in York for about five years. The political controversy attached to the case, then and since, stems from French's failure to gain a pardon. Carroll recalled that Nowlan was 'a reputed bully for the "Compact"' and that 'there were too many and powerful influences in the Council against the prisoner's life.' John Ross Robertson believed that Robinson and John Strachan had 'refused' mercy. Mackenzie's biographer, Charles Lindsey, was more explicit. French had been a 'marked man' for testifying at the type trial. Nowlan, 'as savage as a gorilla and twice as vicious,' was the man 'who undertook to execute vengeance.'

Thus emerged the story that the 'family compact' was unwilling to save one of Mackenzie's employees, a witness to the type riot and a victim of a tory bully-boy. As such, it is of a piece with the charges of partiality hurled by opposition critics against Maitland and Robinson. The main objects of the denunciation have long been familiar: the persecution of Robert Randal, the dismissal of judge John Walpole Willis, and the so-called outrages against John Matthews and William Forsyth. French's execution ranks with such lesser-known incidents as the tarring and feathering of George Rolph and the trial of Michael Vincent. These incidents contributed to the erosion of public trust in the judicial system but, in French's case, surviving documents dissipate the air of villainy present in the popular account. There was no evident animus in Robinson's prosecution or in the council's deliberations. Everything seems to have been proper and above-board. Whether or not manslaughter would have been the more appropriate charge was a question requiring an assumption of judicial responsibility of which Sherwood was incapable.

ROBERT L. FRASER

BENAJAH MALLORY

Colonizer, businessman, militia officer, politician, justice of the peace, and army officer; b. *c.* 1764 in the American colonies; m. first Abia Dayton, and they had five children; m. secondly Sally Bush, and they had no children; d. 9 Aug. 1853 in Lockport, N.Y.

Benajah Mallory may have been the son of Ogden Mallory, an early settler of Wells, Vt, where Benajah was living at the outbreak of the American revolution. He later enlisted in the local militia as a private and saw action in several battles. According to American historian Orasmus Turner, Mallory was the 'first merchant' in the Genesee country of western New York State. He settled in the community founded there in the late 1780s by the followers of Jemima Wilkinson. He was drawn, no doubt, by an 'anticipated' connection to the daughter of one of the sect's prominent members, though Mallory apparently never shared the religious tenets of the group. In 1792 he was listed as an ensign in the Ontario County militia. His father-in-law, Abraham Dayton, was interested in obtaining the grant of a township in Upper Canada near the Grand River lands of the Six Nations. In 1795 he and his associates, including Mallory, settled in Burford Township. Within a year Mallory had built a house and established a tan-yard, 'at a great expence with other Improvements.' Bedridden from the outset, Dayton died in 1797. Mallory assumed the leadership of the small community of 21 settlers and went to 'much Expence towards opening and settling' the township. He hastened to report his intention to bring the number of settlers above the 40 required under the terms of the grant. It was, however, to no avail. Lieutenant Governor John Graves Simcoe had become disenchanted with his experimental system of making township grants, and his successor, Administrator Peter Russell, was determined to rescind them. The Burford Township grant reverted to the crown, but actual settlers were individually confirmed in their lands: Mallory was granted 1,200 acres and his wife was recommended for 200.

Within a regional population of nondescript, semi-literate, non-loyalist Americans, Mallory stood out. He had only cleared 15 acres by 1798, but he was a leader with both ambition and ability. During the reorganization of the region's militia that year Surveyor General David William Smith successfully recommended him for the captaincy of a local company. Mallory's immediate interest, however, was land speculation, particularly within Burford Township. His claim to a lease of lands owned by the Six Nations occasioned a complaint to Smith by Joseph Brant [Thayendanegea] early in 1798. By late 1801 Mallory had acquired stills, which he seems to have leased for some time since he did not possess a licence. On 2 April 1802 he took out a recognizance to maintain order in 'his house of public entertainment.' Soon after, he purchased 560 acres in Burford, an acquisition financed by mortgaging the property to the Kingston merchant Richard Cartwright. Lord Selkirk [Douglas], who visited Mallory in 1803, described him as possessing a 'good frame house' and 'a large stock of Cattle – 50 head or more.' Mallory claimed at that time to have contracted to supply army garrisons with fresh beef and had sent 'last year or before 20,000 lb from his own stock.'

He had thus reinforced his early prominence with economic prosperity. The establishment of the London District in 1800 necessitated the appointment of local officials. For the most part, the positions went to loyalist officers such as Samuel Ryerse and Thomas Welch, rather than to the non-loyalist, largely Methodist Americans who comprised the majority of the new district's population. In May 1802 Smith had recommended Mallory to Ryerse as a likely candidate for the magistracy. Ryerse, 'not being well acquainted with him myself,' soon learned of two incidents that did not reflect 'much honor on his character.' In one case, Mallory had apparently demanded payment to divulge information relating to a robbery; in the second, he had, again apparently, arranged the robbery of one of his creditors, who was anxious to collect on a note. For his part, Mallory had become disenchanted with the officers of the local courts. In December 1802 he complained to Welch, clerk of the district court, about Welch's fees on suits filed by Mallory; at the same time, he criticized the fees taken by the judge, Ryerse. Criticism of this sort was a justifiable and common complaint, especially among small merchants and farmers. But Welch had obviously detected an unsettling quality in Mallory's charges; in his response, he offered the hope that 'you do not mean ... to advance your Popularity by impeaching the Conduct of the Judge of this District, and his Clerk.' Such a course, he suggested, would be inconsistent with the conduct of the 'Religious, the Humane Capt. Mallory.'

Surveyor General Smith was the dominant influence in the area. His decision not to seek re-election to the House of Assembly opened the way for a formal political challenge to the office-holding élite. Mallory and Ryerse contested the riding of Norfolk, Oxford and Middlesex. In May 1804 Selkirk commented, 'Electioneering seems here to go on with no small sharpness – his [Mallory's] adversaries threw out some allegations to which he replied by the Lie direct – and he alledges they pursued him with a view to assassinate.' Mallory's victory, 166 votes to 77, only exacerbated factional strife, which soon erupted in the Court of Quarter Sessions. After shots had been fired into his home in January 1805, Mallory claimed the attempted assassination to be the work of Ryerse or John Backhouse, a justice of the peace; Ryerse, in turn, implied that Mallory had had the shooting staged. The affair degenerated into a skein of charge and countercharge, which spilled over from quarter sessions into the Court of King's Bench, where ultimately the affair came to naught.

The unruliness of local life developed from concrete criticisms of the administration of the district's courts. In a small society, concern about such issues quickly acquired a personal dimension. When factionalism escalated into the political arena, the lines of division broadened. Thomas Welch denounced the Mallory-led group as seditious – Methodists bent on subverting 'good Order.' He noted that one of them had announced that Upper Canada would become 'a very good Country after we have adriven out of it all the old Tories and Half Pay officers, and have a new Constitution like that of the United States.'

Mallory's initial impact on the assembly was negligible; he was, at best, a secondary figure. His support of William Weekes's motion of 1 March 1805 to consider 'the disquietude which prevails ... by reason of the administration of Public Offices' indicated his attraction to the fragmentary opposition in parliament. In the session of 1806 he brought up a petition for the relief of Methodists in their want of full enjoyment of civil and religious rights. More important to him was Ryerse's charge that he had been 'illegally and unduly returned,' being 'a preacher and teacher of the Religious Society or Sect called Methodists.' In 1807 the charge was dismissed by the assembly for want of evidence: Ryerse had simply been unable to marshal his witnesses in York (Toronto). Some, however, such as Richard Cartwright, who was then a legislative councillor, claimed the charge was true.

Mallory had finally become a justice of the peace in December 1806; he was, as well, a captain in the 1st Oxford Militia. But he was identified with political opposition and symbolized the political beliefs frequently associated with the American settlers, whom Lieutenant Governor Francis Gore described as retaining 'those ideas of equality & insubordination much to the prejudice of this Government.' Welch claimed that nine out of ten settlers in Oxford County were Americans. The *Chesapeake* affair of 1807 led him to believe that, in the event of war with the United States, these people would become 'internal enemies' and were therefore 'very much to be dreaded.' When in 1808 leadership of the opposition within the assembly passed to Joseph Willcocks, Mallory became much more active in the day-to-day activities of the house and increasingly supported Willcocks's initiatives. He disagreed with Willcocks, however, on such issues as the bill to give salaries to judges in the Court of Common Pleas, which, although favourites of the opposition, were unpopular in the London District. Mallory was the sole opponent of an amendment to the District School Act because the 'inhabitants were much dissatisfied with the law as it now stood.'

In 1808 he was re-elected for Oxford and Middlesex. Throughout the fifth parliament (1809–12) the opposition became more cohesive. By 1811 Mallory was, with John Willson, one of Willcocks's foremost supporters. They worked together on a range of measures popular with the opposition; they unsuccessfully attempted, for example, to pass a bill restraining sheriffs from packing juries and another preventing government officials from sitting in the assembly. They co-operated too in adopting potentially popular positions on other measures: they opposed the bill to relieve creditors with absconding debtors, voted to reconsider the state of loyalist and military grants, and opposed changes to the Militia Act of 1793. On the one hand, it seems probable that Mallory was politicized by his career as an assemblyman. On the other, he himself felt harassed by members of a vindictive provincial administration. On 15 Jan. 1807 Richard Cartwright had won a massive judgement against Mallory for debt – £1,887 17s. 0d. and costs. No doubt the judgement had an effect on Mallory, for the following year he sought a lease of Six Nations land where he had discovered iron ore and planned to build an ironworks.

He eventually leased about 1,460 acres, but nothing was erected. In 1810–11 he lost three cases involving debts, one for a staggering £1,000 and costs, and two parcels of his land were seized and sold to pay his debt to Cartwright. He was referred to in one case as 'late of Burford, now a merchant and farmer.' In 1810 he was acquitted of assaulting a sheriff. Mallory later claimed it had cost him 'near' $2,000 just to defend himself; financially, he was ruined.

The greatest success of the opposition in the assembly occurred in early 1812 when Administrator Isaac Brock attempted to put the province on a war footing. The resistance to changes in the Militia Act (notably the opposition's refusal to see an oath of abjuration incorporated in the act) was attributed to Willcocks and Mallory. Robert Nichol reported in March 1812 that their efforts 'to create apprehensions respecting the intended operation of the Militia Bill' had produced much alarm among young men at the head of Lake Ontario. A frustrated Brock dissolved parliament in May, hoping to secure, as Archibald McLean put it, a new assembly 'composed of well informed Men who are well *affected* to the Government.'

The old élite had withered in the face of popular opposition. In the ensuing election Mallory was opposed by Mahlon Burwell, a close associate of Thomas Talbot, whose base of power was rooted in what amounted to a personal fiefdom. This alliance was determined to bring Mallory to heel. Years later Asahel Bradley Lewis alleged that the hustings for Oxford and Middlesex in 1812 had been located in 'an *entire wilderness*. So that Mallory and his friends were obliged to travel nearly 60 miles through the woods, to the poll, – there they found the "*Father of the Settlement*" [Talbot], providing votes for his favourite ... by furnishing all who were willing to support the claims of the Young Aspirant to office, and who were not already qualified – with LOCATION TICKETS.' Mallory derided this tactic as 'the most blackest and unConstitutional Designs' and urged electors to 'Repell oppression accompanied with tyreney.' His effort, however, proved futile and Burwell was returned.

Disaffection and treason are among the major themes of the War of 1812 and its effect upon Upper Canada. The population was overwhelmingly non-loyalist American; most, probably, were indifferent to the outcome. Some, such as Michael Smith, returned to the United States while others, Ebenezer Allan and Andrew Westbrook among them, were immediately seditious; a few, such as Elijah Bentley, sought the most propitious moment to declare their real loyalty. But the most sensational cases – Willcocks, Mallory, and Abraham Markle – fall into none of these categories. Each man had had a record of political opposition, but only in the summer of 1813 did any one of the three become actively disloyal. Their treason then has to be understood in the light of changes taking place within the province at that time rather than by interpreting treason as the logical outcome of persistent opposition. Brock had used both Willcocks and Mallory as emissaries to the Six Nations; moreover, Willcocks had served at the battle of Queenston Heights in 1812. In 1829 Francis Collins referred in the *Canadian Freeman* to a statement made in the assembly by Robert Nichol that Willcocks had been 'forced from his allegiance by a vile conspiracy against his life.' Collins reported that this 'assertion was supposed by many' to mean the actions of Judge William Dummer Powell. Like Willcocks and Markle, Mallory could argue that he too had been persecuted, but by none other than Nichol. At some point early in 1812 Mallory protested to Brock that 'many caluminous reports has been advanced to you by a mr Robert Nicol and Some of his Coagiters loath against my Private and Public Character.' The reports had accused him of disloyalty, of attending 'Public Meetings for bad Purposes,' and of having been prosecuted. Mallory denounced the charge of disloyalty but admitted that he had indeed been prosecuted. To him, however, the court actions, both civil and criminal, were tangible evidence of a persecution that had begun after his election in 1804. His public record as a magistrate and militia officer could not be impugned. He had, he said, encouraged the militia to adhere to the crown and offered to lead them 'to Repel the Ravages or intrusion of an invading Enemy.' But he was never given the chance. As concern for maintaining the rule of law withered before the civil élite's fear of disorder after the American occupation of York in the spring of 1813, the three leaders of opposition, one by one, crossed the border.

Willcocks went over to the Americans in July 1813 and offered to raise a corps of expatriate Canadian volunteers 'to assist in changing the government of this province into a Republic.' Mallory may have had some prior commitment to republicanism. Certainly what had begun 10 years previously as reaction to executive maladministration of government, when combined with his perception of military despotism in the summer of 1813, made him draw upon the only rhetoric of opposition that he knew, republicanism. Such language entailed a fundamental clash with the polity of Upper Canada.

Mallory's formal enlistment as a captain in the Company of Canadian Volunteers dates from 14 November; the same day he was reported to have been seen by Major William D. Bowen with a party recruiting on the Grand River. Following the burning of Niagara (Niagara-on-the-Lake) by the Americans and their retreat to Fort Niagara (near Youngstown), N.Y., Mallory was given command at Fort Schlosser (Niagara Falls), N.Y. In late December his detachment fought a spirited rearguard action against British troops advancing south after taking Fort Niagara. Mallory's men again distinguished themselves at Black Rock (Buffalo) as the British continued their drive towards Buffalo.

Mallory was outraged by the United States Army's obstruction of local generals and its resistance to establishing Willcocks's corps as a permanent force. In spite of the opposition of superiors, he continued to recruit and paid his men from his own resources. Finally, as a result of Willcocks's lobbying in Washington, the Volunteers were put on a permanent footing and on 19 April 1814 Mallory was promoted major. During the following summer the unit saw action at the battles of Chippawa and Lundy's Lane. In mid July Mallory barely escaped capture near Beaver Dams (Thorold). Despite their effectiveness, the Volunteers were disintegrating; on 24 August Mallory sought a transfer because of a lack of recruits and a surplus of officers. He hoped to remain on the Niagara frontier where, he explained to John Armstrong, the American secretary of war, 'I have no Doubt from the Knowledge I Possess of the Country ... I can be more usefull.' Mallory urged a more aggressive military stance and the raising of 10,000 or 15,000 militia commanded by a 'few Patriots.' He was convinced that Americans now saw the 'necessity of Exterminating British and Savage tyranny from the Demain of Canada I am Sattisfied our effort will be the Last Struggle of the British in Canada.'

A transfer, however, was not forthcoming. Willcocks died in September and command devolved upon Mallory. He argued in vain for more arms and supplies. The Volunteers were hobbled by desertion and squabbling among the officers. On 15 November Markle and William Biggar, an ensign in the Volunteers and possibly Markle's son-in-law, charged Mallory with embezzlement and felonious conduct. He was suspended and Markle took command. Mallory attributed the accusations to 'Malevolence and black Designs Proceeding from a black heart.' The corps was disbanded on 3 March 1815 although Mallory continued to serve in the army in some capacity until 31 July.

In Upper Canada, Mallory had been convicted of treason at Ancaster in 1814 and his lands were later vested in the crown. He had sacrificed, as he put it, 'both family & property.' According to Joel Stone, his mother-in-law's second husband, Mallory had joined the Americans 'without the Knowledge or assent of his wife who was left in Canada with a family of five children.' She remained 'sincere – as to her Congugal vows' and later 'followed him when Sent for.' Mallory eventually settled in Lockport. On 1 Jan. 1829 a notice in York in the *Canadian Freeman* reported that he 'has since figured in the Newspapers of his country as an adept in the art of converting the property of others to his own use, for which accomplishment he has been honoured with lodgings in a State Prison.' A letter of 28 March 1832 in the *Western Mercury* reported that Mallory, 'one of the basest of the human race,' was 'now lingering out his wretched existence in prison.' His wife remained with him throughout, struggling to support their family, 'until she found that her said Husband ... was,' according to Joel Stone, 'if possible more criminally traitorous to herself than he had been ... capable of being to both Governments.' She renounced him and returned to Upper Canada with her two youngest daughters to live with Stone and her mother in Gananoque. Early in January 1838 Mallory offered his services to William Lyon Mackenzie and 'the brave Patriots' on Navy Island. He drew a parallel between the traitors of 1813 and the rebels of 1837: he 'had once Suffred from my takeing the Same Stand In the british Parliament in opposing dispotic tyrants.' Mallory later remarried and was baptized in Lockport in July 1853. He died there a month later.

ROBERT L. FRASER

JOHN MATTHEWS
Politician; b. probably in England; d. 20 Aug. 1832, perhaps in England.

John Matthews's accounts of his youth hint at a genteel background. He claimed attendance at an English college in Paris and attended, some time after 1779, the Royal Military Academy, Woolwich (London). He served in the Royal Artillery for 27 years until his battalion's reduction in March 1819, when he retired on a pension with the rank of captain. His period of active service was not continuous, though: at some point during the Napoleonic Wars he took up farming 'to retrieve the reduced condition of my family,' only to be ruined by the agricultural crisis that followed the peace. He then rejoined his battalion for the sake of the pay until its disbandment 18 months later, when he emigrated to Canada.

Matthews reached Quebec shortly before the death of the governor-in-chief, the Duke of Richmond [Lennox], in August 1819. He presented himself to Richmond's son-in-law Sir Peregrine Maitland, lieutenant governor of Upper Canada, as an old friend of the duke's and claimed to have come out upon Richmond's promise to put him in charge of a planned military colony. He sought Maitland's aid in settling in Upper Canada and established himself temporarily near Queenston.

Maitland was willing to help, but Matthews proved hard to please and their relationship soon soured. The lieutenant governor successively recommended sites on Lake Simcoe and Rice Lake. Matthews refused these, while asking for an assortment of locations, all of which were either reserved or pre-empted. At last he was summoned before the Executive Council and pressed to accept an 800-acre estate on the Thames River in Lobo Township.

Matthews, his family, and servants proceeded to Lobo in October 1820, forming a train of 'nearly thirty persons ... six waggons, one cart, twenty-four horses, a flock of sheep, and some cows.' As soon as he arrived, he let the government know of his disappointment. He had sold his British properties at a loss of 1,000 guineas in order to speed to Richmond's side, and had been rewarded with stony oak-plains worth a dollar an acre. 'This, Sir, certainly was not the sort of service the Duke proposed or intended to render me.' He feared that Maitland's good intentions were thwarted by influences with which the lieutenant governor could not contend. This was the first murmur of a theme that was to become a staple of Matthews's political discourse.

Matthews now began to covet the estates of a neighbour, the magistrate Daniel Springer, whom he accused of enlarging his holdings by force and fraud. He dropped these charges when told that Springer's allegedly fraudulent claims had been certified by Thomas Talbot, the aristocratic patriarch of the London District, but he continued to pursue the magistrate with charges of official and personal misconduct. A series of letters harped on Springer's indolence, drunkenness, rapacity, and deceit; on his reputed paternity of his associate in villainy, deputy surveyor Roswell Mount; and even, once, on the 'unfortunate condition' of his eldest daughter (a misfortune to which Matthews, with daughters of his own, was no doubt especially sensitive).

Matthews also began feuding with the commissioners for forfeited estates and their secretary, James Buchanan Macaulay, over two lots they had sold him. In one case they had given him a title-deed to a different lot from the one he claimed to have purchased; in the other they were simply unable to supply an adequate deed. In the second case Maitland supported Matthews, while chiding him for his insolence towards the commissioners. The lieutenant governor asked the commissioners to refund the purchase price, but to his chagrin they refused when advised by Solicitor General Henry John Boulton that they had no legal power to do so. Boulton at once was added to Matthews's list of enemies, as was Attorney General John Beverley Robinson for failing to take seriously the charges against Springer. 'There is a jealous connexion of friendship, of family, and of interest throughout the province,' Matthews told Maitland in 1822, 'and under those circumstances every thing I say is misrepresented, and every thing I do is misconceived with a boldness truly astonishing.' His calumniators were encouraged, he wrote, by the knowledge that he was not in Maitland's favour.

Matthews's denunciations of Springer, and his themes of oligarchic misrule and a local usurpation of power, found ready credence among those of his neighbours who felt similarly aggrieved. He made himself the spokesman of these malcontents, including even the local Indians, and enlarged his constituency by espousing the sectional interests of northern Middlesex County. At the general election of 1824 he and John Rolph ousted the sitting members for Middlesex, Mahlon Burwell and John Bostwick, both of whom enjoyed the favour of Talbot. Talbot reported to Major George Hillier, Maitland's civil secretary, that Matthews had been supported 'by all the Old Country and Yankee Radicals.'

A few months later, Talbot had to write to Hillier again. Matthews had taken witnesses to the London District assizes of September 1824 in order to complain of Springer to the grand jury. The resulting presentment apparently persuaded the government that an inquiry was desirable. Talbot advised that the inquiry be confided to three reliable men (whom he named) rather than to the district magistracy as a whole, since most of the magistrates would 'lean to Matthews.' Talbot urged Hillier to discuss his advice only with Maitland and Robinson, 'as I am desirous of not appearing in these dirty works.'

The incident for which Matthews is especially remembered happened on the last day of 1825. In the evening he was among a group of assemblymen who attended a theatrical performance by an American company. While the actors got ready, the musicians played popular airs, starting with 'God Save the King!' and 'Rule, Britannia!' Various members of the assembly competed in calling for a Jacobite song, 'Hail, Columbia!' and 'Yankee Doodle.' That day the assembly, agitated by Robinson's Naturalization Bill, had passed resolutions which humiliated the provincial government by rejecting the official view that post-loyalist American immigrants were aliens. One or two pro-government members took it in bad part when there was a call for 'Yankee Doodle.' A reformer's attempt to remove a tory's cap sparked a momentary scuffle, but the play then proceeded without further fuss.

It was a trifling incident and Matthews did not figure in it with special prominence. Three months later, however, he was officially apprised that Lord Dalhousie [Ramsay], Richmond's successor as governor-in-chief, had read in the newspapers that Matthews and others 'had in a riotous and outrageous manner called for the national tunes and songs of the United States ... urging the audience then assembled to take off their hats, as is usual in the British dominions in honour of the national air of "God Save the King."' Finding these rumours 'fully corroborated,' Dalhousie intended to report the incident to the commander-in-chief of the army but wished to permit

Matthews to transmit through Maitland 'any explanations that may palliate (if possible) such report of his conduct.'

Matthews protested that he had evidently been condemned unheard. There had been nothing 'riotous or outrageous' about the incident; 'it was all fun and frolic.' The construction his traducers put upon it 'must have originated in paltry political vexations, and in great baseness and malignity of Heart.' He did acknowledge, though, that the political events of the day had coloured those of the evening. In forwarding Matthews's reply, Maitland seized on this admission to present Matthews's conduct in the worst light.

In September 1826 the Board of Ordnance ordered that Matthews should return to England by the first ship of the next season, and in the mean time go at once to Quebec. This order was transmitted to him from Quebec on 8 Dec. 1826, three days after the start of the new legislative session. The House of Assembly referred the affair to a select committee, which took evidence from almost every member of the theatre audience. Its report stressed the triviality of the incident, the impossibility that Dalhousie could have obtained 'full corroboration' of misconduct that had not occurred, and the iniquity of condemning Matthews on the evidence of secret informers. It noted the impropriety of trying to place Matthews under arrest at Quebec during the parliamentary session.

Matthews's pension had been suspended, and it is commonly stated that he went to England in order to recover it and died there. In fact, it was restored without his going to England. Re-elected with Rolph in 1828 (after first declining to stand, because of ill health), he played his usual prominent role in the session of 1829 but seems to have missed that of 1830. When his wife died, in April 1830, he was reported to be in England, and he may have stayed there until his death.

Matthews was one of those post-war British immigrants to Upper Canada whose hostility to the provincial government was partly rooted in disappointment of their material expectations and a jealous contempt for the local élite. In the case of Matthews, a Unitarian, as in that of the Quaker Charles Fothergill, religious heterodoxy played a part by fostering an aversion towards the narrow Anglican orthodoxy of the provincial establishment. Matthews has been dismissed as a self-deceiving egoist, often carried away by his own inflated rhetoric, a dissipated malingerer, an advocate of paternalistic social ideals which were old-fashioned, self-contradictory, and hopelessly utopian. There are grounds for believing that these judgements underestimate him.

There is no evidence that he was more dissipated than others of his time and class. His ill health, which he traced in part to a fall from his waggon in 1820, was real enough to alarm his friends. Above all, he shows signs of too much intelligence to be written off as a political nitwit.

Matthews's was in fact a more complex personality than at first appears, and his paternalist rhetoric may at once represent a sincere commitment to the ideal and a satiric comment on society's failure to achieve it. One clue to his complexity is his outspoken Unitarianism – so inconsistent with his character as a simple old soldier – which inspired a fellow assemblyman to call him 'the Reverend John Matthews.' Another is his taste for subversive irony. When Maitland spurned his first charges against Springer, Matthews solemnly announced his conclusion that in future he should keep silent about abuses that were reported to him, 'no matter how imperiously I should feel it my duty to expose them to His Excellency.' When as an assemblyman he was invited by Maitland to dinner, he declined with the dry remark that his attendance could give pleasure to no one, but he punctiliously sent Lady Sarah Maitland (his old patron's daughter) a note regretting the circumstances that kept him from 'once more paying my humble and most dutiful respects to your Ladyship.' Even in the letter that was supposed to exonerate him from the charge of disgraceful conduct at the theatre, he characterized that day's resolutions on the alien question as a decision 'that the King had thousands more of good and excellent subjects than many of his friends were willing to allow him.' It was Matthews who presented Timothy Street's satirical petition against the Marmora Iron Works to the assembly in 1828, and he may well have had a hand in its composition.

Matthews's occasional invasions of the local Court of Requests in order to denounce the presiding magistrates suggest that his subversive instincts were allied with a politically effective sense of theatre. It is likely that this theatricality (somewhat compulsive perhaps, yet not entirely uncontrolled) pervaded his personality, and that his Falstaffian bombast and Shandean emotionalism were at least in part an affectation based on available cultural models. Matthews, in short, who owned a notable library, was more intelligent then he pretended, and his buffoonery was most likely the expression of an authentic English eccentricity rooted in social alienation.

Beneath the grease-paint, a courageous determination is evident in the relentlessness with which, in letter after letter to Maitland, he vilified enemies who enjoyed the lieutenant governor's confidence. 'Captain Matthews is violent,' observed William Lyon Mackenzie in 1828, 'but he is a tower of strength to the people in the Assembly.' 'Matthews political character is of the manly cast,' commented a neutral observer, 'for he has always acted as he said he would.' Certainly Maitland and Talbot were not inclined to dismiss him as a clown. By subverting the established order in Middlesex he had proved himself one of the most dangerous men in the colony.

Here is the essential context for evaluating his treatment in 1826. It is inconceivable that the incident at the theatre came to Dalhousie's attention without the connivance of men close to Maitland. The two known informers against Matthews were John Beikie, clerk of the Executive Council, and Charles Richardson, a law student of Robinson's who was shortly to take part in the wrecking of Mackenzie's printing-shop. Beikie by his own admission had entered the theatre midway through the incident, and his account was completely superficial and disconnected. Richardson's was prejudiced against Matthews but could not disguise the trifling nature of the incident. Both men's extant reports were written by request. Although it is impossible to say whence the initiative came, Maitland made the most of the opportunity by his own disingenuous commentary on Matthews's letter of justification and by enclosing Beikie's and Richardson's tendentious remarks on it. Like the other vindictive blows struck at this time by the government and its supporters against leading critics, this one rebounded on its perpetrators by its effect on public opinion. Its petty vengefulness was typical of Maitland and his advisers, but it also hints at the danger they perceived in Matthews.

PAUL ROMNEY

PETER PERRY

Politician and businessman; b. 14 Nov. 1792 in Ernestown (Bath), Upper Canada, youngest child of Robert Perry and Jemima Gary Washburn; m. 19 June 1814 Mary Polly Ham, and they had seven daughters and two sons; d. 24 Aug. 1851 in Saratoga Springs, N.Y., and was buried near Oshawa, Upper Canada.

The Perry family's North American history was begun by Anthony Perry, who immigrated from England to Massachusetts in 1640. Peter Perry's father, a loyalist who had moved to Vermont in 1772, served during the American revolution in the Queen's Loyal Rangers and in Jessup's Rangers, and subsequently came to Township No.2 (Ernestown). Raised on his father's farm there, Peter married a daughter of another loyalist, John Ham, and settled near by in Fredericksburgh Township.

Public involvement was not new to the Perry family; Peter's uncle Ebenezer Washburn had been an outspoken member of the House of Assembly. Peter Perry first appeared in the public life of Upper Canada in January 1819. He was one of nearly 200 men of Ernestown Township who signed an address to Lieutenant Governor Sir Peregrine Maitland disavowing the activities of Robert Gourlay and repudiating the criticism of government he had aroused, especially among recent American immigrants. That address was consistent with the loyalist political tradition which Perry had inherited and which he maintained throughout the most important years of his career. He accepted the land grants due to him as a reward for his father's decision to remain loyal and he often cited that decision as proof of his own adherence to the British constitution and the imperial connection.

But he had inherited more than loyalty. He was a North American whose family connection with the New World stretched back six generations. The appeal of the crown and the constitution were not, for him, based in any way upon the sentimental nostalgia of the newly arrived Briton. Nor was that appeal part of a tory political ideology.

He was an egalitarian democrat for whom the rights and interests of the people of Upper Canada were the primary reality. He had no fear of American influence and, while he was prepared to defend the constitution against the 'prejudices' of American-born settlers, he did not believe that they should be penalized for uttering them. Thus it was his interest in the alien question that brought him into politics.

In 1823 Perry took the lead in protesting the exclusion of Marshall Spring Bidwell from the ballot in a by-election in Lennox and Addington. On election day, it was later reported in the *Kingston Chronicle*, Perry spoke to a crowd 'from an upper window,' arguing ineffectively that the proceedings were illegal and that British subjects had been deprived of their rights. None the less, in the general election of the following year Perry, a reformer, joined Bidwell as a candidate for the county. The two men, each with American antecedents, led the polls and in January 1825 took their seats in the house. Their political partnership – an association of complementary qualities – lasted until they were both defeated 11 years later; their friendship persisted until Perry's death.

As a result of the election, the colonial assembly was divided between a small reform majority and a minority of conservatives led with consummate ability by Attorney General John Beverley Robinson. The late 1820s were among the best years for the incipient reform party as its optimistic and enthusiastic members threw themselves into the task of reorganizing colonial society. In the attempt, they developed an *esprit de corps* that led them to affirm each legislative success in the house by discarding decorum, standing, waving their hats, and cheering tumultuously.

Perry fitted well into those parliamentary sessions. He was a man with little formal education, whose speeches contained no biblical quotations or classical allusions. Blunt, occasionally emotional, and often enlivened with imaginative, if homely, references to the common experiences of the inhabitants of Upper Canada, his speeches reveal him as an aggressive, sometimes overbearing man whose emphatic sincerity about the purity of his own motives reflects a certain self-righteousness. He conceived of himself as the spokesman of the common people and the defender of their rights. They were, he said, as talented and capable as any people anywhere and needed only 'to have their paps brought out by education' in order to prove it.

When he spoke about Upper Canada, Perry had in mind primarily a society of small agricultural and, latterly, industrial producers. The people, with the farmers the most important group among them, were, he thought, the source of all political sovereignty. To express and protect their rights and interests, Upper Canadian society should, he believed, be democratic and egalitarian. He opposed, therefore, élites of all kinds and considered that the colonial government ought actively to discourage them. During the mid 1830s, for example, he spoke out against the 'great power' enjoyed by the Bank of Upper Canada and believed that bank directors in general should be required to guarantee deposits with their personal assets. When the first railways in Upper Canada were chartered in 1836 he tried to have their charters amended to allow the government to purchase them after 50 years. As well, he favoured local control over local affairs. He supported a decentralized political system with township officials elected by secret ballot. At a higher level he was willing to assert the economic and political interests of the colony over those of both Britain and the United States.

Perry's involvement in the business of the assembly after 1824 established him as an unimpeachable reformer. He moved or seconded the resolutions and voted for the bills – passed repeatedly by the house but rejected by the Legislative Council – that collectively defined the party's identity. On the alien question, he was consistently in favour of removing all restrictions on the civil status of American settlers and, indeed, wanted the colonial government to encourage additional immigration from the United States. He voted to abolish primogeniture in cases of persons dying intestate, for the abolition of imprisonment for debt, for the provision of counsel for accused felons, and for the repeal of the Sedition Act of 1804. Perry wanted to erase doubt about the independence of the judiciary by removing the colony's chief justice from the Executive Council. He was one of the minority in the house who, in the interest of taxpaying farmers, tried unsuccessfully to block government loans to the Welland Canal Company. He supported resolutions, again without success, by which control over colonial trade with the United States would be transferred from London to York (Toronto) and a protective duty on American livestock imports would be established.

Of all the issues that came before the assembly, the ones that most engaged Perry's attention were those complex questions involving the relationship of church and state. Although his family were Methodists and he had been married by a Presbyterian clergyman, Robert McDowall, Perry had no denominational affiliation. He believed in what he called 'pure and undefiled religion,' simple and basic Christianity which, ideally, would be taught by enthusiastic clergy, financially dependent upon their congregations and intent only upon the salvation of souls. It was the ecclesiastical counterpart of the egalitarian community he favoured.

What he found in Upper Canada was quite different. The establishment there of the Church of England implied a society in which religious and social inequality was guaranteed by law. Anglicans constituted an élite and from his first days in the legislature Perry set about the work of levelling their pretensions. He voted consistently for the secularization of the clergy reserves, urging that they be sold and the proceeds be applied either to internal improvements or to popular education. He supported resolutions and formulated addresses to the imperial authorities requesting that all ecclesiastics be removed from the Legislative and Executive councils. He was convinced that King's College (University of Toronto), with its exclusive charter, was intended to produce an educated oligarchy that would oppress the common people of the colony and he was, therefore, determined that the charter's objectionable features be removed. Perry had minimal success in most of these attempts at ecclesiastical reform. But there was one exception. In each session of the legislature during the late 1820s Perry was either the mover or the seconder of a bill designed to permit clergymen of every legally recognized denomination to perform the marriage ceremony. His bills were turned back by the Legislative Council until the session of 1829. The measure he proposed that year was passed by both houses and, after being reserved by Lieutenant Governor Sir John Colborne, it became law in 1831. It was the most important piece of legislation with which he was associated.

Perry was re-elected in 1828, 1830, and 1834. He was a member of the house, therefore, as the political constitution of the colony slowly began to break down. During those stormy years he was intent not on changing the constitution but on desperately striving to make it work. He accepted the result of the election of 1830, which reduced the reformers to a small group, and, unlike William Lyon Mackenzie, was able to reconcile himself to the generally conservative consequences. Throughout the sessions of the 11th parliament (1831–34), the 'glorious minority,' though outvoted scores of times, persistently criticized the proposals of the conservative majority and brought forward its own resolutions and bills, with some success. In 1831 a resolution requesting the removal of Anglican privilege from the charter of King's College was approved by a large majority. The assembly also voted to terminate the salary of its Church of England chaplain. The felon's counsel bill moved successfully through the house, and those amendments to the libel law of which reformers could approve were endorsed by the majority; neither measure, however, received royal assent at that time. In 1834, when confronted by possible imperial disallowance of recent banking legislation, the members voted almost unanimously for a resolution, moved by Bidwell and seconded by Perry, that unambiguously asserted colonial autonomy against imperial interference. There were other minor victories.

Put together with the reformers' triumph in the election of 1834, these successes allowed Perry at times to be mildly optimistic about the progress of reform. Nevertheless, it is quite clear that by 1835 the political constitution of Upper Canada was close to collapse. The balanced constitution of the colony could only operate properly in an atmosphere of moderation, in which divisive issues were avoided and cooperation among the three branches (elected assembly, appointed legislative council, and lieutenant governor) was made possible. What developed instead was political polarization that culminated in a crisis in the spring of 1836, precipitated when Robert Baldwin and the rest of the Executive Council resigned in protest over actions by the new lieutenant governor, Sir Francis Bond Head.

One source of that polarization was the conflict between William Lyon Mackenzie and the conservative majority in the assembly. Mackenzie posed serious problems for Perry. On the one hand, he and Mackenzie had similar ideas about the kind of society that ought to be established in Upper Canada. There was, therefore, a broad range of legislative matters on which they could cooperate. Moreover, from the time of Mackenzie's first expulsion in 1831 until parliament was dissolved in 1834, Perry and Bidwell defended Mackenzie in the house on numerous occasions and urged the angry members to moderate their treatment of him. In the session of 1835 not only did Perry vote to have the record of the expulsions expunged from the *Journal* of the house but he also declared that it ought to be publicly burned by the common hangman.

Nevertheless, Perry ultimately dissociated himself from Mackenzie. One reason was the latter's lack of moderation, his uncompromising intransigence. That was what Perry referred to when he remarked that he and Bidwell disapproved of Mackenzie's 'occasional violence.'

There was another reason. Mackenzie was all too willing to depart from the British constitution. Perry was as dedicated to reform as Mackenzie but he was convinced that it could be achieved within the established constitutional framework. He could not, therefore, accept Mackenzie's suggestion that the Legislative Council be made elective. To do so would be to modify seriously the constitution that his father had sacrificed 'all but life' to defend. When he considered the question during the session of 1835, as chairman of a select committee on the Legislative and Executive councils, he carefully avoided recommending the extension of the elective principle to the upper chamber. To resolve the impasse between the two houses, he urged only that the imperial authorities change the composition of the Legislative Council.

By the time the session of 1836 had begun, Perry had ceased thinking about the upper house and had turned instead to a version of responsible government. In a proposed amendment to the reply to the speech from the throne, he took up the notion that the British constitution operated imperfectly in the colony. He drew a contrast between the convention in London, by which councillors were 'only such men as enjoy the confidence of the people, expressed through their representatives,' and the practice in Upper Canada, where positions of 'trust, honor or emolument,' from executive councillors to militia officers, were 'bestowed on persons belonging to a particular party in politics.' That, Perry said, directly contravened the constitution.

When the assembly rejected his amendment in favour of a more general statement, Perry did not pursue the matter. But when the Executive Council resigned on Saturday, 12 March, he seized upon the issue again. On Monday he immediately moved the preparation of an address to Head affirming approval in principle of a responsible Executive Council and requesting information on the resignations. The lieutenant governor's reply and related documents were laid before the assembly two days later and again Perry forced events. He moved the creation of a committee, of which he would be chairman, to report on the information the house had received. On the next day he also introduced a motion declaring an 'entire want of confidence' in the four new councillors whom Head had appointed: William Allan, Angustus Warren Baldwin, John Elmsley, and Robert Baldwin Sullivan.

Perry presented his report on 15 April and after a long debate the house voted to accept it on the 18th. His solution to the crisis was, essentially, to extend the whole British constitution to Upper Canada. That would involve a system in which the lieutenant governor would be required to appoint executive councillors who had the confidence of the assembly, to consult with them on all important questions, and to follow their advice. In effect, as his critics immediately pointed out, Perry claimed colonial sovereignty over all local affairs. Given his loyalist background and his repeated insistence that he wished to maintain the imperial connection, the conclusion he reached in 1836 demands explanation.

What seems to lie at the bottom of it was that Perry did not see the crisis primarily as one involving an antithesis between colonial interest and imperial authority. He conceived of the crisis as an internal one precipitated by the aggressive behaviour of the executive branch of government. He cited two examples of the way in which the lieutenant governors had acted irrespective of popular wishes: patronage appointments and the creation of rectories as endowments for Anglican clergymen. Moreover, Head had informed the house that, in so far as the colony was concerned, he intended to retain total freedom of action in the future. Within the context of the balanced constitution, Perry saw those actions and that claim as despotism. He turned to the idea of responsibility as a means of restoring the balance and, like his 17th-century counterparts in the British parliament, recommended that the supplies be withheld.

Although Perry welcomed the election of 1836 – in fact he challenged Head to call it – he and Bidwell lost their seats to the conservatives John Solomon Cartwright and George Hill Detlor. By that time Perry had accumulated an impressive list of political liabilities. Like Mackenzie, he had broken with Egerton Ryerson and probably lost the support of some Methodists. He was accused in the Kingston press of using his political position to secure for himself and his friends appointments to government positions which the assembly intended to create. Perry was also an extensive speculator in loyalist land rights and had been a leader in the assembly in attempting to have the requirement of settlement duties removed from them. As well, despite his attempts to distance himself from Mackenzie – Perry voted against the adoption of the *Seventh report on grievances* in 1836 – the association between them remained too close for many. Similarly, the vigour of his denunciation of Head as a deliberate liar and a tyrant who would place 'a yoke of despotism' on Upper Canada, was seen by the Kingston *Chronicle & Gazette* as an insult to the crown and a danger to the imperial connection.

There was another factor in the reaction against Perry which was of greater importance and was, moreover, largely beyond his control. When he and Bidwell had been first elected, the Bay of Quinte area was the most settled and prosperous region of the colony. By the mid 1830s, however, the rapid development of the western part of the province had made it appear a backwater. No politician could do much to improve those circumstances and the situation was made even more damaging politically when it was argued in the *Chronicle & Gazette* in 1834 that new settlers avoided the Quinte region because of its American reputation, the eradication of which demanded the defeat of Perry and Bidwell.

After the election Perry withdrew from public life. There were rumours that he would return but in fact he had decided to leave Lennox and Addington to pursue another career. By the fall of 1836 he had moved to Whitby Township, on the north shore of Lake Ontario, and had begun business as a general merchant. The location was an excellent choice. Its most attractive feature was the harbour at Windsor Bay and Perry was fully aware of its potential; in 1831 it had been made a port of entry. Government engineers reported in 1835 that if improved, Windsor harbour would be the best facility between Toronto and Kingston. In the spring 1836, a few days before he presented his final constitutional report, Perry personally guided legislation through the house that provided £9,000 to pay for improvements to the site. The bill died, however, when Head dissolved parliament and called an election. For a few months in the spring and summer of 1838 Perry may have seriously considered moving to the United States. At that time he was one of a group of reformers who organized the Mississippi Emigration Society; he was, in fact, chosen to act as its president. But a large-scale exodus from Upper Canada failed to materialize and in the end he decided to remain in Whitby Township.

Perry's business prospects were based on the capacity of the harbour to handle the commercial traffic of the extensive area to the north, at least as far as Lake Simcoe. By the 1840s, to exploit that traffic, Perry had constructed warehouses with access to the government wharf. The centre of his enterprise was the general store located slightly north of the port in the village of Windsor (Whitby), which became known as Perry's Corners. He also possessed a store at Port Perry, at the western end of Lake Scugog. In the mid 1840s Perry took the leadership in persuading the government to take over and improve the road from Windsor harbour to Lake Scugog. This Centre Line road was essential because it would direct the traffic of the northern area through Windsor rather than its rival, Oshawa.

Not only was the road built, but in 1850, acting on behalf of a company he had organized, Perry purchased the road from the government along with the harbour facilities at Windsor Bay at a price that was less than half of the original cost. With those components in place, he might well have been optimistic about his commercial future. During the late 1840s Windsor harbour handled a larger volume of traffic than any other Canadian port on Lake Ontario except Toronto and Kingston. But when Perry died in 1851, his personal financial situation seemed precarious. Although he had provided for his family, his will recorded debts of about £10,000 with virtually no assets with which to satisfy them. Perhaps the costs of establishing his enterprise, especially the purchase price of the road and harbour, were more than his resources could absorb.

Although Perry left public life in 1836, he did retain a connection with politics. Throughout the 1840s he worked in the reform interest in the riding to which he had moved, 3rd York. Consistent with his position in 1836, his immediate objective appeared to be the same as that of the reform party, a system of responsible government. To achieve it he was willing to accept the leadership of Robert Baldwin. Indeed, as the election of 1844 approached, he tried to persuade Baldwin to be the riding's candidate. When he declined, Perry threw his influence behind James Edward Small, and four years later worked on behalf of William Hume Blake. In fact, Blake, who did not appear in the riding during the campaign, seems to have owed his election largely to Perry's influence in Whitby Township.

Yet, by the fall of 1849, Perry was in the process of breaking with the reform majority. Although he left no testimony about his reason, his career surely reveals it. He was a North American for whom the interests of the people of Upper Canada were paramount. Those interests, he thought, would best be served by the establishment of a democratic and egalitarian society. But until the late 1840s Perry pursued that goal within the structure of the British constitution. His expectations of the new system of responsible government, however, were far more radical than those of the Baldwinite reformers. The performance of the ministry of Baldwin and Louis-Hippolyte La Fontaine during the sessions of 1848 and 1849, therefore, must have been a bitter disappointment to him. When Blake resigned his seat in late 1849, Perry accepted the nomination in the ensuing by-election. He did so on a platform that could not be approved by the reform party leadership. By the fall of 1849 Perry had become a republican and he refused, despite pressure from Baldwin, Francis Hincks, and George Brown, to declare himself opposed in principle to annexation. Nevertheless, his election campaign was successful and at the convention in Markham in March 1850, he publicly abandoned the British constitution and emerged as one of the leading Clear Grits.

Perry, however, had little time left to work for radical reform. Severely ill in the spring of 1850, he was unable to take his seat in the legislature until early July and even after that his attendance was irregular. His voting record and the resolutions he introduced, notably on the Municipal Corporations Act, reveal his clear opposition to the reform leaders. When the session came to a close in early August, he had achieved little – even a bill he moved which would have created a new county, Ontario, with Whitby as its municipal centre, was refused second reading.

It was his last session. By the spring of 1851 he was again drastically ill. There was a brief recovery in early summer which allowed him to regain sufficient strength for a visit to Marshall Spring Bidwell in New York City. But, before he could return, he died at Saratoga Springs on 24 August.

H.E. TURNER

ROBERT RANDAL
(before about 1809 he signed Randall)
Businessman and politician; b. c. 1766 probably in Harford County, Md; probably unmarried, he had a daughter by Deborah Pettit; d. 2 May 1834 at Gravelly Bay, Niagara District, Upper Canada.

Some secondary sources make Robert Randal a Virginian, but the earliest and best evidence traces him to Harford County in northeastern Maryland. Little is known of him before 1795, when he achieved notoriety as the first person cited for contempt for trying to bribe members of the United States Congress. In September 1795, Randal and two Vermonters had joined seven Detroit merchants, including John Askin and William Robertson, in a partnership to buy the lower Michigan peninsula, now to be open for American settlers, from the United States government. The associates planned to sell their scheme not only by bribing federal legislators with shares in the land but also by urging that, because Major-General Anthony Wayne had not effectually cowed the Indians in the battle of Fallen Timbers, the influence of the Detroit merchants with them was needed to persuade them to surrender their territory.

Randal and his American associates set about lobbying congressmen, Randal indiscreetly enough to be cited for contempt. Apart from the attempted bribery, several legislators took offence at Randal's private claims that 30 or 40 congressmen had already joined in and only a few more were needed. Randal claimed in his defence that he had not thought his proposals improper since the scheme would benefit the public, and complaisant legislators were not to receive any special consideration but merely to take part in the purchase on the same terms as the partners. His punishment was confined to a reprimand and a few days in custody.

When he visited Upper Canada in 1795, Randal had had other business dealings. Lieutenant Governor John Graves Simcoe had recently granted John McGill and Benjamin Canby a 999-year lease of a prime four-acre mill seat on the Niagara River, where they had built a grist-mill and a sawmill. In October, Randal concluded a provisional agreement with Canby to buy a one-third share in this concern. The agreement lapsed, but Randal's interest in the site did not. In November 1798 he reappeared in Upper Canada and petitioned for a 999-year lease of a riparian tract, immediately north of the McGill-Canby grant, on which to erect an iron foundry. He also asked for an adequate wood-lot, the right to mine ore near by, and a 12-year monopoly of iron manufacture to compensate him for his investment.

At the time of the bribery scandal in 1795, Randal was said to have recently been 'insolvent.' Now, however, he produced letters of credit to the amount of £1,950 (Halifax currency) and assured the Executive Council that 'General Christie' (perhaps General Gabriel Christie of Montreal) would extend him credit to any amount. He presented letters of introduction including one from Robert Hamilton, the pre-eminent Niagara merchant, which stated that Randal possessed 'very respectable recommendations' from some of Hamilton's friends in New York. The council turned down Randal's first petition, but when he persisted they authorized him to proceed on the understanding that he would receive the desired lease once he had fulfilled his undertaking to make iron on the site. Randal then contracted to buy the adjoining mills from McGill and Canby's successors in the lease, Elijah Phelps and David Ramsay, as well as 1,200 acres in Wainfleet Township which they owned in fee simple. By these transactions, Randal constructed the cross on which he was to suffer for the rest of his life and inaugurated a train of events that was to make him, in the eyes of many Upper Canadians, the colony's foremost martyr to puissant greed.

Randal erected his forge and began making iron, but he soon ran into financial difficulties. In June 1800 he signed two-thirds of the business over to his Montreal suppliers, Nathaniel Burton and James Maitland McCulloch, in liquidation of a debt of £1,600. In 1802 Burton and McCulloch commissioned Randal to buy and grind enough wheat to ship 6,000 barrels of flour to England, flour which Randal later claimed was the first ever manufactured in Upper Canada for the European market. The speculation was either the ruin of their fortunes or a vain effort to recoup them; either way, by June 1802 Burton and McCulloch were bankrupt. They disposed of their interest in the Bridgewater Works (as Randal had named it) to their British creditors, Caldcleugh, Boyd, and Reid, who sent out James Durand as their agent to assume control of the property.

A subsequent series of transactions in October 1802 left Randal as a one-third partner in the concern, with Durand holding the other two-thirds as agent for Caldcleugh, Boyd, and Reid. For some months Randal continued to manage the property, but in August 1803 he went east, leaving it in the hands of Durand and their clerk, Samuel Street. He bought land on the American side of the St Lawrence River, opposite Cornwall, erecting a tannery and potash works and setting up a ferry. In the summer of 1804 he established a mercantile concern at Cornwall. By his own later account, he undertook all these enterprises virtually on a whim, because he had some spare cash and nothing to do.

From the start, Randal encountered difficulty in receiving the payments due to him from Durand, who bought out his principals in 1804 and took Street into partnership. In 1806 Randal suffered a serious blow when Phelps, who had never surrendered the legal title, resumed possession of the property by ejectment, of which Durand kept Randal in ignorance. Phelps then let the property to Street. It is unclear whether Street and Durand were still partners, or whether any of these transactions constituted a collusive endeavour to dispossess Randal; but it was Durand from whom Street and his new partner, Thomas Clark, were later to claim title by an instrument of 1810.

Far off in Cornwall, Randal was unable to protect his interests. By 1806 he was in debt to the amount of £3,000. He spent the second half of 1807 determinedly dodging the writs of his creditors (mostly Montreal merchants) while nagging them to grant him an amnesty that would let him proceed about his business without fear of arrest. Despite the initial obduracy of the merchant Samuel David (whom Randal accused of 'a Jewish persecution,' citing Shylock's persistent demand for his pound of flesh), the amnesty was obtained in April 1808.

Randal's scheme to recoup his fortunes entailed building an ironworks on a superb site he hoped to acquire by grant from the crown at the Chaudière Falls on the Ottawa River. These works were to be supplied from 'an inexhaustible iron bank, a mountain of the richest & best quality rock ore,' which he had acquired by grant across the river in Hull Township, Lower Canada (for which purpose he claimed to have left the Niagara area in 1803). His hopes were dashed in March 1809 when, just after he had finally acquired the Chaudière property, he was arrested for debt in Montreal. For the next six and a half years he languished in prison at the mercy of whichever of his creditors was to blame. He and his friends always claimed that his oppressor was Thomas Clark. After Clark and Street had forced Durand to sell them the major interest in the Bridgewater property in 1810, Clark visited Randal in prison in 1812 to press him to dispose of his share. While in Montreal, he sued Randal for a debt owed to the concern. Randal always claimed that this was an accounting transaction, but as an incarcerated debtor he was unable to defend himself. A note in his papers records one man's testimony that he had heard Clark and two others exulting at having Randal in their power; and it is additional, circumstantial evidence of Clark's responsibility that Randal was released only in October 1815, just after Clark had procured the Executive Council's fulfilment of an order of the imperial government to grant him the freehold of the Bridgewater site, which until then had been alienated only by lease.

Upon his release, Randal returned to the Niagara area, bent on resuming the Bridgewater property and asserting his right to the expected government compensation for damages in the recent war with the United States. His legal counsel was Attorney General D'Arcy Boulton, whom he had employed when at Cornwall. Randal's first step was to institute an action for damages against Phelps for failing to transfer the legal title to his half of the property as provided by their contract of 1799. Randal could already produce evidence of legal title to Ramsay's half, and he apparently hoped that a successful action against Phelps, affirming his title in equity to the other half, would sustain a petition to the government to void as improvident the freehold grant to Clark, on the grounds that Clark had procured it by falsely representing himself to be the lawful tenant under the lease of 1794.

At the Niagara District Assizes of 1816, Randal won his case and nominal damages, the actual amount to be determined later by arbitration; but his opponents refused to agree to an impartial arbitrator and the matter came to trial again the following year. This time Phelps produced new evidence. In pressing their claim to the Bridgewater freehold, Clark and Street had asserted that the original deed of lease to McGill and Canby had been burnt during a fire in 1806. Now it was brought forward, endorsed with an instrument dated June 1801 by which Phelps and Ramsay had purportedly transferred the lease to Burton and McCulloch. Phelps claimed he had done this at Randal's behest in fulfilment of their contract of 1799, and he supported his claim by the testimony of two local notables, Robert Nichol and William Dickson, that Randal had been present and consenting at the time of the transfer. If valid, this instrument constituted grounds for the argument that Randal had renounced all title to the premises in 1801, and the one-third share he claimed under his agreement with Durand in October 1802 was a new interest which he had later forfeited by failing to fulfil the agreement. Phelps's claim was absurd on the face of it, however, since Randal (who always denied the validity of the instrument) could have transferred the lease by his own hand had he wished. Randal was also able to produce verbal testimony of McCulloch's denial that he and Burton had ever possessed title to the property. The jury awarded Randal £10,000 in damages, but the Court of King's Bench ordered a new trial on the grounds that the award was excessive.

Before the assizes in 1818 D'Arcy Boulton was elevated to the King's Bench and his son, acting solicitor general Henry John Boulton, took over Randal's cause. By now the Boultons had a substantial unpaid bill against their client, who was penniless until he could successfully assert his claim to the property in dispute. The younger Boulton refused to act unless Randal gave him a note of hand for £25 and security for a further £100. After Randal had given him the note and a mortgage on a lot he owned, Boulton went into court; but the presiding judge was his father, who refused to hear the case on the grounds that he had formerly acted in it. The action was held over for another year. Randal and his friends always claimed that H.J. Boulton must have known, or at least guessed, that his father would refuse to hear the case, though the solicitor general denied it.

Before the assizes of 1819, Randal's debt to Boulton fell due. He could not pay it, and Boulton instituted proceedings against him in the Home District. Randal heard nothing further after the initial notice and assumed, he later claimed, that Boulton had not proceeded to trial. In fact, he had done so and obtained judgement without Randal's knowledge. In doing so he broke at least three rules of the Court of King's Bench and unfairly exploited another rule, possibly promulgated *ultra vires*, which allowed a creditor to proceed to judgement without notifying the debtor when the latter lived outside the district in which the action was brought. To satisfy this judgement, Boulton attached the whole of Randal's 1,000-acre property at the Chaudière Falls. In 1820 it was sold for £449: far more than the amount of Randal's debt, but only a tiny fraction of its actual value, which was becoming known as a result of the area's recent opening to settlement. The purchasers were John Le Breton, a half-pay army officer who had tried in 1819 to buy a piece of it from Randal, and Levius Peters Sherwood, a Brockville notable who became in 1825 a judge of the King's Bench. When Randal learned of the sale, in January 1821, he instituted an appeal in *Boulton* v. *Randal*. The case was of such a nature that Alexander Stewart, Randal's attorney and a self-proclaimed 'old Tory,' later said of it that 'a more rascally proceeding never disgraced the administration of justice in any country'; nevertheless, Randal's appeal was in vain. It is noteworthy that, while Randal may not have heard of the *sale* before 1821, he had heard of the judgement (though he later denied it) by December 1819. Perhaps, not imagining it would cause him such loss, he had preferred at the time to let the matter go by default. It is more likely, however, that he had simply become disenchanted with the legal process; for in December 1819 the breach with Boulton had just brought about the ruin of all his hopes.

In August of that year *Randal* v. *Phelps* had come on at the Niagara District Assizes for the fourth year in a row. The plaintiff, bereft of counsel, was forced to conduct his own case; Attorney General John Beverley Robinson represented the defendant. The result of so unequal a contest was a foregone conclusion: the same evidence that had failed Phelps in 1817 now sufficed to secure a verdict in his favour. By Randal's own account, however, this result was achieved only with the help of an extraordinary act of oppression by the presiding judge, Chief Justice William Dummer Powell. In a letter written soon afterwards, Randal asserted that Powell had threatened the jury with a writ of attaint if they found for the plaintiff (i.e., against the evidence as Powell interpreted it). This procedure had fallen into desuetude in England by the end of the 17th century. At the same assizes, Randal was successfully sued by Clark on the judgement he had won in Montreal in 1812. This decision was to lead to a sheriff's sale of Randal's 1,200-acre estate in Wainfleet, which Clark himself bought for the derisory price of £40.

Until now, Randal had evinced little interest in Upper Canadian politics, and such evidence as exists suggests that his predilections in American politics were conservative. Now it appeared that his experiences had radicalized him. A letter to an unidentified friend reveals, though incoherently, his disaffection. 'Every coercive measure has been taken and admitted on the part of Powell and Cambell

[William Campbell] to restrain my legal and equitable rights, to arme Clark, in withholding from me, my property. These are dispotic days; a sort of Mock Military, or tantalized Civil Government, a good deal like the Executive Religion in this Province. ... I have now been a Victim to its influence for Ten Years.' He accused the judges of intending to restrict his movements by exposing him to arrest for debt, and blamed the Executive Council for making an improvident grant of the Bridgewater freehold when Clark had clearly deluded the imperial government into believing that he and Street were the rightful tenants. He swore he would take revenge on the judges and Robinson by pursuing their impeachment in the provincial legislature, on Durand by suing him for breach of contract, and on Durand, Phelps, Clark, Street, Dickson, and Nichol by presenting them for perjury at the next Niagara Assizes.

Randal did none of these things. Instead, in July 1820, he stood in the riding of 4th Lincoln for the House of Assembly. In his election address he appealed to the popular dislike of aristocracy, favouritism, and patronage, assailed abuses in the administration of justice, and asserted the importance of electing men who would not become 'puppets to executive influence.' (This last declaration was a thrust against his opponent Isaac Swayze, MHA for Lincoln in the last legislature, who had instituted the proceedings leading to Robert Gourlay's expulsion under the Sedition Act the previous year.) Observing that 'it is private injuries that produce public grievances,' he called for 'an equal distribution of Justice' and 'a liberal dispensation of rights.' Upper Canada's constitution was mild and its laws just, but both were perverted by a 'Maniac interest; that knows no bounds but the crush of its own weight.' Randal, by now a popular hero, won easily. He was to remain MHA for Lincoln until his death.

In a series of initiatives taken during 1824, Randal continued his personal quest for justice against Clark, Street, and Boulton with the help of the brilliant young advocate, John Rolph. An action for ejectment against Clark and Street failed because Randal could show a legal title to only the Ramsay half of the property. A second attempt to reopen *Boulton v. Randal* foundered because it had already been appealed in vain; a final attempt to do so never came to a decision, because both D'Arcy Boulton and his successor on the bench, Sherwood, were interested parties.

Randal also sought satisfaction by petitions to both the executive and the legislature. The governor-in-chief, Lord Dalhousie [Ramsay], was sympathetic to his case concerning the Chaudière property, because the Lower Canadian government had been anxious to buy part of it at the very moment of the shrieval sale and he believed that Captain Le Breton had bid for it in that knowledge. Petitioning in 1822, when the proposed union of Upper and Lower Canada was a leading political question, Randal noted that the property (which lies immediately west of today's downtown Ottawa) was the most central site for the capital of the united province. In 1828, when the founding of Bytown at last nerved Sherwood to test his title by an action of ejectment against Randal's tenants, Dalhousie ordered Robinson to defend the case, but he found an excuse to refuse. With Chief Justice Campbell absent in England, John Walpole Willis just dismissed from the bench, and judge Sherwood an interested party, the case was heard by the then puisne justice Christopher Alexander Hagerman, who found for Sherwood at the assizes in August and then, a few months later, dismissed the appeal against his own errors in the Court of King's Bench. Randal's petitions to the lieutenant governor in council and the imperial government, seeking avoidance of the Chaudière sale and annulment of the Bridgewater freehold as an improvident grant, also failed. Those to the assembly evoked a swingeing denunciation of H.J. Boulton's conduct but no practical benefit. Since Randal's quest for justice was hampered by the colony's lack of an equity tribunal, the assembly passed bills in 1828 and 1830 erecting a court of chancery for the special purpose of inquiring into his wrongs, but both bills failed in the Legislative Council.

Nevertheless, Randal's persistence made him a popular hero and led his enemies in the Niagara area to make another, and this time ill-judged, effort to crush him in the courts. In swearing to his qualification for parliamentary office at the general election of 1824, he claimed ownership of all the properties of which they had despoiled him. His defiance provoked Samuel Street and William Johnson Kerr to present him for perjury at the Niagara Assizes of 1825. The trial was notable for Rolph's brilliant defence of Randal. After discrediting the prosecution by forcing Clark to confess to his attempts to coerce Randal in prison in Montreal in 1812 (a confession which threw doubt on Clark's claim to have been the lawful tenant of the Bridgewater property from 1810 on), Rolph closed with a speech which implicated the entire judicial establishment in Randal's persecution and secured his client's acquittal despite Chief Justice Campbell's hostile summing-up.

Two years later, Randal enjoyed a more devastating triumph over his enemies. In 1827 the provincial legislature passed an act to confer political and civil rights on all those residents of Upper Canada (the majority of those of North American origin and some foreign military settlers) who had supposedly been adjudged aliens by the English court case *Thomas* v. *Acklam* (1824). The terms of this legislation had been dictated by the Colonial Office and were highly obnoxious to many whom it affected. A petition for its disallowance was got up, and the steering committee, which included Jesse Ketchum, appointed Randal to present the request to the imperial government and parliament. He was courteously received by the colonial secretary, Lord Goderich, and the parliamentary undersecretary, Robert John Wilmot-Horton, and returned with their promise that the colonial government would be instructed to bring in acceptable legislation. If this was not passed at the next session of the provincial legislature, it would be enacted at Westminster.

The success of Randal's mission was a staggering shock to the Upper Canadian political establishment. True, the petitioners had been lucky, in that one of the objectionable clauses – that which made naturalization conditional on the beneficiary's abjuration of his former allegiance – was now unacceptable to the British government for reasons of high policy. Nevertheless, the courteous treatment accorded Randal, whom they particularly despised, and his evident influence on the thinking of the imperial authorities, left Lieutenant Governor Sir Peregrine Maitland and his advisers feeling betrayed (even though Goderich stated publicly that it was not they, but the Colonial Office, who were responsible for the legislation of 1827).

Randal's vendetta with the Niagara area élite persisted. Aided by the vagaries of imperial policy, he managed to postpone payment of most of the war losses compensation for the Bridgewater property to Clark and Street until 1833. This delay was despite the fact that, nine years earlier, Maitland had assigned the task of adjudicating the conflicting claims to their counsel, Attorney General Robinson, who had found in his clients' favour. As the general election of 1828 approached, Randal was threatened that, if by subterfuge he had managed to retain or acquire enough real estate to qualify for re-election, it would be attached by his creditors as soon as he identified it in his qualification oath. None the less, he was returned both in 1828 and in 1830.

It is unclear if these continuing feuds had any bearing on Randal's attitude towards the question of public financial aid to the Welland Canal Company. Until 1830, he consistently opposed such aid. In that year, he voted with the minority against a bill which authorized £25,000 in aid to the canal and appointed him as commissioner to report on the state of the works to the government. He reported very favourably on the future utility of the canal as an artery in the Laurentian trade system and in 1831 supported a measure authorizing a further £50,000 in aid. The measure might be unpopular in the old Niagara River commercial centres of Niagara (Niagara-on-the-Lake), Queenston, St Davids, and Waterloo, he observed, but it would benefit many more people than it harmed. Randal's explanation for his volte-face in 1831 was consistent with his support for the union of Upper and Lower Canada in 1822.

Despite his public prominence, Randal continued all but destitute till his dying day. He had no visible means of support but his salary as MHA during the short parliamentary session and, during the navigation season only, a small stipend as toll collector on the Welland Canal at Port Colborne. It is likely that his friends and fellow radical assemblymen William Lyon Mackenzie, John Johnston Lefferty, and Thomas Hornor helped him with money: all three are named as beneficiaries in his will, along with the impecunious Montrealers who had succoured him during his long incarceration. Jesse Ketchum, named as an executor along with Mackenzie, Lefferty, Hornor and Willis, may also have helped.

An appreciation of Randal's historical importance must start with an assessment of his personality. His role in the Michigan bribery scandal, his deportment towards his creditors in 1807–8, and his contradiction by so many leading Niagara-area personalities in the Bridgewater litigation might suggest that he was merely an unscrupulous trickster who deserved his bleak destiny; yet his career of almost unrelieved failure forbids so glib a judgement. Under closer scrutiny he appears more like a naïve optimist, even a starry-eyed visionary – a simple, amiable man, apt to be deceived by men more designing than he. Yet this is also, perhaps, too superficial a view. There was, conceivably, a self-deceiving quality to his optimism. So often was he gulled and cast down, and so tenacious was his defiance in adversity, that one suspects him of having laid himself open to such disasters by an unconscious masochistic impulse to failure. In this he resembles another opposition politician of the 1820s, Charles Fothergill.

Randal's apparent innocence and amiability, and his defiance in adversity, all contributed to his political importance, which lay chiefly in his symbolic role as martyr *par excellence* to the avarice and oppression of the 'family compact' and its regional affiliates. His experience seemed to typify that of the pioneer farmer, struggling to make a living in a milieu in which both the legal system and the terms of trade favoured the merchant capitalist. To these Bible-drenched pioneers, Randal's story of spoliation by legal process was that of Naboth's vineyard; but it was also their story, and his persistent (and ultimately political) struggle for justice set them an example. Randal also fitted the period's conventional, 'sentimentalist' stereotype of injured innocence, and he was presented in that light by advocates such as Rolph and Mackenzie: a sort of Vicar of Wakefield, a man – as he was described by his contemporaries – of 'romantic history and eminent worth,' 'long accustomed to persecution – the child of misfortune, and the companion of troubles,' at one time 'dressed in a dark-green suit that had long since been threadbare,' at another '*literally* clothed with the approbation of his constituents.' Nothing did more than his sufferings to discredit the legal profession and the administration of justice: H.J. Boulton was so unpopular because of them that Maitland opposed his application to be made a judge in 1825 and Lieutenant Governor Sir John Colborne was dubious about making him attorney general in 1829.

It is paradoxical that Randal, this energetic and tenacious adventurer, should have played such an essentially passive role in public life; yet his political career was of a piece with it. Mackenzie remarked in his obituary that 'few who have sat in the House have given as many good votes as Mr. R.,' but 'if he ever spoke for five minutes I don't recollect it.' Mackenzie is said to have taken up politics under Randal's influence, and he made the cause of Randal and his heirs his own until his dying day. Randal, for his part, persuaded Mackenzie to move the *Colonial Advocate* to York (Toronto) in 1824 and promoted his election to the assembly in 1828. Randal probably owed his selection as the "Aliens"' ambassador in 1827 to Mackenzie and Ketchum, since both men had played leading parts the previous year in a fund-raising campaign to help him travel to London to pursue his case against Clark and Street (he tried in 1827 but was rebuffed by the British government).

Randal's correspondence in London with the Colonial Office shows an uncharacteristic polish which may reflect the counsel of his chief adviser there, the Scottish radical, Joseph Hume. The success of his mission entitles it to be considered as the first of the three great blows the imperial authorities delivered to the Upper Canadian political establishment during the colony's last years, the others being Mackenzie's reception in 1832, which led to the dismissal of H.J. Boulton and Hagerman as attorney general and solicitor general respectively, and the decision in 1839 to unite Upper and Lower Canada.

PAUL ROMNEY

JOSEPH WILLCOCKS (Wilcox)
Diarist, office holder, printer, publisher, journalist, politician, and army officer; b. 1773 in Palmerston (Republic of Ireland), second son of Robert Willcocks and Jane Powell; d. unmarried 4 Sept. 1814 at Fort Erie, Upper Canada.

A man of some education and modest contacts, Joseph Willcocks left Ireland on 1 Dec. 1799 and arrived at York (Toronto), Upper Canada, on 20 March 1800. He stayed first with his kinsman William Willcocks. On 1 May he became private clerk to a distant cousin, Receiver General Peter Russell. Later, as a result of Russell's influence, he became receiver and payer of fees in the Surveyor General's Office. Willcocks petitioned successfully for a town lot in York on 15 July; on 12 August another petition for 1,200 acres was also granted, and he later located this land in Hope Township. On 7 August he moved into the Russell household, remaining there until 23 Aug. 1802 when he was dismissed for courting Russell's half-sister Elizabeth. The same day Willcocks visited Chief Justice Henry Allcock, who remonstrated with Russell, to no avail, on Willcocks's behalf. On 13 October Willcocks moved into the home of Allcock, who proved a worthy patron. He soon received a position engraving deeds for the provincial secretary, William Jarvis. He was appointed registrar of the probate court and marshal of assize on 9 May 1803 and sheriff of the Home District on 4 Sept. 1804.

To this point, there was little indication that Willcocks's career would be controversial. His diary and letters covering his first three years in the province reveal a man interested mainly in social life and good connections who claimed that 'mediocrity ... is the summit of my ambition.' He noted that 'there are not more than 100 Persons of Consequence in the Whole Province,' and he counted many of them among his intimates. Willcocks was not, however, without an interest in politics and was a close observer of events in Ireland. Of Upper Canada, he declared that 'politics never ran higher in Ireland than they do here,' and that he was careful to assure the government of his loyalty. Consequently, he had 'no intercourse with the Republican party.' Willcocks was in the gallery of the House of Assembly on 30 May 1801 when Allcock denounced the claim of Angus Macdonell (Collachie) to continue as that body's clerk. The following month Willcocks and his friend William Weekes were among Allcock's first visitors after his election to the assembly had been voided by the house. In the subsequent by-election Willcocks voted for the administration's candidate, John Small, who, however, lost to Macdonell. Relations between Allcock and Weekes became strained after the by-election, and Weekes soon accused Willcocks of being 'under the Pay of Government as their informer.'

Allcock's influence grew after 1802 as Lieutenant Governor Peter Hunter came to rely more and more upon his judgement. Willcocks basked in the security of his appointment to the shrievalty: 'No Governor or King can dismiss me without [my] having committed some high offence.' Although the 'officers of Government disagree very much,' he noted, 'I have the good fortune to be always at the strongest side.' In the fall of 1804 Allcock left for England and the following year he was appointed chief justice of Lower Canada. Willcocks was no longer on the strongest side.

Willcocks had been contented with his lot in Upper Canada and had expressed no regrets about leaving his native land. However, the equipoise of his life in the colony seems to have been undermined by the loss of Allcock as a patron and by a gradual rethinking (since 1803) of recent events in Ireland. He had not supported the rebellion by the Society of United Irishmen in 1798. He had had doubts about the wisdom of the legislative union of Ireland with Great Britain in 1800 but had accepted it as a matter of loyalty. The immediate post-union period had, however, occasioned even graver doubts. When in 1803 his brother warned authorities in Dublin of imminent uprisings, Willcocks wondered if he were right in doing so. Willcocks became increasingly certain that true loyalty was to withstand arbitrary rule.

Willcocks's views began to crystallize around his understanding of 18th-century whiggism. According to that tradition, the revolution of 1688 represented successful resistance to authoritarian rule. Even though the British parliament was dominated by whigs throughout the 18th century, the concern over arbitrary power remained a dominant thread of their thought. Given the mixed or balanced constitution, in their view any increase in power by the executive or the crown meant a loss of liberty elsewhere. Consequently, the loyal subject needed to be ever vigilant. Willcocks's outlook on these points was influenced by justice Robert Thorpe and Charles Burton Wyatt, the surveyor general.

A successor to Allcock as mentor and friend, Thorpe arrived in Upper Canada in late September or early October 1805. He was Willcocks's neighbour in York, and by coincidence they had cousins who were neighbours in Palmerston. Willcocks was attracted to Thorpe's extraordinary self-confidence, his Irishness, and his clear criticism of the arbitrariness of the administrations of Hunter and his successor, Alexander Grant. In May 1806 Willcocks considered Thorpe 'my most particular friend.' A principle championed by Thorpe and later espoused by Willcocks was that colonial legislatures were independent. Basing his assertion on the authority of Sir William Blackstone's *Commentaries on the laws of England*, Thorpe argued that the legislature of a colony such as Upper Canada, was, as Blackstone put it, 'subject ... to the control of Parliament though (like Ireland, Man, and the rest) not bound by any acts of Parliament, unless particularly named.' Thorpe, following Weekes, was struck by how far removed colonial government seemed to be from that ideal. Indeed, the possibility of misrule seemed to increase with distance from the seat of power. Men such as Willcocks and Thorpe were therefore even more sensitive to supposed abuses of power, and even more certain that the only solution to the problem of misrule was to recognize the legitimate legislative independence of the colony and to ensure that executive councillors considered themselves responsible to the legislature rather than to the governor. Many officials in Upper Canada were surprised by these views, not only because the colonial government seemed to them to be comparatively independent but, more important, because such attitudes seemed to show that critics were abusing the positions of trust they held.

What in practice sparked the rise of a political opposition in Upper Canada was the widespread reaction against government changes in land policy, implemented between 1802 and 1804, which increased the fees on land grants and tightened the rules concerning the eligibility of loyalists for free land grants. That opposition was given a parliamentary focus by Weekes's election to the assembly in 1805. In October 1806 he was killed in a duel, and when Thorpe ran, successfully, in the subsequent by-election Willcocks was active in his campaign. Between 1806 and 1808 an opposition group in the assembly formed around whig ideas and around the leadership of

Thorpe and then Willcocks. This group seems to have derived its support from those with Irish roots and the small farmers and loyalists who had borne the brunt of the so-called reforms in land policy.

Thorpe and Willcocks had a good perspective on the land issue. Willcocks, for instance, had worked at the land office; moreover, as sheriff, he had seen many people forced to sell their land at auction to pay off debts to merchants. Both had been involved in the foundation and proceedings of the Upper Canada Agricultural and Commercial Society, of which Thorpe was chairman, formed to encourage the cultivation of hemp and to report on improvements made in agriculture and on the need for government assistance to farmers. Since the Executive Council had responsibility for land grants, after 1802 it became the focus of criticism and the symbol of arbitrary power. The concern with the council combined with the Irishness of Thorpe and Willcocks to add an overtone of nationality to an issue which was, at heart, one of constitutional proprieties and interpretations of law. Condemning the influence of merchants such as Robert Hamilton, Thorpe characterized the administrations of Hunter, Grant, and Francis Gore as being 'surrounded with the same scotch Pedlars.' To this group could be added such key office holders as John McGill and Thomas Scott, both from Scotland. John Mills Jackson, the author of a pamphlet highly critical of the Gore administration, was reported to have reviled 'that damned Scotch faction, with the Governor at the head.' Willcocks himself denounced the policies originating from the executive since 1802 as nothing less than the 'tyrannical' actions of a Scotch clique.

In the face of this challenge to the structure of authority in the colony, Gore moved swiftly to assert the power of his office. Much to the amazement of Willcocks and his friends, who were confident of the security of their appointments and the importance of their connections in Britain, in a short space of time the British government withdrew the appointments of Thorpe and Wyatt and on 23 April 1807 Gore removed Willcocks from the shrievalty, ostensibly for 'general and notorious bad conduct.' These actions confirmed the group's concern about the dangers of arbitrary authority in the hands of a colonial governor.

Shortly after his dismissal from office, Willcocks moved to Niagara (Niagara-on-the-Lake) where he established the *Upper Canada Guardian; or, Freeman's Journal*. A small four-page sheet, the paper was published from 24 July 1807 to 9 June 1812, 'avowedly calculated,' as he wrote in the last issue, 'to disseminate the principles of political truth, check the progress of inordinate power, and keep alive the sacred flame of a just and rational liberty.' Willcocks's criticism of government was well within the limits of these touchstones of whig canon. Yet such was the world of Upper Canadian politics that many in official circles believed that his paper was financed by the United Irishmen, aided by American editors, and controlled by Thorpe. There were reports that Willcocks intended 'to revolutionize the province,' and that he personally believed the government would censor him within six months of the paper's founding. His friends worried because he was prone to trouble, unaccustomed to business practices, and unlikely to heed advice.

The few issues of the paper that have survived indicate Willcocks's continuing concern with liberty, oppressive land laws, and arbitrary power. Letters in early numbers from 'A Loyalist,' reputedly Thorpe, argued that civic duty did not involve support for bad rulers: 'Surely it would not be loyalty to assist a monarch in rendering himself absolute, who would overturn the constitution, and subvert the law?' The paper received widespread notice. Judge William Dummer Powell complained in 1809 that it was in almost every house, and Gore lamented the 'vulgar attacks' by the 'Seditious Printer' which were 'relished too much, by the good people of Upper Canada.' In fact, however, the paper contained remarkably little editorial matter, and it was premature for Willcocks's enemies to label him and his followers 'Rebels, and supporters of unprincipled demagogues.' In addition to the newspaper, Willcocks carried on a conveyancing business at Niagara. As he explained in the *Guardian* of 14 April 1810, this undertaking was in part an effort to obviate the exorbitant charges of 'the learned and conscientious gentlemen of the Long Robe.' He had problems with the paper and does not seem to have published between July 1810 and July 1811. In June 1812 he sold the press, which he said was 'growing old and crazy,' to Richard Hatt for $1,600. He was certain that he could purchase 'a new and complete set of Types and Press' for a quarter of the price.

Willcocks won the by-election called in 1807 to replace Solomon Hill in the riding of West York, 1st Lincoln, and Haldimand and took his seat on 26 Jan. 1808. The fact of his election was significant. In the Niagara peninsula Thorpe's opposition and particularly his stinging attack in 1806 upon local magistrates such as John Warren had, it seemed, unified a number of disparate, but pro-government, political groupings. Certainly the merchants led by Robert Hamilton had closed ranks with their old opponents, loyalist officers such as Ralfe Clench and small office holders such as Isaac Swayze. Despite this change Willcocks was re-elected in 1808 and 1812.

Willcocks participated briefly in the fourth session of the fourth parliament before being jailed for contempt of the house. In the election held after parliament was dissolved on 21 May 1808, he was re-elected, without opposition, for the constituency of 1st Lincoln and Haldimand. Although the legislative record of the first session of the fifth parliament (February–March 1809) has not survived, it is clear from the observations of contemporaries that Willcocks assumed the leadership of the parliamentary opposition. He may not have been as clever as Thorpe, who once remarked that Willcocks 'did not possess a sufficiency of brains to bait a mouse trap'; none the less, Weekes was dead and Thorpe and Wyatt were no longer on the scene. As the editor of the only newspaper critical of government, Willcocks was in a position to coordinate and sustain the grievances of various groups against the administration. Moreover, as a man who had been dismissed by the governor and jailed by the assembly, he evoked the sympathy of other victims of supposed arbitrariness – small farmers on the one hand and petty loyalists anxious to retain their privileges with respect to land grants on the other. The opposition group for which Willcocks provided a focus throughout his legislative career grew steadily within the assembly; at the peak of its power in 1812 it controlled half the votes in the house. How Willcocks felt about his new political role is not clear. However, this active leadership contrasted sharply with his early years in the colony when as a diarist and a journalist his function was mainly to observe.

Considerable controversy has surrounded the group, and Willcocks in particular, as successive generations of historians have sought to explain the basis of its political opposition. Most often, Willcocks and his associates have been understood simply as 'intriguing spirits' frustrated in their search for political appointment. More probably, the opposition group was held together by pragmatic, but not entirely selfish, responses to legitimate grievances related to land-granting, executive power, and social inequities.

The cohesiveness of the parliamentary opposition and its ability to affect the legislative process have also been the subject of a good deal of historiographical debate. Often that debate has concerned the extent to which it is accurate to label the group a 'party.' It was not a party in the modern political sense. There was no formal structure although, for a time, Thorpe may have used the Upper Canada Agricultural and Commercial Society to provide some cohesion for the group's efforts. Moreover, the parliamentary composition of the group fluctuated over time and, when disagreements occurred, there was not sufficient cohesion to enforce discipline and prevent members from voting independently. But it did mark a departure from the usual pattern of assemblymen working as individuals. The group's composition and behaviour may be examined through a study of the division lists, that is, the recorded votes on individual motions, especially as the number of them increased during Willcocks's career as an MLA. An analysis of the divisions of the second session of the fifth parliament in 1810 indicates that Willcocks had a high percentage of voting agreement with six other members. Among them, David McGregor Rogers, who had given only lukewarm support to Thorpe in 1807, worked closely with Willcocks and sided with him on 18 of the 21 divisions in which he participated. Benajah Mallory supported him on 16 of 21 divisions, Peter Howard on 18 of 23, and John Roblin on 18 of 20. His greatest backing came from John Willson, who voted with him on 25 of 26 divisions. This group made a number of demands which the administration and its supporters in the assembly opposed: a civil list controlled by the legislature, lower salaries for public officials, easier regulations with respect to loyalist and military claims for land, and tighter controls over jury practices and electoral procedures. Particularly noteworthy was the group's resistance to several motions to unseat members on the grounds that they were Methodist ministers, and the motions citing John Mills Jackson for libel.

During the third session in 1811, Willcocks, Howard, Mallory, and Willson were in almost complete accord in 18 recorded divisions. Moreover, there was considerable support from Rogers and from the recently elected Willet Casey, Abraham Marsh, David Secord, and Philip Sovereign. This group continued the fights of the previous session as well as seeking to exclude crown appointees from sitting in the assembly, to broaden the availability of schooling, and to reconsider the rates of assessment.

The high point of the group's opposition came in the last session of the fifth parliament in February and March 1812, under the threat of war with the United States. The colony's administrator, Isaac Brock, was determined to push through the assembly measures calculated to put the province on a war footing. But he was not to have his way. The nine assemblymen of the previous session who had coalesced under Willcocks's leadership were joined by Thomas Dorland and John Stinson. Thus, in a house that contained 23 members Willcocks's group now had a near majority. It received timely support from Thomas Barnes Gough, and the speaker, Samuel Street, who could vote only in instances of a tie, never did. Moreover, the group had considerable legislative experience which Willcocks and Rogers marshalled well. In the face of this strong opposition Brock dissolved parliament on 5 May and called an election, determined to get a loyal (and more pliant) assembly on the eve of war.

Many members were not returned, but Willcocks was among the half-dozen re-elected. He won a resounding victory in 1st Lincoln and Haldimand, defeating Abraham Nelles by 154 votes to 40. Brock had high hopes for the new parliament with its many new members, including his highly regarded attorney general, John Macdonell (Greenfield). He called an emergency session, which was to run from 27 July to 5 August. Yet even during a time of war, the assembly under the influence of Willcocks and the Ancaster miller Abraham Markle refused to grant Brock such controversial legislation as the partial suspension of habeas corpus. Unable to secure the house's cooperation, a disgusted Brock lost no time in proroguing it.

Some historians have judged Willcocks's performance in the assembly as if it were nothing more than a prelude to his treason in 1813. In fact, the invasion of Upper Canada by American forces in the summer of 1812 affected neither his opposition nor his loyalty. It needs to be reiterated that he saw no contradiction between the two. In the last issue of the *Guardian* on 9 June 1812 he maintained that he was an enemy 'of the measures of the Kings Servants in this colony,' asserting at the same time that he was a 'constant adherent to the interests of the Country.' Indeed, Brock appealed to this loyalty in August 1812 when he sought Willcocks's cooperation in securing an alliance with the Six Nations Indians, whose reserve was in his constituency. Brock's concern was that the Niagara peninsula would be flanked on both sides, should the Indians' support go to the Americans. In spite of ill health, Willcocks took up the task willingly. Early in September he reported to John Macdonell (Greenfield), one of Brock's aides-de-camp, that the mission had been completed successfully and that he was prepared to serve again if called upon. He then returned to Niagara, and he was subsequently mentioned in British army dispatches as one of several gentleman volunteers who served at the battle of Queenston Heights.

Nor was Willcocks's loyalty called into question during the first few months of 1813. The second session of the sixth parliament, held from 25 February to 13 March 1813, passed without incident. The Niagara merchant William Hamilton Merritt wrote that Willcocks had become a 'zealous loyalist': 'He has behaved very well on all occasions and so have all his party, altho' they are trusted with no office whatever.' Furthermore, early in April William Warren Baldwin, one of Willcocks's earliest acquaintances in York, noted that his friend was then actively recruiting for the Incorporated Militia. One must either take a cynical approach to Willcocks's actions in the months following the outbreak of the war, or seek another explanation for his treason in the summer of 1813. It is the timing that suggests there was more to his career than a pattern of disloyalty.

His loyalty was shaken when the climate of civil opinion within the province was altered shortly following the capture of York in April 1813 and the invasion of the Niagara peninsula in May. With the stabilization of the military situation after the battle of Stoney Creek on 5 June 1813, local élites, in both the Niagara and the Home districts, were able to demand the imposition of harsh military measures to curb the disaffected. Willcocks, who had accepted with Thorpe the argument that colonial legislatures had, *de jure*, independent powers, had become convinced during his years in the assembly, and particularly during the important legislative sessions of 1812, that the maintenance of those powers required constant vigilance against executive despotism and arbitrary rule; if the legislature were to retain the right to act independently, it must prove itself worthy of the trust. The collapse of virtually all resistance to the erosion of the constitution by the executive dashed his hopes for the province. When during the *Chesapeake* affair of 1807 the British forcibly asserted their right to search American ships for deserters, Willcocks wrote to an American correspondent: 'The honest part of us say that if the States pocket the indignity they can no longer style themselves a nation.' The events of 1813 showed Willcocks that Upper Canadians were willing to pocket the indignity of arbitrary and, what was worse, military rule. No longer were they concerned to defend their liberties. Willcocks was not pro-American. He probably had never overcome his early conviction that the Americans were 'not an honest people.' But he was certain they would never challenge or subvert the supremacy of the local legislature. Some time in July 1813 Willcocks crossed the Niagara River and offered his services to the American forces.

By the end of August 1813 he had raised and was commanding a unit of expatriate Upper Canadians known as the Company of Canadian Volunteers. Among his fellow officers were such prominent figures from the parliamentary opposition in Upper Canada as Mallory and Markle. Indeed most of the unit's 120 or so recruits were from the constituencies that these three men had represented in the assembly. The Americans valued Willcocks for his 'zeal, activity and local knowledge.' In November and December 1813 he led scouting and foraging parties to Stoney Creek and the Forty (Grimsby), aided in the burning of Niagara, and participated in the subsequent retreat to Buffalo, N.Y. 'Surpassed by none in enterprise and bravery,' Willcocks commanded his volunteers at Fort George (Niagara-on-the-Lake) and Fort Erie until on 4 Sept. 1814 he 'received a mortal wound by a shot through the right breast' during an action before the latter.

Willcocks was important as an observer of Upper Canadian politics, as the leader of its first sustained opposition group, and as a traitor. Trying to find a consistent thread in his career, some historians have come to the conclusion that his early professions of loyalty must have been lies. In other words, a traitor must be understood in the light of his treason. But this interpretation fails to take account of the developments in Willcocks's maturing political opinions. During the course of his Upper Canadian career he became convinced that resistance to bad government was a duty demanded of loyal subjects. Individuals, colonies, and even nations had to prove that they deserved their independence through the vigilant defence of their rights. He came to see similarities among the situations in Upper Canada, Ireland, and the United States. Having concluded that the union of Ireland and Great Britain was a mistake, he was persuaded by 1806 that the United Irishmen had been right in their active opposition to misrule and that he himself had let Ireland down when she needed him most. Similarly, in their resistance to the British in the critical tests of 1807 and 1812 the Americans proved themselves worthy of nationhood in Willcocks's eyes. When in the summer of 1813 Upper Canadians failed to defend their constitutional liberties and the maintenance of civil law, they forfeited not only Willcocks's sympathy but also his allegiance. To find a consistent and rational thread in Willcocks's political career it is not necessary to discount his words and emphasize his treason; rather, it may be found by paying closer attention to what he said, when he said it, what he did, and when he did it. Firmly in the opposition whig tradition, Willcocks opposed arbitrary and distant power, valued loyalty to his country rather than to his rulers, and believed in the independence of colonial legislatures. At great inconvenience to his own position, he pursued a public course consistent with those whig principles.

ELWOOD H. JONES

JOHN WILLSON

Politician, office holder, justice of the peace, and judge; b. 5 Aug. 1776 in New Jersey, son of Ann ——; m. 28 Feb. 1799 Elizabeth Bowlby (Boultby, Bowlsby), and they had nine children; d. 26 May 1860 in Saltfleet Township, Upper Canada.

In a land petition dated 16 June 1806, John Willson claimed to have been 'upwards of thirteen years' in Upper Canada; other sources claim that he arrived in 1790. He settled first at Newark (Niagara-on-the-Lake) before moving to Saltfleet Township in 1797. Willson quickly established himself as a prosperous farmer and a leader in local Methodist circles. His chief claim to fame was a political career that began in 1809 when a local deputation encouraged him to contest a by-election for the West Riding of York. As Willson later explained, the 'parties in politics known at that time, were the *"Government"* and the "Opposition." I was called by the latter, – which was chiefly composed of dissenting religious people.' It is also likely that Willson drew support from small farmers frustrated by the monopolistic practices of merchants such as Richard Hatt. Willson's election was protested, unsuccessfully, by Hatt, Richard Beasley, and others, who claimed that he was ineligible as a Methodist 'Teacher and Preacher.'

During the remaining sessions of the fifth parliament, Willson made an enduring reputation as a defender of civil and religious liberty. His voting record in 1810–11 indicates complete support for Joseph Willcocks, the foremost opponent of the administration of Lieutenant Governor Francis Gore. Willson was elected in 1812 to the sixth parliament (1812–16). In the last years of the War of 1812 he became highly critical of the change in the climate of opinion, especially as reflected in the stern measures enacted by successive administrations, which he considered to be military despotism. On 26 Feb. 1814 he cast the sole vote against the bill suspending habeas corpus. In 1816 he supported a more liberal marriage bill. More important, he introduced and, with James Durand, drafted the Common Schools Bill, which provided for public support of elementary education.

There has been some historical confusion with respect to Willson's involvement in the seventh parliament (1817–20), but what happened is really straightforward. At the opening of parliament in February 1817, Gore asked that there be due representation for the recently established Gore District before any business was transacted. The legislature concurred, the requisite bill was passed, and parliament adjourned. Willson then opposed Durand for the new riding of Wentworth. In a handbill printed by Bartemas Ferguson and published in the *Niagara Spectator* by Richard Cockrell, Durand attacked Willson for duplicity, cowardice, and corruption, claiming that the erstwhile champion of liberty had become a tool of government in return for a magistracy in the new district. The election was held about 18 February; Willson attributed Durand's victory to the 'spirit of Radicalism' which had begun 'to diffuse itself more generally.' If anything, that spirit manifested itself even more strongly in the widespread local support for Robert Gourlay's convention of 1818. The tide, however, was turning against Gourlay and his supporters at the Head of the Lake (the vicinity of present-day Hamilton Harbour). When Richard Hatt died in 1819, Willson won the by-election to replace him for the riding of Halton.

Local perception of Willson's politics had been changing since his defeat by Durand. Willson, he himself later recalled, was referred to as 'a thorough-going tory.' Elected along with George Hamilton for Wentworth in 1820, he had the support of 'the Conservative interest, both in and out of office.' He was subsequently re-elected to the ninth (1825–28), tenth (1829–30), and eleventh (1830–34) parliaments, thus emerging as the first major politician from the Head of the Lake. 'Honest John,' as he was usually called, had made a local reputation from his continued advocacy of the interests of farmers, his espousal of universal education, and his unrelenting tirades against the inequity of the civil courts. From a strong regional base he moved to the front ranks of the House of Assembly. In 1824 the first issue of William Lyon Mackenzie's *Colonial Advocate* had lauded him: 'Many members of our legislature get less *useful* the longer they are kept in parliament; but his talents appear to us the more eminent, and his knowledge the more solid and extensive, the longer he is there.'

Willson was at the height of his political power and influence between 1825 and 1834, his prominence being reflected in his election to the speakership of the assembly for the ninth parliament. During his tenure the assembly handled some of the colony's most important and contentious issues: the alien bill, the partiality of the judicial system, and the large-scale provincial support needed for public works, such as the Welland Canal. Increasingly, Willson associated with such men as John Beverley Robinson and John Strachan, the closest advisers of Lieutenant Governor Sir Peregrine Maitland. Slowly but surely, the image of Willson as he had been in opposition changed until he had become the epitome of the political turncoat and double-dealer. In 1828 Mackenzie, who described Willson as 'positively ministerial' and featured him prominently on his legislative 'Black List,' wrote, 'The more I examined his past parliamentary conduct, the more I was satisfied that he was acting a double and deceitful part as a politician.' In his resurrection of the province's political past, Mackenzie, looking for patterns of parliamentary compliance with unpopular administrations, singled out for particular censure the session of 1816; an impression of Willson's role in this session stuck among the reform-minded of the 1820s and 1830s. In 1831 John Rolph claimed the 'Maitland Faction' rivalled 'the ever memorable parliament of 1816: and John Willson appears to act over again the same character which at that time brought upon him the odium of the country.'

Through the latter half of the 1820s and into the 1830s, politics in Hamilton became associated in the opposition press with the abuse of civil liberties: the tar and feathering and then the dismissal, from the position of clerk of the peace, of George Rolph, an ardent reformer and John's brother; the alleged violations of judicial principles by Judge Christopher Alexander Hagerman during the murder trial of Michael Vincent; the failure of local magistrates to act against a tory mob in the so-called 'Hamilton Outrage' in 1829; and the beating of Mackenzie. In the town a distinctive local political culture was emerging, partly in response to attacks by reformers in York (Toronto) such as Mackenzie and Francis Collins. The flashpoint was the decision by Mackenzie and Collins in 1825 to support Peter Desjardins's proposal to build a canal to connect Dundas and Burlington Bay (Hamilton Harbour). The scheme was derided by Willson who saw, in Hamilton's rival Burlington Bay Canal, 'the life and soul of all prosperity to the Gore, the Wellington, and the Brock Districts.' York reformers, especially Mackenzie, not only supported the Desjardins Canal, they sided with the pretensions of Dundas over those of Hamilton to become a commercial and administrative capital at the Head of the Lake. In Hamilton the cause of political reform withered as beleaguered residents, of disparate ethnic, religious, and political backgrounds, came together in common cause over local economic development. In defence of its economic ambitions, Hamilton began with John Willson to turn to political leaders who would represent its interests. Its first newspaper, the *Gore Balance*, begun in 1829 by Bartemas Ferguson, was hostile to radicalism (especially of the York variety), championed development, and ardently boosted John Willson.

For his part, Willson considered himself a conservative independent, a spokesman of the interests of small farmers. In 1819 he had offered himself for the office of district court judge as a means of obviating the 'evil' that could result from the marriage of that office to a man of commerce. Eight years later, during his speakership and at a time when he was being vilified by reformers, he criticized an assembly 'composed of government officers, placemen, and pentioners.' His remedy was more farmers and fewer lawyers in government – in other words, plain, ordinary folk who would attend to useful improvements rather than spending their time 'in levees, balls, and dinners with a view to procure places and pensions.' In 1832, for instance, while Marshall Spring Bidwell was lashing him for being 'opposed to popular measures,' Willson supported Peter Perry's bill for disposing of the clergy reserves. Willson, in fact, went further and argued that the entire proceeds be appropriated to education and, much to Bidwell's displeasure, that all denominations, including Roman Catholics, had a claim on the reserves. Willson had reservations about Perry's attempt to reform the jury laws but sympathized with its main thrust. 'I am not fond of leaving the selection of juries to the Sheriff,' Willson said in the assembly. Finally, he supported a bill to bar dower. Though wives 'might not be actually employed in clearing the land,' he reasoned, 'they were often called upon to assist, and they were therefore as much entitled to a property in the land, and should have the right to dispose of that title.'

Willson did not contest the election of 1834, a date that marks the ascendancy of Allan Napier MacNab as chief advocate of Hamilton's interests. None the less, Willson continued to be a major force. On 11 Dec. 1839 he was appointed to the Legislative Council, just in time for the critical debate on the proposed union with Lower Canada. Willson, who had opposed the scheme when it first came up in 1822 because of the differences between the two colonies in law, language, and religion, voted with the minority against union. That vote cost him the chance of reappointment to the council after the declaration of union on 10 Feb. 1841. He had had enough of politics and decried the rise of party, 'a grasping power exerted to confine ... the whole patronage of the government.' Thereafter, he retired from public life to his farm in Saltfleet.

Locally, Willson served for many years as a justice of the peace, surrogate court judge, road commissioner, inspector of licences and stills, trustee of the Gore District Grammar School, commissioner for the Burlington Bay Canal, and member of the district board of health. He also served as a commissioner for the Welland Canal but was removed in 1840 by Lieutenant Governor Sir George Arthur for urging completion of the work on 'a scale of expence' which Arthur regarded as 'quite improper.' As well, Willson was active in the Gore District Emigrant Society and in the Agricultural Society of the Gore District.

John Willson died in 1860 at his farm and was buried in St Andrew's churchyard in Grimsby. He left a modest estate worth about $6,000; he had sold off most of his lands in the early 1850s to his sons. A Methodist and then a supporter of Henry Ryan, he seems to have become an Anglican in later life. Contemporary political language serves no useful purpose in coming to terms with 'Honest John.' There was a measure of continuity to his politics and it was this continuity that best defines the man. To his mind, it was the times that had changed, not he himself. He was, as he put it, a 'plain farmer,' self-educated, and ever concerned 'to reap the advantages of the country,' by which he meant a due regard for the farmer, moderate constitutional reform, liberal marriage laws, cheap justice, universal and decentralized elementary education, and economic development. In the combination of moderate conservatism and unabashed support for development, one finds the defining characteristics of Hamilton's political culture to the present day. Willson was its first spokesman.

ROBERT L. FRASER

Contributors

ELIZABETH ABBOTT is Dean of Women at St Hilda's College, University of Toronto, Toronto, Ontario.

FREDERICK H. ARMSTRONG is Professor Emeritus of History at the University of Western Ontario, London, Ontario.

PETER BASKERVILLE is a professor of History at the University of Victoria, Victoria, British Columbia.

JOHN D. BLACKWELL is a historian and writer in Antigonish, Nova Scotia.

GERALD E. BOYCE is an author, researcher, and city councillor in Belleville, Ontario.

DANIEL J. BROCK is a teacher at Catholic Central High School, London, Ontario.

ROBERT J. BURNS is a historian with Environment Canada, Parks Service, in Ottawa, Ontario.

DENNIS CARTER-EDWARDS is Area Superintendent with Environment Canada, Parks Service, at Fort Malden National Historic Park, Amherstburg, Ontario.

WILLIAM G. COX is Head of the History Department at Carleton Place High School, Carleton Place, Ontario.

G.M. CRAIG was a professor of History at the University of Toronto, Toronto, Ontario.

MICHAEL S. CROSS is a professor of History at Dalhousie University, Halifax, Nova Scotia.

GORDON DODDS is Associate Provincial Archivist, Government Records, at the Provincial Archives of Manitoba, Winnipeg, Manitoba.

DAVID R. FARRELL is a professor of History at the University of Guelph, Guelph, Ontario.

EDITH G. FIRTH is the former head of the Canadian History Department at the Metropolitan Toronto Library, Toronto, Ontario.

DOUGLAS L. FLANDERS is Director of the Department of Education and Information at the National Offices of the United Church of Canada, Toronto, Ontario.

ROBERT L. FRASER is a historian in Hamilton, Ontario.

H. PEARSON GUNDY is Professor Emeritus of English at Queen's University, Kingston, Ontario.

BRUCE W. HODGINS is a professor of History and Director of the Frost Centre for Canadian Heritage and Development Studies at Trent University, Peterborough, Ontario.

ELWOOD H. JONES is a professor of History at Trent University, Peterborough, Ontario.

JOHN LOWNSBROUGH is a writer in Toronto, Ontario.

RUTH McKENZIE is a freelance writer, editor, and researcher in Ottawa, Ontario.

S.R. MEALING is retired from the Department of History at Carleton University, Ottawa, Ontario.

GEORGE METCALF was a professor of History at the University of Western Ontario, London, Ontario.

ROBERT J. MORGAN is Director of the Beaton Institute at the University College of Cape Breton, Sydney, Nova Scotia.

BRIAN H. MORRISON Toronto, Ontario.

GRAEME H. PATTERSON is a professor of History at the University of Toronto, Toronto, Ontario.

IAN C. PEMBERTON is a professor of History at the University of Windsor, Windsor, Ontario.

RICHARD A. PRESTON is W.K. Boyd Professor of History Emeritus, Duke University, Durham, North Carolina.

COLIN READ is a professor of History at Huron College, University of Western Ontario, London, Ontario.

PAUL ROMNEY is a private scholar in Baltimore, Maryland.

VICTOR L. RUSSELL is Manager of the City of Toronto Archives, Toronto, Ontario.

ROBERT E. SAUNDERS is Chief Executive Officer of the Education Relations Commission and the College Relations Commission, Government of Ontario, Toronto, Ontario.

ELINOR SENIOR was a professor of History at St Francis Xavier University, Antigonish, Nova Scotia.

Contributors 451

HEREWARD SENIOR is a professor of History at McGill University, Montreal, Quebec.

RONALD J. STAGG is a professor and Chair of the Department of History at Ryerson Polytechnical Institute, Toronto, Ontario.

THOMAS H.B. SYMONS is Vanier Professor and President Emeritus at Trent University, Peterborough, Ontario, and Chair of the Historic Sites and Monuments Board of Canada.

WILLIAM TEATERO is a policy analyst at the Ontario Ministry of Health, Kingston, Ontario.

HARRY E. TURNER is Professor Emeritus of History at McMaster University, Hamilton, Ontario.

CAROL M. WHITFIELD is Special Projects Manager with Environment Canada, Parks Service, in Ottawa, Ontario.

ALAN WILSON is Professor Emeritus of History at Trent University, Peterborough, Ontario, and a senior research fellow of the Gorsebrook Research Institute, St Mary's University, Halifax, Nova Scotia.

WILLIAM N.T. WYLIE is a historian with Environment Canada, Parks Service, in Ottawa, Ontario.

Index

Biographies of individuals are indicated by boldface type

alien question, lxviii, 93, 108–9, 158–9, 160, 162–4, 165, 225–6, 257–8, 292, 366–7, 371, 406, 411, 412, 428, 430, 445. *See also* Bidwell, Barnabas
Allan, Ebenezer (businessman), 343, 400
Allan, Ebenezer (convicted criminal), 60–1
Allan, William, 109–10, 222–3, 274, 275, 277, 291, 322, 334, 390, 415
Allcock, Henry, xlix–l, li, lv, **3–7**, 40, 77, 142, 145, 152, 182, 183, 285, 317, 432, 433
allegiance, oath of, 364, 365, 366
American revolution, xxix, xxxii, 136, 176, 253, 254
amnesty: for rebels of 1837–8, 21, 27, 69, 231, 265

Ancaster assizes (1814), xxv, lix, 56, 148–9, 155, 183, 205, 245, 250, 291, 323–6, 341, 403
Anderson, John, 128, 172
Anger family, 320, 321, 324, 325, 326
Anglican rectories question, 111, 416
anti-Catholicism: in Upper Canada, 32
arbitrary power, xxxv, 433, 435, 437, 440, 442
aristocracy: in Upper Canada, xxix, xxx, xxxi, xxxvi, xxxvii, lxiv
arson: cases of, 111, 113
Arthur, Sir George, 96–7, 98, 112, 113, 167, 186, 223, 231, 275, 276, 277, 334, 335, 447
assault: cases of, liv, lvi–lvii, 156, 193. *See also* Sullivan, Daniel

(blacksmith)
assessment laws, 84, 274, 438
assizes, annual: in Upper Canada, 55–6
attaint, writ of, 425
attorney general: appointments as, 41, 19–20, 26–7, 43, 66, 79, 96, 100, 122, 154, 156, 182, 192; duties, 101; fees, 80–1
attorney general (Cape Breton), 52, 54
attorneys and barristers: distinction established, xliii, 193

Baby, François, xxx
Baby, James, 116, 139, 152, 253, 255, 358, 394
Backhouse, John, 398
Badgley, William, 71
Bagot, Sir Charles, 19, 21, 66, 67, 68, 187, 278
Baldwin, Augustus Warren, 218, 274, 277, 415
Baldwin, Robert, xxiv, lxiv, lxvi, lxxi, lxxii, **8–38**, 48, 65, 114, 119, 171, 229, 241, 248, 251, 274–5, 278, 372, 414, 418, 419; and W.W. Baldwin, 204, 205, 206, 211, 218, 220; and responsible government, lxxiii, 214, 215, 217, 219; and John Rolph, 259, 260, 261, 262, 263; and J.H. Samson, 270, 271; and R.B. Sullivan, 272–3, 279–80; and S.E. Washburn, 283, 284; and Willis affair, lxix, lxx, 196, 197, 198, 212–13. See also Baldwin–La Fontaine ministry
Baldwin, William Warren, xxiv, xl, xliii, xlv–xlvi, lxiv, lxix, lxxii, lxxv, xcii n.196, 80, 89, 90, 106, 111, 122, 127, **201–21**, 227, 248, 250, 251, 367, 440; and Robert Baldwin, 8, 9, 11–12, 13, 15, 20; and John Rolph, 259, 261, 262; and R.B. Sullivan, 272, 273, 274–5; and S.E. Washburn, 283, 284; and Willis affair, lxx, lxxi, 196, 197, 198
Baldwin, William Willcocks, 36, 37–8
Baldwin–La Fontaine ministry: first, 19, 67–8, 278; second, 24, 26, 27–8, 49, 71–2, 235, 265–6, 281, 418
ballot: bill to legalize, 228; secret, 412
Bank of Upper Canada, 12, 109–10, 220, 222–3, 224, 239–40, 252, 412; 'pretended,' at Kingston, 91–2
banks: in Upper Canada, 228, 271. *See also* People's Bank
bar: admission to, in Newfoundland, 46
Barclay, John, 95, 96
Bathurst, Henry, 3rd Earl Bathurst, 81, 190, 328, 330, 344, 345
Beamer, Jacob R., 113
Beardsley, Bartholomew Crannell, 92, 323, 327, 330, 379
Beasley, Richard, 207, 333, 443
Bédard, Pierre-Stanislas, 215
Beikie, John, 123, 409
Bell, William, 247, 248
Bentley, Benjamin, 291
Bentley, Elijah, **289–92**, 343, 375, 400
Bentley, Ira, 289, 291
Bently, Samuel, 289, 291

Berczy, William, 133, 179
Berthon, George Theodore, 134
Bethune, Donald, 94, **222-4**
Bidwell, Barnabas, xlv, lxiv, lxviii, 89-90, 108, 158-9, 163, 186, 197, 208, 225, **361-9**
Bidwell, Marshall Spring, xxiv, lxiv, lxvi, lxxi, lxxii, lxxv, 90, 95, 106, 108, 158-9, 163, 196, 198, 213, 216, 217, **225-33**, 240, 241, 251, 367, 368, 411, 416, 417, 419, 446; and Robert Baldwin, 11, 13, 14, 21, 27; and John Rolph, 259, 260, 261, 262
Biggar, William, 402
blacks: Sir William Campbell's views on, 58; convicted of capital crimes, 316
Blackstone, Sir William, xl, 105, 109, 129, 203, 209, 434
Blake, William Hume, 26-7, 74, 101, 102, 235, 280, 283, 418, 419
Bliss v. Street, xlix, l, lv
Bonnycastle, Sir Richard Henry, 390
Boswell, John, xlv-xlvi
Boucher, François-Firmin, 185
Boulton, D'Arcy, **39-42**, 43, 59, 79, 80, 93, 116, 153, 155, 156, 313, 352, 376; and Robert Randal, 423, 424, 426
Boulton, George Strange, 44, 64
Boulton, Henry John, lxx, 26, 31, 41-2, **43-50**, 94, 100, 116, 196, 212, 217, 235, 274, 280-1, 389, 405; cases prosecuted by, 157, 304, 327; Jarvis-Ridout duel, lxix, 164-5, 371-2; and Robert Randal, 424, 426, 427, 430, 431
Boulton, James, 247
Boulton, William Henry, 24, 49, 267
Boulton v. Randal, 424-5, 426
Boyd, Sir John Alexander, 391
Braddock, Edward, 175
Brant, Joseph. *See* Thayendanegea
Brass, William, 113, **293-5**
Breakenridge, John, 234
Briggs, Jacob, 98
British connection, xxxviii, 22-3, 26, 28, 31, 44, 48, 65, 128, 158, 160-1, 162, 173, 190, 219, 374, 410, 416
Brock, Sir Isaac, 55, 123-5, 143-4, 154, 322, 400, 401, 438-9
Brown, George, 27, 32, 34, 37, 73, 74, 419
Brown, John, 385, 386, 387-8
Brown, Paul, 185
Bruce, James, 8th Earl of Elgin, 23, 24, 28, 71, 171, 266, 281
Buell, William, 20, 101, 108, 111
Buell family, 105
Bullock, Richard, 295
burglary: cases of, 148. *See also* York, Jack
Burke, Edmund, 362, 367
Burley, Cornelius Albertson, **296-300**
Burns, David, 84, 203
Burns, Patrick, 349
Burns, Robert Easton, 26, **234-5**
Burns, Mowat, and VanKoughnet, 234
Burton, Nathaniel, 421, 423
Burwell, Adam Hood, 151
Burwell, Mahlon, 151, 297, 298, 366, 400, 406

Bytown College (University of Ottawa), 30

Caldwell, Sir John, 159
Cameron, Duncan, 122, 124, 290
Cameron, John Hillyard, 23, 71, 119
Cameron, Malcolm, 25, 30–1, 248, 266
Campbell, Sir William, xxxiv, 41, **51–63**, 88, 91, 93, 152, 165, 196, 197, 352, 426; at Ancaster assizes, 148, 323; cases heard by, 10, 310–11, 312, 313, 327–8, 330, 332, 344, 346
Canada Company, 165, 219
Canada Trade Act (1822), 159–60
Canadian Alliance Society, 186
Canby, Benjamin, 420, 421
Carey, John, 373, 374
Carleton, Guy, 1st Baron Dorchester, 132, 138, 139, 140, 253
Carmichael, Hugh, 267
Caron, René-Edouard, 25, 70–1, 279–80
Carroll, John Saltkill, 394, 395
Cartier, Sir George-Étienne. *See* Macdonald–Cartier ministry
Cartwright, John Solomon, 66, 98, 113, 240, 294, 416
Cartwright, Richard, xli, xlii, liv, lvii, lix, lxi, 77, 129, 131, 132, 143, 145, 355, 397, 399
Cassady, Henry, 293, 294
Cassidy, John, 306, 307, 308
Caswell, John, 294, 295
Cayley, William, 71, 223
Chancery Bill (1849), 26–7. *See also* Court of Chancery
Charter of Rights and Freedoms, lxxvi
chief justice: appointments as, 4, 62, 76, 129, 145, 165, 183; as president of Executive Council and speaker of Legislative Council, lxxiv, lxxv, lxxvi, xc–xci n.188, 78, 412. *See also* judiciary: independence of
chief justice (Lower Canada), 5, 77–8, 79, 132
chief justice (Newfoundland), 45
chief justice (Prince Edward Island), 188
cholera: epidemics of 1832 and 1834, 251, 259, 270, 283, 347, 373
church and state, separation of, xxxii, 35, 219, 258, 261, 262, 412
church law: violation of, 3
Church of England: in Upper Canada, xxx, lii, 95, 106, 130, 140, 158, 163, 171, 226, 240, 258, 261, 277, 413. *See also* Anglican rectories question; clergy reserves
Church of Scotland: in Upper Canada, 95–6, 127, 241
civil cases: hearing of, 55
civil list: control of, 22, 69, 90, 438
civil rights, xxxiii, xxxiv, xxxv, l, li, lix, lxxi, 19, 106, 183, 271, 322, 443, 445
Clark, Benjamin, 321, 324, 325, 326
Clark, James, 143, 203, **236–8**
Clark, Peter, 236
Clark, Thomas, 157, 208, 327, 328, 329, 382–3, 387–91, 422, 423, 425–8, 430
Clarke, Isaac Winslow, 137
clergy reserves, 30, 33, 65, 93,

Index 457

95–6, 140, 146–7, 165, 168, 169–70, 171, 219, 220, 226, 227, 240, 261, 266, 277, 413, 446
Cloud, Daniel, 310, 311
Cochrane, Thomas, 84
Cochrane, Sir Thomas John, 45
Coffin, Nathaniel, 389
Colborne, Sir John, 1st Baron Seaton, 44, 45, 94, 95, 99, 110, 165, 240, 297, 307–8, 372, 413, 430
Collins, Francis, xxiii–xxiv, lxiii, lxvi, lxviii, lxix, lxx, lxxii, 43, 94, 164–5, 186, 197, 211, 258, 272–3, **370–4**, 381, 392, 393, 401, 445
Columbia Law School, 232
Commercial Bank of the Midland District, 223, 239–40, 241
Common Schools Act (1841): amendments to, 30–1
common schools act (1846), 69
Common Schools Bill (1816), 443
Company of Canadian Volunteers, lix, 292, 401, 441
concealment: in cases of infanticide, 352, 353, 354
conservative party: W.H. Draper's attempts to form, 65, 67, 70, 71–2
constitution: of Upper Canada, xxv, xxxiii–xxxiv, xxxix, l, 58, 63, 89–90, 173. *See also* Constitutional Act (1791)
constitution, British, xxvii, xxviii, xxxiv–xxxv, xxxviii, xlvii, li, lv–lvi, lix, lx, lxi, lxxi, lxxiv–lxxv, 58, 207, 410, 411, 415, 416, 418, 419
Constitutional Act (1791), xxv, xxvi, xxviii–xxxii, xxxv, xxxvi,

xxxviii, lii, lx, lxxiv, xc–xci n.188, 90, 146, 161, 192, 209–10, 211, 214, 254–5, 276, 366
Constitutional Reform Society of Upper Canada, 218
contempt: charges of, 46–7, 84, 371, 389, 420
coroners: appointment of, 29
corporate law, 241
corvée, law of: prosecutions under, 137
Couche, John Rodolph, 303, 304
Couche, Rebecca. *See* Smith, Rebecca (Couche)
Court of Appeal: appointments to, 101, 119, 187
Court of Chancery: attempts to establish, 3, 5, 189, 195–6, 427; bill to abolish, 33; commission to review (1842–3), 102, 119; creation of, xlii; R.S. Jameson vice-chancellor of, 101; not in Judicature Act (1794), 131; jurisdiction, 101; reform of, 26–7, 102–3
Court of Common Pleas: appointments to, 73, 119, 128, 281; bill to give salaries to judges in, 399; case overturned by, 172; creation of, 26; value of, 130, 131
Court of Error and Appeal: appointments to, 73, 119, 128, 174; creation of, 26
Court of King's (Queen's) Bench: appeal issues heard by, 55; appointments to, 3, 40, 41, 54–5, 71, 73, 93, 97, 112, 117, 128, 140, 178, 180, 186, 188, 195, 230, 235, 281; cases heard by, 240–1; creation of, xlii, 131, 193; duties of judges, xlii, 3, 55–6, 98,

117; fees, 80; legality of. See Willis, John Walpole; move to York (Toronto), 76; reform of, 171–2; reporter, 64, 283; value of, 130; violation of rules, 424
court of probate: creation of, 131
Court of Quarter Sessions, xlii, 283
courts, division, 235
courts of common law: bill to transfer equity jurisdiction to, 33
courts of common pleas, district, xli–xlii, 131; Hesse District, 139, 254; Montreal District, 139
Craig, Sir James Henry, 6
Crandall, Reuben, 289, 375–7
criminal cases, 55–6; defence counsel in, lxv; inhumane treatment in, 196
Crooks, James, xlvi, lxi, 317, 322, 323, 328
crown lands: act to remit arrears on, in Lower Canada, 133
Cutler, Thomas, 51
Cuttan (Cutten), Josiah, 316

Dalhousie, Earl of. See Ramsay, George, 9th Earl of Dalhousie
Dalton, Thomas, 90–1
Daly, W.L., lxii–lxiii
De Bonne, Pierre-Amable, 133
debt: bill to relieve creditors, 399; imprisonment for, lxi, 131, 150, 226, 227, 258, 412. See also Randal, Robert
democracy: views on, 89, 173–4, 290, 292
Dempsey, Mary Ann, 293, 294
desertion: cases of. See Seely, Joseph
Desjardins Canal, 173, 445

Despard, John, 52–4
Detroit, battle of. See War of 1812
Dickson, Thomas, 320–1, 323, 324, 379
Dickson, William, lvi, 121, 157, 208, 209, 286, 317, 384, 388, 424, 426
District School Act, 399
Doan, Joel P., 301–2
Doan, Joshua Gwillen, 301–2
Dorchester, Baron. See Carleton, Guy, 1st Baron Dorchester
Dorion, Sir Antoine-Aimé, 74
double majority principle, 71
'double shuffle,' 74
Douglas, Thomas, 5th Earl of Selkirk, liii, 150, 156, 397. See also Red River colony
dower, 23–4, 446
Doxater, Susannah, 333, 334
Draper, William George, 75
Draper, William Henry, 19, 23, 48, 64–75, 96, 97, 119, 128, 187, 240, 241, 277, 279–80, 294, 307, 334
Drew, Andrew, 334, 335
Drummond, Sir Gordon, lxxvii n.3, 56, 87, 312–13, 323, 325, 342
Du Calvet, Pierre, 137
duelling, 4, 130; charges arising from, 164–5. See also Jarvis, Samuel Peters
Duggan, George, 283
Duggan, John, 235
Duncombe, Charles, 256, 301
Dunn, John Henry, 13–14, 218, 229, 260, 279
Dunn, Thomas, 6
Durand, Charles Morrison, lxxii, 85, 221, 349

Index 459

Durand, James, 421, 422, 424, 426, 443, 444
Durham, Earl of; Durham report. See Lambton, John George, 1st Earl of Durham

Early, Thomas, lxxix n.8
Easten, James Christie Palmer, 101, 103
Elgin, Earl of. See Bruce, James, 8th Earl of Elgin
Elmsley, John, xlix, 3, 4, 5, **76–8**, 84, 131, 141, 149, 179–80, 237, 244
Elmsley, John (son), 240–1, 274, 415
English legal models: in Upper Canada, xli, xlii, 3, 77, 130–1, 149, 192
equity law, 33, 100, 101, 129, 130, 195. See also Court of Chancery
established church: in Upper Canada. See Church of England
executions, xxi–xxii, 294–5, 296, 298, 318, 347, 394
executive and judicial powers, separation of. See judiciary: independence of
Executive Council: cases referred to, 335, 394; committee to investigate, 118. See also ministerial responsibility
Executive Council (Cape Breton): legality of ordinances passed by, 54
executive power, 105, 106
extradition: case of, 172

'family compact,' 39, 43, 64, 65, 113, 127, 162, 166, 167, 186, 226, 227, 257, 259, 271, 395, 430; in Massachusetts, 362
Fanning, Edmund, 188
felony: bill to allow counsel for persons tried for, 226, 412, 414
Ferguson, Bartemas, xxiii–xxiv, lxiv–lxv, lxviii, 93–4, 207, 246, 299, **378–81**, 446
Firth, William, 40, 41, **79–82**, 122, 127, 203, 207
Fitzgibbon, James, 128, 284
Fleming, Michael Anthony, 46, 47, 48
Forest, William D., 392, 393
Forsyth, William, lxviii, lxix, 93, 211, **382–91**, 395
Fothergill, Charles, 151, 351, 354, 371, 407, 429
Fraser, John, 137, 138
freedom of the press, 241, 371, 373, 379, 381
free trade, 25, 26, 280
French, Charles, lxviii, **392–5**
French language: repeal of restrictions on, 69
Frichet, Charles, 134
fugitive slaves. See Anderson, John
Fuller, Andrew, 310, 311

Galt, John, 160
Gardiner, Singleton, lxx, 151, 212
Gibbons, Richard Collier Bernard DesBarres Marshall, 53–4
Girty, James, 148, 355, 357, 358
Givins, James, 389
Glenelg, Baron. See Grant, Charles, 1st Baron Glenelg
Gore, Francis, lvii, 40–1, 55, 59, 79, 80, 81, 87, 121, 122–3, 142–4, 145, 183, 189, 190, 203,

204, 207, 238, 286, 290, 399, 435, 436, 443, 444
Goslin, James Pratt, 392, 393, 394
Gourlay, Robert Fleming, lxiv, lxviii, 27, 57, 88–9, 105, 106, 150, 157–8, 185, 196, 197, 207, 209, 258, 330, 365, 378, 379, 380, 410, 426, 444
government officials: bill to prevent from sitting in the House of Assembly, 399, 438
Gowan, Ogle Robert, 68, 101, 109, 110–11
Grant, Alexander, 180, 182–3, 189, 238, 355
Grant, Charles, 1st Baron Glenelg, 96, 167, 230, 231, 251
Grant, William, 137
Gray, James, 111
Gray, Robert Isaac Dey, 4, 40, **83–4**
Gray v. Willcocks, lv
Gurnett, George, 240–1, 380

habeas corpus, 58, 137–8; suspension during the War of 1812, lix, 148, 292, 322, 439, 443
Hagerman, Christopher Alexander, xxxviii, xliv, xlv, lxxii, lxxv, lxxvii, 44, 62, 64, 66, **85–99**, 105, 106, 109, 111, 113, 114, 117, 152, 196, 197, 208, 222, 223, 228, 230, 231, 234, 261, 270, 271, 273, 277, 372, 394, 431; cases heard by, xxiii–xxiv, lxxviii–lxxx n.8, 427, 445; cases prosecuted by, 298, 344
Hagerman, Daniel, 225, 365
Hagerman, Nicholas, 85–6
Haldimand, Sir Frederick, 137, 138
Hamilton, Elizabeth Ann (Anderson), 327, 329, 330
Hamilton, Henry, lxxxix n.166
Hamilton, Robert, xxix, xlii, xlviii, lvii, lxi, 132, 141, 317, 355, 382, 421, 435, 437
Hamilton outrage (1829), 445
Harrison, Samuel Bealey, 18, 19, 66, 67, 68
Hartwell, Joseph K., 108
Hatt, Richard, 323, 436, 443, 444
Hatt, Samuel, 323
Hawe, King Hans, 61
Hawn, Mathias, lvi–lvii
Head, Sir Edmund Walker, 74
Head, Sir Francis Bond, 13–15, 64–5, 96, 112, 113, 118, 166, 218, 220, 228–9, 230, 231, 251, 260, 261–2, 263, 264, 274, 275, 414, 416
Heir and Devisee Commission, 141, 144, 178–9
Higgins, William, 349
High Court of Justice: case referred to, 391
Hillier, George, 91, 109
Hincks, Sir Francis, 15, 17, 19, 21, 22, 25, 26, 29, 32, 34–5, 48, 218, 219, 260, 278, 279–80, 419
Hincks–Morin ministry, 34, 266–7
Hoff, Isaac, lxiii
Holly, Jesse, 149
Hornor, Thomas, 429
Horton, Sir Robert John Wilmot. *See* Wilmot-Horton, Sir Robert John
Horton, William, 344
Howard, Matthew Munsel, 101, 111
Howard, Peter, lxi, 438
Hudson's Bay Company: territorial

Index   461

rights, 73
Hunter, Peter, li–lii, 4, 5, 6, 77, 78, 142, 152, 180, 182, 189, 202, 203, 208, 285, 286, 357, 358, 433, 434, 435

imbecility, 60
immigration: views on, 160, 165, 173, 276, 277
immunity from legal proceedings, Indians' supposed. *See* Indians: and criminal law
imprisonment, false: case of, lvii
Indian affairs: report on, 118; responsibility for, 179
Indian customs: guaranteed under treaty, 344
Indian Department: commission to examine, 102, 118
Indians: and criminal law, 63, 149, 332, 344–5; right to alienate land, 179
infanticide: cases of. *See* Pilotte, Angelique; Thompson, Mary; repeal of statute on, in Upper Canada, 353–4
Inspector General's Office: commission to examine, 102
intestate estates bills, 89, 208, 226, 412
Ironside, George, 344

Jackson, James, 298–9
Jackson, John Mills, lviii, 245, 435, 438
jails: conditions in, 118, 308–9. *See also* Kingston Penitentiary
Jameson, Anna. *See* Murphy, Anna Brownell (Jameson)
Jameson, Robert Sympson, 96, **100–3**, 111, 118
Jarvis, Samuel Peters, lxix, 12, 117, 142, 151, 164, 250, 335, 371, 392
Jarvis, William, 80, 141, 142, 243, 244, 250, 290, 432
Jarvis, William Munson, 308
Jay's Treaty, 178
Jones, Charles, xliv, xlv, lxi, 106, 107, 108, 208, 340
Jones, Jonas, xliv, xlv–xlvi, lxvi–lxvii, 62, 85, 89, 97, 99, **104–14**, 115, 208, 222, 294, 312, 353, 366
judges: salaries of, 59
Judicature Act (1794), xli, xlii, xlvii, 131–2, 193
judicial system, 77; dissatisfaction with, lx, lxiii, lxiv, lxv, lxvii, lxxii, lxxiii, 33, 93, 94; impartiality of, xxii–xxiii, xxiv–xxv, xxxiii, xxxv, lviii, lxxii, lxxv, 57, 444, 445; reform of, 26–7, 84, 280
judicial system (Lower Canada): views on, 6, 78
judicial system (Newfoundland): reform of, 45
judiciary: independence of, xxxii, xxxv, lxxv, xci n.188, 166, 180, 412. *See also* chief justice: as president of Executive Council
juries: bills to regulate, 226, 399, 438, 446; empanelling of, in Newfoundland, 45; tendency to acquit, 61
juries, grand: Sir William Campbell's views on, 58, 60

Kain, William, **303–5**, 318
Kent, John, 45, 47

Kerr, William Johnson, 328, 334, 335, 427
King's College, 29, 65, 70, 102, 171, 226–7, 265, 413, 414. See also University of Toronto
Kingston Penitentiary: commission to investigate, 27

La Fontaine, Sir Louis-Hippolyte, 18, 20, 21, 22, 23, 26, 30, 33, 34, 36, 70, 71, 72, 280, 281. See also Baldwin–La Fontaine ministry
Lambton, John George, 1st Earl of Durham, 15, 29, 65, 97, 167–9, 170, 219, 275
land boards, 139–40
landed property: seizure for debt, xlix, liv, lv, lxi
Landen, Herman, 341–2
land grants, 434, 435; fees on, lii, 80, 194; patents, 182; regulation of, lii, liv, 4, 77, 178–9, 192; unpatented, 102
land grants (Lower Canada), 132–3, 138
law society: act to incorporate, in Newfoundland, 46
Law Society Act (1822), xliii–xlv, lxiii, lxxvi, 106
Law Society of Upper Canada, xliii–xlvi, lxiv, 116, 134, 235, 238, 244, 270, 272, 273, 283; founding in 1797, xliii, 193, 237, 255; treasurers, xl–xli, lxxv, 9, 35, 37, 83, 102, 119, 187, 206, 211, 250. See also Law Society Act (1822); Osgoode Hall
Le Breton, John, 187, 425, 427
Lefferty, John Johnston, 389, 429
legal aid: provided by S.E. Washburn, 284
legal profession: rise of, xl–xlvii, lxi, lxiii, lxiv
Legislative Council (Province of Canada): proposal to make it elective, 31, 49, 415
Legislative Council (Upper Canada), xxxi, lxv
Leonard, Richard, 388
libel: cases of, lxviii, 19, 47, 81, 151, 240–1, 247, 271, 438. See also Collins, Francis; Ferguson, Bartemas; seditious libel
libel law, lxiv; amendments to, 414
London, Bartholomew, 316–17
London, Mary. See Osborn, Mary (London)
Lount, Samuel, 167, 263, 267, 315
loyalism, xxvi–xxix, xxxii, xxxiii, lvii–lviii
loyalty: during the War of 1812, 310–13, 341, 342, 439, 441
Lunatic Asylum, Toronto. See Provincial Lunatic Asylum
Lundy's Lane, battle of. See War of 1812
Lyon, Robert, 248
Lyons, Elijah, 92

Mabane, Adam, 138
Macaulay, Sir James Buchanan, 10, 62, 73, 88, 94, 97, 98, **115–20**, 128, 217, 297, 394, 405; cases heard by, 304, 307–8, 309, 347, 388
Macaulay, John, xxix, 85, 90, 91, 95, 96, 98–9, 104, 107, 110, 114, 158, 275
McCarthy, James Owen, lxxxix n.166, 117, **306–9**

McCulloch, James Maitland, 421, 423
Macdonald, Sir John Alexander, 34, 71, 72, 73, 74, 119, 241–2, 293, 294, 339
Macdonald, John Sandfield, 24, 33, 34, 128
Macdonald–Cartier ministry, 73, 74
McDonell, Alexander, 44, 123, 350, 373
McDonell (Collachie), Alexander, 121, 123, 125
Macdonell (Collachie), Angus, l, 84, 237, 285, 433
Macdonell (Greenfield), John, **121–6**, 143, 154, 204, 250, 439
McGill, John, 143, 182–3, 420, 421, 435
McKee, Alexander, 139, 253, 355, 358
McKee, Thomas, 357
McKenney, Amos, 378, 379
Mackenzie, George, **239–42**
Mackenzie, William Lyon, lxiv, lxvii, lxxi, lxxvi, 11, 12, 32, 33, 34, 89, 105, 108, 109, 116–17, 143, 150, 162, 166, 228–9, 242, 251, 257, 260, 261, 267, 284, 301, 348–9, 373, 380, 381, 385, 386, 390, 392, 393, 409, 413, 414–15, 416, 429, 430, 444, 445; amnesty for, 21, 27; expulsion from the House of Assembly, 44–5, 94–5, 228, 240, 271; and family compact, 39, 42, 44, 395. *See also* rebellion of 1837–8; types riot
McLane, David, 134
McLean, Archibald, xliii, 73, 85, 97, 104, 107, 111, 112, 113, 115, 123, 124, **127–8**, 312, 340, 341, 342, 400
MacNab, Sir Allan Napier, 17, 34, 69, 71, 111, 113, 211, 241, 302, 307, 333, 446
McNab, Archibald, 19, 247
McNiff, Patrick, xxx
McSwiney, Edward, 57, **310–13**
magistrates, lxii–lxiii, lxv
Magowan, Peter, 188
Maitland, Sir Peregrine, lxix, lxxi, 11, 12, 42, 56, 91, 93, 105, 109, 116, 147, 149, 151–2, 157, 158, 160, 163, 165, 196, 197, 210, 211, 213, 344, 345, 346, 351, 352, 373, 376, 378, 386, 388, 390, 393–4, 404, 405, 408, 409, 428, 430
Mallory, Benajah, liii–liv, lix, lxi, lxii, **396–403**, 438, 441
manslaughter, 307–8, 394, 395
Markland, George Herchmer, 13, 14, 89, 91, 104, 353
Markle, Abraham, 183, 322, 323, 343, 401, 402, 439, 441
Marriage Act (1798), 289, 375
marriages: bills to liberalize law on, lii, 84, 106, 131, 226, 227, 413, 443; illegally performed, 148. *See also* Crandall, Reuben
married women: alienation of property, 77
Marshall, Charles, 159
martial law: during the War of 1812, xliv, lix, 148, 183, 292
Mathews, David, 52
Matthews, John, lxviii, lxxi, 258, 273, 388, 389, 395, **404–9**
Matthews, Peter, 167, **314–15**
Maxwell, Elizabeth, 61

Merritt, Thomas, liv
Merritt, William Hamilton, 23, 25, 32, 68, 124, 328, 440
Metcalfe, Sir Charles Theophilus, 1st Baron Metcalfe, 21, 22, 68, 69, 70, 71, 170, 278, 279
Methodists: in Upper Canada, lii, liv, 226, 398, 438
Militia Act (1793): amendments to, 399, 400
Milnes, Sir Robert Shore, 5, 133, 134
ministerial responsibility, xci–xcii n.193, 23, 214–15, 367, 434. *See also* responsible government
Mitchell, James, 298
'moderate' party, 66, 68
Monk, Sir James, 137
monopolies, xlviii–xlix, liv
Moore, Thomas, 320, 321, 324
Morin, Augustin-Norbert, 69, 70–1. *See also* Hincks–Morin ministry
Morris, Patrick, 45, 46, 47
Morris, William, 68, 71, 247
Morrison, Joseph Curran, 283
Morrison, Thomas David, 15, 264, 272–3
Mott, Eliza, 113
Mountain, Jacob, 130, 134
Mowat, Sir Oliver, 234, 280
Municipal Corporations Act, 29, 419
municipal government: bill to provide, in Upper Canada, 18
murder: cases of, xxi, xxiii, 4, 61, 92, 93, 117, 148, 185, 349; difficulty of getting convictions, 192–3, 316. *See also* Burley, Cornelius Albertson; French, Charles; infanticide; Kain, William; McCarthy, James Owen; McSwiney, Edward; Osborn, Mary (London); Powlis, George; Shawanakiskie; Sovereene, Henry
murder, attempted: case of, 172
Murdoch, Sir Thomas William Clinton, 335
Murphy, Anna Brownell (Jameson), 100, 101, 103
Murray, Sir George, 144, 155–6
Murray, John, 52

Naturalization Bill (1825), 406; (1827), 108–9, 258. *See also* alien question
navigation acts, British, 26
Nelles, Robert, 317, 323, 328
Nemiers (Nemire), George, 316, 317–18
Nepean, Nicholas, 54
Newberry, William, 148, 357–8
Niagara Falls outrage (1827), lxix, 211, 386–8
Nichol, Robert, xlv–xlvi, lxi, xcii n.193, 95, 105, 106, 107, 146, 207, 208, 209, 215, 322, 379, 385, 400, 401, 424, 426
North West Company. *See* Red River colony
Norton, John, 92
Nowlan, Edward, 392, 393, 394, 395
Nugent, John Valentine, 47

Oberholser, Jacob. *See* Overholser, Jacob
O'Grady, William John, 44, 94, 218, 309, 373
Orange order, 19, 21–2, 101,

110–11, 117–18, 172, 219, 220, 278, 279, 348, 350. *See also* Secret Societies Bill
O'Reilly, Miles, 333, 334–5
Osborn, Mary (London), **316–19**
Osgoode, William, xxvi, xxix, xli, 5, 78, **129–34**, 140, 141, 177–8, 192
Osgoode Club, 235
Osgoode Hall, 36, 119, 134, 250
Overholser, Jacob, 148, 183, **320–6**
Owen, James. *See* McCarthy, James Owen

Papineau, Denis-Benjamin, 68, 69, 70
Papineau, Louis-Joseph, 21, 31, 227, 229
pardons, 56, 57, 60, 61, 312–13, 331, 335, 342, 353, 372, 376, 379, 394
Park, George Hamilton, 265, 281
Parsons, Robert John, 46–7
partnerships: bill to permit, with limited liability (1847), 23
Party Processions Bill (1843), 278
patronage, xlii
Patterson, Leslie, 151
Paulus Paulus. *See* Powlis, Paul
Pawling, Benjamin, 378
penitence, 60–1
People's Bank, 260
perjury: cases of, 57, 427
Perley, Amos, 302
Perry, Peter, 14, 28, 29, 30, 226, 228, 240, 261, **410–19**, 446
Perry family, 364
Peters, William Birdseye, **243–6**
Phelps, Elijah, 421, 422, 423, 425, 426. See also *Randal v. Phelps*
Phillpotts, George, 388, 390, 391

Pilotte, Angelique, 57, **327–31**, 332, 351, 354
Pollard, Richard, 358
Pomeroy, Timothy Conklin, 296, 297
Powell, Grant, 143
Powell, William Dummer, lxxv, 3, 4, 10, 41, 55, 59, 61–2, 63, 79, 80, 91, 121, 123, 125, 129, 132, **135–52**, 153, 154, 155, 157, 159, 183, 185, 250, 253, 344; cases heard by, xlix, lv, lvi, 323, 324, 351, 352, 353, 355, 356, 357–8, 379, 425; during the War of 1812, 290, 322, 341; and Joseph Willcocks, 401, 436
Powlis, George, **332–6**, 345
Powlis, Joseph, 333–4
Powlis, Noah, 113
Powlis, Paul (Paulus Paulus), 332, 333–4
Prescott, Robert, 132, 133
Prescott, Upper Canada. *See* windmill, battle of the
Prevost, Sir George, 144, 322, 341
Price, James Harvey, 30, 265
Privy Council, 48, 73
property: bill to allow husband to dispose of, without wife's consent, 23. *See also* married women
Provincial Lunatic Asylum, 102, 265–6, 267–8, 281

Quebec Act (1774), 137–8, 254
Queen's College, Kingston, 30, 70
Queenston Heights, battle of, 124–5. *See also* War of 1812

Radenhurst, Thomas Mabon, **247–9**
Railway Guarantee Act (1849), 32

Ramsay, David, 421, 423
Ramsay, George, 9th Earl of Dalhousie, 383, 384, 387, 406, 407, 409, 426–7
Randal, Robert, lxviii, lxxi, 57, 149, 164, 258, 384, 389, 395, **420–31**
Randal v. Phelps, 149, 423–4, 425
rape, 58, 98; cases of, 98, 186, 357. *See also* Brass, William; York, Jack
rebellion losses bill (1845), 69; (1849), 28, 31, 49
rebellion of 1837–8, 15, 65, 96, 112, 118, 128, 166–7, 218–19, 223, 229, 230, 251, 262–5, 267, 269, 301–2, 314–15, 403; trials arising from, 102, 112–13, 167, 186. *See also* amnesty; Mackenzie, William Lyon; Matthews, Peter; windmill, battle of the
Red River colony, 116, 150, 156, 185
Reform Association of Canada, 48, 278–9
Regiopolis College, 30, 339
representation by population, 49
representative government, xxviii
republicanism: in Upper Canada, 189, 285, 290, 301, 362, 363, 368, 372, 401, 433
responsible government, xxxii, lxxiii, lxxx n.13, 11, 14, 15, 18, 19, 22, 28, 33, 48, 49, 67, 71–2, 128, 174, 190, 198, 206, 214–15, 217, 219, 227, 276, 279, 415, 418. *See also* ministerial responsibility
revision of statutes, 119
Ribble, Anthony, 297–8, 299
Ribble, Henry, 296, 297, 299

Richardson, Charles, 409
Ridout, George, 102, 124, 230, 247, **250–2**, 349, 351
Ridout, John, lxix, 164–5, 250, 371
Ridout, Samuel Smith, 252
Ridout, Thomas, 250, 251, 290, 291
Ridout, Thomas Gibbs, 252
Ritchie, John Corbett, 54
Robertson, William, 139, 253, 254, 420
Robinson, Christopher, 84, 153, 355
Robinson, Sir Frederick Philipse, 87
Robinson, Sir John Beverley, xxv, xxix, xxxi, xxxiv, xxxv–xxxix, xliii, xlv, xlvii, lxvi, lxvii, lxviii, lxx–lxxi, lxxiii, lxxv, lxxvii, lxxxiii n.58, 12, 41–2, 43, 63, 64, 85, 86, 89, 94, 99, 104, 105, 106, 107, 112, 113, 115, 116, 119, 121, 124, 128, 147, 150, 152, **153–74**, 184, 187, 196, 197, 208, 209, 211–12, 217, 245, 257, 258, 272, 275, 290, 291, 312, 313, 335, 353, 354, 365, 370, 371, 372, 376, 387, 388, 405, 406, 411, 445; at the Ancaster assizes, lix, 57, 323; cases heard by, 117, 307, 309; cases prosecuted by, xxiv, lxviii, lxix, 298, 324, 325–6, 351, 379, 380, 381, 393, 395; in *Randal v. Phelps*, 425, 426, 427, 428
Robinson, John Beverley (son), 172
Robinson, Peter, 13, 14, 159, 161, 172, 207, 217, 251, 291, 394, 395
Robinson, William Benjamin, 70,

Index   467

71
Roe, Walter, 132, **253–5**
Rogers, David McGregor, xxxiii, xlvi, 79, 84, 89, 143, 208, 438, 439
Rolph, George, lxviii, lxx, lxxi, 211, 212, 256, 259, 395, 445
Rolph, John, xxiii, xxiv, lxiv, lxix, lxx, lxxi, lxxii, lxxv, lxxvii, 10, 11, 13–15, 93, 107, 151, 163–4, 196, 212, 213, 216, 218, 226, 229, **256–69**, 272–3, 281, 372, 389, 406, 407, 426, 427, 430, 445
Rooney, John, 117, 306, 307, 308
Rottenburg, Francis de, Baron de Rottenburg, 155, 290, 291, 312, 322–3, 341, 342
Row, Walter. See Roe, Walter
rule of law, xxxiii, xxxvi, xxxvii, xxxix, xlvii, xlix, lvi, lix, lx, lxxi, lxxiv
Russell, Dennis, 186
Russell, John, 1st Earl Russell, 15–16, 169, 170
Russell, Peter, li, 76–7, 130, 131, 141, **175–81**, 189, 192, 194, 202, 203, 205, 382, 396, 432
Ryckman, John, xxi, xxiii, lxxvii
Ryerse, Samuel, liii, 397, 398
Ryerson, Egerton, 31, 65, 69, 230, 231, 279, 416

St James' Church, Toronto, 6, 118, 284
St Lawrence River: navigation on, 107, 110, 112, 271, 277, 429
Samson, James Hunter, 8–9, **270–1**
schools: in Upper Canada, 21, 30–1, 158, 438. See also Common Schools Act (1841); Common Schools Bill (1816)
schools act for Lower Canada (1845), 69
Schoultz, Nils von, **337–9**
Scott, Thomas, li, 4, 41, 55, 59, 77, 79, 80, 84, 87, 142, 144, **182–4**, 207, 317, 435; at Ancaster assizes, 148, 155, 291, 323, 324
Secret Societies Bill (disallowed), 22, 68, 278
Sedgwick, Theodore, 361
sedition, 245. See also Bentley, Elijah
Sedition Act (1804), li, lxviii, 84, 150, 157, 197, 285; repeal of, lxiv, 106, 209, 412
seditious libel: cases of, 79, 88, 105, 157, 378
Seely, Joseph, **340–3**
Selkirk, Earl of. See Douglas, Thomas, 5th Earl of Selkirk
Semple, Robert, 185. See also Red River colony
sentencing: in criminal cases, 56
Seven Oaks incident. See Red River colony
Sewell, Jonathan, 5, 6
Sewell (Sewall), Jonathan, 136
Shawanakiskie, 63, 149, 332, **344–5**
sheriffs: appointment of, lxv, 29
Sherwood, Henry, 31, 69, 70, 71, 111, 117, 302
Sherwood, Levius Peters, 62, 104, 106, 109, **185–7**, 196, 212, 283, 425, 426, 427; cases heard by, lxx, 333, 334, 335, 372, 392, 393, 394, 395
Sherwood family, 105
Simcoe, John Graves, xxvi, xxix, xli, xlviii, 76, 77, 83, 115, 130,

132, 134, 140, 177, 178, 179, 180, 193, 210, 236, 243, 255, 396, 420
Simms, James, 45
Six Nations: lands held by, 132, 179, 397
slavery: act to abolish in Upper Canada (1793), 132, 193, 355; bill to extend, 84; views on, 128
Small, James Edward, lxix, 12, 64, 164, 205, 279, 349, 371, 418
Small, John, 4, 194, 203, 433
small claims: jurisdiction over, 235
Smith, Sir David William, liii, 84, 141, 177, 193, 194, 244, 397, 398
Smith, Grace, 113
Smith, Sir Henry, 293, 294, 295
Smith, Larratt William Violett, 99
Smith, Rebecca (Couche), 303
Smith, Samuel, 107, 152, 157, 328
Smith, William, 129
solicitor general: acting, 250; appointments as, 16, 40, 43, 65, 83, 94, 155; proposed, 259
solicitor general (Cape Breton): appointment as, 52
Sorel, seigneury of, 138
Sovereene, Henry, **346–7**
Springer, Daniel, 405, 406, 408
Stanton, Robert, xxxiv, 94, 95, 108, 213
Stark, John, 47
Stewart, Alexander, 425
Stewart, John, 247
Stone, Joel, xxix, 403
Strachan, James McGill, 97
Strachan, John, xxxii, xxxiii, xxxv–xxxvi, xxxix, lix, 10, 15, 30, 64, 70, 94, 99, 109, 116, 143,

146–7, 149, 150, 152, 153, 158, 161, 162, 165, 171, 174, 183, 186, 217, 226, 240, 251, 284, 291, 308, 353, 363, 395, 445
Street, Samuel, 84, 439. See also *Bliss v. Street*
Street, Samuel (nephew), 323, 327, 387, 388, 389, 390, 422, 423, 426, 427, 428, 430
Strong, George Templeton, 232
Strong, Bidwell and Strong, 232
Stuart, George Okill, 3
Sullivan, Augustus Baldwin, 273
Sullivan, Daniel (blacksmith), **348–50**
Sullivan, Daniel (law student), 205, 272
Sullivan, Robert Baldwin, 11, 17, 23, 25, 67, 96, 101, 128, 205, 217, 218, 241, 251, **272–82**, 307, 335, 348, 390, 415
supremacy, oath of, 16
Supreme Court of Newfoundland, 45
Swayze, Isaac, xxx, 286, 426, 437
Switzer, Martin, 301
Sydenham, Baron. *See* Thomson, Charles Edward Poulett, 1st Baron Sydenham

Talbot, Thomas, 151, 256–7, 400, 405, 406, 409
tariffs, 77. *See also* Canada Trade Act (1822)
Taylor, Thomas, 379
Telfer, Walter, 265, 281
Ten Broeck, John, 323
Thayendanegea (Joseph Brant), 179, 397
theft: cases of, 113, 156

Thomas v. Acklam (1824), 428
Thompson, Mary, 149, 328, **351–4**
Thomson, Charles Edward Poulett, 1st Baron Sydenham, 15–16, 17, 18, 97, 98, 119, 169, 170, 220, 248, 277
Thomson, Hugh Christopher, lxviii, 371
Thorpe, Robert, liv–lv, lvi–lviii, lx, lxxv, 6, 40, 41, 55, 81, 145, 183, **188–91**, 196, 203, 209, 215, 286, 290, 322, 367, 434, 435, 436, 437, 438
Tiffany, George Sylvester, 333
Tiffany, Silvester, 316, 317, 318
Toronto: incorporation (1834), 252. *See also* York
Toronto Constitutional Society, 187
Toronto Political Union, 218
Toronto School of Medicine, 265, 266, 268
treason: cases of, 246. *See also* Ancaster assizes; Doan, Joshua Gwillen; Mallory, Benajah; Matthews, Peter; Overholser, Jacob; rebellion of 1837–8: trials arising from; Willcocks, Joseph
trespass: cases of, lvii, 388, 389
trial by jury, xxxiv, xli, 58, 131, 137, 138, 148
Trinity College, 102, 171. *See also* Upper Canada School of Medicine
Troup, Robert, 149
Troy, Edward, 48, 50
Tucker, Richard Alexander, 45, 118, 277
Tufflemier, Jacob, 356, 357
Tufflemier, Ruth, 355, 356, 357
types riot, lxviii, lxx, 57–8, 92, 117, 164–5, 212, 371–2, 386, 392, 393, 395, 409. *See also* Mackenzie, William Lyon

Uniformity of Process Act (1832), 134
union: of British North America, 161, 167, 173
union: of Upper and Lower Canada (1841), 15–16, 65–6, 97, 128, 167, 168, 169, 170, 173, 220, 276, 277, 431, 446–7; proposed (1822), 90, 106, 159, 161–2, 210, 429
University Bill (1843), 21, 24, 29; (1845), 69–70; (1849), 29–30, 171
University of Toronto, 21, 29–30, 34–5, 235; medical faculty, 268. *See also* King's College
University of Upper Canada, proposed, 70
Upper Canada: move of the capital to York, 76–7, 180
Upper Canada Academy, 65. *See also* Victoria College
Upper Canada Agricultural and Commercial Society, 435, 438
Upper Canada College, 235
Upper Canada School of Medicine, 268

VanKoughnet, Philip Michael Matthew Scott, 234
Victoria College, 30, 70; medical faculty, 268. *See also* Upper Canada Academy
Viger, Denis-Benjamin, 23, 68, 70
Vincent, Michael, xxi–xxv, lxviii, lxxii, lxxvii, lxxviii–lxxx n.8, 93,

395, 445
voluntary principle. *See* church and state, separation of

Wait, Benjamin, 113
Walker, Edward, 341
war damages, 160
War of 1812, xxxii, lix, 104–5, 115–16, 123–4, 127, 144, 148, 154–5, 156–7, 173, 183, 185, 245, 250, 289, 290, 310–11, 320–3, 340–1, 364, 382–3, 400–2, 438–41, 443. *See also* Ancaster assizes; war damages
Warren, John, lvi, 320, 436
Warren, John (son), 321, 324, 325
Washburn, Daniel, 225, 365
Washburn, Simon Ebenezer, lxx, 122, 205, 212, **283–4**, 393
Weekes, William, l–li, lii, lv, lvi, lx, 4, 189, 190, **285–6**, 322, 398, 433, 434
Welch, Thomas, liii, 397, 398
Welland Canal Company, 107, 112, 173, 219, 412, 429, 445
Westbrook, Andrew, 343, 400
Wetenhall, John, 31, 235
Wheller, Peter, 331
whiggism, 63, 209, 433, 434, 442
whipping: bill to abolish for women, 106
White, John, 4, 84, 129–30, 132, 141, 177, **192–4**, 255, 316
wife beating, 58, 88
Wilcox, Joseph. *See* Willcocks, Joseph

wild land: taxation of, 21, 208
Willcocks, Joseph, lix, lx, 13, 79, 145, 155, 202–3, 207, 209, 245, 292, 322, 323, 399, 400, 401, 402, **432–442**, 443
Willcocks, William, lv, 175, 179, 181, 201, 202, 205, 206, 290, 432
Williams, Jenkin, 6
Willis, John Walpole, lxviii, lxix–lxxi, 11, 12, 57, 62, 93, 117, 164–5, 186, **195–8**, 211, 212–13, 248, 258, 274, 283, 284, 371, 372, 395, 427
Willson, John, xliv, xlv, lxi, lxii, 208, 274, 333, 378, 381, 399, 438, **443–7**
Wilmot-Horton, Sir Robert John, 160
Wilson, Sir Adam, 23, 74
Wilson, John, 248
windmill, battle of the, 338–9
women: right to vote, 24, 130
Wood, Alexander, 149, 152, 291
Woodfall, William, 54
Workman, Joseph, 235, 267
wrecked ship: seizure of goods from, lvi
Wyatt, Charles Burton, 81, 191, 203, 207, 434, 435, 437
Wycliffe College, 74

Yonge Street riot (1839), 220
York, Jack, 148, 316, **355–8**
York: American occupation of. *See* War of 1812; bills to incorporate, 44. *See also* Toronto

www.ingramcontent.com/pod-product-compliance
Lightning Source LLC
Chambersburg PA
CBHW031358290426
44110CB00011B/198